T0183874

Lecture Notes in Computer Science 9466

More information about this series at http://www.springer.com/series/7411

Ahmed Bouajjani · Hugues Fauconnier (Eds.)

Networked Systems

Third International Conference, NETYS 2015
Agadir, Morocco, May 13–15, 2015
Revised Selected Papers

Editors
Ahmed Bouajjani
Université Paris Diderot
Paris Cedex 13
France

Hugues Fauconnier
Université Paris Diderot
Paris Cedex 13
France

ISSN 0302-9743 ISSN 1611-3349 (electronic)
Lecture Notes in Computer Science
ISBN 978-3-319-26849-1 ISBN 978-3-319-26850-7 (eBook)
DOI 10.1007/978-3-319-26850-7

Library of Congress Control Number: 2015954980

LNCS Sublibrary: SL5 – Computer Communication Networks and Telecommunications

Springer Cham Heidelberg New York Dordrecht London

Printed on acid-free paper

Springer International Publishing AG Switzerland is part of Springer Science+Business Media
(www.springer.com)

Message from the Program Chairs

NETYS 2015 received 133 submissions from 25 countries from all over the world. The reviewing process was undertaken by a Program Committee of 31 international experts in the areas of networking, distributed computing, security, formal methods, and verification. This process led to the definition of a strong scientific program. The Program Committee accepted 29 regular papers and 12 short papers. In addition, 22 papers were selected for poster presentations. Besides these high-quality contributions, the program of Netys 2015 included keynotes talks by three world-renowned researchers: Javier Esparza (Technische Universität München), Christoph Kirsch (University of Salzburg), and Madan Musuvathi (Microsoft Research).

We warmly thank all the authors for their great contributions, all the Program Committee members for their hard work and their commitment, all the external reviewers for their valuable help, and the three keynote speakers to whom we are deeply grateful for their support. Special thanks to the two conference general chairs, Mohammed Erradi (ENSIAS, Rabat), and Rachid Guerraoui (EPFL, Lausanne), for their invaluable guidance and tremendous help.

Ahmed Bouajjani
Hugues Fauconnier

Message from the General Chairs

The recent developments in the Internet as well as mobile networks, together with the progress of cloud computing technology, have changed the way people perceive computers, communicate, and do business. Today's Internet carries huge volumes of personal, business, and financial data, much of which are accessed wirelessly through mobile devices. In addition, cloud computing technology is providing a shared pool of configurable computing resources (hardware and software: e.g., networks, servers, storage, applications, and services) that are delivered as services over a diversity of network technologies. Advances in Web technologies, social networking, and middleware platforms have raised new opportunities for the implementation of novel applications and the provision of high-quality services over connected devices. This allows participatory information sharing, interoperability, and collaboration on the World Wide Web. All these technologies can be gathered under the umbrella of networked systems.

After the great success of the previous editions of the International Conference on Networked Systems (NETYS 2013 and NETYS 2014), this year's edition, NETYS 2015, took place in the sunny city Agadir, Morocco, during May 11–15, 2015. It provided a forum to report on the best practices and novel algorithms, results, and techniques in networked systems. To face the challenge of building robust distributed systems and to protect such networked systems and data from attack and abuse, this edition gathered researchers and experts from both the community of distributed systems and the community of formal verification; it also addressed the challenging issues related to networked systems such as multi-core architectures, concurrent and distributed algorithms, middleware environments, storage clusters, social networks, peer-to-peer networks, sensor networks, wireless and mobile networks, as well as privacy and security measures.

We would like to express our cordial thanks to our partners and sponsors for their permanent trust and support. A special thanks goes to Springer, who have ensured that the proceedings, since the first edition of NETYS, reach a wide readership around the world. We are grateful to the Program Committee co-chairs, the session chairs, and the Program Committee members for their excellent work and we wish to take this opportunity to congratulate all the authors for the high quality displayed in their papers and to thank all the participants for their support and interest. Finally, no conference can be a success without the valuable contribution of the Organizing Committee, whom we thank for their dedication and hard work in making this conference a success.

Mohammed Erradi
Rachid Guerraoui

Organization

Program Committee

Parosh Aziz Abdulla	Uppsala University, Sweden
Joffroy Beauquier	LRI, Paris 11, France
Gregor Bochmann	University of Ottawa, Canada
Ahmed Bouajjani	LIAFA, University Paris Diderot, France
Carole Delporte-Gallet	University Paris Diderot, France
Amr El Abbadi	University of California at Santa Barbara, USA
Mohamed El Kamili	LiM, FSDM, USMBA, Fès, Morocco
Mohammed El Koutbi	ENSIAS, Morocco
Hugues Fauconnier	LIAFA, University Paris Diderot, France
Bernd Freisleben	Philipps-Universitaet Marburg, Germany
Mohamed Gouda	The University of Texas at Austin, USA
Vincent Gramoli	The University of Sydney, Australia
Seif Haridi	SICS, Sweden
Maurice Herlihy	Brown University, USA
Claude Jard	University of Nantes, France
Zahi Jarir	Cadi Ayyad University, Marrakech, Morocco
Anne-Marie Kermarrec	Inria, France
Rupak Majumdar	MPI-SWS, Germany
Stephan Merz	Inria Nancy, France
Louise Moser	University of California at Santa Barbara, USA
Hassan Mountassir	FEMTO-ST Institute, France
Guevara Noubir	Northeastern University, USA
Andreas Podelski	Universität Freiburg, Germany
Shaz Qadeer	Microsoft Research, USA
Vivien Quema	INPG, France
Sergio Rajsbaum	Instituto de Matematicas, UNAM, Mexico
Ganesan Ramalingam	Microsoft Research, India
Michel Raynal	IRISA, Rennes, France
Alexander Shvartsman	University of Connecticut, USA
Sebastien Tixeuil	LIP6, Univ Pierre et Marie Curie – Paris 6, France
Martin Vechev	ETH Zurich, Switzerland

Additional Reviewers

Ali, Muqeet
Arora, Vaibhav
Bielik, Pavol
Burckhardt, Sebastian
Burman, Janna
Dan, Andrei
Dimitrov, Dimitar
Dubois, Swan
Erradi, Mohammed
Fernandez, Antonio
Frey, Davide
Georgiou, Theodore
Godard, Emmanuel
Golan-Gueta, Guy
Hadjistasi, Theophanos
Hendler, Danny
Koulali, Mohammed-Amine
Leonardsson, Carl
Melliar-Smith, Peter Michael
Nawab, Faisal
Ngo, Tuan Phong
Pothapu, Kranti
Raychev, Veselin
Reaz, Rezwana
Reinhold, Gregory
Rezine, Othmane
Sahin, Cetin
Shrestha, Amendra
Singh, Gagandeep
Stenman, Jari
Trinh, Cong Quy
Xu, Chuan
Zakhary, Victor
Zhu, Yunyun

Abstracts of Posters

Evaluation of MCR Protocol for WSNs

Bahae Abidi[1], Abdelillah Jilbab[2], and Mohamed El Haziti[3]

[1] LRIT Associated Unit with CNRST, University Mohammed V-Rabat, Morocco
[2] ENSET, University Mohammed V-Rabat, Morocco
[3] EST Salé, University Mohammed V-Rabat, Morocco

Abstract. The networking techniques now allow the easily deployment of sensor networks, even in places with difficult access. The evolution of wireless communication has extended the application of sensor network. The application in a medical context requires operation at a low consumption of energy. Another constraint is related to the quality of information sent by the network. And in order to respond to these criteria, different methods of wireless communication area used. In this work, we evaluate a multi-hop clustering routing protocol to resolve our constraint by comparing his concept with HEED protocol, who is a single hope clustering routing protocol, who reduce the communication overhead by selecting a cluster head to forward data to base station via one hop. Comparing the concept of the MCR with that of HEED, we notice that it offers best performance in terms of network lifetime and consumption of energy and this is due to the concept of the gateway node that is used to transmit data from cluster head to BS. With that the CHs can keep the energy in data transmission and the gateway node by not participating in clustering. In addition CHs rotation is adopted to balance the consumption of energy.

Keywords: WSN · Gateway node · MCR · Clustering · Single hop clustering routing

The First Step Towards Securing a Distributed Collaborative System

Meryeme Ayache[1], Mohammed Erradi[1], and Ahmed Khoumsi[2]

[1] Networking and Distributed Systems Research Group, TIES, SIME Lab, Ensias, Mohammed V University, Rabat, Morocco
{meryemeayache,mohamed.erradi}@gmail.com
[2] Department of Electrical and Computer Engineering, University of Sherbrooke, Sherbrooke, Canada
ahmed.khoumsi@usherbrooke.ca

Abstract. In a distributed collaborative system dedicated to remote diagnosis in eHealth, one fundamental requirement is to secure the data exchange and the interactions among the collaborative users. To tackle this problem, we need first to provide a formal model describing the involved entities and their interactions during a collaborative session. As a formal description of the distributed eHealth system, we propose an emergency medical system containing three organizations (hospitals, university hospitals and emergency medical services). Each organization is composed of subjects (human resources) and objects (medical files, scans …). The collaborative interactions are considered as a sequence of accesses. Each access is modeled by an automaton with four states linked by labeled transitions, and represented by a graph whose nodes and arcs are the states and the transitions of the automaton respectively. The final states of each automaton are associated to a specific action (e.g. read). The proposed model can be used to verify whether the collaborative session answers the security requirements of the involved organizations.

Minimum Interference in Wireless Mesh Networks

Asma Benmohammed and Merniz Salah

Laboratoire LIRE, Université Abdelhamid Mehri-Constantine 2, 25000 Constantine, Algérie
aben_asmal23@yahoo.fr, s_merniz@hotmail.com

Abstract. In this paper, we consider a multi-channel multi-radio wireless mesh network. Most of the work on channel allocation propose to allocate orthogonal channels which will reduce the flow in high-density networks. In our work, we address the problem of channel assignment by using a new metric MICE that uses metric uses partially overlapping channels POC and considers the channel separation and the distance between the nodes to allocate the best channels to the network in order to minimize the overall interference. Compared to metrics as WCETT and MIC, our metric considers both: inter-flow and intra-flow interference, and both the distance between nodes and channel separation which will allow us to choose the best set of channels that will reduce the network overall interference. It has been shown that considering different factors that affects the interference will positively affects the overall interference problem in a mesh network. In our future work, we plan to extend the interference metric for multicast routing in multi-radio/multi-channel mesh networks.

Keywords: Multi-channel · Multi-radio · Mesh · Interference · Channel assignment

A Routing Algorithm for Wireless Sensor Networks Based on Ant Colony Optimization and Multi-criteria Decision Aid

Amine Kada and Mohammed Ouzzif

RITM Laboratory, Ecole Nationale Supérieure D'électricité et de Mécanique, Hassan II University of Casablanca, Morocco
a.kada@outlook.com, ouzzif@gmail.com

Abstract. Wireless Sensor Networks (WSN) are becoming a key building block of our communication infrastructure; as they find applications in several military as well as civilian domains. Examples range from target tracking to monitoring and environmental scenarios. Due to their use and design, WSN are facing many problems, which can be categorized as optimization problems such as energy consumption, routing and quality of service. Many researchers have done research to solve these problems and recently new class of routing algorithms came up which is based on Swarm Intelligence. In this poster, we propose a routing algorithm for WSN based on Ant Colony Optimization (ACO) heuristic and Multi-criteria Decision Aid (MCDA) methods. Allying ACO heuristic to MCDA methods result in an approach that facilitate tackling complex decision problems that are characterized by a great number of possible choices as in routing in WSN. The basic idea would be to perform the search through the solution space in a more directed manner, already taking valuable information into account. This will result in an improved routing protocol for WSN; designed to optimize the node power consumption and increase network lifetime as long as possible, while data transmission is attained efficiently.

Keywords: Ad-hoc networks · Wireless sensor networks · Ant colony optimization · Multi-criteria decision aid · Routing · Swarm intelligence

Hybrid Intrusion Detection System in Cloud Computing (Hy-CIDS)

Ali Azougaghe[1], Hicham Boukhriss[2], Mustapha Hedabou[2], and Mostafa Belkasmi[1]

[1] SIME Lab, National School of Computer Science and Systems Analysis Mohammed V University, Rabat, Morocco
azaling@gmail.com

[2] MTI Lab. ENSA School, Cadi Ayyad University, Safi, Morocco

Abstract. Actually, Cloud Computing is an exciting field, but security and privacy is a major obstacle to its success because of its open and distributed architecture that is vulnerable to intruders. In this context, Intrusion Detection System (IDS) is the most common mechanism used to detect attacks in the cloud environment. This article gives an overview of different intrusions, IDS types and techniques, as we proposed a hybrid IDS architecture (Hy-CIDS) that uses three techniques to know the artificial neural networks, Bayesian networks and genetic algorithms. This architecture aims to increase the detection accuracy with low false positive rate.

Keywords: Cloud computing · Security · Attacks · Intrusion detection system

An Overview of VANET: Architectures, Challenges and Routing Protocols

Bayad Kanza, Rziza Mohammed, and Oumsis Mohammed

LRIT Associated Unit with CNRST,
Mohammed V-Agdal University, B.P 1014, Rabat, Morocco
bayadkanza17@gmail.com, rziza@fsr.ac.ma,
oumsis@yahoo.com

Abstract. Vehicular ad hoc networking (VANET) is relatively a new environment compared to other wireless networks. In the last years, it has gained in popularity because of its practice in a wide range of applications, mainly in transferring information between auto-mobiles. Therefore the network topology changes rapidly and has a special mobility pattern. The features of vehicular ad hoc routing protocols are crucial and represent an important issue for the intelligent transportation system (ITS). As a condition to communication, the VANET routing protocols must adjust efficiently to the varying route between network nodes and the rapidity of moving vehicles. In this paper, we describe the principal characteristics and discuss the research challenges of routing in this type of networks. We also discuss routing protocols in VANETs. In addition, the advantages and disadvantages of the current protocols in this field are presented.

Keywords: VANET · ITS · V2V · V2I · Routing protocols

Performance Evaluation of Routing Protocols in VANET

El Houssine Bourhim and Mohammed Oumsis

LRIT Associated Unit with CNRST,
Mohammed V University, Faculty of Sciences Rabat, Morocco

Abstract. Vehicular Ad Hoc Network (VANET) is an instance of MANETs that establishes wireless connections between vehicles and vehicle to road side equipments to provide scalable and cost-effective solutions for the applications of the Intelligent Transportation System (ITS) such as traffic safety, dynamic route planning, and context-aware advertisement using short range wireless communication. to function properly, these applications require efficient routing protocols adapted to vehicular specific characteristics and requirements. the routing performance in VANET is dependent to the availability and stability of wireless links, which makes it a crucial parameter in order to obtain accurate performance measurements. In this paper, we evaluate AODV and DSDV performance under varying metrics such as node mobility and traffic load in realistic urban environment.

Keywords: Urban environment · VANET · Routing protocols · Simulation · Performance

Architecture of Remote Virtual Labs as a Service in the Cloud Computing

Naoual Boukil[1] and Abdelali Ibriz[2]

[1] University Sidi Mohamed Ben Abdellah, Faculty of Science and Technology, Fez, Morocco
Naoual.boukil@gmail.com
[2] University Sidi Mohamed Ben Abdellah, High school of Technology, Fez, Morocco
a.ibriz@gmail.com

Abstract. Today, Cloud Computing is becoming an attractive technology used in virtualization of resources even in education filed. In fact, it's used in e-learning scenarios due to dynamic scalability offered by the different services of Cloud Computing. we propose an architecture of using Cloud computing to delivering labs as a solution of limited availability of resources in classical labs, it can be viewed as a service in the cloud computing, This architecture fits very well to remote virtual labs requirement like using remote services to provide on-demand access to lab's documentations, lab's resources or lab's realization; we show in this paper that how and why the development of a platform of labs and integrate it into the "cloud computing" is essential.

Keywords: Cloud computing · E-learning · Remote virtual labs · Remote services

Dynamic Integration of Security Requirements in Web Service Composition

Ilyass El Kassmi and Zahi Jarir

Laboratory LISI, Computer Science Department, Faculty of Sciences, Cadi Ayyad University, BP 2390, Marrakech, Morocco
Ilyass.elkassmi@ced.uca.ma, jarir@uca.ma

Abstract. Most of the current researches in the web service composition domain are mainly focused on issues about how to ensure desired functional requirements and how to fulfill them. However, it's highly recommended to provide, in addition to functional needs satisfaction, more support for security requirements especially for web services exchanging sensitive information. In this work we propose an approach that generates automatically a composite web service according to user's functional requirements and security constraints. This generation is based on our previous developed DIVISE Framework (DIscovery and Visual Interactive web Service Engine). This framework has the capability to generate a BPEL code of the needed composite web services according to expressed functional requirements. However, to secure the generated composite web services and especially the selected sensitive web services, the current contribution consists on enhancing our DIVISE framework by adding a security layer. This layer has the faculty to inject specific security tags into the generated BPEL code. These tags are related to security requirements in term of web services such as Authentication, Authorization, etc.

Keywords: Web service composition · Security requirements · DIVISE framework

Modeling Wireless Sensor Networks

Younes Driouch[1,2], Abdellah Boulouz[1,*], Mohamed Ben Salah[1], and Congduc Pham[3]

[1] LabSIV, Faculty of Science, Ibn ZOHR University Agadir
abdellah.boulouz@gmail.com
[2] Faculty of Science and Techniques, Hassan Premier University Settat
[3] LIUPPA, UFR Sciences et Techniques, PAU, France

Abstract. Wireless Sensor Network (WSN) is a network made of autonomous nodes (sensors) that collect information about its environment and send it back to a central point (base station, or a sink), WSN has so much potentials and possibilities in automation especially data collection. RFID is a technology that allows a verity of items to be automatically identified through small microchips attached to them. Petri Net is a sophisticated graphical modeling technique that relies on three components (places, transitions and tokens) to model complex systems on different levels of abstraction. This poster try to present the main challenges facing the process of modeling WSN using Petri Nets and the integration of RFID technology to form a hybrid network which would lead the ground for the Internet of Things (IoT).

Keywords: Wireless sensor network · Modeling · Petri net · IoT · RFID · QoS

Geographical Query Reformulation Based on Spatial Taxonomies Constructed Using the Apriori Algorithm

Omar El Midaoui[1], Abderrahim El Qadi[2], Moulay Driss Rahmani[1], and Driss Aboutajdine[1]

[1] LRIT Associated Unit to the CNRST - URAC n°29 Faculty of Science Mohammed V-Agdal University Rabat, Morocco
omarelmidaoui@gmail.com, {mrahmani, aboutaj}@fsr.ac.ma
[2] TIM, High School of Technology Moulay Ismaïl University Meknes, Morocco
elqadi_a@yahoo.com

Abstract. Geographical queries needs a special treatment by Information Retrieval systems (IRS) due to their specificities. Most of search engines are ignoring this fact. In this paper, we propose an approach for building a geographical taxonomy of adjacency automatically in order to use it for reformulating the spatial part of the query. This approach exploit the best-ranked documents retrieved when submitting the spatial entities, which are composed of the spatial relation and a noun of a city. Then, we construct a database of transactions, considering each document extracted as a transaction containing the nouns of the cities sharing the same country of the query's city. The association rules algorithm Apriori is applied to this database in order to extract rules that will form the country's taxonomy. Experiments shows that query reformulation using the taxonomy resulted from our proposed approach improves the effectiveness and the precision of the IRS.

Counting Spanning Trees in Bipartite and Reduced Pseudofractal Scale-Free Network

Raihana Mokhlissi, Mohamed El Marraki, and Dounia Lotfi

LRIT, Associated Unit to CNRST (URAC No 29)
Mohammed V-Rabat University, B.P.1014 RP, Agdal, Morocco
mokhlissiraihana@gmail.com, marraki@fsr.ac.ma, doun.lotfi@gmail.com

Abstract. The number of spanning trees is an important measure of the reliability of a wireless sensor network (WSN) in order to reduce energy consumption and improve network capacity. In this paper, we are interested by the pseudo fractal scale-free network. This type of fractal is considered as a self-similar pattern, it has found applications in many areas of science and engineering... We propose two very important combinatorial approaches facilitating the enumeration of spanning trees of a network containing a large number of nodes and links such as the bipartition and reduction. These techniques allow changing the topological nature of a network, by multiplying the number of nodes in the case of the bipartion approach, or by multiplying the number of links in the case of the reduction approach. The aim of these approaches is the evaluation of the complexity of an infinite network which cannot be find by using the existing methods.

Keywords: WSN · Spanning trees · Pseudofractal scale-free · Bipartition · Reduction

Prosumers Integration and the Hybrid Communication in Smart Grid Context

Youssef Hamdaoui

Departement of Computer Science, Mohamed 5 University, Rabat, Morocco
hamdaouiyoussef@gmail.com

Abstract. The success of the smart grid depends on the integration of the prosumers into the grid and his Reactivity, Many stakeholders are involved in, but the role of consumes is neglected, recently the prosumers has been became a very important entity to migrate to Smart Grids because he can consume, produce and powering the electrical grid. In this context, Smart grids, smart meters, demand side management and smart appliances play a crucial role, Inefficient use of these appliances causes a waste of energy and bad management of the electricity, leading to a reduction of this energy wasting behavior. The DSM helps to reduce peak demand and energy consumption while still allowing for the same level of comfort within the household. The challenge is to ensure the interoperability of the PLC, WSN and RFID into an hybrid communication using a mix of technologies, collection data from a heterogeneous platform, analysis of data, save for statistic and offer the information to the end user like a service appliances. This makes it possible to understand the origin of its electricity consumption, identify energy savings, reduce consummation, real-time eco-feedback displays in the home, help to make decision to turn on/off the electrical machine in the peak hours and the most important is to estimate the electrical energy demand.

Keywords: Smart grid · Smart meter · Smart appliances · NIALM · Prosumers · Communications · WSN · Demand management

Integrating Communication-Centric Programming in the Design of Distributed Systems

Karam Younes Kharraz and Mohammed Erradi

Networking and Distributed Systems Research Group,
TIES, SIME Lab, ENSIAS,
Mohammed V University, Rabat, Morocco
kkharraz@acm.org, erradi@ensias.ma

Abstract. Distributed Systems are mainly built to provide services; this is why the design is often focused on Service Oriented Architecture. Thus, after the design process, developers find themselves dealing with complex and discrete problems like live locks, race conditions, and deadlocks. Distributed Systems are concurrent by definition, and neglecting concurrency can lead to a complete system re-engineering. In this poster, we will discuss the importance of handling the process view during the design of Distributed Systems. Communication-Centric Programming techniques describe the communication behavior of systems components using formal calculi. Using it during the modeling phase can help to detect problems and then address the right local or global solutions; the final goal of the proposed approach is to achieve a derivation of design components from a distributed system global specification before starting the development phase. In order to illustrate this, we will show step by step, an example of how to integrate Communication Centric Programming while using a Service oriented approach for the design.

Keywords: Distributed systems design · Communication centric programming · Software architecture · Service oriented architecture

Mobility Models Impact on the Throughput in MANET

Nisrine Ibadah[1], Mohammed Rziza[1], Khalid Minaoui[1], and Mohammed Oumsis[2]

[1] LRIT Associated Unit with CNRST (URAC 29)
nisrine.ibadah@gmail.com,
{rziza, khalid.minaoui}@fsr.ac.ma
[2] Superior School of Technology – Salé
Mohammed V University, B.P.1014 RP, Agdal, Morocco
oumsis@yahoo.com

Abstract. Mobile ad hoc network (MANET) has become an interesting field of the Next Generation Network. It includes several interconnected nodes in charge of delivering information from a given node to another. Routing allows, using routing protocols, choosing the suitable path to reach the destination with the minimum delay. Therefore, it is important to have knowledge about the appropriate protocol for the studied scenarios. The current study is dedicated to performance analysis of the Throughput using five protocols and four mobility models under two different sizes of area. Simulation results demonstrate that, in all mobility models used the throughput works better in the small area than it does in the large one because the number of the received packets is important. Each one of the proposed routing protocol provides high performance for different strategies for a given network scenario. This study has proven that, in the case of throughput, the reactive routing protocols outperform the proactive and hybrid protocols in small and large areas. Moreover, it can be noted that the AODV is the most suitable protocol for throughput in all used mobility models.

Keywords: MANET · Routing protocols · Mobility models · NS2 · BoonMotion

Performance Analysis of ARQ and FEC in WBANs

Nabila Samouni[1], Abdelilah Jilbab[2], and Driss Aboutajdine[1]

[1] LRIT Associated Unit with CNRST, Mohammed V-Agdal University, Rabat, Morocco
[2] ENSET, University Mohamed V-Rabat, Morocco

Abstract. Recent developments in wireless sensor network and integrated circuits has enabled physiological, intelligent and micro-components sensors nodes strategically are attached on clothing of human body or even implanted under the skin. This exciting new area of research is called Wireless Body Area Networks (WBANs). One of the major challenges in this network is to prolong the lifetime of network. In addition, the data transmitted from the sensors are vulnerable to corruption by noisy channels and others. To deal with these two problems of instability of the radio channel and the energy consumption, several solutions have been proposed in literature, and that they can be grouped into two majors error control modes: ARQ (Automatic Repeat reQuest) and FEC (Forward Error correction). In this context, we evaluated the performances in terms of energy consumption provided by ARQ and FEC in WBAN to show who performs the best. We consider the fountain codes that derives from the FEC, due to its low encoding/decoding complexity and its adaptation with all channels. Our result show that the use of the fountain code in wireless body area networks can significantly increase the node and network lifetime, compared to ARQ.

Keywords: WBAN · ARQ · FEC · Fountain code · Energy consumption

A Generic Natural Language Interface for Database Interface Based on Machine Learning Approach

Hanane Bais, Mustapha Machkour, and Lahcen Koutti

Information Systems and Vision Laboratory, Department Computer Sciences, Faculty of Sciences, Ibn Zohr University, Agadir, Morocco
baishanan@gmail.com, machkour@hotmail.com, lkoutti@yahoo.fr

Abstract. In the world of modern computing, one of the main sources of information is the database. For extracting information from a database system, it is necessary to formulate a query using database query languages such as SQL (Structured Query Language). However casual users who don't understand SQL can't write such queries. So, asking questions to databases in natural language is a very important method. But without any help, computers cannot understand this language; that is why it is essential to develop an interface that can be able to translate user's query given in natural language to an equivalent one in database query language.

In this paper we present the Architecture and the implementation of a generic natural language query interface for relational database based on machine learning approach. The interface functions independently of the database domain and automatically improves through experience its knowledge base. These properties will certainly provide an interface respecting the qualities of software such as genericity, adaptability and extensibility.

Keywords: Databases · Natural language · XML · Machine learning

Impact of Malicious Behavior on AODV Routing Protocol

Houda Moudni[1], Mohamed Er-rouidi[1], Hicham Mouncif[2], and Benachir El Hadadi[2]

[1] Computer Science Department, Faculty of Sciences and Technology, Sultan Moulay Slimane University, Beni Mellal, Morocco
{h.moudni, m.errouidi}@usms.ma
[2] Faculty Polydisciplinary, Sultan Moulay Slimane University, Beni Mellal, Morocco
{hmouncif, benachirelhadadi}@yahoo.fr

Abstract. Mobile Ad-Hoc Networks (MANETs) is a collection of autonomous nodes that are self-managed without any existing infrastructure and centralized administration. However, the lack of centralized monitoring and the dynamic topology makes the routing protocol more vulnerable and defenseless to different security attacks. In this paper, we focus on the behavior of the Ad hoc Ondemand Distance Vector (AODV) routing protocol under attacks which are mainly Black Hole attack, Flooding attack and Rushing attack in the network layer. Also, we simulate these routing attacks to analyze their impact on AODV protocol using various performance parameters like throughput, packet delivery ratio and end to end delay using different simulation parameters with the NS-2 network simulator. The simulation results show that the black hole and flooding attacks have a severe impact on the network performance while the rushing attack have a less significant effect on the network performance.

Keywords: MANETs · AODV · Black hole attack · Flooding attack · Rushing attack

An Access Control Model for Collaborative Cloud Environment

Mohamed Amine Madani and Mohammed Erradi

Networking and Distributed Systems Research Group, SIME Lab, ENSIAS, University Mohammed V of Rabat, Morocco
madani.medamin@gmail.com, erradi@ensias.ma

Abstract. Nowadays, collaborative applications are among services that can be provided by the cloud computing. They enable collaboration among users from the same or different tenants of a given cloud provider. During collaborations, the participants need to access and use resources held by other collaborating users. These resources often contain sensitive data. They are meant to be shared only during specific collaboration sessions. In this context, the security of the shared resources in collaborative session becomes an important issue that must be addressed. After analyzing the access control approaches related to the collaboration in the cloud environment, we noticed that the existing access control models do not provide concepts to secure resources shared among users in collaborative sessions. Moreover, the problem becomes more complex when the shared resources reside in different tenants within the cloud environment. In our work, we propose an approach that ensures access control to the shared resources in a collaborative session in multi-tenants environments. We suggest CBAC, the Collaboration-based Access Control. CBAC consists of an extended version of the OrBAC model. CBAC defines new entities to support access control in collaborative sessions. The suggested model has been implemented within Swift component in the open source cloud-computing platform OpenStack. Currently, we are enforcing CBAC by adding new entities and trust relationships in order to support access control when the collaboration involves resources of multiples tenants.

Keywords: Cloud computing · Multi-tenancy · Trust · Collaborative session · Access control · OpenStack

Social Networks: For Increase More Interactions and Feedbacks

Mohcine Kodad[1], El Miloud Jaara[1], and Mohammed Erramdani[2]

[1] Research in Computer Science Laboratory (LARI), University Mohammed 1st (UMP), Oujda, 60000, Morocco
[2] High School of Technology (ESTO), University Mohammed 1st (UMP), Oujda, 60000, Morocco

Abstract. This paper tackles the social networks. It actually gives an analysis about the reliability of Facebook pages according to fans' feedback, to figure out Facebook users' needs and recognize their satisfactions according to their posts. In order to check this strategy we felt the need to create an online survey, which was conducted from November 17th, 2014 to November 21st, 2014 by Computer Science Research Laboratory (LARI) at the Mohammed first University-Oujda. The paper presents all results of this survey and also presents an experimentation that we have achieved, so as to know the most attractive types of posts by which we set a strategy to increase the feedback rate.

Keywords: Social networks · Increase of feedbacks · Facebook · Reach rate

Clustering Algorithm in Vehicular Networks

Bouchra Marzak[1], Hicham Toumi[1], Elhabib Benlahmar[2], and Mohamed Talea[1]

[1] Laboratory of Information Processing, University Hassan II, Cdt Driss El Harti, BP 7955 Sidi Othman Casablanca, 20702, Morocco
{marzak8bouchra, toumi.doc}@gmail.com
taleamohamed@yahoo.fr
[2] Information Technology and Modeling Laboratory, University Hassan II, Cdt Driss El Harti, BP 7955 Sidi Othman Casablanca, 20702, Morocco
h.benlahmer@gmail.com

Abstract. Vehicular networks have moved from simple curiosity to become today an interest both from the point of view of the automotive industry as networks and service operators. These networks are indeed an emerging class of wireless networks for the exchange of data between vehicles and between vehicles and infrastructure. VANETs will enhance driver safety and will enable the dissemination of traffic and road condition. VANETs suffer from high mobility, high node density and the hidden nodes problem. VANETs have a highlymobile environment with a rapidly changing network topology. In cluster-based routing, a virtual network infrastructure must be created through the clustering of nodes in order to provide scalability [1]. Cluster-based approaches have been applied in VANETs, because the clusters reduce the overhead, delay, and minimize collisions, providing load balance in large scale networks. Clusters are formed by a clustering algorithm. In a high mobility environment the clusters usually are unstable. Cluster stability is an important goal that clustering algorithms try to achieve and is considered as a measure of performance of a clustering algorithm. Cluster stability can be defined in different ways. In this paper, we propose a model which seeks to determine the value of stability of nodes from the average speed, density of the nodes, and the difference in distance parameters. The proposed model possesses a better cluster stability, where stability is defined by long cluster-head duration, long cluster member duration, and low rate of cluster-head change.

Keywords: VANET · Vehicular ad hoc networks · Clustering · Stability

Evaluation of Association Rules Extraction Algorithms

Ait-Mlouk Addi[2], Gharnati Fatima[1], and Agouti Tarik[2]

[1] Department of Physics, Faculty of Science Semlalia, Cadi Ayyad University
gharnati@uca.ma
[2] Department of Computer Science, Faculty of Science Semlalia, Cadi Ayyad University, Marrakech, Morocco
addi.aitmlouk@edu.uca.ma, t.agouti@uca.ma

Abstract. Association rules Extraction is a leading task, which attracted the attention of researchers, it generally spend two important steps, in the first is the extraction of frequent items, and the second is extracting association rules from this frequent items. This extraction is a difficult task, costly in terms of response time and memory space as the number of frequent items is exponential to the number of items in database. Many algorithms have been designed to answer these problems. Nevertheless, the high number of algorithms is itself an obstacle to the ability of expert choice. In this context we propose an approach to make a good choice of extraction algorithm based on multiple criteria analysis.

Keywords: Algorithms · Data mining · Knowledge discovery in database

Contents

Scal: A Benchmarking Suite for Concurrent Data Structures

Andreas Haas, Thomas Hütter, Christoph M. Kirsch(✉), Michael Lippautz, Mario Preishuber, and Ana Sokolova

University of Salzburg, Salzburg, Austria
{andreas.haas,thomas.hutter,ck,michael.lippautz, mario.preishuber,ana.sokolova}@cs.uni-salzburg.at

Abstract. Concurrent data structures such as concurrent queues, stacks, and pools are widely used for concurrent programming of shared-memory multiprocessor and multicore machines. The key challenge is to develop data structures that are not only fast on a given machine but whose performance scales, ideally linearly, with the number of threads, cores, and processors on even bigger machines. Part of that challenge is to provide a common ground for systematically evaluating the performance and scalability of new concurrent data structures and comparing the results with the performance and scalability of existing solutions. For this purpose, we have developed Scal which is an open-source benchmarking framework that provides (1) software infrastructure for executing concurrent data structure algorithms, (2) workloads for benchmarking their performance and scalability, and (3) implementations of a large set of concurrent data structures. We discuss the Scal infrastructure, workloads, and implementations, and encourage further use and development of Scal in the design and implementation of ever faster concurrent data structures.

1 Introduction

We describe Scal[1], an open-source benchmarking framework for evaluating performance and multicore scalability of concurrent data structures such as concurrent queues, stacks, and pools. With (multicore) scalability we mean that performance grows (ideally linearly) with the number of threads increasing.

Scal provides:

1. Infrastructural software for scalable memory allocation and computational load generation, as well as tagging for atomicity and operation logging. Here, by scalable memory allocation and computational load generation we mean constant overhead independent of the number of threads.
2. Workloads for benchmarking concurrent data structures such as, for example, producer-consumer scenarios.

[1] The Scal homepage is at http://scal.cs.uni-salzburg.at, the Scal code is publicly available at http://github.com/cksystemsgroup/scal.

A. Bouajjani and H. Fauconnier (Eds.): NETYS 2015, LNCS 9466, pp. 1–14, 2015.
DOI: 10.1007/978-3-319-26850-7_1

3. Concurrent data structure implementations, like (relaxed) queues, stacks, and pools, listed in Table 1.

Each pair of a workload and a concurrent data structure defines a *configuration*. Hence, Scal provides infrastructure and configurations, as shown in Fig. 1.

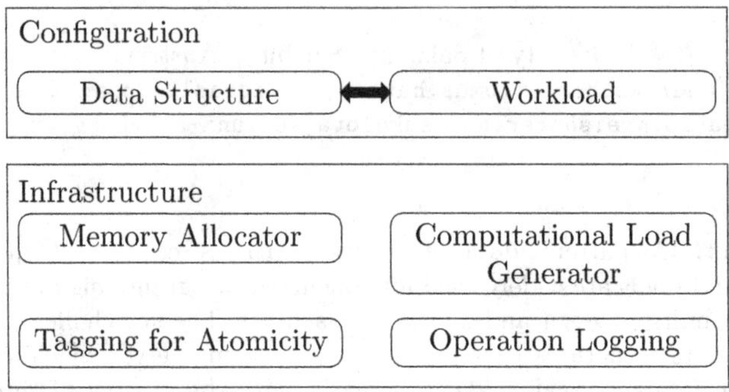

Fig. 1. Architecture of Scal

Scal requires an x86 machine and Posix threads. It has been successfully run on Intel and AMD machines with Linux Ubuntu 12.04 and 14.04. Porting Scal to other architectures and operating systems should be easily possible.

Scal reports temporal performance by measuring total execution time and calculating throughput. Time is measured (using standard OS primitives) from the moment that all threads are created and configured, until the moment that the last thread terminates. Creation and configuration is done sequentially by a single initialization thread. All other threads wait on a barrier after they have been created. As soon as the configuration is complete, the initialization thread records the (start) time and releases the barrier. The last thread that terminates records the (end) time again right before terminating. Total execution time is then reported as the difference between the end time and the start time. Throughput is the total execution time divided by the total number of data-structure operations performed by all threads. All Scal workloads determine (configure) the total number of operations to be performed, which enables throughput calculation. Obtaining meaningful temporal performance results requires disabling CPU frequency scaling (in addition to using scalable memory allocation and load generation).

The Scal benchmarking framework was originally designed for the evaluation of concurrent (relaxed) data structures [3,7–9,12,15,16]. Note that Scal not only contains our newly developed data structure algorithms, but also many other state-of-the-art concurrent data structure implementations (cf. Table 1). We are aware of two other recently developed benchmarking frameworks for a similar purpose. The sim-universal-construction framework has been designed to develop and evaluate wait-free algorithms [4]. It has also been used to evaluate

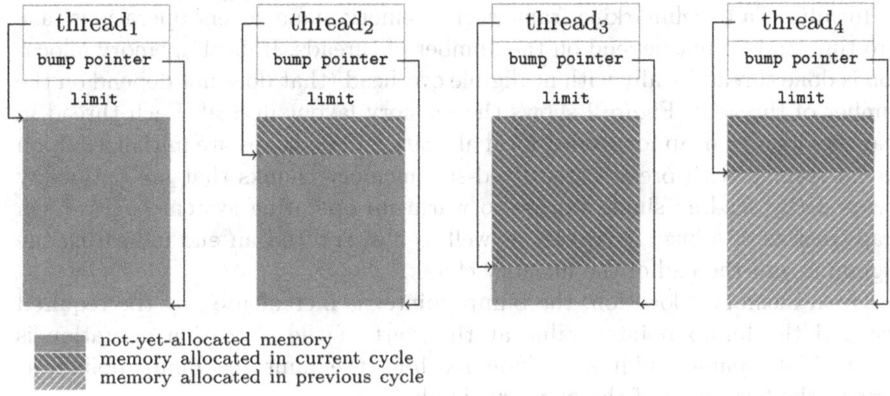

Fig. 2. Memory allocation in Scal

lock-free data structures [23]. The framework provides a subset of Scal's capabilities such as portable abstractions for atomic operations like `fetch-and-inc` or `compare-and-swap` (covered by tagging for atomicity in Scal) and implements lock-free queues such as the Michael-Scott queue [21]. However, there is no scalable memory allocation, computational load generation, and predefined workloads. The SynchroBench [5] framework has been designed with the same goals as Scal. It provides a broad spectrum of concurrent data structure implementations such as linked lists, skiplists, trees, and hash tables. SynchroBench uses transactional memory libraries and does not provide scalable memory allocation, which makes the framework less suitable for high-performance benchmarking. SynchroBench also does not provide predefined workloads.

2 Scal Infrastructure

Next we describe the Scal infrastructure, in particular memory allocation, computational load generation, tagging for atomicity, and operation logging.

All experiments reported here ran on a unified memory architecture (UMA) machine with four 10-core 2 GHz Intel Xeon E7-4850 processors supporting two hardware threads (hyperthreads) per core, 128 GB of main memory, and Linux kernel version 3.8.0. All measurements are averaged over ten runs and reported as arithmetic mean including the 95 % confidence interval (based on corrected sample standard deviation).

To this end, let us note that Scal is open-source and publicly available, and hence also open to improvement and extensions. New utilities may be developed as the demand grows.

2.1 Memory Allocator

The memory allocator of Scal is a special purpose concurrent allocator that performs cyclic allocation [24].

Ideally, in a benchmarking framework, memory management operations take zero time and do not depend on the number of threads. In Scal, memory allocation is done thread-locally with negligible overhead (that does not depend on the number of threads). Figure 2 shows the memory layout in Scal. Each thread in Scal gets its own heap for thread-local allocation. The heaps are initialized upon thread startup with preallocated fixed-size memory chunks that are optionally accessed (by reading single words) to warm up operating system pages. Each heap consists of a `bump pointer`, as well as a `start` and an `end` indicating the beginning and the end of the memory chunk.

Upon memory allocation, the bump pointer is incremented by the required size and the bump pointer value at the start of the allocation operation is returned as memory address[2]. Upon reaching the limit the bump pointer is reset to the beginning of the memory chunk.

Cyclic allocation is sound as long as no allocated and still live memory gets reallocated, i.e., the bump pointer returns addresses to dead memory. For any benchmark that terminates in finite time, there is a heap size such that cyclic allocation with that heap size is sound. In order to determine the heap size sufficient for sound cyclic allocation, Scal provides a configuration mode in which, instead of resetting the bump pointer (cyclic allocation), the heap expands by obtaining another memory chunk from the OS. This configuration mode is not scalable because of the overhead involved in obtaining memory chunks.

Cyclic allocation does not require explicit deallocation. Nevertheless, for saving memory, Scal provides a limited form of explicit deallocation: A free call (without arguments) rolls back the bump pointer to the value before the last allocation. Consecutive free calls without allocation in between have no effect. This form of explicit deallocation provides the benefit of keeping the size of the needed heap for sound cyclic allocation small, in particular with algorithms where many threads allocate memory within concurrent operations of which only one succeeds. The failing threads can then roll back, i.e., deallocate the most recently allocated memory.

In order to demonstrate the scalability of the allocator in Scal we designed a benchmark where each thread executes ten million allocation operations of the size required to accommodate a node of a Michael-Scott queue [21]. After each allocation operation, a computation is performed that simulates application activity and reduces the load on the allocator. Note that for many allocators, there is a computational load that renders them scalable. However, the smaller that load is, the more load can be put on the benchmarked concurrent data structure without introducing performance artifacts of the allocator. The computational load for which Scal's memory allocator is scalable is small. Figure 3a illustrates the scalability (constant overhead) of the allocator. We discuss computational load generation and the computational load used in Fig. 3a in the next section.

---

[2] This is standard bump pointer allocation.

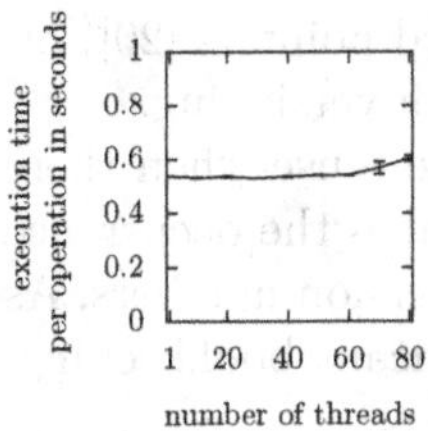

(a) Memory allocation: Scalability for an increasing number of threads

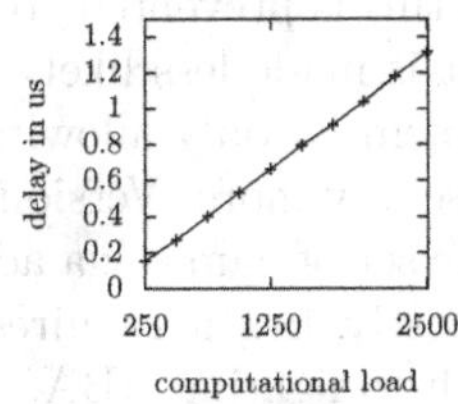

(b) Computational load: Delay for varying computational load

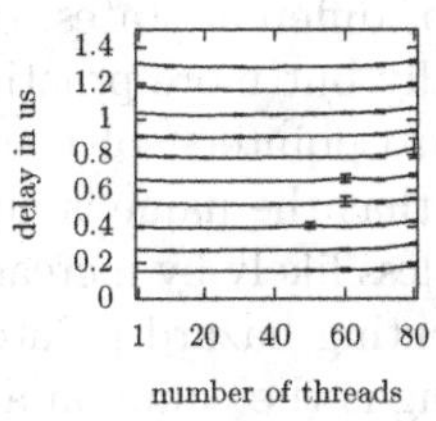

(c) Computational load: Scalability for an increasing number of threads

Fig. 3. Evaluation of Scal's infrastructure

2.2 Computational Load

Scal provides a primitive that simulates computational load resulting in a time delay. This enables exercising the concurrent data structures in different contention scenarios: In between any two data structure operations, the computational load imitates application behavior, i.e., a real computation. The higher the load, the lower the contention on the data structure.

The computational load primitive has a unit-less input that translates to a time delay that is close to linear in the input, as shown in Fig. 3b. Moreover, the linear relationship remains the same independent of the number of threads concurrently using the primitive as shown in Fig. 3c, even on hyper-threaded machines. In the figure we present many (pretty straight) curves, one for each data point of Fig. 3b. Each curve shows the time delay for a given unit-less input value of the computational load for an increasing number of threads. The linearity is demonstrated as the curves are close to equally distant for equally distant inputs. The scalability is demonstrated by the fact that each curve is close to a constant line.

Our computational load primitive uses the x86 CPU instruction (RDTSC) that reads the time stamp counter (TSC) from the corresponding register of the processor. The counter represents the number of cycles since the last processor reset. Note that TSC only relates linearly to actual time for a constant clock speed. This is one of the reasons for disabling CPU frequency scaling in Scal.

The computational load primitive implements a busy wait on the value of TSC obtained from RDTSC. Additionally, the processor is informed that it currently executes a busy wait, potentially reducing CPU resources needed to execute the code fragment, making the computational load primitive scalable for hyper-threaded machines.

2.3 Pointer Tagging

Concurrent programs may be subject to the ABA problem: Finitely many names (memory addresses) for an infinite state space which requires eventual reuse of names for different states. Ideally, this is prevented (by hazard pointers [20]) or, less ideally but more practically, it is made less likely through versioning.

Hazard pointers solve the problem by only allowing name reuse when there is proof that the name is not in use any more. Versioning makes the occurrence of ABA less likely by increasing the set of names via adding version numbers. As implementing hazard pointers is costly, i.e., it requires significant bookkeeping, versioning is the common approach to fighting ABA.

Most concurrent data-structure algorithms, in particular the lock-free ones, use versioning to address ABA [19]. To ease the programming of algorithms that require versioning, Scal provides a versioning utility, that we refer to as *pointer tagging*, as part of its infrastructure.

In particular, Scal provides 16-bit version tags for values with up to 48 bits, assembling value and tag in a single 64-bit word so that all standard atomic operations still work atomically on the pair of a value and a version tag. Note that this indeed enlarges the set of names, as current 64-bit operating systems limit address spaces to 48 bits.

Note that taking care of versioning by hand in concurrent algorithms is a common source of bugs. The pointer tagging of Scal relieves the programmer from such a burden, and the careful handling of version tags is implicitly done by Scal itself.

2.4 Operation Logging

In order to investigate the detailed behavior of a single run, and even individual operations, Scal provides the utility of *operation logging*.

For each concurrent data-structure operation, Scal provides functions for thread-locally logging the type of an operation, e.g., insert or remove, the invocation time, the response time, a linearization point. Some of these functions are added automatically as soon as operation logging is enabled, e.g., logging of invocation and response time. For others, the programmer can use the Scal functions to annotate the code of a concurrent algorithm, e.g., if linearization points are known within the code. Operation logging only incurs negligible overhead, since all data is stored in pre-allocated memory at runtime and only output into a file upon termination.

Operation logging allows to experimentally validate different metrics on concurrent executions. See [9] for definitions and experimental evaluation of such metrics. Last but not least, operation logging may be useful to the programmer (and has been useful to some of us) when debugging concurrent algorithms.

3 Scal Workloads

There are two generic configurable workloads in Scal, a classical producer-consumer workload, and a sequential alternating workload. We describe both below.

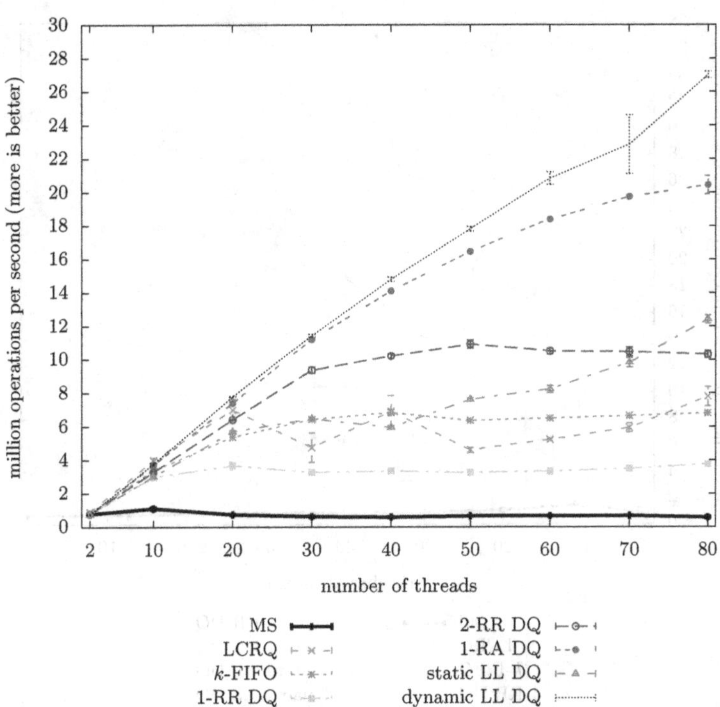

Fig. 4. Performance and scalability in a producer-consumer benchmark for a number of queue and queue-like data structures, for an increasing number of threads

3.1 Producer-Consumer

In the producer-consumer workload, as usual, some threads are producers and some consumers. Scal allows configuring the number of producers, consumers, the computational load, and the number of elements to be produced per producer thread. Each producer then inserts its produced elements into the concurrent data structure. Each consumer retrieves its fair share of elements (equal to the total number of elements produced divided by the number of consumers). Residual elements are discarded, i.e., they are left in the data structure. The configured computational load is executed in between any two operations performed. Additionally, the producer-consumer benchmark allows to insert a barrier between producing and consuming threads, for measuring either producing or consuming (or both) of elements separately.

Figure 4 shows the results of an exemplary scalability measurement of the producer-consumer benchmark for an increasing number of threads of which half are producers and half consumers, for a computational load of 1000, and 1 million elements inserted per producer thread.

In this benchmark, Scal reports the total number of performed operations divided by the total execution time. To this end, we note that changing Scal to

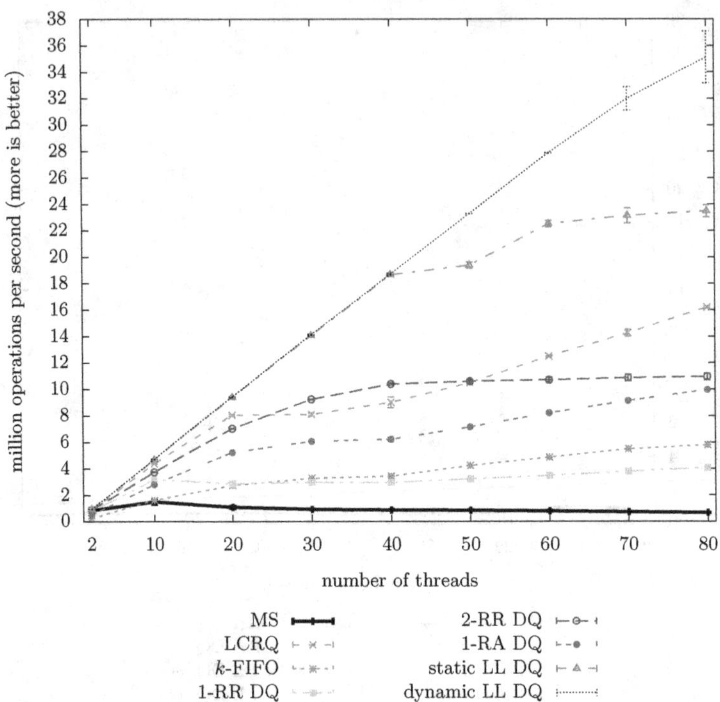

Fig. 5. Performance and scalability in a sequential alternating benchmark for a number of queue and queue-like data structures, for an increasing number of threads

report other data, e.g. (average) number of operations per thread per unit of time, is a matter of changing one line of code.

3.2 Sequential Alternating

The sequential alternating workload is designed so that each thread alternates between an insert operation and a remove operation.

For sequential alternating, similar to the producer-consumer workload, Scal allows configuring the number of threads, the computational load, and the number of operations (pairs of consecutive insert and remove operation) per thread. Additionally, the sequential alternating workload allows the data structure to be prefilled with a specified amount of elements. Such an option could easily be added to the producer-consumer benchmark as well, it was just never needed for our experimental purposes. The computational load is again computed in between any two operations.

Figure 5 shows the results of an exemplary scalability measurement of the sequential alternating benchmark for an increasing number of threads, computational load of 1000, and 1 million pairs of consecutive insert and remove operations per thread.

Table 1. Concurrent data structures in Scal

Name	Semantics	Year	Ref.
Lock-based Singly-linked List Queue	strict queue	1968	[17]
Michael Scott (MS) Queue	strict queue	1996	[21]
Flat Combining Queue	strict queue	2010	[10]
Wait-free Queue	strict queue	2012	[18]
Linked Cyclic Ring Queue (LCRQ)	strict queue	2013	[23]
Timestamped (TS) Queue	strict queue	2015	[3]
Cooperative TS Queue	strict queue	2015	[6]
Segment Queue	k-relaxed queue [1,12]	2010	[1]
Random Dequeue (RD) Queue	k-relaxed queue [1,12]	2010	[1]
Bounded Size k-FIFO Queue	k-relaxed queue [1,12], pool	2013	[15]
Unbounded Size k-FIFO Queue	k-relaxed queue [1,12], pool	2013	[15]
b-RR Distributed Queue (DQ)	k-relaxed queue [12], pool	2013	[8]
Least-Recently-Used (LRU) DQ	k-relaxed queue [12], pool	2013	[8]
Locally Linearizable DQ (static, dynamic)	locally linearizable queue [7], pool	2015	[7]
Locally Linearizable k-FIFO Queue	locally linearizable queue [7], k-relaxed queue [12], pool	2015	[7]
Relaxed TS Queue	quiescently consistent queue (conjectured)	2015	[6]
Lock-based Singly-linked List Stack	strict stack	1968	[17]
Treiber Stack	strict stack	1986	[26]
Elimination-backoff Stack	strict stack	2004	[11]
Timestamped (TS) Stack	strict stack	2015	[3]
k-Stack	k-relaxed stack [12]	2013	[12]
b-RR Distributed Stack (DS)	k-relaxed stack [12], pool	2013	[8]
Least-Recently-Used (LRU) DS	k-relaxed stack [12], pool	2013	[8]
Locally Linearizable DS (static, dynamic)	locally linearizable stack [7], pool	2015	[7]
Locally Linearizable k-Stack	locally linearizable stack [7], k-relaxed queue [12], pool	2015	[7]
Timestamped (TS) Deque	strict deque (conjectured)	2015	[6]
d-RA DQ and DS	strict pool	2013	[8]

4 Concurrent Data Structure Implementations in Scal

All Scal implementations of concurrent data structures are listed in Table 1. We distinguish between strict queues, relaxed queues, strict stacks, relaxed stacks, a strict deque (conjectured), and strict pools. By strict we mean data structures that are linearizable [14] with respect to a sequential specification of a queue, stack, deque, or pool, respectively. Strict concurrent data structures often lack performance and scalability [25] as they require significant synchronization [2]. A common trend in the design of concurrent data structures chooses to relax the semantics for gain in performance and scalability. The relaxations could affect the sequential specification [1,12,22] or the consistency condition [7,13]. Note that most data structures in Scal are lock free [13]. In the sequel, we discuss all implemented data structures in some detail. The table shows references for each data structure, which we omit in the text below.

4.1 Strict Queues

As baseline for queues, there is a standard lock-based implementation of a queue based on a singly-linked list. As lock-free baseline for queues, we have implemented the Michael-Scott queue. The flat combining queue is another well-known strict queue. The wait-free queue is a strict queue based on the Michael-Scott queue whose wait freedom is achieved by faster threads helping slower ones to complete their operations. The linked list cyclic ring queue is a fast lock-free queue that operates on very large cyclic buffers and uses fetch-and-add as basic synchronization primitive. The (cooperative) timestamped queue is a fast lock-free queue that uses timestamps to achieve queue order.

4.2 Relaxed Queues

There are several variants of relaxed queues in Scal:

- A number of k-relaxed queues that are linearizable with respect to the k-out-of-order relaxation of the sequential specification of a queue [12]. In a k-relaxed queue, one of the $k+1$-oldest elements is returned upon a dequeue operation.
- Several queues that are locally linearizable with respect to the sequential specification of a queue, and a relaxed queue that is conjectured to be quiescently consistent.

The segment queue and the random dequeue queue are k-relaxed but do not provide a linearizable emptiness check and hence are not linearizable pools. All other relaxed queues in Scal are linearizable pools.

The bounded and unbounded size k-FIFO queues are lock-free k-relaxed queues related to the segment queue. They implement a Michael-Scott queue of segments of size k.

The b-RR distributed queue and the least-recently-used distributed queue are members of the distributed queues (DQ) family. All data structures in the DQ family implement an array of Michael-Scott queues which are accessed using various load balancers. For these particular DQs, the load balancers enable proving a bound k for a k-relaxation.

The locally linearizable queues are variants of DQ and the k-FIFO queue. The locally linearizable DQ comes in two variants: with a static or dynamic array size (number of Michael-Scott queues). It is the load balancer(s) that make them locally linearizable. Finally, the relaxed TS queue is a relaxed timestamped queue that is conjectured to provide quiescent consistency.

4.3 Strict Stacks

As baseline for stacks, we have implemented a lock-based stack based on a singly linked list. As lock-free baseline for stacks, there is the Treiber stack. The elimination-backoff stack is a fast stack that utilizes the possibility of elimination, i.e., popping any element that is being concurrently pushed. The timestamped stack is a fast lock-free stack that uses timestamps to achieve stack order and also benefits from elimination.

4.4 Relaxed Stacks

Just like relaxed queues, also relaxed stacks come in two flavors:

- k-Relaxed stacks that relax the sequential specification to a k-out-of-order stack that allows for removing one of the $k+1$-youngest elements in the stack.
- Locally linearizable stacks.

All relaxed stacks in Scal are linearizable pools, in particular they provide linearizable emptiness checks.

The k-Stack is a typical k-relaxed stack implemented as a Treiber stack of segments of size k. The k-Stack has a linearizable emptiness check and is hence a linearizable pool. Just like for queues, there is a family of distributed stacks (DS) implemented as an array of Treiber stacks with different load balancers of which b-RR DS and least-recently-used DS are proven to be k-relaxed for a particular bound k depending on the parameters of the data structure.

Also here we have the same locally linearizable variants of stacks, namely the locally linearizable DQ with static and dynamic array size, and the locally linearizable k-Stack.

4.5 Strict Deque

The implementation of a strict deque in Scal is a timestamped implementation, combining the timestamped stack and timestamped queue. Proving the correctness (linearizability with respect to the data structure) was a highly nontrivial task for the timestamped stack, leading to a new theorem that provides sufficient conditions for stack linearizability. We conjecture that this combined deque implementation is linearizable with respect to a deque. The proof still remains to be done.

4.6 Strict Pools

All other variants of DQ and DS are very much relaxed queue-like or stack-like data structures, i.e., they can only be proven to be linearizable with respect to a pool. Currently *d*-RA DQ and DS are implemented in Scal. We have experimented with other implementations of pools as well. Their code is currently not part of Scal but will be added in the future.

5 Conclusions

We have presented Scal, an open-source benchmarking framework for evaluating the performance and scalability of concurrent data structures. Scal provides implementations of many concurrent data structures as well as the necessary infrastructure and relevant workloads for executing and benchmarking them. The framework has already enabled research that has lead to some of the concurrent data structures mentioned here. Scal is nevertheless only the starting point of a comprehensive benchmarking suite for concurrent data structures. The code is open source and may easily be extended with implementations of other concurrent data structures and enhanced with more infrastructure and workloads.

Acknowledgements. This work has been supported by a Google PhD Fellowship and the National Research Network RiSE on Rigorous Systems Engineering (Austrian Science Fund (FWF): S11404-N23 and S11411-N23).

References

1. Afek, Y., Korland, G., Yanovsky, E.: Quasi-linearizability: relaxed consistency for improved concurrency. In: Lu, C., Masuzawa, T., Mosbah, M. (eds.) OPODIS 2010. LNCS, vol. 6490, pp. 395–410. Springer, Heidelberg (2010)
2. Attiya, H., Guerraoui, R., Hendler, D., Kuznetsov, P., Michael, M.M., Vechev, M.: Laws of order: expensive synchronization in concurrent algorithms cannot be eliminated. In: Proceedings of Principles of Programming Languages (POPL), pp. 487–498. ACM (2011)
3. Dodds, M., Haas, A., Kirsch, C.M.: A scalable, correct time-stamped stack. In: Proceedings of Symposium on Principles of Programming Languages (POPL), pp. 233–246. ACM (2015)
4. Fatourou, P., Kallimanis, N.D.: A highly-efficient wait-free universal construction. In: Proceedings of Symposium on Parallelism in Algorithms and Architectures (SPAA), pp. 325–334. ACM (2011)
5. Gramoli, V.: More than you ever wanted to know about synchronization: synchrobench, measuring the impact of the synchronization on concurrent algorithms. In: Proceedings of Symposium on Principles and Practice of Parallel Programming (PPoPP), pp. 1–10. ACM (2015)
6. Haas, A.: Fast Concurrent Data Structures Through Timestamping. Ph.D. thesis, University of Salzburg, Salzburg, Austria (2015)

7. Haas, A., Henzinger, T.A., Holzer, A., Kirsch, C.M., Lippautz, M., Payer, H., Sezgin, A., Sokolova, A., Veith, H.: Local linearizability. CoRR, abs/1502.07118 (2015)
8. Haas, A., Henzinger, T.A., Kirsch, C.M., Lippautz, M., Payer, H., Sezgin, A., Sokolova, A.: Distributed queues in shared memory–multicore performance and scalability through quantitative relaxation. In: Proceedings of International Conference on Computing Frontiers (CF). ACM (2013)
9. Haas, A., Kirsch, C.M., Lippautz, M., Payer, H.: How FIFO is your concurrent FIFO queue? In: Proceedings of Workshop on Relaxing Synchronization for Multicore and Manycore Scalability (RACES), pp. 1–8. ACM (2012)
10. Hendler, D., Incze, I., Shavit, N., Tzafrir, M.: Flat combining and the synchronization-parallelism tradeoff. In: Proceedings of Symposium on Parallelism in Algorithms and Architectures (SPAA), pp. 355–364. ACM (2010)
11. Hendler, D., Shavit, N., Yerushalmi, L.: A scalable lock-free stack algorithm. In: Proceedings of Symposium on Parallelism in Algorithms and Architectures (SPAA), pp. 206–215. ACM (2004)
12. Henzinger, T.A., Kirsch, C.M., Payer, H., Sezgin, A., Sokolova, A.: Quantitative relaxation of concurrent data structures. In: Proceedings of Symposium on Principles of Programming Languages (POPL), pp. 317–328. ACM (2013)
13. Herlihy, M., Shavit, N.: The Art of Multiprocessor Programming. Morgan Kaufmann Publishers Inc., San Francisco (2008)
14. Herlihy, M., Wing, J.M.: Linearizability: a correctness condition for concurrent objects. ACM Trans. Program. Lang. Syst. **12**(3), 463–492 (1990)
15. Kirsch, C.M., Lippautz, M., Payer, H.: Fast and scalable, lock-free k-FIFO queues. In: Malyshkin, V. (ed.) PaCT 2013. LNCS, vol. 7979, pp. 208–223. Springer, Heidelberg (2013)
16. Kirsch, C.M., Payer, H., Röck, H., Sokolova, A.: Performance, scalability, and semantics of concurrent FIFO queues. In: Xiang, Y., Stojmenovic, I., Apduhan, B.O., Wang, G., Nakano, K., Zomaya, A. (eds.) ICA3PP 2012, Part I. LNCS, vol. 7439, pp. 273–287. Springer, Heidelberg (2012)
17. Knuth, D.E.: The Art of Computer Programming. Fundamental Algorithms, vol. 1, 3rd edn. Addison Wesley, Redwood City (1997)
18. Kogan, A., Petrank, E.: A methodology for creating fast wait-free data structures. In: Proceedings of Symposium on Principles and Practice of Parallel Programming (PPoPP), pp. 141–150. ACM (2012)
19. Michael, M.M.: ABA prevention using single-word instructions. Technical report RC 23089, IBM Research Center (2004)
20. Michael, M.M.: Hazard pointers: safe memory reclamation for lock-free objects. IEEE Trans. Parallel Distrib. Syst. **15**(6), 491–504 (2004)
21. Michael, M.M., Scott, M.L.: Simple, fast, and practical non-blocking and blocking concurrent queue algorithms. In: Proceedings of Symposium on Principles of Distributed Computing (PODC), pp. 267–275. ACM (1996)
22. Michael, M.M., Vechev, M.T., Saraswat, V.A.: Idempotent work stealing. In: Proceedings of Symposium on Principles and Practice of Parallel Programming (PPoPP), pp. 45–54. ACM (2009)
23. Morrison, A., Afek, Y.: Fast concurrent queues for x86 processors. In: Proceedings of Symposium on Principles and Practice of Parallel Programming (PPoPP), pp. 103–112. ACM (2013)

24. Nguyen, H.H., Rinard, M.: Detecting and eliminating memory leaks using cyclic memory allocation. In: Proceedings of International Symposium on Memory Management (ISMM), pp. 15–30. ACM (2007)
25. Shavit, N.: Data structures in the multicore age. Commun. ACM **54**(3), 76–84 (2011)
26. Treiber, R.K.: Systems programming: Coping with parallelism. Technical report RJ-5118, IBM Research Center (1986)

Verification of Buffered Dynamic Register Automata

Parosh Aziz Abdulla[1], Mohamed Faouzi Atig[1], Ahmet Kara[2], and Othmane Rezine[1](✉)

[1] Uppsala University, Uppsala, Sweden
{parosh,mohamed_faouzi.atig,othmane.rezine}@it.uu.se
[2] TU Dortmund University, Dortmund, Germany
ahmet.kara@cs.tu-dortmund.de

Abstract. We consider the verification problem for Communicating Register Automata (BDRA) which extend classical register automata by process creation. In this setting, each process is equipped with a mailbox (i.e., a channel) in which received messages can be stored. Moreover, each process has a finite number of registers in which IDs of other processes can be stored. A process can send messages to the mailbox of the processes whose IDs are stored in its registers and can send them the content of its registers. The state reachability problem asks whether a BDRA reaches a configuration where at least one process is in an error state. In this paper, we study the decidability of the reachability problem for different kind of channels and we provide a complete characterisation of the (un)decidable subclasses in this generalised setting.

Keywords: Formal verification · Distributed systems

1 Introduction

Register automata [14] were introduced as a reasonable extension of finite automata to deal with languages over infinite alphabets. The expressiveness and computational properties of different versions of this model are intensively studied (see e.g. [4,12,17–19]). A register automaton is a finite state automaton equipped with a finite number of registers in which symbols from an infinite domain can be stored for later comparison. There are many papers investigating the strong relationship between logics on structures over infinite alphabets and register automata [8,10,13,15].

In [5,6] register automata with process creation are proposed to describe the behavior of parallel processes. In this approach registers are used to store the IDs of other processes in the network. Every process can spawn new processes and communicate asynchronously with processes whose IDs are stored in its

Supported by the Uppsala Programming for Multicore Architectures Research Center (UPMARC) and the Programming Platform for Future Wireless Sensor Networks Project (PROFUN). The third author acknowledges the financial support by the German DFG under grant SCHW 678/4-2.

A. Bouajjani and H. Fauconnier (Eds.): NETYS 2015, LNCS 9466, pp. 15–31, 2015.
DOI: 10.1007/978-3-319-26850-7_2

registers through unbounded channels. This extended register automata model is used as an (implementation) model for ad-hoc networks [6] and dynamic message sequence charts [5].

In [3], we studied the *state reachability problem* for *Dynamic Register Automata* (DRA) which is basically the automata model in [5,6] adapted to rendezvous-based communication and equipped with a reset transition for deleting register contents. Given a DRA and an (error) state q_{err} the sate reachability problem asks whether the network induced by the DRA reaches a configuration where at least one process is in state q_{err}. The reachability problem for DRA is in general not decidable. Searching for decidable sub-classes and inspired by recent investigations on ad-hoc networks [1,7], we set several restrictions on the configuration graphs induced by DRA and considered *degenerative* DRA, i.e. DRA which are able to reset registers nondeterministically.

In this paper we consider *Buffered Dynamic Register Automata* (BDRA) which, compared to the model we studied in [3], is closer to the original model in [5,6] in terms of communication. Besides finitely many registers, a BDRA is equipped with an (un)bounded FIFO buffer. A process described by a BDRA can create new processes and send messages to the buffers of other processes whose IDs are stored in its registers. An exchanged message can contain a symbol from a finite alphabet along with a process ID (from one of the process registers for instance). Moreover, the process can read messages from its own buffer and store incoming IDs in its own registers. Thus, the number of processes involved in the network induced by a BDRA and the communication topology of the network are not fixed a priori but change dynamically during the run of the system. Note also, that message sending and message receiving occur asynchronously. Finally, processes may execute a disconnect action, which will detach them from the whole network. As a result of this action, the content of the process registers and the process buffer are deleted.

We investigate the decidability borders of the state reachability problem for both BDRA and *lossy* BDRA, a sub-class of BDRA in which any process in the network can non deterministically disconnect itself. We show first that, in terms of reachable states, every BDRA is equivalent to its lossy counterpart.

Note that in order to simulate rendezvous communication through buffered systems, acknowledgement messages from receiver to sender are needed. This requires the existence of communication cycles in the graph of the network, which in turn makes the state reachability problem undecidable. In fact, we show that the reachability problem for (lossy) BDRA is undecidable even in the case where only configurations of which the graph of the network contains at most one edge are allowed.

We consider therefor a new restriction on (lossy) BDRA that would diminish the power of the model coming from the buffer: bounding the process buffers. We show that the problem remains undecidable for this case, even if the buffer is set to contain at most one message. The undecidability result still holds when only acyclic configurations are allowed and even if we bound the simple paths of the communication graph.

Finally, we concentrate on *strongly bounded* BDRA with bounded buffers. A BDRA is called strongly bounded if the only configurations allowed are those in which the simple paths of the underlying undirected graph of the network is bounded by some constant. While the reachability problem for strongly bounded BDRA with bounded buffer is still undecidable, we get decidability when we consider lossy BDRA. The proof comes from a non-trivial instantiation of the well-structured transition system framework. It is worth mentioning here that, due to the channel semantics we considered in our model (non-lossy FIFO), messages with IDs can not be dropped. Therefor, there is no trivial reduction from strongly bounded lossy BDRA with bounded buffers to strongly bounded degenerative DRA considered in [3]. Furthermore, the definitions of the graph encoding of configurations and the well-quasi ordering needed in order to instantiate the framework of well-structured transition systems to show decidability for strongly bounded lossy BDRA with bounded buffer are different from the ones used to prove the decidability of strongly bounded degenerative DRA in [3] and more involved.

Related Work. For related work concerning register automata and wireless Ad-Hoc networks, we refer the reader to the related work section in [3]. In the following, we mainly compare our work with [3].

The main difference between the two works is the communication modality. In [3], the communication is done via rendezvous, while in our work, we consider asynchronous communication through the use of buffers. Both models are Turing powerful. Also, as it is not obvious how reset transitions can be simulated by disconnect transitions, there is no simple reduction of the reachability problem from one model to the other. Moreover, our model allows a more fine-grained analysis since we can reason about the acyclicity of the communication graph while the rendezvous communication requires the synchronisation of sender and receiver and consequently the creation of an implicit cycle in the communication graph.

We show that our general undecidability result and the undecidability result for BDRA with bounded buffer hold even in the case where the communication graph is acyclic and all its simple paths are bounded. Our undecidability proofs are more involved and complicated than in the case of DRA [3] due to the acyclicity restriction of the communication graph. We show also the decidability of the reachability problem for strongly bounded BDRA when the underlying undirected graphs of the network are acyclic. This case was not considered in [3]. Finally, the graph encoding used for the configurations and the well-quasi ordering for strongly bounded lossy BDRA are different and more involved than the ones used in the case of strongly bounded degenerative DRA in [3].

2 Preliminaries

Let A and B be two sets. We use $|A|$ to denote the cardinality of A ($|A| = \omega$ if A is infinite). Let $\mathbb{N}$ be the set of natural numbers. For a partial function $g : A \rightharpoonup B$ and $a \in A$, we write $g(a) = \bot$ if g is undefined on a. We use $\bot_A$ to denote the partial function which is undefined on all elements of A, i.e. $\bot_A(a) = \bot$ for all $a \in A$. Given a (partial) function $f : A \rightharpoonup B$, $a \in A$ and $b \in B$, we denote by

$f[a \leftarrow b]$ the function f' defined by $f'(a) = b$ and $f'(a') = f(a')$ for all $a' \in A$ with $a \neq a'$.

Let Σ be an alphabet. We denote by Σ^* (resp. Σ^+) the set of all finite words (resp. finite non-empty words) over Σ, and by ε the empty word. Let w be a word over Σ. The length of w is denoted by $|w|$; we assume that $|\varepsilon| = 0$. For every $j : 1 \leq j \leq |w|$, we use $w(j)$ to denote the jth letter of w. For every letter $a \in \Sigma$, we use $a \in w$ to denote that there is an index j such that $1 \leq j \leq |w|$ and $w(j) = a$. Let $A = \langle Q_A, q_A^0, \delta_A, F_A \rangle$ be a finite state automaton over the alphabet Σ, with Q_A being the set of *control states*, q_A^0 the *initial state*, $\delta_A \subseteq Q_A \times \Sigma \times Q_A$ the *transition relation*, and F_A the set of *accepting states*. We use $L(A)$ to denote the regular language accepted by A.

A *transducer* T over the alphabet Σ is a tuple $\langle Q_T, q_T^0, \delta_T, F_T \rangle$ where Q_T is the set of control states, q_T^0 is the initial state, $\delta_T \subseteq Q \times (\Sigma \cup \{\varepsilon\}) \times (\Sigma \cup \{\varepsilon\}) \times Q$ is the transition relation and F_T is the set of accepting states. A transducer T induces a binary relation $\mathtt{Rel}_T$ over Σ^* where two words $w_1, w_2 \in \Sigma^*$ are in relation $(w_1 \, \mathtt{Rel}_T \, w_2)$ if T outputs w_2 when accepting w_1. If $(w_1 \, \mathtt{Rel}_T \, w_2)$ we say that w_2 is a *transduction* of w_1 by T. Given a word $w \in \Sigma^*$, we use $T(w) := \{w' \in \Sigma^* | \, w \, \mathtt{Rel}_T \, w'\}$ to denote the set of all possible transductions of the word w by T. We define the transduction of a language $L \subseteq \Sigma^*$ as $T(L) := \{w' \in \Sigma^* | \, \exists w \in L, w \, \mathtt{Rel}_T \, w'\}$. By induction, we define the ith transduction of L as follows: $T^0(L) := L$ and $T^{i+1}(L) := T(T^i(L))$.

Given two finite state automaton A and B and a transducer T, all over the same alphabet Σ, the *transduction problem* TRANSD consists in checking whether there exits $i \in \mathbb{N}$ such that $T^i(L(A)) \cap L(B) \neq \varnothing$.

We define a *directed labeled graph* (or simply *graph*) G as a tuple $\langle V, L_v, L_e, l, E \rangle$ composed of a finite set of vertices V, a set of vertex labels L_v, a set of edge labels L_e, the vertex labeling function $l : V \to L_v$ and the set of labeled edges $E \subseteq V \times L_e \times V$. A *path* in G is a finite sequence of vertices $\pi = v_1 v_2 \ldots v_k$, $k \geq 1$, where, for every $i : 1 \leq i < k$, there is an $a \in L_e$ such that $\langle v_i, a, v_{i+1} \rangle \in E$. The path is a cycle if $v_1 = v_k$ and $k \geq 2$. The path π is *simple* if all vertices in π are distinct, i.e. $v_i \neq v_j$ for all $i, j : 1 \leq i < j \leq k$. We define $\mathtt{length}(\pi) := k - 1$. The largest k such that there is a simple path π in G with $\mathtt{length}(\pi) = k$ is called the *diameter* of G, and is denoted by $\varnothing(G)$.

We define a *transition system* T as a triple $\langle C, C_{init}, \longrightarrow \rangle$, where C is a set of *configurations*, $C_{init} \subseteq C$ is a set of *initial* configurations, and $\longrightarrow \subseteq C \times C$ is a *transition relation*. We write $c_1 \longrightarrow c_2$ if $\langle c_1, c_2 \rangle \in \longrightarrow$ and $\longrightarrow^*$ to denote the reflexive transitive closure of $\longrightarrow$. A configuration $c \in C$ is *reachable* in T if there is some $c_{init} \in C_{init}$ such that $c_{init} \longrightarrow^* c$.

3 Buffered Dynamic Register Automata

A network induced by a *Buffered Dynamic Register Automaton* (BDRA or buffered DRA) consists of a set of processes. Each process has a unique ID and is modelled as a finite-state system equipped with a mailbox and a finite number of registers. The mailbox is the recipient of all messages addressed to that process. In this paper, we assume that the mailbox is described by a (bounded) perfect FIFO buffer. The finitely many registers of a process are used to store the IDs of other processes in the network. A process is allowed to send a message (together with a possible content of one of its registers) to the mailbox of another process only if the ID of the receiver is stored in one of its registers. A process can receive a message from its mailbox and store a received ID in one of its registers. Finally, a process can also create (or spawn) a new process, allowing the number of processes in the network to increase over time.

In the following, we describe the syntax and semantics of BDRA. We introduce its subclass of *Lossy* BDRA where any process can be disconnected from the network in a non-deterministic way. Finally, we define the state reachability problem

Syntax. A BDRA D is a tuple $\langle Q, q_0, M, X, \delta\rangle$ where Q is a finite set of control states, $q_0 \in Q$ is the initial state, M is a finite set of messages, $X = \{x_1, \ldots, x_n\}$ is a finite set of registers, and δ is a set of transitions, each of the form $\langle q_1, \texttt{action}, q_2\rangle$ where $q_1, q_2 \in Q$ are control states and $\texttt{action}$ is of one of the following forms:

(i) τ which corresponds to a local action,
(ii) $x \leftarrow\!\!\dashv \texttt{create}(q)$ where $x \in X$ and $q \in Q$, which creates a new process with a fresh ID in state q, and stores this fresh ID in the register x of the creating process,
(iii) $m(v)\,!\,y$ where $m \in M$, $v \in X \cup \{\perp, \texttt{self}\}$, and $y \in X$. This transition sends the message m together with the value pointed by v to the mailbox of the process whose ID is stored in register y. Observe that the value pointed by v is either the content of register v if $v \in X$ and v is assigned to a process ID, the ID of the sending process if $v = \texttt{self}$ or the null value otherwise. This transition can not be performed if the register y is undefined (i.e. containing the value $\perp$).
(iv) $m?x$ where $m \in M$ and $x \in X$, receives a message of the form $m(id)$ and stores id in its register x if id is a process ID or deletes the content of x otherwise.
(v) $\texttt{disconnect}$ which disconnects the process from the network by disabling any possible future communication with any other process. This is done by (1) reseting (to $\perp$) all registers belonging to the disconnecting process or containing its ID, (2) emptying the buffer of the process, and (3) resetting the ID field in all the messages containing the ID of the process to undefined.

A BDRA D is said to be *lossy* if for every state $q \in Q$ the transition $\langle q, \texttt{disconnect}\,\langle x\rangle\,, q\rangle$ is contained in δ (i.e. any process can be disconnected from the network at any time). Given a BDRA $D = \langle Q, q_0, M, X, \delta\rangle$, we define its lossy counterpart $\texttt{Lossy}\,(D)$ as the tuple $\langle Q, q_0, M, X, \delta'\rangle$ with $\delta' = \delta \cup \{\langle q, \texttt{disconnect}, q\rangle \mid q \in Q\}$.

Configuration. We use $\mathcal{P}$ to denote the domain of all possible process IDs. In the following, we sometimes refer to a process by its ID. We define a configuration

c of a BDRA $D = \langle Q, q_0, M, X, \delta \rangle$ as a tuple $\langle \texttt{procs}, \texttt{s}, \texttt{r}, \texttt{ch} \rangle$, where $\texttt{procs} \subseteq \mathcal{P}$ is a finite set of processes, $\texttt{s} : \mathcal{P} \rightharpoonup Q$ is a partial function that associates each process $p \in \texttt{procs}$ with its current state, $\texttt{r} : \mathcal{P} \rightharpoonup \{X \rightharpoonup \texttt{procs}\}$ is a partial function that maps every process $p \in \texttt{procs}$ to its register contents and $\texttt{ch} : \mathcal{P} \rightharpoonup (M \times (\mathcal{P} \cup \{\bot\}))^*$ maps each process $p \in \texttt{procs}$ to the content of its channel. We use $\texttt{msg}\,(m\,(id)) = m$ (respectively $\texttt{Id}\,(m\,(id)) = id$) to denote the message part (respectively the ID part) of a message tuple $m\,(id)$. For two processes $p_1, p_2 \in \texttt{procs}$ and $x \in X$, $\texttt{r}\,(p_1)\,(x) = p_2$ means that register x of p_1 contains the ID of p_2. If $\texttt{r}\,(p_1)\,(x)$ is not defined then register x of p_1 is empty. We use $q \in c$ to denote that there is a process $p \in \texttt{procs}$ such that $\texttt{s}\,(p) = q$. The set of all possible configurations of D is denoted by $C(D)$. A configuration $c = \langle \texttt{procs}, \texttt{s}, \texttt{r}, \texttt{ch} \rangle \in C(D)$ is said to be *initial* if it contains exactly one process (i.e., $\texttt{procs} = \{p\}$ for some $p \in \mathcal{P}$) in the initial state ($\texttt{s}\,(p) = q_0$), whose registers are empty ($\texttt{r}\,(p)\,(x) = \bot, \forall x \in X$) and whose mailbox is empty ($\texttt{ch}\,(p) = \varepsilon$). The set of initial configurations is denoted by $C_{init}(D)$.

Graph Representation. Let $c = \langle \texttt{procs}, \texttt{s}, \texttt{r}, \texttt{ch} \rangle$ be a configuration. We propose a graph encoding for c in order to show the communication possibilities between processes. In this encoding, every process is represented by a vertex labeled with its state. Moreover, if register $x \in X$ of a process p_1 contains the ID of another process p_2, then there is an edge from the vertex representing p_1 to the vertex representing p_2 and the edge is labeled with x. Furthermore, we add edges that represent the potential connectivity between processes that comes from the message-ID tuples contained in the process mailboxes, and we label them with the symbol $-$. Formally, the *encoding* of the configuration c is defined as the graph $\texttt{enc}\,(c) := \langle \texttt{procs}, Q, X \cup \{-\}, \texttt{s}, E \rangle$ with $E = \{\langle p, x, p' \rangle | \; \texttt{r}\,(p)\,(x) = p' \neq \bot\} \cup \{\langle p, -, p' \rangle | \; m(p') \in \texttt{ch}\,(p) \text{ and } p' \neq \bot\}$.

Operational Semantics. We define a transition relation $\longrightarrow_D$ on the set of configurations $C\,(D)$ of D. Let $c = \langle \texttt{procs}, \texttt{s}, \texttt{r}, \texttt{ch} \rangle, c' = \langle \texttt{procs}', \texttt{s}', \texttt{r}', \texttt{ch}' \rangle \in C\,(D)$ be two configurations. We have $c \longrightarrow_D c'$ if one of the following conditions holds:

`Local`: There is a transition $\langle q_1, \tau, q_2 \rangle \in \delta$ and a process $p \in \texttt{procs}$ such that (i) $\texttt{s}\,(p) = q_1$, (ii) $\texttt{s}' = \texttt{s}[p \leftarrow q_2]$, and (iii) $\texttt{procs}' = \texttt{procs}$, $\texttt{r}' = \texttt{r}$ and $\texttt{ch}' = \texttt{ch}$, i.e. processes, registers and mailboxes are left unchanged. A local transition changes the state of at most one process.

`Process Creation`: There is a transition $\langle q_1, x \leftarrow \texttt{create}(q), q_2 \rangle \in \delta$ and a process $p \in \texttt{procs}$ such that: (i) $\texttt{s}\,(p) = q_1$, (ii) $\texttt{procs}' = \texttt{procs} \cup \{p'\}$ for some process $p' \notin \texttt{procs}$, i.e. a new process p' is created, (iii) $\texttt{s}' = \texttt{s}[p \leftarrow q_2][p' \leftarrow q]$, i.e. process p' is spawned in state q, while the new state of process p is q_2, (iv) $\texttt{r}' = \texttt{r}[p \leftarrow \texttt{r}(p)[x \leftarrow p']]$, i.e. register x of process p is assigned the ID of the new process p', and (v) $\texttt{ch}'[p' \leftarrow \varepsilon]$, i.e. the new process p' gets an empty buffer.

`Message Sending`: There are two distinct processes $p, p' \in \texttt{procs}$ and a transition $\langle q_1, m(v)\,!\,y, q_2 \rangle \in \delta$ such that: (i) $\texttt{s}\,(p) = q_1$ and $\texttt{s}' = \texttt{s}[p \leftarrow q_2]$, (ii) $\texttt{r}\,(p)\,(y) = p'$, i.e. register y of p contains the ID of p', (iii) $\texttt{procs}' = \texttt{procs}$

and $\mathtt{r}' = \mathtt{r}$, and (iv) $\mathtt{ch}' = \mathtt{ch}[p' \leftarrow \mathtt{ch}(p') \cdot m(id)]$, where $id = \mathtt{r}(p)(v)$ if $v \in X$, $id = p$ if $v = \mathtt{self}$ and $id = \perp$ otherwise. Observe that this transition can not be performed when y is undefined since there is no process $p' \in \mathtt{procs}$ such that $\mathtt{r}(p)(y) = p'$.

`Message Receiving`: There is a process $p \in \mathtt{procs}$ and a transition $\langle q_1, m?x, q_2\rangle \in \delta$ such that: (i) $\mathtt{s}(p) = q_1$ and $\mathtt{s}' = \mathtt{s}[p \leftarrow q_2]$, (ii) $\mathtt{ch} = \mathtt{ch}'[p \leftarrow m(id) \cdot \mathtt{ch}'(p)]$, i.e. channel $\mathtt{ch}(p)$ of process p in configuration c contains a message of the form $m(id)$ that will be read, (iii) $\mathtt{r}' = \mathtt{r}[p \leftarrow \mathtt{r}(p)[x \leftarrow id]]$, and (iv) $\mathtt{procs}' = \mathtt{procs}$.
Note that id can be empty ($id = \perp$) or contain the ID of another process $p'' \in \mathtt{procs}$.

`Process Disconnection`: There is a transition $\langle q_1, \mathtt{disconnect}, q_2\rangle \in \delta$ and a process $p \in \mathtt{procs}$ such that: (i) $\mathtt{s}(p) = q_1$ and $\mathtt{s}' = \mathtt{s}[p \leftarrow q_2]$, (ii) $\mathtt{procs}' = \mathtt{procs}$, (iii) $\mathtt{r}'(p) = \perp_X$ i.e. all registers of process p are reset, (iv) for every other process $p' \in \mathtt{procs}$ we have, for every register $x \in X$, either $\mathtt{r}(p')(x) \neq p$ and the value of the register is preserved ($\mathtt{r}'(p')(x) = \mathtt{r}(p')(x)$), or $\mathtt{r}'(p')(x) = p$ and the register is reset ($\mathtt{r}'(p')(x) = \perp$), (v) $\mathtt{ch}'(p) = \varepsilon$, i.e. the channel of process p is emptied, and (vi) for every other process $p' \in \mathtt{procs}$, every message of the form $m(p)$ in $\mathtt{ch}(p')$ is replaced by $m(\perp)$.

For $c, c' \in C(D)$, we use $c \xrightarrow{\mathtt{action}} c'$ to denote that c' can be obtained from c by the execution of a transition $\langle q_1, \mathtt{action}, q_2\rangle \in \delta_D$.

State Reachability. We use $\mathcal{T}(D)$ to denote the transition system defined by the triple $\langle C(D), C_{init}(D), \longrightarrow_D\rangle$. We say that a state $\mathtt{target} \in Q$ is reachable in $\mathcal{T}(D)$ if there exists a reachable configuration $c = \langle \mathtt{procs}, \mathtt{s}, \mathtt{r}, \mathtt{ch}\rangle$ with $p \in \mathtt{procs}$ and $\mathtt{s}(p) = \mathtt{target}$. The problem of checking whether the state $\mathtt{target}$ is reachable or not is the *state reachability problem*. We use $\mathtt{Reach}(D, \mathtt{target})$ to denote the state reachability of $\mathtt{target}$ in D.

Any lossy BDRA is an over-approximation of its non-lossy counterparts in terms of reachable states. Lemma 1 states that this approximation is exact.

Lemma 1. *Let D be a* BDRA*. Then, D and $\mathtt{Lossy}(D)$ reach the same set of control states.*

The idea of the proof is that a buffered BDRA D can simulate any run of its lossy counterpart $\mathtt{Lossy}(D)$ by ignoring any of its disconnecting processes. More precisely, the simulation is done by letting the network of D follow each step of the run of the $\mathtt{Lossy}(D)$ besides the process disconnecting transitions that are not present in D.

4 BDRA State Reachability is Undecidable

We give in this section a proof to the following theorem:

Theorem 1. *Given a (lossy)* BDRA $D = \langle Q, q_0, M, X, \delta\rangle$ *and a control state $\mathtt{target} \in Q$, the problem $\mathtt{Reach}(D, \mathtt{target})$ is undecidable.*

Observe that the reduction used in this proof generates configurations of which graph encodings contain at most one edge.

Proof Sketch. The proof is carried out by a reduction from the TRANSD problem introduced in Sect. 2 which has been proven to be undecidable in [1]. Given two finite state automata A and B and a transducer T, we first define a BDRA D that we use in order to build a *transduction chain*. A transduction chain is a chain of processes $p_0, p_1, \ldots, p_m$, $m \geq 1$, where the first process p_0 simulates automaton A, the last process p_m simulates automaton B and all processes in between (i.e. $p_2, \ldots, p_{m-1}$) simulate transducer T. Note that the length of the chain should be as big as desired. We show in the rest of this section how to reduce TRANSD problem to $\texttt{Reach}(D, \texttt{target})$ for some control state $\texttt{target}$ that we will define. Note that the graph representations of the configurations generated by D contain no cycles and that their simple paths are bounded by 1 (Fig. 1 shows the configurations used during the simulation).

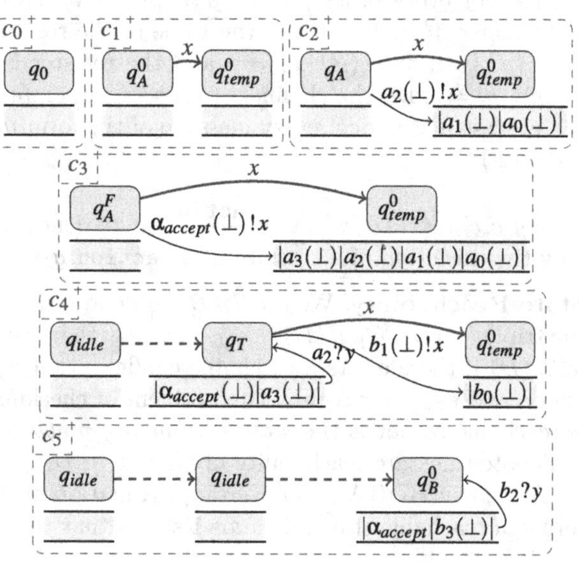

Fig. 1. TRANSD encoding into BDRA.

Reduction. Let $A = \langle Q_A, q_A^0, \delta_A, F_A \rangle$ and $B = \langle Q_B, q_B^0, \delta_B, F_B \rangle$ be two finite state automaton and $T = \langle Q_T, q_T^0, \delta_T, F_T \rangle$ be a transducer, all over the same alphabet Σ. We construct the BDRA $D = \langle Q, q_0, M, X, \delta \rangle$ as follows. Process p_0 of the initial configuration (c_0 in Fig. 1) is in the initial state q_0. Process p_0 starts the simulation by creating a new process p_1 and moves to a state q_A^0. The new process p_1 is spawned in state q_{temp}^0 and its ID is saved into register x of p_0 (c_1 in Fig. 1). Simulation of automaton A by process p_0 can now start: p_0 sends all letters generated by the traversal of automaton A to the channel of the created process p_1 (c_2 in Fig. 1). If p_0 reaches an accepting state of A, it chooses non-deterministically to either send an accepting symbol to p_1 or to keep traversing A. If p_0 decides to send the accepting symbol, then it stops traversing A and disconnects itself from the rest of the network (c_3 and then c_4 in Fig. 1). In state q_{temp}^0, the spawned process p_1 makes the non-deterministic choice of either simulating automaton B or simulating transducer T. It does so by moving either to state q_B^0 or to state q_T^0. If it moves to state q_B^0 (c_5 in Fig. 1), it will simulate automaton B by reading from its channel the word sent by p_0 and simultaneously traversing automaton B. When reading the acceptance symbol, process p_1 checks if it reached an accepting state of B. If it is the case, the process moves to state `target`. If not, it moves to an error state q_{error}. If instead process p_1 made the initial choice of simulating transducer T (c_4 in Fig. 1), then it creates a new process p_2 and moves to state q_T^0. From state q_T^0, process p_1 will simulate transducer T by reading the input letters from its channel, traversing T and sending the output letters to the channel of the next process, here p_2. When reading the acceptance symbol from its channel, process p_1 checks if it reached an accepting state in T. If it is the case, it sends the acceptance symbol to the next process p_2, stops simulating T and disconnects itself from the rest of the network. If not, it moves to an error state q_{error}. The newly created process p_2 is spawned in state q_{temp}^0 from which, again, the choice between simulating B or T will be non-deterministically made.

5 Bounded Buffer BDRA

We saw in the previous section that the undecidability result holds for configurations of which the graph encodings contain at most one single edge. This means that bounding the simple paths in the graph representation of the configurations or not allowing cycles will not bring decidability to the reachability problem. We consider therefor a rather different direction: bounding the channels, i.e. we only consider runs of the BDRA where the communication buffers are under a certain bound $l \in \mathbb{N}$. In the following, we first formally define the state reachability problem with this new restriction. Then we show that the problem is still undecidable even if buffers are bounded by 1.

Bounded Buffer State Reachability. Let $l \geq 1$, D be a BDRA and $\mathcal{T}(D) = \langle C(D), C_{init}(D), \longrightarrow_D \rangle$ be its corresponding transition system. We define the l-*bounded buffer* transition system associated with D as the tuple $\mathcal{T}^{\mathtt{buf}\leq l}(D) = \left\langle C^{\mathtt{buf}\leq l}(D), C_{init}^{\mathtt{buf}\leq l}(D), \xrightarrow{\mathtt{buf}\leq l}_D \right\rangle$ where (i) $C^{\mathtt{buf}\leq l}(D) \subseteq C(D)$ is the set of all possible configurations $c = \langle \mathtt{procs}, \mathtt{s}, \mathtt{r}, \mathtt{ch} \rangle$ of which channels are bounded by l (i.e. $|\mathtt{ch}(p)| \leq l$ for every $p \in \mathtt{procs}$), (ii) $C_{init}^{\mathtt{buf}\leq l}(D) = C_{init}(D)$ is the set of initial configurations, and finally (iii) $\xrightarrow{\mathtt{buf}\leq l}_D \subseteq \longrightarrow_D \cap \left(C^{\mathtt{buf}\leq l}(D) \times C^{\mathtt{buf}\leq l}(D)\right)$ is the transition relation. We say that a state `target` $\in Q$ is reachable in $\mathcal{T}^{\mathtt{buf}\leq l}(D)$ if there is a reachable configuration $c = \langle \mathtt{procs}, \mathtt{s}, \mathtt{r}, \mathtt{ch} \rangle$ in $\mathcal{T}^{\mathtt{buf}\leq l}(D)$ and a process $p \in \mathtt{procs}$ with $\mathtt{s}(p) = \mathtt{target}$. Checking whether `target` is reachable or not in $\mathcal{T}^{\mathtt{buf}\leq l}(D)$ is the l-*bounded buffer state reachability* problem that we denote hereafter by $\mathtt{BufReach}(D, \mathtt{target}, l)$.

Theorem 2. *Given a* BDRA D *and a state* $\mathtt{target} \in Q$, *the* 1-*bounded buffer state reachability problem* $\mathtt{BufReach}(D, \mathtt{target}, 1)$ *is undecidable.*

This result holds even if we forbid cycles and if we impose a bound on the length of the simple paths in the graph encoding of the configurations.

Proof sketch. The proof is carried out by a reduction from the TRANSD problem. More precisely, given two finite state automata A and B and a transducer T, we define a 1-bounded buffer BDRA D that we use in order to build a transduction chain $p_0, p_1, \ldots, p_m$ of arbitrary length $m + 1$. Since we dispose of channels of bounded size, we cannot transmit a word in one chunk and then transmit its transduction. Instead, we adopt a *continuous* communication flow, i.e. words are transmitted symbol by symbol and the transduction operates at the level of a symbol. One simple way to build the transduction chain consists in letting process p_0 of the initial configuration create a new process p_1, then letting p_1 create the next process p_2, and so on until some process p_m decides non deterministically to stop the chain construction. We obtain then a chain of length $m+1$. Although this approach fulfils our goal of building a transduction chain, configurations corresponding to these chains do not have a bound on the simple paths of their graph encoding. We consider therefor a more intricate chain building method that generates configurations for which the simple paths of their graph encoding is bounded (by two). The shape of the generated chain is shown in Fig. 2. Building such a transduction chain represents the first part of the proof.

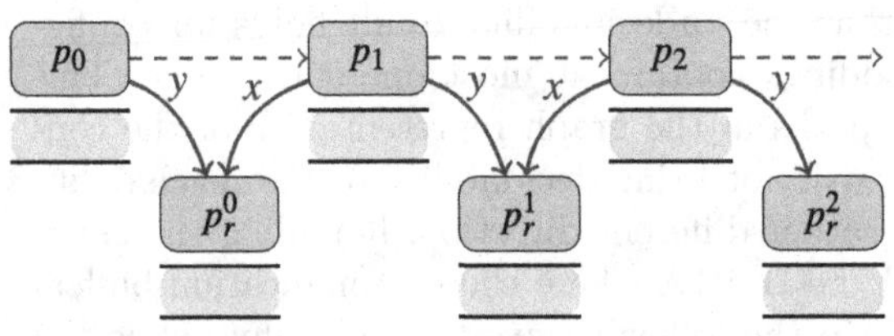

Fig. 2. Transduction chain $(p_0, p_1, p_2, \ldots)$.

The second part of the proof consists in showing how the communication is carried through the chain. The idea here is to let processes p_r^i, $0 \leq i \leq m$, play the role of *relays* between each pair of consecutive processes (p_i, p_{i+1}) of the chain. They do so by by making use of the *boundedness of the buffer* and ensuring that messages they receive from p_i and p_{i+1} match.

6 Strongly Bounded BDRA with Bounded Buffer

Attempts to get decidability for the state reachability problem by bounding the size of the channels or by bounding the simple paths of the graph encoding of the configurations were vain. We consider therefor another direction, which consists, together with bounding the channels, in bounding the simple paths of the *underlying* undirected graph of the encoding of the configurations. By underlying undirected graph, we mean the undirected graph that we obtain after removing the direction and the labels from the edges. Formally, we define an undirected graph as a tuple $\langle V, L_v, l, E\rangle$, where V is a finite set of vertices, L_v is a set of vertex labels, $l : V \mapsto L_v$ is a vertex labeling function and $E \subseteq \{\{v, u\}|\ v, u \in V\}$ is a set of edges. Let $G = \langle V, L_v, L_e, l, E\rangle$ be a labeled directed graph. We use $\texttt{closure}(G) := \langle V, L_v, l, F\rangle$ to denote its underlying undirected graph with $F := \{\{u, v\}|\ \langle u, e, v\rangle \in E\}$. We extend in a straightforward manner the definition of diameter to undirected graphs.

In the following, we first define the transition system where only configurations that are bounded in their buffer size and in their undirected graph are allowed. Then, we give the undecidability result for this subclass.

Strongly Bounded State Reachability with Bounded Buffer. Let $k \geq 1$ and $l \geq 1$, $D = \langle Q_b, q_b^0, \delta_b, F_b \rangle$ *eaBDRAandD* $\mathcal{T}(D) = \langle C, (D), C_{init}(D), \rightarrow_D$ its corresponding transition system. We define the *l-bounded buffer, k-strongly bounded* (l, k-strong) transition system associated to D as the tuple $\mathcal{T}^{(l,k)}(D) = \left\langle C^{(l,k)}(D), C_{init}^{(l,k)}(D), \longrightarrow_D^{(l,k)} \right\rangle$ composed of the set of (l,k)-strong configurations $C^{(l,k)}(D) := C^{\text{buf} \leq l}(D) \cap \{c \in C(D) | \varnothing(\texttt{closure}(\texttt{enc}(c))) \leq k\}$, the set of initial configurations $C_{init}^{(l,k)}(D) := C_{init}(D)$ and the transition relation $\longrightarrow_D^{(l,k)} := \longrightarrow_D \cap \left(C^{(l,k)}(D) \times C^{(l,k)}(D)\right)$. Given a control state $\texttt{target} \in Q_D$, checking whether there is a reachable configuration $c = \langle \texttt{procs}, \texttt{s}, \texttt{r}, \texttt{ch} \rangle$ in the transition system $\mathcal{T}^{(l,k)}(D)$ such that there is a process $p \in \texttt{procs}$ with $\texttt{s}(p) = \texttt{target}$ is the (l,k)-strong state reachability problem and is denoted by $\texttt{StrongReach}(D, \texttt{target}, k, l)$.

Theorem 3. *Given $l \geq 1$, $k \geq 4$, a* BDRA $D = \langle Q_D, q_D^0, \delta_D, F_D \rangle$ *and a control state* $\texttt{target} \in Q_D$, $\texttt{StrongReach}(D, \texttt{target}, l, k)$ *is undecidable.*

Proof Idea. The proof proceeds by a reduction from *Minsky's two counter machines* to the $(1,4)$-strong state reachability problem. A counter is simulated by a process to which a set of processes are attached. The value of the counter is defined by the number of such processes. In order to test if a counter is equal to zero, we make use of the fact that configurations are strongly bounded, i.e. transition to a configuration for which a simple path is over the bound is forbidden.

7 Lossy Strongly Bounded BDRA with Bounded Buffer

In this section, we show that the bounded buffer, strongly bounded state reachability problem becomes decidable if we consider lossy BDRA. To that purpose, we start by providing a more precise graph encoding of configurations where mailboxes are bounded by some $l \in \mathbb{N}$. Then, we state our result and dedicate the rest of this section to prove it.

Graph Representations for Bounded Buffered Configurations. Let $l \geq 1$ be natural number and $c = \langle \texttt{procs}, \texttt{s}, \texttt{r}, \texttt{ch} \rangle$ be a configuration with l-bounded buffers, i.e. $|\texttt{ch}(p)| \leq l$ for every process $p \in \texttt{procs}$. We propose a new graph encoding $\texttt{extenc}(c)$ of configuration c in the form of an extension of the previous encoding $\texttt{enc}(p)$. The new encoding takes into account the presence (and absence) of every message contained in the mailboxes. Besides representing processes as vertices and register contents as edges, we encode mailboxes as follows. Let $p \in \texttt{procs}$ be a process. Each message $m(id) \in \texttt{ch}(p)$ of index j, $1 \leq j \leq |\texttt{ch}(p)| \leq l$, is encoded with (i) a vertex v_p^j labeled with (m, j), (ii) an edge going from the vertex representing p to v_p^j and (iii) an edge going from v_p^j to the vertex representing process p', if $id = p' \neq \perp$. Furthermore, we encode every empty message place holder of index j, $|\texttt{ch}(p)| < j \leq l$ with

(i) a vertex v_p^j labeled by (ε, j) and (ii) an edge going from the vertex representing p to v_p^j. Formally, the extended encoding is defined by $\texttt{extenc}(c) := \langle \texttt{procs} \cup \{v_p^j | \, p \in \texttt{procs}, 1 \leq j \leq l\}, Q \cup \{(m, j) | \, m \in (M \cup \{\varepsilon\}), 1 \leq j \leq l\}, X \cup \{-\}, L_c, E_c\rangle$ where the vertex labeling function is given by, $L_c(p) = \texttt{s}(p)$ for every process $p \in \texttt{procs}$, $L_c(v_p^j) = (\texttt{msg}(\texttt{ch}(p)(j)), j)$ for every $j : 1 \leq j \leq |\texttt{ch}(p)|$ and $L_c(v_p^j) = (\varepsilon, j)$ for every $j : |\texttt{ch}(p)| < j \leq l$, and the set of edges is given by $E_c = \{\langle p, x, p'\rangle | \, \texttt{r}(p)(x) = p'\} \cup \{\langle p, -, v_p^j\rangle\} \cup \{\langle v_p^j, -, p'\rangle | \, \exists m \in M, \texttt{ch}(p)(j) = m(p')\}$.

Observe that if the diameter of the closure of the graph encoding of some bounded buffer configuration is bounded by k, i.e. $\varnothing(\texttt{closure}(\texttt{enc}(c))) \leq k$, then the diameter of the closure of the extended graph encoding of the same configuration is bounded by at most $2 * k$, i.e. $\varnothing(\texttt{closure}(\texttt{extenc}(c))) \leq 2 * k$.

The rest of this section is devoted to the proof of the following theorem.

Theorem 4. *The strongly bounded state reachability problem for lossy* BDRA *with bounded buffers is decidable.*

We show the decidability of the strongly bounded state reachability problem for lossy BDRA with bounded buffers by a non-trivial instantiation of the framework of Well-Structured Transition Systems (WSTS) [2,11]. We proceed to that end in several steps. First, we list the three main ingredients required in order to instantiate the WSTS framework on any transition system $\mathcal{T} = \langle C, C_{init}, \longrightarrow\rangle$. Then, we introduce the notion of *coverability* and show how to reduce the state reachability problem to it. Finally, we show the applicability of the main ingredients to our problem.

Ordering, Predecessors and Monotonicity. We present in this paragraph the three main components required for the instantiation of the WSTS framework.

Well-Quasi Ordering: First, we need to define a *Well-Quasi Ordering* (WQO) over the set of configurations C, i.e. a reflexive and transitive binary relation $\preceq$ over C such that, for every infinite sequence of configurations $(c_k)_{k \geq 0}$, there exist $i, j \in \mathbb{N}$ such that $i < j$ and $c_i \preceq c_j$. Let $U \subseteq C$ be a set of configurations. Using the notion of well-quasi ordering, we can define the following notions:

- The *upward closure* of U is the set $U\uparrow := \{c \in C | \, \exists c' \in U \text{ with } c' \preceq c\}$.
- U is *upward closed* if $U = U\uparrow$.

It has been shown that every upward closed set U can be characterised by a finite *minor set* $M \subseteq U$ such that (i) for every $c' \in U$ there is $c \in M$ with $c \preceq c'$, and (ii) if $c, c' \in M$ and $c \preceq c'$ then $c = c'$. We use $\texttt{min}$ to denote the function which for a given upward closed set U returns one minor set of U.

Computing the $\texttt{minpre}$: We use $\texttt{Pre}(U) := \{c | \, \exists c_1 \in U, c \longrightarrow c_1\}$ to denote the set of predecessors of U. Given a configuration c, we denote by $\texttt{minpre}(c)$ the set $\texttt{min}(\texttt{Pre}(\{c\}\uparrow) \cup \{c\}\uparrow)$. Providing an algorithm that computes a finite $\texttt{minpre}(c)$ represents the second ingredient.

Monotonicity: The third ingredient consists in showing that the transition relation $\longrightarrow$ is monotonic with regard to the ordering $\preceq$, i.e. for every three configurations $c_1, c_2, c_3 \in C$ such that $c_1 \preceq c_2$ and $c_1 \longrightarrow c_3$ there should be a configuration $c_4 \in C$ such that $c_3 \preceq c_4$ and $c_2 \longrightarrow c_4$.

Coverability. Given a configuration $c_{\mathtt{target}} \in C$, the *coverability problem* asks whether there is a configuration $c' \succcurlyeq c_{\mathtt{target}}$ reachable in $\mathcal{T}$. Given that the three ingredients are provided, the following conditions are sufficient for the decidability of this problem: (i) For every $c \in C$, we can check whether $\{c\}\uparrow \cap\, C_{init} \neq \emptyset$, and (ii) for every two configurations c_1 and c_2, it is decidable whether $c_1 \preceq c_2$. The solution for the coverability problem of WSTS suggested in [2,11] is based on a backward analysis approach. It is shown that starting from $U_0 := \{c_{\mathtt{target}}\}$, the sequence $(U_i)_{i\geq 0}$ with $U_{i+1} := \mathtt{min}\,(\mathtt{Pre}\,(U_i)\!\uparrow \cup\, U_i\!\uparrow)$, for $i \geq 0$ reaches a fix-point and is computable.

In the following, we instantiate the framework of WSTS to show the decidability of the state reachability problem for strongly bounded lossy BDRA with bounded buffer, but first we need to introduce some notations.

Let l and k be two natural numbers, $D = \langle Q, q_0, M, X, \delta\rangle$ a lossy BDRA, $\mathtt{target} \in Q$ a target state and $C = C^{(l,k)}(D)$. We introduce the *disconnect prefix* transition relation $\dashrightarrow := \xrightarrow{\mathtt{disconnect}}{}^{*}_{D} \circ \longrightarrow^{(l,k)}_{D}$. Note that the reflexive transitive closures of $\dashrightarrow$ and $\longrightarrow^{(l,k)}_{D}$ are identical. Thus, the state reachability of $\mathtt{target}$ in $\left\langle C, C_{init}, \longrightarrow^{(l,k)}_{D}\right\rangle$ is equivalent to its corresponding problem in $\langle C, C_{init}, \dashrightarrow\rangle$. Next, we will prove the decidability of the latter problem.

We will show that $\langle C, C_{init}, \dashrightarrow\rangle$ is a well-structured transition system. Let $C_{\mathtt{target}}$ denote the set of all configurations of the form $\langle\{p\}, \mathtt{s}, \mathtt{r}, \mathtt{ch}\rangle$, composed of a single process in state $\mathtt{target}$ ($\mathtt{s}\,(p) = \mathtt{target}$), whose registers are empty, and whose channel contains any (finitely many) possible word $w \in (M \times \{\bot\})^*$ of length $|w| \leq l$. We will define the well-quasi ordering on C in such a way that the upward closure of C_{target} consists of all configurations $c \in C$ with $\mathtt{target} \in c$. It becomes then clear that the coverability of any configuration $c \in C_{\mathtt{target}}$ in $\langle C, C_{init}, \dashrightarrow\rangle$ is equivalent to the reachability of $\mathtt{target}$ in the same transition system. We define in the next paragraph an ordering on the set of configurations C and show that it is a well-quasi ordering.

A Well-Quasi Order on Configurations. We define in this paragraph a well-quasi ordering on the set of configurations C. The ordering is defined by using the notion of *induced sub-graph* embedding $\sqsubseteq_{ind}$ on directed graphs defined as follows. Let $G_1 = \langle V_1, L_v, L_e, l_1, E_1\rangle$ and $G_2 = \langle V_2, L_v, L_e, l_2, E_2\rangle$ be two directed graphs. We say that G_1 is an induced sub-graph of G_2, and we write $G_1 \sqsubseteq_{ind} G_2$, if there is an injective mapping $t : V_1 \rightarrow V_2$ such that (i) for all $v \in V_1$ we have $l_1\,(v) = l_2\,(t\,(v))$, and (ii) for all $v, u \in V_1$ and $a \in L_e$ we have $\langle v, a, u\rangle \in E_1 \Leftrightarrow \langle t\,(v), a, t\,(u)\rangle \in E_2$. The induced sub graph relation on undirected graphs is defined in a similar manner.

Let $c_1 = \langle \mathtt{procs}_1, \mathtt{s}_1, \mathtt{r}_1, \mathtt{ch}_1\rangle$ and $c_2 = \langle \mathtt{procs}_2, \mathtt{s}_2, \mathtt{r}_2, \mathtt{ch}_2\rangle$ be two configurations from C. We define the ordering $\preceq$ on configurations by $c_1 \preceq c_2$ if $\mathtt{extenc}\,(c_1) \sqsubseteq_{ind} \mathtt{extenc}\,(c_2)$. We can show that, if $c_1 \preceq c_2$, then there should be an injective mapping $t : \texttt{procs}_1 \mapsto \texttt{procs}_2$ such that (i) $\texttt{s}_2(t(p)) = \texttt{s}_1(p)$ for every $p \in \texttt{procs}_1$, (ii) $\texttt{r}_2(t(p))(x) = t(p') \Leftrightarrow \texttt{r}_1(p)(x) = p'$ for every $p, p' \in \texttt{procs}_1$ and every $x \in X$, and (iii) for every $p \in \texttt{procs}_1$ with $\texttt{ch}_1(p) = m_1(id_1)\ldots m_n(id_n)$ for some n we have $\texttt{ch}_2(t(p)) = m_1(id'_1)\ldots m_n(id'_n)$ and for every $i : 1 \leq i \leq n$, if $id_i = p_i \in \texttt{procs}_1$ then $id'_i = t(p_i)$, otherwise $id_i = id'_i = \perp$.

Based on a result by Ding in [9] and using the fact that the underlying undirected graph of the configuration encoding is bounded, we can show the following lemma:

Lemma 2. *The relation $\preceq$ is a well-quasi ordering on C.*

Monotonicity. Let $c_1, c_2, c_3 \in C$ be three configurations such that: $c_1 \preceq c_2$ and $c_1 \dashrightarrow c_3$. The goal here is to find a fourth configuration $c_4 \in C$ such that $c_3 \preceq c_4$ and $c_2 \dashrightarrow c_4$. This can be achieved by disconnecting as many processes as necessary in c_2 in order to obtain a configuration c_{sub} equal to c_1 modulo disconnected processes. From there, we let c_{sub} take the same transition as the one taken by c_1 to get to c_3 and we obtain a configuration c_4 such that $c_3 \preceq c_4$, $c_2 \xrightarrow{\texttt{disconnect}}{}^{*}_{D} c_{sub}$ and $c_{sub} \dashrightarrow c_4$, thus $c_2 \dashrightarrow c_4$.

Lemma 3. *The transition relation $\dashrightarrow$ is monotonic w.r.t. $\preceq$.*

Summary of the WSTS ***Instantiation.*** The first sufficient condition for the decidability of the coverability problem, namely checking whether the upward closed set $\{c\}\uparrow$ of some configuration c contains an initial configuration, is trivial (we check that c contains one process only, that the process is in state q_{init} and that its registers and channels are empty). The second sufficient condition is also trivial (checking whether $c_1 \preceq c_2$ amount to checking graph embedding, which is decidable). The first ingredient needed in order to use the WSTS transition system has been provided with Lemma 2, which states that the induced subgraph relation on the extended graph encoding of the configurations is a well-quasi ordering. The second ingredient, i.e. computability of the `minpre`, is given by the following lemma.

Lemma 4. *Given a configuration $c \in C$, we can effectively compute* $\texttt{minpre}(c)$.

The third ingredient, i.e. the monotonicity of the ordering wrt. the transition relation, is given by lemma 3.

Thus, Lemmas 2, 3 and 4 show that the coverability of the finite set C_{target} is decidable. Hence, the state reachability problem for strongly bounded lossy BDRA with bounded buffers is decidable. □

8 Acyclic Strongly Bounded BDRA with Bounded Buffer

In the following we show the decidability of the reachability problem for strongly bounded BDRA when the *underlying* undirected graph of configurations is acyclic.

Acyclic Strongly Bounded State Reachability with Bounded Buffer. Let $k, l \geq 1$, $D = \langle Q_D, q_D^0, \delta_D, F_D \rangle$ be a BDRA and $\mathcal{T}(D) = \langle C, (D), C_{init}(D), \rightarrow_D \rangle$ its corresponding transition system. We define the *l-bounded buffer, k-strongly bounded* acyclic ((l,k)-strong acyclic) transition system associated to D as the tuple $\mathcal{T}^{a(l,k)}(D) = \left\langle C^{a(l,k)}(D), C_{init}^{a(l,k)}(D), \longrightarrow_D^{a(l,k)} \right\rangle$ composed of the set of (l,k)-strong acyclic configurations $C^{a(l,k)}(D) := \{c \in C^{(l,k)} | \ \texttt{closure}(\texttt{enc}(c)) \text{ is acyclic}\}$, the set of initial configurations $C_{init}^{a(l,k)}(D) := C_{init}(D)$ and the transition relation $\longrightarrow_D^{a(l,k)} := \longrightarrow_D \cap \left(C^{a(l,k)}(D) \times C^{a(l,k)}(D)\right)$. Let $\texttt{target} \in Q_D$ be a control state. Checking whether there is reachable configuration $c = \langle \texttt{procs}, \texttt{s}, \texttt{r}, \texttt{ch} \rangle$ in the transition system $\mathcal{T}^{a(l,k)}(D)$ such that there is a process $p \in \texttt{procs}$ with $\texttt{s}(p) = \texttt{target}$ is the (l,k)-strong acyclic state reachability problem and is denoted by $\texttt{AStrongReach}(D, \texttt{target}, l, k)$.

Theorem 5. *Given $l \geq 1$, $k \geq 1$, a buffered* DRA $D = \langle Q_D, q_D^0, \delta_D, F_D \rangle$ *and a control state $\texttt{target} \in Q_D$, $\texttt{AStrongReach}(D, \texttt{target}, l, k)$ is decidable.*

Proof Sketch. The proof of Theorem 5 is based on the simple observation that the processes cannot exchange IDs, otherwise there will be a creation of a cycle in the *underlying* undirected graph configuration encodings. Hence, each process can only receive plain messages (without an ID) from its creator. Furthermore, at any time each process can send plain messages to a finite number of other processes (i.e. bounded by the number of registers). Since simple paths are also bounded, we have that the graph representation of any reachable configuration is a disjoint union of finite trees. Furthermore, any two processes in two different disjoint trees can never communicate with each other. This implies that the acyclic strongly bounded state reachability problem with bounded buffer can be reduced to the standard reachability problem for finite-state systems. Such a finite-state system keeps track of at most one tree in which each node corresponds to a process and its channel. When a tree is split into a finite number of subtrees due to the creation of new processes or disconnect operations, the finite-state system can decide in non-deterministic manner, to follow one of these sub-trees.

9 Conclusion

In this paper, we studied the state reachability problem for the class of buffered DRA. This work is a continuation of [3] where the analysis was carried for DRA with rendez-vous communication. The problem is undecidable even if we bound the simple paths and even if we forbid cycles in the communication graph of the network. Our goal was to investigate sub-classes where state reachability becomes decidable. To that end, we considered different directions including bounding the size of the buffers, bounding the simple paths of the underlying (un)directed communication graph of the network and / or disallowing cycles in the network. It turned out that many of these restrictions, even combined, were not sufficient. However, we proved that the problem becomes decidable in two particular and interesting cases. In the first one, we considered the class of *lossy* buffered DRA, in which processes are allowed to disconnect themselves from the network in a non-deterministic fashion, where we bounded both the size of the buffers and the simple paths of the undirected communication graph. The proof was obtained through a non-trivial instantiation of well-structured transition systems. In the second case, we showed that the number of possible shapes of the network is finite if we bound the size of the buffers, disallow cycles and bound the simple paths in the communication graph. As future work, we think that it is worth checking whether decidability boundary can be lowered by considering other channel semantics, such as the unordered and the lossy ones. As future work, we think that it is worth checking whether decidability can be obtained for more general classes by considering other channel semantics, such as the unordered and the lossy ones. We also think that an important line of work would be to study the link between register automata and π-calculus and to study the relation between our results using the DRA formalism and the work of Meyer [16] in which π-calculus has been used.

References

1. Abdulla, P.A., Atig, M.F., Rezine, O.: Verification of directed acyclic ad hoc networks. In: Beyer, D., Boreale, M. (eds.) FORTE 2013 and FMOODS 2013. LNCS, vol. 7892, pp. 193–208. Springer, Heidelberg (2013)
2. Abdulla, P., Cerans, K., Jonsson, B., Tsay, Y.: General decidability theorems for infinite-state systems. In: LICS 1996, pp. 313–321. IEEE Computer Society (1996)
3. Abdulla, P.A., Atig, M.F., Kara, A., Rezine, O.: Verification of dynamic register automata. In: FSTTCS 2014, pp. 653–665 (2014)
4. Benedikt, M., Ley, C., Puppis, G.: Automata vs. logics on data words. In: Dawar, A., Veith, H. (eds.) CSL 2010. LNCS, vol. 6247, pp. 110–124. Springer, Heidelberg (2010)
5. Bollig, B., Cyriac, A., Hélouët, L., Kara, A., Schwentick, T.: Dynamic communicating automata and branching high-level MSCs. In: Dediu, A.-H., Martín-Vide, C., Truthe, B. (eds.) LATA 2013. LNCS, vol. 7810, pp. 177–189. Springer, Heidelberg (2013)
6. Bollig, B., Hélouët, L.: Realizability of dynamic MSC languages. In: Ablayev, F., Mayr, E.W. (eds.) CSR 2010. LNCS, vol. 6072, pp. 48–59. Springer, Heidelberg (2010)
7. Delzanno, G., Sangnier, A., Zavattaro, G.: Parameterized verification of ad hoc networks. In: Gastin, P., Laroussinie, F. (eds.) CONCUR 2010. LNCS, vol. 6269, pp. 313–327. Springer, Heidelberg (2010)
8. Demri, S., Lazic, R.: LTL with the freeze quantifier and register automata. In: LICS, pp. 17–26. IEEE Computer Society (2006)
9. Ding, G.: Subgraphs and well quasi ordering. J. Graph Theory **16**(5), 489–502 (1992)
10. Figueira, D.: Alternating register automata on finite words and trees. Logical Methods in Computer Science **8**(1), 22 (2012)
11. Finkel, A., Schnoebelen, P.: Well-structured transition systems everywhere!. Theor. Comput. Sci. **256**(1–2), 63–92 (2001)

12. Grigore, R., Distefano, D., Petersen, R.L., Tzevelekos, N.: Runtime verification based on register automata. In: Piterman, N., Smolka, S.A. (eds.) TACAS 2013 (ETAPS 2013). LNCS, vol. 7795, pp. 260–276. Springer, Heidelberg (2013)
13. Jurdzinski, M., Lazic, R.: Alternation-free modal mu-calculus for data trees. In: LICS, pp. 131–140. IEEE Computer Society (2007)
14. Kaminski, M., Francez, N.: Finite-memory automata. Theor. Comput. Sci. **134**(2), 329–363 (1994)
15. Lazić, R.S.: Safely freezing LTL. In: Arun-Kumar, S., Garg, N. (eds.) FSTTCS 2006. LNCS, vol. 4337, pp. 381–392. Springer, Heidelberg (2006)
16. Meyer, R.: On boundedness in depth in the pi-calculus. In: IFIP TCS, pp. 477–489 (2008)
17. Neven, F., Schwentick, T., Vianu, V.: Finite state machines for strings over infinite alphabets. ACM Trans. Comput. Log. **5**(3), 403–435 (2004)
18. Sakamoto, H., Ikeda, D.: Intractability of decision problems for finite-memory automata. Theor. Comput. Sci. **231**(2), 297–308 (2000)
19. Tzevelekos, N.: Fresh-register automata. In: POPL. ACM (2011)

Precise and Sound Automatic Fence Insertion Procedure under PSO

Parosh Aziz Abdulla(✉), Mohamed Faouzi Atig, Magnus Lång, and Tuan Phong Ngo

Department of Information Technology, Uppsala University, Uppsala, Sweden
{parosh,mohamed_faouzi.atig,magnus.lang.7837,tuan-phong.ngo}@it.uu.se

Abstract. We give a sound and complete procedure for fence insertion for concurrent finite-state programs running under the PSO memory model. This model allows "write to read" and "write-to-write" relaxations corresponding to the addition of an unbounded store buffers between processors and the main memory. We introduce a novel machine model, called the Hierarchical Single-Buffer (HSB) semantics, and show that the reachability problem for a program under PSO can be reduced to the reachability problem under HSB. We present a simple and effective backward reachability analysis algorithm for the latter, and propose a counter-example guided fence insertion procedure. The procedure infers automatically a minimal set of fences that ensures correctness of the program. We have implemented a prototype and run it successfully on all standard benchmarks, together with several challenging examples.

1 Introduction

For performance reasons, most of the modern architectures implement *weak memory models* [5,16]. Such models allows the reordering of memory instructions issued by the set of processes. For instance, the most common reordering is "write to read" which allows that writes to shared memory may be delayed past subsequent reads from memory. The "write to read" reordering leads to the *Total Store Order* (TSO) memory model that is adopted by Sun's SPARC and x86 architectures [22,23]. Adding the "write to write" reordering to TSO leads to the *Partial Store Order* (PSO) memory model (described in the Sun's SPARC architecture [24]). The "write to write" reordering may swap the order between two writes of the same process if they concern different variables.

The gain in the performance through the use of weak memory models comes with a price since reasoning about the behavior of even very small programs running under weak memory models is more difficult and counter-intuitive than under the usual *Sequentially Consistent* (SC) memory model. In fact, the SC memory model is the one that is usually assumed by the programmers where

This work was supported in part by the Swedish Research Council and carried out within the Linnaeus centre of excellence UPMARC, Uppsala Programming for Multicore Architectures Research Center.

A. Bouajjani and H. Fauconnier (Eds.): NETYS 2015, LNCS 9466, pp. 32–47, 2015.
DOI: 10.1007/978-3-319-26850-7_3

the program instructions of different processes should appear as if these instructions are interleaved in a consistent global order. This means that a program under weak memory models can deviate from its intended behaviour (under the SC model) and hence violates its specifications. For example, several mutual exclusion algorithms and produce-consumer protocols become incorrect when executed under weak memory models. To avoid such undesired behaviours, programmers can use special *memory fence* instructions that prevent some reordering of instructions issued before and after the fence. Then, an important problem is to find the set of fences that ensures the correctness of programs when run under a weak memory model without compromising the performance. In fact, inserting too many fences would result in a degradation of program performance.

In this paper, we present the first *precise* and *sound* method for automatic fence insertion for concurrent finite-state programs running under the PSO memory model. To this end, we make the following contribution:

- We propose a *new model*, called the *Hierarchical Single-Buffer* (HSB), that is equivalent to the PSO memory model and allows the application of efficient infinite state model-checking techniques.
- A *simple* and *effective algorithm* to solve the reachability problem under HSB, using a backward analysis algorithm.
- A *fence insertion procedure* that infers a minimal fence set in order to correct programs under PSO.
- A *prototype* that is integrated to Memorax [1–3]. We evaluate our prototype on a wide range of benchmarks. The download link can be seen in Sect. 6.

Related Work. Weak memory models are an active research area today. Many techniques have been developed to help programmers, in the form of precise model-checking algorithms (e.g., [9,10,12]), monitoring and testing tools (e.g., [13,14,21]), explicit state-space exploration (e.g., [19,20]), bounded model checking (e.g., [8,17,25]) and program transformations (e.g., [7,11,12]). Most of these works have focused on different memory models than PSO and thus are not directly comparable. Almost all the existed works on the PSO memory model are either (i) based on under-approximation techniques and which leads to sound but potentially imprecise analysis (e.g., [14,20]), or (ii) based on over-approximations techniques and which leads to potentially unsound analysis (e.g., [6,15,19]). Finally, checking safety property for finite-state programs running under TSO and PSO memory models has been shown to be decidable with a non-primitive recursive complexity [9,10]. A tool implementing an exact procedure for checking safety properties for programs running under TSO was presented in [1–3]. Our reachability algorithms can be seen as an efficient instance of the work [10] to the PSO memory model. Moreover, [10] does not discuss fence insertion.

2 Preliminaries

In this section, we introduce some notations and definitions that we use later.

Notation. We use $\mathbb{N}$ to denote the set of natural numbers. For sets A and B, we use $[A \mapsto B]$ to denote the set of all total functions from A to B and $f : A \mapsto B$ to denote that f is a total function that maps A to B. For $a \in A$ and $b \in B$, we use $f[a \hookleftarrow b]$ to denote the function f' defined as follows: $f'(a) = b$ and $f'(a') = f(a')$ for all $a' \neq a$.

Let Σ be a finite alphabet. We denote by Σ^* (resp. Σ^+) the set of all *words* (resp. non-empty words) over Σ, and by ϵ the empty word. The length of a word $w \in \Sigma^*$ is denoted by $|w|$; we assume that $|\epsilon| = 0$. For every $i : 1 \leq i \leq |w|$, let $w(i)$ be the symbol at position i in w. For $a \in \Sigma$, we write $a \in w$ if a appears in w, i.e., $a = w(i)$ for some $i : 1 \leq i \leq |w|$. For words w_1, w_2, we use $w_1 \cdot w_2$ to denote the concatenation of w_1 and w_2. For a word $w \neq \epsilon$ and $i : 0 \leq i \leq |w|$, we define $w \odot i$ to be the suffix of w that we get by deleting the prefix of length i, i.e., the unique w_2 such that $w = w_1 \cdot w_2$ and $|w_1| = i$.

Set Ordering. Given an ordering $\sqsubseteq$ on C, we say that $\sqsubseteq$ is a *well-quasi ordering* if for every (infinite) sequence $c_0, c_1, \ldots$ in C, there are $i < j$ with $c_i \sqsubseteq c_j$. The *upward closure* of a set C wrt. $\sqsubseteq$ is defined as $C\!\uparrow := \{c' \mid \exists c \in C, c \sqsubseteq c'\}$. A set C is *upward closed* if $C = C\!\uparrow$. We use $\mathtt{Min}\,(C)$ to denote the *minor set* of a given set C wrt. $\sqsubseteq$, that satisfies the following conditions: (i) for all $c \in C$ there is a $c' \in \mathtt{Min}\,(C)$ such that $c' \sqsubseteq c$, and (ii) for all $c, c' \in \mathtt{Min}\,(C)$, $c \neq c'$ implies $c \not\sqsubseteq c'$.

Transition System. A transition system $\mathcal{T}$ is a triple $(C, \mathtt{Init}, \rightarrow)$ where C is a (infinite) set of *configurations*, $\mathtt{Init} \subseteq C$ is a set of *initial configurations*, and $\rightarrow \subseteq C \times C$ is a reflexive *transition relation*. We write $c \rightarrow c'$ to denote that $(c, c') \in \rightarrow$, and $\xrightarrow{*}$ to denote the reflexive transitive closure of $\rightarrow$. A *run* π of $\mathcal{T}$ is of the form $c_0 \rightarrow \cdots \rightarrow c_n$, where $c_i \rightarrow c_{i+1}$ for all $i : 0 \leq i < n$. Then, we write $c_0 \xrightarrow{\pi} c_n$. We use *target* (π) to denote c_n. Notice that, for configurations c, c', we have that $c \xrightarrow{*} c'$ iff $c \rightarrow \pi c'$ for some run π. The run π is said to be a *computation* if $c_0 \in \mathtt{Init}$. A configuration c is said to be reachable if there is a computation π such that $c =$ *target* (π). Two runs $\pi_1 = c_0 \rightarrow c_1 \rightarrow \cdots \rightarrow c_m$ and $\pi_2 = c_{m+1} \rightarrow c_{m+2} \rightarrow \cdots \rightarrow c_n$ are said to be *compatible* if $c_m = c_{m+1}$. Then, we write $\pi_1 \bullet \pi_2$ to denote the run $\pi_1 = c_0 \rightarrow c_1 \rightarrow \cdots \rightarrow c_m \rightarrow c_{m+2} \rightarrow \cdots \rightarrow c_n$. Given an ordering $\sqsubseteq$ on C, we say that $\rightarrow$ is *monotonic* wrt. $\sqsubseteq$ if whenever $c_1 \rightarrow c_1'$ and $c_1 \sqsubseteq c_2$, there exists a c_2' such that $c_2 \xrightarrow{*} c_2'$ and $c_1' \sqsubseteq c_2'$. We say that $\rightarrow$ is *effectively monotonic* wrt. $\sqsubseteq$ if, given the configurations c_1, c_1', c_2 described above, we can compute c_2' and a run π such that $c_2 \xrightarrow{\pi} c_2'$.

3 Concurrent Programs under PSO

A *concurrent program* $\mathcal{P}$ has a finite number of finite-state processes, each with its own program code. Communication between processes is performed by reading and writing through a shared-memory with finite number of shared variables and finite domains. First, we introduce the PSO semantics (similar to the one described in [20]) and its reachability problem. Then we propose a new model, the HSB model, that we use to analyse programs under the PSO model.

3.1 Syntax

We assume a finite set X of *variables* ranging over a finite data domain V. A *concurrent program* is a pair $\mathcal{P} = (P, A)$ where P is a finite set of *processes* and $A = \{A_p | \, p \in P\}$ is a set of extended finite-state automata (one automaton A_p for each process $p \in P$). The automaton A_p is a triple $(Q_p, q_p^{init}, \Delta_p)$ where Q_p is a finite set of *local states*, $q_p^{init} \in Q_p$ is the *initial* local state, and Δ_p is a finite set of *transitions*. Each transition is a triple $(q, op, ,')$ where $q,' \in Q_p$ and op is an *operation*. An operation is of one of the following six forms: (i) the *"no operation"* nop, (ii) the *read operation* $\mathsf{r}(x, v)$, (iii) the *write operation* $\mathsf{w}(x, v)$, (iv) the *full fence operation* mfence, (v) the *write-write fence operation* sfence, and (vi) the *atomic read-write operation* $\mathsf{arw}(x, v, v')$, where $x \in X$, and $v, v' \in V$. For a transition $t = (q, op,')$, we use *source* (t), *operation* (t), and *target* (t) to denote q, op, and q' respectively. We define $Q := \cup_{p \in P} Q_p$ and $\Delta := \cup_{p \in P} \Delta_p$. A *local state definition* $\underline{q}$ is a mapping $P \mapsto Q$ such that $\underline{q}(p) \in Q_p$ for each $p \in P$.

3.2 PSO Semantics

Transition System. We define the transition system induced by a program running under the PSO semantics. To do that, we define the set of configurations and transition relation. A *PSO-configuration* c is a triple $(\underline{q}, \underline{b}, mem)$ where $\underline{q}$ is a local state definition, $\underline{b} : P \mapsto [X \mapsto (V \cup \{\star\})^*]$, and $mem : X \mapsto V$. Intuitively, $\underline{q}(p)$ gives the local state of process p. The value of $\underline{b}(p)(x)$ is the content of the buffer belonging to variable x of p. This buffer associates a sequence of values from V to the variable x, where each value v represents a write operation that assigns v to the variable x. The buffer may also contain the *write-write fence* symbol $\star$ that restricts the ordering of writes. In our model, writes will be appended to *the tail of buffer* (the right most one), and fetched from *the head of buffer* (the left most one). The head of buffer $\underline{b}(p)(x)$ is at the index 1, and the tail of buffer is at the index $|\underline{b}(p)(x)|$. Finally, *mem* defines the state of the memory (defines the value of each variable in the memory). We use C_{PSO} to denote the set of PSO-configurations.

We define the transition relation $\rightarrow_{PSO}$ on C_{PSO}. The relation is induced by (i) members of Δ; (ii) a set $\Delta' := \{\mathsf{update}_{p,x} | \, p \in P, x \in X\}$ where $\mathsf{update}_{p,x}$ is an operation that updates the memory using the message at the head of the buffer for variable x of process p; and (iii) a set $\Delta'' := \{\mathsf{update}_{p,\star} | \, p \in P\}$ where $\mathsf{update}_{p,\star}$ removes the write-write fence symbol from the head of all the buffers of process p. For configurations $c = (\underline{q}, \underline{b}, mem)$, $c' = (\underline{q}', \underline{b}', mem')$, a process $p \in P$, and $t \in \Delta_p \cup \{\mathsf{update}_{p,x}, \mathsf{update}_{p,\star}\}$, we write $c \rightarrow t_{PSO} c'$ to denote that one of the following conditions is satisfied.

- Nop: $t = (q, \mathsf{nop}, q')$, $\underline{q}(p) = q$, $\underline{q}' = \underline{q}[p \hookleftarrow q']$, $\underline{b}' = \underline{b}$, and $mem' = mem$. The process changes its state while the buffer contents and the memory remain unchanged.
- Write to store: $t = (q, \mathsf{w}(x, v), q')$, $\underline{q}(p) = q$, $\underline{q}' = \underline{q}[p \hookleftarrow q']$, $\underline{b}' = \underline{b}[p \hookleftarrow \underline{b}(p)[x \hookleftarrow \underline{b}(p)(x) \cdot v]]$, and $mem' = mem$. The write operation is appended to the tail of the buffer for variable x of process p.

- Memory update: $t = \mathsf{update}_{p,x}$, $\underline{q}' = \underline{q}$, $\underline{b} = \underline{b}'\left[p \hookleftarrow \underline{b}'(p)\left[x \hookleftarrow v \cdot \underline{b}'(p)(x)\right]\right]$, and $mem' = mem\left[x \hookleftarrow v\right]$. The write at the head of the buffer for x of p is removed and the memory is updated accordingly.
- Write-write fence update: $t = \mathsf{update}_{p,\star}$, $\underline{q}' = \underline{q}$, $\forall x \in X : \underline{b} = \underline{b}'\left[p \hookleftarrow \underline{b}'(p)\right]\left[x \hookleftarrow \star \cdot \underline{b}'(p)(x)\right]$, and $mem' = mem$. The write-write fence symbol $\star$ is removed from the head of all buffers of process p.
- Read: $t = (q, \mathsf{r}(x,v), q')$, $\underline{q}(p) = q$, $\underline{q}' = \underline{q}\left[p \hookleftarrow q'\right]$, $\underline{b}' = \underline{b}$, $mem' = mem$, and one of the following conditions is satisfied. (i) Read own write: There is an $i : 1 \leq i \leq |\underline{b}(p)(x)|$ such that $\underline{b}(p)(x)(i) = v$, and $v' \notin (\underline{b}(p)(x) \odot i)$ for all $v' \in V$. If there is a write in the buffer for x of p then we consider the write at the tail of the buffer (the right most one of the buffer). This operation should assign v to x. (ii) Read memory: $v' \notin \underline{b}(p)(x)$ for all $v' \in V$ and $mem(x) = v$. If there is no write operation in the buffer for x of p then the value v of x is fetched from the memory.
- Full fence: $t = (q, \mathsf{mfence}, q')$, $\underline{q}(p) = q$, $\underline{q}' = \underline{q}\left[p \hookleftarrow q'\right]$, $\forall x \in X : \underline{b}(p)(x) = \epsilon$, $\underline{b}' = \underline{b}$, and $mem' = mem$. A full fence operation may be performed by a process only if all its buffers are empty.
- Write-write fence: $t = (q, \mathsf{sfence}, q')$, $\underline{q}(p) = q$, $\underline{q}' = \underline{q}\left[p \hookleftarrow q'\right]$, $\forall x \in X : \underline{b}' = \underline{b}\left[p \hookleftarrow \underline{b}(p)\left[x \hookleftarrow \underline{b}(p)(x) \cdot \star\right]\right]$, and $mem' = mem$. A write-write fence operation adds the symbol $\star$ to the tail of all buffers of process p.
- ARW: $t = (q, \mathsf{arw}(x, v, v'), q')$, $\underline{q}(p) = q$, $\underline{q}' = \underline{q}\left[p \hookleftarrow q'\right]$, $\underline{b}(p)(x) = \epsilon$, $\underline{b}' = \underline{b}$, $mem(x) = v$, and $mem' = mem\left[x \hookleftarrow v'\right]$. The operation $\mathsf{arw}(x, v, v')$ is performed atomically. It may be performed by a process only if its buffer for x is empty. The operation checks whether the value of variable x is v. In such a case, it changes its value to v'. Note this operation permits to model instructions like compare-and-swap (or test-and-set) under SPARC [24].

We use $c \rightarrow_{PSO} c'$ to denote the reflexive closure of $c \xrightarrow{t}_{PSO} c'$ for some $t \in \Delta \cup \Delta' \cup \Delta''$. The set $\mathtt{Init}_{PSO}$ of *initial* PSO-configurations contains all configurations of the form $\left(\underline{q_{init}}, \underline{b_{init}}, mem_{init}\right)$ where, for all $p \in P$, we have that $\underline{q_{init}}(p) = q_p^{init}$ and $\underline{b_{init}}(p)(x) = \epsilon$ for all $x \in X$. In other words, each process is in its initial local state and all the buffers are empty. On the other hand, the memory may have any initial value. The transition system induced by a concurrent system under the PSO semantics is then given by $(C_{PSO}, \mathtt{Init}_{PSO}, \rightarrow_{PSO})$.

The PSO Reachability Problem. Given a set $\mathtt{Target}$ of local state definitions, we use *Reachable*$(PSO)\,(\mathcal{P})\,(\mathtt{Target})$ to be a predicate that indicates the reachability of one of the following configurations $\left\{\left(\underline{q}, \underline{b}, mem\right) \mid \underline{q} \in \mathtt{Target}\right\}$, i.e., whether a configuration c, where the local state definition of c belongs to $\mathtt{Target}$, is reachable. The reachability problem for PSO is to check, for a given $\mathtt{Target}$, whether *Reachable*$(PSO)\,(\mathcal{P})\,(\mathtt{Target})$ holds or not. We use $\mathtt{Target}$ to denote *"bad configurations"* that we do not want to occur during the execution of the system. Therefore, we often say that the *"program is correct (or safe)"* to indicate that $\mathtt{Target}$ is not reachable.

3.3 Hierarchical Single-Buffer Semantics

The PSO semantics make use of *unbounded perfect FIFO buffers* that induces an infinite transition system. However, the reachability problem under PSO is still decidable as shown in [9,10]. In fact, it can be solved using the framework of well-structured transition systems [4]. For the case of TSO, the paper [2] proposes an ordering partly based on the sub-word relations of the configuration's buffer contents. However, because PSO configurations can contain the $\star$ symbol (which can not be lost), a similar ordering is not monotonic wrt. the PSO semantics. Therefore, our goal is to derive a new semantical model, called the *Hierarchical Single-Buffer model (HSB)*, that is both equivalent to PSO wrt. reachability problems and monotonic wrt. some ordering. The buffer contents of HSB configurations will not contain $\star$ symbol.

Formal Semantics. A *HSB-configuration* c is a quadruple $(\underline{q}, \underline{b}, m, \underline{z})$ where $\underline{q}$ is (as in the case of the PSO semantics) a local state definition, $\underline{b} : P \mapsto [X \mapsto V^*]$, $m \in ([X \mapsto V] \times P \times X)^+$, and $\underline{z} : P \mapsto \mathbb{N}$. Intuitively, $\underline{b}(p)(x)$ is a per process and variable buffer, the *channel* m contains *messages* as triples of the form (mem, p, x) where mem defines the values of the variables (encoding a memory snapshot), x is the latest variable that has been written by the process p. Furthermore, $\underline{z}$ represents a set of *pointers* (one for each process) where, from the point of view of p, the word $m \odot \underline{z}(p)$ is the sequence of write operations that have not yet been used for memory updates and the first element of the triple $m(\underline{z}(p))$ represents the memory content. We use C_{HSB} to denote the set of HSB-configurations. As we shall see below, the channel will never be empty, since it is not empty in an initial configuration, and since no messages are ever removed from it during a run of the system (in HSB semantics, the update operation moves a pointer to the right instead of removing a message in the channel). This implies (among other things) that the invariant $\underline{z}(p) > 0$ is always maintained. Messages are appended to *the tail of the channel* (the right most one) that has index $|m|$. The *bottom of channel*, index 1, is the *initial message*.

Let $c = (\underline{q}, \underline{b}, m, \underline{z})$ be a HSB-configuration. For every $p \in P$ and $x \in X$, we use $\texttt{LastWrite}(c, p, x)$ to denote the index of *the most recent channel message* where p writes to x or the message with the current memory of p if the aforementioned type of message does not exist in the channel. Formally, $\texttt{LastWrite}(c, p, x)$ is the largest index $i : \underline{z}(p) \leq i \leq |m|$, such that $m(i) = (mem, p, x)$ for some mem, or $i = \underline{z}(p)$ if such $m(i)$ does not exist.

We define the transition relation $\rightarrow_{HSB}$ on the set of HSB-configurations as follows. For configurations $c = (\underline{q}, \underline{b}, m, \underline{z})$, $c' = (\underline{q}', \underline{b}', m', \underline{z}')$, and $t \in \Delta_p \cup \{\mathsf{update}_p, \mathsf{serialize}_{p,x}\}$ where update_p is an operation that updates memory from the view point of p by increasing $\underline{z}(p)$ by one, and $\mathsf{serialize}_{p,x}$ is an operation that serialises the write (the left most one) at the head of the buffer $\underline{b}(p)(x)$ into a new message at the tail of m, we write $c \rightarrow t_{HSB} c'$ to denote that one of the following conditions is satisfied:

- Nop: $t = (q, \mathsf{nop}, q')$, $\underline{q}(p) = q$, $\underline{q}' = \underline{q}\,[p \hookleftarrow q']$, $\underline{b}' = \underline{b}$, $m' = m$, and $\underline{z}' = \underline{z}$. The operation changes only local states.

- Write to store: $t{=}(q, \mathsf{w}(x,v), q')$, $\underline{q}(p){=}q$, $\underline{q}'{=}\underline{q}\,[p \hookleftarrow q']$, $\underline{b}' = \underline{b}\,[p \hookleftarrow \underline{b}(p)\,[x \hookleftarrow \underline{b}(p)(x)\cdot v]]$, $m' = m$, and $\underline{z}' = \underline{z}$. The write operation is added to the tail of $\underline{b}(p)(x)$.
- Serialize: $t{=}\mathsf{serialize}_{p,x}$, $\underline{q}' = \underline{q}$, $\underline{b} = \underline{b}'\,[p \hookleftarrow \underline{b}'(p)\,[x \hookleftarrow v \cdot \underline{b}'(p)(x)]]$, $m(|m|)$ is of the form (mem_1, p_1, x_1), $m' = m \cdot (mem_1\,[x \hookleftarrow v]\,, p, x)$, and $\underline{z}' = \underline{z}$. A new message is serialised to the head of the channel. The values of the variables in the new message are identical to those in the previous last message except that the value of x has been updated to v. Moreover, we include the updating process p and the updated variable x.
- Update: $t = \mathsf{update}_p$, $\underline{q}' = \underline{q}$, $\underline{b}' = \underline{b}$, $m' = m$, $\underline{z}(p) < |m|$ and $\underline{z}' = \underline{z}\,[p \hookleftarrow \underline{z}(p) + 1]$. An update operation performed by a process p is simulated by moving the pointer of p one step to the right. This means that we remove the oldest write operation that is yet to be used for a memory update. The removed element will now represent the memory contents from the point of view of p.
- Read: $t = (q, \mathsf{r}(x,v), q')$, $\underline{q}(p) = q$, $\underline{q}' = \underline{q}\,[p \hookleftarrow q']$, $\underline{b}' = \underline{b}$, $m' = m$, $\underline{z}' = \underline{z}$, and one of the following conditions is satisfied: (i) Read own write: $\underline{b}(p)(x)(|\underline{b}(p)(x)|) = v$. If there is a write on x in the buffer for x of p then we consider the most recent of such write operations (the right most one in the buffer). (ii) Read memory: $m(\texttt{LastWrite}\,(c, p, x)) = (mem_1, p_1, x_1)$ for some mem_1, p_1, x_1 with $mem_1(x) = v$, $\underline{b}(p)(x) = \epsilon$. If there is no write operation in the buffer for x of p then the value v of x is fetched from the memory. Note that $\underline{b}(p)(x)$ always does not contain the symbol $\star$.
- Full fence: $t = (q, \mathsf{mfence}, q')$, $\underline{q}(p) = q$, $\underline{q}' = \underline{q}\,[p \hookleftarrow q']$, $\underline{b}' = \underline{b}$, $\forall x \in X$: $\underline{b}(p)(x) = \epsilon$, $\underline{b}' = \underline{b}$, $m' = m$, $\underline{z}' = \underline{z}$, and $\underline{z}(p) = |m|$. A full fence operation may be performed by a process p only if all its buffers are empty, and process p is observing the most recent message.
- Write-write fence: $t = (q, \mathsf{sfence}, q')$, $\underline{q}(p) = q$, $\underline{q}' = \underline{q}\,[p \hookleftarrow q']$, $\underline{b}' = \underline{b}$, $\forall x \in X$: $\underline{b}(p)(x) = \epsilon$, $m' = m$, and $\underline{z}' = \underline{z}$. A write-write fence operation requires all previous writes of p to be serialised before continuing, hence a write of p cannot reorder past a sfence.
- ARW: $t = (q, \mathsf{arw}(x, v, v'), q')$, $\underline{q}(p) = q$, $\underline{q}' = \underline{q}\,[p \hookleftarrow q']$, $\underline{b}' = \underline{b}$, $\underline{b}(p)(x) = \epsilon$, $\underline{z}(p) = |m|$, $m(|m|)$ is of the form (mem_1, p_1, x_1), $mem_1(x) = v$, $m' = m \cdot (mem_1\,[x \hookleftarrow v']\,, p, x)$, and $\underline{z}' = \underline{z}\,[p \hookleftarrow \underline{z}(p) + 1]$. The fact that the buffer is empty from the point of view of p is encoded by the equality $\underline{z}(p) = |m|$. The content of the memory can then be fetched from the right most element $m(|m|)$ in the channel. To encode that the buffer is still empty after the operation (from the point of view of p) the pointer of p is moved one step to the right.

We define the sets $\mathsf{update} := \cup_{p \in P}\mathsf{update}_p$, $\mathsf{serialize}_x := \cup_{p \in P}\mathsf{serialize}_{p,x}$, and $\mathsf{serialize} := \cup_{x \in X}\mathsf{serialize}_x$. We use $c \rightarrow_{HSB} c'$ to denote that $c \rightarrow t_{HSB} c'$ for some $t \in \Delta \cup \{\mathsf{update}, \mathsf{serialize}\}$. The set $\texttt{Init}_{HSB}$ of *initial* HSB-configurations of the form $(\underline{q_{init}}, \underline{b_{init}}, m_{init}, \underline{z_{init}})$ where $|m_{init}| = 1$, and for all $p \in P$, we have that $\underline{q_{init}}(p) = q_p^{init}$, $\underline{b_{init}}(p)(x) = \epsilon$, and $\underline{z_{init}}(p) = 1$. In other words, each process is in its initial local state. The channel contains a single message, say of the form $(mem_{init}, p_{init}, x_{init})$, where mem_{init} represents the initial value of the memory. The memory may have any initial value. Also, the values of p_{init} and x_{init} are not relevant since they will not be used in the computations of the system. The pointers of all processes point to the first position in the channel. Moreover, all buffers are all empty. The transition system induced by a concurrent system under the HSB semantics is then given by $(C_{HSB}, \texttt{Init}_{HSB}, \rightarrow_{HSB})$.

The HSB Reachability Problem. In a similar manner to the case of PSO, we define the predicate *Reachable*(*HSB*) ($\mathcal{P}$) (Target), and define the reachability problem for the HSB semantics. The following theorem states equivalence of the reachability problems under the PSO and HSB semantics.

Theorem 1. *For a finite-state program $\mathcal{P}$ and a local state definition* Target*, the reachability problems are equivalent under the PSO and HSB semantics.*

4 The HSB Reachability Algorithm

We present an algorithm to check HSB reachability problem for a given set Target. Then according to Theorem 1, we can solve the PSO reachability problem. First, we define an ordering $\sqsubseteq$ on the set of HSB-configurations. We then show that it satisfies two properties: (i) it is well-quasi ordering (wqo), and (ii) the HSB relation $\rightarrow_{HSB}$ is effectively monotonic wrt. $\sqsubseteq$. Recall that the term *well-quasi ordering* and *effectively monotonic* are defined in Sect. 2.

4.1 Ordering

We define $\texttt{Active}(c) := min\{\underline{z}(p)|\, p \in P\}$ for a HSB-configuration $c = (\underline{q}, \underline{b}, m, \underline{z})$. In other words, the part of m to the right of (and including) $\texttt{Active}(c)$ is *"active"*, while the left part is *"dead"* in the sense that it is not needed for computations starting from c.

Given two HSB configurations $c = (\underline{q}, \underline{b}, m, \underline{z})$ and $c' = (\underline{q}', \underline{b}', m', \underline{z}')$. Define $j := \texttt{Active}(c)$ and $j' := \texttt{Active}(c')$. We write $c \sqsubseteq c'$ to denote that: • (i) $\underline{q} = \underline{q}'$; • (ii) for every $p \in P$ and $x \in X$, there is a mapping $g_{p,x} : \{1, 2, \ldots, |\underline{b}(p)(x)|\} \mapsto \{1, 2, \ldots, |\underline{b}'(p)(x)|\}$ such that the following conditions are satisfied: for every $i, i_1, i_2 \in \{1, 2, \ldots, |\underline{b}(p)(x)|\}$, (1) $i_1 < i_2$ implies $g_{p,x}(i_1) < g_{p,x}(i_2)$, and (2) $\underline{b}(p)(x)(i) = \underline{b}'(p)(x)(g_{p,x}(i))$; • (iii) there is a mapping $h : \{j, j+1, \ldots, |m|\} \mapsto \{j', j'+1, |m'|\}$ such that the following conditions are satisfied: for every $i, i_1, i_2 \in \{j, j+1, \ldots, |m|\}$, (1) $i_1 < i_2$ implies $h(i_1) < h(i_2)$, (2) $m(i) = m'(h(i))$, (3) $\texttt{LastWrite}(c', p, x) = h(\texttt{LastWrite}(c, p, x))$ for all $p \in P$ and $x \in X$, (4) $\underline{z}'(p) = h(\underline{z}(p))$ for all $p \in P$; • (iv) For every $p \in P$ and $x \in X$, one of the following condition holds: (1) if $\underline{b}(p)(x)(|\underline{b}(p)(x)|) = v$ then $\underline{b}'(p)(x)(|\underline{b}'(p)(x)|) = v$, or (2) if $\underline{b}(p)(x) = \epsilon$ then $\underline{b}'(p)(x) = \epsilon$.

The conditions (ii-1) and (iii-1) mean that g and h are strictly monotonic. The condition (ii) indicates that $\underline{b}(p)(x)$ is a *sub-word* of $\underline{b}'(p)(x)$. The conditions (iii-1,2) present the active part of m is a *sub-word* of the active part of m'. The conditions (iii-2,3) ensure the last write indices wrt. all processes and variables are consistent. The conditions (iii-2,4) ensure each process points to identical elements in m and m'. The last condition (iv) shows that the two buffer are empty or contains the same element at the tail of buffers (the right most ones).

We get the following lemma about the ordering on HSB-configurations.

Lemma 1. *The relation $\sqsubseteq$ is a well-quasi ordering on HSB-configurations.*

Proof. The lemma is an immediate consequence of the fact that: (1) the subsequence relations (ii) and (iii) are well-quasi orderings on finite words [18], and (2) the number of states (i), pointers (iii-4), observed memory states (iii-2), and last writes (iii-3) and (ii) that should be equal, is finite.

The following lemma shows the effectively monotonicity of HSB-transition relation wrt. $\sqsubseteq$.

Lemma 2. $\rightarrow_{HSB}$ *is effectively monotonic wrt.* $\sqsubseteq$.

Proof. We show that give HSB-configurations c_1, c_1', and c_2 such that $c_1 \rightarrow_{HSB} c_1'$ and $c_1 \sqsubseteq c_2$, there exists an HSB-configuration c_2' and a run π satisfying: $c_2 \rightarrow \pi_{HSB} c_2'$ and $c_1' \sqsubseteq c_2'$. Let h and $g_{p,x}$ be the mappings defined by $c_1 \sqsubseteq c_2$. We will consider each transition $t \in \Delta_p \cup \{\mathsf{update}_p, \mathsf{serialize}_p\}$ for some $p \in P$ such that $c_1 \rightarrow t_{HSB} c_1'$, and show that $c_2 \rightarrow \pi_{HSB} c_2'$ for some c_2' and π. Then because a run is a concatenation of some transitions, we have the proof.

- Nop: $t = (q, \mathsf{nop}, q')$, select c_2' such that $c_2 \rightarrow t_{HSB} c_2'$. Because nop operation only change the local state of c_1 to c_1' and of c_2 to c_2', and $c_1 \sqsubseteq c_2$, we have $c_1' \sqsubseteq c_2'$.
- Write to store: $t = (q, \mathsf{w}(x, v), q')$, select c_2' such that $c_2 \rightarrow t_{HSB} c_2'$. We add a value to $\underline{b}(p)(x)$ of c_1, and we add the same value to $\underline{b}(p)(x)$ of c_2. Hence the condition (ii) and (iv) hold. Because in this transition we only change the buffers and local states, and $c_1 \sqsubseteq c_2$, we have $c_1' \sqsubseteq c_2'$.
- Read: $t = (q, \mathsf{r}(x, v), q')$, select c_2' such that $c_2 \rightarrow t_{HSB} c_2'$. We do not change the buffers and channel, and require process p to observe x with value v. Because conditions (iii-3) and (iv), c_2' exists. Because of $c_1 \sqsubseteq c_2$, we have $c_1' \sqsubseteq c_2'$.
- Serialize: t=$\mathsf{serialize}_{p,x}$. This transition takes an element from buffer for x of p and send a message to channel. The same element exists in c_2 and will make the same message when serialised. However, there might be more elements in buffer for x of p of c_2 that must be serialised before that element can be reached. Select a run π as a sequence of serialised transitions of p on x will do this work. Formally, select $\pi = c_2 \underbrace{\xrightarrow{\mathsf{serialize}_{p,x}} \cdots \xrightarrow{\mathsf{serialize}_{p,x}}}_{g_{p,x}(1) \text{ times}} c_2'$. In other words, π will serialise all p's writes to x up to and including the one that corresponds to the one that is being serialised in c_1. Because π only removes the element from buffer for x of p, the same message is created at the end of channels of both c_1 and c_2. Since neither t nor π change the local states or pointers, and the serialised operation changes the `LastWrite`(c_1, p, x) and `LastWrite`(c_2, p, x) in both two configurations to a new consistent message, we have $c_1' \sqsubseteq c_2'$.

- Update: $t = \mathsf{update}_p$. This transition advances the pointer of p to a more recent message. However, the corresponding message in c_2 might not be immediately following the message currently pointed by p. But by performing several updates, the pointer in c_2 can be advanced to the message corresponding to the more recent message in c_1. Formally, select $\pi = c_2 \underbrace{\xrightarrow{\mathsf{update}_p} \cdots \xrightarrow{\mathsf{update}_p}}_{h(\underline{z}(p)+1)-h(\underline{z}(p))\text{ times}} c_2'$. Since the pointer of p in c_1 has been forwarded from $\underline{z}(p)$ to $\underline{z}(p)+1$, and the pointer of p in c_2 has moved from $h(\underline{z}(p))$ to $h(\underline{z}(p)+1)$, (iii-4) holds. Also (iii-3) holds between c_1' and c_2' because of (iii-3,4) and $c_1 \sqsubseteq c_2$. Then we have $c_1' \sqsubseteq c_2'$.
- ARW: $t = (q, \mathsf{arw}(x, v, v'), q')$, select c_2' such that $c_2 \rightarrow t_{HSB} c_2'$. This transition performs all read, write, serialise, and update as a single operation. Above we show that any operation of read, write, serialise, and update operations is an effectively monotonic operation. The arw requires p's buffer of x to be empty in c_2. This requirement holds because the p's buffer of x is empty in c_1 and because of (ii). The arw also requires the p's pointer to be on the last message, but it must be the case in c_2 if it is in c_1. Suppose that this requirement does not hold. Then because the pointer of p points to the last message in channel in c_1 (the one at the tail of channel), (1) the last message in channel of c_2 (the one at the tail of channel) does not have a corresponding message in channel of c_1. But (2) the last message of c_2 must be the $\texttt{LastWrite}\,(c_2, p', y)$ for some $p' \in P, y \in X$ (because some process must add more messages after the position $\texttt{LastWrite}\,(c_2, p, x)$). (1) and (2) make (iii-3) not hold. This is a contradiction. Thus c_2' exists, and $c_1' \sqsubseteq c_2'$.
- Full fence and write-write fence cases are trivial, because we do not change anything for buffers and channels.

4.2 Reachability Algorithm

Recall that the terms *upward closure*, *upward closed set*, and *minor set* are defined in Sect. 2. We define the *pre-set* $\texttt{Pre}\,(C)$ of a set C as $\texttt{Pre}\,(C) := \{c'|$

Algorithm 1: Reachability Algorithm.

input : A concurrent program $\mathcal{P}$, and a finite set $\texttt{Target}$ of local state definitions.
output: "u" if $\neg \mathit{Reachable}(HSB)\,(\mathcal{P})\,(\texttt{Target})$, "r" otherwise.

$\mathcal{W} \leftarrow \texttt{Min}\left(\left\{\left(\underline{q}, \underline{b}, \mathit{mem}\right) \mid \underline{q} \in \texttt{Target}\right\}\right)$;
$\mathcal{F} \leftarrow \emptyset$;
while $\mathcal{W} \neq \emptyset$ **do**
    Pick, remove a configuration c' from $\mathcal{W}$;
    $\mathcal{O} \leftarrow \texttt{Min}\,(\texttt{Pre}\,(\{c'\}\uparrow) \cup \{c'\})$;
    foreach $c \in \mathcal{O}$ **do**
        if $\exists c_0 \in \texttt{Init}_{HSB} : c \sqsubseteq c_0$ **then return** "r";
        if $\exists f \in \mathcal{F} : f \sqsubseteq c$ **then** discard c;
        else
            $\mathcal{W} \leftarrow \mathcal{W} \setminus \{w \in \mathcal{W} \mid c \sqsubseteq w\} \cup \{c\}$;
            $\mathcal{F} \leftarrow \mathcal{F} \cup \{c\}$;
return "u";

$\exists c \in C, t \in \Delta \cup \{\mathsf{update}, \mathsf{serialize}\}, c' \rightarrow t_{HSB} c\}$. Bellow we present our algorithm to check the HSB reachability problem using the ordering $\sqsubseteq$ that is well-quasi and monotonic wrt. $\rightarrow_{HSB}$. The algorithm performs backward reachability analysis from the set of configurations that are defined by `Target`. It inputs a finite set `Target`, and checks the predicate $\mathit{Reachable}(HSB)(\mathcal{P})(\mathtt{Target})$. If the predicate does not hold then Algorithm 1 returns *"u"* (unreachable), otherwise it returns *"r"* (reachable). It maintains a *working set* $\mathcal{W}$ that contains *detected* configurations that need to be checked. If one of configuration in $\mathcal{W}$ can be reached by a configuration c *smaller* than the initial configurations (in the sense that there exists a computation c_0 from $\mathtt{Init}_{HSB}$ such that $c \sqsubseteq c_0$), the finite set `Target` also can be reachable (line 7). The set $\mathcal{F}$ is a set of all analysed configurations.

Initially, $\mathcal{W}$ has all elements from a minor set of `Target`, and $\mathcal{F}$ is an empty set. At the beginning of each iteration, the algorithm picks and removes a configuration c' from the set $\mathcal{W}$. Then it computes the set $\mathcal{O}$ that is a minor set of c' and all configurations that can reach a configuration in $\{c'\}\uparrow$ in one transition t, $t \in \Delta \cup \{\mathsf{update}, \mathsf{serialize}\}$. For each minor element c, it checks whether the element is smaller than an initial configuration. If *yes*, it returns *"r"*. If not, it checks whether c is *presented* in $\mathcal{F}$ (in the sense that $\mathcal{F}$ already has a configuration f such that $f \sqsubseteq c$). If *yes* then c can be discarded. Otherwise the algorithm performs the following operations: (i) discards all elements w of $\mathcal{W}$ that $c \sqsubseteq w$, (ii) adds to $\mathcal{W}$ the configuration c, and (iii) adds c to $\mathcal{F}$. The algorithm terminates when $\mathcal{W}$ is empty and return *"u"*.

Theorem 2. *The reachability algorithm always terminates.*

Proof. An immediate consequence of the framework of well-structured transition systems from [4] and the fact that it is possible to compute the finite sets $\mathtt{Min}\left(\left\{\left(\underline{q}, \underline{b}, mem\right) \mid \underline{q} \in \mathtt{Target}\right\}\right)$ and $\mathtt{Min}\left(\mathtt{Pre}\left(\{c'\}\uparrow\right) \cup \{c'\}\right)$ for a configuration c' in the same manner as done in [2].

We can modify the Alg. 1 to return a *trace* (if exists) from a configuration in $\mathtt{Init}_{HSB}$ to a configuration in $\mathtt{Bad} = \left\{\left(\underline{q}, \underline{b}, mem\right) \mid \underline{q} \in \mathtt{Target}\right\}$ in the form $t_0 \cdot t_1 \ldots t_{n-1}$ such that there is a computation: $\pi = c_0 \xrightarrow{t_0} c_1 \xrightarrow{t_1} \cdots \xrightarrow{t_{n-1}} c_n$ with $c_0 \in \mathtt{Init}_{HSB}$ and $c_n \in \mathtt{Bad}$. Indeed, in the algorithm for each configuration c we keep the trace from this configuration to one configuration in Bad. Initially, all configurations in $\mathcal{W}$ have empty traces (line 1). There are two more positions in the algorithm we need to modify. At line 5, when we calculate the list of configurations $\mathtt{Pre}\left(\{c'\}\uparrow\right)$, we add the corresponding transition to the current trace of c'. We do the similar modification in line 10.

5 Fence Insertion

In this section we describe our fence insertion procedure that given a set of *bad configurations*, we can find a minimal set of fences to avoid these configurations under PSO. A *minimal fence set* is the one sufficient for *correctness*; and if we remove any fences from this set, we violate the correctness. There are cases when these fence sets do not exist because the program can reach to bad configurations *even* under SC semantics. In this case we return an empty set. Bellow we fix a configuration $c_i = \left(\underline{q}_i, \underline{b}_i, m_i, \underline{z}_i\right)$ with $0 \leq i \leq n$.

Fence Inference. We will identify the set of points along a trace returned by Algorithm 1, $\pi = c_0 \xrightarrow{t_0} c_1 \xrightarrow{t_1} \cdots \xrightarrow{t_{n-1}} c_n$ with $c_0 \in \texttt{Init}_{HSB}$ and $c_n \in \texttt{Bad}$ with $\texttt{Bad} = \left\{(\underline{q}, \underline{b}, mem) \mid \underline{q} \in \texttt{Target}\right\}$, in which (i) read operations overtake write operations, or (ii) write operations overtake write operations, and derive the set of fences such that any one of them forbids an overtaking, $\mathsf{NewFences}(\pi) := \mathsf{NewFences}_{\mathsf{mfence}}(\pi) \cup \mathsf{NewFences}_{\mathsf{sfence}}(\pi)$. The set $\mathsf{NewFences}_{\mathsf{mfence}}(\pi)$ (or $\mathsf{NewFences}_{\mathsf{sfence}}(\pi)$) can prevent write-read overtaking (or write-write overtaking) in π.

First, we show how to find the set of $\mathsf{NewFences}_{\mathsf{mfence}}(\pi)$ for π. Define $n_i := |m_i| + \Sigma_{p\in P, x\in X} \underline{b}_i(p)(x)$. We define a sequence of functions $\alpha_0, \alpha_1, \ldots, \alpha_n$ where $\alpha_i(j)$ (with $1 \leq j \leq n_i$) associates to each element in the channel m_i or buffers $\underline{b}_i$ the position in π of the corresponding write transition. Note that the lowest index element (index 1) is the initial message in the channel, and the highest index element (index n_i) is the newest element added to buffers. We define $\alpha_0, \alpha_1, \ldots, \alpha_n$ in a recursive way. (i) At the beginning, c_0 contains only initial values in the channel, and all buffers are empty, $\alpha_0(j)$ is undefined for all $1 \leq j \leq n_0$. (ii) The first element in buffers and channel is the initial message in channel, therefore $\alpha_i(1)$ is undefined also. (iii) If t_{i+1} is not a *write operation* then the number of elements in buffers and channel are not changed, define $\alpha_{i+1} := \alpha_i$. (iv) Otherwise, we define $\alpha_{i+1}(j) := \alpha_i(j)$ if $2 \leq j \leq n_i$, and define $\alpha_{i+1}(n_i + 1) := i + 1$. The definition (iv) means that a new write operation will add a new element to the tail of one buffer, and for this element we associate $i+1$. Next, we find the write transitions that have been overtaken by *read operations.* We define a function $\texttt{OverRead}$ such that if t_i (with $1 \leq i \leq n$) is a read transition then $\texttt{OverRead}(\pi)(i)$ gives the positions of write transitions in π that have been overtaken by t_i. Formally, if t_i is not a read then define $\texttt{OverRead}(\pi)(i) := \emptyset$. Otherwise, $t_i = (q, \mathsf{r}(x, v), q') \in \Delta_p$ for some $p \in P$, define $\texttt{OverRead}(\pi)(i) := \left\{\alpha_i(j) \mid \texttt{LastWrite}(c_i, p, x) < j \leq n_i \wedge t_{\alpha_i(j)} \in \Delta_p\right\}$. In other words, we consider the process p that performed t_i and the variable x that is read by p in t_i. We search for pending write operations are issued by p and associated with elements in buffers and channel that are not updated to the memory. Now define $\mathsf{NewFences}_{\mathsf{mfence}}(\pi) := \left\{\underline{q}_k(p) \mid \exists i, j : 1 \leq i \leq n, j \in \texttt{OverRead}(\pi)(i), j \leq k < i\right\}$. In other words, it is necessary to insert a mfence fence at least one position between a pair (j, i) for each $i : 1 \leq i \leq n$ and each $j \in \texttt{OverRead}(\pi)(i)$ in order to eliminate at least one of write-read overtaking.

Second, we show how to find the set of $\mathsf{NewFences}_{\mathsf{sfence}}(\pi)$ for π in a similar way. Define $n'_i := |m_i|$. We define a sequence of function $\gamma_0, \gamma_1, \ldots, \gamma_n$ where $\gamma_i(j)$ (with $1 \leq j \leq n'_i$) associates to each element in the channel m_i the position in π of the write transition that is correspond to the element. We define $\gamma_0, \gamma_1, \ldots, \gamma_n$ in a recursive way. (i) $\gamma_0(j)$ is undefined for all $1 \leq j \leq n'_i$. (ii) $\gamma_i(1)$ is undefined also. (iii) If t_{i+1} is not a *serialised operation* then define

$\gamma_{i+1} := \gamma_i$. (iv) Otherwise, we define $\gamma_{i+1}(j) := \gamma_i(j)$ if $2 \leq j \leq n'_i$, and define $\gamma_{i+1}(n'_i + 1) := i + 1$. Next, we find the write transitions that have been overtaken by *write operations*. We define a function $\mathtt{OverWrite}$ such that if t_i (with $1 \leq i \leq n$) is a write transition then $\mathtt{OverWrite}(\pi)(i)$ gives the positions of write transitions in π that have been overtaken by t_i. Formally, if t_i is not a write then define $\mathtt{OverWrite}(\pi)(i) := \emptyset$. Otherwise, $t_i = (q, \mathsf{w}(x, v), q') \in \Delta_p$ for some $p \in P$, define $\mathtt{OverWrite}(\pi)(i) := \{\alpha_i(j) \| \mathtt{LastWrite}\,(c_i, p, x) < j \leq n_i, t_{\alpha_i(j)} \in \Delta_p, \exists 1 \leq k_1 < k_2 \leq n'_n : \gamma_n(k_1) = t_i \wedge \gamma_n(k_2) = t_{\alpha_i(j)}\}$. Now define $\mathsf{NewFences}_{\mathsf{sfence}}(\pi) := \left\{\underline{q}_k(p) \middle| \, \exists 1 \leq i \leq n, j \in \mathtt{OverWrite}(\pi)(i), j \leq k < i\right\}$.

Algorithm 2: Fence Insertion.

input : A concurrent program $\mathcal{P}$, and a finite set $\mathtt{Target}$ of local state definitions.
output: A minimal set of fences if it exists, or an empty set.

$\mathcal{W} \leftarrow \{\emptyset\}$;
while *true* **do**
    Pick and remove a set F from $\mathcal{W}$;
    if *Reachable(HSB)* $(\mathcal{P} \oplus F)$ $(\mathtt{Target})$ **then**
        $\mathsf{N} \leftarrow \mathsf{NewFences}(\pi)$;
        if $\mathsf{N} = \emptyset$ **then return** $\emptyset$;
        foreach $\mathfrak{f} \in \mathsf{N}$ **do**
            $F' \leftarrow F \cup \{\mathfrak{f}\}$;
            if $\exists F'' \in \mathcal{W} : F'' \subseteq F'$ **then discard** F';
            else $\mathcal{W} \leftarrow \mathcal{W} \cup \{F'\}$;
    else
        return F;

Algorithm. We present our fence insertion algorithm (Algorithm 2). The algorithm takes a concurrent finite-state program $\mathcal{P}$, a finite set $\mathtt{Target}$, and returns a minimal set of fences that is sufficient to make the program safe wrt. $\mathtt{Target}$. If this set is empty then we conclude that the program cannot be corrected by placing fences. It means that the program is *not safe* (i.e. can reach to $\mathtt{Target}$) even under SC semantics. The algorithm uses a set, namely $\mathcal{W}$, for sets of fences that have been *partially* constructed (but not yet large enough to make the program correct). During each iteration, a set F is picked and removed from $\mathcal{W}$. We use the HSB reachability analysis algorithm (Algorithm 1) to check whether the set F is sufficient to make the program correct. If *yes*, we return F as a possible set of minimal fences. If *no*, we compute the set of fences N such that inserting a member of N will eliminate one overtaking in the trace generated by Algorithm 1. We use $\mathcal{P} \oplus F$ to denote the program we get by inserting a set of fences F to $\mathcal{P}$, and use π for the trace. For each $\mathfrak{f} \in \mathsf{N}$ we add $F' = F \cup \{\mathfrak{f}\}$ back to $\mathcal{W}$ unless there is already a subset of F' in $\mathcal{W}$.

Theorem 3. *For a concurrent finite-state program $\mathcal{P}$ and a finite set* $\mathtt{Target}$, *Algorithm 2 terminates and returns a minimal set of fences wrt. $\mathcal{P}$ if the set exists, or an empty one otherwise.*

6 Experimental Results

Tool. We have implemented our techniques from Sects. 3–5 for reachability analysis and fence insertion of programs under PSO semantics to Memorax[1].

[1] https://github.com/margnus1/memorax

The current version of Memorax only applies for TSO semantics [2]. We compare our method with state-of-the-art tools: Remmex [20] (a tool based on state-space verification with acceleration for program analysis wrt. safety properties under TSO and PSO), and Musketeer [6] (a static analysis tool for correctness analysis wrt. robustness property under weak memory model). We compare based on two criteria: *number of fences* and *the running time*. We run the experiments using an Intel x86-32 Core2 2.4 Ghz machine and 4GB of RAM on 16 programs used as benchmarks in [2,6,19,20]. The results are given in Table 1. For each experiment, we report the number of processes (#P), the number of detected fences (#F) (including mfence and sfence if possible), the running time in seconds (#T). Musketeer does not make difference between mfence and sfence, so we put the total number of fences for it.

Table 1. Analyzed concurrent program.

Program	#P	Memorax		Remmex		Musketeer	
		#F	#T	#	#T	#F	#T
SimDek	2	2 m,0 s	1.0	2 m,0 s	2.2	6	1.0
Dekker	2	4 m,0 s	2.2	4 m,0 s	4.8	10	1.0
LamBak	2	4 m,2 s	1253.7	4 m,2 s	9.3	8	1.0
Dijkstra	2	2 m,0 s	5.0	2 m,0 s	5.5	8	1.0
LamFast2	2	4 m,2 s	241.6	4 m,2 s	12.9	12	1.0
Peterson	2	2 m,2 s	4.1	2 m,2 s	7.6	6	1.0
Burns	2	2 m,0 s	1.0	2 m,0 s	4.2	6	1.0
IncSeq	2	0 m,0 s	1.0	0 m,0 s	104.3	0	1.0
Szymanski	2	3 m,0 s	3.3	3 m,0 s	5.8	10	1.0
AltBit	2	0 m,0 s	49.4	0 m,0 s	2.2	4	1.0
CLHQLock	2	•	OM	0 m,0 s	3.1	•	TO
TaskSched	2	0 m,0 s	153.2	0 m,0 s	3.0	0	1.0
Pgsql	2	2 m,1 s	5.4	2 m,1 s	22.82	4	1.0
TickSLock	2	0 m,0 s	24.5	0 m,0 s	5.03	2	1.0
RevBarrier	2	0 m,0 s	2.4	0 m,0 s	1.5	4	1.0
SpinLock	2	0 m,0 s	1.0	0 m,0 s	1.4	1	1.0

For all experiments, we set up the time out to 1800 seconds. If a tool runs out of time (resp. memory), we put "TO" (resp. "OM") in the #T column, and • in #F column. We use "m" for mfence and "s" for sfence. Bellow we summarise the main observations: (i) Memorax successfully finds the minimal fence sets in 15/16 experiments, and only fails in one test because of running out memory (CLHQLock). The minimal fence sets of Memorax and Remmex are the same. (ii) The running time of Memorax and Remmex are compatable (Memorax is better in 9 examples, and Remmex is better in 7 ones). (iii) Musketter is the fastest tool, but also fails in CLHQLock test as Memorax does. However, in most cases (13/15), Musketter returns redundant fences that are not optimal. Especially, AltBit, TickSLock, RevBarrier, and SpinLock are declared to be safe under PSO according to Memorax and Remmex, but still need fences using Musketter.

7 Conclusion

We have presented a precise and sound automatic fence insertion method for concurrent finite-state programs under PSO memory model. We have introduced a new HSB semantics that is equivalent to PSO semantics in the sense of reachability problems, we use a backward analysis to solve the HSB reachability problem. In the case of an unsafe program under PSO but safe under SC, we propose a counter-example algorithm to find a minimal fence set to correct it. We prove the efficiency of our approach by running several benchmarks including challenging ones in existed methods.

References

1. Abdulla, P.A., Atig, M.F., Chen, Y.-F., Leonardsson, C., Rezine, A.: Automatic fence insertion in integer programs via predicate abstraction. In: Miné, A., Schmidt, D. (eds.) SAS 2012. LNCS, vol. 7460, pp. 164–180. Springer, Heidelberg (2012)
2. Abdulla, P.A., Atig, M.F., Chen, Y.-F., Leonardsson, C., Rezine, A.: Counter-example guided fence insertion under TSO. In: Flanagan, C., König, B. (eds.) TACAS 2012. LNCS, vol. 7214, pp. 204–219. Springer, Heidelberg (2012)
3. Abdulla, P.A., Atig, M.F., Chen, Y.-F., Leonardsson, C., Rezine, A.: MEMORAX, a precise and sound tool for automatic fence insertion under TSO. In: Piterman, N., Smolka, S.A. (eds.) TACAS 2013 (ETAPS 2013). LNCS, vol. 7795, pp. 530–536. Springer, Heidelberg (2013)
4. Abdulla, P.A., Cerans, K., Jonsson, B., Tsay, Y.-K.: General decidability theorems for infinite-state systems. In: LICS, pp. 313–321 (1996)
5. Adve, S., Gharachorloo, K.: Shared memory consistency models: a tutorial. Computer **29**(12), 66–76 (1996)
6. Alglave, J., Kroening, D., Nimal, V., Poetzl, D.: Don't sit on the fence. In: Biere, A., Bloem, R. (eds.) CAV 2014. LNCS, vol. 8559, pp. 508–524. Springer, Heidelberg (2014)
7. Alglave, J., Kroening, D., Nimal, V., Tautschnig, M.: Software verification for weak memory via program transformation. In: Felleisen, M., Gardner, P. (eds.) ESOP 2013. LNCS, vol. 7792, pp. 512–532. Springer, Heidelberg (2013)
8. Alglave, J., Kroening, D., Tautschnig, M.: Partial orders for efficient bounded model checking of concurrent software. In: Sharygina, N., Veith, H. (eds.) CAV 2013. LNCS, vol. 8044, pp. 141–157. Springer, Heidelberg (2013)
9. Atig, M.F., Bouajjani, A., Burckhardt, S., Musuvathi, M.: On the verification problem for weak memory models. In: POPL, pp. 7–18. ACM (2010)
10. Atig, M.F., Bouajjani, A., Burckhardt, S., Musuvathi, M.: What's decidable about weak memory models? In: Seidl, H. (ed.) ESOP 2012. LNCS, vol. 7211, pp. 26–46. Springer, Heidelberg (2012)

11. Atig, M.F., Bouajjani, A., Parlato, G.: Getting rid of store-buffers in TSO analysis. In: Gopalakrishnan, G., Qadeer, S. (eds.) CAV 2011. LNCS, vol. 6806, pp. 99–115. Springer, Heidelberg (2011)
12. Bouajjani, A., Derevenetc, E., Meyer, R.: Checking and enforcing robustness against TSO. In: Felleisen, M., Gardner, P. (eds.) ESOP 2013. LNCS, vol. 7792, pp. 533–553. Springer, Heidelberg (2013)
13. Burckhardt, S., Musuvathi, M.: Effective program verification for relaxed memory models. In: Gupta, A., Malik, S. (eds.) CAV 2008. LNCS, vol. 5123, pp. 107–120. Springer, Heidelberg (2008)
14. Burnim, J., Sen, K., Stergiou, C.: Testing concurrent programs on relaxed memory models. In: ISSTA, pp. 122–132. ACM (2011)
15. Dan, A., Meshman, Y., Vechev, M., Yahav, E.: Effective abstractions for verification under relaxed memory models. In: D'Souza, D., Lal, A., Larsen, K.G. (eds.) VMCAI 2015. LNCS, vol. 8931, pp. 449–466. Springer, Heidelberg (2015)
16. Gharachorloo, K., Gupta, A., Hennessy, J.: Performance evaluation of memory consistency models for shared-memory multiprocessors. In: ASPLOS 1991, pp. 245–257 (1991)
17. Gopalakrishnan, G.C., Yang, Y., Sivaraj, H.: QB or not QB: an efficient execution verification tool for memory orderings. In: Alur, R., Peled, D.A. (eds.) CAV 2004. LNCS, vol. 3114, pp. 401–413. Springer, Heidelberg (2004)
18. Higman, G.: Ordering by divisibility in abstract algebras. Proc. London Math. Soc. (3) **2**(7), 326–336 (1952)
19. Kuperstein, M., Vechev, M.T., Yahav, E.: Partial-coherence abstractions for relaxed memory models. In: PLDI, pp. 187–198. ACM (2011)
20. Linden, A., Wolper, P.: A verification-based approach to memory fence insertion in PSO memory systems. In: Piterman, N., Smolka, S.A. (eds.) TACAS 2013 (ETAPS 2013). LNCS, vol. 7795, pp. 339–353. Springer, Heidelberg (2013)
21. Liu, F., Nedev, N., Prisadnikov, N., Vechev, M.T., Yahav, E.: Dynamic synthesis for relaxed memory models. In: PLDI, pp. 429–440. ACM (2012)
22. Owens, S., Sarkar, S., Sewell, P.: A better x86 memory model: x86-TSO. In: Berghofer, S., Nipkow, T., Urban, C., Wenzel, M. (eds.) TPHOLs 2009. LNCS, vol. 5674, pp. 391–407. Springer, Heidelberg (2009)
23. Sewell, P., Sarkar, S., Owens, S., Nardelli, F.Z., Myreen, M.O.: X86-TSO: a rigorous and usable programmer's model for x86 multiprocessors. Commun. ACM **53**(7), 89–97 (2010)
24. SPARC International, Inc., The SPARC Architecture Manual Version 9 (1994)
25. Yang, Y., Gopalakrishnan, G., Lindstrom, G., Slind, K.: Nemos: a framework for axiomatic and executable specifications of memory consistency models. In: IPDPS. IEEE Computer Society (2004)

Model Checking Dynamic Distributed Systems

C. Aiswarya(✉)

Uppsala University, Uppsala, Sweden
aiswarya.cyriac@it.uu.se

Abstract. We consider distributed systems with dynamic process creation. We use data words to model behaviors of such systems. Data words are words where positions also contain some data values from an infinite domain. The data values are seen as the process identities. We use an automata with a stack and registers to model a distributed system with dynamic process creation. The non-emptiness checking of these automata is NP-Complete. While satisfiability of first order logic over data words is undecidable, we show that model checking such an automata against full MSO logic (with data equality and comparison predicates) is decidable.

1 Introduction

Distributed systems with a pre-defined finite set of processes have been studied extensively. However, verification of distributed systems with unbounded set of processes or those with dynamic process creation has received relatively little attention. One reason might be the additional difficulty in modeling and model checking caused by the unbounded set of processes. Most of the distributed systems we encounter in our everyday life, like internet, creates processes dynamically. Hence verification of distributed systems with dynamic process creation has become a necessity, needless to say it is interesting in its own with the scope of extending the frontiers from bounded number of processes to a dynamic setting.

There has been an increasing interest in the verification of systems with unbounded number of processes in the recent years. Most of these works describe the system by describing the local processes in the system. For obtaining decidability in the shared memory setting (1) the processes are assumed to be anonymous, and (2) often a bound on the number of context switched per process is assumed to obtain decidability (cf. [3]). In the message passing setting, such systems have been considered as parametrised systems (see [1,6,8,9]). In the parametrized setting, each individual process has a finite control and fixed set of registers to store the identities of some of the other processes and possibly a stack to model recursion.

A global description of such systems is interesting, mainly for protocol specifications. In [14], grammars were used to model global descriptions of systems with dynamic process creation. It was shown that model checking these grammars against MSO is decidable. In [10] the authors study how to synthesize the local implementations of processes from a global grammar specification.

A. Bouajjani and H. Fauconnier (Eds.): NETYS 2015, LNCS 9466, pp. 48–61, 2015.
DOI: 10.1007/978-3-319-26850-7_4

Instead of the grammars of [14], a very powerful automata based formalism was proposed in [7] for global descriptions of systems with dynamic process creation. The formalism called data-multi-pushdown automata has registers and *multiple* stacks which can store (an unbounded number of) process identities. This model supported dynamic process creation by injecting "fresh" process identities into the system (values that have not been used in the history). The main (and surprising) result of [7] states that model checking of these automata against monadic second order logic (MSO) augmented with predicates for data-(dis)equality tests is decidable.

This paper is closely related to [7]. We consider a model which is a restriction and at the same time an extension of the data-multi-pushdown system. We restrict to models with only one stack (instead of multiple stacks). On the other hand, we extend the transition guards to perform data inequality tests (in addition to the (dis)equality tests if [7]). We demonstrate the modelling power of this formalism with several examples. We show that the decidability of model checking against MSO holds for this model as well, even though the MSO has predicates for data equality/disequality/inequality tests. We study control state reachability problem for this model (as opposed to full MSO model checking) in hope of obtaining better complexity. We show that it is in fact NP complete.

There has been many works on languages of data-words and logics for them which do not assume freshness (cf. [4,5,11–13]).

2 Data Words to Model Protocols

Notation. The set of natural numbers $\{1, 2, \ldots\}$ is denoted by $\mathbb{N}$. A ranked alphabet is a pair $(A, \mathsf{arityOf})$ where A is a set, and $\mathsf{arityOf} : A \mapsto \mathbb{N}$ is a mapping. Abusing notations, we sometimes write A to denote the ranked alphabet $(A, \mathsf{arityOf})$. Given a ranked alphabet $(A, \mathsf{arityOf})$ and a (potentially infinite) set B, we denote by A_B the set $\{a(b_1, \ldots, b_n) \mid a \in A, n = \mathsf{arityOf}(a) \text{ and } b_i \in B\}$.

2.1 Data Words

A (multi-dimensional) data word, over a finite ranked alphabet $(A, \mathsf{arityOf})$ and an infinite data domain D, is a sequence of elements from Σ_D. Consider a data word $w \in \Sigma_D^*$. By $\mathsf{symAt}(i)(w)$ we denote the letter at position i of w. For $k \leq \mathsf{arityOf}(\mathsf{symAt}(i))$, we denote the kth data value at position i by $\mathsf{dataAt}(k)(i)(w)$. For example, suppose $w = a_1(d_1^1, \ldots, d_{n_1}^1)a_2(d_1^2, \ldots, d_{n_2}^2)a_3(d_1^3, \ldots, d_{n_3}^3)\ldots$. Then $\mathsf{symAt}(i)(w) = a_i$ and $\mathsf{dataAt}(k)(i)(w) = d_k^i$ if $k < n_i$.

2.2 Dynamic Distributed Systems (DDS)

A Dynamic Distributed Systems (DDS) consists of a collection of processes. Each process in the system has a unique identifier (called pid). We fix the set of process identifiers of any DDS to be $\mathbb{N}$.

We consider DDS capable of performing two types of atomic events: (a) create, and (b) message. Each of these events have two participating processes. For create, we have the creating process and the created process. For message, we have the sender and the receiver. The created process will be a fresh (non existing) process, while the creating process as well as the sender and the receiver are assumed to be already existing in the system.

We assume the pid of the created process to be bigger (in the natural order) than that of any existing process. This is in accordance with the pid assigning conventions in Unix. This convention facilitates determining which process is more recent by comparing their process ids.

A message can have the message contents, which we denote by a predefined message type and the set of (existing) process ids appearing in the message. The number of process ids that appear in a message is determined by the message type. Let the finite ranked alphabet $(\mathsf{Messages} = \{a, b, \ldots\}, \mathsf{arityOf})$ be the predefined message types. For each $a \in \mathsf{Messages}$ we have $\mathsf{arityOf}(a) \geq 2$, since two pids are required to specify the sender and the receiver. In fact $\mathsf{arityOf}(a) - 2$ gives the number of process ids that are transmitted from the sender to the receiver in a message of type a.

The set of events of DDS is given by finite ranked alphabet $(\textsc{Events} = \{\texttt{create}\} \cup \mathsf{Messages}, \mathsf{arityOf})$. We have $\mathsf{arityOf}(\texttt{create}) = 2$, and $\mathsf{arityOf}(a)$ for $a \in \mathsf{Messages}$ is inherited from the ranked alphabet $(\mathsf{Messages}, \mathsf{arityOf})$ defined before.

An event is an element of $\textsc{Events}_{\mathbb{N}}$. The behavior of a DDS is a data word from $\textsc{Events}^*_{\mathbb{N}}$.

Example 1. Consider the following data word over $(\{\texttt{create}, \texttt{msg}\}, \mathsf{arityOf})$ where $\mathsf{arityOf}(\texttt{create}) = \mathsf{arityOf}(\texttt{msg}) = 2$.

$$\begin{aligned} w_1 = \quad & \texttt{create}(1,2) \;\; \texttt{create}(2,3) \;\; \texttt{msg}(3,1) \;\; \texttt{create}(3,4) \\ & \texttt{msg}(2,1) \;\; \texttt{create}(4,5) \;\; \texttt{msg}(5,1) \;\; \texttt{msg}(4,1). \end{aligned}$$

This behaviour can be visualised graphically as depicted in Fig. 1. The sequence of events taking place on process i is given in the left to right order on the horizontal line next to i. □

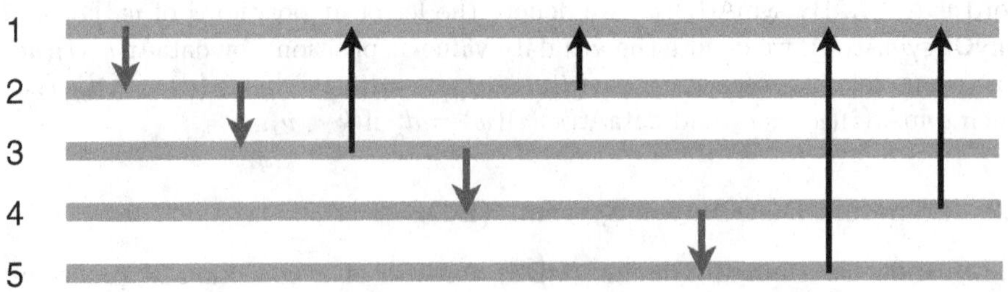

Fig. 1. A trace

Example 2 (Peer-to-peer protocol). Consider the set of data words of the form (where $m, n \in \mathbb{N}$ and $m < n$)

$$\begin{aligned} w_{n,m} = \quad & \mathtt{create}(1,2) \;\; \mathtt{create}(2,3) \;\; \ldots \;\; \mathtt{create}(n-1,n) \\ & \mathtt{req}(n,n-1,n) \;\; \mathtt{req}(n-1,n-2,n) \;\; \ldots \;\; \mathtt{req}(m-1,m,n) \\ & \mathtt{msg}(m,n)\mathtt{msg}(n,m) \;\; \mathtt{msg}(m,n)\mathtt{msg}(n,m) \;\; \ldots \;\; \mathtt{msg}(m,n)\mathtt{msg}(n,m). \end{aligned}$$

These set of words describe a dynamic peer to peer protocol. The informal description of the protocol is as follows. There is a creation phase in which the processes are created in a cascade fashion. After that the last created process is in search for a peer and requests its parent to be one. It can either accept, or refuse by passing the request from its child on to its parent. This continues for a while until one process decided to be the peer, and then peer-peer communication takes place between these two (by msg events). If the request reached the process 1, it is forced to be a peer, since it cannot forward the request to its parent. Note that the messages in the request phase needs to carry the identity of the requesting process in its contents.

Figure 2 depicts the peer-to-peer protocol with $n = 6$ and $m = 2$. The data word is obtained by writing down the events in the left to right order. □

Example 3. Consider a DDS which creates processes to form a tree architecture like in Fig. 3. This word can be represented by a *depth-first-search* listing of the create events. For e.g. in Fig. 3 it is given by the dataword tree:

$$\begin{aligned} \mathit{tree} = \quad & \mathtt{create}(1,2) \;\; \mathtt{create}(2,3) \;\; \mathtt{create}(3,4) \;\; \mathtt{create}(3,5) \;\; \mathtt{create}(2,6) \\ & \mathtt{create}(1,7) \;\; \mathtt{create}(7,8) \;\; \mathtt{create}(8,9) \;\; \mathtt{create}(8,10) \;\; \mathtt{create}(10,11). \end{aligned}$$

This can be followed by a request propagating from the leftmost leaf to the right most leaf only through the leafs (i.e. the request message scans the yield of the tree from left to right). This is similar to the seeking phase in the peer-to-peer protocol. A data word for this phase in the example is seek:

$$\mathit{seek} \;=\; \mathtt{req}(4,5,4) \;\; \mathtt{req}(5,6,4) \;\; \mathtt{req}(6,9,4) \;\; \mathtt{req}(9,11,4).$$

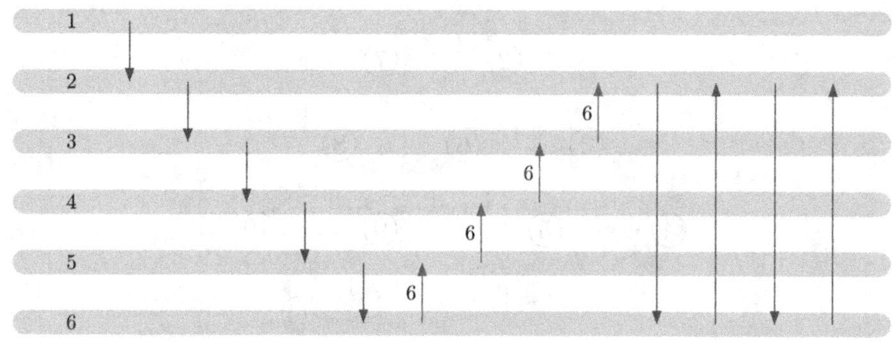

Fig. 2. A peer-to-peer protocol.

Finally, the rightmost leaf (peer) sends a message directly to the leftmost leaf ($\texttt{msg}(11,4)$). Thus a data word representation of Fig. 3 is *tree seek* $\texttt{msg}(11,4)$.

This example can be seen as modeling the search for a distant relative in a social network. The green part of the tree shows the family tree. The leaves are the current generation. The leaves know only their closest relatives in the current generation (their left and right neighbors in the left-to-right ordering of the leaves). A person in the present generation (process 4) wants to find a kin peer. The request for such a peer must be propagated along the current generation. (Older generations are perhaps dead!) □

Remark 1. The behaviors of DDS are data words over $\text{Events}_{\mathbb{N}}$. However any data word over $\text{Events}_{\mathbb{N}}$ need not have an interpretation as the behavior of a DDS. For example, $\texttt{create}(1,2)\texttt{create}(2,1)$ is a valid data word, but it cannot be seen as the behavior of a DDS since an existing process cannot be created. The dataword $\texttt{create}(2,1)$ is also not a valid behavior, since the pid of the newly created process needs to be bigger than the existing processes.

Remark 2. It might be a bit annoying to see that we have used sequences to represent the behaviors of a DDS. This looks like it captures only *linearzations* of the distributed behavior. However, as we will shortly see, the specification language we use is powerful enough to recover the concurrency information from a linearization.

2.3 Monadic Second Order Logic over Data Words

Now we describe a powerful specification language to reason about the properties of data words. We use an extension of MSO over words to data words. In addition to the MSO over words, it allows comparison of data values.

We assume countably infinite supplies of first-order and second-order variables. We let $x, y, \ldots$ denote first-order variables, which vary over positions in

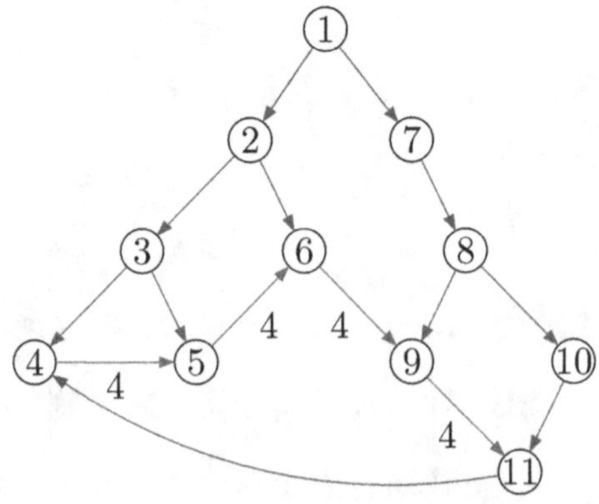

Fig. 3. A distant-relative search (Colour figure online).

the word, and we use $X, Y, \ldots$ to denote second-order variables, which vary over sets of positions in the word.

Definition 1 (MSO logic over data words). *The class* $\mathrm{MSO}_d(\textsc{Events})$ *of* monadic second-order (MSO) formulas *over data words is given by the following grammar, where* a *ranges over* $\textsc{Events}$, *and* k, ℓ *are at most the maximum rank of any letter in* $\textsc{Events}$*:*

$$\varphi ::= a(x) \mid d^{<}_{k,\ell}(x,y) \mid d^{=}_{k,\ell}(x,y) \mid x \leq y \mid x \in X \mid \neg\phi \mid \phi \vee \phi \mid \exists x\phi \mid \exists X\phi$$

If the free variable x is interpreted as position i of a data word w, then the formula $a(x)$ holds if $\mathsf{symAt}(i)(w) = a$. If the free variable x and y are interpreted as positions i and j respectively, then the formula $d^{=}_{k,\ell}(x,y)$ holds if $\mathsf{dataAt}(k)(i)(w) = \mathsf{dataAt}(k)(\ell)(w)$. Semantics of Formula $d^{<}_{k,\ell}(x,y)$ is similar but requires $\mathsf{dataAt}(k)(i)(w) < \mathsf{dataAt}(k)(\ell)(w)$ instead of $\mathsf{dataAt}(k)(i)(w) = \mathsf{dataAt}(k)(\ell)(w)$. Formula $x \leq y$, the boolean connectives, and quantifiers are self-explanatory. We may use the usual abbreviations $x < y$, $\forall x\phi$, $\phi \rightarrow \psi \ldots$

If ϕ is a sentence, i.e., it does not have any free variable, then we set $L(\phi)$ to be the set of data words w such that $w \models \phi$.

Example 4. Consider the property that any process which requests for a peer eventually gets a peer. This can be said by the following formula: $\forall x\, req(x) \rightarrow \exists y(y > x \wedge msg(y) \wedge d^{=}_{3,2}(x,y))$. That is, if there is a "*req*" event, then there is a "*msg*" event in the future such that the parameter of "req" event and the receiver of the "msg" event are the same.

Example 5. Consider a property that the participants of any message are always leaves, i.e., they do not create other processes. This can be said by the formula $\forall x\, \neg create(x) \rightarrow \neg\exists y\, create(y) \wedge (d^{=}_{1,2}(y,x) \vee d^{=}_{1,1}(y,x))$

Example 6. Messages are always sent from younger processes to older processes can be said by the formula $\forall x\, msg(x) \rightarrow d^{<}_{2,1}(x,x)$

Example 7. Every created process eventually sends a message to the "root" process. This can be said by the formula $\exists x\, (\min(x) \wedge \forall y\, (\mathtt{create}(y) \rightarrow \exists y'\, (d^{=}_{2,1}(y,y') \wedge d^{=}_{1,2}(x,y'))))$. The formula holds in the data word w of Example 1 (Fig. 1).

Example 8. This example demonstrates that the our logic is powerful enough to express causal dependencies, though it is evaluated on linearizations. The property that every two events are causally dependent can be said by the following formula. $\forall x \forall y(x \preceq y \vee y \preceq x)$ where $x \preceq y := (x \leq y \wedge \bigvee_{i,j \in \{1,2\}} d^{=}_{i,j}(x,y))^*$. We do not explicitly give this formula, but transitive closure is definable in MSO.

3 Data Pushdown Automata

A data pushdown automata is a finite state automaton equipped with a stack and a finite set of registers. It can remember data values by either storing it in registers or by pushing it to the stack.

All registers except one are undefined in the beginning. The undefined registers hold a special value $\perp$. The defined registers hold the pid of the initial (root) process.

The stack symbols come from a ranked alphabet $\mathcal{Z}$, and the stack contains words from $\mathcal{Z}_{\mathbb{N}}^*$. Only the contents of those registers with a proper pid can be pushed onto the stack. Thus the stack does not contain $\perp$. Similarly the registers can be rewritten by only pids. Thus a register if ever gets to store a pid, it will never hold $\perp$ again.

At any state the automaton may (optionally) pop the topmost letter on the stack, while storing the associated data-values (pids) to some registers. Then it can perform an event involving the data values in the registers. Then it may (optionally) push another letter from $\mathcal{Z}_{\mathbb{N}}$ to the stack where the data-values come from the current register contents. Finally it reassigns the register values, and updates its state.

The infinite set of transition labels allow a finite abstraction by writing the register name which contains the data value rather than the actual data value. Let $\mathcal{R}$ be the finite set of register names. The set of such abstract events is $\text{Events}_{\mathcal{R}}$. That is, $\text{Events}_{\mathcal{R}} = \{a(r_1, \ldots r_n) \mid a \in \text{Events},\ n = \mathsf{arityOf}(a)$ and r_i is a register name from the set $\mathcal{R}\}$. The abstract pop and push actions can be described using $\mathcal{Z}_{\mathcal{R}}$. The letter $Z(r_1, \ldots, r_n) \in \mathcal{Z}_{\mathcal{R}}$ for a pop action means that, upon popping the letter $Z(d_1, \ldots, d_n) \in \mathcal{Z}_{\mathbb{N}}$ the data-values $d_1, \ldots, d_n$ are stored in registers $r_1, \ldots, r_n$ respectively. Similarly, for a push action denoted by the letter $Z(r_1, \ldots, r_n) \in \mathcal{Z}_{\mathcal{R}}$ means that that the letter $Z(d_1, \ldots, d_n) \in \mathcal{Z}_{\mathbb{N}}$ is actually pushed into the stack where $d_1, \ldots, d_n$ are the data-values stored in registers $r_1, \ldots, r_n$ respectively.

A subtle point in our model is the semantics of `create` event. If it executes a `create` event, the data value in the target register is rewritten by a "fresh" value which is higher than any of the data values used so for. This freshness is very crucial for our decidability results.

We define these notions formally.

Definition 2 (Data pushdown automaton). *Let* $\Bbbk \geq 0$. *A* $\Bbbk$*-register data pushdown automaton (DPA) over* Events *is a 7-tuple* $\mathcal{A} = (S, \mathcal{Z}, s_0, r_0, Z_0, F, \Delta)$ *where* S *is a finite* set of states, $\mathcal{Z}$ *is a finite ranked alphabet of* stack symbols, $s_0 \in S$ *is the* initial state, r_0 *is the initial state,* $Z_0 \in \mathcal{Z}$ *is the* start symbol *with* $\mathsf{arityOf}(Z_0) = 0$, *and* $F \subseteq S$ *is the set of* final states. *Moreover,* Δ *is a set of* transitions *of the form* $\tau = (s, A(r_1, \ldots, r_n), \alpha, \mathsf{upd}, \rho, s')$ *where* $s, s' \in S$ *are states,* $A(r_1, \ldots, r_n) \in \mathcal{Z}_{\mathcal{R}}$, $\alpha \in \text{Events}_{\mathcal{R}}$ *and* $\mathsf{upd} \in \mathcal{Z}_{\mathcal{R}}^*$ *and* $\rho : [\Bbbk] \mapsto [\Bbbk]$ *is an injective partial functions.*

We let $Conf_{\mathcal{A}} := S \times (\mathbb{N} \cup \{\perp\})^{\Bbbk} \times \mathbb{N} \times \mathcal{Z}_{\mathbb{N}}^*$ denote the set of *configurations* of $\mathcal{A}$. Configuration $\gamma = [s, \mathbf{r}, \mathtt{max}, w]$ with $\mathbf{r} = (d_1, \ldots, d_{\Bbbk})$ says that the current state is s, the content of register r_i is d_i, all the data values which have already been used are at most $\mathtt{max}$, and the stack content is $w \in \mathcal{Z}_{\mathbb{N}}^*$ where we assume that the topmost symbol is written last. If some d_i is $\perp$, then the register r_i is undefined.

Now, consider a transition $\tau = (s, A(r_{i^1}, \ldots, r_{i^n}), \alpha, \mathsf{upd}, \rho, s')$. It is enabled at a configuration $\gamma = [s, \mathbf{r}, \mathtt{max}, w]$ if the conditions E1 ... E5 are satisfied.

E1 $w = w'\, A(d''_1, \ldots, d''_n)$

Before listing the remaining conditions, we first define an auxiliary register assignment $\mathbf{r}'$ which represents the effect of the pop on $\mathbf{r}$. Define $\mathbf{r}' = (d'_1, \ldots, d'_{\Bbbk})$ where $d'_i = \begin{cases} d''_j & \text{if } i = i^j \\ d_i & \text{otherwise.} \end{cases}$

E2 If $r_i \in \mathsf{pre\text{-}image}(\rho)$, then one of the following must hold:
- $d'_i \neq \bot$ or
- $\alpha = \mathtt{create}(\text{-}, r_i)$.

E3 If $\alpha = \mathtt{create}(r_i, -)$, then $d'_i \neq \bot$.
E4 If $\alpha = a(r_{j^1}, r_{j^2}, \ldots r_{j^\ell})$, then for all $k \in \{1, \ldots \ell\}$, we have $d'_{j^k} \neq \bot$.
E5 if $B(r_{k^1}, r_{j^2}, \ldots r_{k^m})$ is present in upd then for each $i \in \{k^1, \ldots, k^m\}$, either $d'_i \neq \bot$ or $\alpha = \mathtt{create}(\text{-}, r_i)$.

That is, for τ to be enabled at γ (1) the top stack symbol of γ should match that of the transition, (2) the register assignment should not overwrite a defined register with $\bot$, (3) and (4) the pids executing the event and message contents must exist (or the corresponding register names must be defined), and (4) the symbol $\bot$ is never written to the stack.

Now, we define the effect of an enabled transition τ at a configuration γ. Consider a register assignment function $\sigma : \mathcal{R} \mapsto \mathbb{N}$. We say that σ is suitable for γ and τ, if it can represent the effect of a $\mathtt{create}$ event (if applicable). That is σ is suitable for γ and τ if $\sigma(r_i) = \begin{cases} d > \mathtt{max} & \text{if } \alpha = \mathtt{create}(\text{-}, r_i) \\ d'_i & \text{otherwise.} \end{cases}$. That is, the in the case of a $\mathtt{create}$ event, the target register should be assigned a value larger than $\mathtt{max}$.

For every γ and τ there exists infinitely many suitable register assignment functions. If $\alpha = a(r_1, \ldots, r_n) \in \text{EVENTS}_{\mathcal{R}}$, we let $\sigma(\alpha)$ be $a(\sigma(r_1), \ldots, \sigma(r_n))$. We lift this notion to words in $\text{EVENTS}^*_{\mathcal{R}}$ as well: $\sigma(uv) = \sigma(u)\sigma(v)$.

If τ is enabled at γ and if σ is a suitable register assignment function, the automaton $\mathcal{A}$ can execute τ under σ generating $\sigma(\alpha)$. Then it moves into a new configuration $\gamma' = [s', \mathbf{r}', \mathtt{max}', w'']$ with $\mathtt{max}' = \mathtt{max}(\mathtt{max}, \mathtt{max}_i \sigma(r_i))$, $w'' = w'\sigma(\mathsf{upd})$ and $\mathbf{r}' = (\sigma(\rho^{-1}(r_1)), \ldots, \sigma(\rho^{-1}(r_{\Bbbk})))$ where we set $\rho(r_i) = r_i$ if $r_i \notin \mathsf{image}(\rho)$. In this case we write $\gamma \xRightarrow{\sigma(\alpha)}_{\sigma,\tau} \gamma'$.

A configuration of the form $[s_0, (d, \bot, \ldots, \bot), d, Z]$ with $d \in \mathbb{N}$ is called *initial*, and a configuration $[s, \mathbf{r}, d, w]$ such that $s \in F$ is called *final*. A *run* of $\mathcal{A}$ on $u \in \text{EVENTS}^*_{\mathbb{N}}$ is a sequence $\gamma_0 \xRightarrow{\alpha_1}_{\sigma_1,\tau_1} \gamma_1 \xRightarrow{\alpha_2}_{\sigma_2,\tau_2} \cdots \xRightarrow{\alpha_n}_{\sigma_n,\tau_n} \gamma_n$ such that $u = \alpha_1 \cdots \alpha_n$ and γ_0 is initial. The run is *accepting* if γ_n is final. We let $L(\mathcal{A}) := \{u \in \text{EVENTS}^*_{\mathbb{N}} \mid \text{there is an accepting run of } \mathcal{A} \text{ on } u\}$ be the *language* of $\mathcal{A}$.

Example 9. A DPA for the peer-to-peer protocol (cf. Example 2) is given in Fig. 4. It uses three registers. We need only one extra stack symbol with arityOf 1. Hence we remove this symbol in the figure for readability.

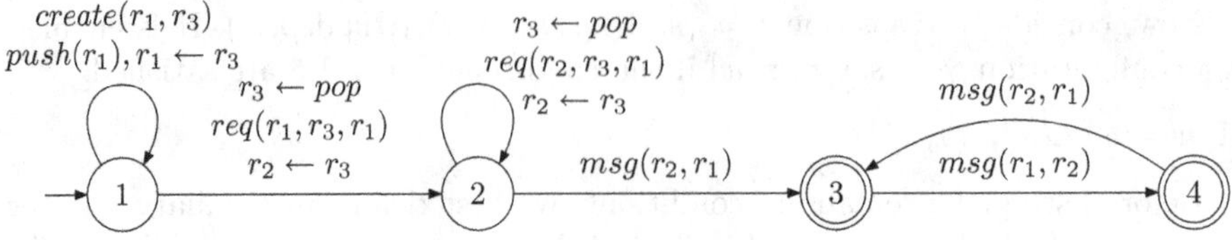

Fig. 4. A DPA for peer-to-peer

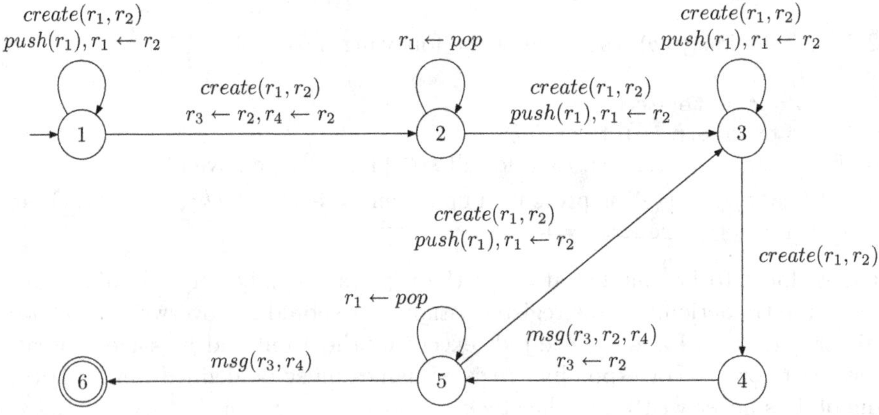

Fig. 5. A DPA for distant-relative search

Example 10. The DPA given in Fig. 5 accepts the distant-relative search example (cf. Example 3).

The *control state reachability problem* asks, given a data pushdown automata $\mathcal{A} = (S, \mathcal{Z}, s_0, r_0, Z_0, F, \Delta)$ and a state $\texttt{target} \in S$, whether there is an initial run of $\mathcal{A}$ of the form $\gamma_0 \xRightarrow{\alpha_1}_{\sigma_1,\tau_1} \gamma_1 \xRightarrow{\alpha_2}_{\sigma_2,\tau_2} \cdots \xRightarrow{\alpha_n}_{\sigma_n,\tau_n} \gamma_n$ where γ_n is of the form $[\texttt{target}, \mathbf{r}, d, w]$. The non-emptiness problem asks, given a data pushdown automata $\mathcal{A} = (S, \mathcal{Z}, s_0, r_0, Z_0, F, \Delta)$, whether the language of $\mathcal{A}$ is non-empty (i.e., $L(\mathcal{A}) \neq \emptyset$). The control state reachability problem and the non-emptiness problem are inter-reducible.

4 Non-emptiness of DPA

We show the complexity of non-emptiness of DPAs in this section.

Theorem 1. *Non-emptiness checking of data pushdown automata is NP-Complete*

Proof. We show the NP hardness by reducing 3-CNF-SAT to the non-emptiness problem of DPA. The problem 3-CNF-SAT which is given below is a well known NP-Complete problem. Let $V = \{v_1, \ldots v_n\}$ be a set of propositional variables.

By $\overline{V}$, we denote the set $\{\overline{v_1}, \ldots, \overline{v_n}\}$, the set of negations of propositional variables. Let $\mathsf{Lit} = V \cup \overline{V}$ be the set of literals.

> Input: $\varphi \equiv \bigwedge_{i=1}^{m} C_i$ where $C_i = \ell_1^i \vee \ell_2^i \vee \ell_3^i$ and $\ell_j^i \in \mathsf{Lit}$ for $1 \leq j \leq 3$.
> Question: Is there a satisfying truth assignment of the variables V such that φ evaluates to `true`?

Our reduction is as follows. On the input φ, we construct an DPA $\mathcal{A}_\varphi$ as given in the Fig. 6. Remember that ℓ_j^i is actually some v_k or $\overline{v_k}$. Thus $\mathcal{A}_\varphi$ uses $2n+1$ registers: $\mathcal{R} = \{x_0\} \cup \mathsf{Lit}$. On going from state s_{i-1} to state s_i the run defines one and only one of the two registers v_i and $\overline{v_i}$. Thus on reaching state s_n, the configuration corresponds to a unique truth assignment: The register v_i is defined if and only if the propositional variable v_i is set to `true` by the truth assignment, and the register $\overline{v_i}$ is defined if and only if the propositional variable v_i is set to `false` by the truth assignment. Thus there is a run from s_0 to s_n corresponding to every truth assignment, and there is a truth assignment corresponding to every run from s_0 to s_n. The run can be extended to reach the state s_1' if and only if the current truth assignment satisfies the clause C_1. Inductively, the run can be extended to reach the state s_i' if and only if all the clauses $C_1, \ldots C_i$ are satisfiable by the current truth assignment. Hence there is an accepting run of the DPA $\mathcal{A}_\varphi$ if and only if ϕ is satisfiable. This proves the NP-hardness. Notice that, non-emptiness is NP hard without using the stack.

We now describe the NP algorithm.

From the DPA $\mathcal{A} = (S, \mathcal{Z}, s_0, r_0, Z_0, F, \Delta)$, we obtain a classical pushdown automata (over finite alphabet) as follows. The set of states of the pushdown automata is $S^{\mathcal{R}}$. The set of stack symbols of the pushdown automata is the unranked alphabet $\mathcal{Z}$ (i.e., only the symbols of the ranked alphabet $(\mathcal{Z}, \mathsf{arityOf})$). Intuitively, a state (s, R) corresponds to a configuration of $\mathcal{A}$ where the state is s and the set of defined registers is precisely $R \subseteq \mathcal{R}$. If the DPA has a transition $\tau = (s, A(r_{i^1}, \ldots, r_{i^n}), \alpha, \mathsf{upd}, \rho, s')$, then the pushdown automata has transition of the form $((s, R), A, \alpha, \mathsf{symAt}(\mathsf{upd}), (s', R'))$ where

- $\mathsf{symAt}(\mathsf{upd})$ corresponds to the word in $\mathcal{Z}^*$ obtained by projecting to the $\mathsf{symAt}()$ of upd.
- If α is of the form $\mathtt{create}(r_i, r_j)$ then $r_i \in R \cup \{r_{i^1}, \ldots, r_{i^n}\}$, i.e. r_i must be defined. Further $R' = R \cup \{r_{i^1}, \ldots, r_{i^n}\} \cup \{r_j\}$.
- If α is of the form $\alpha(r_{j^1}, \ldots, r_{j^m})$ where $\alpha \neq \mathtt{create}$, then for each r_{j^k}, $r_{j^k} \in R \cup \{r_{i^1}, \ldots, r_{i^n}\}$, i.e. r_{j^k} must be defined. Further $R' = R \cup \{r_{i^1}, \ldots, r_{i^n}\}$.

Since we do not have any guards with data value comparisons in the transitions of the DPA $\mathcal{A}$, if this pushdown automata has an accepting run, then the DPA also has an accepting run.

However, since the pushdown automata is exponential sized, the construction of this pushdown automata is too expensive for an NP algorithm. Hence, instead of constructing the automata, we will make some clever guesses to remain in NP.

Notice that the set of defined registers is monotonously non decreasing along any run. Our NP procedure guesses an ordering among the registers and assume that the registers are added into the "defined" set only in this order. Let $X_1 \subsetneq X_2 \subsetneq \ldots \subsetneq X_{\Bbbk}$ be the sequence of defined registers in this order. That is, X_i be the set of first i registers that are defined according to this guessed order.

First we translate the given DPA into another one which on each transition either (a) pops a symbol from the stack but does not push, or (b) push one symbol to the stack, but does not pop, or (c) does not push or pop. This translation causes only a linear blowup in the size of the input DPA. Then, for each transition τ, we pre-compute $\min(\tau)$ the minimum set of registers needed to be defined in order to enable τ. We also compute $\mathsf{fin}(\tau)$, which is the resulting set of defined registers if τ was executed at $\min(\tau)$. The pre computation can be done in polynomial time, since we are associating just two sets to every transition of the DPA $\mathcal{A}$.

Then we have a saturation based reachability algorithm which tries to populate sets $R_i^j \subseteq S \times S$ with $1 \leq i < j \leq \Bbbk$. Note that, the number of sets R_i^j is $\Bbbk(\Bbbk+1)/2$. These sets can be populated simultaneously in polynomial time. The intended meaning of the set R_i^j is that, if $(s, s') \in R_i^j$, then if the all registers in X_i are defined, then the automaton can reach state s' from s, resulting in a new defined set of registers which is exactly X_j. We explain the computation of R_i^j below.

The set R_i^j is initiated to the reflexive relation on states. Then for each pair of complementary transitions $\tau = (s, , -, A, , s')$ and $\tau' = (t, A, -, , -, t')$, the pair (s, t') is added to all sets R_i^j such that there exists i', j' with (a) $\min(\tau) \subseteq X_i$, (b) $X_{i'} \subseteq X_i \cup \mathsf{fin}(\tau)$, (c) $(s', t) \in R_{i'}^{j'}$, (d) $\min(\tau') \subseteq X_{j'}$ and (e)$X_j \subseteq X_{j'} \cup \mathsf{fin}(\tau')$. After each iteration, if no new pair could be added to *any* set R_i^j, the procedure terminates as it has reached the fixed point. The number of iterations needed is polynomial ($|S|^2 \times \Bbbk^2$) since the maximum size of these sets is bounded. Finally, the automaton is non-empty if (s_0, s_f) is present in some R_i^j for some $s_f \in F$.

Thus our NP procedure guesses an ordering of the registers in which they are defined. Once this ordering is guessed, it verifies in polynomial time whether this guess can indeed lead to an accepting run.

Remark 3. Notice that, our convention of keeping the registers undefined in the beginning is very crucial for our NP-completeness. We could imagine a different semantics for DPA where the registers hold arbitrary but distinct values at the initial configuration. With such a definition, the non-emptiness checking odd DPA would be in P. We can indeed construct a pushdown automata abstracting away from pids. The pushdown automata checks whether a transition is enabled by checking the top symbol of the stack. The register values are irrelevant. Thus the emptiness checking of this variant of the DPA boils down to the emptiness checking of a polynomial sized pushdown automata.

5 MSO Model Checking

In fact, not only reachability but also model checking against powerful MSO_d turns out to be decidable for data pushdown automata.

Theorem 2. *Given a DPA $\mathcal{A}$ and an* MSO_d *formula ϕ, it decidable to check whether $L(\mathcal{A}) \subseteq L(\phi)$.*

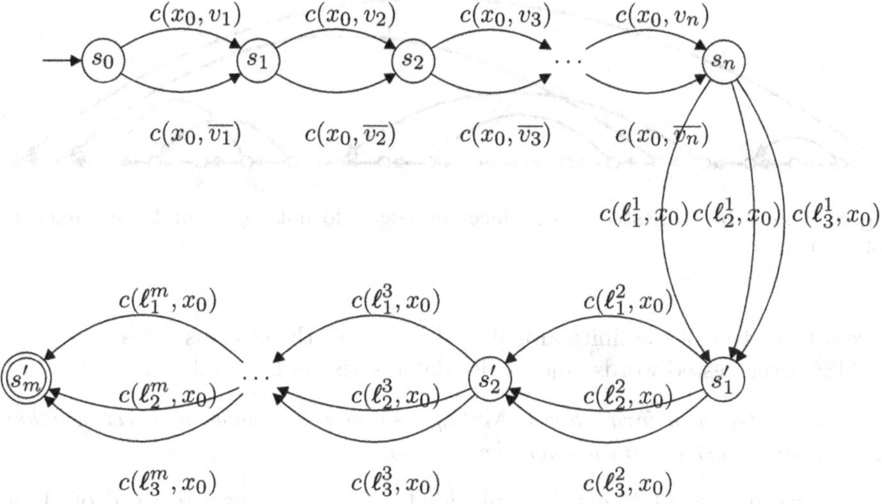

Fig. 6. Reduction from 3-CNF-SAT to non-emptiness of DPA

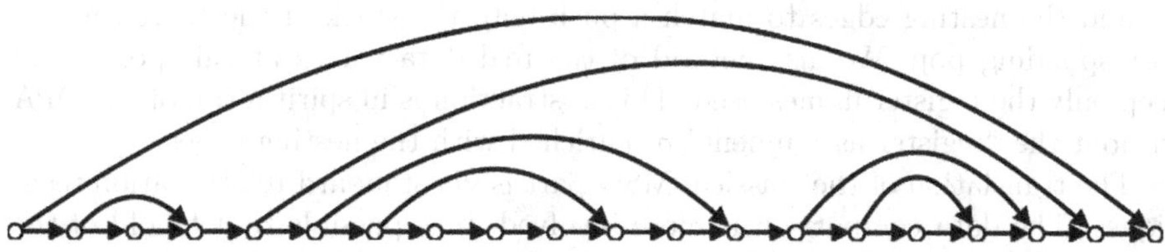

Fig. 7. A nested word

We give the proof outline in this section. The proof is essentially by abstracting the runs of a DPA as the runs of a Pushdown automata over a finite alphabet. Then the formula ϕ can be translated to an "equivalent" formula over the runs of PDA. The main challenge in obtaining a translation is to recover the data value comparisons. The proof is given in enough detail in [7]. However only data equality is considered in [7]. Hence we revisit the proof technique quickly.

We would like to see the runs of a pushdown automata as *Nested Words*. Nested words are words enriched with an additional binary relation (see Fig. 7). The additional binary relation is used to match a push with the corresponding pop. We write $x \curvearrowright y$ to denote that there is a push at position x which is matched by a pop at position y. Indeed, $\curvearrowright$ is the additional binary matching relation. In order to comply with the last-in-first-out policy of stacks, we require that the nesting edges do not cross each other. For example, Fig. 8 has a crossing of the additional edges, and hence it is not a nested word.

The MSO over nested words $\text{MSO}_{nw}(A)$ extends the classical MSO over words to incorporate the nesting edges. Its syntax is given by:

$$\varphi ::= a(x) \mid x \curvearrowright y \mid x \leq y \mid x \in X \mid \neg\phi \mid \phi \vee \phi \mid \exists x\phi \mid \exists X\phi$$

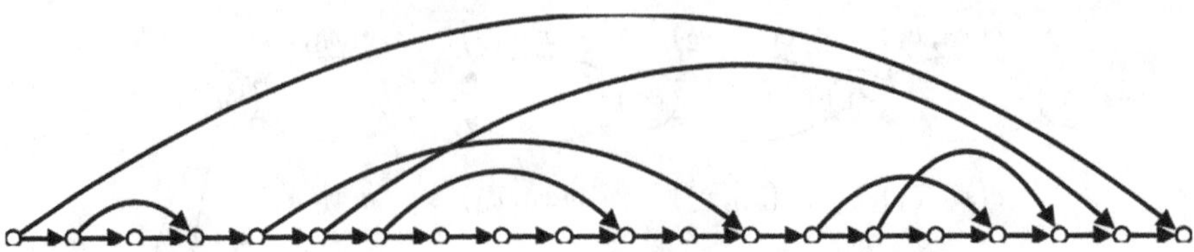

Fig. 8. This is not a nested word, since the edges do not represent last-in-first-out policy of stacks

Here a is a letter of the finite alphabet A. We omit the obvious semantics.

MSO over nested words enjoy a decidable satisfiability problem.

Fact 3. *[2] Given a formula $\phi \in \text{MSO}_{nw}(A)$, it is decidable to check whether there exists a nested word w such that $w \models \phi$.*

Any word $w \in L(\mathcal{A})$ can be embedded in an accepting run word of $\mathcal{A}$. A run word contains several consecutive nodes corresponding to a node in w, in order to carry the information of which transition it has taken. In the next step, we add the nesting edges to match a push onto the stack of the DPA with its corresponding pop. We also get rid of the real data values at this point, and keep only the register names used. This abstraction is in spirit a run of the DPA without the "register assignment" σ, enriched with the nesting edges.

The translation of the classical MSO part is via standard relativisation techniques. The data comparison is more involved. It is possible to get hold of the first position where a data value appears. We can do this by backtracking the way of this data value via registers (moving to the preceding transition via a linear edge) and stacks (moving to the transition where the value was pushed via a $\curvearrowright$ edge), and keeping the register name at which it occurred by means of second order variable. We continue the backtracking until we hit a create action with the intended register as its second argument.

Thus, we can obtain a MSO_{nw} formula $\mathsf{first}_i(x,)$ which uniquely identifies the position y at which $data_i(x)$ was created. Then $d^{=}_{k,\ell,(}(x,y)$ is equivalent to $\exists z.\mathsf{first}_k(x,z) \wedge \mathsf{first}_\ell(y,z)$. Also $d^{<}_{k,\ell,(}(x,y)$ is equivalent to $\exists z_1 z_2\, \mathsf{first}_k(x,z_1) \wedge \mathsf{first}_\ell(y,z_2) \wedge z_2 < z_1$.

Thus every MSO_d formula ϕ can be translated to an "equivalent" MSO_{nw} formula ϕ'. Indeed the set of all (abstract) valid runs of a DPA as a set of nested words is expressible in MSO_{nw}. Thus by Fact 3, Theorem 2 follows.

6 Discussions

The MSO model checking result could be extended to a DPA that runs over arbitrary data words (that is, not necessarily over `create` and `msg` alphabet). Indeed, we need to require the fresh data values to be higher than any of the previously used values. Perhaps it is also possible, instead of requiring the fresh data value to be higher, to allow guards involving data inequality comparisons of the register contents and the fresh value for the transitions.

To conclude, we have considered a special case of the Data Multi-pushdown automata defined in [7]. We have extended this restriction to include data comparison, while restricting the application domain to Dynamic Distributed Systems. This model is powerful enough to model several interesting examples. We retain all the results of [7], but also show a tight bound on the complexity of deciding non-emptiness for this particular class of automata.

References

1. Abdulla, P.A., Atig, M.F., Kara, A., Rezine, O.: Verification of dynamic register automata. In: Raman, V., Suresh, S.P. (eds.) FSTTCS 2014. LIPIcs, vol. 20, pp. 653–665. Leibniz-Zentrum für Informatik (2014)
2. Alur, R., Madhusudan, P.: Adding nesting structure to words. J. ACM **56**(3), 1–43 (2009)
3. Atig, M.F., Bouajjani, A., Qadeer, S.: Context-bounded analysis for concurrent programs with dynamic creation of threads. In: Kowalewski, S., Philippou, A. (eds.) TACAS 2009. LNCS, vol. 5505, pp. 107–123. Springer, Heidelberg (2009)
4. Bojańczyk, M., David, C., Muscholl, A., Schwentick, T., Segoufin, L.: Two-variable logic on data words. ACM Trans. Comput. Log. **12**(4), 27 (2011)
5. Bollig, B.: An automaton over data words that captures EMSO logic. In: Katoen, J.-P., König, B. (eds.) CONCUR 2011. LNCS, vol. 6901, pp. 171–186. Springer, Heidelberg (2011)
6. Bollig, B.: Logic for Communicating Automata with Parameterized Topology. In: CSL/LICS 2014, chap. 18. ACM Press (2014)
7. Bollig, B., Cyriac, A., Gastin, P., Narayan Kumar, K.: Model checking languages of data words. In: Birkedal, L. (ed.) FOSSACS 2012. LNCS, vol. 7213, pp. 391–405. Springer, Heidelberg (2012)
8. Bollig, B., Gastin, P., Kumar, A.: Parameterized communicating automata: complementation and model checking. In: Raman, V., Suresh, S.P. (eds.) FSTTCS 2014. LIPIcs, vol. 20, pp. 625–637. Leibniz-Zentrum für Informatik (2014)
9. Bollig, B., Gastin, P., Schubert, J.: Parameterized verification of communicating automata under context bounds. In: Ouaknine, J., Potapov, I., Worrell, J. (eds.) RP 2014. LNCS, vol. 8762, pp. 45–57. Springer, Heidelberg (2014)
10. Bollig, B., Hélouët, L.: Realizability of dynamic MSC languages. In: Ablayev, F., Mayr, E.W. (eds.) CSR 2010. LNCS, vol. 6072, pp. 48–59. Springer, Heidelberg (2010)
11. Demri, S., Lazić, R.: LTL with the freeze quantifier and register automata. ACM Trans. Comput. Logic **10**(3), 16 (2009)
12. Demri, S., Lazić, R.S., Sangnier, A.: Model checking freeze LTL over one-counter automata. In: Amadio, R.M. (ed.) FOSSACS 2008. LNCS, vol. 4962, pp. 490–504. Springer, Heidelberg (2008)
13. Demri, S., Sangnier, A.: When model-checking freeze LTL over counter machines becomes decidable. In: Ong, L. (ed.) FOSSACS 2010. LNCS, vol. 6014, pp. 176–190. Springer, Heidelberg (2010)
14. Leucker, M., Madhusudan, P., Mukhopadhyay, S.: Dynamic message sequence charts. In: Agrawal, M., Seth, A.K. (eds.) FSTTCS 2002. LNCS, vol. 2556, pp. 253–264. Springer, Heidelberg (2002)

Efficient State-Based CRDTs by Delta-Mutation

Paulo Sérgio Almeida, Ali Shoker(✉), and Carlos Baquero

HASLab/INESC TEC and Universidade Do Minho, Braga, Portugal
{psa,shokerali,cbm}@di.uminho.pt

Abstract. CRDTs are distributed data types that make eventual consistency of a distributed object possible and non ad-hoc. Specifically, state-based CRDTs ensure convergence through disseminating the entire state, that may be large, and merging it to other replicas; whereas operation-based CRDTs disseminate operations (i.e., small states) assuming an exactly-once reliable dissemination layer. We introduce *Delta State Conflict-Free Replicated Datatypes* (δ-CRDT) that can achieve the best of both worlds: small messages with an incremental nature, disseminated over unreliable communication channels. This is achieved by defining *δ-mutators* to return a *delta-state*, typically with a much smaller size than the full state, that is joined to both: local and remote states. We introduce the δ-CRDT framework, and we explain it through establishing a correspondence to current state-based CRDTs. In addition, we present an anti-entropy algorithm that ensures causal consistency, and two δ-CRDT specifications of well-known replicated datatypes.

Keywords: Replicated data types · State-based CRDT · Delta mutation

1 Introduction

Eventual consistency (EC) is a relaxed consistency model that is often adopted by large-scale distributed systems [11,13,24] where availability must be maintained, despite outages and partitioning, whereas delayed consistency is acceptable. A typical approach in EC systems is to allow replicas of a distributed object to temporarily diverge, provided that they can eventually be reconciled into a common state. To avoid application-specific reconciliation methods, costly and error-prone, *Conflict-Free Replicated Data Types* (CRDTs) [22,23] were introduced, allowing the design of self-contained distributed data types that are always available and eventually converge when all operations are reflected at all replicas. Though CRDTs are being deployed in practice [11], more work is still required to improve their design and performance.

This work is co-financed by the North Portugal Regional Operational Programme (ON.2, O Novo Norte), under the National Strategic Reference Framework (NSRF), through the European Regional Development Fund (ERDF), within project NORTE-07-0124-FEDER-000058; and by EU FP7 SyncFree project (609551).

A. Bouajjani and H. Fauconnier (Eds.): NETYS 2015, LNCS 9466, pp. 62–76, 2015.
DOI: 10.1007/978-3-319-26850-7_5

CRDTs support two complementary designs: *operation-based* (or op-based) and *state-based*. In op-based designs [17,23], the execution of an operation is done in two phases: *prepare* and *effect*. The former is performed only on the local replica and looks at the operation and current state to produce a message that aims to represent the operation, which is then shipped to all replicas. Once received, the representation of the operation is applied remotely using *effect*. On the other hand, in a state-based design [4,23] an operation is only executed on the local replica state. A replica periodically propagates its local changes to other replicas through shipping its entire state. A received state is incorporated with the local state via a *merge* function (designed as a least upper bound over a join-semilattice [4,23]) that deterministically reconciles both states.

Op-based CRDTs have more advantages as they can allow for simpler implementations, concise replica state, and smaller messages; however, they are subject to some limitations: First, they assume a message dissemination layer that guarantees reliable exactly-once causal broadcast (required to ensure idempotence); these guarantees are hard to maintain since large logs must be retained to prevent duplication even if TCP is used [15]. Second, membership management is a hard task in op-based systems especially once the number of nodes gets larger or due to churn problems, since all nodes must be coordinated by the middleware. Third, the op-based approach requires operations to be executed individually (even when batched) on all nodes.

The alternative is to use state-based systems which are deprived from these limitations. However, a major drawback in current state-based CRDTs is the communication overhead of shipping the entire state, which can get very large in size. For instance, the state size of a *counter* CRDT (a vector of integer counters, one per replica) increases with the number of replicas; whereas in a *grow-only Set*, the state size depends on the set size, that grows as more operations are invoked. This communication overhead limits the use of state-based CRDTs to data-types with small state size (e.g., counters are reasonable while sets are not). Recently, there has been a demand for CRDTs with large state sizes (e.g., in RIAK DT Maps [6] that can compose multiple CRDTs).

In this paper, we rethink the way state-based CRDTs should be designed, having in mind the problematic shipping of the entire state. Our aim is to ship a *representation of the effect* of recent update operations on the state, rather than the whole state, while preserving the idempotent nature of *join*. This ensures convergence over unreliable communication (on the contrary to op-based). To achieve this, we introduce *Delta State-based CRDTs* (δ-CRDT): a state is a join-semilattice that results from the join of multiple fine-grained states, i.e., *deltas*, generated by what we call δ-*mutators* which are new versions of the datatype mutators that return the effect of these mutators on the state. Thus, deltas can be temporarily retained in a buffer to be shipped individually (or joined in groups) instead of shipping the entire object. The local changes are then incorporated at other replicas by joining the shipped deltas with their own states.

The use of "deltas" (i.e., incremental states) may look intuitive in state dissemination; however, this is not the case for state-based CRDTs. The reason is that once a node receives an entire state, merging it locally is simple since there is no need to care about causality, as both states are self-contained (including meta-data). The challenge in δ-CRDT is that individual deltas are now "state fragments" and must be causally merged to maintain the correct semantics. This raises the following questions: is merging deltas semantically equivalent to merging entire states in CRDTs? If not, what are the sufficient conditions to make this true in general? And under what constraints causal consistency is maintained? This paper answers these questions and presents corresponding solutions.

We address the challenge of designing a new δ-CRDT that conserves the correctness properties and semantics of an existing CRDT by establishing a relation between the novel δ-mutators with the original CRDT mutators. We then show how to ensure causal consistency using deltas through introducing the concept of *delta-interval* and the *causal delta-merging condition.* Based on these, we then present an anti-entropy algorithm for δ-CRDT, where sending and then joining delta-intervals into another replica state produces the same effect as if the entire state had been shipped and joined.

As the area of CRDTs is relatively new, we illustrate our approach by explaining a simple *counter* δ-CRDT specification; then we introduce a challenging non-trivial specification for a widely used datatype: Optimized Add-Wins Observed-Remove Sets [5]; and finally we present a novel design for an Optimized Multi-Value Register with meta-data reduction. In addition, we make a basic δ-CRDT C++ library available online [2] for various CRDTs: GSet, 2PSet, GCounter, PNCounter, AWORSet, RWORSet, MVRegister, LWWSet, etc. Our experience shows that a δ-CRDT version can be devised for most CRDTs, however, this requires some design effort that varies with the complexity of different CRDTs. This is referred to the ad-hoc way CRDTs are designed in general (which is also required for δ-CRDTs). To the best of our knowledge, no model has been introduced so far to make designing CRDTs generic rather than type-specific.

2 System Model

Consider a distributed system with nodes containing local memory, with no shared memory between them. Any node can send messages to any other node. The network is asynchronous; there is no global clock, no bound on the time a message takes to arrive, and no bounds are set on relative processing speeds. The network is unreliable: messages can be lost, duplicated or reordered (but are not corrupted). Some messages will, however, eventually get through: if a node sends infinitely many messages to another node, infinitely many of these will be delivered. In particular, this means that there can be arbitrarily long partitions, but these will eventually heal. Nodes have access to durable storage; they can crash but will eventually recover with the content of the durable storage just before crash the occurred. Durable state is written atomically at each state transition. Each node has access to its globally unique identifier in a set $\mathbb{I}$.

3 A Background of State-Based CRDTs

Conflict-Free Replicated Data Types [22,23] (CRDTs) are distributed datatypes that allow different replicas of a distributed CRDT instance to diverge and ensures that, eventually, all replicas converge to the same state. State-based CRDTs achieve this through propagating updates of the local state by disseminating the entire state across replicas. The received states are then merged to remote states, leading to convergence (i.e., consistent states on all replicas).

A state-based CRDT consists of a triple (S, M, Q), where S is a join-semilattice [12], Q is a set of query functions (which return some result without modifying the state), and M is a set of mutators that perform updates; a mutator $m \in M$ takes a state $X \in S$ as input and returns a new state $X' = m(X)$. A join-semilattice is a set with a *partial order* $\sqsubseteq$ and a binary *join* operation $\sqcup$ that returns the *least upper bound* (LUB) of two elements in S; a *join* is designed to be commutative, associative, and idempotent. Mutators are defined in such a way to be *inflations*, i.e., for any mutator m and state X, the following holds:

$$X \sqsubseteq m(X)$$

In this way, for each replica there is a monotonic sequence of states, defined under the lattice partial order, where each subsequent state subsumes the previous state when joined elsewhere.

Both query and mutator operations are always available since they are performed using the local state without requiring inter-replica communication; however, as mutators are concurrently applied at distinct replicas, replica states will likely diverge. Eventual convergence is then obtained using an *anti-entropy* protocol that periodically ships the entire local state to other replicas. Each replica merges the received state with its local state using the *join* operation in S. Given the mathematical properties of *join*, if mutators stop being issued, all replicas eventually converge to the same state. i.e. the least upper-bound of all states involved. State-based CRDTs are interesting as they demand little guarantees from the dissemination layer, working under message loss, duplication, reordering, and temporary network partitioning, without impacting availability and eventual convergence.

Example. Figure 1 represents a state-based increment-only counter. The CRDT state Σ is a map from replica identifiers to positive integers. Initially, σ_i^0 is an empty map (assuming that unmapped keys implicitly map to zero, and only non zero mappings are stored). A single mutator, i.e., inc, is defined that increments the value of the local replica i (returning the updated map). The query operation

$$\begin{aligned}
\Sigma &= \mathsf{I} \hookrightarrow \mathsf{N} \\
\sigma_i^0 &= \{\} \\
\mathsf{inc}_i(m) &= m\{i \mapsto m(i) + 1\} \\
\mathsf{value}_i(m) &= \sum_{i \in \mathsf{I}} m(i) \\
m \sqcup m' &= \{(i, \max(m(i), m'(i))) \mid i \in \mathsf{I}\}
\end{aligned}$$

Fig. 1. State-based Counter CRDT; replica i.

value returns the counter value by adding the integers in the map entries. The join of two states is the point-wise maximum of the maps.

Weaknesses. The main weakness of state-based CRDTs is the cost of dissemination of updates, as the full state is sent. In this simple example of counters, even though increments only update the value corresponding to the local replica i, the whole map will always be sent in messages though the other map values remained intact (since no messages have been received and merged).

It would be interesting to only ship the recent modification incurred on the state. This is, however, not possible with the current model of state-based CRDTs as mutators always return a full state. Approaches which simply ship operations (e.g., an "increment n" message), like in operation-based CRDTs, require reliable communication (e.g., because increment is not idempotent). In contrast, our approach allows producing and encoding recent mutations in an incremental way, while keeping the advantages of the state-based approach, namely the idempotent, associative, and commutative properties of join.

4 Delta-State CRDTs

We introduce *Delta-State Conflict-Free Replicated Data Types*, or δ-CRDT for short, as a new kind of state-based CRDTs, in which *delta-mutators* are defined to return a *delta-state*: a value in the same join-semilattice which represents the updates induced by the mutator on the current state.

Definition 1 (Delta-mutator). *A delta-mutator m^δ is a function, corresponding to an update operation, which takes a state X in a join-semilattice S as parameter and returns a delta-mutation $m^\delta(X)$, also in S.*

Definition 2 (Delta-group). *A delta-group is inductively defined as either a delta-mutation or a join of several delta-groups.*

Definition 3 (δ-CRDT). *A δ-CRDT consists of a triple (S, M^δ, Q), where S is a join-semilattice, M^δ is a set of delta-mutators, and Q a set of query functions, where the state transition at each replica is given by either joining the current state $X \in S$ with a delta-mutation:*

$$X' = X \sqcup m^\delta(X),$$

or joining the current state with some received delta-group D:

$$X' = X \sqcup D.$$

In a δ-CRDT, the effect of applying a mutation, represented by a delta-mutation $\delta = m^\delta(X)$, is decoupled from the resulting state $X' = X \sqcup \delta$, which allows shipping this δ rather than the entire resulting state X'. All state transitions in a δ-CRDT, even upon applying mutations locally, are the result of some join with the current state. Unlike standard CRDT mutators, delta-mutators do not need to be inflations in order to inflate a state; this is however ensured by joining their output, i.e., deltas, into the current state.

In principle, a delta could be shipped immediately to remote replicas once applied locally. For efficiency reasons, multiple deltas returned by applying several delta-mutators can be joined locally into a delta-group and retained in a buffer. The delta-group can then be shipped to remote replicas to be joined with their local states. Received delta-groups can optionally be joined into their buffered delta-group, allowing transitive propagation of deltas. A full state can be seen as a special (extreme) case of a delta-group.

If the causal order of operations is not important and the intended aim is merely eventual convergence of states, then delta-groups can be shipped using an unreliable dissemination layer that may drop, reorder, or duplicate messages. Delta-groups can always be re-transmitted and re-joined, possibly out of order, or can simply be subsumed by a less frequent sending of the full state, e.g. for performance reasons or when doing state transfers to new members. Due to space limits, we only address causal consistency in this paper, while information about state convergence can be found in the associated technical report [1].

4.1 Delta-State Decomposition of Standard CRDTs

A δ-CRDT (S, M^δ, Q) is a *delta-state decomposition* of a state-based CRDT (S, M, Q), if for every mutator $m \in M$, we have a corresponding mutator $m^\delta \in M^\delta$ such that, for every state $X \in S$:

$$m(X) = X \sqcup m^\delta(X)$$

This equation states that applying a delta-mutator and joining into the current state should produce the same state transition as applying the corresponding mutator of the standard CRDT.

Given an existing state-based CRDT (which is always a trivial decomposition of itself, i.e., $m(X) = X \sqcup m(X)$, as mutators are inflations), it will be useful to find a non-trivial decomposition such that delta-states returned by delta-mutators in M^δ are smaller than the resulting state:

$$\mathsf{size}(m^\delta(X)) \ll \mathsf{size}(m(X))$$

4.2 Example: δ-CRDT Counter

Figure 2 depicts a δ-CRDT specification of a counter datatype that is a delta-state decomposition of the state-based counter in Fig. 1. The state, join and value query operation remain as before. Only the mutator inc^δ is newly defined, which increments the map entry corresponding to the local

$$\begin{aligned}
\Sigma &= \mathsf{I} \hookrightarrow \mathsf{N} \\
\sigma_i^0 &= \{\} \\
\mathsf{inc}_i^\delta(m) &= \{i \mapsto m(i) + 1\} \\
\mathsf{value}_i(m) &= \sum_{i \in \mathsf{I}} m(i) \\
m \sqcup m' &= \{(i, \mathsf{max}(m(i), m'(i))) \mid i \in \mathsf{I}\}
\end{aligned}$$

Fig. 2. A δ-CRDT counter; replica i.

replica and only returns that entry, instead of the full map as inc in the state-based CRDT counter does. This maintains the original semantics of the counter while allowing the smaller deltas returned by the delta-mutator to be sent, instead of the full map. As before, the received payload (whether one or more deltas) might not include entries for all keys in $\mathbb{I}$, which are assumed to have zero values. The decomposition is easy to understand in this example since the equation $\mathsf{inc}_i(X) = X \sqcup \mathsf{inc}^\delta_i(X)$ holds as $m\{i \mapsto m(i)+1\} = m \sqcup \{i \mapsto m(i)+1\}$. In other words, the single value for key i in the delta, corresponding to the local replica identifier, will overwrite the corresponding one in m since the former maps to a higher value (i.e., using max). Here it can be noticed that: (1) a delta *is* just a state, that can be joined possibly several times without requiring exactly-once delivery, and without being a representation of the "increment" operation (as in operation-based CRDTs), which is itself non-idempotent; (2) joining deltas into a delta-group and disseminating delta-groups at a lower rate than the operation rate reduces data communication overhead, since multiple increments from a given source can be collapsed into a single state counter.

5 Causal Consistency

Traditional state-based CRDTs converge using joins of the full state, which implicitly ensures per-object causal consistency [8]: each state of some replica of an object reflects the causal past of operations on the object (either applied locally, or applied at other replicas and transitively joined).

Therefore, it is desirable to have δ-CRDTs offer the same causal-consistency guarantees that standard state-based CRDTs offer. This raises the question about how can delta propagation and merging of δ-CRDT be constrained (and expressed in an anti-entropy algorithm) in such a manner to give the same results as if a standard state-based CRDT was used. Towards this objective, it is useful to define a particular kind of delta-group, which we call a *delta-interval*:

Definition 4 (Delta-interval). *Given a replica i progressing along the states $X_i^0, X_i^1, \ldots$, by joining delta d_i^k (either local delta-mutation or received delta-group) into X_i^k to obtain X_i^{k+1}, a delta-interval $\Delta_i^{a,b}$ is a delta-group resulting from joining deltas $d_i^a, \ldots, d_i^{b-1}$:*

$$\Delta_i^{a,b} = \bigsqcup \{d_i^k \mid a \leq k < b\}$$

The use of delta-intervals in anti-entropy algorithms will be a key ingredient towards achieving causal consistency. We now define a restricted kind of anti-entropy algorithm for δ-CRDTs.

Definition 5 (Delta-interval-based anti-entropy algorithm). *A given anti-entropy algorithm for δ-CRDTs is delta-interval-based, if all deltas sent to other replicas are delta-intervals.*

Moreover, to achieve causal consistency the next condition must satisfied:

Definition 6 (Causal delta-merging condition). *A delta-interval based anti-entropy algorithm is said to satisfy the causal delta-merging condition if the algorithm only joins* $\Delta_j^{a,b}$ *from replica* j *into state* X_i *of replica* i *that satisfy:*

$$X_i \sqsupseteq X_j^a.$$

This means that a delta-interval is only joined into states that at least reflect (i.e., subsume) the state into which the first delta in the interval was previously joined. The causal delta-merging condition is important since any delta-interval based anti-entropy algorithm of a δ-CRDT that satisfies it, can be used to obtain the same outcome of standard CRDTs; this is formally stated in Proposition 1.

Proposition 1. *(CRDT and* δ*-CRDTcorrespondence) Let* (S, M, Q) *be a standard state-based CRDT and* (S, M^δ, Q) *a corresponding delta-state decomposition. Any* δ*-CRDT state reachable by an execution* E^δ *over* (S, M^δ, Q)*, by a delta-interval based anti-entropy algorithm* A^δ *satisfying the causal delta-merging condition, is equal to a state resulting from an execution* E *over* (S, M, Q)*, having the corresponding data-type operations, by an anti-entropy algorithm* A *for state-based CRDTs.*

Proof. Please see the associated technical report [1].

Corollary 1. *(*δ*-CRDT causal consistency) Any* δ*-CRDT in which states are propagated and joined using a delta-interval-based anti-entropy algorithm satisfying the causal delta-merging condition ensures causal consistency.*

Proof. From Proposition 1 and causal consistency of state-based CRDTs.

5.1 Anti-entropy Algorithm for Causal Consistency

Algorithm 1 is a delta-interval based anti-entropy algorithm which enforces the causal delta-merging condition. It can be used whenever the causal consistency guarantees of standard state-based CRDTs are needed. For simplicity, it excludes some optimizations that are important, but easy to derive, in practice. The algorithm distinguishes neighbor nodes, and only sends them delta-intervals that are joined at the receiving node, obeying the delta-merging condition.

Each node i keeps a contiguous sequence of deltas $d_i^l, \ldots, d_i^u$ in a map D from integers to deltas, with $l = \min(\mathsf{dom}(D))$ and $u = \max(\mathsf{dom}(D))$. The sequence numbers of deltas are obtained from the counter c_i that is incremented when a delta (whether a delta-mutation or delta-interval received) is joined with the current state. Each node i keeps an acknowledgments map A that stores, for each neighbor j, the largest index b for all delta-intervals $\Delta_i^{a,b}$ acknowledged by j (after j receives $\Delta_i^{a,b}$ from i and joins it into X_j).

Node i sends a delta-interval $d = \Delta_i^{a,b}$ with a (delta, d, b) message; the receiving node j, after joining $\Delta_i^{a,b}$ into its replica state, replies with an acknowledgment message (ack, b); if an ack from j was successfully received by node i, it

```
inputs:
    n_i ∈ P(I), set of neighbors
durable state:
    X_i ∈ S, CRDT state; initially X_i = ⊥
    c_i ∈ N, sequence number; initially c_i = 0
volatile state:
    D_i ∈ N ↪ S, sequence of deltas; initially
    D_i = {}
    A_i ∈ I ↪ N, acknowledges map; initially
    A_i = {}
on receive_{j,i}(delta, d, n)
    if d ⋢ X_i then
        X'_i = X_i ⊔ d
        D'_i = D_i{c_i ↦ d}
        c'_i = c_i + 1
    send_{i,j}(ack, n)
on receive_{j,i}(ack, n)
    A'_i = A_i{j ↦ max(A_i(j), n)}
on operation_i(m^δ)
    d = m^δ(X_i)
    X'_i = X_i ⊔ d
    D'_i = D_i{c_i ↦ d}
    c'_i = c_i + 1
periodically // ship delta-interval or state
    j = random(n_i)
    if D_i = {} ∨ min(dom(D_i)) > A_i(j) then
        d = X_i
    else
        d = ⊔{D_i(l) | A_i(j) ≤ l < c_i}
    if A_i(j) < c_i then
        send_{i,j}(delta, d, c_i)
periodically // garbage collect deltas
    l = min{n | (_, n) ∈ A_i}
    D'_i = {(n, d) ∈ D_i | n ≥ l}
```

Algorithm 1. Anti-entropy algorithm ensuring causal consistency of δ-CRDT.

updates the entry of j in the acknowledgment map, using the max function. This handles possible old duplicates and messages arriving out of order.

Like the δ-CRDT state, the counter c_i is also kept in a durable storage. This is essential to avoid conflicts after potential crash and recovery incidents. Otherwise, there would be the danger of receiving some delayed ack, for a delta-interval sent before crashing, causing the node to skip sending some deltas generated after recovery, thus violating the delta-merging condition.

The algorithm for node i periodically picks a random neighbor j. In principle, i sends the join of all deltas starting from the latest delta acked by j and forward. Exceptionally, i sends the entire state in two cases: (1) if the sequence of deltas D_i is empty, or (2) if j is expecting from i a delta that was already removed from D_i (e.g., after a crash and recovery, when both deltas and the ack map, being volatile state, are lost); i tracks this in $A_i(j)$. To garbage collect old deltas, the algorithm periodically removes the deltas that have been acked by *all* neighbors.

Proposition 2. *Algorithm 1 produces the same reachable states as a standard algorithm over a CRDT for which the δ-CRDT is a decomposition.*

Proof. Please see the associated technical report [1].

6 δ-CRDTs for Add-Wins OR-Sets

An Add-wins Observed-Remove Set (OR-set) is a well-known CRDT datatype that offers the same sequential semantics of a sequential set and adopts a specific resolution semantics for operations that concurrently add and remove the same element. Add-wins means that an add prevails over a concurrent remove. Remove operations, however, only affect elements added by causally preceding adds. The purpose of these δ-CRDT OR-set versions is to design δ-mutators that return small deltas to be lightly disseminated, as discussed above, instead of shipping the entire state as in classical CRDTs [5,22,23].

$$
\begin{aligned}
\Sigma &= \mathcal{P}(\mathbb{I} \times \mathbb{N} \times E) \times \mathcal{P}(\mathbb{I} \times \mathbb{N}) \\
\sigma_i^0 &= (\{\}, \{\}) \\
\mathsf{add}_i^\delta(e, (s, t)) &= (\{(i, n+1, e)\}, \{\}) \\
&\quad \text{with } n = \max(\{k \mid (i, k, \_) \in s\}) \\
\mathsf{rmv}_i^\delta(e, (s, t)) &= (\{\}, \{(j, n) \mid (j, n, e) \in s\}) \\
\mathsf{elements}_i((s, t)) &= \{e \mid (j, n, e) \in s \land (j, n) \notin t\} \\
(s, t) \sqcup (s', t') &= (s \cup s', t \cup t')
\end{aligned}
$$

(a) With Tombstones

$$
\begin{aligned}
\Sigma &= \mathcal{P}(\mathbb{I} \times \mathbb{N} \times E) \times \mathcal{P}(\mathbb{I} \times \mathbb{N}) \\
\sigma_i^0 &= (\{\}, \{\}) \\
\mathsf{add}_i^\delta(e, (s, c)) &= (\{(i, n+1, e)\}, \{(i, n+1)\}) \\
&\quad \text{with } n = \max(\{k \mid (i, k) \in c\}) \\
\mathsf{rmv}_i^\delta(e, (s, c)) &= (\{\}, \{(j, n) \mid (j, n, e) \in s\}) \\
\mathsf{elements}_i((s, c)) &= \{e \mid (j, n, e) \in s\} \\
(s, c) \sqcup (s', c') &= ((s \cap s') \cup \{(i, n, e) \in s \mid (i, n) \notin c'\} \\
&\quad \cup \{(i, n, e) \in s' \mid (i, n) \notin c\}, c \cup c')
\end{aligned}
$$

(b) Without Tombstones (optimized)

Fig. 3. Add-wins observed-remove δ-CRDT set, replica i.

6.1 Add-Wins OR-Set with Tombstones

Figure 3a depicts a simple, but inefficient, δ-CRDT implementation of a state-based add-wins OR-Set. The state Σ consists of a set of tagged elements and a set of tags, acting as tombstones. Globally unique tags of the form $\mathbb{I} \times \mathbb{N}$ are used and ensured by pairing a replica identifier in $\mathbb{I}$ with a monotonically increasing natural counter. Once an element $e \in E$ is added to the set, the delta-mutator add^δ creates a globally unique tag by incrementing the highest tag present in its local state and that was created by replica i itself ($\max$ returns 0 if no tag is present). This tag is paired with value e and stored as a new unique triple in s. Since an "add" wins any concurrent "remove", removing an element e should only be tombstoned if it was preceded by an add operation (i.e., the element is in s), otherwise it has no effect. Consequently, the delta-mutator rmv^δ retains in the tombstone set all tags associated to element e, being removed from the local state. This is essential to prevent a removed element to reappear once the local state is merged with another replica state that still have that element (i.e., it has not been removed yet remotely as replicas are loosely coupled). The function $\mathsf{elements}$ returns only the elements that are added but not yet tombstoned. Join $\sqcup$ simply unions the respective sets that are, therefore, both grow-only.

6.2 Optimized Add-Wins OR-Set

A more efficient design is presented in Fig. 3b allowing also the set of tagged elements (i.e., tombstone set above) to shrink as elements are removed. This design offers the same semantics and have a similar state structure to the former; however, it has a different behavior. Now, $\mathsf{elements}$ returns all the elements in the tagged set s, without consulting t as before. Added and removed items are now tagged in the *causal context set* c. Although, the set c and t look similar in structure, they have a different behavior (we call it c instead of t to remove this confusion): a tombstone set t simply stores all removed elements tags, while c retains only the causal information needed to add/remove an element. For presentation simplicity, c in Fig. 3b simply retains all removed elements tags; however, after compression, c will be very concise and look different from t; this is explained in the next section.

Adding an element creates a unique tag by resorting to the causal context c (instead of s). The tag is paired with the element and added to s (as before). The difference is that the new tag is also added to the causal context set c. The delta-mutator rmv^δ is the same as before, adding all tags associated to the element being removed to c. The desired semantics are maintained by the novel join operation $\sqcup$. To join two states, their causal contexts c are simply unioned; whereas, the new element set s only preserves: (1) the triples present in both sets (therefore, not removed in either), and also (2) any triple present in one of the sets and whose tag is not present in the causal context of the other state.

Causal Context Compression. In practice, the causal context c can be efficiently compressed without any loss of information. When using an anti-entropy algorithm that provides causal consistency, e.g., Algorithm 1, then for each replica state $X_i = (s_i, c_i)$ and replica id $j \in \mathbb{I}$, we have a contiguous sequence:

$$1 \le n \le \mathsf{max}(\{k \mid (j,k) \in c_i\}) \Rightarrow (j,n) \in c_i.$$

Thus, the causal context can always be encoded as a compact version vector [21] $\mathbb{I} \hookrightarrow \mathbb{N}$ that keeps the maximum sequence number for each replica. Even under non-causal anti-entropy, compression is still possible by keeping a version vector that encodes the offset of the contiguous sequence of tags from each replica, together with a set for the non-contiguous tags. As anti-entropy proceeds, each tag is eventually encoded in the vector, and thus the set remains typically small. Compression is less likely for the causal context of delta-groups in transit or buffered to be sent, but those contexts are only transient and smaller than those in the actual replica states. Moreover, the same techniques that encode contiguous sequences of tags can also be used for transient context compression [19].

7 Optimized Multi-value Register δ-CRDT

Multi-Value Registers (MVR) are popular constructions in which a read operation returns the set of values concurrently written, but not causally overwritten; these values are then reduced to a single value by applications [13]. Until now, these types have been implemented by assigning a version vector to each written value [8,22]. In Fig. 4, we show that the optimization that was developed for Sets, can also be used to compactly tag the values in a multi-value register. On a write operation wr, it is enough to assign a new scalar tag, from $\mathbb{I} \times \mathbb{N}$,

$$\begin{aligned}
\Sigma &= \mathcal{P}(\mathbb{I} \times \mathbb{N} \times V) \times \mathcal{P}(\mathbb{I} \times \mathbb{N}) \\
\sigma_i^0 &= (\{\}, \{\}) \\
\mathsf{wr}_i^\delta(v, (s,c)) &= (\{(i, n+1, v)\}, \{(i, n+1)\} \cup \{(j,m) \mid (j,m,_) \in s\}) \text{ with } n = \mathsf{max}(\{k \mid (i,k) \in c\}) \\
\mathsf{rd}_i((s,c)) &= \{v \mid (j,n,v) \in s\} \\
(s,c) \sqcup (s',c') &= ((s \cap s') \cup \{(i,n,v) \in s \mid (i,n) \notin c'\} \cup \{(i,n,v) \in s' \mid (i,n) \notin c\}, c \cup c')
\end{aligned}$$

Fig. 4. Optimized δ-CRDT multi-value register, replica i.

using a replica id i and counter to uniquely tag the written value v. To ensure that values overwritten are deleted, the produced causal context c lists all tags associated to those values. Since those values are absent from the payload set s they will be deleted in replicas that still have them, applying join definition $\sqcup$ (that is in common with Fig. 3b). The causal context compression techniques defined earlier also apply here.

8 Message Complexity

Our delta-based framework, δ-CRDT, clearly introduces significant cost improvements on messaging. Despite being a generic framework, δ-CRDT requires delta mutators to be defined per datatype. This makes the bit-message complexity datatype-based rather than generic. To give an intuition about this complexity, we address the three datatypes introduced above: *counter*, OR-Set, and MVR.

Counters. In classical state-based CRDTs, the entire map of a *counter* is shipped. As the map-size grows with the number of replicas, this leads a bit-message complexity of $\widetilde{O}(|\mathbb{I}|)$[1]. In the δ-CRDT case, only recently updated map entries α are shipped yielding a bit-complexity $\widetilde{O}(\alpha)$, where $\alpha \ll |\mathbb{I}|$.

OR-set. Shipping in classical OR-set CRDTs delivers the entire state which yields a bit-message complexity of $O(S)$, where S is the state-size. In δ-CRDT, only deltas are shipped, which renders a bit-message complexity $O(s)$ where s represents the size of the recent updates occurred since the last shipping. Clearly, $s \ll S$ since the updates that occur on a state in a period of time are often much less than the total number of items.

MVR. In classical MVR, the worst case state is composed of $|\mathbb{I}|$ concurrently written values, each associated with a $|\mathbb{I}|$ sized version vector. This makes the bit-message complexity $\widetilde{O}(|\mathbb{I}|^2)$. In the novel delta design in Fig. 4, no version vector is used, whereas the number of possible values remain the same (summing up the values set s and meta-data in c), this reduces the bit-message complexity to $\widetilde{O}(|\mathbb{I}|)$ as well as the worst case state complexity.

9 Related Work

Eventually Convergent Data Types. The design of replicated systems that are always available and eventually converge can be traced back to historical designs in [16,25], among others. More recently, replicated data types that always eventually converge, both by reliably broadcasting operations (called operation-based) or gossiping and merging states (called state-based), have been formalized as CRDTs [4,17,22,23]. These are also closely related to Bloom^L [10] and Cloud Types [7].

[1] $\widetilde{O}$ is a variant of big O ignoring logarithmic factors in the size of integers and ids.

Deltas. A key feature of δ-CRDT is message size reduction (not improving local state lower bounds [8]), by using small-sized deltas, while preserving the advantages of classical state-based CRDTs. The general old idea of using differences between things, called "deltas" in many contexts, can lead to many designs, depending on how exactly a delta is defined. The state-based deltas introduced for Computational CRDTs [20] require an extra delta-specific merge (in addition to the standard join) which does not ensure idempotence. In [14], an improved synchronization method for non-optimized OR-set CRDT [22] is presented, where delta information is propagated; in that paper deltas are a collection of items (related to update events between synchronizations), manipulated and merged through a protocol, as opposed to normal states in the semilattice. No generic framework is defined (that could encompass other data types) and the protocol requires several communication steps to compute the information to exchange.

Operation-Based CRDTs. These CRDTs [3,22,23] also support small message sizes, and in particular, *pure* flavors [3] that restrict messages to the operation name, and possible arguments. Though pure operation-based CRDTs allow for compact states and are very fast at the source (since operations are broadcast without consulting the local state), the model requires more systems guarantees than δ-CRDT do, e.g., exactly-once reliable delivery and membership information, and impose more complex integration of new replicas. The work in [9] shows a different trade-off among state deltas and pure operations, by tagging operations and creating a globally stable log of operations while allowing local transient logs to preserve availability. While having other advantages, the creation of this global log requires more coordination than our gossip approach for causally consistent delta dissemination, and can stall dissemination.

Encoding Causal Histories. State-based CRDT are always designed to be causally consistent [4,23]. Optimized implementations of sets, maps, and multi-value registers can build on this assumption to keep the meta-data small [8]. In δ-CRDT, however, deltas and delta-groups are normally not causally consistent, and thus the design of *join*, the meta-data state, as well as the anti-entropy algorithm used must ensure this. Without causal consistency, the causal context in δ-CRDT can not always be summarized with version vectors, and consequently, techniques that allow for gaps are often used. A well known mechanism that allows for encoding of gaps is found in Concise Version Vectors [18]. Interval Version Vectors [19], later on, introduced an encoding that optimizes sequences and allows gaps, while preserving efficiency when gaps are absent.

10 Conclusion

We introduced the new concept of δ-CRDTs and devised *delta-mutators* over state-based datatypes which can detach the changes that an operation induces on the state. This brings a significant performance gain as it allows only shipping small states, i.e., *deltas*, instead of the entire state. The significant property in δ-CRDT is that it preserves the crucial properties (idempotence, associativity and commutativity) of standard state-based CRDT. In the worst case, deltas can be forgotten and the entire state can always be shipped, allowing scenarios such as long duration partitions, which would be problematic for op-based CRDTs.

In addition, we have shown how δ-CRDT can achieve causal consistency; and we presented an anti-entropy algorithm that allows replacing classical state-based CRDTs by more efficient ones, while preserving their properties. As an application for our approach, we designed two novel δ-CRDT specifications for two well-known datatypes: an optimized observed-remove set [5] and an optimized multi-value register [13].

References

1. Almeida, P.S., Shoker, A., Baquero, C.: Efficient state-based crdts by delta-mutation. CoRR abs/1410.2803 (2014). http://arxiv.org/abs/1410.2803
2. Baquero, C.: Delta-enabled-crdts. http://github.com/CBaquero/delta-enabled-crdts
3. Baquero, C., Almeida, P.S., Shoker, A.: Making operation-based CRDTs operation-based. In: Magoutis, K., Pietzuch, P. (eds.) DAIS 2014. LNCS, vol. 8460, pp. 126–140. Springer, Heidelberg (2014)
4. Baquero, C., Moura, F.: Using structural characteristics for autonomous operation. Oper. Syst. Rev. **33**(4), 90–96 (1999)
5. Bieniusa, A., Zawirski, M., Preguiça, N., Shapiro, M., Baquero, C., Balegas, V., Duarte, S.: An optimized conflict-free replicated set. Rapp. Rech. RR-8083, INRIA, Rocquencourt, France, October 2012. http://hal.inria.fr/hal-00738680
6. Brown, R., Cribbs, S., Meiklejohn, C., Elliott, S.: Riak DT map: a composable, convergent replicated dictionary. In: Proceedings of the First Workshop on Principles and Practice of Eventual Consistency, PaPEC 2014, pp. 1:1–1:1. ACM, New York (2014). http://doi.acm.org/10.1145/2596631.2596633
7. Burckhardt, S., Fähndrich, M., Leijen, D., Wood, B.P.: Cloud types for eventual consistency. In: Noble, J. (ed.) ECOOP 2012. LNCS, vol. 7313, pp. 283–307. Springer, Heidelberg (2012)
8. Burckhardt, S., Gotsman, A., Yang, H., Zawirski, M.: Replicated data types: specification, verification, optimality. In: Jagannathan, S., Sewell, P. (eds.) POPL, pp. 271–284. ACM (2014)
9. Burckhardt, S., Leijen, D., Fahndrich, M.: Cloud types: Robust abstractions for replicated shared state. Technical report. MSR-TR-2014-43, March 2014. http://research.microsoft.com/apps/pubs/default.aspx?id=211340
10. Conway, N., Marczak, W.R., Alvaro, P., Hellerstein, J.M., Maier, D.: Logic and lattices for distributed programming. In: Proceedings of the Third ACM Symposium on Cloud Computing, p. 1. ACM (2012)
11. Cribbs, S., Brown, R.: Data structures in Riak. In: Riak Conference (RICON), San Francisco, CA, USA, October 2012
12. Davey, B.A., Priestley, H.A.: Introduction to Lattices and Order, 2nd edn. Cambridge University Press, Cambridge (2002)

13. DeCandia, G., Hastorun, D., Jampani, M., Kakulapati, G., Lakshman, A., Pilchin, A., Sivasubramanian, S., Vosshall, P., Vogels, W.: Dynamo: amazon's highly available key-value store. In: Symposium on Operating Systems Principles (SOSP). Operating Systems Review, vol. 41, pp. 205–220. Assoc. for Computing Machinery, Stevenson, October 2007
14. Deftu, A., Griebsch, J.: A scalable conflict-free replicated set data type. In: Proceedings of the 2013 IEEE 33rd International Conference on Distributed Computing Systems, ICDCS 2013, pp. 186–195. IEEE Computer Society, Washington, DC (2013). http://dx.doi.org/10.1109/ICDCS.2013.10
15. Helland, P.: Idempotence is not a medical condition. Queue **10**(4), 30–46 (2012). http://doi.acm.org/10.1145/2181796.2187821
16. Johnson, P.R., Thomas, R.H.: The maintenance of duplicate databases. Internet Request for Comments RFC 677, Information Sciences Institute, January 1976. http://www.rfc-editor.org/rfc.html
17. Letia, M., Preguiça, N., Shapiro, M.: CRDTs: Consistency without concurrency control. Rapp. Rech. RR-6956, INRIA, Rocquencourt, France, June 2009. http://hal.inria.fr/inria-00397981/
18. Malkhi, D., Terry, D.: Concise version vectors in winfs. Distrib. Comput. **20**(3), 209–219 (2007)
19. Mukund, M., Shenoy R., G., Suresh, S.P.: Optimized OR-sets without ordering constraints. In: Chatterjee, M., Cao, J., Kothapalli, K., Rajsbaum, S. (eds.) ICDCN 2014. LNCS, vol. 8314, pp. 227–241. Springer, Heidelberg (2014)
20. Navalho, D., Duarte, S., Preguiça, N., Shapiro, M.: Incremental stream processing using computational conflict-free replicated data types. In: Proceedings of the 3rd International Workshop on Cloud Data and Platforms, pp. 31–36. ACM (2013)
21. Parker, D.S., Popek, G.J., Rudisin, G., Stoughton, A., Walker, B.J., Walton, E., Chow, J.M., Edwards, D., Kiser, S., Kline, C.: Detection of mutual inconsistency in distributed systems. IEEE Trans. Softw. Eng. **9**(3), 240–247 (1983). http://dx.doi.org/10.1109/TSE.1983.236733
22. Shapiro, M., Preguiça, N., Baquero, C., Zawirski, M.: A comprehensive study of Convergent and Commutative Replicated Data Types. Rapp. Rech. 7506, INRIA, Rocquencourt, France, January 2011. http://hal.archives-ouvertes.fr/inria-00555588/
23. Shapiro, M., Preguiça, N., Baquero, C., Zawirski, M.: Conflict-free replicated data types. In: Défago, X., Petit, F., Villain, V. (eds.) SSS 2011. LNCS, vol. 6976, pp. 386–400. Springer, Heidelberg (2011)
24. Terry, D.B., Theimer, M.M., Petersen, K., Demers, A.J., Spreitzer, M.J., Hauser, C.H.: Managing update conflicts in Bayou, a weakly connected replicated storage system. In: Symposium on Operating Systems Principles (SOSP), pp. 172–182. ACM SIGOPS, ACM Press, Copper Mountain, CO, USA, December 1995
25. Wuu, G.T.J., Bernstein, A.J.: Efficient solutions to the replicated log and dictionary problems. In: Symposium on Principles of Distributed Computing (PODC), Vancouver, BC, Canada, pp. 233–242, August 1984

Concurrency in Snap-Stabilizing Local Resource Allocation

Karine Altisen, Stéphane Devismes, and Anaïs Durand(✉)

VERIMAG UMR 5104, Université Grenoble Alpes, Grenoble, France
{karine.altisen,stephane.devismes,anais.durand}@imag.fr

Abstract. In distributed systems, resource allocation consists in managing fair access of a large number of processes to a typically small number of reusable resources. As soon as the number of available resources is greater than one, the efficiency in concurrent accesses becomes an important issue, as a crucial goal is to maximize the utilization rate of resources. In this paper, we tackle the concurrency issue in resource allocation problems. We first characterize the maximal level of concurrency we can obtain in such problems by proposing the notion of *maximal-concurrency*. Then, we focus on Local Resource Allocation problems (LRA). Our results are both negative and positive. On the negative side, we show that it is impossible to obtain maximal-concurrency in LRA without compromising the fairness. On the positive side, we propose a snap-stabilizing LRA algorithm which achieves a high (but not maximal) level of concurrency, called here *strong partial maximal-concurrency*.

1 Introduction

Mutual exclusion [14,25] is a fundamental resource allocation problem, which consists in managing fair access of all (requesting) processes to a unique non-shareable reusable resource. This problem is inherently sequential, as no two processes should access this resource concurrently. There are many other resource allocation problems which, in contrast, allow several resources to be accessed simultaneously. In those problems, parallelism on access to resources may be restricted by some of the following conditions:

1. The maximum number of resources that can be used concurrently, *e.g.*, the *ℓ-exclusion* problem [19] is a generalization of the mutual exclusion problem which allows use of ℓ identical copies of a non-shareable reusable resource among all processes, instead of only one, as standard mutual exclusion.
2. The maximum number of resources a process can use simultaneously, *e.g.*, the *k-out-of-ℓ-exclusion* problem [27] is a generalization of *ℓ-exclusion* where a process can request for up to k resources simultaneously.
3. Some topological constraints, *e.g.*, in the *dining philosophers* problem [16], two neighbors cannot use their common resource simultaneously.

This work has been partially supported by the ANR Persyval Project DACRAW.

A. Bouajjani and H. Fauconnier (Eds.): NETYS 2015, LNCS 9466, pp. 77–93, 2015.
DOI: 10.1007/978-3-319-26850-7_6

For efficiency purposes, algorithms solving such problems must be as parallel as possible. As a consequence, these algorithms should be, in particular, evaluated at the light of the level of concurrency they permit, and this level of concurrency should be captured by a dedicated property. However, most of the solutions to resource allocation problems simply do not consider the concurrency issue, *e.g.*, [5,7,9,20,22,24,26]

Now, as quoted by Fischer *et al.* [19], specifying resource allocation problems without including a property of concurrency may lead to degenerated solutions, *e.g.*, any mutual exclusion algorithm realizes the safety and the fairness of ℓ-exclusion. To address this issue, Fischer *et al.* [19] proposed an ad hoc property to capture concurrency in ℓ-exclusion. This property is called *avoiding ℓ-deadlock* and is informally defined as follows: "if fewer than ℓ processes are executing their critical section,[1] then it is possible for another process to enter its critical section, even though no process leaves its critical section in the meantime." Some other properties, inspired from the avoiding ℓ-deadlock property, have been proposed to capture the level of concurrency in other resource allocation problems, *e.g.*, k-out-of-ℓ-exclusion [11] and committee coordination [6]. However, until now, all existing properties of concurrency are specific to a particular problem.

In this paper, we first propose to generalize the definition of avoiding ℓ-deadlock to any resource allocation problems. We call this new property the *maximal-concurrency*. Then, we consider the maximal-concurrency in the context of the *Local Resource Allocation (LRA)* problem, defined by Cantarell *et al.* [9]. LRA is a generalization of resource allocation problems in which resources are shared among neighboring processes. Dining philosophers, local reader-writers, local mutual exclusion, and local group mutual exclusion are particular instances of LRA. In contrast, local ℓ-exclusion and local k-out-of-ℓ-exclusion cannot be expressed with LRA although they also deal with neighboring resource sharing.

Now, we show that algorithms for any instance of this important problem cannot achieve maximal-concurrency. This impossibility result is mainly due to the fact that fairness of LRA and maximal-concurrency are incompatible properties: it is impossible to implement an algorithm achieving both properties. As unfair resource allocation algorithms are clearly unpractical, we propose to weaken the property of maximal-concurrency. We call *partial maximal-concurrency* this weaker version of maximal concurrency. The goal of *partial maximal-concurrency* is to capture the maximal level of concurrency that can be obtained in LRA without compromising fairness.

We propose a LRA algorithm achieving (strong) partial maximal-concurrency in bidirectional identified networks of arbitrary topology. As additional feature, this algorithm is *snap-stabilizing* [8]. *Snap-stabilization* is a versatile property which enables a distributed system to efficiently withstand transient faults. Informally, after transient faults cease, a snap-stabilizing algorithm *immediately* resumes correct behavior, without external intervention. More precisely, a snap-

[1] The *critical section* is the code that manages the access of a process to its allocated resources.

stabilizing algorithm guarantees that any computation started after the faults cease will operate correctly. However, we have no guarantees for those executed all or a part during faults. By definition, snap-stabilization is a strengthened form of *self-stabilization* [15]: after transient faults cease, a self-stabilizing algorithm *eventually* resume correct behavior, without external intervention.

There exist many algorithms for particular instances of the LRA problem. Many of these solutions have been proven to be self-stabilizing, *e.g.*, [5,7,9,20,22, 24,26]. In [7], Boulinier *et al.* propose a self-stabilizing unison algorithm which allows to solve local mutual exclusion, local group mutual exclusion, and the local reader-writers problem. There are also many self-stabilizing algorithms for the local mutual exclusion [5,20,24,26]. In [22], Huang proposes a self-stabilizing algorithm solving the dining philosophers problem. A self-stabilizing drinking philosophers algorithm is given in [26]. In [9], Cantarell *et al.* generalize the above problems by introducing the LRA problem. They also propose a self-stabilizing algorithm for that problem. To the best of our knowledge, no other paper deals with the general instance of LRA and no paper proposes snap-stabilizing solution for any particular instance of LRA. Finally, none of the aforementioned papers (especially [9]) consider the concurrency issue. Finally, note that there exist weaker versions of the LRA problem, such as the (local) *conflict managers* proposed in [21] where the fairness is replaced by a progress property.

Roadmap. The next section introduces the computation model and the specification of the LRA problem. In Sect. 3, we define the property of maximal-concurrency, show the impossibility result, and then circumvent this impossibility by introducing the partial maximal-concurrency. Our algorithm is presented in Sect. 4. We outline the proofs of its correctness and (strong) partial maximal-concurrency in Subsect. 4.4. A detailed proof is available in the technical report [3]. We conclude in Sect. 5.

2 Computational Model and Specifications

2.1 Distributed Systems

We consider *distributed systems* composed of n *processes.* A process p can (directly) communicate with a subset $\mathcal{N}_p$ of other processes, called its *neighbors.* These communications are assumed to be *bidirectional*, *i.e.*, for any two processes p and q, $q \in \mathcal{N}_p$ *if and only if* $p \in \mathcal{N}_q$. Hence, the topology of the network can be modeled by a simple undirected graph $G = (V, E)$, where V is the set of processes and E is the set of edges representing (direct) communication relations. Moreover, we assume that each process has a unique ID, a natural integer. By abuse of notation, we identify the process with its own ID, whenever convenient.

2.2 Locally Shared Memory Model

We consider the *locally shared memory model* in which processes communicate using a finite number of locally shared registers, called *variables.* Each process can read its own variables and those of its neighbors, but can only write to its own variables. The *state* of a process is the vector of values of all its variables. A configuration γ of the system is the vector of states of all processes. We denote by $\gamma(p)$ the state of a process p in a configuration γ.

A *distributed algorithm* consists of one *program* per process. The program of a process p is composed of a finite number of *actions*, where each action has the following form: $(\langle\text{priority}\rangle)\ \ \langle\text{label}\rangle : \langle\text{guard}\rangle \rightarrow \langle\text{statement}\rangle$. The *labels* are used to identify actions. The *guard* of an action in the program of process p is a Boolean expression involving the variables of p and its neighbors. *Priorities* are used to simplify the guards of the actions. The actual guard of an action "$(j)\ L\ :\ G\ \rightarrow\ S$" at p is the conjunction of G and the negation of the disjunction of all guards of actions at p with priority $i < j$. An action of priority i is said to be of *higher priority* than any action of priority $j > i$. If the actual guard of some action evaluates to true, then the action is said to be *enabled* at p. By definition, a process p is not enabled to execute any (lower priority) action if it is enabled to execute an action of higher priority. If at least one action is enabled at p, p is also said to be enabled. We denote by $Enabled(\gamma)$ the set of processes enabled in configuration γ. The *statement* of an action is a sequence of assignments on the variables of p. An action can be executed only if it is enabled. In this case, the execution of the action consists in executing its statement.

The asynchronism of the system is materialized by an adversary, called the *daemon*. In a configuration γ, if there is at least one enabled process (*i.e.*, $Enabled(\gamma) \neq \emptyset$), then the daemon selects a non empty subset S of $Enabled(\gamma)$ to perform an *(atomic) step*: Each process of S atomically executes one of its enabled action in γ, leading the system to a new configuration γ'. We denote by $\mapsto$ the relation between configurations such that $\gamma \mapsto \gamma'$ *if and only if* γ' can be reached from γ in one (atomic) step. An *execution* is a maximal sequence of configurations $\gamma_0, \gamma_1, \ldots$ such that $\forall i > 0$, $\gamma_{i-1} \mapsto \gamma_i$. The term "maximal" means that the execution is either infinite, or ends at a *terminal* configuration γ in which $Enabled(\gamma)$ is empty.

In this paper, we assume a *distributed weakly fair* daemon. "Distributed" means that while the configuration is not terminal, the daemon should select at least one enabled process, maybe more. "Weakly fair" means that there is no infinite suffix of execution in which a process p is continuously enabled without ever being selected by the daemon.

2.3 Snap-Stabilizing Local Resource Allocation

In resource allocation problems, a typically small amount of reusable *resources* is shared among a large number of processes. A process may spontaneously request for one or several resources. When granted, the access to the requested resource(s) is done using a special section of code, called *critical section.* The process can only hold resources for a finite time: eventually, it should release these resources to the system, in order to make them available for other requesting processes. In particular, this means that the critical section is always assumed to be finite. In the following, we denote by $\mathcal{R}_p$ the set of resources that can be accessed by a process p.

Local Resource Allocation. The *Local Resource Allocation (LRA)* problem [9] is based on the notion of compatibility: two resources X and Y are said to be *compatible* if two neighbors can concurrently access them. Otherwise, X and Y are said to be *conflicting*. In the following, we denote by $X \rightleftharpoons Y$ (resp. $X \not\rightleftharpoons Y$) the fact that X and Y are compatible (resp. conflicting). Notice that $\rightleftharpoons$ is a symmetric relation.

Using the compatibility relation, the *local resource allocation* problem consists in ensuring that every process which requires a resource r eventually accesses r while no other conflicting resource is currently used by a neighbor. Notice that the case where there are no conflicting resources is trivial: a process can always use a resource whatever the state of its neighbors. So, from now on, we will always assume that there exists at least one conflict, *i.e.*, there are (at least) two neighbors p, q and two resources X, Y such that $X \in \mathcal{R}_p, Y \in \mathcal{R}_q$ and $X \not\rightleftharpoons Y$.

Specifying the relation $\rightleftharpoons$, it is possible to define some classic resource allocation problems in which the resources are shared among neighboring processes.

Example 1: Local Mutual Exclusion. In the *local mutual exclusion* problem, no two neighbors can concurrently access the unique resource. So there is only one resource X common to all processes and $X \not\rightleftharpoons X$.

Example 2: Local Readers-Writers. In the *local readers-writers* problem, the processes can access a file in two different modes: a read access (the process is said to be a *reader*) or a write access (the process is said to be a *writer*). A writer must access the file in local mutual exclusion, while several reading neighbors can concurrently access the file. We represent these two access modes by two resources at every process: R for a "read access" and W for a "write access." Then, $R \rightleftharpoons R$, but $W \not\rightleftharpoons R$ and $W \not\rightleftharpoons W$.

Snap-Stabilization. Let $\mathcal{A}$ be a distributed algorithm. A *specification SP* is a predicate over all executions of $\mathcal{A}$. In [8], snap-stabilization has been defined as follows: $\mathcal{A}$ is *snap-stabilizing w.r.t. SP* if starting from any arbitrary configuration, all its executions satisfy SP.

Of course, not all specifications — in particular their safety part — can be satisfied when considering a system which can start from an arbitrary configuration. Actually, snap-stabilization's notion of safety is *user-centric*: when the user initiates a computation, then the computed result should be correct. So, we express a problem using a *guaranteed service specification* [2]. Such a specification consists in specifying three properties related to the computation start, computation end, and correctness of the delivered result. (In the context of LRA, this latter property will be referred to as "resource conflict freedom.")

To formally define the guaranteed service specification of the local resource allocation problem, we need to introduce the following four predicates, where p is a process, r is a resource, and $e = (\gamma_i)_{i \geq 0}$ is an execution:

- $Request(\gamma_i, p, r)$ means that an application at p requires r in configuration γ_i. We assume that if $Request(\gamma_i, p, r)$ holds, it continuously holds until p accesses r.
- $Start(\gamma_i, \gamma_{i+1}, p, r)$ means that p starts a computation to access r in $\gamma_i \mapsto \gamma_{i+1}$.
- $Result(\gamma_i \ldots \gamma_j, p, r)$ means that p obtains access to r in $\gamma_{i-1} \mapsto \gamma_i$ and p ends the computation in $\gamma_j \mapsto \gamma_{j+1}$. Notably, p released r between γ_i and γ_j.
- $NoConflict(\gamma_i, p)$ means that, in γ_i, if a resource is allocated to p, then none of its neighbors is using a conflicting resource.

These predicates will be instantiated with the variables of the local resource allocation algorithm. Below, we define the guaranteed service specification of LRA.

Specification 1 (Local Resource Allocation). *Let $\mathcal{A}$ be an algorithm. An execution $e = (\gamma_i)_{i\geq 0}$ of $\mathcal{A}$ satisfies the guaranteed service specification of LRA, noted SP_{LRA}, if the three following properties hold:*

Resource Conflict Freedom: *If a process p starts a computation to access a resource, then there is no conflict involving p during the computation:* $\forall k \geq 0, \forall k' > k, \forall p \in V, \forall r \in \mathcal{R}_p, \left[Result(\gamma_k \ldots \gamma_{k'}, p, r) \wedge (\exists l < k, Start(\gamma_l, \gamma_{l+1}, p, r))\right] \Rightarrow \left[\forall i \in \{k, \ldots, k'\}, NoConflict(\gamma_i, p)\right]$

Computation Start: *If an application at process p requests resource r, then p eventually starts a computation to obtain r:* $\forall k \geq 0, \forall p \in V, \forall r \in \mathcal{R}_p, \left[\exists l > k, Request(\gamma_l, p, r) \Rightarrow Start(\gamma_l, \gamma_{l+1}, p, r)\right]$

Computation End: *If process p starts a computation to obtain resource r, the computation eventually ends (in particular, p obtained r during the computation):* $\forall k \geq 0, \forall p \in V, \forall r \in \mathcal{R}_p, Start(\gamma_k, \gamma_{k+1}, p, r) \Rightarrow \left[\exists l > k, \exists l' > l, Result(\gamma_l \ldots \gamma_{l'}, p, r)\right]$

Thus, an algorithm $\mathcal{A}$ is snap-stabilizing *w.r.t.* SP_{LRA} (*i.e.*, snap-stabilizing for LRA) if starting from any arbitrary configuration, all its executions satisfy SP_{LRA}.[2]

3 Concurrency

Many existing resource allocation algorithms, especially self-stabilizing ones [5, 7,9,20,22,24,26], do not consider the concurrency issue. In [19], authors propose a concurrency property *ad hoc* to ℓ-exclusion. We now define the *maximal-concurrency*, which generalizes the definition of [19] to any resource allocation problem.

3.1 Maximal-Concurrency

Informally, maximal-concurrency can be defined as follows: if there are processes that can access some resource they are requesting without violating the safety

[2] By contrast, a non-stabilizing algorithm achieves LRA if all its executions starting from *predefined initial* configurations satisfy SP_{LRA}.

of the considered resource allocation problem, then at least one of them should eventually access one of its requested resources, even if no process releases the resource it holds in the meantime.

Let $P_{CS}(\gamma)$ be the set of processes that are executing their critical section in γ, *i.e.*, the set of processes holding resources in γ. Let $P_{Req}(\gamma)$ be the set of processes that are requesting in γ. Let $P_{Free}(\gamma) \subseteq P_{req}(\gamma)$ be the set of requesting processes that can access their requested resource(s) in γ without violating the safety of the considered resource allocation problem. We denote by $\gamma(p).req$ the resource(s) requested by process p in γ. Let $continuousCS(\gamma_i \dots \gamma_j) \equiv \forall k \in \{i, \dots, j-1\}, P_{CS}(\gamma_k) \subseteq P_{CS}(\gamma_{k+1})$

Definition 1 (Maximal-Concurrency). *An algorithm is* maximal-concurrent *if and only if* $\forall e = (\gamma_i)_{i \geq 0} \in \mathcal{E}$, $\forall i \geq 0$, $\exists N \in \mathbb{N}$, $\forall j > N$, $continuousCS((\gamma_i \dots \gamma_{i+j}) \wedge P_{Free}(\gamma_i) \neq \emptyset) \Rightarrow (\exists k \in \{i, \dots, i+j-1\}, \exists p \in V, p \in P_{Free}(\gamma_k) \cap P_{CS}(\gamma_{k+1}))$.

The two examples below show the versatility of our property: we instantiate the set P_{Free} according to the considered problem.

Example 1: ℓ-Exclusion Maximal-Concurrency. In the ℓ-exclusion problem, up to ℓ processes can execute their critical section concurrently. Hence,

$$P_{Free}(\gamma) = \emptyset \text{ if } |P_{CS}(\gamma)| = \ell; \quad P_{Free}(\gamma) = P_{Req}(\gamma) \text{ otherwise}$$

Using this latter instantiation, we obtain a definition of maximal concurrency which is equivalent to the "avoiding ℓ-deadlock" property of Fischer *et al.* [19].

Example 2: Local Resource Allocation Maximal-Concurrency. In the local resource allocation problem, a requesting process is allowed to enter its critical section if all its neighbors in critical section are using resources which are compatible with its request:

$$P_{Free}(\gamma) = \{p \in P_{Req}(\gamma) \mid \forall q \in \mathcal{N}_p, (q \in P_{CS}(\gamma) \Rightarrow \gamma(q).req \rightleftharpoons \gamma(p).req)\}$$

The maximal-concurrency property can also be defined using the following alternative definition:

Definition 2 (Maximal Concurrency). An algorithm is *maximal concurrent if and only if* $\forall e = (\gamma_i)_{i \geq 0} \in \mathcal{E}$, $\forall i \geq 0$, $\exists T \in \mathbb{N}$, $\forall t \geq T$,

$$continuousCS(\gamma_i \dots \gamma_{i+t}) \Rightarrow P_{Free}(\gamma_{i+t}) = \emptyset$$

Definitions 1 and 2 are equivalent using induction arguments (see [3]). Using the latter definition, remark that an algorithm is not maximal concurrent if and only if $\exists e = (\gamma_i)_{i \geq 0} \in \mathcal{E}$, $\exists i \geq 0$, $\forall T \in \mathbb{N}$, $\exists t \geq T$, $continuousCS(\gamma_i \dots \gamma_{i+t}) \wedge P_{Free}(\gamma_{i+t}) \neq \emptyset$.

3.2 Maximal Concurrency Vs. Fairness

Definition 3 below gives a definition of fairness classically used in resource allocation problems. Notably, Computation Start and End properties of Specification 1 trivially implies this fairness property. Next, Theorem 1 states that no LRA algorithm (stabilizing or not) can achieve maximal-concurrency. Actually, its proof is based on the incompatibility between fairness and maximal-concurrency.

Definition 3 (Fairness). *Each time a process is (continuously) requesting a resource r, it eventually accesses r.*

Theorem 1. *It is impossible to design a LRA algorithm for arbitrary networks that satisfies maximal-concurrency.*

Proof. Assume, by contradiction, that there is a local resource allocation algorithm $\mathcal{A}$ (stabilizing or not) which satisfies maximal-concurrency. Let consider the following graph: $G = (V, E)$ where $V = \{p_1, p_2, p_3\}$ and $E = \{(p_1, p_2), (p_2, p_3)\}$. Let X and Y be two resources such that $X \not\rightleftharpoons Y$, $X \in \mathcal{R}_{p_1}$, $Y \in \mathcal{R}_{p_2}$, and $X \in \mathcal{R}_{p_3}$ (notice that we can have $X = Y$). We assume that, when p_1 and p_3 request a resource, they request X, and, when p_2 requests a resource, it requests Y. Below, we exhibit a possible execution e of $\mathcal{A}$ on G where fairness is violated if maximal-concurrency is achieved. Figure 1 illustrates the proof.

First, assume that p_1 continuously requests X while p_2 and p_3 are idle (Configuration 1.(a)). As $\mathcal{A}$ satisfies the fairness property, p_1 eventually executes its critical section to access X. This critical section can last an arbitrary long (yet finite) time (Fig. 1.(b)).

Then, p_2 and p_3 start continuously requesting (Y for p_2 and X for p_3). To satisfy the maximal-concurrency property, p_3 must eventually obtain resource X, even if p_1 does not finish its critical section in the meantime. In this case, the system reaches the configuration given in Fig. 1.(d).

Then, it is possible that p_1 ends its critical section and releases resource X right after Configuration 1.(d). But, in this case, p_2 still cannot access Y because Y is conflicting with the resource X currently used by p_3. So, the system can reach Configuration 1.(e). If p_1 continuously requests X again right after Configuration 1.(e), we obtain Configuration 1.(f). Now, the execution of the critical section of p_3 may last an arbitrary long (yet finite) time, and p_1 should again access X, even if p_3 does not finish its critical section in the meantime, by maximal-concurrency. So, the system can reach Configuration 1.(g).

Now, if p_3 releases its resource and then continuously requests it again, we retrieve a configuration similar to the one of Fig. 1.(c). We can repeat this scheme infinitely often so that p_2 continuously requests Y but never access it: the fairness property is violated, a contradiction.

3.3 Partial Maximal-Concurrency

To circumvent the previous impossibility result, we propose a weaker version of maximal concurrency, called *partial maximal-concurrency*.

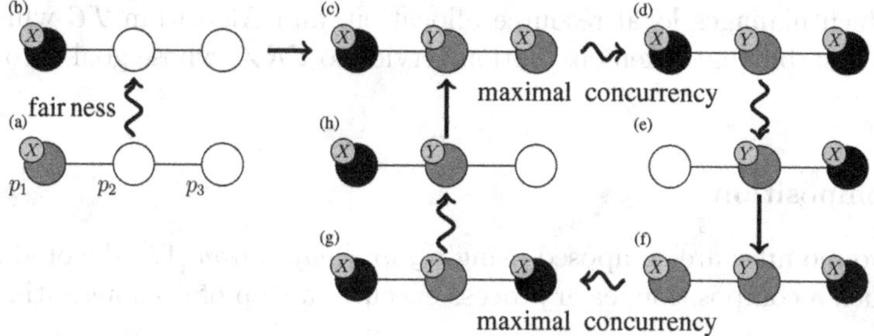

Fig. 1. Maximal concurrency *vs.* fairness. The processes in black are executing their critical section. The processes in gray are requesting resources. The processes in white are idle. Requested resources are given in the bubbles next to the nodes.

Definition 4 (Partial Maximal-Concurrency). *Analgorithm $\mathcal{A}$ is* partially maximal-concurrent *if and only if* $\forall e = (\gamma_i)_{i \geq 0} \in \mathcal{E}$, $\forall i \geq 0$, $\exists T \in \mathbb{N}$ such that $\forall t \geq T$, $\exists X \subseteq V$ such that $continuousCS(\gamma_i \dots \gamma_{i+t}) \Rightarrow P_{Free}(\gamma_{i+t}) \subseteq X$.

Notice that, by definition, a maximal-concurrent algorithm is also partially maximal-concurrent.

The proof of Theorem 1 reveals that fairness and maximal concurrency are contradictory in the following situation: some neighbors of a process alternatively use resources which are conflicting with its own request. So, to achieve fairness, we must relax the expected level of concurrency in such a way that at least in that situation p eventually satisfies its request. To ensure this, any LRA algorithm should then eventually allow p to prevent its requesting neighbors from entering their critical section, even if p cannot currently satisfies its request (*i.e.*, even if one of its neighbor is using a conflicting resource) and even if some of its requesting neighbors can enter critical section without creating any conflict. Hence, in the worst case, p has one neighbor holding a conflicting resource and it should prevent all other neighbors to satisfy their requests, in order to eventually satisfy its own request (and so to ensure fairness).

We derive the following refinement of partial maximal concurrency based on this latter observation: this seems to be the finest concurrency we can expect in LRA algorithm.

Definition 5 (Strong Partial Maximal-Concurrency). *An algorithm $\mathcal{A}$ is* strongly partially maximal-concurrent *if and only if* $\forall e = (\gamma_i)_{i \geq 0} \in \mathcal{E}$, $\forall i \geq 0$, $\exists T \in \mathbb{N}$ such that $\forall t \geq T$, $\exists p, q \in V$, $q \in \mathcal{N}_p$ such that $continuousCS(\gamma_i \dots \gamma_{i+t}) \Rightarrow P_{Free}(\gamma_{i+t}) \subseteq \mathcal{N}_p \backslash \{q\}$.

In the next section, we show that strong partial maximal-concurrency can be realized by a snap-stabilizing LRA algorithm.

4 Local Resource Allocation Algorithm

We now propose a snap-stabilizing LRA algorithm which achieves the strong partial maximal concurrency. This algorithm consists of two modules: Algorithm

$\mathcal{LRA}$, which manages local resource allocation, and Algorithm $\mathcal{TC}$ which provides a self-stabilizing token circulation service to $\mathcal{LRA}$, whose goal is to ensure fairness.

4.1 Composition

These two modules are composed using a *fair composition* [17], denoted $\mathcal{LRA} \circ \mathcal{TC}$. In such a composition, each process executes a step of each algorithm alternately.

Notice that the purpose of this composition is only to simplify the design of the algorithm: a composite algorithm written in the locally shared memory model can be translated into an equivalent non-composite algorithm. Such a translation can be done using the rewriting rule given in the technical report [3].

4.2 Token Circulation Module

We assume that $\mathcal{TC}$ is a self-stabilizing black box which allows $\mathcal{LRA}$ to emulate a self-stabilizing token circulation. $\mathcal{TC}$ provides two outputs to each process p in $\mathcal{LRA}$: the predicate $Token(p)$ and the statement $PassToken(p)$. The predicate $Token(p)$ expresses whether the process p holds a token or not. The statement $PassToken(p)$ can be used to pass the token from p to one of its neighbor. Of course, it should be executed (by $\mathcal{LRA}$) only if $Token(p)$ holds. Precisely, we assume that $\mathcal{TC}$ satisfies the following properties.

Property 1 (Stabilization). $\mathcal{TC}$ stabilizes, *i.e.*, reaches and remains in configurations where there is a unique token in the network, independently of any call to $PassToken(p)$ at any process p.

Property 2. Once $\mathcal{TC}$ has stabilized, $\forall p \in V$, if $Token(p)$ holds, then $Token(p)$ is continuously true until $PassToken(p)$ is invoked.

Property 3 (Fairness). Once $\mathcal{TC}$ has stabilized, if $\forall p \in V$, $PassToken(p)$ is invoked in finite time each time $Token(p)$ holds, then $\forall p \in V$, $Token(p)$ holds infinitely often.

To design $\mathcal{TC}$ we proceed as follows. There exist several self-stabilizing token circulations for arbitrary rooted networks [10,12,23] that contain a particular action, $T : Token(p) \rightarrow PassToken(p)$, to pass the token, and that stabilizes independently of the activations of action T. Now, the networks we consider are not rooted, but identified. So, to obtain a self-stabilizing token circulation for arbitrary identified networks, we can fairly compose any of them with a self-stabilizing leader election algorithm [1,4,13,18] using the following additional rule: if a process considers itself as leader it executes the token circulation program for a root; otherwise it executes the program for a non-root. Finally, we obtain $\mathcal{TC}$ by removing action T from the resulting algorithm, while keeping $Token(p)$ and $PassToken(p)$ as outputs, for every process p.

Algorithm 1. Algorithm $\mathcal{LRA}$ for every process p

Variables

$p.status \in \{\mathsf{Out}, \mathsf{Wait}, \mathsf{Blocked}, \mathsf{In}\}$, $p.token \in \mathbb{B}$

Inputs

$p.req \in \mathcal{R}_p \cup \{\bot\}$: Variable from the application
$Token(p)$: Predicate from $\mathcal{TC}$, indicate that p holds the token
$PassToken(p)$: Statement from $\mathcal{TC}$, pass the token to a neighbor

Macros

$WaitingNeigh(p) \equiv \{q \in \mathcal{N}_p \mid q.status = \mathsf{Wait}\}$
$LocalMax(p) \equiv \max\{q \in WaitingNeigh(p) \cup \{p\}\}$
$LocalTokens(p) \equiv \{q \in \mathcal{N}_p \cup \{p\} \mid q.token\}$
$TokenMax(p) \equiv \max\{q \in LocalTokens(p)\}$

Predicates

$ResourceFree(p) \equiv \forall q \in \mathcal{N}_p, (q.status = \mathsf{In} \Rightarrow p.req \rightleftharpoons q.req)$
$IsBlocked(p) \equiv \neg ResourceFree(p) \vee (\exists q \in \mathcal{N}_p, q.status = \mathsf{Blocked} \wedge q.token)$
$TokenAccess(p) \equiv LocalTokens(p) \neq \emptyset \wedge p = TokenMax(p)$
$MaxAccess(p) \equiv LocalTokens(p) = \emptyset \wedge p = LocalMax(p)$

Guards

$Requested(p) \equiv p.status = \mathsf{Out} \wedge p.req \neq \bot$
$Block(p) \equiv p.status = \mathsf{Wait} \wedge IsBlocked(p)$
$Unblock(p) \equiv p.status = \mathsf{Blocked} \wedge \neg IsBlocked(p)$
$Enter(p) \equiv p.status = \mathsf{Wait} \wedge \neg IsBlocked(p) \wedge (TokenAccess(p) \vee MaxAccess(p))$
$Exit(p) \equiv p.status = \mathsf{In} \wedge p.req = \bot$
$ResetToken(p) \equiv Token(p) \neq p.token$
$ReleaseToken(p) \equiv Token(p) \wedge p.status \in \{\mathsf{Out}, \mathsf{In}\} \wedge \neg Requested(p)$

Actions

(1) RsT-$action$ :: $ResetToken(p) \rightarrow p.token \leftarrow Token(p)$;
(3) RlT-$action$ :: $ReleaseToken(p) \rightarrow PassToken(p)$;
(4) R-$action$ :: $Requested(p) \rightarrow p.status \leftarrow \mathsf{Wait}$;
(4) B-$action$ :: $Block(p) \rightarrow p.status \leftarrow \mathsf{Blocked}$;
(4) UB-$action$ :: $Unblock(p) \rightarrow p.status \leftarrow \mathsf{Wait}$;
(4) E-$action$ :: $Enter(p) \rightarrow p.status \leftarrow \mathsf{In}$; **if** $p.token$ **then** $PassToken(p)$ **fi**;
(2) Ex-$action$ :: $Exit(p) \rightarrow p.status \leftarrow \mathsf{Out}$;

4.3 Resource Allocation Module

The code of $\mathcal{LRA}$ is given in Algorithm 1. Priorities and guards ensure that actions of Algorithm 1 are mutually exclusive. We now informally describe Algorithm 1, and explain how Specification 1 is instantiated with its variables.

First, a process p interacts with its application through two variables: $p.req \in \mathcal{R}_p \cup \{\bot\}$ and $p.status \in \{\mathsf{Out}, \mathsf{Wait}, \mathsf{In}, \mathsf{Blocked}\}$. $p.req$ can be read and written by the application, but can only be read by p in $\mathcal{LRA}$. Conversely, $p.status$ can be written by p in $\mathcal{LRA}$, but the application can only read it. Variable $p.status$ can take the following values:

- Wait, which means that p requests a resource but does not hold it yet;
- Blocked, which means that p requests a resource, but cannot hold it now;
- In, which means that p holds a resource;
- Out, which means that p is currently not involved into an allocation process.

When $p.req = \bot$, this means that no resource is requested. Conversely, when $p.req \in \mathcal{R}_p$, the value of $p.req$ informs p about the resource requested by the application. We assume two properties on $p.req$. Property 4 ensures that the application (1) does not request for resource r' while a computation to access resource r is running, and (2) does not cancel or modify a request before the request is satisfied. Property 5 ensures that any critical section is finite.

Property 4. $\forall p \in V$, the updates on $p.req$ (by the application) satisfy the following constraints:

- The value of $p.req$ can change from $\bot$ to $r \in \mathcal{R}_p$ *if and only if* $p.status = \mathsf{Out}$,
- The value of $p.req$ can change from $r \in \mathcal{R}_p$ to $\bot$ *if and only if* $p.status = \mathsf{In}$.
- The value of $p.req$ cannot directly change from $r \in \mathcal{R}_p$ to $r' \in \mathcal{R}_p$ with $r' \neq r$.

Property 5. $\forall p \in V$, if $p.status = \mathsf{In}$ and $p.req \neq \bot$, then eventually $p.req$ becomes $\bot$.

Consequently, the predicate $Request(\gamma_i, p, r)$ in Specification 1 is true if and only if $p.req = r$ in γ_i; the predicate $NoConflict(\gamma_i, p)$ is expressed by $p.status = \mathsf{In} \Rightarrow (\forall q \in \mathcal{N}_p, q.status = \mathsf{In} \Rightarrow (q.req \rightleftharpoons p.req))$ in γ_i. (We set $\bot$ compatible with every resource.)

The predicate $Start(\gamma_i, \gamma_{i+1}, p, r)$ becomes true when process p takes the request for resource r into account in $\gamma_i \mapsto \gamma_{i+1}$, *i.e.*, when the status of p switches from Out to Wait in $\gamma_i \mapsto \gamma_{i+1}$ because $p.req = r \neq \bot$ in γ_i.

Assume that $\gamma_i \ldots \gamma_j$ is a computation where $Result(\gamma_i \ldots \gamma_j, p, r)$ holds: process p accesses resource r, *i.e.*, p switches its status from Wait to In in $\gamma_{i-1} \mapsto \gamma_i$ while $p.req = r$, and later switches its status from In to Out in $\gamma_j \mapsto \gamma_{j+1}$.

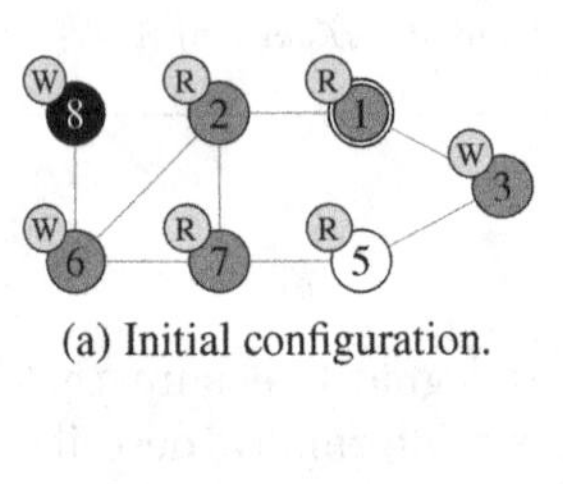

(a) Initial configuration.

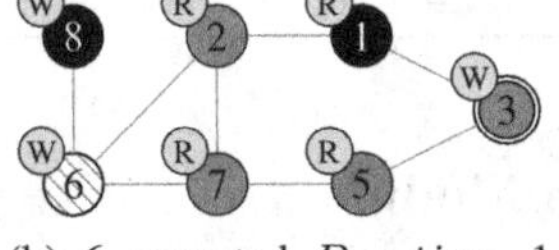

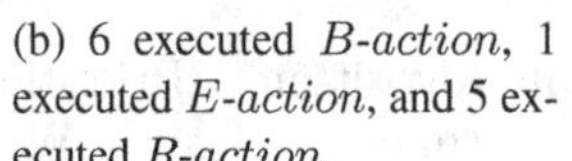

(b) 6 executed *B-action*, 1 executed *E-action*, and 5 executed *R-action*.

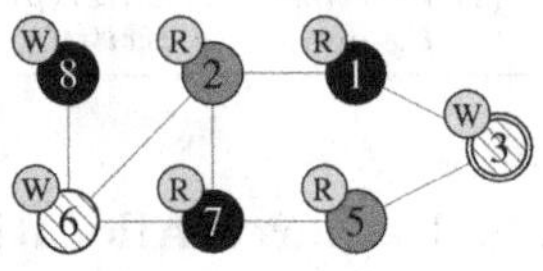

(c) 3 executed *B-action* and 7 executed *E-action*.

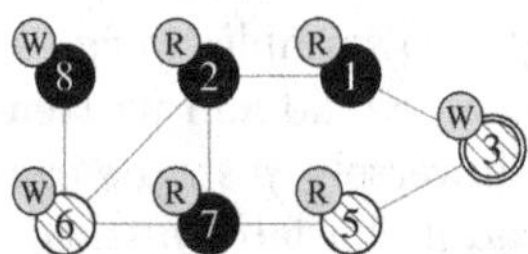

(d) 2 executed *E-action* and 5 executed *B-action*.

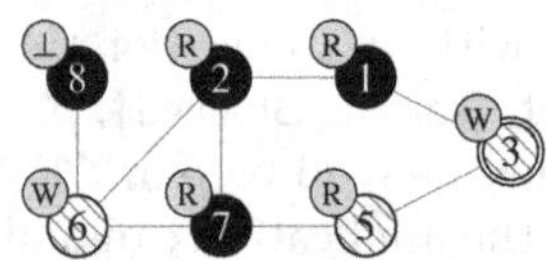

(e) The application of 8 does not need the write access anymore.

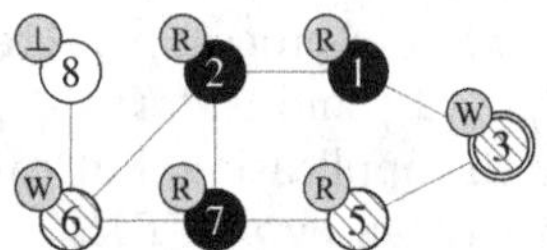

(f) 8 executed *Ex-action*.

Fig. 2. Example of execution of $\mathcal{LRA} \circ \mathcal{TC}$.

We now illustrate the principles of $\mathcal{LRA}$ with the example given in Fig. 2. In this example, we consider the local reader-writer problem. In the figure, the numbers inside the nodes represent their IDs. The color of a node represents its status: white for Out, gray for Wait, black for In, and crossed out for Blocked. A double circled node holds a token. The bubble next to a node represents its request. Recall that we have two resources: R for a reading access and W for a writing access.

When the process is idle ($p.status$ = Out), its application can request a resource. In this case, $p.req = r \neq \bot$ and p sets $p.status$ to Wait by *R-action*: p starts the computation to obtain r. For example, 5 starts a computation to obtain R in (a)$\mapsto$(b). If one of its neighbors is using a conflicting resource, p cannot satisfy its request yet. So, p switches $p.status$ from Wait to Blocked by *B-action* (see 6 in (a)$\mapsto$(b)). If there is no more neighbor using conflicting resources, p gets back to status Wait by *UB-action*.

When several neighbors request for conflicting resources, we break ties using a token-based priority: Each process p has an additional Boolean variable $p.token$ which is used to inform neighbors about whether p holds a token or not. A process p takes priority over any neighbor q *if and only if* $(p.token \wedge \neg q.token) \vee (p.token = q.token \wedge p > q)$. More precisely, if there is no token in the neighborhood of p, the highest priority process is the waiting process with highest ID. Otherwise, the token holders (there may be several tokens during the stabilization phase of $\mathcal{TC}$) blocked all their requesting neighbors, even if they request for non-conflicting resources, and until the token holders obtain their requested resources. This mechanism allows to ensure fairness by slightly decreasing the level of concurrency. (The token circulates to eventually give priority to blocked processes, *e.g.*, processes with small IDs.)

The highest priority waiting process in the neighborhood gets status In and can use its requested resource by *E-action*, *e.g.*, 7 in step (b)$\mapsto$(c) or 1 in (a)$\mapsto$(b). Moreover, if it holds a token, it releases it. Notice that, as a process is not blocked when one of its neighbors is using a compatible resource, several neighbors using compatible resources can concurrently enter and/or execute their critical section (see 1, 2, and 7 in Configuration (d)). When the application at process p does not need the resource anymore, *i.e.*, when it sets the value of $p.req$ to $\bot$, p executes *Ex-action* and switches its status to Out, *e.g.*, 8 during step(e)$\mapsto$(f).

RlT-action is used to straight away pass the token to a neighbor when the process does not need it, *i.e.*, when its status is either Out or In. (Hence, the token can eventually reach a process of status Wait or Blocked and help it to satisfy its request.)

The last action, *RsT-action*, ensures the consistency of variable *.token* so that the neighbors realize whether or not a process holds a token.

4.4 Correctness and Partial Maximal-Concurrency

In this subsection, we sketch the proof of snap-stabilization of Algorithm $\mathcal{LRA} \circ \mathcal{TC}$. Then, we give the proof outline which shows that $\mathcal{LRA} \circ \mathcal{TC}$ is strongly partially maximal-concurrent. Recall that we assume a distributed weakly fair daemon.

Theorem 2 (Resource Conflict Freedom). *Every execution of $\mathcal{LRA} \circ \mathcal{TC}$ satisfies the resource conflict freedom property.*

Proof Outline. Immediate from the guard of *E-action*. □

In $\mathcal{LRA}\circ\mathcal{TC}$, the token circulation is used to ensure fairness. Hence, a crucial point to show that $\mathcal{LRA}\circ\mathcal{TC}$ satisfies the computation start and end properties (Theorems 3 and 4) consists in showing that no process can keep a token forever.

Lemma 1. *No process can keep a token forever.*

Proof Outline. Assume, by contradiction, that a process p holds a token forever. Then, eventually p is the only token holder forever, by Property 1. If $p.status \in \{\mathsf{Out}, \mathsf{In}\}$ forever, p does not need the token and straightaway releases it by *RlT-action*, a contradiction. Otherwise, the token gives priority to p over all of its neighbors. So, p eventually enters in critical section by *E-action* and so releases the token, a contradiction. □

Theorem 3 (Computation End). *Every execution of $\mathcal{LRA}\circ\mathcal{TC}$ satisfies the computation end property.*

Proof Outline. Assume a computation starts at process p to obtain resource r.

Assume, by contradiction, that r is never allocated to p. By Property 1, a unique token eventually exists in the network. Moreover, p eventually gets the token, by Lemma 1 and Property 3. Again by Lemma 1, p eventually releases the token. Now, p can only release the token by executing *E-action*. In this case, p obtains resource r, a contradiction.

Hence, r is allocated to p in finite time. Now, by Property 5, in finite time, the application does not need the resource r anymore and sets $p.req$ to $\perp$. So p eventually executes *Ex-action* and ends its computation. □

We illustrate the previous proof with an example given in Fig. 3. We consider the local mutual exclusion problem. In this example, we try to delay as much as possible the critical section of process 2. First, process 2 has two neighbors (7 and 8) that also request the resource and have greater IDs. So, they will execute their critical section before 2 (in steps (a)↦(b) and (e)↦(f)). But, the

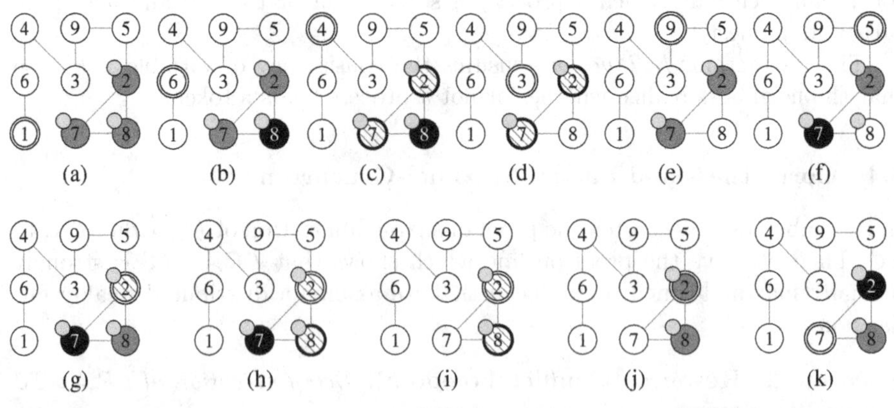

Fig. 3. Example of execution of $\mathcal{LRA}\circ\mathcal{TC}$ on the local mutual exclusion problem. The bubbles mark the requesting processes.

token circulates and eventually reaches 2 (see Configuration (g)). Then, 2 has priority over its neighbors (even though it has a lower ID) and eventually starts executing its critical section in (j)$\mapsto$(k)).

Theorem 4 (Computation Start). *Every execution of $\mathcal{LRA} \circ \mathcal{TC}$ satisfies the computation start property.*

Proof Outline. A process p eventually obtains status Out. Indeed, if $p.status \neq$ Out, p is computing and, by Theorem 3, this computation eventually ends. Hence, if the application of p requests some resource r, *i.e.*, $p.req = r \neq \bot$, p eventually executes *R-action* and a computation for r starts. □

Theorem 5 below is immediate from Theorems 2, 3, and 4.

Theorem 5 (Correctness). *Algorithm $\mathcal{LRA} \circ \mathcal{TC}$ is snap-stabilizing* w.r.t. *SP_{LRA} assuming a distributed weakly fair daemon.*

We now show that $\mathcal{LRA} \circ \mathcal{TC}$ is strongly partially maximal-concurrent. We instantiate the sets P_{CS} and P_{Req} as follows: $P_{Req}(\gamma) = \{p \in V, p.req \neq \bot \wedge p.status \neq \mathsf{In} \text{ in } \gamma\}$ and $P_{CS}(\gamma) = \{p \in V, p.status = \mathsf{In} \wedge p.req \neq \bot \text{ in } \gamma\}$.

Theorem 6 (Strong Partial Maximal-Concurrency). *Algorithm $\mathcal{LRA} \circ \mathcal{TC}$ is a strong partial maximal concurrent local resource allocation algorithm.*

Proof Outline. After stabilization of $\mathcal{TC}$, $\exists T$ from which, if $continousCS$ holds until γ_T, then every process does not change the values of its variables $.req$ and $.status$. After γ_T (and if $continuousCS$ still holds), if P_{Free} is not empty, every process in P_{Free} has status Blocked. Indeed, otherwise there is a finite sequence of processes in P_{Free} with increasing priorities such that the last process is allowed to execute *E-action* and change its $.status$ to In, a contradiction with the definition of T.

A process p is blocked because $\neg ResourceFree(p)$ or $(\exists q \in \mathcal{N}_p, q.status = \mathsf{Blocked} \wedge q.token)$. Now, in the former case, $p \notin P_{Free}$. So, $p \in P_{Free}$ is blocked because of the unique token holder, say q. Then, $p \in \mathcal{N}_q$ and $P_{Free}(\gamma_T)$ contains all the requesting neighbors of q. In the worst case, it contains all the neighborhood of q except one process s that is in critical section, namely, the one that blocks q. Hence, $P_{Free}(\gamma_T) \subseteq \mathcal{N}_q \backslash \{s\}$, and $\mathcal{LRA} \circ \mathcal{TC}$ is strongly partially maximal-concurrent. □

5 Conclusion

We characterized the maximal level of concurrency we can obtain in resource allocation problems by proposing the notion of *maximal-concurrency*. This notion is versatile, *e.g.*, it generalizes the avoiding ℓ-deadlock [19] and (k,ℓ)-liveness [11] defined for the ℓ-exclusion and k-out-of-ℓ-exclusion, respectively. From [11,19], we already know that *maximal-concurrency* can be achieved in some important global resource allocation problems.[3] Now, perhaps surprisingly, our results show that *maximal-concurrency* cannot be achieved in problems that can be expressed with the LRA paradigm. However, we showed that *strong partial maximal-concurrency* (an high, but not maximal, level of concurrency) can be achieved by a snap-stabilizing LRA algorithm. We have to underline that the level of concurrency we achieve here is similar to the one obtained in the committee coordination problem [6]. Defining the exact class of resource allocation problems where *maximal-concurrency* (resp. *strong partial maximal-concurrency*) can be achieved is a challenging perspective.

References

1. Altisen, K., Cournier, A., Devismes, S., Durand, A., Petit, F.: Self-stabilizing leader election in polynomial steps. In: Felber, P., Garg, V. (eds.) SSS 2014. LNCS, vol. 8756, pp. 106–119. Springer, Heidelberg (2014)
2. Altisen, K., Devismes, S.: On probabilistic snap-stabilization. In: Chatterjee, M., Cao, J., Kothapalli, K., Rajsbaum, S. (eds.) ICDCN 2014. LNCS, vol. 8314, pp. 272–286. Springer, Heidelberg (2014)
3. Altisen, K., Devismes, S., Durand, A.: Concurrency in Snap-Stabilizing Local Resource Allocation. Research report, VERIMAG, December 2014. https://hal.archives-ouvertes.fr/hal-01099186
4. Arora, A., Gouda, M.G.: Distributed reset. IEEE Trans. Comput. **43**(9), 1026–1038 (1994)
5. Beauquier, J., Datta, A.K., Gradinariu, M., Magniette, F.: Self-stabilizing local mutual exclusion and daemon refinement. Chicago J. Theor. Comput. Sci. **2002**, 1–19 (2002)
6. Bonakdarpour, B., Devismes, S., Petit, F.: Snap-stabilizing comittee coordination. In: IPDPS, pp. 231–242 (2011)
7. Boulinier, C., Petit, F., Villain, V.: When graph theory helps self-stabilization. In: PODC, pp. 150–159 (2004)
8. Bui, A., Datta, A.K., Petit, F., Villain, V.: Snap-stabilization and PIF in tree networks. Dist. Comp. **20**(1), 3–19 (2007)
9. Cantarell, S., Datta, A.K., Petit, F.: Self-stabilizing atomicity refinement allowing neighborhood concurrency. In: Huang, S.-T., Herman, T. (eds.) SSS 2003. LNCS, vol. 2704, pp. 102–112. Springer, Heidelberg (2003)
10. Cournier, A., Devismes, S., Villain, V.: Light enabling snap-stabilization of fundamental protocols. ACM TAAS **4**(1), 1–27 (2009)
11. Datta, A.K., Hadid, R., Villain, V.: A self-stabilizing token-based k-out-of-l-exclusion algorithm. Concurrency Comput. Pract. Exp. **15**(11–12), 1069–1091 (2003)
12. Datta, A.K., Johnen, C., Petit, F., Villain, V.: Self-stabilizing depth-first token circulation in arbitrary rooted networks. Dist. Comp. **13**(4), 207–218 (2000)
13. Datta, A.K., Larmore, L.L., Vemula, P.: Self-stabilizing leader election in optimal space under an arbitrary scheduler. Theor. Comput. Sci. **412**(40), 5541–5561 (2011)
14. Dijkstra, E.W.: Solution of a problem in concurrent programming control. Commun. ACM **8**(9), 569 (1965)

[3] By "global" we mean resource allocation problems where a resource can be accessed by any process.

15. Dijkstra, E.W.: Self-stabilizing systems in spite of distributed control. Commun. ACM **17**(11), 643–644 (1974)
16. Dijkstra, E.W.: Two Starvation-Free Solutions of a General Exclusion Problem. Technical report EWD 625, Plataanstraat 5, 5671, AL Nuenen, The Netherlands (1978)
17. Dolev, S.: Self-Stabilization. MIT Press, Cambridge (2000)
18. Dolev, S., Herman, T.: Superstabilizing protocols for dynamic distributed systems. Chicago J. Theor. Comput. Sci. **3**, 1–40 (1997)
19. Fischer, M.J., Lynch, N.A., Burns, J.E., Borodin, A.: Resource allocation with immunity to limited process failure (Preliminary Report). In: FOCS, pp. 234–254 (1979)
20. Gouda, M.G., Haddix, F.F.: The alternator. Dist. Comp. **20**(1), 21–28 (2007)
21. Gradinariu, M., Tixeuil, S.: Conflict managers for self-stabilization without fairness assumption. In: ICDCS, p. 46 (2007)
22. Huang, S.: The fuzzy philosophers. In: IPDPS, pp. 130–136 (2000)
23. Huang, S., Chen, N.: Self-stabilizing depth-first token circulation on networks. Dist. Comp. **7**(1), 61–66 (1993)
24. Kakugawa, H., Yamashita, M.: Self-stabilizing local mutual exclusion on networks in which process identifiers are not distinct. In: SRDS, pp. 202–211 (2002)
25. Lamport, L.: A new solution of dijkstra's concurrent programming problem. Commun. ACM **17**(8), 453–455 (1974)
26. Nesterenko, M., Arora, A.: Stabilization-preserving atomicity refinement. J. Parallel Distrib. Comput. **62**(5), 766–791 (2002)
27. Raynal, M.: A distributed solution to the k-out of-M resources allocation problem. In: ICCI 1991, pp. 599–609 (1991)

Distributed Privacy-Preserving Data Aggregation via Anonymization

Yahya Benkaouz[1](✉), Mohammed Erradi[1], and Bernd Freisleben[2]

[1] Networking and Distributed Systems Research Group, ENSIAS, Mohammed V University, Rabat, Morocco
y.benkaouz@um5s.net.ma, erradi@ensias.ma

[2] Department of Mathematics and Computer Science, Philipps-Universität Marburg, Marburg, Germany
freisleb@informatik.uni-marburg.de

Abstract. Data aggregation is a key element in many applications that draw insights from data analytics, such as medical research, smart metering, recommendation systems and real-time marketing. In general, data is gathered from several sources, processed, and publicly released for data analysis. Since the considered data might contain personal and sensitive information, special handling of private data is required.

In this paper, we present a novel distributed privacy-preserving data aggregation protocol, called ADiPA. It relies on anonymization techniques for protecting personal data, such as k-anonymity, l-diversity and t-closeness. Its purpose is to allow a set of entities to derive aggregate results from data tables that are partitioned across these entities in a fully decentralized manner while preserving the privacy of their individual sensitive inputs. ADiPA neither relies on a trusted third party nor on cryptographic techniques. The protocol performs accurate aggregation when communication links and nodes do not fail.

Keywords: Data aggregation · Privacy · Anonymization

1 Introduction

During the last decade, the production, collection, processing and storage of data has expanded at an astonishing pace. Remarkable insights that enable novel applications and support decision-making processes are expected from the analysis of large volumes and varying types of data. However, this potential comes with the responsibility to protect the subjects referenced in the data, otherwise the willingness of stakeholders to contribute their data will probably decrease significantly. In general, data should be classified and assigned to a level of sensitivity based on who should have access to it and how much harm would be done if it were disclosed. Sensitive information requires special care, especially when

This work is supported by the BMBF (PMARS Programme) and the DAAD (German-Arab Transformation Partnership).

A. Bouajjani and H. Fauconnier (Eds.): NETYS 2015, LNCS 9466, pp. 94–108, 2015.
DOI: 10.1007/978-3-319-26850-7_7

inappropriate handling of information could result in a violation of privacy due to unauthorized access.

Combining data coming from different sources represents an interesting input to research and decision-making processes. In some scenarios, companies need to perform computations on data held by a set of other companies in the same business domain. Typically, these companies are competitors that do not want to disclose their own data. For instance, assume that there is a set of companies in the medical and pharmaceutical domains that each have relevant data and need data of other companies for developing effective treatments for different diseases. The companies should collaborate with each other by delivering and aggregating data for their individual analysis tasks, but they are only willing to cooperate if their sensitive data is adequately protected.

Data aggregation is a straightforward task in the case where a trusted aggregator collects the data and shares the results. The problem is to find such a trusted entity. In distributed data aggregation, individual entities want to derive aggregate results from data sets that are partitioned across these entities. While the individual entities may not want to share their entire data sets, they may consent to limited information sharing, based on using particular protocols. The overall effect of such protocols is to maintain privacy for each individual entity, while deriving aggregate results over the entire data.

The key contribution of this paper is a distributed privacy-preserving data aggregation protocol that makes use of anonymization techniques. The proposed protocol is an extension of the DiPA *"Distributed Privacy-preserving Aggregation"* protocol [4]. DiPA is a protocol that allows a set of partners to compute a class of aggregation functions that are derived from an *Abelian group* without revealing the partners' inputs. DiPA has been designed to aggregate numerical inputs. The new protocol, called ADiPA ("Anonymized Distributed Privacy-preserving Aggregation"), allows a set of participants to construct a unique aggregated data table based on their distinct private data. ADiPA is based on an overlay construction. It has the following advantages: (1) it preserves data privacy such that a participant's data is only known to its owner, with a given probability; (2) the aggregation result is computed by the participants themselves, in a self-organized and cooperative manner, without interacting with a dedicated aggregator; (3) the aggregation result is accurate when there is no data loss, and (4) it neither relies on cryptographic techniques nor on the trustworthiness of a third party.

The remainder of this paper is structured as follows: Sect. 2 describes the system model. Section 3 briefly summarizes the DiPA protocol. The considered problem is defined in Sect. 4. Fundamental anonymization techniques are discussed in Sect. 5. The new distributed data aggregation protocol is presented in Sect. 6. Finally, Sect. 7 concludes the paper and outlines areas for future work.

2 System Model

The proposed protocol is based on a system model that consists of N participants. Each participant is represented as a uniquely identified node (in the rest of this paper, we call a node a participant). Each participant p_i has its private input q_i. The global outcome is the aggregated data.

As shown in Fig. 1, the N nodes are clustered into r ordered groups, from g_0 to g_{r-1}. All groups virtually form a ring, g_0 being the successor of g_{r-1}. Each group contains N_j nodes ($\sum_{j=0}^{r-1} N_j = N$). Each node in the system maintains three sets of nodes: Officemates, Proxies and Clients. For a given node p_i in a group g_j, these sets are defined as follows:

- The set of officemates ($\mathcal{P}_o$) contains all nodes belonging to the same group ($\mathcal{P}_o = \{p\} \in g_j \backslash p_i$), i.e. the set p of participants in g_j except p_i.
- The set of proxies ($\mathcal{P}_p$) contains a subset of nodes in the next group ($\mathcal{P}_p \subseteq g_{j+1 \bmod r}$). The proxies of each node are selected uniformly at random from nodes in the successor group. The size of this set, for each node, is chosen according to a parameter k such that $| \mathcal{P}_p |= 2k+1$ with $k \in \{0, 1, \ldots, k_{max}\}$, and k_{max} is a system parameter.
- The set of clients ($\mathcal{P}_c$) contains a subset of nodes in the previous group ($\mathcal{P}_c \subseteq g_{j-1 \bmod r}$). A client is defined in such a way that if p is a proxy of q, then q is one of p's clients.

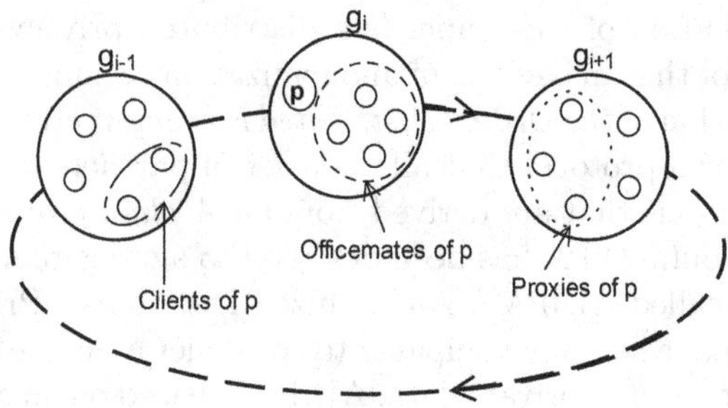

Fig. 1. System model

For security reasons, nodes discard every message originating from a node that does not belong to the set $\mathcal{P}_c \cup \mathcal{P}_o$. The distribution of nodes across the r groups is uniform. Note that the proposed protocol is designed for systems where N is sufficiently large. For practical usage, the system should consist of at least 9 participants.

3 The DiPA Protocol

This section gives a brief description of the DiPA *"Distributed Privacy-preserving Aggregation"* protocol [4], which enables participants to have the precise aggregate of their numerical inputs while no user should learn anything about the inputs of other users.

DiPA considers numerical inputs and aggregation functions expressed as Abelian group. Assuming that an aggregation function is a triplet (f, S, G), where S and G are two arbitrary sets and f is a composition law $f : S^* \rightarrow G$, DiPA is only suitable for functions where $S \subseteq G$ and (G, f) is an Abelian group.

As shown in Fig. 2, DiPA consists of three steps: Sharing, Counting and Broadcasting.

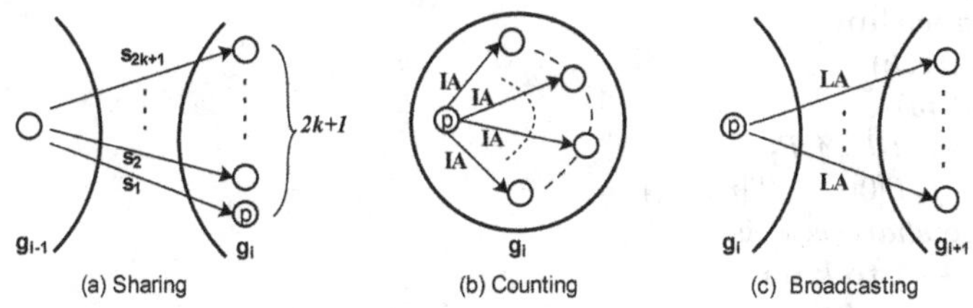

Fig. 2. DiPA steps: Sharing, Counting and Broadcasting

Step 1: Sharing. Each node casts its input as $2k + 1$ shares where $k \in \{0, 1, \ldots, k_{max}\}$. The set of $2k + 1$ shares is generated as follows: k values are randomly chosen from the set of possible entries. The other k values represent the inverses of the first k chosen values with respect to the considered aggregation function, and a single share that represents the real participant's input. Thus, aggregating the generated shares outputs the actual initial value. Note that in the case where $k = 0$, only one share will be generated representing the real input. Once a node has generated its $2k + 1$ shares, it sends each of them to a distinct proxy. Therefore, when a proxy receives a message from a given client node, the proxy could not distinguish if such share was generated as a single one or it is one among the previously generated $2k + 1$ shares with $k \in \{1, 2, \ldots, k_{max}\}$. Once every node in the system has received one share from each of its clients, the sharing round is over (Algorithm 1, Lines 05 – 11).

Step 2: Counting. In the counting step, each proxy within the receiving group g_j aggregates the received shares from its clients in the group g_{j-1}. The resulted value is designated as the Individual Aggregate (IA). Note that each proxy will have its own individual aggregate. Once a participant node has received the expected number of shares from its clients, it broadcasts the computed individual aggregate to its officemates. Each officemate will compute the aggregation of the received individual aggregates resulting in a Local Aggregate (LA) of its group. Then, each officemate will forward the computed local aggregate to a randomly chosen node from its proxies in the next group (Algorithm 1, Lines 12 – 15).

Step 3: Broadcasting. During this step, once a proxy receives a local aggregate from a given client, it broadcasts the received local aggregate within its officemates and send this aggregate to a randomly chosen proxy in the next group g_{j+1}. In the same way, local aggregates are then forwarded along the ring. Note that when a node receives a local aggregate from its officemates, this node does not forward the received aggregate to other participants. Once a participant node in the group g_j

Algorithm 1. DiPA protocol: Node p in group g_j, $j \in \{0, \ldots, r-1\}$

```
Variables:
   The set of possible inputs, S
   An individual aggregate, ia = null
   A local aggregate, la = null
   A local aggregate array, T[0, ..., r − 1]
Input: A private input, v ∈ S
Output: The global aggregate, ga
DiPA Algorithm
01.  share(v, k)
02.  count(ia)
03.  broadcast(la, j, P_p)
04.  ga ← f(T[0], ..., T[r − 1])
Procedure share(v, k) is
05.  for i ← 1 to k do
06.     s_i ← rand(S)
07.     s_{i+k} ← inv(s_i)
08.  end for
09.  s_{2k+1} ← v
10.  for i ← 1 to 2k + 1 do
11.     send([share, s_i], proxy)
Upon event < receive|[share, s_i] > do
12.  ia ← f(ia, s_i)
Procedure count(ia)
13.  foreach officemate ∈ P_o do
14.     send([IndividualAggregate, ia], officemate)
Upon event < receive|[IndividualAggregate, ia] > do
15.  la ← f(la, ia)
Procedure broadcast(la, i_group, P_p)
16.  proxy ← selectOneRandom(P_p)
17.  send([LocalAggregate, i_group, la], proxy)
Upon event < receive|[LocalAggregate, i_group, la] > do
18.  if (i_group ≠ j and la_src ∈ P_c) then
19.     T[i_group] ← la
20.     broadcast(la, i_group, P_p)
21.  end if
```

receives back the local aggregate of its group, this local aggregate is no longer forwarded. Each node, separately, computes the global aggregate (GA), after reception of local aggregates of all groups. This global aggregate represents the final outcome of the protocol (Algorithm 1, Lines 16 – 21).

4 Problem Definition

In this work, we consider a set of N participants $P = \{p_1, p_2, \ldots, p_N\}$ involved in a data aggregation task. Each participant stores its own input locally. The input is assumed to be a data table of rows and columns. Columns represent distinct attributes. Attributes consist of identifiers, quasi-identifiers and sensitive attributes. Each row is a tuple that contains relationships among the set of attributes values. The subjects referenced in different participants' data tables are assumed to be different, e.g., records in two distinct data tables of health information do not refer to the same person.

The aim is to aggregate the entire data tables supplied by the N participants, while preserving data privacy. We assume that the data tables have the same structure (i.e., the same attributes and same data types). Furthermore, we assume that identifiers, quasi-identifiers and sensitive attributes do not intersect. This means that an attribute cannot be both sensitive and a quasi-identifier.

A data table is defined as $D = (\langle id \rangle, \langle qId \rangle, \langle sensInfo \rangle)$, where $\langle id \rangle$, $\langle qId \rangle$ and $\langle sensInfo \rangle$ are lists of identifiers, quasi-identifiers and sensitive attributes, respectively. Each row of the table is an ordered $s + t + n$-tuple of values $\langle id_1, \ldots, id_s, q_1, \ldots, q_t, s_1, \ldots, s_n \rangle$ where s is the number of identifiers, t is the number of quasi-identifiers and n is the number of sensitive attributes.

The aggregation consists of the application of a set of operators on data table attributes (i.e., columns). We define an *aggregation vector* as a set of operators $av = \langle op_1, \ldots, op_n \rangle$, where n is the number of sensitive attributes. The proposed approach assumes that operators op_i are commutative and associative when the attribute is numerical. Also, op_i will be the *union* for categorical attributes. The aggregation vector is only associated with the sensitive attributes.

Since the objective of our work is to support the aggregation of data tables with different types of data, we have to consider techniques that help protecting data while allowing operations on the data. In the next section, we present data anonymization techniques to achieve this goal. Unlike cryptographic techniques that could also be used for this purpose, data anonymization techniques produce human-readable outputs that are more convenient for many distributed data aggregation tasks.

5 Data Anonymization

In order to release data tables to other stakeholders while preserving data privacy, data holders often de-identify the data. Data de-identification consists of the process of removing or masking explicit identifiers to prevent a person's identity from being connected to sensitive information. Table 1 shows an example of a de-identified table in which the SSN ("Social Security Number") and the names were deleted. In this example, we consider medical data records where the available records do not identify the person suffering from a given disease.

Deleting explicit identifiers does not provide any data protection guarantees. This is due to the fact that the released data might contain information, referred to as *quasi-identifiers*, that can be linked to publicly available data (i.e., a so-called linking attack). Sweeney [17] has shown that he could uniquely identify the medical records of the governor of Massachusetts in an anonymized medical data set, based on the publicly available Massachusetts voter registration

Table 1. Medical Records

Identifiers		Quasi-identifiers			Sensitive Info
SSN	Name	Date of Birth	Sex	Zip Code	Disease
-	-	2000/07/05	M	20364	Meningitis
-	-	2002/03/23	F	31443	Diabetes
-	-	2002/03/05	F	31442	Epilepsy
-	-	1990/11/14	M	30079	Influenza
-	-	2000/07/10	M	20368	HIV
-	-	1990/11/26	M	30077	Stroke
-	-	1990/11/30	M	30073	Epilepsy

records. This was possible because both the medical data and the voter records contain the same set of attributes: gender, zip code and date of birth. In addition, it has been shown [16] that it was possible to uniquely identify 87 % of the population in the United States based only on gender, 5-digit zip code and date of birth (63 % of the population according to a recent study [8]). For this reason, different techniques have been proposed to protect identities while releasing useful data. In the following, we will focus on three main anonymization techniques: k-anonymity, l-diversity and t-closeness.

5.1 k-Anonymity

The technique of k-anonymity has been defined by Sweeney [17] as follows: Given a data table T and the set of quasi-identifiers associated with it. The data table is said to satisfy k-anonymity if and only if each sequence of values of the quasi-identifiers appears with at least k occurrences in T. In other words, a data table satisfies the k-anonymity requirement if and only if: i) each tuple in the released table cannot be related to less than k individuals in the population; and ii) each individual in the population cannot be related to less than k tuples in the table [6]. For instance, the data presented in Table 1 is k-anonymous with $k = 1$, because each combination of quasi-identifiers refers only to a unique tuple. Consequently, the aim is to construct a table in which each combination of the values of quasi-identifiers appears with zero or at least k occurrences with the largest possible value of k. It is trivial to note that having a larger value of k improves the anonymity ensured. Note that to verify whether a data table satisfies the k-anonymity requirement, the data holder should know in advance any possible external source of information that an observer could exploit for re-identification.

k-anonymity is mainly based on generalization and suppression [15]. Suppression consists of removing data from the table. It is applied at the tuple level where a record can be suppressed in its entirety. Generalization consists of making some quasi-identifiers less informative by replacing their values with more general ones. For example, the zip code can be generalized by removing the last digits. Instead of the original value 20054, the new value will be 2005*. The date of birth can generalized by removing the day.

Table 2. 2-anonymous medical records

SSN	Name	Date of Birth	Sex	Zip Code	Disease
-	-	2000/07/*	M	2036*	Meningitis
-	-	2002/03/*	F	3144*	Diabetes
-	-	2002/03/*	F	3144*	Epilepsy
-	-	1990/11/*	M	3007*	Influenza
-	-	2000/07/*	M	2036*	HIV
-	-	1990/11/*	M	3007*	Stroke
-	-	1990/11/*	M	3007*	Epilepsy

Table 2 shows an anonymized version of Table 1 with $k = 2$. Each combination of the values of quasi-identifiers refers to at least $k = 2$ rows in the table. This was achieved by generalizing the values of the zip code and the date of birth. The "*" denotes a suppressed value, "date of birth = 2002/03/*" means that the day is not defined. Thus, having external information that a specific combination of quasi-identifiers values belongs to a given person does not help to link the exact sensitive information to that person (e.g., knowing that Bob was born on 2000/07 and lives in the 2036* area results in $k = 2$ diseases: HIV and Meningitis).

In general, different levels of generalization are possible. For example, considering the date of birth, a first generalization consists of deleting only the date and a second generalization consists of removing the month and the day. It is clear that going from one generalization level to another, more information is lost. In this direction, different algorithms have been proposed to find the best generalization in which less information is lost while ensuring k-anonymity.

Table 3 presents several k-anonymity algorithms proposed in the literature. One difference between these algorithms consists of the level (Tuple, Column, Cell) on which generalization and the suppression can be applied. Generalization can be applied to the entire column or to a specific cell. Regarding suppression, it is possible to delete the whole record (tuple), a column, or a cell. Columns Gen. and Supp. indicate on which level the generalization and the suppression were applied. A survey of these algorithms has been presented by Ciriani et al. [5].

In different scenarios, k-anonymity can produce tables that are still sensitive to different attacks: *homogeneity attack* and *background knowledge attack* [12]. The homogeneity attack consists of situations where a set of tuples, with the same quasi-identifiers values, has the same value for the sensitive attribute. For instance, assume that the k-anonymous table contains 2 tuples with the same values of {zip code, date of birth, sex} and the same disease. Knowing that Bob's

Table 3. k-anonymity algorithms [5] ($|Q_i|$: the number quasi-identifiers)

Algorithm	Gen.	Supp.	Type of Algorithm	Time Complexity
Samarati [14]	column	row	Exact	exponential in $\|Q_i\|$
Sweeney [18]	column	row	Exact	exponential in $\|Q_i\|$
Bayardo-Agrawal [3]	column	row	Exact	exponential in $\|Q_i\|$
LeFevre et al. [10]	column	row	Exact	exponential in $\|Q_i\|$
Aggarwal et al. [1]	-	cell	$O(k)$-Approx	$O(kn^2)$
Meyerson-Williams [13]	-	cell	$O(klogk)$-Approx	$O(n^{2k})$
Aggarwal et al. [2]	cell	-	$O(k)$-Approx	$O(kn^2)$
Iyengar [9]	column	row	Heuristic	limited nbr. of iter.
Winkler [19]	column	row	Heuristic	limited nbr. of iter.
Fung-Wang-Yu [7]	column	-	Heuristic	limited nbr. of iter.

data corresponds to these quasi-identifier values, Bob's disease becomes easily identifiable.

The background knowledge attack occurs when the attacker exploits additional knowledge, in order to reduce her uncertainty about the value of the sensitive attribute of a given targeted person. Assume that Alice knows that Bob was born on 2000/07 and is living in 2036*. If Alice also knows that in the school where she studies with Bob, no one suffers from HIV, then it becomes clear that Bob has meningitis.

5.2 l-Diversity

As mentioned in the previous section, the data holder should know in advance any possible external source of information that an observer could exploit for re-identification. The concept of l-diversity has been proposed by Machanavajjhala et al. [12] to provide privacy even when the data publisher does not know what kind of knowledge is possessed by the adversary. The main idea behind l-diversity is the requirement that the values of the sensitive attributes are well-represented in each set of records with the same quasi-identifier values. A given set of sensitive attributes values are considered as well-represented, if there are at least l different values. Table 4 is 4-anonymous. However, it suffers from the *homogeneity attack*, since all females born in March 2003 and living in the 3144* area suffer from epilepsy. Considering the l-diversity requirement, the last four tuples of Table 4 have well-represented values of sensitive attributes (there are four different values of the disease attribute). An example of a 4-anonymous and 3-diverse Table is shown in Table 5. This table is 3-diverse because in the worst case, we have three different diseases associated with a given combination of quasi-identifiers attributes.

L-diversity takes into account the diversity of sensitive values in the group, but does not take into account the *semantical* closeness of the values. That makes

Table 4. 4-anonymous medical records

SSN	Name	Date of Birth	Sex	Zip Code	Disease
-	-	2000/07/*	M	2036*	Meningitis
-	-	2000/07/*	M	2036*	Cancer
-	-	2000/07/*	M	2036*	Meningitis
-	-	2000/07/*	M	2036*	HIV
-	-	2002/03/*	F	3144*	Epilepsy
-	-	2002/03/*	F	3144*	Epilepsy
-	-	2002/03/*	F	3144*	Epilepsy
-	-	2002/03/*	F	3144*	Epilepsy
-	-	1990/11/*	M	3007*	Stroke
-	-	1990/11/*	M	3007*	Diabetes
-	-	1990/11/*	M	3007*	Influenza
-	-	1990/11/*	M	3007*	Epilepsy

Table 5. 3-diverse medical records

SSN	Name	Date of Birth	Sex	Zip Code	Disease
-	-	2000/07/*	M	2036*	Epilepsy
-	-	2000/07/*	M	2036*	Cancer
-	-	2000/07/*	M	2036*	Meningitis
-	-	2000/07/*	M	2036*	HIV
-	-	2002/03/*	F	3145*	Viral infection
-	-	2002/03/*	F	3145*	Epilepsy
-	-	2002/03/*	F	3145*	Stroke
-	-	2002/03/*	F	3145*	Epilepsy
-	-	1990/11/*	M	3007*	Stroke
-	-	1990/11/*	M	3007*	Diabetes
-	-	1990/11/*	M	3007*	Influenza
-	-	1990/11/*	M	3007*	Epilepsy

l-diversity suffer from two attacks: the *similarity attack* [11] and the *skewness attack* [11]. The similarity attack occurs when, in an l-diverse table, the values of the sensitive attribute associated with the tuples of the same quasi-identifiers are semantically similar. Also, l-diversity does not care about the global distribution of sensitive attributes, which leads to the *skewness attack* [11]. The skewness attack exploits the possible difference in the frequency distribution of the sensitive attribute values within an equivalence class, with respect to the frequency distribution of sensitive attribute values in the population [6]. Considering Table 5, if an attacker knows that a given female lives in the 3145* area and was born on 2002/03, then the attacker can infer that the considered person has an epilepsy with probability 50 %, compared to a probability of 25 % when considering the whole table. To counter these attacks, t-closeness was introduced by Li et al. [11].

5.3 t-Closeness

An equivalence class (set of tuples with the same quasi-identifiers) is said to have t-closeness if the distance between the distribution of a sensitive attribute in this class and the distribution of the attribute in the whole table is no more than a threshold t. A table is said to have t-closeness if all equivalence classes have t-closeness [11]. t-closeness reduces also the effectiveness of the similarity attack, because the presence of semantically similar values in an equivalence class can only be due to the presence, with similar relative frequencies, of the same values in the original data table. The enforcement of t-closeness requires to evaluate the distance between the frequency distribution of the sensitive attribute values in the released table and in each equivalence class. Such distances can be computed based on different metrics, such as the Earth Mover Distance (EMD) used in t-closeness [11].

6 ADiPA: Anonymized Distributed Privacy-Preserving Data Aggregation

In this section, we present ADiPA, a new distributed privacy-preserving data aggregation protocol that makes use of the discussed anonymization techniques in order to privately aggregate data held by multiple parties.

In addition to the main steps of Sharing, Counting and Broadcasting (see Sect. 3), a new *Pre-processing* step will initially take place in ADiPA. The aim of the pre-processing step is to produce anonymized data from the raw data of each participant. The anonymized data tables are then split into a set of shares. These shares are then sent to the set of proxies of each participant (*Sharing*). Each proxy computes the individual aggregate of the received shares. The computed individual aggregates are then broadcast within officemates (nodes of the same group). Then, each participant aggregates the received individual aggregates, resulting in local aggregates (*Counting*). The computed local aggregates are then forwarded along the ring. Once a participant receives local aggregates of all groups, she computes the global aggregate which is the outcome of the protocol (*Broadcasting*).

Pre-processing. Each node prepares locally the data table to be used as input of the aggregation protocol. Thus, each node separately produces an anonymized version of its data. By applying a particular anonymization technique, the resulting data ensures either k-anonymity, l-diversity or t-closeness. Then, the sensitive values of each equivalence class are aggregated as shown in Fig. 3 (*Pre-Processing*). In this example, sensitive attributes are: disease and medical cost. Within each equivalence class, diseases are aggregated via the *union*

DoB	Gender	Zip code	Disease	Medical costs
2000/07/*	M	2036*	Epilepsy	20
2000/07/*	M	2036*	Cancer	80
2000/07/*	M	2036*	Meningitis	50
2000/07/*	M	2036*	HIV	100
2002/03/*	F	3145*	Viral Infection	30
2002/03/*	F	3145*	Epilepsy	20
2002/03/*	F	3145*	Stroke	50
2002/03/*	F	3145*	Epilepsy	20

Pre-Processing

DoB	Gender	Zip code	Disease	Medical costs
2000/07/*	M	2036*	{Epilepsy, Meningitis, Cancer, HIV}	250
2002/03/*	F	3145*	{Viral Infection, Epilepsy, Stroke}	120

Sharing

Share 1:

DoB	Gender	Zip code	Disease	Medical costs
2000/07/*	M	2036*	{Epilepsy}	40
2002/03/*	F	3145*	{Stroke}	80

Share 2:

DoB	Gender	Zip code	Disease	Medical costs
2000/07/*	M	2036*	{Cancer, HIV}	110
2002/03/*	F	3145*	{Viral Infection, Stroke}	20

Share 3:

DoB	Gender	Zip code	Disease	Medical costs
2000/07/*	M	2036*	{Meningitis}	100
2002/03/*	F	3145*	{Epilepsy}	20

Fig. 3. Data table pre-processing and construction of shares

operator. The medical cost is a numerical attribute, and we consider the *sum* function as the operator of this attribute.

Sharing. Once the anonymized table is prepared, each node casts its input as $2k + 1$ shares. To construct the shares, the quasi-identifier values remain unchanged, while the values of the sensitive attributes are shared as follows: the values (s_i) are split in such a way that the application of the operator op_i on the split values results in the original value of the sensitive attribute ($s_i = op_i(s_i^1, \ldots, s_i^{2k+1})$). Figure 3 (Sharing) illustrates an example of the generated shares in the case where $k = 1$. Thus, 3 shares are created. The sum of medical costs of the constructed shares equals the initial medical cost. In the same way, the union of the diseases in the shares results in the initial set of diseases. Once a node has generated its $2k+1$ shares, it sends each of them to a distinct proxy.

Table 1

DoB	Gender	Zip code	Disease	Medical costs
2000/07/*	M	2036*	{Epilepsy}	40
2002/03/*	F	3145*	{Stroke}	80

Table 2

DoB	Gender	Zip code	Disease	Medical costs
2000/07/*	M	2036*	{Cancer, HIV}	110
2002/02/*	F	3145*	{Viral Infection, Stroke}	20

Table 3

DoB	Gender	Zip code	Disease	Medical costs
2000/01/*	M	2036*	{Meningitis, Cancer}	100
2002/03/*	F	3145*	{Epilepsy}	20

Aggregation

DoB	Gender	Zip code	Disease	Medical costs
2000/07/*	M	2036*	{Epilepsy, Cancer, HIV}	150
2002/03/*	F	3145*	{Stroke, Epilepsy}	100
2002/02/*	F	3145*	{Viral Infection, Stroke}	20
2000/01/*	M	2036*	{Meningitis, Cancer}	100

Fig. 4. Aggregating data tables

The remaining steps of ADiPA (Counting and Broadcasting) remain unchanged, except for the aggregation function used to compute the individual aggregates, the local aggregates and the global aggregate (see Sect. 3). In ADiPA, given a set of data tables, the aggregation vector will be applied to the sensitive attribute values, whenever the sequences of the quasi-identifiers values intersect. Otherwise, the aggregation will be the union of the different data tables. An example is shown in Fig. 4. Note that these data tables might be: shares, individual aggregates, or local aggregates. They are gathered to produce individual aggregates, local aggregates or the global aggregate, respectively.

Discussion. The communication cost of ADiPA is $O(r.k + N_i)$ where r is the number of groups in the overlay and N_i is the number of participants per group. No message is exchanged during pre-processing, since it is a local step. Then, each node sends $2k+1$ shares during the sharing step, N_i-1 individual aggregates during the counting step, and finally forwards $r(2k+1)$ local aggregates. Given the set of N participants, by organizing the nodes into $r = \sqrt{N}$ groups where each group contains $\sqrt{N}$ nodes, the communication complexity is $O(k\sqrt{N})$.

Assuming that communication links and nodes do not fail, the protocol is accurate. Since each node maintains the lists of clients, proxies and officemates, each node knows the number of messages it is supposed to receive. Thus, each step completes. Since the protocol has a finite number of steps, the protocol terminates. The local aggregate reflects the aggregation of the data tables of participants in the previous group (i.e., a local aggregate is the aggregation of individual aggregates which consists of the aggregation of participants' shares). During the last step, each node gathers local aggregates of all groups, so the global aggregate correctly reflects the aggregation of all participants' data tables.

The combination of anonymization techniques, sharing, and the overlay construction helps ADiPA to ensure the privacy of the participants. First, anonymization techniques help to protect identities while releasing data tables. Thus, the released records will not be linkable to external information. Then, the participants split their data tables into shares. A given proxy receives only a unique share from a given participant. Thus, a proxy has access to only a partial view of the anonymized data table of its client. This makes attacks on anonymization techniques inefficient for proxies, unless proxies that receive shares from the same participant collude. Later, once the individual aggregate is computed, the association between the participant and the records it supplied is lost, since the individual aggregate is based on shares coming from different clients. Following the protocol steps, more aggregations take place. This results in making the association of a given record to the participant who supply it a harder task. Moreover, the global result represents the aggregation of the anonymized data tables of all participants. Thus, in the worst case, the aggregated data tables will ensure k-anonymity with k equal to the value of k of the initial anonymized data table with the lowest k-anonymity.

7 Conclusions

In this paper, we have presented a novel distributed privacy-preserving data aggregation protocol, called ADiPA, which makes use of anonymization techniques. Its purpose is to allow a set of parties to aggregate their private data tables in a fully decentralized manner while preserving the privacy of their inputs. The proposed approach does neither rely on a third party nor on cryptographic techniques. The communication cost of ADiPA is $O(r.k + N_i)$ where r is the number of groups in the overlay and N_i is the number of participants per group. The protocol is accurate when communication links and nodes do not fail.

There are several areas for future research. Currently, we are working on the implementation of ADiPA and its evaluation based on medical datasets. An interesting aspect is to study what would be the privacy property of the aggregated data in the case where the supplied data ensures different privacy properties (k-anonymity, l-diversity, t-closeness). Also, we plan to compare the ensured privacy against the privacy level of Secure Multiparty Computation protocols under different attack scenarios. On the other hand, a natural follow up of our research consists of the relaxation of the considered assumptions, especially regarding the intersection of data held by multiple parties. Finally, the use of ADiPA in different application scenarios should be investigated, such as sensor network aggregation, smart metering, public health and clinical research, population monitoring and sensing, and Cloud services.

References

1. Aggarwal, G., Feder, T., Kenthapadi, K., Motwani, R., Panigrahy, R., Thomas, D., Zhu, A.: Anonymizing tables. In: Eiter, T., Libkin, L. (eds.) ICDT 2005. LNCS, vol. 3363, pp. 246–258. Springer, Heidelberg (2005)
2. Aggarwal, G., Feder, T., Kenthapadi, K., Motwani, R., Panigrahy, R., Thomas, D., Zhu, A.: Approximation algorithms for k-anonymity. In: Proceedings of the International Conference on Database Theory (ICDT 2005), November 2005

3. Bayardo, R.J., Agrawal, R.: Data privacy through optimal k-anonymization. In: Proceedings of the 21st International Conference on Data Engineering, ICDE 2005, pp. 217–228. IEEE Computer Society, Washington, DC (2005)
4. Benkaouz, Y., Erradi, M.: A distributed protocol for privacy preserving aggregation. In: Gramoli, V., Guerraoui, R. (eds.) NETYS 2013. LNCS, vol. 7853, pp. 221–232. Springer, Heidelberg (2013)
5. Ciriani, V., De Capitani di Vimercati, S., Foresti, S., Samarati, P.: k-anonymity. In: Yu, T., Jajodia, S. (eds.) Secure Data Management in Decentralized Systems. Advances in Information Security, vol. 33, pp. 323–353. Springer, US (2007)
6. Di Vimercati, S.D.C., Foresti, S., Livraga, G., Samarati, P.: Data privacy: definitions and techniques. Int. J. Uncertainty Fuzziness Knowl. Based Syst. **20**(06), 793–817 (2012)
7. Fung, B.C.M., Wang, K., Yu, P.S.: Top-down specialization for information and privacy preservation. In: Proceedings of the 21st International Conference on Data Engineering, ICDE 2005, pp. 205–216. IEEE Computer Society, Washington, DC (2005)
8. Golle, P.: Revisiting the uniqueness of simple demographics in the us population. In: WPES 2006, Alexandria, Virginia, USA, October 30, 2006
9. Iyengar, V.S.: Transforming data to satisfy privacy constraints. In: Proceedings of the Eighth ACM SIGKDD International Conference on Knowledge Discovery and Data Mining, KDD 2002, pp. 279–288. ACM, New York (2002)
10. LeFevre, K., DeWitt, D.J., Ramakrishnan, R.: Incognito: Efficient full-domain k-anonymity. In: Proceedings of the 2005 ACM SIGMOD International Conference on Management of Data, SIGMOD 2005, pp. 49–60. ACM, New York (2005)
11. Li, N., Li, T., Venkatasubramanian, S.: t-closeness: privacy beyond k-anonymity and l-diversity. In: ICDE 2007, IEEE 23rd International Conference on Data Engineering, 2007, pp. 106–115, April 2007
12. Machanavajjhala, A., Kifer, D., Gehrke, J., Venkitasubramaniam, M.: L-diversity: privacy beyond k-anonymity. ACM Trans. Knowl. Discov. Data **1**(1), 3 (2007)
13. Meyerson, A., Williams, R.: On the complexity of optimal k-anonymity. In: Proceedings of the Twenty-Third ACM SIGMOD-SIGACT-SIGART Symposium on Principles of Database Systems, PODS 2004, pp. 223–228. ACM, New York (2004)
14. Samarati, P.: Protecting respondents' identities in microdata release. IEEE Trans. Knowl. Data Eng. **13**(6), 1010–1027 (2001)
15. Samarati, P., Sweeney, L.: Protecting privacy when disclosing information: k-anonymity and its enforcement through generalization and suppression. Technical report, CMU, SRI (1998)
16. Sweeney, L.: Uniqueness of simple demographics in the U.S. population. Technical report, Carnegie Mellon University, Laboratory for International Data Privacy (2000)
17. Sweeney, L.: k-anonymity: a model for protecting privacy. Int. J. Uncertainty Fuzziness Knowl. Based Syst. **10**(05), 557–570 (2002)
18. Sweeney, L.: Guaranteeing anonymity when sharing medical data, the datafly system. In: Journal of the American Medical Informatics Association. Hanley and Belfus Inc, Washington, DC (1997)
19. Winkler, W.E.: Using simulated annealing for k-anonymity. Technical report, Statistical Research Division, U.S. Bureau of the Census, Washington D.C. (2002)

Gracefully Degrading Consensus and k-Set Agreement in Directed Dynamic Networks

Martin Biely[1], Peter Robinson[2], Ulrich Schmid[3], Manfred Schwarz[3](✉), and Kyrill Winkler[3]

[1] EPFL, Lausanne, Switzerland
martin.biely@epfl.ch
[2] National University of Singapore, Singapore, Singapore
robinson@comp.nus.edu.sg
[3] ECS Group, TU Wien, Vienna, Austria
{s,mschwarz,kwinkler}@ecs.tuwien.ac.at

Abstract. We present (This work has been supported the Austrian Science Fund (FWF) project P26436 (SIC) and S11405 (RiSE).) the first consensus/k-set agreement algorithm for synchronous dynamic networks with unidirectional links, controlled by an omniscient message adversary, which automatically adapts to the actual network properties in a run: If the network is sufficiently well-connected, it solves consensus, while it degrades gracefully to general k-set agreement in less well-connected communication graphs. The actual number k of system-wide decision values is determined by the number of certain vertex-stable root components occurring in a run, which are strongly connected components without incoming links from outside. Related impossibility results reveal that our condition is reasonably close to the solvability border for k-set agreement.

1 Introduction

In sharp contrast to conventional wireline networks, communication in *wireless dynamic networks* like sensor networks and mobile ad-hoc networks is adequately modeled by time-varying directional links only: Fading and interference phenomena such as capture effects and near-far problems are *local* effects, which affect the receiver but not the sender of a particular message. Mobility and duty-cycling for energy saving purposes are additional causes for irregular communication patterns in dynamic networks. Consequently, according to [13], 80 % of the links in a typical wireless network are sometimes asymmetric. In this paper, we hence consider synchronous distributed systems consisting of a possibly unknown number of processes that never fail. All communication links are controlled by an omniscient *message adversary* RS13:PODC, which effectively determines the sequence of *directed* per-round communication graphs occuring in a run.

A. Bouajjani and H. Fauconnier (Eds.): NETYS 2015, LNCS 9466, pp. 109–124, 2015.
DOI: 10.1007/978-3-319-26850-7_8

A natural approach to build robust services despite the dynamic nature of such systems is to use consensus to agree system-wide on (fundamental) parameters like action schedules. Clearly, such solutions rest on the ability to (efficiently) reach consensus in dynamic systems. Unfortunately, solving consensus requires well-connected communication graphs: In [5], we provided a consensus algorithm that works under the assumption that, in every round, the communication graph is both (i) weakly connected and (ii) contains a single *root component*, i.e., a *strongly connected component* (SCC) without incoming links (note that every weakly connected graph has at least one root component). For termination, the root component must eventually consist of the same members for a certain number of rounds, even though their interconnection topology may perpetually change. As these assumptions do not guarantee bidirectional reachability system-wide, the model in BRS12:sirocco falls between the weakest and second weakest class of models defined in [8].

However, in larger-scale dynamic networks, it is unrealistic to assume that the above properties can always be guaranteed. In this paper, we therefore provide a consensus algorithm that gracefully degrades to k-set agreement, for some k determined by the actual network properties, in case of less favorable conditions. Recall that, in the k-set agreement problem, processes may decide on one of at most k different values system-wide; 1-set agreement is equivalent to consensus.

In sharp contrast to classic k-set agreement algorithms, our algorithm is *k-uniform*, i.e., the parameter k does not appear in its code, and is even *worst-case k-optimal*: The number of system-wide decision values is bounded by the number k of (certain) *vertex-stable root components* (VSRC) occurring in the particular run. If the network partitions into k SCCs, for example,[1] each partition may obtain its own decision value. On the other hand, if the network is well-connected, the algorithm will guarantee a unique decision value. Viewed from the applications perspective, our gracefully degrading solution is perfectly fine if processes that cannot communicate with each other do not need to agree on a common value, as is the case for agreeing on communication schedules or frequencies, for example.

Main Contributions. In Sect. 3, we provide a fairly weak natural message adversary VSRC(k,d) (where k specifies the maximum number of root components per round and d is the duration of vertex-stability), which is still too strong for solving k-set agreement if d of just one VSRC is too small. Moreover, even *eventual* stability of *all* VSRCs is not enough for solving k-set agreement, not even when it is guaranteed that (substantially) less than k VSRCs exist simultaneously. On the other hand, we also provide a message adversary VSRC(n, d) + MAJINF(k), which combines VSRC(n, d) with some information flow guarantee MAJINF(k) between certain VSRCs, that is sufficient for solving

[1] It is important to note, however, that the network properties required by our algorithm to reach k decision values need *not* involve k isolated partitions: Obviously, k isolated partitions in the communication graph also imply k root components, but k root components do not imply a partitioning of the communication graph into k components — it may still be weakly connected.

k-set agreement: In Sect. 4, we provide a k-uniform, worst-case k-optimal k-set agreement algorithm that works correctly under VSRC(n, d) + MAJINF(k). To the best of our knowledge, it is the first gracefully degrading consensus algorithm proposed so far.

Related Work. Agreement problems in dynamic networks with undirected communication graphs have been studied in [11]; agreement in directed graphs has been considered in [1,5,14,15]. Whereas [15] considerably restrict the dynamicity of the communication graphs, e.g., by not allowing stabilizing behavior, which effectively causes them to belong to quite strong classes of network assumptions in the classification of Casteigts et al. [8], our previous work [5] allows to solve consensus under very weak network assumptions. Afek and Gafni [1] introduced message adversaries for relating problems solvable in wait-free read-write shared memory systems to those solvable in message-passing systems. Raynal and Stainer [14] used message adversaries for exploring the relationship between round-based models and failure detectors.

Regarding k-set agreement in dynamic networks, we are not aware of any previous work except [16], where bidirectional links are assumed, and our previous paper [4], where we assumed the existence of an underlying *static* skeleton graph (a non-empty common intersection of the communication graphs of all rounds) with at most k *static* root components. Note that this essentially implies a directed dynamic network with a static core. By contrast, in this paper, we allow the directed communication graphs to be fully dynamic.

Albeit we are not aware of related work exploring gracefully degrading consensus, there have been several attempts to weaken the semantics of consensus. Vaidya and Pradhan introduced the notion of *degradable* agreement [17], where processes are allowed to also decide on a (fixed) default value in case of excessive faults. The *almost everywhere agreement* problem introduced by [9] allows a small linear fraction of processes to remain undecided. Aguilera et al. [2] considered quiescent consensus in partitionable systems, which requires processes outside the majority partition not to terminate.

2 Model

We consider a synchronous distributed system made up of a fixed set of distributed processes $\Pi = \{p_1, \dots, p_n\}$ with $|\Pi| = n \geq 2$, which have fixed unique ids and communicate via unreliable message passing. For convenience, we assume that the unique id of $p_i \in \Pi$ is i, and use both p_i and i for denoting this process; "generic" processes will also be denoted by p, q etc.

Processes execute an infinite number of rounds $r = 1, 2, \dots$ (conceptually) in lock-step. In every round r, processes first broadcast a round r message of arbitrary content, determined by some message sending function, and then perform some deterministic local computation based on the received round r messages and their current (local) state. The actual communication in the system is modeled as an infinite sequence of simple directed graphs $\mathcal{G}^1, \mathcal{G}^2, \dots$, which is determined by an omniscient *message adversary* [1,14] that has access to the processes' states. $\mathcal{G}^r$ contains a directed edge $(p \to q)$ from process p to q iff q receives p's round r broadcast in round r. The set $\mathcal{N}_p^r$ denotes p's (in-)*neighbors* in round r. We emphasize that p does not know (a bound on) n and does not have any *a priori* knowledge of its neighbors, i.e., p does not know who receives its round r broadcast, and does not know who it will receive from in round r before its round r computation.

Definition 1 (Message adversary). *A message adversary* Adv *(for our system Π of n processors) is a set of sequences of communication graphs $(\mathcal{G}^r)_{r>0}$. A particular sequence of communication graphs $(\mathcal{A}^r)_{r>0}$ is* feasible *for* Adv, *if $(\mathcal{A}^r)_{r>0} \in$ Adv.*

For our system Π of n processes, this introduces a natural partial order of message adversaries, where A is weaker than B (denoted $A \leq B$) iff $A \subseteq B$, i.e., if it can generate at most the communication graph sequences of B. As a consequence, an algorithm that works correctly under message adversary B will also work under A. We say that some message adversary Adv guarantees some property, called a *network assumption*, if every $(\mathcal{G}^r)_{r>0} \in Adv$ satisfies this property.

To define the *k-set agreement problem*, we assume some finite set $\mathcal{V}$ satisfying $|\mathcal{V}| > k$ and $n > k$ (to rule out trivial solutions). Each process p_i starts with an initial value x_i taken from $\mathcal{V}$ and must irrevocably decide on some y_i, such that the following properties hold in all runs:

Definition 2 (k-set agreement). *Algorithm $\mathcal{A}$ solves k-*set agreement, *if the following properties hold in every run of $\mathcal{A}$:*

(k-Agreement) At most k different decision values are obtained system-wide.
(Validity) If $y_i = v$, then v is some p_j's initial value x_j.
(Termination) Every process must eventually decide.

Consensus is the special case of 1-set agreement; set agreement is a short-hand for $n-1$-set agreement. A k-set agreement algorithm is *uniform* if it does not have any a priori knowledge of the network (and hence of n); it is called *k-uniform* if it does not require a priori knowledge of k.

We will now define the cornerstones of the message adversaries defined in our paper. They will rest on the pivotal concept of *root components*, which are strongly connected components in $\mathcal{G}^r$ without *incoming* edges from processes outside the component.

Definition 3 (Root Component). *A* root component *R^r, with non-empty set of vertices $R \subseteq \Pi$, is a* strongly connected component *(SCC) in $\mathcal{G}^r$ that has no incoming edges from other components, formally $\forall p \in R, \forall q \in \mathcal{G}^r : (q \to p) \in \mathcal{G}^r \Rightarrow q \in R$.*

By contracting SCCs, it is easy to see that every weakly connected directed simple graph $\mathcal{G}$ has at least one root component. Hence, if $\mathcal{G}$ has k root components, it has at most k weakly connected components (with disjoint root components, but possibly overlapping in the remaining processes).

Some root components generated by our message adversaries will be required to be vertex-stable, i.e., to consist of the same *set* of nodes (with possibly varying interconnect) during a sufficiently large number of consecutive rounds.

Definition 4 (Vertex-Stable Root Component). *A sequence of consecutive rounds with communication graphs $\mathcal{G}^x$ for $x \in I = [a,b]$, $b \geq a$, contains an* I-vertex-stable root component R^I, *if, for $x \in I$, every $\mathcal{G}^x$ has a root component R^x with the same set of nodes R (but possibly varying interconnect).*

We will abbreviate R^I as an I-VSRC or $|I|$-VSRC if only the length of I matters, and sometimes denote an I-VSRC R^I just by its vertex set R if I is clear from the context. Note carefully that we assume $|I| = b - a + 1$ here, since $I = [a,b]$ ranges from the *beginning* of round a to the *end* of round b; hence, $I = [r,r]$ is not empty but rather represents round r.

The most important property of a VSRC R^I is that information is guaranteed to spread to all its vertices R if the interval I is large enough, c.f. Lemma 1 below. To express this formally, we need a few basic definitions and lemmas.

Similarly to the classic "happened-before" relation, we say that a process p *causally influences q in round r*, denoted by $(p \overset{r}{\rightsquigarrow} q)$, iff either (i) q has an incoming edge $(p \to q)$ from p in $\mathcal{G}^r$, or (ii) if $q = p$, i.e., we assume that p always influences itself in a round. Given a sequence of communication graphs $\mathcal{G}^r, \mathcal{G}^{r+1}, \ldots$, we say that there is an *causal influence chain* of length $\ell \geq 1$ starting from p in round r to q, denoted by $(p \overset{r[\ell]}{\rightsquigarrow} q)$, if there exists a sequence of not necessarily distinct processes $p = p_0, \ldots, p_\ell = q$ such that $p_i \overset{r+i}{\rightsquigarrow} p_{i+1}$ for $0 \leq i < \ell$. If ℓ is irrelevant, we just write $(p \overset{r}{\rightsquigarrow} q)$ or just $(p \rightsquigarrow q)$ and say that p (in round r) causally influences q. This allows us to define the notion of a dynamic causal distance between processes as given in Definition 5.

Definition 5 (Dynamic causal distance). *Given a sequence of communication graphs $\mathcal{G}^r, \mathcal{G}^{r+1}, \ldots$, the* dynamic causal distance $cd^r(p,q)$ *from process p (in round r) to process q is the length of the shortest causal influence chain starting in p in round r and ending in q, formally $cd^r(p,q) := min\{\ell\colon (p \overset{r[\ell]}{\rightsquigarrow} q)\}$. We define $cd^r(p,p) = 1$ and $cd^r(p,q) = \infty$ if p never influences q after round r.*

Note that, in contrast to the similar notion of dynamic distance defined in [11], the dynamic causal distance in our *directed* graphs is not necessarily symmetric. Corresponding to the dynamic diameter defined for undirected communication graphs in [11], we define the *dynamic causal diameter* $\varnothing^x(R^I)$ for round x in a I-VSRC R^I as the largest round x dynamic causal distance $cd^x(p,q)$ between any pair of processes $p, q \in R$:

Definition 6 (Dynamic causal diameter). *Given a sequence of communication graphs $\mathcal{G}^r, \mathcal{G}^{r+1}, \ldots$, let $I = [a,b]$, $r \leq a \leq b$, be a nonempty interval of indices in this sequence. Assume that the subsequence of communication graphs*

$\mathcal{G}^x$ for $x \in I$ contains an I-VSRC R^I with node set R. Then, the dynamic causal diameter *of R^I for round x is defined as $\varnothing^x(R^I) := \max_{p,q \in R}\{cd^x(p,q)\}$.*

Obviously, it may be the case that $\varnothing^x(R^I) = \infty$ in general. However, if $|I|$ is sufficiently large, the following Lemma 1 reveals that

Lemma 1 (Bound on dynamic causal diameter). *Given some $I = [a,b]$ and a VSRC R^I with $|R| \geq 2$, if $b \geq a + |R| - 2$, then $\forall x \in [a, b - |R| + 2]\colon \varnothing^x(R^I) \leq |R| - 1$.*

Proof. Fix some process $p \in R$ and some x where $a \leq x \leq b - |R| + 2$. Let $\mathcal{P}_0 = \{p\}$, and define for each $i > 0$ the set $\mathcal{P}_i = \mathcal{P}_{i-1} \cup \{q : \exists q' \in \mathcal{P}_{i-1} : q' \in \mathcal{N}_q^{x+i-1} \cap R\}$. $\mathcal{P}_i$ is hence the set of processes $q \in R$ such that $(p \overset{x[i]}{<} q)$ holds. Using induction, we will show that $|\mathcal{P}_k| \geq \min\{|R|, k+1\}$ for $k \geq 0$. Induction base $k = 0$: $|\mathcal{P}_0| \geq \min\{|R|, 1\} = 1$ follows immediately from $\mathcal{P}_0 = \{p\}$. Induction step $k \rightarrow k+1$, $k \geq 0$: Clearly the result holds if $|\mathcal{P}_k| = |R|$, thus we consider round $x+k$ and $|\mathcal{P}_k| < |R|$: It follows from strong connectivity of $\mathcal{G}^{x+k} \cap R$ that there is a set of edges from processes in $\mathcal{P}_k$ to some non-empty set $\mathcal{L}_k \subseteq R \setminus \mathcal{P}_k$. Hence, we have $\mathcal{P}_{k+1} = \mathcal{P}_k \cup \mathcal{L}_k$, which implies $|\mathcal{P}_{k+1}| \geq |\mathcal{P}_k| + 1 \geq k + 1 + 1 = k + 2 = \min\{|R|, k+2\}$ by the induction hypothesis.

Thus, in order to guarantee $R = \mathcal{P}_k$ and thus $|R| = |\mathcal{P}_k|$, choosing k such that $|R| = 1 + k$ and $k \leq b - x + 1$ is sufficient. Since $b \geq x + |R| - 2$, both conditions can be fulfilled by choosing $k = |R| - 1$. Moreover, due to the definition of $\mathcal{P}_k$, it follows that $\mathsf{cd}^x(p,q) \leq |R| - 1$ for all $q \in R$. Since this holds for any p and any $x \leq s - |R| + 2$, the statement of Lemma 1 follows. □

Lemma 1 reveals that, in the worst case, $|I|$ must be as large as $|R| - 1$ to ensure that messages sent by any process in R reach all members of R within I. To be able to also model faster information propagation in a VSRC, our message adversaries will be based on Definition 7. It guarantees a dynamic causal diameter of $D > 0$, such that messages sent by any process in R, in any but the last $D - 1$ rounds of I, reach all members of R within I.

Definition 7 (D-bounded I-VSRC). *An I-vertex-stable root component R^I with $I = [a,b]$ is D-bounded with* dynamic causal diameter *$D > 0$, if either $|I| < D$ [2] or else $\forall x \in [a, b - D + 1]\colon \varnothing^x(R^I) \leq D$.*

To formalize information propagation from root components to the entire network, one has to account for the fact that a process q outside any root component may be reachable from *multiple* root components in general. Intuitively speaking, this models dynamic networks that do not "cleanly" partition. Given a sequence of communication graphs $\mathcal{G}^r, \mathcal{G}^{r+1}, \ldots$ containing a set $S^I = \{R_1^I, \ldots, R_\ell^I\}$ of $\ell \geq 1$ I-VSRCs, all vertex-stable in the same interval $I = [a,b]$, let the round x *dynamic network causal distance* h^x be the maximum, taken over all processes

[2] That is, by convention, we also call a VSRC D-bounded if its duration is too short to be interesting.

$q \in \Pi$, of the minimal dynamic causal distance $cd^x(p,q)$ from *some* process $p \in \bigcup_{i=1}^{\ell} R_i^I$ in round x, formally $h^x(S^I) := \max_{q\in\Pi}\{\min_{p\in\cup_{i=1}^{\ell} R_i}\{cd^x(p,q)\}\}$. Definition 8 will be used in the sequel to guarantee that every process in the network receives a message from some member of at least one VSRC in $S^I = \{R_1^I, \ldots, R_\ell^I\}$ within H rounds provided $|I| \geq H$.

Definition 8 (H-network-bounded I-VSRCs). *A set $S^I = \{R_1^I, \ldots, R_\ell^I\}$ of $\ell \geq 1$ I-VSRCs with $I = [a,b]$ is H-network-bounded, with* dynamic network causal distance *$H > 0$, if either $|I| < H$ or else $\forall x \in [a, b-H+1] : h^x(S^I) \leq H$.*

Note that Definition 8 guarantees $(p \overset{x[H]}{\rightsquigarrow} q)$ for *at least one* but not for all $p \in R_i$. Moreover, p (and hence R_i) may be different for different starting rounds x in I.

Analogous to Lemma 1, it can be shown that H is bounded by $n-1$ if $b - a \geq n - 2$ (see [6, Lemma 4] for the proof).

3 A Message Adversary for k-Set Agreement

We first define the generic message adversary $\mathrm{VSRC}_{D,H}(k,d)$, which allows at most k VSRCs per round and guarantees a common window of vertex stability of duration at least d. Note that it involves both the dynamic causal diameter D and the dynamic network causal distance H according to Definitions 7 and 8 (that have to be enforced by the message adversary). To keep the notation simple, however, we will abbreviate $\mathrm{VSRC}_{D,H}(k,d)$ by $\mathrm{VSRC}(k,d)$ subsequently.

Definition 9 (Message adversary VSRC(k, d)=VSRC$_{D,H}$(k, d)). *The message adversary VSRC(k,d) is the set of all sequences of communication graphs $(\mathcal{G}^r)_{r>0}$, where*

(i) for every round r, $\mathcal{G}^r$ contains at most k root components,
(ii) all vertex-stable root components occurring in any $(\mathcal{G}^r)_{r>0}$ are D-bounded,
(iii) for each $(\mathcal{G}^r)_{r>0}$, there exists some $r_{ST} > 0$ and an interval of rounds $J = [r_{ST}, r_{ST}+d-1]$ where $1 \leq \ell \leq k$ H-network-bounded vertex-stable root components $R_1^J, \ldots, R_\ell^J$ exist simultaneously.

Theorem 1 below shows that it is impossible to solve k-set agreement for $1 \leq k < n-1$ under the message adversary $\mathrm{VSRC}(k, \min\{n-k, H\} - 1)$. Its proof (which has been omitted due to lack of space but can be found in [6]) uses the generic impossibility theorem provided in [3, Theorem 1], which exploits the fact that k-set agreement is impossible if k sufficiently disconnected components may occur and consensus cannot be solved in some component.

Theorem 1 [6, Theorem 7]. *No algorithm can solve k-set agreement with $n > k+1$ processes under the message adversary VSRC($k, \min\{n-k, H\} - 1$) stated in Definition 9, for any $1 \leq k < n-1$, even if there are $k-1$ root components $R_1, \ldots, R_{k-1}$ that are vertex-stable all the time, i.e., in $[1,\infty]$ (and only root component R_k is vertex-stable for at most $\min\{n-k, H\} - 1$ rounds).*

In addition, the following Theorem 2 reveals that even much less than k root components per round before stabilization and a single perpetually stable root component after stabilization are insufficient for solving k-set agreement. Consult [6] for its proof, which employs a lossy-link consensus impossibility [15].

Theorem 2 [6, Theorem 9]. *There is no algorithm that solves k-set agreement for $n \geq k+1$ processes under the message adversary for every $1 < k < n$, even if $\mathcal{G}^r = \mathcal{G}$, $r \geq r_{ST}$, where $\mathcal{G}$ contains only a single root component.*

We will now provide a message adversary MAJINF(k) that is sufficiently weak for solving k-set agreement if combined with VSRC($k, 3D+H$) and even with VSRC($n, 3D+H$).

We obtained this combination by adding some additional properties to the necessary network conditions implied by our impossibility Theorems 1 and 2: To avoid non-terminating (i.e., forever undecided) executions as predicted by Theorem 1, we require the *stable interval* constraint guaranteed by the message adversary VSRC($n, 3D+H$) to hold. In order to also circumvent executions violating the k-agreement property established by Theorem 2, we introduce the *majority influence* constraint guaranteed by the message adversary MAJINF(k) given in Definition 12 below. It guarantees some (minimal) information flow between sufficiently long-lasting vertex-stable root components that exist at different times. It implies that the information available in any such VSRC originates in at most k "initial" VSRCs. Thereby, it enhances the very limited information propagation that could occur in our model solely under VSRC($k, 3D+H$), which is too strong for solving k-agreement.

Given some run ρ, we denote by $\mathbb{V}_d$ the set of all root components that are vertex-stable for at least d consecutive rounds in ρ. Let $R^v \in \mathbb{V}_1$ consisting of processes in R_v be vertex-stable in $V = [a_v, b_v]$ and $R^W \in \mathbb{V}_1$ consisting of processes in R_W be vertex-stable in $W = [a_W, b_W]$ with $a_W > b_v$; note that $\mathbb{V}_d \subseteq \mathbb{V}_1$ for every $d \geq 1$.

Definition 10 (Causal Influence Sets). *Given $R^v, R^W \in \mathbb{V}_1$ with sets of processes R_v, R_W, their causal influence set $CS(R^v, R^W)$ consists of those processes q of $\mathcal{R}^W$ for which there exists a causal chain from some process p of $\mathcal{R}^v$ starting after V that ends before or at the beginning of W. That is, $CS(R^v, R^W) := \{q \in R_W \mid \exists p \in R_v \colon cd^{b_v+1}(p,q) \leq a_W - b_v\}$.*

The *majority influence* between R^v and R^W guarantees that R^v influences a set of nodes in R^W, which is greater than any set influenced by VSRCs not already known by the processes in R^v (and greater than or equal to any set influenced by VSRCs already known by the processes in R^v).

Definition 11 (Majority influence). *We say that a VSRC $R^v \in \mathbb{V}_{2D+1}$ exercises a* majority influence *on a VSRC $R^W \in \mathbb{V}_{2D+1}$, denoted $R^v \hookrightarrow_{\mathtt{m}} R^W$ with $\hookrightarrow_{\mathtt{m}} \subseteq \mathbb{V}^2_{2D+1}$, iff $\forall R^I \in \mathbb{V}_{D+1}$ with $CS(R^I, R^v) = \emptyset$ we have $|CS(R^v, R^W)| > |CS(R^I, R^W)|$ and $\forall R^I \in \mathbb{V}_{D+1}$ with $CS(R^I, R^v) \neq \emptyset$ we have $|CS(R^v, R^W)| \geq |CS(R^I, R^W)|$.*

We can now specify the message adversary MAJINF(k) given in Definition 12.

Definition 12 (k-majority influence message adversary). *The message adversary MAJINF(k) is the set of all communication graph sequences $(\mathcal{G}^r)_{r>0}$, where in every run there is a set $K \subseteq \mathbb{V}_{2D+1}$ of $|K| \leq k$ VSRCs s.t. $\forall R^I \in \mathbb{V}_{2D+1} \setminus K\ \exists R^J \in \mathbb{V}_{2D+1}$ with $R^J \hookrightarrow_{\mathrm{m}} R^I$.*

Informally speaking, Definition 12 ensures that all but at most k "initial" VSRCs in $\mathbb{V}_{2D+1}$ are majority-influenced by some earlier VSRC in $\mathbb{V}_{2D+1}$. Note carefully, though, that Definition 12 neither prohibits partitioning of the system in more than k simultaneous VSRCs nor directly exhibits a k-quorum property, cf. the well-known quorum failure detector Σ_k [7] that is known to be necessary (but not sufficient!) for solving k-set agreement:[3] After all, choosing any $Q \subseteq \mathbb{V}_{2D+1}$ with $|Q| = k + 1$ does not imply that there exist two VSRCs in Q that are majority-influenced by a common VSRC. As MAJINF(k) alone is hence too strong for solving k-set agreement, VSRC($n, 3D + H$) + MAJINF(k) is indeed reasonably close to the k-set agreement solvability border.

We conclude this section with some straightforward stronger assumptions, which also imply Definition 12 and can hence be handled by the algorithm introduced in Sect. 4:

(i) Replacing majority influence in Definition 11 by majority intersection $|R_v \cap R_W| > |R_I \cap R_W|$, which is obviously the strongest form of influence.
(ii) Requiring $|R_v \cap R_W| > |R_W|/2$, i.e., a majority intersection with respect to the number of processes in R_W. This could be interpreted as a changing VSRC, in the sense of "R_W is the result of changing a minority of processes in R_v". Although this restricts the rate of growth of VSRCs in a run, it would apply, for example, in case of random graphs where the giant component has formed [10].

4 Gracefully Degrading Consensus/k-Set Agreement

In this section, we provide a k-set agreement algorithm and prove that it works correctly under the message adversary VSRC($n, 3D + H$) + MAJINF(k), i.e., the conjunction of Definitions 9 and 12. Note that the algorithm needs to know D, but neither n, k nor H. It consists of a "generic" k-set agreement algorithm, which relies on a function `InStableRoot(I)` that returns the member set of the VSRC R^I (or $\emptyset$ if none) provided by a network approximation algorithm, and a function `GetLock` that extracts candidate decision values from history information. Our implementation of `GetLock` uses a vector-clock-like mechanism for maintaining "causally consistent" history information, which can be guaranteed to lead to proper candidate values thanks to VSRC($n, 3D + H$) + MAJINF(k).

Properties. Our algorithm is in fact not only k-uniform but even worst-case k-optimal, in the sense that (i) it provides at most k decisions system-wide in all runs that are feasible for VSRC($n, 3D + H$) + MAJINF(k), and (ii) that there is

[3] Working out the intricacies of relating our message adversaries to failure detectors (in the spirit of [14]) is part of our current research.

at least one feasible run under VSRC$(n, 3D + H)$+MAJINF(k) where no correct k-set agreement can guarantee less than k decisions. (i) will be proved below, and (ii) follows immediately from the fact that a run consisting of k isolated partitions is also feasible for VSRC$(n, 3D + H)$ + MAJINF(k). Our algorithm can hence indeed be viewed as a consensus algorithm that degrades gracefully to k-set agreement, for some k determined by the actual network properties.

Network Approximation. Our k-set agreement algorithm relies on the network approximation algorithm already used in [5]. As detailed in [6, Sec. 5.1], it maintains *network estimate* A_p at process p, which holds p's local knowledge of every communication graph $\mathcal{G}^r$ that occurred so far: Whenever p gets evidence that some communication link $(v \to w)$ was present in round $\mathcal{G}^r$, e.g., by receiving some other process's A_q containing this edge, it also adds $(v \to w)$ with label r to A_p. For the joint algorithm, we assume that the complete round r computing step of the network approximation algorithm is executed just before the round r computing step of the k-set algorithm, and that the round r message of the former is piggybacked on the round r message of the latter. This implies that the round r computing step of the k-set core algorithm, which terminates round r, can already access the *result* of the round r computation of the network approximation algorithm, i.e., its state at the *end* of round r.

Detailed Description. The general idea of our core k-set agreement algorithm in Alg. 1 is to generate new decision values only at members of $2D+1$-VSRCs, and to disseminate those values throughout the remaining network. Using the local information provided by the network approximation algorithm, our algorithm causes process p_i to make a transition from the initially *undecided* state to a *locked* state when it detects some minimal "stability of its surroundings", namely, its membership in some $D+1$-VSRC D rounds in the past (line 17). Note that the latency of D rounds is inevitable here, since information propagation within a $D+1$-VSRC may take up to D rounds due to D-boundedness as guaranteed by item (ii) in Definition 9. If process p_i, while in the locked state, observes some period of stability that is sufficient for locally inferring a consistent view among *all* VSRC members (which occurs when the $D+1$-VSRC has actually extended to a $2D+1$-VSRC), p_i can safely make a transition to the *decided* state (line 24). The decision value is then broadcast in all subsequent rounds, and adopted by any not-yet decided process in the system that receives it later on (line 9). Note that VSRC$(n, 3D + H)$ (Definition 9) guarantees that this will eventually happen.

Since locking is done optimistically, however, it may also happen that the $D+1$-VSRC does not extend to a $2D+1$-VSRC (or, even worse, is not recognized to have done so by some members) later on. In this case, p_i makes a transition from the locked state back to the undecided state (line 22). Unfortunately, this possibility has severe consequences: Mechanisms are required that, despite possibly inconsistently perceived unsuccessful locks, ensure both (a) an *identical* decision value among all members of a $2D+1$-VSRC who successfully detect this $2D+1$-VSRC and thus reach the decided state, and (b) no more than k different decision values originating from different $2D+1$-VSRCs.

Algorithm 1. k-uniform k-set agreement algorithm, code for process p_i

```
Variables and Initialization:
hist_i[*][*] := ∅ /* hist_i[j][r] holds p_i's estimate of the locks learned by p_j in round r */
hist_i[i][0] := {({p_i}, x_i, 0)} /* virtual first lock (V(R) := {p_i}, v := x_i, τ_create := 0) at p_i */
ℓ := ⊥ // most recent lock round, ⊥ if none
decision_i := ⊥ // p_i's decision, ⊥ if undecided
Emit round r messages:
send ⟨hist_i, decision_i⟩ to all neighbors
Receive round r messages:
for all p_j in p_i's neighborhood N^r_{p_i}, receive ⟨hist_j, decision_j⟩
Round r computation:
if decision_i = ⊥ then
   if received any message m containing m.decision ≠ ⊥ then
      decide m.decision and set decision_i := m.decision
   else
      // update hist_i with hist_j received from neighbors
      for p_j ∈ N^r_{p_i}, where p_j sent hist_j do
         hist'_i := hist_i // remember current history
         for all non-empty entries hist_j[x][r'] of hist_j, x ≠ i do
            hist_i[x][r'] := hist_i[x][r'] ∪ hist_j[x][r']
         hist_i[i] := hist_i \ hist'_i // locally add all newly learned locks
      // perform state transitions (undecided, locked, decided):
      myRoot := InStableRoot([r − 2D, r − D])
      if ℓ = ⊥ and myRoot ≠ ∅ then
         ℓ := r − 2D
         lock := GetLock(myRoot, ℓ)
         hist_i[i][r] := hist_i[i][r] ∪ lock // create new lock
      else if ℓ ≠ ⊥ and myRoot = ∅ then
         ℓ := ⊥ // release unsuccessful lock
      else if ℓ ≠ ⊥ and InStableRoot([ℓ, ℓ + 2D]) ≠ ∅ then
         decide lock.v and set decision_i := lock.v

function GetLock(R, r')
   Let S be the multiset ⋃_{p_j ∈ R, r'' ≤ r'} hist_i[j][r'']
   Let mfrq(S) be the set of the most frequent elements in S
   Let mfrq_latest(S) := {x ∈ mfrq(S) | ∀y ≠ x ∈ mfrq(S): x.τ_create > y.τ_create}
   if |mfrq_latest(S)| = 1 then
      Let v be s.v of the single element s ∈ mfrq_latest(S)
      newLock := (R, v, r)
   else
      newLock := (R, max_{s∈S} {s.v}, r) // deterministic choice
   return newLock
```

Both goals are accomplished by a particular selection of the decision values (using function GetLock), which ultimately relies on an intricate utilization the network properties guaranteed by our message adversary VSRC$(n, 3D+H)$ + MAJINF(k) (Definitions 9 and 12): Our algorithm uses a suitable *lock history* data structure for this purpose, which is continuously exchanged and updated among all reachable processes. It is used to store sets of *locks* $L = (R, v, \tau_{create})$, which are created by every process that enters the locked state: R is the vertex-set of the detected $D+1$-VSRC, v is a certain proposal value (determined as explained below), and τ_{create} is the round when the lock is created.

Maintaining History. In more detail, the lock history at process p_i consists of an array $\texttt{hist}_i[j][r]$ that holds p_i's (under)approximation of the locks process p_j got to know in round r. It is maintained using the following simple update rules:

(i) *Local lock creation:* Apart from the single *virtual* lock $(\{p_i\}, x_i, 0)$ created initially by p_i in line 2 (which guarantees a non-empty lock history right from the beginning), all regular locks created upon p_i's transition from the undecided to the locked state are computed by the function `GetLock` in line 19. Any lock locally created at p_i in round r (that is, in the round r computing step of the core k-set agreement algorithm that terminates round r) is of course put into $\texttt{hist}_i[i][r]$.

(ii) *Remote lock learning:* Since all processes exchange their lock histories, p_i may learn about some lock L created by process p_x in round r' from the lock history $\texttt{hist}_j[x][r']$ received from some p_j later on. In this case, L is just added to $\texttt{hist}_i[x][r']$ (line 14).

(iii) *Local lock learning:* In order to ensure that the lock histories of all members of a $2D+1$-VSRC are eventually consistent, which will finally ensure identical decision values, *every* newly learned remote lock $L \in \texttt{hist}_i[x][r']$ obtained in (ii) is also added to $\texttt{hist}_i[i][r]$.

Note that the update rules (i)+(ii) resemble the ones of vector clocks [12].

Clearly, $\texttt{hist}_i[i][r']$ will always be accurate for current and past rounds $r' \leq r$, while $\texttt{hist}_i[j][r']$ may not always be up-to date, i.e., may lack some locks that are present in $\texttt{hist}_j[j][r']$. Nevertheless, if p_i and p_j are members of the same $2D+1$-VSRC R^I with $I = [r-2D, r]$, Definition 7 ensures that p_i and p_j have consistent histories $\texttt{hist}_i[j][r']$ and $\texttt{hist}_j[i][r']$ at latest by (the end of) round $r'+D$, for any $r' \in [r-2D, r-D]$. Hence, if p_i creates a new lock L when it detects, in its round r computing step, that it was part of a $D+1$-VSRC that was stable from $r-2D$ to $r-D$, it is ascertained that any other member p_j will have locally learned the same lock L in the same round r, provided that the $D+1$-VSRC in fact extended to a $2D+1$-VSRC.

Consistent Decisions. The resulting consistency of the histories is finally exploited by the function $\texttt{GetLock}(R, \ell)$, which computes (the value of) a new local lock (line 19) created in round r. As its input parameters, it is provided with the members R of the detected $D+1$-VSRC and its starting round $\ell = r-2D$. `GetLock` first determines a multiset S, which contains all locks locally known to the members $p_j \in R$ by round $r-2D$ (line 26). Note that the multiplicity of some lock $L = (R', v, r')$ in S is just the number of members of R who got to know L by round $r-2D$, which is just $|CS(R', R)|$ according to Definition 10. In order to determine a proper value for the new lock to be computed by `GetLock`, we exploit the fact that MAJINF(k) (given in Definition 12) ensures majority influence according to Definition 11: If the set $mfrq_{latest}(S)$, containing the most frequent locks in S with the same maximal lock creation round, contains a single lock L only, its value $L.v$ is used. Note that the restriction to the maximal lock creation date automatically filters unwanted, outdated locks that have merely been disseminated in preceding $2D+1$-VSRCs. Otherwise, i.e., if $mfrq_{latest}(S)$ contains multiple candidate locks, a consistent deterministic choice, namely, the maximum among all lock values in S, is used (line 32). As a consequence, at most k different decision values will be generated system-wide.

In the remainder of this section, we will prove the following Theorem 3:

Theorem 3. *Algorithm 1 solves k-uniform k-set agreement in a dynamic network under the message adversary VSRC($n, 3D + H$) + MAJINF(k), which is the conjunction of Definitions 9 and 12.*

The proof consists of a sequence of technical lemmas, which will finally allow us to establish all the properties of k-set agreement given in Sect. 2.

Validity according to Definition 2 is straightforward to see. To establish termination, we start with Lemmas 2, 3 and 4 (the proofs can again be found in [6]) that are related to setting locks at all members of vertex stable root components. They all rely on the guarantees provided by the network approximation algorithm, which have already been established in [5]:

Corollary 1 [6, Corollary 1]. *If the function* `InStableRoot(`I`)` *evaluates to $R \neq \emptyset$ at process p in round r, then $\forall x \in I$ where $x < r$, it holds that p is a member of R^x, i.e., $p \in R$.*

Corollary 2 [6, Corollary 2]. *Consider an interval of rounds $I = [a, b]$, with $|I| = b - a + 1 > D$, such that there is a D-bounded vertex-stable root component R^I. Then, from the end of round b on, a call to* `InStableRoot(`$[a, b-D]$`)` *returns R at every process in R.*

Lemma 2 [6, Lemma 19]. *Apart from processes adopting a decision sent by another process, only processes part of a vertex stable root with interval length greater than D (resp. $2D$) lock (resp. decide).*

Lemma 3 [6, Lemma 20]. *All processes part of a vertex stable root $R^{[a,b]}$ with interval length greater than $2D$, which did not start already before a, lock, i.e. set $l = a$, in round $a + 2D$.*

Lemma 4 [6, Lemma 21]. *All processes part of a vertex stable root $R^{[a,b]}$ with interval length greater than $3D$, which did not start already before a, have decided by round $a + 3D$.*

Lemma 5. *The algorithm eventually terminates at all processes.*

Proof. Pick any process p_j. If p_j is part of a root component during the stable interval guaranteed by Definition 9, Lemma 3 ensures termination by $r_{ST} + 3D$ at the latest. If p_j is not part of a root component during the stable interval, it follows from Definition 8 that there exists a causal chain of length at most H to p_j from some member p_i of some terminating VSRC. Therefore, p_j must receive the decide message and decide via line 9 by $r_{ST} + 3D + H$ at latest. □

Although we now know that all members of a VSRC that is vertex stable for at least $3D$ rounds will decide, we did not prove anything about their decision values yet. In the sequel, we will prove that they decide on the *same* value.

Lemma 6. *Given some VSRC R^I with $I = [a, b]$ and $b \geq a + D$, in all rounds $x \in [a + D, b]$ it holds that $\forall p_i, p_j \in R$: $\bigcup_{r' \leq a} \texttt{hist}_i[j][r'] = \bigcup_{r' \leq a} \texttt{hist}_j[j][r']$*

Proof. By the D-boundedness of R^I, a message from round a has reached every member of R by round $a + D$. Moreover, no message sent by a process not in R during I can reach a member of R during I because R^I is a root component. Therefore, since $\texttt{hist}_i$ is sent by each process p_i in every round (line 5) and p_i adds only newly learned entries to $\texttt{hist}_i$ (lines 15 and 20), all these updates of $\texttt{hist}_i$ during I, regarding any round $r' \leq a$, occur at the latest in round $a + D$. □

Lemma 7. *All processes of a VSRCs R^I of $\mathbb{V}_{2D+1}$ with $I = [a, b]$ adopt the same lock (and hence decide the same).*

Proof. Such a lock is created by $p_i \in R$ in round $a + 2D$, when it recognizes R^I as having been vertex-stable for $D+1$ rounds according to Lemma 3. As the lock (value) is computed based on $\texttt{hist}_i$ present in round $a+2D$, which is consistent among all VSRC members by Lemma 6, the lemma follows. □

Finally, we show that, given that the system satisfies Definition 12, there will be at most k decision values in any run of Algorithm 1, which proves k-agreement: Since there are at most k VSRCs of $\mathbb{V}_{2D+1}$ that are not majority-influenced by other VSRCs, it remains to show that any majority-influenced VSRC decides the same as the VSRC it is majority-influenced by. In order to do so, we will first establish a key property of our central data structure $\texttt{hist}_i$.

Lemma 8. *Given R^v, $V = [a_v, b_v]$, and R^W, $W = [a_W, b_W]$, where $|v| > 2D$ and $|W| \geq 1$, let L be a lock known to all members of R^v by b_v, i.e., for all $p_i \in R_v$ it holds that, by the end of round b_v, $L \in \bigcup_{r' \leq b_v} \texttt{hist}_i[i][r']$. For any process $p_j \in CS(R^v, R^W)$, it holds that $L \in \bigcup_{r' \leq a_W} \texttt{hist}_j[j][r']$.*

Proof. Assume the contrary, i.e., there exists some $p_j \in CS(R^v, R^W)$ but $L \notin \bigcup_{r' \leq a_W} \texttt{hist}_j[j][r']$. Definition 10 implies that there exists a causal chain from some $p_i \in R^v$ to p_j that ends before p_j becomes a part of R_W. Since processes send their own history in every round according to line 5, every message in this causal chain consisted of a $\texttt{hist}$ containing L and thus p_j put L into its $\texttt{hist}_j[j][r]$ via line 14 if $\bigcup_{r' \leq r} \texttt{hist}_j[j][r']$ did not already contain L. □

Lemma 9. *Given $R^v \in \mathbb{V}_{2D+1}$, $V = [a_v, b_v]$, and $R^W \in \mathbb{V}_{2D+1}$, $W = [a_W, b_W]$, assume that the processes of R_v created the (same) lock L when locking. If $R^v \hookrightarrow_{\mathtt{m}} R^W$, then the processes in R_W will choose a lock L' where $L.v = L'.v$ (and hence decide the same as the processes in R_v).*

Proof. From the definition of $\hookrightarrow_{\mathtt{m}}$ (Definition 11), it follows that no VSRC R^I of $\mathbb{V}_{D+1}$ has a larger influence set on R^W than R^v. By Lemma 2, this implies that no lock that was generated by some R^I in $\mathbb{V}_{D+1}$ can be known to more members of R^W than the lock L generated by R^v. Since process p_i puts only newly learned locks into $\texttt{hist}_i$ (line 15 and 20), by Lemma 8, this means that in round a_W no "bad" lock L_b is present in more elements of $S = \bigcup_{p_i \in R_W, r' \leq a_W} \texttt{hist}_i[i][r']$ than L. We now show that $L.\tau_{create} > L_b.\tau_{create}$ for all L_b occuring in as many elements of S as L with $L_b \neq L$. Obviously, the only locks L_b that could occur in as many elements of S as L are locks that have been in $\texttt{hist}_i$ of some $p_i \in R_v$ at the beginning of round r_v already. Since for any such L_b, L was created after L_b, by line 30 and 32, we have that $L.\tau_{create} > L_b.\tau_{create}$, as claimed. Because in round $a_W + 2D$, at all processes p_i, p_j of R_W, Lemma 6 implies that $\bigcup_{r' \leq a_W} \texttt{hist}_i[j][r'] = \bigcup_{r' \leq a_W} \texttt{hist}_j[i][r']$, when locking in round $a_W + 2D$ according to Lemma 3, every p_i of R_W will find L as the unique most common lock in the elements of S with maximal τ_{create}. This leads to the evaluation of the if-statement in line 28 to true and to the creation of a new lock L', where $L'.v = L.v$ in line 30, as asserted. □

5 Conclusions

We provided the first consensus algorithm for synchronous dynamic networks, which degrades gracefully to general k-set agreement in unfavorable runs; k is related to the number of mutually independent vertex-stable root components occuring in the run. Related impossibility results show that the network assumptions (eventual stability and majority influence) required by our algorithm are reasonably close to the solvability border.

References

1. Afek, Y., Gafni, E.: Asynchrony from synchrony. In: Frey, D., Raynal, M., Sarkar, S., Shyamasundar, R.K., Sinha, P. (eds.) ICDCN 2013. LNCS, vol. 7730, pp. 225–239. Springer, Heidelberg (2013)
2. Aguilera, M.K., Chen, W., Toueg, S.: Using the heartbeat failure detector for quiescent reliable communication and consensus in partitionable networks. Theor. Comput. Sci. **220**(1), 3–30 (1999)
3. Biely, M., Robinson, P., Schmid, U.: Easy impossibility proofs for k-set agreement in message passing systems. In: Fernàndez Anta, A., Lipari, G., Roy, M. (eds.) OPODIS 2011. LNCS, vol. 7109, pp. 299–312. Springer, Heidelberg (2011)
4. Biely, M., Robinson, P., Schmid, U.: Solving k-set agreement with stable skeleton graphs. In: Proceedings of the IPDPS Workshops, pp. 1488–1495 (2011)
5. Biely, M., Robinson, P., Schmid, U.: Agreement in directed dynamic networks. In: Even, G., Halldórsson, M.M. (eds.) SIROCCO 2012. LNCS, vol. 7355, pp. 73–84. Springer, Heidelberg (2012)
6. Biely, M., Robinson, P., Schmid, U., Schwarz, M., Winkler, K.: Gracefully degrading consensus and k-set agreement in directed dynamic networks, January 2015. arXiv:1501.02716
7. Bonnet, F., Raynal, M.: On the road to the weakest failure detector for k-set agreement in message-passing systems. Theor. Comput. Sci. **412**(33), 4273–4284 (2011)
8. Casteigts, A., Flocchini, P., Quattrociocchi, W., Santoro, N.: Time-varying graphs and dynamic networks. IJPEDS **27**(5), 387–408 (2012)
9. Dwork, C., Peleg, D., Pippenger, N., Upfal, E.: Fault tolerance in networks of bounded degree. SIAM J. Comput. **17**(5), 975–988 (1988)

10. Janson, S., Knuth, D.E., Luczak, T., Pittel, B.: The birth of the giant component. Random Struct. Algorithms **4**, 233–358 (1993)
11. Kuhn, F., Oshman, R., Moses, Y.: Coordinated consensus in dynamic networks. In: Proceedings of the PODC 2011 (2011)
12. Mattern, F.: Virtual time and global states of distributed systems. In: Parallel and Distributed Algorithms, pp. 215–226. North-Holland (1989)
13. Newport, C., Kotz, D., Yuan, Y., Gray, R.S., Liu, J., Elliott, C.: Experimental evaluation of wireless simulation assumptions. SIMULATION: Trans. Soc. Model. Simul. Int. **83**(9), 643–661 (2007)
14. Raynal, M., Stainer, J.: Synchrony weakened by message adversaries vs asynchrony restricted by failure detectors. In: Proceedings of the PODC 2013, pp. 166–175 (2013)
15. Schmid, U., Weiss, B., Keidar, I.: Impossibility results and lower bounds for consensus under link failures. SIAM J. Comput. **38**(5), 1912–1951 (2009)
16. Sealfon, A., Sotiraki, A.A.: Brief announcement: agreement in partitioned dynamic networks. In: Kuhn, F. (ed.) DISC 2014. LNCS, vol. 8784, pp. 555–556. Springer, Heidelberg (2014)
17. Vaidya, N.H., Pradhan, D.K.: Degradable agreement in the presence of Byzantine faults. In: Proceedings of ICDCS 1993, pp. 237–244 (1993)

Homonym Population Protocols

Olivier Bournez[1(✉)], Johanne Cohen[2], and Mikaël Rabie[1]

[1] LIX, Ecole Polytechnique, 91128 Palaiseau Cedex, France
{olivier.bournez,mikael.rabie}@lix.polytechnique.fr
[2] LRI, Université de Paris-Sud, Bâtiment 425, 91405 Orsay Cedex, France
Johanne.Cohen@lri.fr

Abstract. Angluin *et al.* introduced Population protocols as a model in which n passively mobile anonymous finite-state agents stably compute a predicate on the multiset of their inputs via interactions by pairs. The model has been extended by Guerraoui and Ruppert to yield the community protocol models where agents have unique identifiers but may only store a finite number of the identifiers they already heard about. The Population protocol model only computes semi-linear predicates, whereas the community protocol model provides the power of a Turing machine with a $O(n \log n)$ space.

We consider variations on the above models and we obtain a whole landscape that covers and extends already known results. By considering the case of homonyms, that is to say the case when several agents may share the same identifier, we provide a hierarchy that goes from the case of no identifier (population protocol model) to the case of unique identifiers (community protocol model).

We obtain in particular that any Turing Machine on space $O(\log^{O(1)} n)$ can be simulated with at least $O(\log^{O(1)} n)$ identifiers, a result filling a gap left open in all previous studies.

Our results also extend and revisit in particular the hierarchy provided by Chatzigiannakis *et al.* on population protocols carrying Turing Machines on limited space, solving the problem of the gap left by this work between per-agent space $o(\log \log n)$ (proved to be equivalent to population protocols) and $O(\log n)$ (proved to be equivalent to Turing machines).

1 Introduction

Angluin *et al.* [3] proposed a model of distributed computation called *population protocols*. It can be seen as a minimal model that aims at modeling large sensor networks with resource-limited anonymous mobile agents. The mobility of the agents is assumed to be unpredictable (given by any fair scheduler) and pairs of agents can exchange state information when they are close together.

The population protocol model can be considered as a computational model, in particular computing predicates: Given some input configuration, the agents have to decide whether this input satisfies the predicate. More precisely, the population of agents has to eventually stabilize to a configuration in which every

A. Bouajjani and H. Fauconnier (Eds.): NETYS 2015, LNCS 9466, pp. 125–139, 2015.
DOI: 10.1007/978-3-319-26850-7_9

agent is in an accepting state or a rejecting one. This must happen with the same program for all population sizes, i.e. for any size of input configuration.

The seminal work of Angluin *et al.* [1,3] proved that predicates computed by population protocols are precisely those on counts of agents definable by a first-order formula in Presburger arithmetic (equivalent to a semilinear set). Subsets definable in this way are rather restricted, as for example multiplication is not expressible in Presburger arithmetic. Several variants of the original model have been considered in order to strengthen the population protocol model with extra realistic and implementable assumptions, in order to gain more computational power. Variants also include natural restrictions like modifying the assumption between agent's interactions (one-way communications [1], particular interaction graphs [2]). This also includes the Probabilistic Population Protocol model that makes a random scheduling assumption for interactions [3]. Various kinds of fault tolerance have been considered for population protocols [10], including the search for self-stabilizing solutions [4]. We refer to [6,8] for a survey.

Among many variants of population protocols, the *passively mobile (logarithmic space) machine model* introduced by Chatzigiannakis *et al.* [7] constitutes a generalization of the population protocol model where finite state agents are replaced by agents that correspond to arbitrary Turing machines with $O(S(n))$ space per-agent, where n is the number of agents. An exact characterization [7] of computable predicates is given: this model can compute all symmetric predicates in $NSPACE(nS(n))$ as long as $S(n) = \Omega(\log n)$. Chatzigiannakis *et al.* establish that with a space in agent in $S(n) = o(\log \log n)$, the model is equivalent to population protocols, i.e. to the case $S(n) = O(1)$.

In parallel, *community protocols* introduced by Guerraoui and Ruppert [13] are closer to the original population protocol model, assuming *a priori* agents with individual very restricted computational capabilities. In this model, each agent has a unique identifier and can only remember $O(1)$ other agent identifiers, and only identifiers from agents that it met. Guerraoui and Ruppert [13] using results about the so-called storage modification machines [15], proved that such protocols simulate Turing machines: Predicates computed by this model with n agents are precisely the predicates in $NSPACE(n \log n)$.

In this paper, we obtain a whole landscape that covers and extends already known results. We do so by considering that the capabilities of agents is even more restricted. Indeed, we drop the hypothesis of unique identifiers. That is to say, we consider that agents may have homonyms. We obtain a hierarchy that goes from the case of no identifier (i.e. population protocol model) to the case of unique identifiers (i.e. community protocol model). In what follows, $f(n)$ denotes the number of distinct available identifiers on a population with n agents. Notice that the idea of having less identifiers than agents, that is to say of having "homonyms", has already been considered in other contexts or with not closely related problematics [5,9,11,12].

Basically, Tables 1 and 2 summarize our results, where $MNSPACE(S(n))$ (respectively: $SMNSPACE(S(n))$) is the set of f-symmetric[1] (resp. also stable

[1] These classes are defined in Sect. 3.4.

Table 1. Homonym population protocols with n agents and $f(n)$ identifiers.

$f(n)$ identifiers	Computational power
$O(1)$	Presburger's definable subsets [1,3]
$\Theta(\log^r n)$ with $r \in \mathbb{R}_{>0}$	$\bigcup_{k\in\mathbb{N}} MNSPACE\,(\log^k n)$ Theorem 5
$\Theta(n^\epsilon)$ with $\epsilon > 0$	$MNSPACE(n \log n)$ Theorem 6
n	$NSPACE(n \log n)$[13]

Table 2. Passively mobile machine model [7] with n agents and space $S(n)$ per agent.

Space per agent $S(n)$	Computational power
$O(1)$	Presburger's definable subsets [1,3]
$o(\log\log n)$	Presburger's definable subsets [7]
$\Theta(\log\log n)$	$\bigcup_{k\in\mathbb{N}} SNSPACE(\log^k n)$ Theorem 7
$\Omega(\log n)$	$SNSPACE(nS(n))$ [7]

under the permutation of the input multisets) languages recognized by Non Deterministic Turing Machines on space $O(S(n))$.

Our results also extend the *passively mobile machine model*. In particular, Chatzigiannakis *et al.* [7] solved the cases $S(n) = o(\log\log n)$ (equivalent to population protocols) and $S(n) = O(\log n)$ (equivalent to Turing machines). We provide a characterization for the case $S(n) = O(\log\log n)$: the model is equivalent to $\bigcup_{k\in\mathbb{N}} SNSPACE(\log^k n)$ (see Table 2).

The document is organized as follows. Section 2 introduces the formal definitions of the different models and some already known main results. Section 3 is devoted to the case where an order is available on identifiers. The number of identifiers $f(n)$ is possibly less than the number n of agents (see Table 1). Section 4 treats the case $S(n) = O(\log\log n)$ in the passively mobile machine model [7] (see Table 2). Section 5 is then a summary of our results with some open questions.

2 Models

Population protocols have been, to date, mostly considered as computing predicates: one considers protocols such that starting from some initial configuration, any fair sequence of pairwise interactions must eventually yield to a state where all agents agree and either accept or reject. The corresponding predicate then corresponds to the inputs that eventually lead to accept. Algorithms are assumed to be uniform: the protocol descriptions are independent of the number n of the agents.

The models we consider are variations of the *community protocol* model [13]. This latter model is in turn considered as an extension of the population protocols. In all these models, a system is a collection of agents. Each agent has a finite number of possible states and has an input value, that determines its initial state. Evolution of states of agents is the product of pairwise interactions between agents: when two agents meet, they exchange information about their states and simultaneously update their own states according to a joint transition function, which corresponds to the algorithm of the protocol. The precise sequence of agents involved under the pairwise interactions is under the control of any fair scheduler. The considered notion of fairness for population protocols states that every system configuration that can be reached infinitely often is eventually reached.

To avoid multiplication of names, we will write community protocols for the model of [13], and homonym population protocols for our version, precising sometimes with $f(n)$ distinct identifiers.

Let U be the infinite set containing the possible identifiers. Compared to [13], we do not consider that the set is arbitrary: we assume that $U \subset \mathbb{N}$. We also assume these identifiers are not necessarily unique: several agents may have the same identifier. We only assume that they share $f(n)$ distinct identifiers.

More formally, a community protocol / homonym population protocol algorithm is then specified by:

1. an infinite set U of the possible identifiers. In the Homonym case, $U = \mathbb{N}$.
2. a function f associating to the size of the population the number of *identifiers* appearing in this population;
3. a finite set B of possible basic states;
4. an integer $d \geq 0$ representing the number of identifiers that can be remembered by an agent;
5. some input alphabet Σ and some output alphabet Y;
6. an input map $\iota : \Sigma \to B$ and an output map $\omega : B \to Y$;
7. a transition function $\delta : Q^2 \to Q^2$, with $Q = B \times U \times (U \cup \{\_\})^d$.

Remark 1. We assume to simplify writing in the following that δ is a function, but this could be a relation as in [13], without changing our results.

The state of an agent stores an element of B, the agent's identifier, together with up to d identifiers. If any of the d slots is not currently storing an identifier, it contains the *null* identifier $\_ \notin U$. In other words, $Q = B \times U \times (U \cup \{\_\})^d$ is the set of possible agent states. The transition relation indicates the result of a pairwise interaction: when agents in respective state q_1 and q_2 meet, they move to respectively state q_1' and q_2' whenever $\delta(q_1, q_2) = (q_1', q_2')$.

As in [13], we assume that agents store only identifiers they have learned from other agents (otherwise, they could be used as an external way of storing arbitrary information and this could be used as a space for computation in a non interesting and trivial way): if $\delta(q_1, q_2) = (q_1', q_2')$, and *id* appears in q_1', q_2' then *id* must appear in q_1 or in q_2.

As in [13], we assume that the identifiers of agents are chosen by some adversary, and not under the control of the program.

We add a hypothesis to the community model [13]: agents need to know when an identifier is equal to 0 and when two identifiers are consecutive (i.e. $id_1 = id_2 + 1$).

As we want to be minimal, we hence assume that this is the only hypothesis we make on identifiers in the following section. More formally, whenever $\delta(q_1, q_2) = (q'_1, q'_2)$, let $u_1 < u_2 < \cdots < u_k$ be the distinct identifiers that appear in any of the four states q_1, q_2, q'_1, q'_2. Let $v_1 < v_2 < \cdots < v_k$ be identifiers such that $u_1 = 0 \Leftrightarrow v_1 = 0$ and $v_i + 1 = v_{i+1} \Leftrightarrow u_i + 1 = u_{i+1}$. If $\rho(q)$ is the state obtained from q by replacing all occurrences of each identifier u_i by v_i, then we require that $\delta(\rho(q_1), \rho(q_2)) = (\rho(q'_1), \rho(q'_2))$.

From now on, an agent in state q with initial identifier k and $L = k_1, \ldots, k_d$ the list storing the d identifiers is denoted by $q_{k,L}$ or $q_{k,k_1,\ldots,k_d}$. If the list L is not relevant for the rule, we sometimes write q_k.

Remark 2. – This weakening of the original model does not change the computational power in the case where all agents have distinct identifiers.
- Our purpose is to establish results with minimal hypothesis. Our results work when identifiers are consecutive integers, say $\{0, 1, 2, \ldots, f(n) - 1\}$. This may be thought as a restriction. This is why we weaken to the above hypothesis, which seems to be the minimal hypothesis to make our proofs and constructions correct.
  We conjecture that without the possibility to know if an identifier is the successor of another one, the model is far too weak. Without this asumption, our first protocol (in Proposition 1) does not work.
- Notice that knowing whether an identifier is equal to 0 is not essential, but ease the explanation of our counting protocol of Proposition 1.

A configuration of the algorithm then consists of a finite vector of elements from Q. An input of size $n \geq 2$ is $f(n)$ non empty multisets X_i over alphabet Σ, one for each of the $f(n)$ identifiers. An initial configuration for n agents is a vector in Q^n of the form $((\iota(x_j), i-1, \_, \ldots, \_))_{1 \leq i \leq f(n), 1 \leq j \leq |X_i|}$ where x_j is the jth element of X_i: in other words, every agent starts in a basic state encoding $\iota(x_j)$, its associated identifier and no other identifier stored in its d slots.

If $C = (q^{(1)}, q^{(2)}, \ldots, q^{(n)})$ and $C' = (p^{(1)}, p^{(2)}, \ldots, p^{(n)})$ are two configurations, then we say that $C \to C'$ (C' is reachable from C in a unique step) if there are indices $i \neq j$ such that $\delta(q^{(i)}, q^{(j)}) = (p^{(i)}, p^{(j)})$ and $p^{(k)} = q^{(k)}$ for all k different from i and j. An execution is a sequence of configurations $C_0, C_1, \ldots$, such that C_0 is an initial configuration, and $C_i \to C_{i+1}$ for all i. An execution is fair if for each configuration C that appears infinitely often and for each C' such that $C \to C'$, C' appears infinitely often.

Example 1 (Leader Election). We adapt here a classical example of Population Protocol. We want a protocol that performs a leader election, with the additional hypothesis that when the election is terminated, all agents know the identifier of the leader (for the classical Population Protocol, it is not possible to store the identifier of the leader). If one prefers, each agent with identifier k starts with state $L_{k,\_}$, considering that it is a leader, with identifier k. We want that eventually at some time (i.e. in a finite number of steps), there will be a unique agent in state L_{k_0,k_0}, where k_0 is the identifier of this unique agent, and all the other agents in state N_{i,k_0} (where i is its identifier).

A protocol that solves the problem is the following: $f(n) = n$, $B = \{L, N\}$, $d = 1$ (only the identifier of the current leader is stored), $\Sigma = \{L\}$, $Y = True$, $\iota(L) = L$, $\omega(L) = \omega(N) = True$, and δ such that the rules are:

$$
\begin{array}{lll}
L_{k,\_} \; q \to L_{k,k} \; q & & \forall k \in \mathbb{N}, \forall q \in Q \\
L_{k,k} \; L_{k',k'} \to L_{k,k} \; N_{k',k} & & \forall k, k' \\
L_{k,k} \; N_{i,k'} \to L_{k,k} \; N_{i,k} & & \forall k, k', i \\
N_{i,k'} \; L_{k,k} \to N_{i,k} \; L_{k,k} & & \forall k, k', i \\
N_{i,k} \; N_{i',k'} \to N_{i,k} \; N_{i',k'} & & \forall k, k', i, i'
\end{array}
$$

By the fairness assumption, this protocol will reach a configuration where there is exactly one agent in state L_{k_0,k_0} for some identifier k_0. Then, by fairness again, this protocol will reach the final configuration $L_{k_0,k_0} \bigcup_{i \neq k_0} N_{i,k_0}$.

A configuration has an *Interpretation* $y \in Y$ if, for each agent in the population, its state q is such that $\omega(q) = y$. If there are two agents in state q_1 and q_2 such that $\omega(q_1) \neq \omega(q_2)$, then we say that the configuration has *No Interpretation.* A protocol is said to *compute the output* y from an input x if, for each fair sequence $(C_i)_{i \in \mathbb{N}}$ starting from an initial condition C_0 representing x, there exists i such that, for each $j \geq i$, C_j has the interpretation y. The protocol is said to compute function h if it computes $y = h(x)$ for all inputs x. A predicate is a function h whose range is $Y = \{0, 1\}$.

Observe that population protocols [1,3] are the special case of the protocols considered here where $d = 0$ and $f(n) = 1$. The following is known for the original model [1,3]:

Theorem 1 (Population Protocols [1]**).** *Any predicate over* $\mathbb{N}^k$ *that is first order definable in Presburger's arithmetic can be computed by a population protocol. Conversely, any predicate computed by a population protocol is a subset of* $\mathbb{N}^k$ *first order definable in Presburger's arithmetic.*

For the community protocols, Guerraoui and Ruppert established in [13] that computable predicates are exactly those of $NSPACE(n \log n)$, i.e. those of the class of languages recognized in non-deterministic space $n \log n$.

Notice that their convention of input in [13] requires that the input be distributed on agents ordered by identifiers.

Theorem 2 (Community Protocols [13]**).** *Community protocols can compute any predicate in* $NSPACE(n \log n)$*. Conversely, any predicate computed by such a community protocol is in the class* $NSPACE(n \log n)$*.*

Notice that Guerraoui and Ruppert [13] established that this holds even with Byzantine agents, under some rather strong conditions. We now determine what can be computed when the number of identifiers $f(n)$ is smaller than n. This will be done by first considering some basic protocols.

3 When Identifiers are Missing

3.1 Computing the Size of the Population

The population has its size in unary: each agent counting itself. However, the protocol can not use the value of the population size with this encoding. Indeed, there is always the possibility that an agent was not counted, and it looks not possible to track that. We introduce here a way to track the size the population permitting, at some point, to be sure to work on the whole population, not missing anyone anymore.

We first construct a protocol that computes n, that is to say the size of the population. Of course, since agents have a finite state, no single agent can store the whole size. We mean by "that computes n", the fact that the size of the population will be encoded by the global population.

Indeed, the protocol will perform a leader election over each identifier. We will call the set of leaders a *chain*. The size of the population will be written in binary on this chain (it will be possible as $f(n) \geq \log n$ in this part).

Clearly, once such a chain has been constructed, it can be used to store numbers or words, and can be used as the tape of a Turing Machine. We will often implicitly use in our description this trick in what follows. This will be used to simulate Turing machines in an even trickier way, in order to reduce space or identifiers.

Proposition 1 (Counting Protocol). *When we have $f(n)$ identifiers with $f(n) \geq \log n$, there exists an homonym population protocol that computes n: At some point, there are exactly $f(n)$ agents not in a particular state $\bot$, all having distinct identifiers. If we align these agents from the highest identifier to the lowest one, we get n written in binary.*

Remark 3. At that point, no agent knows the value of n (nor that the computation is over as usual for population protocol models). However, at that point, the population collectively encodes n.

Proof. Informally, the protocol initializes all agents to a particular state A. In parallel, it performs a leader election inside subsets of agents with same identifier. It also counts the number of agents: an agent that has already been counted is marked in a state different from A, and will not be used in the protocol anymore. An agent in state 1 (respectively 0, or 2) with identifier k represents 2^k (respectively 0, or 2^{k+1}) agents counted. Interactions between agents update those counts.

More formally, here is the protocol. The rules are as follows:

$A_0\ q_k \to 1_0\ q_k$	$\forall q, k$	$0_k\ 1_k \to \bot_k\ 1_k$	$\forall k$
$A_k\ 0_0 \to 0_k\ 1_0$	$\forall k \geq 1$	$1_k\ 1_k \to \bot_k\ 2_k$	$\forall k$
$A_k\ 1_0 \to 0_k\ 2_0$	$\forall k \geq 1$	$2_k\ 0_{k+1} \to 0_k\ 1_{k+1}$	$\forall k$
$0_k\ 0_k \to \bot_k\ 0_k$	$\forall k$	$2_k\ 1_{k+1} \to 0_k\ 2_{k+1}$	$\forall k$

This protocol has 3 steps. (i) At the beginning, all agents are in state A. A state A is transformed into a state 1, by adding 1 to an agent of identifier 0 (the 3 first rules). (ii) Rules 4 to 6 perform a leader election for each identifier, by merging the counted agents. (iii) The remaining rules correspond to summing together the counted agents, carrying on to the next identifier the 1.

Let v be the function over the states defined as follows for any k: $v(A_k) = 1$, $v(0_k) = v(\perp_k) = 0$, $v(1_k) = 2^k$, $v(2_k) = 2^{k+1}$. We can notice that the sum (of v values) over all the agents remains constant over the rules. Thus the sum always equals the number of agents in the population. By fairness, this protocol reaches the desired end. □

Remark 4.
- The previous counting protocol also works with $f(n) = \Omega(\log n)$. If $f(n) \geq \alpha \log n$ with $\alpha < 1$, then, using a base $\lceil e^{1/\alpha} \rceil$ instead of a base 2 ensures that n can be written on $f(n)$ digits.
- We use here the fact that the population knows if an identifier is equal to 0. We can work with identifiers in $[a, a + f(n) - 1]$. For this, agents store an identifier Id_m corresponding to the minimal one he saw (called here Id_m). An agent with identifier Id and state $i \in \{0, 1, 2\}$ stores $i \cdot 2^{Id-Id_m}$. When it meets an identifier equals to $Id_m - 1$, it looks for a leader with identifier $Id - 1$ to give it its stored integer.

From now on, when a proof says that the population uses its size, we suppose that the counting protocol has been performed and the protocol uses the chain to access to this information. Once again, the value of the size is encoded in the population (no agent knows it by itself).

3.2 Resetting a Computation

The computation of the value of size n (encoded as above) is crucial for the following protocols. From now on, we will call *the leader* the (or an) agent with identifier 0 not in state $\perp$ even if the previous protocol (computing the size of the population) has not yet finished.

We now provide a Reset protocol. This protocol has the goal to reach a configuration such that (i) the previous protocol is over, (ii) all agents but the leader are in state R, and (iii) the leader knows when this configuration is reached. This protocol then permits to launch the computation of some other protocols using the chain created and the size of the population computed (i.e. encoded globally in the population).

Proposition 2 (Reset Protocol). *There exists a Reset protocol containing the states F and R such that, once the counting protocol is finished, only one agent will reach state F at some point. As soon as this agent is in state F, all the other agents are in state R.*

This configuration permits to know for sure that all agents are at the same step, with a leader being aware of that, being in state F.

Proof. The idea of this protocol is to reset each time the leader sees that the counting protocol (of the previous proposition) has not finished yet. There are two possible states for the non-leader agents: S and R. First, the leader turn to state S other agents, and second turns agents in state S into state R and count them (by the same way to counting protocol). When the leader manages to turn m agents (where m is the computed size with the counting protocol), it knows that if the counting protocol has finished, the reset protocol is over. It turns its own state into F. □

3.3 Counting Agents in a Given State

We use the previous constructions to create a protocol that can write in its chain[2], with the request of an input symbol $s \in \Sigma$ and an *identifier* Id, the number of agents that started with this *identifier* and this input symbol.

Proposition 3. *When we have $f(n) = \Omega(\log n)$ identifiers, if the reset protocol has finished, for all input $s \in \Sigma$ and for all $Id \leq f(n)$, there exists a protocol that encodes the number of agents initialised as s_{Id}.*

Proof. Recall that s_{Id} means input s with identifier Id. We cannot use directly the counting protocol. We cannot store forever this value if the request is done for each s_{Id}, as agents have a finite memory. Because of that, the protocol will need to be sure that the computation is over to move forward and clean the computation. We will use here the fact that the total number of agents is known (as the computation is reset until this knowledge is reached), by counting the number of agents in the initial state s_k and, at the same time, counting again the whole population. Once we have reached the right total for the population, we know that we have counted all the agents in the requested initial state. □

Remark 5. In other words, if at some moment, the population needs to know the number of agents which started in the state s_{Id}, this is possible.

3.4 Simulating the Reading Tape

With all these ingredients we will now simulate a tape of a Turing machine. First, we need to define which kind of Turing machines we consider. Basically, we are only stating that from the definitions of the models, only symmetric predicates or data can be processed or computed. Our definitions are an adaptation of the usual models to fit to our inputs.

Definition 1 (f-Symmetry). *A Language $L \in (\Sigma \cup \#)$ is f-symmetric if and only if:*

- $\# \notin \Sigma$;
- *Words of L are all of the form $w = x_1\#x_2\#\ldots\#x_{f(n)}$, with $|x_1| + |x_2| + \ldots + |x_{f(n)}| = n$ and $\forall i$, $x_i \in \Sigma^+$;*
- *If, $\forall i$, x'_i is a permutation of x_i, and if $x_1\#x_2\#\ldots\#x_{f(n)} \in L$, then $x'_1\#x'_2\#\ldots\#x'_{f(n)} \in L$;*

Each x_i is a non-empty multiset over alphabet Σ.

[2] Recall the concept of the chain defined in page 7.

Definition 2 (*$MNSPACE(S(n))$*). *Let S be a function $\mathbb{N} \to \mathbb{N}$. We write $MNSPACE(S(n), f(n))$, or $MNSPACE(S(n))$ when f is unambiguous, for the set of $f-$symmetric languages recognized by Non Deterministic Turing Machines on space $O(S(n))$.*

Definition 3 (*$SMNSPACE(S(n))$*). *We write $SMNSPACE(S(n), f(n))$, or $SMNSPACE(S(n))$ when f is unambiguous, for the set of $f-$symmetric languages recognized by Non Deterministic Turing Machines on space $O(S(n))$, where languages are also stable under the permutation of the multisets (i.e. for any permutation σ, $x_1\#x_2\#\ldots\#x_{g(n)} \in L \Leftrightarrow x_{\sigma(1)}\#x_{\sigma(2)}\#\ldots\#x_{\sigma(g(n))} \in L$).*

Remark 6. We have $NSPACE(S(n)) = MNSPACE(S(n), n)$ and $SNSPACE(S(n)) = MNSPACE(S(n), 1)$.

Here is a weaker bound than the one we will obtain. The idea of this proof helps to understand the stronger result.

Proposition 4. *Any language in $MNSPACE(\log n, \log n)$ can be recognized by an homonym population protocol with $\log n$ identifiers.*

Proof. The main idea of this proof is to use the chain as a tape for a Turing Machine. To simulate the tape of the Turing machine, we store the position where the head of the Turing machine is by memorizing on which multiset the head is (via the corresponding identifier) and its relative position inside this multiset: the previous protocol will be used to find out the number of agents with some input symbol in the current multiset, in order to update all these information and simulate the evolution of the Turing Machine step by step.

More precisely, let $M \in MNSPACE(\log n, \log n)$. There exists some $k \in \mathbb{N}$ such that M uses at most $k \log n$ bits for each input of size n. To an input $x_1\#x_2\#\ldots\#x_{f(n)}$ we associate the input configuration with, for each $s \in \Sigma$ and for each $i \leq f(n)$, $|x_i|_s$ agents in state k with the identifier $(i-1)$, $|x_i|_s$ being the number of s in x_i.

The idea is to use the chain as the tape of the Turing Machine. We give k bits to each agent, so that the protocol has a tape of the good length (the chain is of size $\log n$). We just need to simulate the reading of the tape. The protocol starts by counting the population and resetting agents after that.

We assume that symbols on Σ are ordered. Since the language recognized by M is $\log n$-symmetric, we can reorganize the input by permuting the x_is such that the input symbols are ordered.

Here are the steps to perform the simulation of reading the tape:

0. The chain contains two counters. The leader also stores an identifier Id and a state s. The first counter stores the total of s_{Id} computed at some point by the protocol of Proposition 3. The second counter c_2 is the position the reading head. The simulated head is on the c_2th s of x_{Id+1}.
1. At the beginning of the protocol, the population counts the number of S_0, where S_0 is the minimal element of Σ. c_2 is initialized to 1.

2. When the machines needs to go right on the reading tape, c_2 is incremented. If c_2 equals c_1, then the protocol looks for the next state s' in the order of Σ, and count the number of s'_{Id}. If this value is 0, then it takes the next one. If s was the last one, then the reading tape will consider to be on a #. If the reading head was on a #, then it looks for the successor identifier of Id, and counts the number of S_0. If Id was maximal, the machine knows it has reached the end of the input tape.
3. The left movement process is similar to this one.

This protocol can simulate the writing on a tape and the reading of the input. To simulate the non deterministic part, each time the leader needs to make a non deterministic choice between two possibilities, it looks for an agent. If the first agent the leader meets has its identifier equal to 1, then the leader does the first choice, otherwise it choses the second one.

This protocol simulates M. □

Corollary 1. *Let f such that $f(n) = \Omega(\log n)$. Any language in $MNSPACE$ $(f(n),\ f(n))$ can be recognized by an homonym population protocol with $f(n)$ identifiers.*

Proof. We use the same protocol (which is possible as the size of the population can be computed). Since the chain of *identifiers* has a length of $f(n)$, we have access to a tape of size $f(n)$. □

3.5 Recognizing Polylogarithmic Space

Proposition 5. *Let f such that $f = \Omega(\log n)$. Let k be a positive integer.*

Any language in $MNSPACE\left(\log^k n, f(n)\right)$ can be recognized by a protocol with $f(n)$ identifiers.

Proof. The idea here is that, by combining several *identifiers* together, we get much more identifiers available, increasing the chain and space of computation: if we combine m *identifiers* together, we get $f(n)^m$ possible *identifiers*.

First the population performs the computation of the size of the population. Second, it gets a chain of all the identifiers. Third, the leader then creates a counter of m identifiers, initialized at 0^m (seen as the number $0 \dots 0$ written in base $f(n)$). Four, it looks for a $\perp$ agent and gives him its stored m-tuple, then increases its m-tuple. As soon as it has finished (by giving $f(n)^m$ or n identifiers, depending on what happens first), the protocol can work on a tape of space $f(n)^m$.

Since $f(n) = \Omega(\log n)$, there exists some m such that $f(n)^m \geq \log^k n$. □

Theorem 3. *Let f such that there exists some real $r > 0$ such that we have $f(n) = \Omega(\log^r n)$.*

Any language in $\bigcup_{k \geq 1} MNSPACE(\log^k n, f(n))$ can be recognized by an homonym population protocol with $f(n)$ identifiers.

Proof. We only need to treat the counting protocol when $r < 1$ (the case $r = 1$ is treated in Proposition 5, the case $r > 1$ is a direct corollary of this proposition). Let $l = \lceil \frac{1}{r} \rceil$. We will use a l-tuple for each agent. When agents realize that $f(n)$ might be reached and they need more space, they use the tuple, storing the maximal *identifier* Id_1. If at some point, they realize that a bigger *identifier* Id_2 exists, they just do a translation of the numbers stored in the chain.

With $f(n)^l = \Omega(\log n)$ identifiers and the right basis to write the size, we can be sure to have enough space to compute the size of the population. We can then use previous protocols using $(k \cdot l)$-uples to use the required space. □

3.6 Only Polylogarithmic Space

Theorem 4. *Consider a predicate computed by a protocol with $f(n)$ identifiers. Assume that $f(n) = O(\log^l n)$ for some $l \geq 1$.*

The predicate is in $MNSPACE(\log^k n, f(n))$ for some positive integer k.

Proof. We need to prove that there exists a Turing Machine that can compute, for any given input x, the output of the protocol P.

From definitions, given some input x, P outputs the output y on input x if and only if there exists a finite sequence $(C_i)_{i \in \mathbb{N}}$, starting from an initial condition C_0 representing x, that reaches at some finite time j some configuration C_j with interpretation y, and so that any configuration reachable from C_j has also interpretation y.

This latter property can be expressed as a property on the graph of configurations of the protocol, i.e. on the graph whose nodes are configurations of size n, and whose edges corresponds to unique step reachability: one must check the existence of a path from C_0 to some C_j with interpretation y so that there is no path from C_j to some other C' with interpretation different from y.

Such a problem can be solved in $NSPACE(\log N)$ where N denotes the number of nodes of this graph. Indeed, guessing a path from C_0 to some C_j can easily be done in $NSPACE(\log N)$ by guessing intermediate nodes (configurations) between C_0 and C_j. There remains to see that testing if there is no path from C_j to some other C' with interpretation different from y can also be done in $NSPACE(\log N)$ to conclude.

But observe that testing if there is a path from C_j to some other C' with interpretation different from y is clearly in $NSPACE(\log N)$ by guessing C'. From Immerman-Szelepcsnyi's Theorem [14,16] we know that $NSPACE(\log N) = coNSPACE(\log N)$. Hence, testing if there is no path from C_j to some other C' with interpretation different from y is indeed also in $NSPACE(\log N)$.

It remains now to evaluate N: For a given identifier i, an agent encodes basically some basic state $b \in B$, and d identifiers $u_1, u_2, \ldots, u_d$. There are at most n agents in a given state $(i, b, u_1, u_2, \ldots, u_d)$. Hence $N = O(n^{|B| \cdot f(n)^{d+1}})$. In other words, the algorithm above in $NSPACE(\log N)$ is hence basically in $MNSPACE((|B| \cdot f(n)^{d+1}) \log n, f(n)) \subset MNSPACE(\log^k n, f(n))$ for some k. □

Theorem 5. *Let f such that for some r, we have $f(n) = \Omega(\log^r n)$. The set of functions computable by homonym population protocols with $f(n)$ identifiers corresponds exactly to $\bigcup_{k\geq 1} MNSPACE(\log^k n, f(n))$.*

3.7 When We Have n^ϵ Identifiers

One can go from n^ϵ (with $\epsilon > 0$) to a space of computation equivalent to the case where $f(n) = n$: We just need to use a k-tuple of identifiers.

Theorem 6 ($n^{1/k}$ Identifiers). *Let f such that there exists some $k \in \mathbb{N}$ such that $f(n) \geq n^{1/k}$. The set of functions computable by homonym population protocols with $f(n)$ identifiers corresponds exactly to $MNSPACE(n \log n, f(n))$.*

Remark 7. This result does not need the two restrictions of knowing if an identifier is equal to 0 or if two identifiers are consecutive. The result holds when U is chosen arbitrarily and when the restrictions over the rules are those in [13].

4 Passively Mobile Machines

We now show how previous constructions improve the results about the model from [7]:

Definition 4 ($PMSPACE(S(n))$). *[7] Let S be a function.*

We write $PMSPACE(S(n))$ for the set of languages recognized by population protocols where each agent has a Turing Machine with a tape of size at least $S(n)$.

Theorem 7. $PMSPACE(\log \log n) = \bigcup_{k\geq 1} SNSPACE(log^k n)$.

Proof. **1.** $\bigcup_{k\geq 1} SNSPACE(log^k n) \subset PMSPACE(\log \log n)$.

The idea of this proof is quite simple: Let $M \in SNSPACE(log^k n)$. We can notice that $SNSPACE(log^k n) \subset MNSPACE(log^k n, \log n)$. From Theorem 5, there is a population protocol computing M. We will simulate it. With space $O(\log \log n)$, we can simulate a population protocol with $O(2^{\log \log n}) = O(\log n)$ identifiers.

To create $\log n$ identifiers, we adapt a bit the counting protocol. At the beginning, each agent has the identifier 0. When two agents with the same *identifier* meet, if each one contains the integer 1, the first switch its integer to 0, the other increases its own *identifier*.

We then just need to simulate the behavior of each agent as if they have started with their created *identifier*. It requires a space of size $|B|+(d+1) \log \log n$ plus some constant, which is enough.

2. $PMSPACE(\log \log n) \subset \bigcup_{k\geq 1} SNSPACE(log^k n)$: The proof is similar to the one of Theorem 4. □

With a similar proof, we can get the following result that gives a good clue for the gap between $\log \log n$ and $\log n$:

Corollary 2. *Let f such that $f(n) = \Omega(\log \log n)$ and $f(n) = o(\log n)$.*

$SNSPACE(2^{f(n)} f(n)) \subset PMSPACE(f(n)) \subset SNSPACE(2^{f(n)} \log n)$.

5 Summary

From the model given by Guerraoui and Ruppert [13], we introduced a hierarchy according to the number of accessible identifiers in the population:

- With a constant number of the identifiers, the existence of identifiers is useless.
- With $\Theta(\log^r n)$ identifiers, homonym population protocols can exactly recognize any language in $\bigcup_{k\in\mathbb{N}} MNSPACE\left(\log^k n\right)$.
- Homonym population protocols with $\Theta(n^\epsilon)$ identifiers have same power that homonym population protocols with n identifiers.

It remains an open question: is the knowledge of consecutive values of two identifiers crucial or not? Our guess is that it is essential to be able to compute for sure the size of the population. Protocols without this assumption have not been found yet.

Chatzigiannakis *et al.* [7] started a hierarchy over protocols depending on how much space of computation each agent has. The paper left an open question on the gap between $o(\log\log n)$ and $O(\log n)$. We provided an answer, stating that with $\Theta(\log\log n)$ space, we compute exactly $\bigcup_{k\in\mathbb{N}} SNSPACE\left(\log^k n\right)$.

It remains the gap between $O(\log\log n)$ and $O(\log n)$, where we currently just have the following bounds:
$SNSPACE(2^{f(n)}f(n)) \subset PMSPACE(f(n)) \subset SNSPACE(2^{f(n)}\log n)$.

References

1. Angluin, D., Aspnes, J., Eisenstat, D., Ruppert, E.: The computational power of population protocols. Distrib. Comput. **20**(4), 279–304 (2007)
2. Angluin, D., Aspnes, J., Chan, M., Fischer, M.J., Jiang, H., Peralta, R.: Stably computable properties of network graphs. In: Prasanna, V.K., Iyengar, S.S., Spirakis, P.G., Welsh, M. (eds.) DCOSS 2005. LNCS, vol. 3560, pp. 63–74. Springer, Heidelberg (2005)
3. Angluin, D., Aspnes, J., Diamadi, Z., Fischer, M.J., Peralta, R.: Computation in networks of passively mobile finite-state sensors. In: Twenty-Third ACM Symposium on Principles of Distributed Computing, pp. 290–299. ACM Press (2004)
4. Angluin, D., Aspnes, J., Fischer, M.J., Jiang, H.: Self-stabilizing population protocols. In: Anderson, J.H., Prencipe, G., Wattenhofer, R. (eds.) OPODIS 2005. LNCS, vol. 3974, pp. 103–117. Springer, Heidelberg (2006)
5. Arévalo, S., Fernández Anta, A., Imbs, D., Jiménez, E., Raynal, M.: Failure detectors in homonymous distributed systems (with an application to consensus). In: 2012 IEEE 32nd International Conference on Distributed Computing Systems (ICDCS), pp. 275–284 (2012)
6. Aspnes, J., Ruppert, E.: An introduction to population protocols. In: Bulletin of the EATCS, vol. 93, pp. 106–125 (2007)
7. Chatzigiannakis, I., Michail, O., Nikolaou, S., Pavlogiannis, A., Spirakis, P.G.: Passively mobile communicating machines that use restricted space. Theoret. Comput. Sci. **412**(46), 6469–6483 (2011). please check and confirm inserted volume number and page range is correct in Ref. [7]

8. Chatzigiannakis, I., Michail, O., Spirakis, P.G.: Algorithmic verification of population protocols. In: Dolev, S., Cobb, J., Fischer, M., Yung, M. (eds.) SSS 2010. LNCS, vol. 6366, pp. 221–235. Springer, Heidelberg (2010)
9. Delporte-Gallet, C., Fauconnier, H., Guerraoui, R., Kermarrec, A., Ruppert, E., Tran-The, H.: Byzantine agreement with homonyms. In: 30th Annual ACM SIGACT-SIGOPS Symposium on Principles of Distributed Computing, PODC 2011, pp. 21–30 (2011)
10. Delporte-Gallet, C., Fauconnier, H., Guerraoui, R., Ruppert, E.: When birds die: making population protocols fault-tolerant. In: Gibbons, P.B., Abdelzaher, T., Aspnes, J., Rao, R. (eds.) DCOSS 2006. LNCS, vol. 4026, pp. 51–66. Springer, Heidelberg (2006)
11. Delporte-Gallet, C., Fauconnier, H., Tran-The, H.: Homonyms with forgeable identifiers. In: Even, G., Halldórsson, M.M. (eds.) SIROCCO 2012. LNCS, vol. 7355, pp. 171–182. Springer, Heidelberg (2012)
12. Di Luna, G.A., Baldoni, R., Bonomi, S., Chatzigiannakis, I.: Counting the number of homonyms in dynamic networks. In: Higashino, T., Katayama, Y., Masuzawa, T., Potop-Butucaru, M., Yamashita, M. (eds.) SSS 2013. LNCS, vol. 8255, pp. 311–325. Springer, Heidelberg (2013)
13. Guerraoui, R., Ruppert, E.: Names trump malice: tiny mobile agents can tolerate byzantine failures. In: Albers, S., Marchetti-Spaccamela, A., Matias, Y., Nikoletseas, S., Thomas, W. (eds.) ICALP 2009, Part II. LNCS, vol. 5556, pp. 484–495. Springer, Heidelberg (2009)
14. Immerman, N.: Nondeterministic space is closed under complementation. In: Structure in Complexity Theory Conference, Third Annual, pp. 112–115. IEEE (1988)
15. Schönhage, A.: Storage modification machines. SIAM J. Comput. **9**(3), 490–508 (1980)
16. Szelepcsényi, R.: The method of forced enumeration for nondeterministic automata. Acta Inf. **26**(3), 279–284 (1988)

Aspect-Based Realization of Non-functional Concerns in Business Processes

Anis Charfi(✉) and Haolin Zhi

SAP SE, Bleichstrasse 8, 64283 Darmstadt, Germany
{anis.charfi,haolin.zhi}@sap.com

Abstract. While functional concerns are well supported in current business process modeling languages such as the Business Process Modeling Notation (BPMN), many important non-functional concerns such as security and quality of service (QoS) cannot be expressed. Some works proposed specific extensions to business process modeling languages to express certain non-functional concerns. However, most related works focus only on expressing non-functional properties in business process models without considering their realization on the implementation level. In this paper, we present a generic approach to non-functional concerns in business processes and bridge the gap between process modeling and process implementation by generating AO4BPEL aspects that enforce and realize the non-functional properties specified in the business process model. The functional part of the processes is realized by generating executable WS-BPEL code out of BPMN process models. The approach is not specific to a particular non-functional concern and the usage of aspects ensures a modular implementation of the business process.

Keywords: Business process modeling · Non-functional concerns · Aspects · BPMN · AO4BPEL · WS-BPEL

1 Introduction

Current business process modeling languages such as the Business Process Modeling Notation (BPMN) [9] provide good support for expressing the functional concerns in a business process. However, they do not allow expressing important non-functional concerns such as security and quality of service. To address this limitation, several works [7,11,13,18] proposed extensions to business process modeling languages in order to express certain non-functional concerns. However, these proposals are generally specific to a particular non-functional concern. Further, they mostly focus only on the modeling level and do not consider the realization of non-functional properties on the implementation level. In most state of the art approaches the designers enrich the business process model with additional information about non-functional properties by means of the above mentioned extensions. Then, the enriched process models are taken as a reference by the technical developers implementing the business process. The manual

A. Bouajjani and H. Fauconnier (Eds.): NETYS 2015, LNCS 9466, pp. 140–154, 2015.
DOI: 10.1007/978-3-319-26850-7_10

realization of the non-functional properties can result in a different implementation from what the designers specified. Furthermore, the lack of an appropriate approach and of tool support for the realization of non-functional properties makes their implementation difficult and error-prone.

In a previous work of the first author of this paper [16] a generic meta-model and an approach for expressing non-functional properties in business process models were presented. In the current paper we focus on the realization of non-functional concerns in business processes using a model-driven and generative approach. In particular we generate executable processes in WS-BPEL [8] for the functional part of the business process model and AO4BPEL [2] aspects for the non-functional concerns.

Our contributions in this paper are many-fold. First, we define a mapping from non-functional properties in BPMN business processes to AO4BPEL aspects. Second, we present code generators supporting the realization of the BPMN business processes including a WS-BPEL generator and an aspect generator. Third, we extend the approach presented in [16] into a holistic approach supporting both the specification and realization of non-functional concerns in business processes. Fourth, we present an integrated Eclipse-based tool set supporting our approach and model-driven development of service based business processes.

The remainder of this paper is organized as follows. Section 2 presents a motivating example. Section 3 presents the proposed approach and gives examples for illustration. Section 4 presents the toolset supporting our approach. Section 5 reports on related work and Sect. 6 concludes the paper.

2 Motivating Example

In this section we introduce a simple business process for travel booking in a travel agency to illustrate the modeling of functional and non-functional concerns in business processes. This process is shown in Fig. 1 using the BPMN notation. To keep this example simple and clear only the key elements are specified and error handling is not shown.

This process starts when a customer sends a travel booking request to the travel agency. The request contains the necessary data for the booking such as the dates and the destination. After receiving this request, a flight booking activity and a hotel booking activity are started in parallel. The flight booking activity calls a web service of airline companies to find a flight that satisfies the customer criteria. At the same time, the hotel booking activity is started, which calls a service for finding the accommodation. The created offer is then sent to the customer for review and approval. Once the customer accepts the offer he is asked to enter the credit card details for payment and a bank web service is called to charge the credit card. Once the payment is completed successfully a confirmation mail is sent to the customer with all booking details.

There are several non-functional requirements in this simple business process. First, the credit card information has to be handled confidentially to protect it

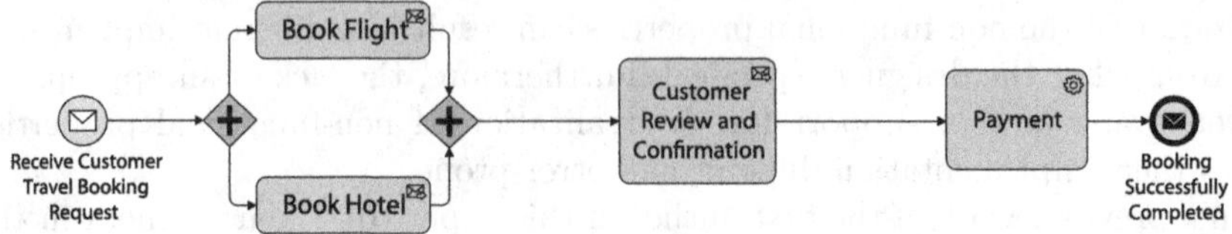

Fig. 1. Travel booking process

when the respective messages are sent to the bank over the Internet. Second, once the customer accepts the offer he should not be able to deny having done this. Third, since user experience is nowadays a key factor in online transactions the response time of the booking service should be acceptable. The travel agency is interested in monitoring the total execution time of the flight and hotel booking activities to ensure a good quality of service (QoS). If that execution time exceeds 10 seconds an alert message has to be raised and the current process instance information needs to be logged down.

Existing process modeling languages lack appropriate means for expressing non-functional concerns such as the ones mentioned above. Several works [11,13, 18] defined extensions of BPMN to express particular non-functional concerns. With respect to the modeling level, most extensions modify the BPMN meta-model in a heavy-weight manner. Furthermore, the extensions are not based on a common meta-model and therefore they cannot be composed with each other. This means that these extensions cannot be used together in a same business process model. In addition, most existing extensions are specific to a particular concern and are not directly applicable to other non-functional concerns. With respect to process implementation, we observe that most existing works focus on the modeling level (i.e., on specifying non-functional requirements) without addressing the realization of those requirements.

3 Proposed Solution

To address the problems explained in the previous sections we propose a model-driven and generative approach for specifying and realizing non-functional properties in business process models. Figure 2 gives a high-level overview of that approach. On the modeling level our approach expects business process models in BPMN including a specification of non-functional properties based on the profile concept we presented in [16]. For bridging the gap between modeling and execution of business processes and at the same time supporting non-functional concerns we defined two mappings. The first mapping is for the non-functional part and it maps non-functional requirements to aspect code in AO4BPEL [2,6]. The second mapping is for the functional part and it maps the BPMN process to a WS-BPEL process. Based on these two mappings we implemented two code generators as Eclipse plugins using the Xpand[1] framework for Model-to-Text

[1] http://www.eclipse.org/modeling/m2t/?project=xpand.

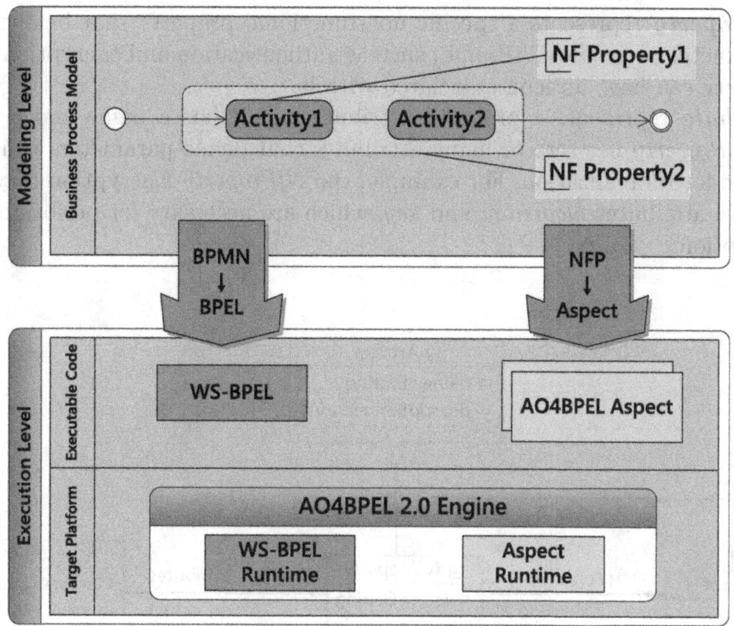

Fig. 2. Approach in a nutshell

transformation. The generated process and aspect code can then be deployed on the AO4BPEL 2.0 Server[2], which is an aspect-oriented extension of the Apache ODE Server[3]. This engine supports the dynamic weaving of aspects and processes and thus executes the WS-BPEL process while realizing the non-functional requirements. The proposed approach and the respective tool set allow a modular implementation of service based business processes.

3.1 Expressing Non-functional Requirements

To express non-functional concerns in BPMN business process models we used non-functional profiles [16], which were proposed in a previous work of the first author of this paper in analogy to the profile concept of UML.

Non-functional Profiles. The meta-model for non-functional profiles is shown in Fig. 3. It defines three main concepts:

- ***NfProfile*** represents a group of non-functional properties related to one concern, such as security and quality of service (QoS).

[2] https://github.com/alook/ao4bpel2.
[3] http://ode.apache.org.

- ***NfProperty*** represents a specific non-functional property that belongs to a non-functional profile (*NfProfile*) such as authentication and encryption. Each property can have an icon associated with it.
- ***Attribute*** represents a property attribute and it has a name and a value. An *NfProperty* has zero or many attributes that define parameters which are needed for its realization. For example, the *NfProperty* Encryption may have the two attributes *algorithm* and *key*, which are necessary for performing the encryption.

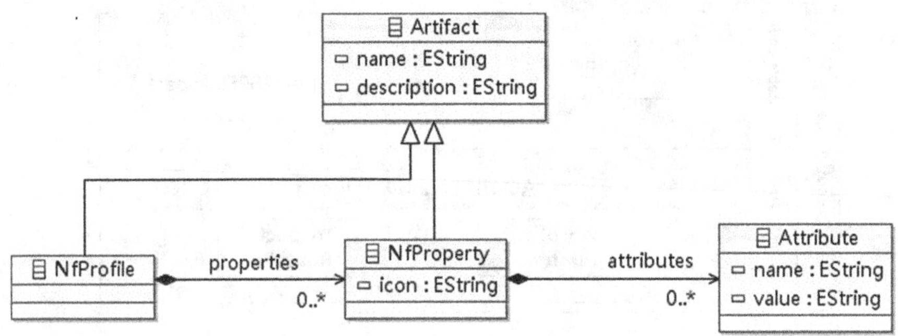

Fig. 3. Meta-model for non-functional profiles

Based on this meta-model, non-functional profiles can be defined using an EMF based editor that we developed. Then the profiles can be imported in an extended version of the Eclipse STP BPMN Editor[4], which provides a graphical annotation for each property in the profile and which allows editing the property attributes using property sheets. The annotations expressing non-functional properties can be then connected with BPMN elements using associations. In this approach the meta-model of BPMN is unchanged as we only define an extension of the artifact text annotation according to BPMN extensibility guidelines.

As examples, we show two simple profiles for expressing quality of service (QoS) and security. The non-functional properties in each profile and their attributes are shown respectively in Tables 1 and 2.

Associating Annotations to Process Elements and Execution Order. The annotations, which represent the non functional properties, can be associated with a single activity or with a group of activities as shown in Fig. 4. In that figure the property *NF-Property1* is associated with the activities *Activity1* and *Activity2*, which means that this property applies individually to each of these two activities. The property *NF-Property2* is associated with a group which contains the three activities *Activity1*, *Activity2* and *Activity3*, which means that the property *NF-Property2* applies around this group of activities.

[4] http://wiki.eclipse.org/STP/BPMN_Component/STP_BPMN_Presentation.

Table 1. Monitoring profile

QoS property	**Attributes** [Possible Values]	**Notation**
Logging: This property expresses that the runtime information of the associated activity should be logged.	**parameters** [true/false]: indicates whether the parameters should be logged at runtime. **soapMessage** [true/false]: indicates whether the soap messages exchanged with the partner service should be logged.	
ExecTime: This property expresses that the execution time of this activity should not be under the minimum value or exceed the maximum value, otherwise an alert will be raised.	**min:** minimum value in ms. **max:** maximum value in ms. **alert** [DB/File/WS]: where the alert message is to be delivered: store in Database, Log File, or invoke a Web Service.	
NumberOfExec: This property expresses that the number of executions of an activity should not be under the minimum threshold or exceed the maximum threshold, otherwise an alert will be raised.	**min:** minimum number of executions. **max:** maximum number of executions. **alert** [DB/File/WS]: where the alert message should be delivered: store in Database, Log File or invoke a Web Service call.	

Table 2. Security profile

Security property	**Attributes**	**Notation**
Timestamp: This property expresses the period after which the message expires.	**timeToLive** (ms)	
Authentication: This property expresses the user credentials.	**username** **password**	
Encryption: This property expresses that the message should be encrypted.	**keyIdentifierType** **symmetricEncAlgorithm** **keyEncAlgorithm** **transportKeyId**	
Signature: This property expresses that the message should be signed.	**keyIdentifierType** **signatureAlgorithm** **signatureCanonicalization** **digestAlgorithm**	

As it is possible to associate several non-functional properties with the same BPMN element we need to specify the order of those properties. For that purpose, we use numbers on the associations of non-functional properties to process

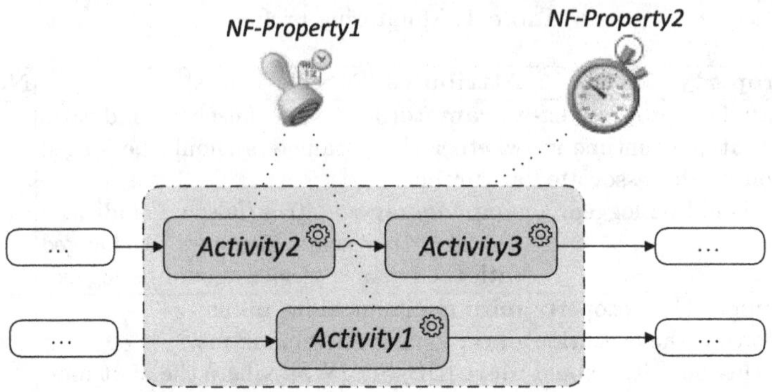

Fig. 4. Association of non-functional properties to BPMN elements

elements. Non-functional properties with lower numbers on their associations will be executed before the ones with higher numbers.

Revisiting the Motivation Example. In Fig. 5 we use non-functional properties from the QoS and security profiles to express some non-functional requirements of the travel agency business process. We associate the encryption annotation to the payment activity to express that the respective data should be encrypted according to WS-Security. We also associate the execution time annotation to the group containing the activities book flight and book hotel to express that both activities should be executed in less than 10 s.

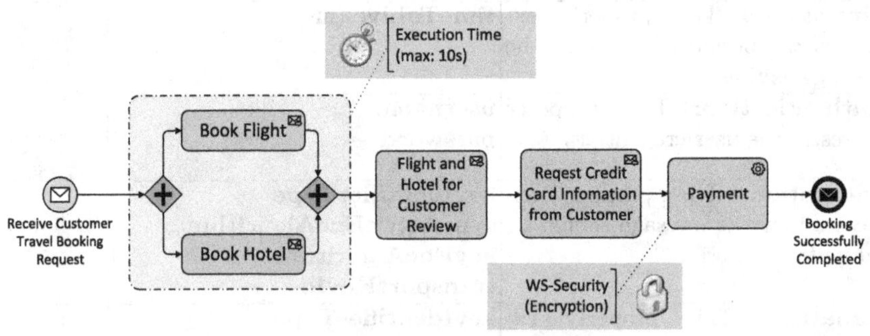

Fig. 5. Travel booking process with non-functional annotations

3.2 Realizing the Non-functional Properties

As shown in Fig. 2, the business process model, which is annotated with non-functional properties, is realized by generating an executable process in WS-BPEL [8] for the functional part and generating AO4BPEL aspects [2] for the non-functional part. The choice of this aspect-based realization ensures a modular implementation, in which the functional and non-functional parts are separated. In this way, understanding and maintaining the WS-BPEL code and the aspect code will be easier. For example, the security expert would just need to focus on the security aspect and does not need to understand aspects implementing other concerns. Furthermore, when the implementation of a non-functional property changes, for example, when an encryption module is upgraded or replaced, then only the respective aspect needs to be regenerated and redeployed. In all these cases the core business process in WS-BPEL remains unchanged.

AO4BPEL [2] is an aspect-oriented extension of WS-BPEL. Like WS-BPEL this extension is also based on XML, i.e., aspects are XML documents. An aspect can contain one or more pointcut and advice elements. Pointcuts are queries that select one or more join points, i.e., activities defined in one or several WS-BPEL processes. AO4BPEL supports XPath and recently Prolog also as pointcut languages. The advice language of AO4BPEL is standard WS-BPEL with some extensions such as the *proceed* activity and constructs for accessing the context of the join point activity. The advice activity can be executed before, after, or instead of the activities selected by the respective pointcut. To execute the generated WS-BPEL process and AO4BPEL aspects we use the orchestration engine AO4BPEL 2.0 Server [6]. This engine is an aspect-aware extension of the Apache ODE Server, which can weave aspects and processes at runtime.

For the realization of the business process including non-functional properties we defined two mappings: one from BPMN to WS-BPEL and one from non-functional properties to AO4BPEL. For each mapping we implemented a corresponding Xpand-based code generator. Regarding the mapping of BPMN to WS-BPEL we observe that various works [10,17] addressed that topic from a conceptual perspective by proposing mapping algorithms. However, the existing mappings are based on older versions of BPMN and WS-BPEL and there are no available code generators supporting those mappings. The only available open source tool is BPMN2BPEL[5], which is very limited in its scope and also based on the old BPMN 1.0 version. This tool is not developed anymore since five years. Due to space limitations we focus in this paper on the mapping of non-functional properties to AO4BPEL aspects.

Mapping Non-functional Properties to Aspects. For each non-functional property in a profile a corresponding AO4BPEL aspect template has to be defined by the expert in a given non-functional domain. Each aspect template is responsible for realizing a specific property and consists of two parts: a static part and a dynamic part. The static part is common among all aspects that enforce the same type of property. The dynamic part is the variable part of the aspect, which contains the missing information in the aspect template. It depends on the concrete association of the non-functional property to an element in the business process model and also on the concrete attribute values.

[5] http://code.google.com/p/bpmn2bpel.

The mapping of a non-functional property to an AO4BPEL aspect consists of two steps:

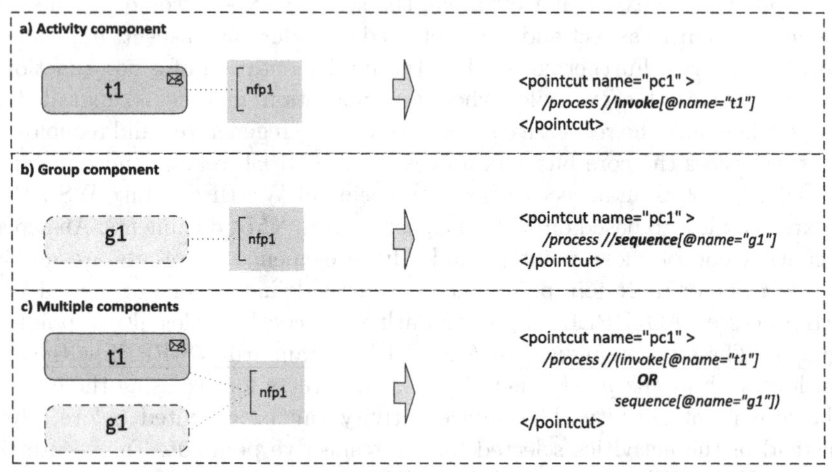

Fig. 6. Cases for pointcut mapping

1. The association between the non-functional property modeled as annotation and the BPMN process elements is transformed to an XPath pointcut expression in the respective AO4BPEL aspect. Figure 6 depicts different cases of mapping from the association in BPMN to the corresponding pointcut expression in AO4BPEL. The non-functional property in the business process model can be associated with a single activity or with a group of activities. In addition, each non-functional property can have one or multiple associations with elements of the process model. As a result, there are three different cases to be distinguished:
   - **Association with a single activity:** The association with an activity in BPMN is transformed into an XPath expression selecting the corresponding WS-BPEL activity by its name.
   - **Association with a group:** The group of activities in BPMN is transformed into the structured activity *sequence* in WS-BPEL. The association with this group in BPMN is transformed into an XPath expression selecting the corresponding *sequence* in WS-BPEL by its name.
   - **Association with multiple elements:** The association with multiple elements is translated to multiple XPath expressions that are later combined with the logical operator **or**.
2. All attribute values of the non-functional property are copied to the corresponding variables and their parts in the respective AO4BPEL aspect. These variables are then used as container of input data for service calls to middleware web services that enforce the different non-functional properties.

Mapping Example. Figure 7 illustrates the mapping of a non-functional property to an AO4BPEL aspect using *Encryption* as an example. The property *encryption* is associated with the *Payment* activity of the travel agency process. In this figure the dynamic part of the aspect is denoted in boldface. The generation of the AO4BPEL aspect in this example works as follows:

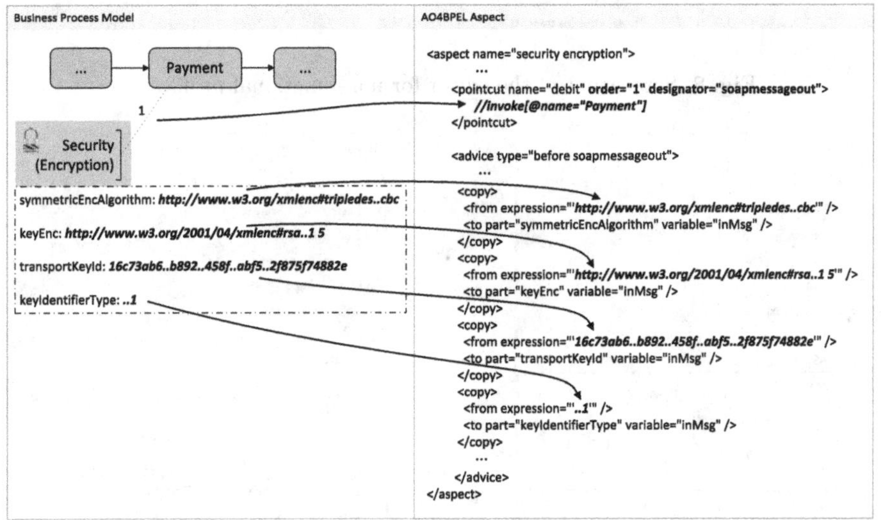

Fig. 7. Mapping example

1. The association between the non-functional property *Encryption* and the activity *Payment* is transformed to the XPath pointcut expression *//invoke[@name=payment]*, which selects the invoke activity corresponding to the payment activity in the WS-BPEL process by its name.
2. The attribute *execution order* of the pointcut element is set to the value 1 as specified in the association.
3. The values of the attributes *symmetricEncAlgorithm*, *keyEnc*, *transportKeyId* and *keyIdentifierType* of the non-functional property are copied to the corresponding variables and parts in the AO4BPEL aspect.

4 Implementation and Tools

We provide an integrated Eclipse-based tool set that supports our proposed approach. This tool set includes:

- an EMF-based editor for creating and editing the non-functional profiles as shown in Fig. 8. In that figure this editor is used to add a new attribute to the encryption property of the security profile.

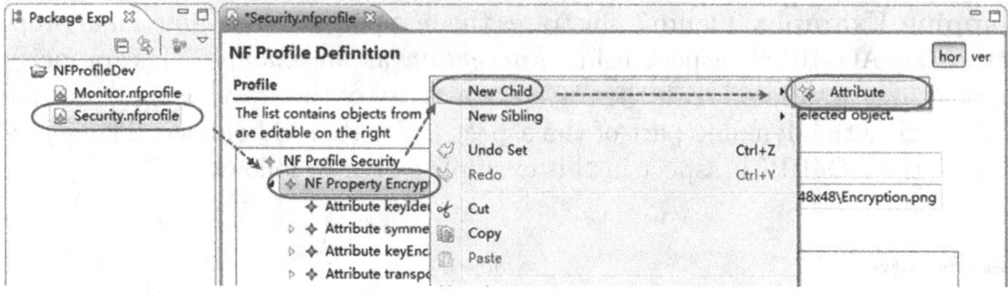

Fig. 8. Screenshot of the editor for non-functional profiles

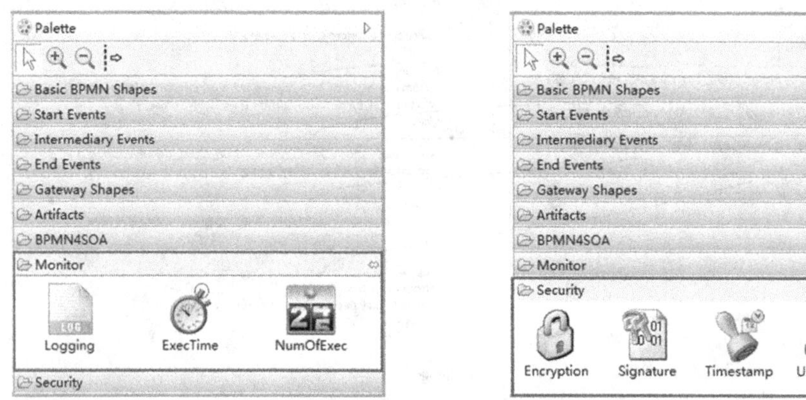

Fig. 9. Palette of the enhanced BPMN editor after profile import

- an enhanced BPMN editor that extends the STP BPMN editor and can import the non-functional profiles. Furthermore, this editor provides an additional group in the palette for each imported non-functional profile. In Fig. 9 we see the new palette groups after importing the QoS and security profiles. The editor allows associating elements of the BPMN process models with the graphical annotations corresponding to the non-functional properties. The attributes of each property can be edited using the property sheet as shown in Fig. 10.
- two Xpand-based code generators which respectively output WS-BPEL and AO4BPEL code. These generators are integrated with the enhanced BPMN editor and can be started by selecting a diagram and right-clicking the respective menu entries as shown in Fig. 11.

5 Related Work

This section presents related work on modeling and realizing non-functional concerns in business processes.

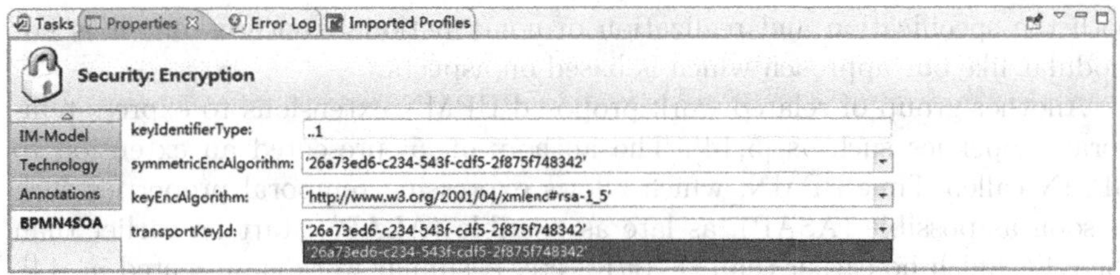

Fig. 10. Editing the attribute values of the encryption property

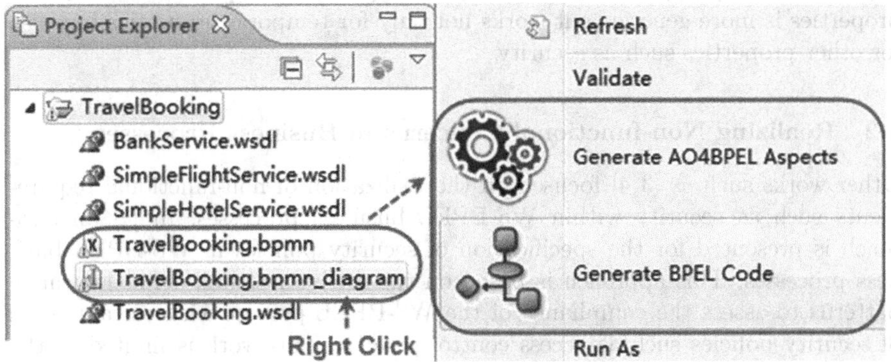

Fig. 11. Starting the code generators from the modeling environment

5.1 Modeling Non-functional Concerns in Business Processes

The work presented in [12] proposes a model-driven approach to specify security requirements in BPMN business processes. In that work the authors extend the BPMN meta-model to express requirements such as integrity, privacy, and non-repudiation. A similar approach is taken in [19], which extends BPMN to specify access control constraints in business process models such as role-based access control and separation of duties. Both works [12,19] extend the BPMN meta-model in a heavy-weight manner, which makes the resulting models no longer compliant with the BPMN standard. In contrast to those, our proposal is based on the extensibility mechanisms of BPMN. Furthermore, both works are specific to security and do not support other non-functional concerns.

SecureBPMN [1] is another work that extends BPMN to express access control requirements including policies such as separation of duty and binding of duty. This work also shares the limitations of the other two proposals mentioned above. However, it goes one step beyond the modeling phase and addresses policy enforcement by generating XACML policies, which will be enforced at runtime by policy enforcement points (PEP). In [15] an approach called Sec-MoSC is presented to address security requirements in web service composition at different abstraction levels such as business process specification, composite service design and development, and business process execution. That approach covers both the specification and realization of non-functional concerns but it is not modular like our approach which is based on aspects.

Another group of related work proposed BPMN extensions to express temporal properties such as [5,14]. The authors of [5] presented an extension to BPMN called Time-BPMN, which allows expressing temporal properties such as soon as possible (ASAP), as late as possible (ALAP), start no earlier than (SNET), finish no earlier than (FNET), etc. A similar work is presented in [14], which defines BPMN extensions to express time, cost and reliability properties. Both works are limited to the modeling level and do no address the realization of the specified properties. In addition, our approach to express non-functional properties is more generic as it works not only for temporal properties but also for other properties such as security.

5.2 Realizing Non-functional Concerns in Business Processes

Other works such as [3,4] focused on the realization of non-functional requirements such as security within WS-BPEL business processes. In [4] an approach is presented for the specification of security policies in WS-BPEL business processes. This approach is based on the analysis of well-defined security patterns to assess the compliance of the WS-BPEL process with certain types of security policies such as access control policies. This work is limited to the analysis of the business process and no policy enforcement is supported.

In [3], the authors use AO4BPEL aspects to realize non-functional concerns in WS-BPEL such as security, reliable messaging, and transactions. In that work, a declarative XML-based deployment descriptor was used to express non-functional requirements and aspects are generated from that deployment descriptor. In all three works the modeling phase is not considered and the focus in only on realizing the non-functional requirements at the technical implementation level.

In [20] the authors present a similar work to the one presented in the current paper. However the mappings and the generators presented in that work target Java for the functional part of the business process and AspectJ for the non-functional parts. Both works nicely complement each other by providing two alternative implementation technology for business processes while covering non-functional concerns.

6 Conclusion

In this paper, we presented a generic and holistic model-driven approach for the specification and realization of non-functional concerns in business processes. The approach is not specific to a particular non-functional concern and we showed its instantiation in this paper using security and QoS as example. It is holistic as it covers both functional and non-functional concerns and it also covers the modeling and the realization levels. Through its generative nature our approach bridges the gap between the modeling and the implementation of business processes while covering functional and non-functional aspects. Furthermore, our approach is modular as the code that is responsible for enforcing non-functional properties is separated from the code that realizes the functional part of the business process. We also presented an integrated Eclipse-based tool set that supports our approach including an editor for non-functional profiles, an extended BPMN editor supporting the expression of non-functional concerns, and two code generators for process and aspect generation.

Acknowledgments. This work was performed in the context of the Software-Cluster projects EMERGENT and SINNODIUM (www.software-cluster.org). It was partially funded by the German Federal Ministry of Education and Research (BMBF) under grant no. "01IC10S01" and "01IC12S01". The authors assume responsibility for the content.

References

1. Brucker, A.D., Hang, I., Lückemeyer, G., Ruparel, R.: SecureBPMN: modeling and enforcing access control requirements in business processes. In: Proceedings of the 17th ACM Symposium on Access Control Models and Technologies (SACMAT), pp. 123–126. ACM, June 2012
2. Charfi, A.: Aspect-Oriented Workflow Management. VDM Verlag, Saarbrücken (2008)
3. Charfi, A., Schmeling, B., Heizenreder, A., Mezini M.: Reliable, secure, and transacted web service compositions with AO4BPEL. In: 4th European Conference on Web Services (ECOWS), pp. 23–34, December 2006
4. Fischer, K.P., Bleimann, U., Fuhrmann, W., Furnell, S.M.: Security policy enforcement in BPEL-defined collaborative business processes. In: Proceedings of the 23rd International Conference on Data Engineering (ICDE), pp. 685–694. IEEE, April 2007
5. Gagne, D., Trudel, A.: Time-BPMN. In: Proceedings of the 11th IEEE International Conference on Commerce and Enterprise Computing (CEC), pp. 361–367. IEEE, July 2009
6. Look, A.: Expressive scoping and pointcut mechanisms for aspect-oriented web service composition. Vorgelegt Diplomarbeit von Alexander Look, Technische Universitaet Darmstadt, September 2011
7. Menzel, M., Thomas, I., Meinel, C.: Security requirements specification in service-oriented business process management. In: International Conference on Availability, Reliability and Security (ARES), pp. 41–48. IEEE, March 2009
8. OASIS: Web Services Business Process Execution Language Version 2.0, April 2007. http://docs.oasis-open.org/wsbpel/2.0/wsbpel-v2.0.pdf
9. OMG: Business Process Model and Notation (BPMN) OASIS Standard 2.0, January 2011. http://www.omg.org/spec/BPMN/2.0/
10. Ouvans, C., Dumas, M., Ter Hofstede, A.H.M., Van Der Aalst, W.M.P.: From BPMN Process models to BPEL web services. In: Proceedings of the International Conference on Web Services (ICWS), pp. 285–292. IEEE (2006)
11. Paja, E., Giorgini, P., Paul, S., Meland, P.H.: Security requirements engineering for secure business processes. In: Niedrite, L., Strazdina, R., Wangler, B. (eds.) BIR Workshops 2011. LNBIP, vol. 106, pp. 77–89. Springer, Heidelberg (2012)

12. Rodríguez, A., Fernández-Medina, E., Piattini, M.: A BPMN extension for the modeling of security requirements in business processes. IEICE Trans. Inf. Syst. **90**(4), 745–752 (2007)
13. Rodríguez, A., Fernández-Medina, E., Piattini, M.: A BPMN extension for the modeling of security requirements in business processes. IEICE - Trans. Inf. Syst. **E90–D**(4), 745–752 (2007)
14. Saeedi, K., Zhao, L., Sampaio, P.R.F.: Extending BPMN for supporting customer-facing service quality requirements. In: Proceedings of the 8th IEEE International Conference on Web Services (ICWS), pp. 616–623. IEEE, July 2010
15. Souza, A.R.R., Silva, B.L.B., Lins, F.A.A., Damasceno, J.C., Rosa, N.S., Maciel, P.R.M., Medeiros, R.W.A., Stephenson, B., Motahari-Nezhad, H.R., Li, J., Northfleet, C.: Incorporating security requirements into service composition: from modelling to execution. In: Baresi, L., Chi, C.-H., Suzuki, J. (eds.) ICSOC-ServiceWave 2009. LNCS, vol. 5900, pp. 373–388. Springer, Heidelberg (2009)
16. Turki, S.H., Bellaaj, F., Charfi, A., Bouaziz, R.: Modeling security requirements in service based business processes. In: Bider, I., Halpin, T., Krogstie, J., Nurcan, S., Proper, E., Schmidt, R., Soffer, P., Wrycza, S. (eds.) EMMSAD 2012 and BPMDS 2012. LNBIP, vol. 113, pp. 76–90. Springer, Heidelberg (2012)
17. Weidlich, M., Decker, G., Großkopf, A., Weske, M.: BPEL to BPMN: the myth of a straight-forward mapping. In: Tari, Z., Meersman, R. (eds.) OTM 2008, Part I. LNCS, vol. 5331, pp. 265–282. Springer, Heidelberg (2008)
18. Wolter, C., Menzel, M., Schaad, A., Miseldine, P., Meinel, C.: Model-driven business process security requirement specification. J. Syst. Archit. **55**(4), 211–223 (2009)
19. Wolter, C., Schaad, A.: Modeling of task-based authorization constraints in BPMN. In: Alonso, G., Dadam, P., Rosemann, M. (eds.) BPM 2007. LNCS, vol. 4714, pp. 64–79. Springer, Heidelberg (2007)
20. Yahya, I., Turki, S.H., Charfi, A., Kallel, S., Bouaziz, R.: An aspect-oriented approach to enforce security properties in business processes. In: Ghose, A., Zhu, H., Yu, Q., Delis, A., Sheng, Q.Z., Perrin, O., Wang, J., Wang, Y. (eds.) ICSOC 2012. LNCS, vol. 7759, pp. 344–355. Springer, Heidelberg (2013)

Verifying Concurrent Data Structures Using Data-Expansion

Tong Che(✉)

École Polytechnique Fédérale de Lausanne, Lausanne, Switzerland
tong.che@epfl.ch

Abstract. We present the first thread modular proof of a concurrent binary search tree. This proof tackles the problem of reasoning about complicated thread interferences using thread modular invariants. The key tool in this proof is the Data-Expansion Lemma, a novel lemma that allows us to reason about search operations in any state. We highlight the power of this lemma when combined with our generalized version of the Hindsight Lemma, which enables us to prove linearizability by reasoning about the temporal properties of the operations instead of reasoning about the linearization points directly.

The Data-Expansion Lemma provides an interesting solution to the proof blowup problem when reasoning about concurrent data structures by separating the verification of effectful and effectless operations. We show that our proof methodology is applicable to several algorithms and argue that many advanced concurrent data structures can be easy to verify using thread-modular arguments.

1 Introduction

Highly concurrent algorithms are extremely hard to design and verify. On one hand, the vast number of interference possibilities makes formal proof impractical and human proof error-prone. On the other hand, thread modular proofs are usually impossible dreams, even for very simple algorithms. Hence, the verification of concurrent algorithms is a major research challenge and an important step to boost the reliability of concurrent programming.

Sophisticated concurrent objects, such as concurrent binary search trees, are becoming popular and are promising to replace traditional search structures, for example, singly linked lists and skip lists. However, because of their complexity, many of these algorithms are published without rigorous mathematical proofs, not to mention formal ones. Meanwhile, the verification community spends most of its efforts on relatively simple data structures, such as linked lists and stacks.

This paper presents a simple proof strategy for the linearizability of advanced concurrent algorithms, which is purely thread modular. Our proof strategy covers a number of algorithms, but in this paper, we focus on one simple example for concreteness — an external binary tree. This algorithm is simple but powerful, because many concurrent algorithms [5,11] use similar mechanisms.

A. Bouajjani and H. Fauconnier (Eds.): NETYS 2015, LNCS 9466, pp. 155–169, 2015.
DOI: 10.1007/978-3-319-26850-7_11

For the verification of highly complicated advanced algorithms, thread modular proofs which allow us to reason about each thread separately seem to be the only feasible solution. Because of their complexity, the linearization points of such algorithms are in many cases non-fixed. In traditional methods [7,13], reasoning about such linearization points was done by tracking the set of pending invocations and auxiliary states, which lead to non-local proofs. In such proofs, one has to construct the set of linearization points before reasoning about the data abstraction. However, these methods are not adapted to advanced data structures, because the behavior of the pending calls are highly complicated, and it is hard, if not impossible, to avoid proof blowup.

A first purely thread modular proof of a simple linked list algorithm with non-fixed linearization point was presented in [12]. It was shown that for linked lists, reasoning about invariants of tiny steps of every thread can lead to important mathematical conclusions, such as the Hindsight Lemma [12], and finally to proofs. In this work, our main purpose is to argue that this idea is actually widely applicable to many advanced data structures, some of which were previously considered too complicated for rigorous or formal proofs.

Our proof strategy proceeds as follows. First, we identify a set of thread local invariants preserved by every computation step of each thread. Then we prove that a small subset of these invariants implies our Generalized Hindsight Lemma as well as a new lemma: the Data-Expansion Lemma. Each lemma captures a specific aspect of the reason why the tree traversal works in both cases no matter whether the traversal encounters its target or not. At last, we prove the operations are linearizable using abstraction functions. The two lemmas give us direct explanations of the non-fixed linearization points, avoiding thereby the use of extra auxiliary states.

The Data-Expansion Lemma is the main technical contribution of this work. It allows us to infer the non-existence of a key in some past state when the tree traversal failed to encounter it without explicit construction of the linearization points. Combined with our generalized version of the Hindsight Lemma, Our Data-Expansion Lemma provides powerful tools to reason about operations with non-fixed linearization points in advanced concurrent data structures.

The rest of this paper is organized as follows: In Sect. 2, we briefly explain our verification strategy. In Sect. 3, we present the verification target, a highly concurrent binary search tree algorithm. In Sect. 4, we introduce our computation models. In Sect. 5, we present our verification. In Sect. 6, we prove the generalized version of Hindsight Lemma, and discuss its applications. Due to space limitations, we put the extension to other algorithms and formal proofs in the technical report.

2 Verification Strategy

We describe the idea underlying our verification strategy intuitively, using the example of a concurrent set algorithm implemented with an optimistic external binary search tree. An external binary search tree is a variant of ordinary BST.

Its keys are stored only in leaf nodes, and the internal nodes are used for routing. We further assume that for all nodes u, v, w, where u is an ancestor of v, w and v/w is located in the left/right subtree of u, then we have $v.key \leq u.key < w.key$.

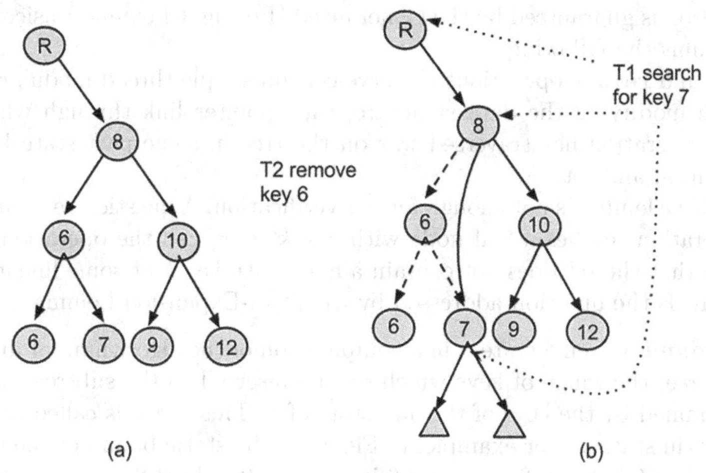

Fig. 1. Concurrent BST

Heap Representation. The shared data of the threads underlying the set algorithm is an external binary search tree composed of dynamic allocated nodes of two types, leaf and internal, which we refer to as *heap*. Each internal node contains three fields, two pointer fields `child(1)`, `child(2)` pointing to its left and right children, and an integer field `key` storing the key of this node. Each leaf node contains only an integer field `key`. The internal node `Root` contains key $-\infty$. For each state, some portion of the heap is *reachable* by following a sequence of child pointers from `Root`. We refer to this portion of the heap as *reachable heap*.

We view a computation of the algorithm as a sequence of shared program states. In each state, each leaf node in the reachable heap corresponds to a key in the set. The unreachable portion of the heap contains removed nodes.

Set Operations. There are three set operations, `add`, `remove`, and `contains`. Intuitively, they correspond to operations that add, remove or search for a key in a sequential set algorithm. All these operations need to traverse the tree first.

Generalized Hindsight Lemma. We use the example of the `contains` operation for illustration. We assume several threads are running the set algorithm. One of them is a `contains` operation, looking for key k in the binary search tree. If the operation reaches a leaf node with key k, can the operation return and claim that the set contains a node with key k at some linearization point? We can separate two cases here:

- The leaf node is currently on the tree.
- The leaf node is removed from the tree in current state and is not in the reachable heap.

The first case is trivial. In the second case, the correctness (linearizability) of the operation is guaranteed by the Generalized Hindsight Lemma. Basically, this lemma claims the following:

If `add` and `remove` operations preserve certain simple thread modular invariants when modifying the data structure, each pointer link through which the `contains` operation has traversed was on the tree in some past state between the invocation and return.

The above lemma is not enough for our verification. A question remains open: if the operation reaches a leaf node with key $k' \neq k$, can the operation return and claim that the set does not contain a node with key k at some linearization point? This is the question addressed by the Data-Expansion Lemma.

Static Bound. Given a state σ in a computation of the algorithm, for any node u on the tree, the range of keys which can be inserted to the subtree rooted at u is determined by the keys of the ancestors of u. This range is called the *static bound* at u in state σ. For example, in Fig. 1(a), the static bound of the internal node with key 6 is $(-\infty, 8]$, because 6 is on the left side of 8.

Data-Expansion Lemma. The intuition behind our Data-Expansion Lemma is that a tree traversal should not miss the target node on the tree in the presence of thread interference. We assume a tree traversal targeting at key k arrives at an internal node u at state σ. If the leaf node with key k is on the tree but not on the subtree rooted at u, then the traversal would miss it.

Our Data-Expansion Lemma states that this will never happen if certain thread modular invariants are preserved. Namely, key k lies in the static bound of node u at state σ if some invariants are preserved by `add` and `remove` operations when they modify the heap. For example, in Fig. 1(b), thread T_1 is searching for node with key 7, while T_2 is concurrently removing the node with key 6. If T_1 reaches the internal node with key 6 before the removal of T_2, the static bound of the node with key 7 is $(6, 8]$, after the removal the static bound of the node with key 7 is $(-\infty, 8]$. So the search target 7 is always contained in the static bound in the presence of thread interference.

Verification of Linearizability. Our verification is a combination of formal proofs of the thread modular invariants and rigorous mathematical arguments, such as the Data-Expansion Lemma and Generalized Hindsight Lemma.

We treat two kinds of operations separately. *Effectful* operations are operations which successfully modify the heap. *Effectless* operations are read-only to the shared heap. Effectless operations do not have fixed linearization points, so reasoning about their linearization points using auxiliary states in such a complicated logic brings severe proof blowup. We will use our two lemmas to deal with two aspects of effectless operations, no matter the traversal encounters its target or not.

3 Verification Target

Our verification target is Fig. 2. The algorithm implements a concurrent dictionary using binary search trees. It is essentially similar to [5], but is simpler, since this algorithm excludes mechanisms in [5] to achieve lock-freedom using only *CAS*. This algorithm can be viewed as a "template" implementation of concurrent binary search trees. In fact, many tree algorithms use similar mechanisms to achieve concurrency. The algorithm is optimistic and highly concurrent, for its atomic sections access only a very small portion (three nodes) of the data structure.

```
struct Leaf : Node {
    Key key;
    bool marked;
}

struct Internal : Node {
    Key key;
    Node * child[2];
    bool marked;
}

Node*,Node*,Node* search(KeyType k) {
    Node *n := Root;
    while (n is not leaf node) {
        dir = k.compareTo(n.key);
        gp := p;
        p := n;
        n = n.getChild(dir);
    }
    return gp, p, n;
}

void init() {
    Root = new Internal(-infty);
    Root.left = new Leaf(-infty);
    Root.right = new Leaf(+infty);
    }

bool contains(KeyType k) {
    while(true) {
        _,_,n := search(k);
        if(k.compareTo(n.key) != 0)
            return false;
        return true;
    }
}

bool add(KeyType k){
    while(true){
        gp,p,n := search(k);
        dir = k.compareTo(n.key);
        if(dir == 0)
            return false;
        na = new Leaf(k);
    // create a node with the smaller key and two children
        n1 = new Internal(min(k, n.key), n, na);
        atomic{
            if( !p->marked && p.isParentOf(n)){
        // change p's child from n to n1.
                p.changeChild(n,n1);
                return true;
    }}}}

int KeyType::compareTo(KeyType k) {
    // return the sign of this - k.
    return sgn(this-k);
}

bool remove(KeyType k){
    while(true){
        gp,p,n := search(k);
        if(k.compareTo(n.key)!=0)
            return false;
        atomic{
            if(gp.isParentOf(p) &&p.isParentOf(n)
&& !gp.marked) {
                n.marked = true;
                p.marked = true;
//gp change its child from p to the child of p other than n.
        gp.changeChild(p,p.getOtherChild(n));
                return true;
                }
    }}}
```

Fig. 2. Concurrent set algorithm

We make several remarks of the algorithm in Fig. 2. First, `compareTo` is a method to compare keys. The method `k1.compareTo(k2)` returns 0 if two keys are equal, or it returns -1 when $k1 < k2$, or 1 when $k1 > k2$. Second, the children choosing function `n.getChild(dir)` for internal node n returns the left child if $dir == 0$ or $dir == -1$, and the function returns the right child otherwise.

The most surprising part of this algorithm is the `search` operation. It traverses the data structure without any synchronization or retry. Many recent tree-based algorithms such as [2] share this property, and many of these algorithms can be verified with our method [3].

Dictionary Operations. The algorithm implements three common operations, `contains`, `add` and `remove`. Their sequential specifications are listed in the table below. They all use the helper operation `search` to locate the position where the operations take place. `add` and `remove` operations modify the heap under the protection of atomic sections. The atomic sections first check a set of validity conditions and retry if they are violated. After these validity checks, atomic sections perform the heap modification safely.

The sequential specification of the concurrent object can be viewed as a set of operations which operate on an abstract set S of keys.

Precondition	operation	Postcondition
$S = A$	`contains(k)`	$S' = A \wedge ret = k \in A$
$S = A$	`add(k)`	$S' = A \cup \{k\} \wedge ret = k \notin A$
$S = A$	`remove(k)`	$S' = A \setminus \{k\} \wedge ret = k \in A$

4 Basic Definitions

States and Transitions. Program states are combinations of local stores and a shared heap. The ith local store s_i is a map from the local variables of thread i to values. A shared heap h is a finite map from memory locations L to values. The heap can be accessed by all threads. A memory state can be written as $\sigma = (s, h)$. In our specific setting, $h = h_a \cup h_b$, where h_a is the set of memory locations which can be accessed by following heap pointer links starting from `Root`, h_b is the locations which cannot be accessed from `Root`.

Backbone Nodes/Links. For a state σ, a link $u \rightarrow_\sigma v$ is a pair of nodes such that for some $i \in 1, 2$, $u.getChild(i) = v$ in state σ. A node/link is called a backbone node/link in state σ, if and only if in state σ, there is a link path from `Root` to the node/link. In any state σ, for two backbone nodes u, v we say that $u <_\sigma v$, if and only if there is a link path from v to u. The state may be omitted if it can be inferred from the context. A node is called a removed node if it was a backbone node in some past state, but not on the backbone in current state.

Computation Steps and Executions. For any thread t, we define a computation step s of t as a transition κ from state σ to σ'. We write $s = \sigma \rightarrow_\kappa^t \sigma'$, and denote $src(s) = \sigma$, $trg(s) = \sigma'$. A computation step of thread t is either an invocation of an operation, a return from an operation, or an atomic action in an operation invoked by thread t. A heap computation step is defined as an atomic action in an operation that modifies the shared heap.

An execution Π is an alternating sequence of states and computation steps $\sigma_0, s_0, \sigma_1, s_1, \cdots$, where $\sigma_i = src(s_i)$ and $\sigma_{i+1} = trg(s_i)$. We define an execution trace of the execution by omiting all the computation step symbols, namely

$\sigma_0, \sigma_1, \cdots$. An execution trace π can be simplified if we consider only heap computation steps, these simplified execution traces are called heap execution traces, they are simplifications of corresponding full execution traces.

Temporal Node Path, Temporal Backbone. In an execution trace $\sigma_0, \sigma_1, \cdots \sigma_n$, a sequence of consecutive pairs of different nodes $(u_0, u_1), (u_1, u_2), \cdots (u_{m-1}, u_m)$ is called a node path. It is called a temporal node path / backbone, if there is a sequence of integers $0 \leq i_1 \leq i_2 \cdots i_m \leq n$, such that (u_{k-1}, u_k) is a link / backbone link in state σ_{i_k} for each $1 \leq k \leq m$. Sometimes, we also call the sequence $u_0, u_1, \cdots u_m$ a temporal node path / backbone going through the subsequence $T_s = \{\sigma_{i_1}, \cdots \sigma_{i_m}\}$.

Bounds. For every state $\sigma = (s, h)$, from the state invariants in Fig. 1, we know that the reachable heap h_0 is actually a binary search tree. For every unmarked node u in heap h_0, there is a unique link path ($u_0 = \texttt{Root}, u_1, u_2 \cdots u_m = u$) from `Root`. We associate to u a real interval $S_\sigma(u) = (a, b]$, where $a = \max\{u_i.key | u_i.key < k, i \in [1, k]\}$, and $b = \min\{u_i.key | u_i.key \geq k, i \in [1, m]\}$. We refer to this interval as *Static Bound* of u at state σ.

Given a temporal node path $P = (v_0, \cdots, v_n)$ going through states T_s such that v_0 is `Root`, we define intervals $D_l(P) = (c, d]$ for $l \in \{1, 2 \cdots n\}$, where $c = \max\{v_i.key | v_i.key < k, i \in [1, l]\}$, and $d = \min\{v_i.key | v_i.key \geq k, i \in [1, l]\}$. $D_n(l)$ is called the *Dynamic Search Bound* of P_l.

Linearizability. Linearizability [7] is a widely-used correctness property of concurrent objects. Intuitively, it means each operation can be viewed as taking effect at some unique point in time between the invocation and response.

Definition 1. *A history H is an execution trace containing only invocations and responses. A sequential history is a history where for each invocation, follows by a corresponding response. A partial history H_t of thread t w.r.t history H is the subsequence of H which is invoked by thread t. A history H is called well-formed when for every thread t, H_t is sequential. A sequential specification S_p is a set of sequential histories.*

Definition 2. *Suppose H is a well formed history, it is linearizable with sequential history H_S, if there is a map τ from operations in H to the same operations in H_S that preserves real time order(Namely, if two operations t_1, t_2 with the response of t_1 is before the invocation of t_2, then $\tau(t_1)$ before $\tau(t_2)$), then H is linearizable w.r.t H_S. If every execution of an algorithm is a linearizable history w.r.t a sequential history in its sequential specification S_p, the algorithm is said to be linearizable w.r.t. S_p.*

5 Verification of the Algorithm

5.1 Thread-Local Invariants Needed for the Proof

Our proof relies on a set of thread modular invariants. Basically, we classify two main classes of invariants: state invariants and step invariants. State invariants are predicates $p(\sigma_0)$ on the state of shared heap σ_0, which can be written as separation logic formulas. Step invariants are predicates on single computation steps. Step invariants can also be written as separation logic formulas, taking account in both pre- and post-program states.

These invariants are natural to concurrent binary search tree algorithms, and most algorithms preserve at least some of these invariants. These invariants can all be formally verified using separation logic. We list these invariants in Table 1. State invariants are named using ϕ, while step invariants are named using δ.

Table 1. Invariants of an external binary search tree.

Shape	ϕ_R	`Root` node exists
Shape	ϕ_{loop}	Shared heap does not contain any loop
Shape	ϕ_{c2}	Every internal node has two children
Data	ϕ_∞	`Root` node has key $-\infty$
Data	$\phi_<$	Data preserves tree order, for any node u, the keys on the left subtree $\leq u.key <$ the keys on the right subtree
Mark	ϕ_R	A node is marked $\Leftrightarrow$ it is a removed node
Shape	δ_e	Child fields of removed nodes never change
Shape	δ_o	For a computation step (σ_1, σ_2), if u, v are two backbone nodes in both σ_1, σ_2, and $u <_{\sigma_2} v$, then $u <_{\sigma_1} v$
Shape	δ_R	`Root` never changes
Shape	δ_{sn}	If a computation step removes a backbone node, the successors of the node remain unchanged in the next state
Shape	δ_{Re}	A marked node can never become backbone again
Data	δ_K	Key of any node can never change

5.2 Generalized Hindsight Lemma

Lemma 1. ***Tree Version Hindsight Lemma***

Consider an execution trace satisfying the shape invariants in Table 1, $\sigma_0, \sigma_1, \cdots \sigma_n$. For $0 \leq i \leq j \leq n$, if there is a backbone link $u \rightarrow_{\sigma_i} v$, and a link $v \rightarrow_{\sigma_j} w$ (u, v, w are different nodes), then there is $i \leq k \leq j$, such that $v \rightarrow_{\sigma_k} w$ is a backbone link.

Proof. See proof of Lemma 7.

Lemma 2. ***Tree Version Temporal Backbone Lemma***

Given an execution trace $T = (\sigma_0, \sigma_1, \cdots, \sigma_n)$ satisfying the shape invariants and a temporal node path $N = \{(u_0 = \texttt{Root}, u_1), (u_1, u_2), \cdots (u_{m-1}, u_m)\}$ going through $T_s = \{\sigma_{i_1}, \cdots \sigma_{i_m}\}$. Then there is another subsequence of execution trace $T'_s = \{\sigma_{j_1}, \cdots \sigma_{j_m}\}$ such that for all $1 \leq k \leq m-1$, $j_{k-1} \leq j_k \leq i_k$, and N is a temporal backbone going through T'_s.

Proof. Apply the Tree version Hindsight Lemma n times, and the theorem follows.

For a `search` operation invoked by any thread t, the operation crosses the links to reach a leaf node. The search path of thread t is defined as a temporal node path $N = u_0, u_1, \cdots u_m$ of all the nodes visited by the search operation.

Corollary 1. *Consider an execution trace of the algorithm in Fig. 2 satisfying shape invariants, $T = (\sigma_0, \sigma_1, \cdots \sigma_n)$. If this execution trace has an invocation to the search operation of a thread t, its search path is $N = u_0, u_1, \cdots u_m$. Then there is a subsequence $T_s = \{\sigma_{i_1}, \cdots \sigma_{i_m}\}$, such that N is a temporal backbone that goes through T_s.*

5.3 Data-Expansion Lemma

To state the Data-Expansion Lemma, we reconsider our definition of static bound $S_\sigma(u)$ of a backbone node u in a state σ. We want to extend the definition to removed nodes. Since a removed node v must be on the backbone at some past state, we denote τ the last state when v was on the backbone. Then we define $S_\sigma(v) = S_\tau(v)$. Note this static bound will never change after a node is removed. We can prove the static and temporal versions of Data-Expansion Lemma.

Lemma 3. ***Static Data-Expansion Lemma***

Given an execution trace $\sigma_0, \sigma_1, \cdots \sigma_n$ satisfying shape, data and mark invariants, then for each $0 \le i \le j \le n$, if internal node u exists from state σ_i, then we have

$$S_{\sigma_i}(u) \subseteq S_{\sigma_j}(u)$$

Proof. We only have to prove $S_{\sigma_i}(u) \subseteq S_{\sigma_{i+1}}(u)$ for each i. We distinguish 2 cases:

1. If u is a backbone node in both σ_i and σ_{i+1}. Let $A_k = \{v | v < u \text{ in } \sigma_k\}$. Then $A_{i+1} \subseteq A_i$, because from δ_o, each node such that $u <_{\sigma i+1} v$ satisfied $u < v_{\sigma_i}$.
   So $A_{i+1} \subseteq A_i$. Since the static bound is determined by the set A_i, and the key of u remain the same, so the static bound of u is non-decreasing.
2. If u is not a backbone node in σ_{i+1}, then the static bound is obviously the same in σ_i and σ_{i+1}.

Lemma 4. ***Data-Expansion Lemma***

Let T be an execution trace $\sigma_0, \sigma_1, \cdots \sigma_n$ satisfying shape, data and mark invariants. Let P be a temporal node path $P = \{v_0 = \texttt{Root}, v_1, \cdots v_m\}$ that goes through subsequence $T_s = \{\sigma_{\tau(1)}, \cdots \sigma_{\tau(m)}\}$. For simplicity we assume v_m is a leaf node. Then the dynamic search bound $D_i(P)$ of the temporal node path is contained in the static bound $S_{\sigma_{\tau(i)}}(v_i)$. Namely, we have

$$D_i(P) \subseteq S_{\sigma_{\tau(i)}}(v_i), 0 \le i < m$$

Proof. Because $v_0 = \texttt{Root}$, the temporal node path is also a temporal backbone that goes through subsequence $T'_s = \{\sigma_{\gamma(1)}, \cdots \sigma_{\gamma(m)}\}$, such that $\gamma(k-1) \leq \gamma(k) \leq \tau(k)$ for each k.

We prove a stronger form of the lemma:

$$D_i(P) \subseteq S_{\sigma_{\gamma(i)}}(v_i), 0 \leq i < m$$

Due to the static Data-Expansion lemma, we have $S_{\sigma_{\gamma(i)}}(v_i) \subseteq S_{\sigma_{\tau(i)}}(v_i)$, so this stronger form implies our lemma.

We prove this lemma by induction on i. For $i = 0$, the lemma holds trivially, because $D_0(P) = S_{\sigma_{\gamma(0)}}(v_0) = (-\infty, +\infty)$.

We assume $i = k$, $D_k(P) \subseteq S_{\sigma_{\gamma(k)}}(v_k)$. Because of the static Data-Expansion Lemma, we have $D_k(P) \subseteq S_{\sigma_{\gamma(k)}}(v_k) \subseteq S_{\sigma_{\gamma(k+1)}}(v_k)$.

For $i = k+1$, in state $\sigma_{\gamma(k+1)}$, the link $l : u_k \rightarrow u_{k+1}$ is a backbone link. Crossing the link would put the same constraint on both dynamic search bound and static bound, for example, if link l is a right child pointer of u_k, then $D_{k+1}(P) = D_k(P) \cap (u_k.key, +\infty)$, and also $S_{\sigma_{\gamma(k+1)}}(v_k) = S_{\sigma_{\gamma(k+1)}}(v_{k+1}) \cap (u_k.key, +\infty)$. So we have $D_{k+1}(P) \subseteq S_{\sigma_{\gamma(k+1)}}(v_{k+1})$.

So the lemma holds for every $0 \leq i < m$.

Corollary 2. *Suppose a search path $P = \{v_0, v_1, \cdots v_m\}$ is visited by a search operation in an execution trace $\sigma_0, \sigma_1, \cdots \sigma_n$ satisfying shape, data and mark invariants. For simplicity we assume the search operation invoked at state σ_0 and return at σ_n. We assume at state σ_i, the search operation is visiting node $v_{\phi(i)}$ (namely pointer $n = v_{\phi(i)}$), then the dynamic search bound $D_{\phi(i)}(P)$ of node v is contained in the static bound $S_{\sigma_i}(v_{\phi(i)})$. Since the search key k always lies in the dynamic search bound, we have*

$$k \in D_{\phi(i)}(P) \subseteq S_{\sigma_i}(v_{\phi(i)})$$

Proof. A search path is a temporal node path from `Root` that goes through a sequence of states $T_s = \{\sigma_{\tau(1)}, \cdots \sigma_{\tau(m)}\}$. So we have from above lemma:

$$D_{\phi(i)}(P) \subseteq S_{\sigma_{\tau(\phi(i))}}(v_{\phi(i)}) \subseteq S_{\sigma_i}(v_{\phi(i)})$$

This is because obviously we can make $\phi(\tau(k)) = k$ for $k \leq m$.

5.4 Verification of Linearizability

We define an effectless operation as one of three types: `contains` operations, `remove` operations returning false, and `add` operations returning false. In these three cases, the linearization points of these operations are non-fixed. Namely, the linearization point of one thread running an effectless operation is sometimes in another thread. However, the linearizability of effectless operations can be directly deduced from the thread modular invariants, which simplifies our verification.

Lemma 5. *Effectless operations are linearizable with respect to their sequential specifications.*

Proof. All effectless operations invoke the `search` operation as a sub-procedure. We assume the search path of one effectless procedure is $v_0 = \texttt{Root}, v_1, \cdots v_m$, v_m is a leaf node. The execution trace is $T = (\sigma_0, \sigma_1, \cdots \sigma_n)$. According to the temporal backbone lemma, we know that link $L_m = (v_{m-1}, v_m)$ was a backbone link in some past state. We denote σ_d the last state when the L_m is on backbone before the `search` operation crosses the link. (If it remains a backbone till the search crosses the link, we take σ_d to be the last state before the algorithm decides no further search is needed) We claim that σ_d is the right linearization point.

We distinguish two cases: If a search operation actually "finds" a node with the search key, namely $v_m.key = k$, then in σ_d, v_m was on the backbone. If search operation finds $v_m.key \neq k$, then node with key k is not in the tree on σ_d. We can prove this as follows:

Without loss of generality, we assume $k > v_{m-1}.key$. The "$\leq$" case follows the same argument. From the Data-Expansion lemma, we know that $k \in S_{\sigma_d}(v_{m-1})$. Namely, if a leaf node k is present in the tree, it should be found in the subtree rooted at node v_{m-1}, namely, on the right subtree of v_{m-1}.

If in σ_{d+1}, L_m is still a backbone link, then the computation step $s = (\sigma_d, \sigma_{d+1})$ is the link crossing of the `search` operation, the heap $h_{\sigma_d} = h_{\sigma_{d+1}}$. Then since $v_m.key \neq k$, so k is not in $Abs(\sigma_d)$.

If in σ_{d+1}, L_m is not a backbone link. The invariants δ_{sn} and δ_e guarantee that in σ_{d+1} and subsequent states, the right child of node v_{m-1} remains the same as in state σ_d. If node with key k exists in state σ_d, it should be on the right subtree of node v_{m-1}. However, the right child of v_{m-1} is a leaf node v_m with $v_m.key \neq k$. So we know that no leaf node with key k exists in state σ_d.

The linearizability of effectful operations, which have fixed linearization points, are not hard to prove.

Lemma 6. *The External BST algorithm implemented above is correct with respect to the sequential specification.*

Proof. It is easy to verify the invariants of Table 1 using separation logic [8]. This verification can be done in a purely thread modular way. The rest is to define the linearization points of each operation. The linearization point of a effectful operation is the state before the execution of the last atomic section. The linearization points of effectless operations is defined above. The linearizability of effectless operations is implied by the thread-modular invariants, which we have already proved in the lemma above. Now we only have to prove the linearizability of effectful operations.

We consider the abstract set function on states, $Abs(\sigma)$. $Abs(\sigma)$ is the set of keys of all reachable (unmarked) leaf nodes in the tree. The formal definition of $Abs(\sigma)$ is included in [3].

For effectful add operations, let $s = (\sigma_a, \sigma'_a)$ be the computation step of the execution of last atomic section. The validation condition ensures $l_1 : *p \rightarrow n$ is a backbone link in σ_a. Using this validation condition and the state invariants in Table 1, and the definition of abstraction function, it is obvious to check the computation step modifies the heap according to its specification: all leaf nodes reachable from Root in σ_a remain reachable in σ'_a, and a single new leaf node with key k become reachable.

The case for effectful remove operations is similar. Let $s = (\sigma_r, \sigma'_r)$ be the computation step of the execution of last atomic section. The validation condition ensures $l_1 : *p \rightarrow n$ and $l_2 : *gp \rightarrow p$ are backbone links in σ_r. It is obvious to check the computation step modifies the heap according to its specification: all leaf nodes reachable from Root in σ_a remain reachable in σ'_a, except the leaf node pointed by n.

6 Generalized Hindsight Lemma

In this section, we generalize Hindsight Lemma to a very general form. The lemma plays an essential role in the verification of both linked list and trees, and interestingly, it is still valid on a large class of linked data structures. We use the concept of *search data structure* to express the lemma.

Definition 3. *A data node is a fixed-size dynamic-allocated heap object consisting of a boolean mark field, a data field and several successor pointers to other data nodes. A search data structure is a heap object consisting of several data nodes with a specific node H, called the entry node. A concurrent search structure is a concurrent object whose shared heap is a search data structure. We assume that the concurrent object also satisfies the thread-modular invariant that a node is marked if and only if it is unreachable from H.*

For a concurrent search structure T, we assume the object also satisfies the step invariant that when or after nodes are removed from reachable heap, they cannot become backbone again and their successor pointers remain unchanged. We call this assumption "Removed Unchanged Assumption (*RUA*)". On a concurrent search structure, we define link, backbone link, temporal backbone, temporal node path as we do in Sects. 4 and 5. We formalize all the conditions of the Generalized Hindsight Lemma and the Generalized Temporal Backbone Lemma in [3].

Lemma 7. ***Generalized Hindsight Lemma***
For a concurrent search structure T_g, assume T_g satisfies RUA. *Consider an execution trace $\sigma_0, \sigma_1, \cdots \sigma_n$. For $0 \leq i \leq j \leq n$, if there is a backbone link $u \rightarrow_{\sigma_i} v$, and a link $v \rightarrow_{\sigma_j} w$ (u, v, w are different nodes), then there is $i \leq k \leq j$, such that $v \rightarrow_{\sigma_k} w$ is a backbone link.*

Proof. If in state σ_j, node v is a backbone node, then choose $k = j$ and we are done. If not, then v is not a backbone node in σ_j, let l be the largest index such that v is a backbone node in σ_l, so $l \geq i$. In σ_{l+1}, v is removed from backbone.

But the link $v \rightarrow_{\sigma_j} w$ exists, according to δ_e and δ_{sn}, $v \rightarrow w$ exists from state σ_l to σ_j. But in state σ_l, v is a backbone node, so the link $v \rightarrow_{\sigma_k} w$ is a backbone link.

7 Remarks

7.1 Related Works

The proof strategy used in this paper is essentially based on the idea of Herlihy and Wing [6]. In their fundamental paper, a proof of linearizability using data abstraction function is presented.

Our work is related to the recent advances [1,4,5] in concurrent binary search tree algorithms. The algorithm we set as our verification target is similar to [5], except that we use locks or atomic sections instead of non-blocking primitives. We find the idea of our verification may also be applicable to many of these algorithms. Our work also shares commonalities with the Hindsight Lemma paper [12]. We go one significant step forward by providing purely thread modular proofs for advanced concurrent algorithms such as trees. In fact, most tree algorithms are extremely complicated and hard to prove correct or verify rigorously. There are some recent proofs for tree algorithms [5], However, their proofs are mathematical (not formal) and do not use explicit thread modular arguments, making their proofs much longer than ours, and it is very hard (if not impossible) to refine their proofs into formal ones. There are also several interesting works on automatically verification of linearizability, such as [10,14]. In [10], a novel approach for thread-modular verification of linearizability using observational refinement is presented. However, it is not clear whether their approach is suitable for dealing with more advanced data structures such as binary search trees.

As the verification of the lazy linked list algorithm in [12], our verification of the invariants can also be viewed as taking place in simple Owicki-Gries logic [13], namely, we do not use complex mechanisms such as these used in rely-guarantee reasoning [9]. In order to express our verification in a clean way, we use small atomic sections instead of locks. This technical limitation, however, is by no means essential. In the price of more complicated proofs, we can actually allow the verification of lazy counterpart of these algorithms with some extra complexity.

In [2], a new abstraction to implement concurrent search trees is presented, together with several mathematical proofs of correctness. Also, in the correctness proof, the author proved a result similar to the Generalized Hindsight Lemma in the context of their implementation. However, their correctness results rely on specialized implementation techniques and do not rely on explicit thread local invariants. So they cannot be used as a basis for thread modular formal verification.

7.2 Conclusions

Formal verification of shared memory concurrent algorithms is a hard but important problem in the multicore era. The main difficulty is to prove the correctness of the algorithms in the presence of complicated thread interferences. Existing methods such as [13] usually need to introduce many auxiliary states, which lead to over-complicated proofs. So they cannot be adapted to some advanced concurrent data structures, such as binary search trees. In [12], O'Hearn etc. have shown that for a special concurrent linked list algorithm, thread modular verification can be established. In this paper, we make a surprising observation that for some advanced concurrent data structures, such as binary search trees, thread modular proofs are also achievable, thus can greatly simplify formal verification of concurrent algorithms.

In [13], Owicki and Gries argued that using auxiliary states is sometimes a must, and many simple concurrent programs cannot admit purely thread modular proofs without auxiliary states. Although Owicki and Gries' work limits the use of thread modular proofs, it is interesting to see that many advanced highly concurrent data structures do not fall into this limitation. Thanks to the Data-Expansion lemma and the Generalized Hindsight Lemma, we can see that some advanced concurrent algorithms can admit purely thread modular formal verification. This observation makes the goal of formal verification of many advanced concurrent objects actually achievable.

On the bright side, the Generalized Hindsight Lemma is proved correct on a large class of data structures satisfying only the Removed Unchanged Assumption, which is easy to formalize and, hopefully, to automate. On the other side, the Data-Expansion Lemma is more data structure specific. It is shown in our running example to hold on the binary search trees. However, the lemma is very promising for generalization to other data structures.

The Data Expansion Lemma combined with the Generalized Hindsight Lemma eliminates the needs of constructing linearization points in other threads before carrying out formal proofs. This is particularly important for advanced concurrent data structures, such as binary search trees, whose internal logic is highly complicated. These lemmas give an direct formal explanation of why the tree traversal can work without any synchronization. They may play an important rule in the design and verification of concurrent algorithms.

References

1. Bronson, N.G., Casper, J., Chafi, H., Olukotun, K.: A practical concurrent binary search tree. ACM Sigplan Not. **45**, 257–268 (2010)
2. Brown, T., Ellen, F., Ruppert, E.: A general technique for non-blocking trees. In: Proceedings of the 19th ACM SIGPLAN Symposium on Principles and Practice of Parallel Programming, PPoPP 2014, pp. 329–342. ACM, New York (2014)
3. Che, T.: Verifying concurrent data structures using data-expansion, Technical report. EPFL (2014)

4. Drachsler, D., Vechev, M., Yahav, E.: Practical concurrent binary search trees via logical ordering. In: Proceedings of the 19th ACM SIGPLAN Symposium on Principles and Practice of Parallel Programming, PPoPP 2014, pp. 343–356. ACM, New York (2014)
5. Ellen, F., Fatourou, P., Ruppert, E., van Breugel, F.: Non-blocking binary search trees. In: Proceedings of the 29th ACM SIGACT-SIGOPS Symposium on Principles of Distributed Computing, pp. 131–140. ACM (2010)
6. Herlihy, M.P., Lev, Y., Luchangco, V., Shavit, N.N.: A simple optimistic skiplist algorithm. In: Prencipe, G., Zaks, S. (eds.) SIROCCO 2007. LNCS, vol. 4474, pp. 124–138. Springer, Heidelberg (2007)
7. Herlihy, M.P., Wing, J.M.: Linearizability: a correctness condition for concurrent objects. ACM Trans. Program. Lang. Syst. (TOPLAS) **12**(3), 463–492 (1990)
8. Ishtiaq, S.S., O'Hearn, P.W.: Bi as an assertion language for mutable data structures. ACM SIGPLAN Not. **36**, 14–26 (2001)
9. Jones, C.B.: Specification and design of (parallel) programs. In: IFIP Congress, pp. 321–332 (1983)
10. Liang, H., Feng, X.: Modular verification of linearizability with non-fixed linearization points. In: Proceedings of the 34th ACM SIGPLAN Conference on Programming Language Design and Implementation, PLDI 2013, pp. 459–470. ACM, New York (2013)
11. Natarajan, A., Mittal, N.: Fast concurrent lockfree binary search trees. In: Proceedings of the 19th ACM Symposium on Principles and Practice of Parallel Programming (2014)
12. O'Hearn, P.W., Rinetzky, N., Vechev, M.T., Yahav, E., Yorsh, G.: Verifying linearizability with hindsight. In: Proceedings of the 29th ACM SIGACT-SIGOPS Symposium on Principles of Distributed Computing, pp. 85–94. ACM (2010)
13. Owicki, S., Gries, D.: An axiomatic proof technique for parallel programs I. Acta Informatica **6**(4), 319–340 (1976)
14. Vafeiadis, V.: Automatically proving linearizability. In: Touili, T., Cook, B., Jackson, P. (eds.) CAV 2010. LNCS, vol. 6174, pp. 450–464. Springer, Heidelberg (2010)

Improving Cognitive Radio Wireless Network Performances Using Clustering Schemes and Coalitional Games

Imane Daha Belghiti(✉), Ismail Berrada, and Mohamed El Kamili

LIMS, Faculty of Sciences, Sidi Mohammed Ben Abdellah University, BP 1796, Fez, Morocco
imanedaha@gmail.com, {ismail.berrada,mohamed.elkamili}@usmba.ac.ma

Abstract. In this paper, we consider the problem of improving the performances of large Cognitive Radio Wireless Networks (CRWN). The lack of network infrastructure and heterogeneous spectrum availability in cognitive radio wireless networks require the self-organization of secondary users (SUs) for efficient spectrum assignment. The cluster structure can be an adequate solution in both guaranteeing system performance and reducing communication overhead in CRWN. The approach considered in this paper relays on the use of a coalitional game in every cluster to preserve energy loss in the sensing phase and to reduce the interference with primary users (PUs) and between SUs. First, we study the coalitional formation process in partition form with non-transferable utility (NTU). In order to reduce the coalition formation cost, a cluster scheme is considered. Then, we use a strategic learning algorithm to learn the Nash equilibrium. At the end, simulation results demonstrate the preference of our CRWN compared to standard wireless cognitive network.

Keywords: Cluster · Overhead · Spectrum sensing · Cognitive wireless network · Energy consumption · Network performance · Coalitional game · Partition form · Opportunistic access

1 Introduction

Cognitive Radio (CR) has enjoyed a powerful interest by the researchers in recent years. CR is a flexible, intelligent radio and network technology that can automatically detect unused channels in spectrum band and changes transmission parameters to enhance radio functioning behavior. In cognitive radio settings, secondary users (SUs) can operate in the same area with primary users (PUs). Using spectrum sensing, SUs can detect the spectrum holes and hence can use the unoccupied licensed channels for communication [1].

A Cognitive radio network is able to search automatically idle channels in wireless spectrum and use learning and decision making algorithms to adaptively change the working parameters of the system. In the case of distributed cognitive radio wireless networks, the system is composed of large number of SUs nodes

A. Bouajjani and H. Fauconnier (Eds.): NETYS 2015, LNCS 9466, pp. 170–182, 2015.
DOI: 10.1007/978-3-319-26850-7_12

and one or multiple base stations. With the absence of the central network control utilities, CR users have to execute multi-hop communications. The end-to-end performance is challenged by the distributed multi-hop architecture, the dynamic network topology, the quality of service QoS requirements and time/location varying spectrum availability.

Clustering [2] can be a good management methodology in distributed CRWN for its capacity of guaranteeing system performances in dynamic network environments with the benefits of providing virtual backbones, reducing network sizes and ensuring more stability to each CR node. Grouping physical network nodes into a small number of logical associations forms clusters. Each cluster performs a leader election procedure to select a cluster head (CH). In a centralized approach, every CR sends its data to the Base Station (BS). Consequently, the amount of energy of a CR decreases rapidly as the distance from the BS increases. A clustering scheme can greatly reduce the energy consumption of nodes and lengthen the network lifetime because data is transmitted to cluster heads. They, transfer data to the BS through the CH backbone.

Another challenge to be addressed by a distributed CRWN is the spectrum availability. In fact, the connectivity of the network depends not only on the geographical locations of nodes but also on the interference with PUs networks from SUs. Several approaches for sensing the channel exist (for more details, refer to the survey of [3]). In this paper, we propose a coalitional game approach to prevent unnecessary energy loss in the sensing phase and to reduce the interference with PUs and between SUs. A coalitional game is when a number of players cooperate in order to enhance their position in the game. The game is defined by (M,V), where M is the players set and V is the coalition value (utility). This value can be in a characteristic or in a partition form. Von Neumann and Morgenstern introduced the first definition of the characteristic form. A coalition game is in characteristic form if the utility of any coalition is independent of the others outside coalitions. It is in partition form if the utility of the coalition depends; both on the coalition players as well as on the players of the others coalitions.

The main contributions of this paper are:

- Improving the system views and performances. By using clusters, we split wide network into small one and thus reduce the communication overhead in large CRWN. Also, by using small networks with clusters every nodes location and available channels is known. From a routing point of view, clusters and coalition games limit the broadcast storm involved in the route establishment process.
- Reducing interference between SUs and PUs by using a coalitional game approach (NTU coalitional game in partition form). We studied the users utilities through a mathematical model.

The remainder of this paper is organized as follows. Section 2 is devoted to the related works. Section 3 presents the system architecture and assumptions. Numerical results are presented in Sect. 4. Finally, the paper is concluded in Sect. 5.

2 Related Works

In [4], the authors propose a three independent transceiver node physical platform, and introduce a dynamic control channel. The gain of SUs in the cognitive radio setting is the arrangement between sensing the channel and enhancing channel access performances. In order to detect the presence of PUs, [5] uses a central point for exchanging information between SUs and this central. However, this concept involves an additional overhead.

A non-cooperative game is a game where every user operates independently of the others. In [6], a Nash equilibrium strategy is a solution of spectrum sensing and access for multiple SUs. In [7], the players carry out cooperation in a non-cooperative environment with no information exchange. The authors consider the minority game (MG), for the sensing phase. In this game, an odd number of players is considered. Each player must choose one of two choices independently at each round. The players, who end up on the minority side, win the game. At each round, *SU* decides on the action that maximizes its payoff through Linear Reward Inaction (LRI) updating rule.

Coalitional game is also a central concept for many papers that investigate the spectrum sensing issue in cognitive radio network. The groups of SUs forming a coalition collaborate in order to reduce the interference with the PUs through collaborative sensing. In [8], a new algorithm is proposed wherein each SUs can autonomously collaborate, while maximizing their detection probability taking into account the false alarm as cooperation costs. The utilization of cooperative games for joint sensing and access models is illustrated [9]. In [10], the authors propose an algorithm for coalition formation to improve system performances, to avoid interference with the licensed users and to permit a better access by using the partition form. However, this algorithm suffers from severe scalability, as it does not take into account large networks.

3 System Architecture and Assumption

The system setup used in this work contains PU transmitters, k channels, M secondary users in network, and N_l of SUs (transceivers pairs) in each cluster Q_l with $l = \{1, 2, .., L\}$. Each primary user uses its licensed channels. The PUs and SUs are both supposed to use a time slotted manner with exact time synchronization [11,12]. Hence, at the beginning of a time-slot, every secondary user can make sensing operation in all primary channels. We assume that each SU always has data to send and no traffic requirement is imposed. In other words, SU transmits data in a best-effort manner.

Each SU is equipped with two transceivers. The first transceiver, called SDR transceiver, consists of a Software Defined Radio module that can tune to any k channels to sense, receive, and transmit signals/packets. The second transceiver, called control transceiver, is devoted to operate over the control channel. The SUs use the control transceiver to obtain the information of available channels and to negotiate with others.

A coalition is a subset of SUs and a coalition structure, $G_i = \{C_1, C_2, .., C_n\}$ is a partition of SUs. The partition $G_i = \{\{1\}, \{2\}, .., \{N_l\}\}$ defines the solo-coalitions at the beginning of the game.

In each coalition, an elected user for transmission starts negotiations with other SUs in other coalitions using the CSMA/CA mechanism. After that, only one winner starts the packets transmission on the channel. The CSMA/CA protocol consists of RTS/CTS mechanism. Each elected user begins by sensing the channel. If idle, SU sends RTS packet over the channel. The receiving user detects RTS and responds with CTS after a SIFS. On the other hand, if the channel is busy, the receiving node pursues checking until it becomes idle. More details in CSMA/CA process can be found in [13].

The proposed spectrum aware clustering structure is depicted in the network and presented under cluster format $Q = \{Q_1, Q_2, .., Q_L\}$. When a node is unable to reach base station, the cluster head collect data from all nodes in a cluster and transmits it to base station (BS) over long distances. It is assumed that each node has a long range communication and it is able to reach cluster head (CH) directly and thereafter the BS. PUs occupying different channels are represented. Neighboring nodes who share common channels form a cluster and one node has to be selected as cluster head (CH) in each cluster. The network communication can be categorized into two classes: intra-cluster communication and inter-cluster communication. During the inter-cluster communication phase, all SUs nodes send their information to their CH through the local common channel. During the intra-cluster communication phase, the CH first compress the information, then transmits it to the upstream neighbor CH using maximal power. Every node knows its coordinates which are embedded in the interaction message. Node mobility is assumed to be slow and the channel availability changes at a relatively low rate such that the topology does not change during the clustering process.

3.1 Cluster Border Determination

In order to scale up the larger networks, an interesting approach is to split the network in clusters. However, this approach faces additional challenges regarding how the clustering should be performed. In order to participate in the cluster formation, each SU needs to have informations on which other SUs are in its neighborhood and their local spectrum availability. To get those informations, a SU broadcast packets in order to solicit packet exchange from all its neighbors. For neighbor discovery, several works was proposed in the literature [14]. In the following, we present a distributed algorithm which divides the CRWN network into clusters, based on local spectrum availability.

Our algorithm is inspired from the [15]. After the neighbor discovery phase, all distributed SUs run the clustering algorithm independently and inspire their decisions on the information in the key, defined by a set $\{K_j, D_j, ID_j\}$. Where ID_j is the SU identification, D_j is the SU_j connectivity. The connectivity is the available information concerning b-hop neighbors, which are at most b-hop away from user j (including node j itself). The term K_j defines the minimum of common channels that SU_j has with each of its neighbors and V_j is SU_j neighbors. We calculate K_j by the formula below:

$$K_j = \min_{i \in V_j} |k_j \cap k_i| \tag{1}$$

Based on this information key, each SU calculates a priority value P_j that will be used during the cluster formation to determine the CH. A SU_j is elected as cluster head if its priority is the maximum of neighbors priority, which mean that the weighted priority of cluster head is the highest among its neighbors. We illustrate that by a formula:

$$P_j = \max_{i \in V_j} (P_i) \tag{2}$$

All node whose weighted priority key is the highest among its neighbors request the creation of a cluster with their ID as cluster ID, nodes that receive the request join the cluster if their priority is lower. Otherwise, they elect themselves as cluster heads. If they receive multiple request from different CH, they choose the CH with the low communication overhead.

After the CH selection, routing paths are established and a protocol of routing is defined. The users in the same cluster can exchange network setup and maintenance messages instead of the first request defined before. Informations about topological changes (because of dead nodes or node mobility) can be exchanges during this phase.

3.2 Scenario of Forming Coalition in Clusters

In this paper, we model the coalition formation as a game with complete information. At the beginning, we have solo-coalitions. Every user sends a proposal to neighbors in the same cluster Q_l. All players in vicinity respond to the offer. Recent works investigate different methods for multi-agent system in cognitive radio [16] (Fig. 1).

At each stage, a player becomes the proposer of forming a coalition. The others players, who received offers make their response to accept or to decline the offer. After the approbation of the request, the coalition will be formed. Every user sends the same proposal that contains a comprehensive offer for all QoS parameters which are: saving energy, delay and enhancing throughput. After that, the users start forming coalitions based on a strategic learning algorithm to learn the best coalition until Nash equilibrium (NE). By using clusters, the node will easily and quickly decide on a winner and send a confirmation message to the winning coalition and a cancellation message to all others. Next, the user j and other members of the coalitions fit contracts such as SLA (Service Level Agreement).

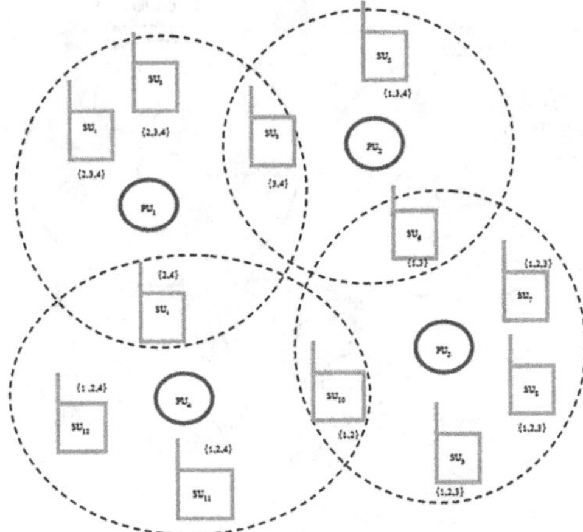

Fig. 1. Cluster formation schema in CRWN

Algorithm 1. Forming coalition Algorithm in clusters

Phase 0

The network starts with solo-coalitions $G = \{\{1\}, \{2\}, .., \{M\}\}$ and no clusters $Q = \emptyset$.

Phase 1

Clusters formation $Q = \{Q_1, Q_2, .., Q_L\}$.

Phase 2: Coalition formation process

repeat

Execute Algorithm 2 (see below) with input j and Q_l.

until convergence to a Nash-stable partition.

A contract is made between users.

Phase 3: Joint spectrum sensing and access

The sensing and access are joined in the formed coalition.

In this section, a cooperative model is proposed in every cluster to preserve the energy of every node in the sensing phase and enhance their performances in the access phase. This layout used a coalitional game in partition form. Indeed, after forming coalitions within each coalition only one *SU* senses the channel according to a discrete distribution probability and broadcast channel occupation information to every *SU* in the same coalition. After that, only one *SU* is elected according to the discrete distribution probability to transmit its data using the unoccupied channel. The others SUs will not sense the channel and so preserve their energy.

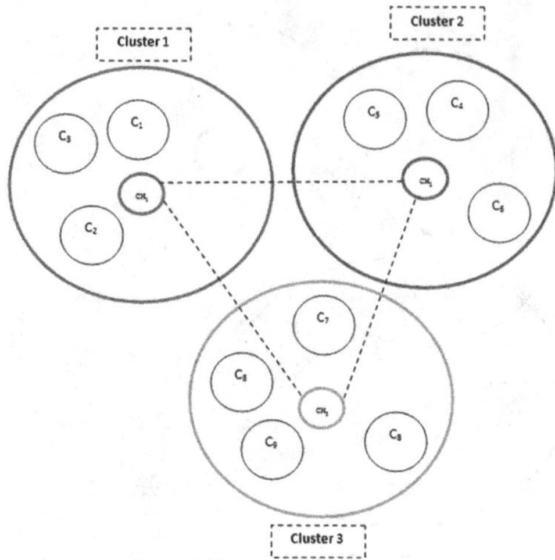

Fig. 2. Cluster formation using coalitional approach in CRWN

The beginning of our Algorithm 1, is with solo coalitions and without clusters. This case corresponds to the non cooperative state of all secondary users and no cluster is defined. A user in our system decides to join the coalition C_i in the same cluster, if this coalition improves its utility. The algorithm terminates when no player wants to join another coalition (Nash Equilibrium). The convergence of the algorithm, is guaranteed because the set C_i can only increase in size and is maximally limited to the grand coalition. The grand coalition is the coalition of all the users in network.

At the end of clusters and coalitions formation, an inter-cluster communication is started, see Fig. 2. The clusters are in different colors and the communication between clusters head is presented by dotted lines.

3.3 User's Utility Function in Clusters

In coalitional game theory, we distinguish between two entities: the value of a coalition and the payoff received by a player. The value of a coalition represents the amount of utility that a coalition, as a whole, can obtain. The payoff of a player represents the amount of utility that a player, member of a certain coalition and cluster can obtain. Using our model, our main goal consists of enhancing throughput with reducing energy consumption. For this purpose, we define our utility based on this two criteria. So, the utility of user j in coalition C_i, partition G_i and cluster Q_l is expressed by:

$$\begin{aligned} U_j(C_i, G_i, Q_l) = F_j(C_i, G_i, Q_l) - \gamma.(E_{T_j}(C_i, G_i, Q_l) + E_{N_j}(C_i, G_i, Q_l) \\ + E_{S_j}(C_i, G_i, Q_l) + E_{f_j}(C_i, G_i, Q_l) + E_Q) \end{aligned} \quad (3)$$

Where:

- $E_{S_j}(C_i, G_i, Q_l)$ and $E_{T_j}(C_i, G_i, Q_l)$ are the energy wasted in sensing and transmitting.
- $F_j(C_i, G_i, Q_l)$ is the throughput of user j in coalition C_i and cluster Q_l. By using the symmetric channels this throughput is equal for all users in the same cluster.
- E_Q is the energy wasted in cluster formation.
- $E_{f_j}(C_i, G_i, Q_l)$ is the energy wasted in coalition formation and it depends on users numbers. It is clear that in large network this cost will be very high, our cluster scheme decreases the cost of coalition formation and thus enhance the users utilities.
- $E_{N_j}(C_i, G_i, Q_l)$ is the energy wasted in negotiation between users in various coalition, same partition and same cluster.
- γ is a constant.

$$\begin{aligned} F_j(C_i, G_i, Q_l) = (1 - R_j(C_i, G_i, Q_l)).(1 - z_k(C_i, G_i, Q_l)) \\ r_j(C_i, G_i, Q_l).t_{T_j}(C_i, G_i, Q_l) \end{aligned} \quad (4)$$

$R_j(C_i, G_i)$ is the probability of collision with another coalition in the same cluster, $t_{T_j}(C_i, G_i, Q_l)$ is time spent in transmission. Finally, $r_j(C_i, G_i, Q_l)$ represents the transmission rate of the user j to its receiver when the PU is absent and $z_k(C_i, G_i, Q_l)$ is the probability of collision with the primary.

3.4 Learning Algorithm in Clusters

In game theory, the term of complete information describes a game in which knowledge about other players is available to all participants in the cluster Q_l. Every player knows the payoffs and strategies available to other players.

Algorithm 2. Learning coalition of informed players in clusters

Initialization

- For each player $j \in M$ and cluster Q_l.
  - Observe state G_0
  - Choose coalition C_0, in cluster Q_l.

Learning patterns

- For each time slot t
  - For each informed player.
    - Observe the current state G_i.
    - Choose coalition C_{i_t} according to the randomized action $A_j(G_i, C_i)$.
    - Observe the realized vector of utility $U_{j,t}(C_i, G_i, Q_l)$ in all coalitions.
- Update strategy $A_j(G_i, C_i)$ according to Eq. (5).

In the proposed game, a coalition is a set of distinct, autonomous players that may cooperate in order to increase their individual gains, noted as selfish cooperation. We have to use an algorithm that converge to Nash equilibrium (NE). In the paper in [10], the authors discuss the convergence with mathematical analysis. They use a strategic learning as solution for coalition formation when the number of coalition are finite. By using strategic Learning Algorithm, each SU learns the coalition with best reward until a Nash equilibrium is reached (Algorithm 2).

The Eq. (5) for the update can be expressed like below:

$$A_j(G_i, C_i) : x_{j,t}\,(G_i, C_i) = \frac{x_{j,t-1}(G_i, C_i)(1 + v_{j,t}(G_i))^{-y_{j,t-1}(G_i,C_i)}}{\sum_{C_i'} x_{j,t-1}(G_i, C_i')(1 + v_{j,t}(G_i))^{-y_{j,t-1}(G_i,C_i')}} \quad (5)$$

With $y_{j,t-1}\,(G_i, C_i)$ is the invert of the utility received and $x_{j,t}(G_i, C_i)$ is the probability of choosing the coalition by the user j being in state G_i. Also, $v_{j,t}(G_i) > 0$ is the learning rate taking into account how many times the same action has been chosen.

4 Numerical Results

In this section, we adopt a simulation approach to evaluate the performance of the proposed clustering algorithm. We consider a CRWN scenario in which SUs are randomly deployed in a 20 m × 20 m square domain.

We have $M = 80$, $Q = \{1, 2, ..., 20\}$, and each cluster contains $N = 4$ secondary users $K = \{1, 2\}$. The possible strategies of four users in each cluster

Table 1. Possible coalition strategies for four players in one cluster

$G_1 = \{1, 2, 3, 4\}$	$G_7 = \{\{1, 3\}, \{2\}, \{4\}\}$
$G_2 = \{\{1, 2, 3\}, \{4\}\}$	$G_8 = \{\{1, 4\}, \{2\}, \{3\}\}$
$G_3 = \{\{1, 2, 4\}, \{3\}\}$	$G_9 = \{2, 3\}, \{1\}, \{4\}\}$
$G_4 = \{\{1, 3, 4\}, \{2\}\}$	$G_{10} = \{2, 4\}, \{1\}, \{3\}\}$
$G_5 = \{\{2, 3, 4\}, \{1\}\}$	$G_{11} = \{\{3, 4\}, \{1\}, \{2\}\}$
$G_6 = \{\{1, 2\}, \{3\}, \{4\}\}$	$G_{12} = \{\{1\}, \{2\}, \{3\}, \{4\}\}$

Table 2. Parameters used in numerical simulations for one cluster

Initial Battery $B = [100, 80, 60, 40]$
$RTS = 352$, $z = 0.3$
$R = [0.3, 0.4, 0.5, 0.6]$
$r = 112$, $m = 3$
$t_{slot} = 3000$, $t_s = 15$

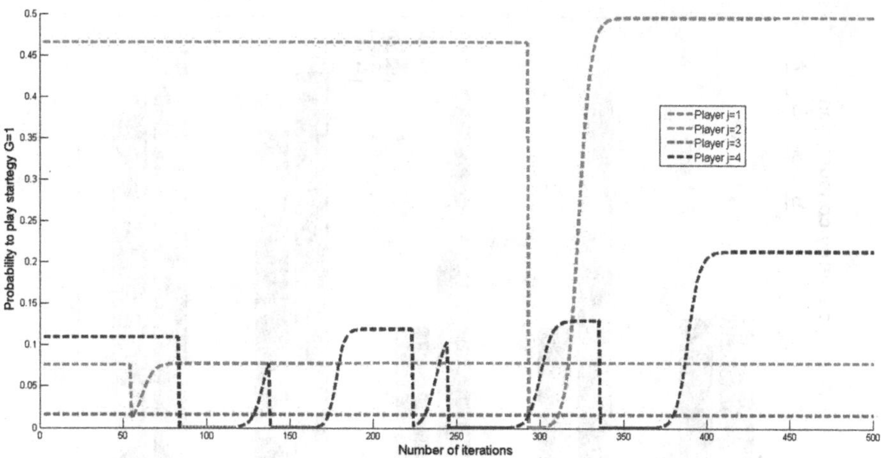

Fig. 3. Probability to play strategy G_1 for $N = 4$ in one cluster

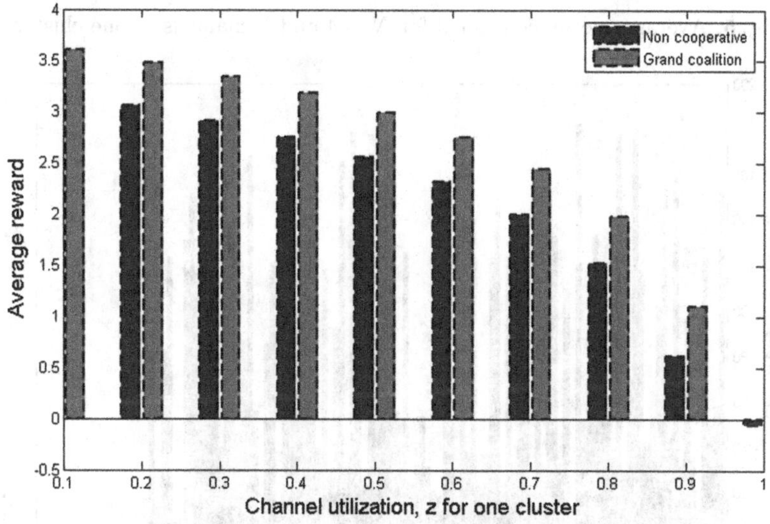

Fig. 4. Average reward in one cluster using different value of channel utilization, $z_k(C_i, G_i, Q_l)$

is presented in Table 1. All others parameters are presented in Table 2. For the equal number of players, we used the learning Algorithm 2. Figure 3 shows the convergence of the algorithm and how all players select the first partition among the twelve possible partitions as mentioned in Table 1. We notice that our algorithm converges after a number of iterations (<400). All players prefer the grand coalition (coalition of all users in the system).

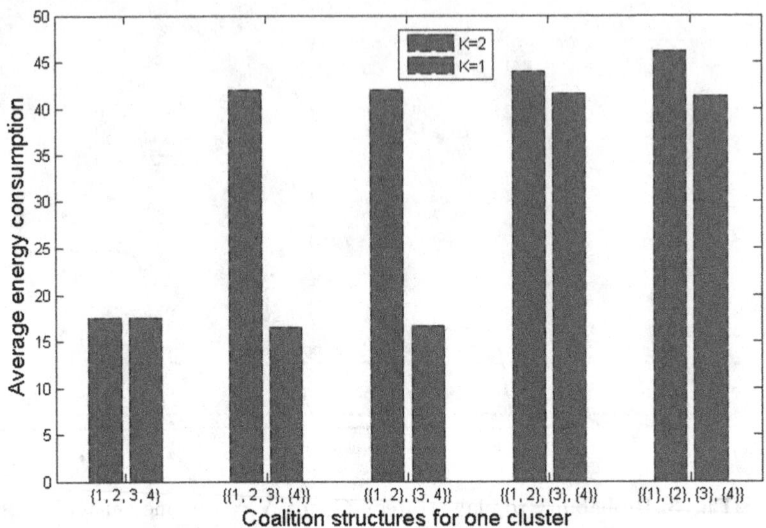

Fig. 5. Average energy consumed for $N = 4$ and k channels in one cluster

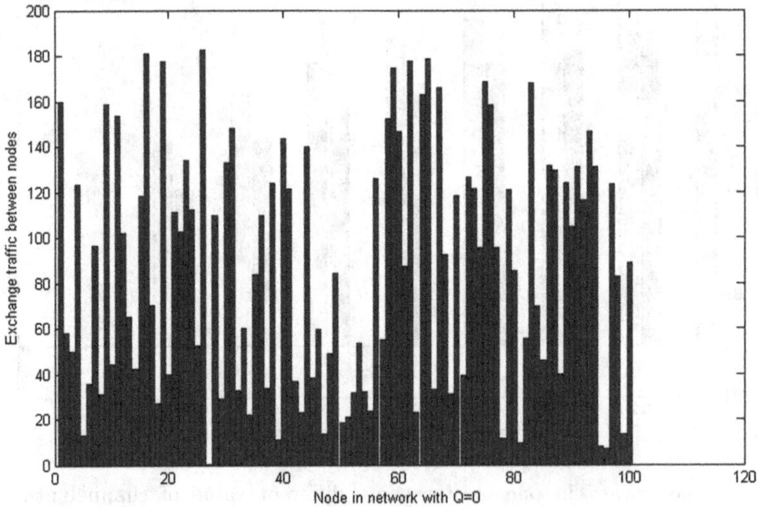

Fig. 6. Communication exchange in CRWN without clusters for $M = 100$

In Fig. 4, the average reward of secondary users, in each cluster, is plotted. The non cooperative state is found by strategy (G_{12}). This is the case where all secondary users are allowed to access all sub-channels. This figure shows clearly, that the cooperative strategy (G_1) gives a very good rewards comparing to strategy (G_{12}) for all channels utilizations values.

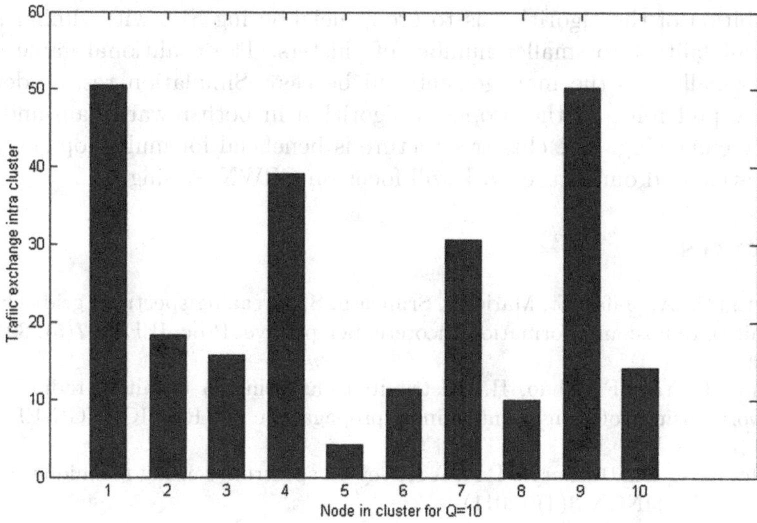

Fig. 7. Communication exchange intra-cluster for $N = 10$, $Q = 10$

Next, we try to evaluate the energy consumption using a coalitional game approach. Note that, secondary users seeking to improve their performances have intention of cooperating.

We plot In Fig. 5, the average energy consumed by coalitions in each cluster using different strategies. This figure shows the average energy consumption as a function of coalition structure. The decrease of energy consumption using strategy G_1 is very clear; when SU cooperate they consume three times less energy than if they use strategy G_{12} and stay alone.

So, comparing with the energy consumption numerical results, for different k values, the difference between the coalitional and non cooperative in clusters is rather important and thus the proposed CRWN using clusters and coalitional approach achieves a good energy consumption.

Our model reduces communication overhead. Figure 6 gives the amount of messages exchanged between nodes in CRWN for $M = 100$ and $Q = \emptyset$. Figure 7, gives the amount of messages exchanged between clusters in CRWN for $N = 10$ and $Q = 10$. The simulation clearly shows that the communication exchange cost in our CRWN is too low by using the clusters (<50) compared to the case of a classic large CRWN (>180).

5 Conclusion

In this work, we propose a new architecture of CRWN by combining two approaches: the clustering scheme and the coalitional game model. We design a distributed coalition algorithm in clusters based on imitative strategic learning.

The ambition of the algorithm is to group neighboring SUs with similar spectrum availability into smaller number of clusters. The coalitional game make network smaller, so the management will be easy. Simulation results demonstrate the preference of the proposed algorithm in both reward gain and performance enhancing. The cluster structure is beneficial for multi-hop spectrum collaboration and our future work will focus on CRWN routing.

References

1. Goldsmith, A., Jafar, S., Maric, I., Srinivasa, S.: Breaking spectrum gridlock with cognitive radios: an information theoretic perspective. Proc. IEEE **97**(5), 894–914 (2009)
2. Zhang, J., Yao, F., Zhao, H.: Distributed clustering in cognitive radio ad hoc networks using soft-constraint affinity propagation. In: RADIOENGINEERING (2012)
3. Garhwal, A., Bhattacharya, P.P.: A survey on spectrum sensing techniques in cognitive radio. IJNGN **3**(4) (2011)
4. Chen, J., Zhang, C.: Channel allocation strategy based on cognitive radio network. IRECOS **7**(7), 3704–3709 (2012)
5. Ghasemi, A., Sousa, E.: Collaborative spectrum sensing for opportunistic access in fading environments. In: Proceedings of the IEEE DySPAN, pp. 131–136 (2005)
6. Scutari, G., Pang, J.-S.: Joint sensing and power allocation in non convex cognitive radio games: nash equilibria and distributed algorithms. IEEE Trans. Inf. Theory **59**(7), 4626–4661 (2013)
7. Elmachkour, M., Daha Belghiti, I., Kobbane, A., Sabir, E., Ben-Othman, J.: Green Opportunistic Access for Cognitive Radio Networks: A Minority Game Approach, ICC (2013)
8. Yan, L., Zeng, Y.: Collaborative Spectrum Sensing Using Coalitional Games in Cognitive Radio Networks. IEEE (2008)
9. Saad, W., Han, Z., Zheng, R., Hjorungnes, A., Basar, T., Poor, H.V.: Coalitional games in partition form for joint spectrum sensing and access in cognitive radio networks. IEEE J. Sel. Topics Signal Process. **6**(2), 195–209 (2012)
10. Daha Belghiti, I., Elmachkour, M., Berrada, I., Omari, L.: Green cognitive radio networks by using coalitional game approach in partition form. IRECOS, vol. 9(10) (2014)
11. Zhao, Q., Tong, L., Swami, A., Chen, Y.: Decentralized cognitive mac for opportunistic spectrum access in ad hoc networks: a pomdp frame- work. IEEE J. Sel. Areas Commun. **25**(3), 589–600 (2007)
12. Fan, R., Jiang, H.: Optimal multi-channel cooperative sensing in cognitive radio networks. IEEE Trans. Wirel. Commun. **9**, 1128–1138 (2010)
13. El Machkour, M., Kobbane, A., Sabir, E., El Koutbi, M.: New insights from a delay analysis for cognitive radio networks with and without reservation. In: IWCMC (2012)
14. Arachchige, C., Venkatesan, S., Mittal, N.: An asynchronous neighbor discovery algorithm for cognitive radio networks. In: Proceedings of IEEE DySPAN, October 2008
15. Lin, C.R., Gerla, M.: Adaptive clustering for mobile wireless networks. IEEE J. Sel. Areas Commun. **15**(7), 1265–1275 (1997)
16. Trigui, E., Esseghir, M., Boulahia, L.M.: On using multi agent systems in cognitive radio networks: a Survey. Int. J. Wirel. Mob. Netw. (IJWMN) **4**(6) (2012)

Optimal Torus Exploration by Oblivious Robots

Stéphane Devismes[1(✉)], Anissa Lamani[2], Franck Petit[3,4], and Sébastien Tixeuil[3,5]

[1] VERIMAG, Université Joseph Fourier, Saint-martin-d'hères, France
stephane.devismes@imag.fr
[2] Kyushu University, Fukuoka, Japan
[3] LIP6, UPMC Sorbonne Universités, Paris, France
[4] INRIA, Projet-Team REGAL, Paris, France
[5] Institut Universitaire de France, Paris, France

Abstract. We consider autonomous robots that are endowed with motion actuators and visibility sensors. The robots we consider are weak, *i.e.*, they are anonymous, uniform, unable to explicitly communicate, and oblivious (they do not remember any of their past actions). In this paper, we propose an optimal (*w.r.t.* the number of robots) solution for the terminating exploration of torus-shaped networks by a team of k such robots in the SSYNC model.

In more details, we first show that it is impossible to explore any simple torus of arbitrary size with (strictly) less than four robots, even if the algorithm is probabilistic. If the algorithm is required to be deterministic, four robots are also insufficient. This negative result implies that the only way to obtain an optimal algorithm (*w.r.t.* the number of robots participating to the algorithm) is to make use of probabilities.

Then, we propose a probabilistic algorithm that uses four robots to explore all simple tori of size $\ell \times L$, where $7 \leq \ell \leq L$. Hence, in such tori, four robots are necessary and sufficient to solve the (probabilistic) terminating exploration. As a torus can be seen as a 2-dimensional ring, our result shows, perhaps surprisingly, that increasing the number of possible symmetries in the network (due to increasing dimensions) does not necessarily come at an extra cost *w.r.t.* the number of robots that are necessary to solve the problem.

1 Introduction

We consider autonomous robots that are endowed with motion actuators and visibility sensors, but that are otherwise unable to communicate. They evolve in a discrete environment, *i.e.*, the space is partitioned into a finite number of locations, conveniently represented by a graph, where the nodes represent the possible locations that a robot can take and the edges the possibility for a robot to move from one location to another.

Those robots must collaborate to solve a collective task despite being limited with respect to inputs from the environment, asymmetry, memory, *etc.* In particular, the robots we consider are anonymous, uniform, yet they can sense their environment and take decisions according to their own ego-centered view.

A. Bouajjani and H. Fauconnier (Eds.): NETYS 2015, LNCS 9466, pp. 183–199, 2015.
DOI: 10.1007/978-3-319-26850-7_13

In addition, they are oblivious, *i.e.*, they do not remember their past actions. Robots operate in *cycles* that include three phases: *Look*, *Compute*, and *Move* (L-C-M, for short). The Look phase consists in taking a snapshot of the other robots positions using its visibility sensors. During the Compute phase, a robot computes a target destination based on the previous observation. The Move phase simply consists in moving toward the computed destination using motion actuators. Using L-C-M cycles, three models has been introduced in the literature, capturing the various degrees of synchrony between robots. According to a recent taxonomy [11], they are denoted FSYNC, SSYNC, and ASYNC, from the stronger to the weaker. The former stands for *fully synchronous*. In this model, all robots execute the L-C-M cycle synchronously and atomically. In the SSYNC (*semi-synchronous*) model, robots are asynchronously activated to perform cycles, yet at each activation, a robot executes one cycle atomically. With the weaker model, ASYNC (stands for *asynchronous*), robots execute L-C-M in a completely independent manner.

In this context, typical problems are *terminating exploration* [4,7–10], *exclusive perpetual exploration* [1,2,5], *exclusive searching* [5,6], and *gathering* [5,12,13]. In this paper, we address the *terminating exploration* (or simply *exploration*) problem, which requires that robots collectively explore the whole graph and stop upon completion. We focus on the case where the network is an *anonymous unoriented torus* (or simply *torus*, for short). The terms *anonymous* and *unoriented* mean that no robot has access to any kind external device (*e.g.*, node identifiers, oracle, local edge labeling) allowing to identify nodes or to determine any (global or local) direction, such as North-South/East-West.

A question naturally arises: "*Why addressing an abstract topology such as torus?*" To answer this question, we must emphasize that robots are unable to communicate explicitly and have no persistent memory. So, they are unable to remember the various steps taken before. Therefore, the positions of the other robots are the only way to distinguish the different stages of the exploration process. Torus belongs to the class of *regular* graphs, *i.e.*, graphs where each vertex has the same number of neighbors. Such graphs are of particular interest because they are topologies for which the symmetry of configurations with respect to robot positions is the most frequently observed, making the exploration problem hard to solve. So far, ring-shaped network is the only *regular* topology that has been studied [8,10,14]. As a result, an immediate question arises: "*Does the increase of the number of possible symmetries in the network (mainly due to increasing dimensions) make the problem harder to solve?*" Terminating exploration has been studied in other topologies than rings, namely the tree [9] and grid [7]. However, none of them are regular networks. Torus can be seen as a 2-dimensional ring. Compared to the ring, the main difficulty lies in the additional axes of symmetry. It appears to be the most natural candidate among regular graphs to study the impact of strong topological symmetry on the complexity to solve the problem.

Furthermore, as previously stated, the exploration (with stop) process is intrinsically related to the ability to differentiate consecutive phases of the exploration. More possible symmetries hint that more robots than in rings are required to complete exploration: As robots have no way to distinguish and agree on some kind of orientation, *e.g.*, North-South/East-West, somehow the current robot configuration has to encode consistent information so that robots agree on both axes. Since numerous symmetric configurations induce a large number of required robots, minimizing the number of robots turns out to be a difficult problem.

Related Work. With respect to the (terminating) exploration problem, minimizing the number of robots for exploring particular classes of graphs led to contrasted results.

The only result available for exploration in general graphs [4] considers that edges are labeled in such a way that the network configuration (made of the topology, the edge labeling, and the robot positions) is asymmetric. In this extended model, three robots are not sufficient to explore all asymmetric configurations, and four robots are sufficient to explore all asymmetric configurations. Note that exploring the set of asymmetric configurations is strictly weaker than exploring the complete underlying graph, especially when the graph is highly symmetric.

The rest of the literature is thus dedicated to a weaker model, where edges are not labeled (or equivalently, the labeling is decided by an adversary anytime a robot is activated). One extreme case in this weak model is the set of tree-shaped networks, as in general, $\Omega(n)$ robots are necessary and sufficient to explore a tree network of n nodes deterministically [9]. The other extreme case is the set of grid-shaped networks [7], where three robots are necessary and sufficient to explore deterministically any grid of at least three nodes (except for the grids of size 2×2 and 3×3, where four – respectively five – robots are necessary and sufficient). However, this result is mainly due to the fact that grids are not regular graphs: they contain nodes of degrees 2, 3, and 4. This topological property implies less symmetries.

In contrast, rings and tori are regular graphs, and consequently more intricate. In ring-shaped networks [10], the fact that the number k of robots and the ring size n must be coprime yields to the lower bound $\Omega(\log n)$ on the number of robots required to explore a n-size ring. Indeed, the smallest non-divisor of n evolves as $\log n$ in the worst case. However, notice that Lamani *et al.* also provide in [14] a protocol that allows 5 robots to deterministically explore any ring whose size is coprime with 5. The large number of robots and the constraint on the ratio between the number of robots and the ring size induced by the deterministic setting in ring-shaped networks hinted at a possible more efficient solutions when robots can make use of probabilities [8]. As a matter of fact, four robots are necessary and sufficient to probabilistically explore any ring of size at least four. While the gain in going probabilistic is only one robot when n is not divisible by 5, a logarithmic factor is obtained in the general case. Aforementioned deterministic solutions typically operate in the ASYNC model, while probabilistic ones can only cope with the weaker SSYNC model. Actually, an impossibility result [8] explicitly states that randomization does not help in the ASYNC model (that is, there exists a scheduling such that random choices are all nullified).

So far, no research explored the feasibility of exploring a torus-shaped network with a team of k robots. The exploration of tori is a step forward toward exploration of other (maybe more complex) *unoriented periodic 2D discrete spaces*, *e.g.*, spheres.

Contribution. We propose an optimal (*w.r.t.* the number of robots) solution for the terminating exploration of torus-shaped networks by a team of k such robots. In more details, we first show that it is impossible to explore any simple torus of arbitrary size with less than four robots, even if the algorithm is probabilistic. If the algorithm is required to be deterministic, four robots are also insufficient. This negative result implies that the only way to obtain an optimal algorithm (*w.r.t.* the number of robots participating to the algorithm) is to make use of probabilities, and thus, within the SSYNC model, due to aforementioned impossibility [8].

So, we propose a probabilistic algorithm designed for the SSYNC model that uses four robots to explore all simple tori of size $\ell \times L$, where $7 \leq \ell \leq L$. Hence, in such tori, four robots are necessary and sufficient to solve the (probabilistic) terminating exploration. As a torus can be seen as a 2-dimensional ring, our result shows, perhaps surprisingly, that increasing the number of possible symmetries in the network (due to increasing dimensions) does not necessarily bring an extra cost with respect to the number of robots that are necessary to solve the problem.

Roadmap. Section 2 presents the system model and the problem to be solved. Lower bounds are shown in Sect. 3. The general solution using four robots is given in Sect. 4. Section 5 gives some concluding remarks.

2 Preliminaries

We consider systems of autonomous mobile entities called *robots* evolving in a *simple unoriented connected graph* $G = (V, E)$, where V is a finite set of n nodes and E a finite set of edges. Nodes represent locations that robots can take and edges represent the possibility for a robot to move from one location to another. Two nodes u and v are *neighbors* in G *iff* $\{u, v\} \in E$.

We assume that G is an (ℓ, L)-*Torus* (or a *Torus*, for short), where ℓ and L are two positive integers, *i.e.*, G satisfies the following two conditions: (i) $n = \ell \times L$ and (ii) there exists an order $v_1, \ldots, v_n$ on the nodes of V such that $\forall i \in [1..n]$:

- If $i + \ell \leq n$, then $\{i, i + \ell\} \in E$, else $\{i, (i + \ell) \bmod n\} \in E$.
- If $i \bmod \ell \neq 0$, then $\{i, i + 1\} \in E$, else $\{i, i - \ell + 1\} \in E$.

Given the previous order $v_1, \ldots, v_n$, for every $j \in [0..(L-1)]$, the sequence $v_{1+j\times\ell}, v_{2+j\times\ell}, \ldots, v_{\ell+j\times\ell}$ is called an ℓ-ring. Similarly, for every $k \in [1..\ell]$, $v_k, v_{k+\ell}, v_{k+2\times\ell}, \ldots, v_{k+(L-1)\times\ell}$ is called an L-ring. Note that when $\ell = L$, any ℓ-ring is also an L-ring and conversely. More generally, we use the term *ring* to arbitrarily designate an ℓ-ring or an L-ring.

Nodes are anonymous (they have no access to identifiers or other symmetry breaking capabilities). Moreover, given two neighboring nodes u and v, there is no explicit or implicit labeling allowing robots to determine whether u is either on the left, on the right, above, or below v. However, for the purpose of explanations, we may use indices for nodes or robots.

An *isomorphism* of graphs G and H is a bijection f between the vertex sets of G and H such that any two nodes u and v of G are neighbors in G *iff* $f(u)$ and $f(v)$ are neighbors in H. When G and H are one and the same graph, f is called an *automorphism* of G. An (ℓ, L)-*Torus* and an (L, ℓ)-*Torus* are isomorphic. Hence, as nodes are anonymous, an (ℓ, L)-*Torus* cannot be distinguished from an (L, ℓ)-*Torus*. So, with loss of generality, we will always consider (ℓ, L)-*Tori*, where $\ell \leq L$.

Remark 1. As an (ℓ, L)-torus is a simple graph, every node has four *distinct* neighbors, and consequently we have: $3 \leq \ell \leq L$ and $n = \ell \times L \geq 9$.

Operating on G are k robots. The robots do not communicate in an explicit way; however they see the position of all other robots in their ego-centered coordinate system and can acquire knowledge from this information. Each robot operates according to its (local) *program.* We call *protocol* a collection of k *programs*, each one operating on a single robot. Robots are *uniform* and *anonymous*, *i.e.*, they all have the same program using no parameter allowing to differentiate them. We assume that robots cannot remember any previous observation or computation. Such robots are called *oblivious.* The program of a robot consists in executing *Look-Compute-Move cycles* infinitely many times. That is, a robot $\mathcal{R}$ first observes its environment (Look phase). Based on its observation, $\mathcal{R}$ then (probabilistically or deterministically) decides to move or stay idle (Compute phase). If $\mathcal{R}$ decides to move, it moves toward its destination during the Move phase. During the Compute phase, the decision between moving or staying idle is either deterministic or probabilistic. In the latter case, the robot decides between moving and staying idle using some fixed probability $p \in (0, 1)$, and we say that the robot *tries to move.*

We consider the SSYNC model, where time is represented by an infinite sequence of instants 0, 1, 2, ... No robot has access to this global time. At each instant, a non-empty subset of robots is *activated.* Every robot that is activated at instant t *atomically* executes a full cycle between t and $t + 1$. Activations are determined by an *adversary.* Note that in this model, any robot performing a Look operation sees all other robots on nodes and not on edges.

We assume that during the Look phase, every robot can perceive whether several robots are located on the same node. This ability is called *(global) multiplicity detection.* We shall indicate by $d_i(t)$ the multiplicity of robots present in node v_i at instant t. We consider two versions of multiplicity detection: the *strong* and *weak* multiplicity detections. Under the *weak* multiplicity detection, for every node v_i, d_i is a function $\mathbb{N} \mapsto \{\circ, \bot, \top\}$ defined as follows: $d_i(t)$ is equal to either $\circ$, $\bot$, or $\top$ according to v_i contains none, one or several robots at instant t. If $d_i(t) = \circ$, then we say that v_i is *free* at instant t, otherwise v_i is *occupied* at instant t. If $d_i(t) = \top$, then we say that v_i contains a *tower* at instant t. Under the *strong* multiplicity detection, for every node v_i, d_i is a function $\mathbb{N} \mapsto \mathbb{N}$, where $d_i(t) = x$ indicates that there are x robots in node v_i at instant t. If $d_i(t) = 0$, then we say that v_i is *free* at instant t, otherwise v_i is *occupied* at instant t. If $d_i(t) > 1$, then we say that v_i contains a *tower (of $d_i(t)$ robots)* at instant t.

To define the notion of *configuration* (of the system), we use an arbitrary order $\prec$ on nodes. The system being anonymous, robots do not know this order. Let $v_1, \ldots, v_n$ be the list of the nodes in G ordered by $\prec$. The configuration at instant t is $d_1(t), \ldots, d_n(t)$. We denote by *initial configurations* the configurations from which the system can start at instant 0. Every configuration from which no robot moves or tries to move if activated is said to be *terminal*. Two configurations $d_1, \ldots, d_n$ and $d'_1, \ldots, d'_n$ are *indistinguishable* (resp., *distinguishable* otherwise) *iff* there exists an automorphism on G, $f : V \mapsto V$ such that $\forall i \in \{1, \ldots, n\}$, $d_i = d'_j$ where $v_j = f(v_i)$.

The *view* of robot $\mathcal{R}$ at instant t is a labeled graph isomorphic to G, where every node v_i is labeled by $d_i(t)$, except the node where $\mathcal{R}$ is currently located, this latter node v_j is labeled by $d_j(t), *$. (Indeed, the coordinate system is ego-centered.) Hence, from its view, a robot can compute the view of each other robot, and decide whether some other robots have the same view as its own. The views $\mathcal{V}$ and $\mathcal{V}'$ are *identical iff* there exists an isomorphism f of $\mathcal{V}$ and $\mathcal{V}'$ such that every node v of $\mathcal{V}$ has the same label in $\mathcal{V}$ as node $f(v)$ in $\mathcal{V}'$.

Every decision to move is based on the view obtained during the last Look action. However, it may happen that some edges incident to a node v currently occupied by the deciding robot look identical in its view, *i.e.*, v lies on a symmetric axis of its view. In this case, if the robot decides to take one of these edges, it may take any of them. We assume the worst-case decision in such cases, *i.e.*, the actual edge among the identically looking ones is chosen by the adversary.

A *scheduling* is a list of activation's choices that can be made by the adversary, *i.e.*, a scheduling is any infinite list of non-empty subset of robots $\sigma_0, \sigma_1, \ldots$, where $\forall i \geq 0$, σ_i is the set of robots activated at instant i. An infinite list of configurations $\gamma_0, \gamma_1, \ldots$ can be *generated* from the scheduling $\sigma_0, \sigma_1, \ldots$ *iff* $\forall i \geq 0$, γ_{i+1} can be obtained from γ_i after each robot in σ_i is activated at instant i to atomically perform a cycle (in this case, $\gamma_i\gamma_{i+1}$ is *step*). We call *execution* any infinite list of configurations $\gamma_0, \gamma_1, \ldots$ that can be *generated* from an arbitrary scheduling and such that γ_0 is a possible initial configuration. An execution e *terminates* if e contains a terminal configuration.

We restrict the power of the adversary by assuming that schedulings are *fair*: a scheduling $\sigma_0, \sigma_1, \ldots$ is *fair iff* for every robot $\mathcal{R}$, for every instant i, there exists an instant $j \geq i$ such that $\mathcal{R} \in \sigma_j$. An execution e is *fair iff* e can be generated by a fair scheduling. A particular case of fair scheduling is the *sequential* fair scheduling: a scheduling $\sigma_0, \sigma_1, \ldots$ that is fair and such that $\forall i \geq 0$, $|\sigma_i| = 1$. An execution e is *sequential fair* if it can be generated from a sequential fair scheduling.

We consider the *exploration* problem, where k robots, initially placed at different nodes of G, collectively explore G before stopping moving forever. By "collectively" we mean that every node of G is eventually visited by at least one robot. More formally, a protocol $\mathcal{P}$ *deterministically* (resp., *probabilistically*) solves the exploration problem assuming a fair scheduling *iff* every fair execution e of $\mathcal{P}$ starting from a *towerless* configuration satisfies: *(1)* e reaches a terminal configuration *in finite time* (resp., *with probability one*), and *(2)* every node is visited by at least one robot during e. Note that the previous definition implies that every initial configuration are *towerless.* Note also that in case of probabilistic exploration, termination is not certain, however the overall probability of non-terminating executions is 0. Observe that the exploration problem is not defined for $k > n$ and is straightforward for $k = n$. (In this latter case, the exploration is already accomplished in the initial towerless configuration.)

3 Lower Bound

To be as general as possible, in this section we assume the strongest possible multiplicity. Moreover, we consider any (deterministic or probabilistic) exploration protocol $\mathcal{P}$ using a team of k robots in an *arbitrary* topology $G = (V, E)$ of n nodes (*i.e.*, $n = |V|$).

Assume first that $n > k$. Then, the exploration is not (trivially) accomplished in an initial configuration. As robots are oblivious, any terminal configuration of $\mathcal{P}$ in that case should be different from any possible initial configuration. Remark 2 follows from the fact that the set of possible initial configurations is exactly the set of all towerless configurations:

Remark 2. If $n > k$, any terminal configuration of $\mathcal{P}$ contains at least one tower.

Our approach is based on Theorem 1, which is a generalization to arbitrary topologies of a theorem from [8] (this latter was given for rings). The intuitive idea behind this result is that when $n > k$, the memory of explored nodes can only be encoded with configurations that (i) contain at least one tower of less than k robots (Remark 2) and that (ii) are pairwise distinguishable–no robot can remember any past move or action, but still needs to distinguish between visited and unvisited nodes. Moreover, assuming a sequentially fair execution, the actual exploration process (which is, of course, preceded by some setup phase) starts in such a configuration where one can memorize that at most k nodes are already visited. Then, as the execution is assumed to be sequential, at least $n-k$ additional configurations are required to memorize the visit of all remaining nodes. Hence, overall there should exist at least $n - k + 1$ configurations that contain a tower of less than k robots and that are pairwise distinguishable.

Theorem 1. *Considering any (probabilistic or deterministic) exploration protocol for k robots on a graph of $n > k$ nodes working under any fair scheduling, there exists a set $\mathcal{S}$ of at least $n - k + 1$ configurations such that:*

1. *Any two different configurations in $\mathcal{S}$ are distinguishable, and*
2. *In every configuration in $\mathcal{S}$, there is a tower of less than k robots.*

A tower involving at least 2 robots, Corollary 1 directly follows from Theorem 1:

Corollary 1. *Under fair schedulings, $\forall k, 0 \leq k < 3$, no protocol exists to (deterministically or probabilistically) explore any torus of n nodes using k robots.*

The previous corollary excludes that $\mathcal{P}$ works with $k < 3$. Now, let assume that $k = 3$ and consider any arbitrary (ℓ, L)-torus (remember that by Remark 1, $n = \ell \times L \geq 9$). Then, by Theorem 1, we should be able to exhibit a set $\mathcal{S}$ of $n-2$ configurations such that: (1) any two different configurations in $\mathcal{S}$ are distinguishable, and (2) in every configuration in $\mathcal{S}$, there is a tower of 2 robots. Such configurations differ according to the relative positions of the tower and the robot which is alone. Two cases are then possible depending on whether $\ell = L$ or $\ell < L$. In the former case, the size of $\mathcal{S}$ is bounded by $\sum_{i=2}^{\lfloor \frac{L}{2} \rfloor + 1} i = \frac{\lfloor \frac{L}{2} \rfloor \times (\lfloor \frac{L}{2} \rfloor + 3)}{2}$. In the latter case, the size of $\mathcal{S}$ is bounded by $(\lfloor \frac{\ell}{2} \rfloor + 1)(\lfloor \frac{L}{2} \rfloor + 1) - 1$.

Two illustrative examples are given in Figs. 1 and 2. In these examples, for every value i inside a white node, every two configurations where (1) the black node contains the tower of two robots and (2) any white node of number i contains the single robot are indistinguishable. In the $(5,5)$-torus of Fig. 1, the size of $\mathcal{S}$ is at most 5. In the $(5,6)$-torus of Fig. 2, the size of $\mathcal{S}$ is at most 11.

Let first study the case where $\ell = L$. Then, $\frac{\lfloor \frac{L}{2} \rfloor \times (\lfloor \frac{L}{2} \rfloor + 3)}{2}$ should be greater or equal to $n - 2$, *i.e.*, $L^2 - 2$. From this inequality, we have: $7L^2 - 6L - 16 \leq 0$. $\Delta = 484 > 0$, so $7L^2 - 6L - 16 = 0$ has two solutions: $\frac{6-\sqrt{484}}{14}$ and $\frac{6+\sqrt{484}}{14}$; and $7L^2 - 6L - 16 \leq 0$ for $L \in [\frac{6-\sqrt{484}}{14}; \frac{6+\sqrt{484}}{14}]$. By Remark 1, $L \geq 3$. Moreover,

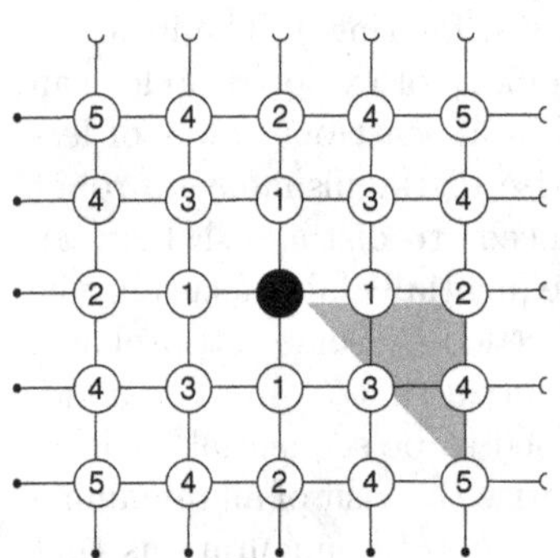

Fig. 1. A $(5,5)$-torus.

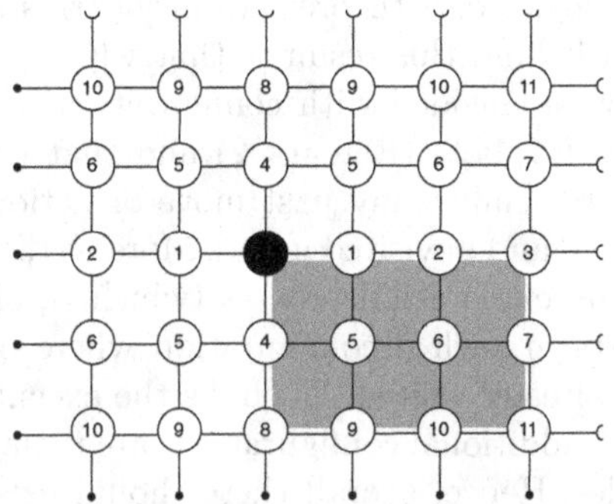

Fig. 2. A $(5,6)$-torus.

$\frac{6+\sqrt{484}}{14} = 2$. So, we obtain a contradiction: there is neither probabilistic nor deterministic exploration protocol in that case, even assuming a fair scheduling.

Let now study the case where $\ell < L$. Then, $(\lfloor \frac{\ell}{2} \rfloor + 1)(\lfloor \frac{L}{2} \rfloor + 1) - 1$ should be greater or equal to $n - 2$, *i.e.*, $\ell \times L - 2$. From this inequality, we have: $2\ell + 2L + 8 \geq 3\ell \times L$. As $3 \leq \ell < L$ (Remark 1), $2\ell + 2L + 8 \geq 3\ell \times L$ has no solution: there is neither probabilistic nor deterministic exploration protocol in that case, even assuming a fair scheduling.

Hence, there is neither probabilistic nor deterministic protocol to explore any torus with 3 robots and, with Corollary 1, we can conclude:

Theorem 2. *Under fair schedulings, $\forall k, 0 \leq k < 4$, there is no protocol to (deterministically or probabilistically) explore any torus of n nodes using k robots.*

Consider now the *deterministic* exploration with $k = 4$ robots. Assume any (ℓ, L)-*Torus* such that $\ell = L$ and ℓ is even. Then, it is possible to initially place the four robots in such way that they have all identical views and all their possible destinations looked identical (just form a square whose adjacent sides have length $\frac{\ell}{2}$). In this case, the adversary can choose to synchronously activate all robots at each step in such way that the initial symmetry continues: we obtain a non-terminating fair execution. Hence:

Theorem 3. *Under fair schedulings, $\forall k, 0 \leq k \leq 4$, there is no protocol to* deterministically *explore all torus of n nodes using k robots.*

Notice that the previous impossibility result can be circumvented, for example, by making restrictions on possible initial configurations [6].

4 Optimal Algorithm

We propose a probabilistic algorithm to explore with 4 robots any (ℓ, L)-torus such that $7 \leq \ell \leq L$, assuming weak multiplicity detection. Before providing informal explanations, we first need to define some terms.

Let v_1 and v_2 be two nodes containing robot r_1 and r_2, resp. r_1 is a neighboring robot of r_2, and conversely. A *block* is a maximal elementary path along some ring of the torus $B = u_i, u_{i+1}, \ldots, u_{i+m}$ with $m > 0$, where each node is occupied by exactly one robot. A robot that does not belong to a block is said to be *isolated.* A *hole* is any maximal non-empty elementary path of free nodes $H = u_i, u_{i+1}, \ldots, u_{i+m}$ that is along some ring of the torus. The *size* of a block (resp., a hole) is the number of nodes it contains. A block (resp. a hole) of size x is said to be an x-*block* (resp., a x-hole). Given the block B (resp., the hole H), the nodes u_i and u_{i+m} are termed as the *extremities* of B (resp., H). We call *neighbor* of a hole (resp. a block) any node that does not belong to the hole (resp. the block) but is neighbor of one of its nodes. In this case, we also say that the hole (resp. the block) is a *neighboring hole* (resp. *neighboring block*) of the node. By extension, any robot that is located at a neighboring node of a hole (resp. a block) is also referred to as a neighbor of the hole (resp. the block).

A node u is said to be *safe* if there is at most one robot that is located within distance one from u. We call *Couple* any ℓ-ring that contains exactly two robots.

We are now ready to sketch our algorithm. Our algorithm works in three distinct successive phases, respectively called **SetUp**, **Tower**, and **Exploration**. Starting from any towerless configuration, the aim of the **SetUp Phase** is to arrange the robots in such a way that they eventually form a $\diamondsuit$.*Configuration* (see Fig. 3), without creating any tower during the process. This first phase is probabilistic. A $\diamondsuit$.Configuration is a configuration, where (1) there are two ℓ-rings of the torus that both contain a 2-block, and (2) there are two robots that have two robots in their neighborhood.

Once a $\diamondsuit$.Configuration is built, **Tower Phase** begins. This phase is also probabilistic and consists in creating a tower using the two neighboring robots that have exactly two robots in their neighborhood. Once the tower is created, the location of robots give an explicit orientation to the torus; and the last phase, **Exploration Phase**, begins. This phase is deterministic. The two isolated robots collaborate together to deterministically explore the torus and eventually stop. We now explain the three successive phases in more details.

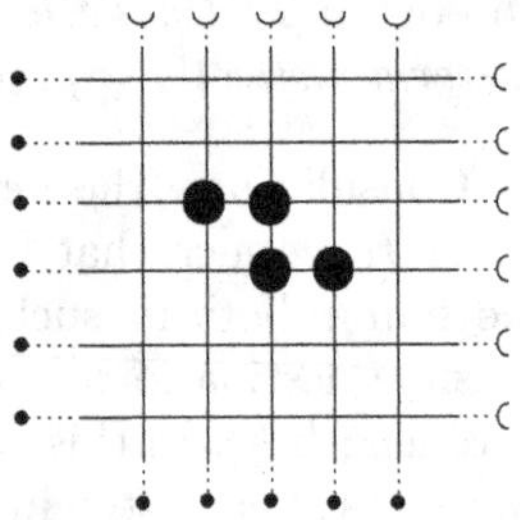

Fig. 3. $\diamondsuit$.Configuration.

SetUp Phase. Let us begin with some definitions. A configuration is said to be a *Double-Trap1* (refer to Fig. 4) if there exists an ℓ-ring R that contains a 3-block having exactly one extremity with a neighboring robot that is not in R. A configuration is a *Double-Trap2* (Fig. 5) if there is one isolated robot at some node z and two 2-blocks $B1 = u, v$ and $B2 = x, y$ such that (1) $v = x$, (2) $B1$ is on a ℓ-ring, (3) z and y are on a ℓ-ring parallel to the one containing $B1$, and (4) z is at distance 2 of both u and y. A configuration C is said to be *Regular* if C contains no tower, C is not a $\diamondsuit$.configuration, and the robots can be split in two pairs $\{r_1, r_2\}$ and $\{r_3, r_4\}$ such that the views of r_1 and r_2 (resp. the views of r_3 and r_4) are identical. (A particular case of configuration Regular is a configuration where all robots have identical views.) A configuration C is said to be *Triplet* if C is not a Double-Trap1 and there is a ℓ-ring R that contains exactly 3 robots. When R contains neither a 3-block nor a 2-block, we define the *Wall* as the ring perpendicular to R that contains the robot not in R, see Fig. 6. A configuration C is said to be *Twin* (Fig. 7) if C contains a couple, but is neither Double-Trap1, nor Double-Trap2, nor $\diamondsuit$, nor Regular, not Triplet. A configuration C is said to be *Isolated* if C is not Regular and there exists at most one robot on each ring of size ℓ. Finally, a configuration C is said to be *Quadruplet* if C is not Regular and there exists an ℓ-ring R that contains 4 robots.

Phase Setup is probabilistic, but as far as possible, robots move deterministically. However, there are symmetric configurations that require robots to move probabilistically. The main one is the following:

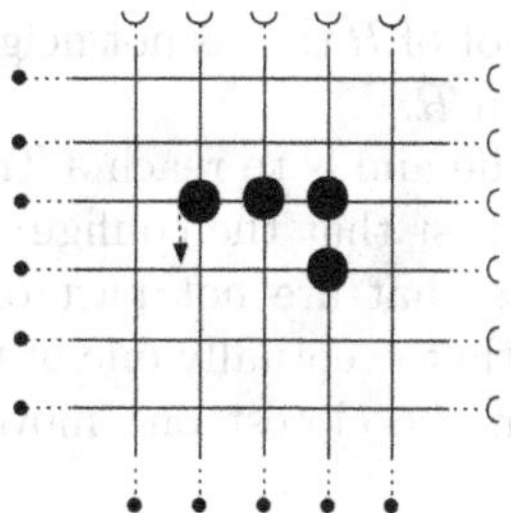

Fig. 4. *Double-Trap1.*

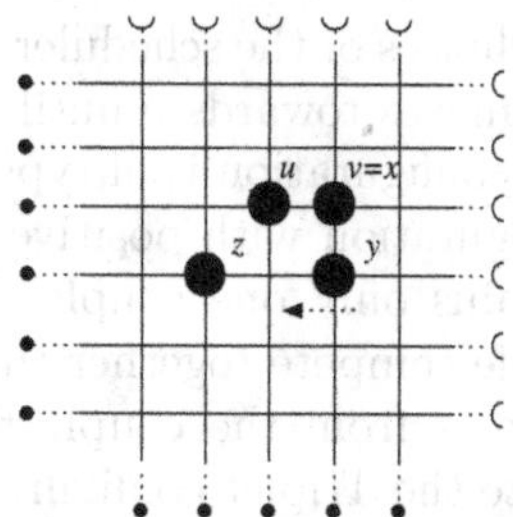

Fig. 5. *Double-Trap2.*

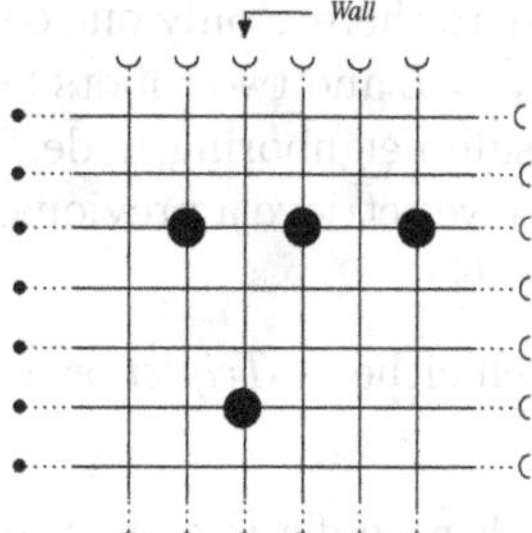

Fig. 6. A *wall* in a *Triplet.*

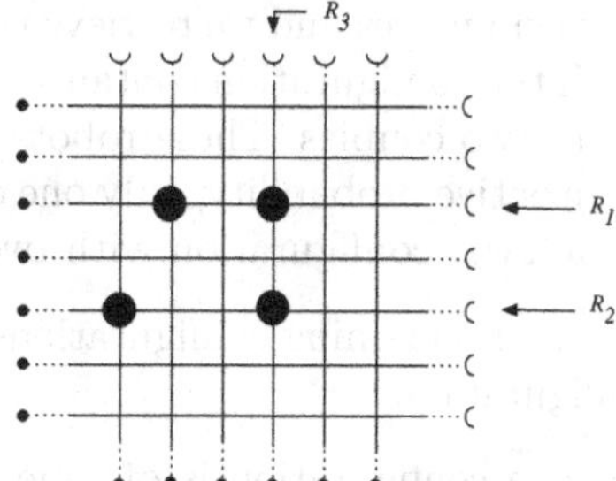

Fig. 7. *Twin.*

(a) *The configuration is of type Regular.* To break this symmetry, each robot tries to move to a safe node. Doing so, the symmetry is broken without creating tower after one step with positive probability.

So, with probability one, the system eventually leaves Case (a) to a configuration that matches one of the following cases:

(b) The configuration is of type *Double-Trap2* or *Double-Trap1*. In the former case, by moving one robot as shown in Fig. 5, the system reaches a ◊.Configuration. In the latter case, we easily obtain a *Double-Trap2* by moving only one robot as shown in Fig. 4.

(c) The configuration is of type *Triplet.* In this case, there are three robots in the same ℓ-ring R and we deterministically build a Double-Trap1 configuration. There are several cases to consider. (i) Three robots on R already forms a 3-block. Then, the remaining robot moves to the adequate position to build a *Double-Trap1.* (ii) R contains a 2-block. Then, the robot in R that is not part of the 2-block moves to create the 3-block. Otherwise (iii), a *Wall* is defined and we use it to create a 2- or 3-block on R as follows: If a node v that intersects both the Wall and R is occupied by some robot, the two other robots on R move towards the Wall to create a 2- or a 3-block (depending on the choices of the scheduler). Otherwise, each robot of R that is not neighbor of v moves towards v until a 2-block is created on R.

(d) The configuration is of type *Twin*. In this case, the aim is to reach a Triplet configuration with positive probability. Assume first that the configuration contains only one couple. Then, the two robots that are not part of the couple compete together (using try to move) so that eventually one of them is closer from the couple than the other. Then, the closest one moves to create the Triplet configuration.
Otherwise, the configuration may also contain two or three couples, but not four, otherwise we would be in Case (a). If the configuration contains two couples, then each robot that is neighbor of a safe node outside any couple tries to move to that safe node. Then, with a positive probability, only one of them moves and we retrieve the previous case where there is only one couple. If the configuration contains three couples, then $\ell = L$ and two robots belong to two couples. These robots try to move to a safe neighboring node. With positive probability, only one of them moves, and we retrieve a previous case: a Twin configuration with two couples.

In all remaining configurations, the aim is to reach either a *Triplet* or a *Twin* configuration.

(e) The configuration is of type *Quadruplet*. In such a configuration, the four robots belong to some ℓ-ring R. We then consider the subgraph G_R induced by the nodes of R. This graph is isomorphic to an elementary cycle. Now, as not all robots have identical views, we can discriminate either one unique robot or two robots (using the sizes of the holes in G_R). We let those robots move outside R. Hence, the system reaches either a Twin or a Triplet configuration.

(f) The configuration is of type *Isolated*. We consider two subcases:
   - $\ell < L$. In this case, we discriminate L-rings according to the number of robots on them. When some but not all robots are alone in their L-rings, they move along their L-ring to eventually form a Triplet or a Twin configuration with the blocked ones.
     In the case where there are two L-rings that contain 2 robots, robots try to move to a neighboring safe node (if any) outside the L-ring they belong to. Hence, with a positive probability, we retrieve the previous case.
     In the case where every L-ring contains at most one robot. We first make robots probabilistically move to discriminate a unique smallest rectangle that encloses the 4 robots. When there are several possible smallest enclosing rectangles (SER), we decrease their number by proceeding as follows: if a robot r that is neighbor of a safe node u such that if it moves to u and it is the only one to move, the number of SER decreases, then r tries to move to u. In this case, with positive probability, only one robot moves, reducing the number of possible smallest enclosing rectangles or leading directly the system to a Twin configuration. If we have a unique smallest rectangle, s, that encloses the 4 robots and the configuration is

not Twin, we discriminate the robots according to their place in s: at a corner, on a side, or inside of s. This allows us to block some of them. The other ones move (or try to move, in case of possible symmetry) to create either a Triplet or a Twin configuration.
Finally, in the case where there is a single L-ring R that contains the four robots, we proceed as in Case (e), but this time we operate on a L-ring: one or two robots eventually leave the L-ring and we retrieve one of the previous cases.

- $\ell = L$. We probabilistically discriminate, as previously, a unique smallest rectangle that encloses the 4 robots. Once the system reaches a configuration containing a unique smallest enclosing rectangle, we proceed as in case $\ell < L$. However, note that this case is simpler than the previous one because all rings have the same size (ℓ), while in the previous case we had to take care that robots gather on a "small" ring.

We have proven the convergence with probability one from any towerless configuration to a $\Diamond$.Configuration (without creating any tower during the process) by showing that the transitions given in Fig. 8 can be made in finite number of steps and with positive probability. Notice that some of them are made deterministically. Note also that there are many other possible transitions.

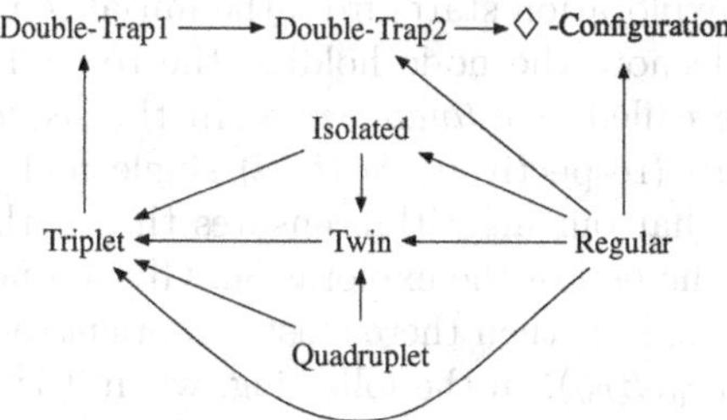

Fig. 8. Possible transitions during SetUp.

Tower Phase. This phase starts in $\Diamond$.Configuration. Let u_1 and u_2 be the two occupied neighboring nodes having themselves two occupied neighboring nodes. Let r_1 and r_2 be the two robots located at u_1 and u_2, respectively. During this phase, r_1 and r_2 *try to move* towards each other anytime they are activated. By scheduler fairness, both of them eventually created a tower T with probability one on either u_1 or u_2 (Fig. 9) and the phase is finished.

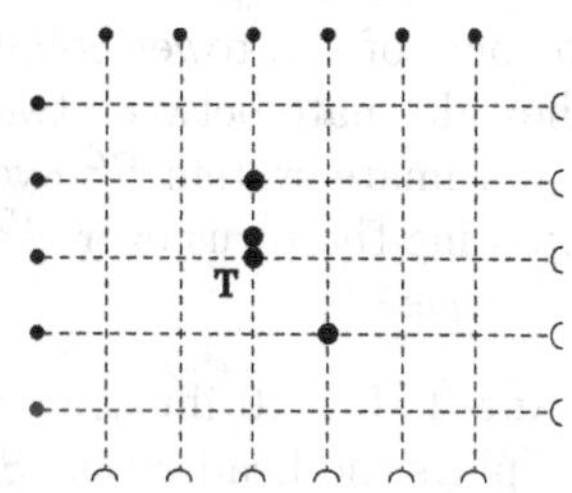

Fig. 9. Initial configuration for the Exploration phase.

Exploration Phase. We first need some definitions. Given two nodes u and v, let R_{uv} be the *smallest enclosing rectangle* that includes both u and v. Let α_{uv} (β_{uv}) be the length

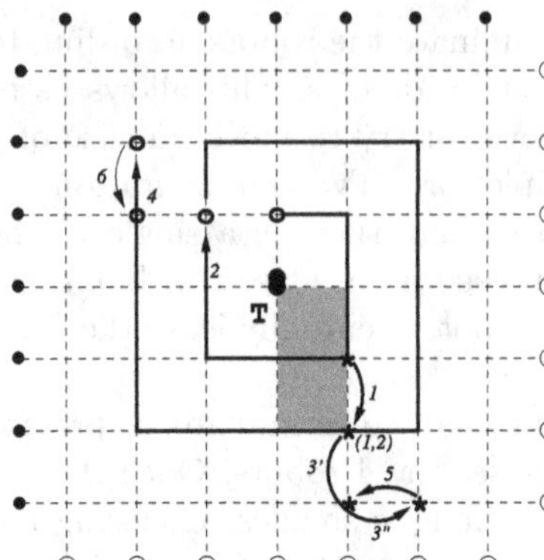

Fig. 10. First phase of exploration, The integers show the move order.

in terms of hops of one of the smallest (resp., greatest) side of R_{uv}, R_{uv} is an $(\alpha_{uv}, \beta_{uv})$-rectangle. The (Manhattan) *distance* between two nodes u and v, denoted by d_{uv}, is equal to $\alpha_{uv} + \beta_{uv}$. We define a total order on distances as follows: given four nodes u, v, u', and v', $d_{uv} \leq d_{u'v'}$ *iff* either $d_{uv} < d_{u'v'}$ or $d_{uv} = d_{u'v'}$ and $\beta_{uv} \leq \beta_{u'v'}$.

The deterministic exploration starts from the initial configuration built during the tower phase. Denote the node holding the tower by T. The two rings passing through T are called *coordinate rings.* In the sequel, 'o' (respectively, '*') denotes the *nearest* (respectively, *farthest*) single node (or robot) from T, *i.e.*, $d_{oT} < d_{*T}$. Note that our algorithm ensures that both 'o' and '*' remain the same robots until the end of the exploration. Given a node u, if $\alpha_{Tu} < \beta_{Tu}$ and $\{\alpha_{Tu}, \beta_{Tu}\} \neq \{\lfloor \frac{\ell}{2} \rfloor, \lfloor \frac{L}{2} \rfloor\}$, then there exists an orientation of the coordinate rings such that $u = (\alpha_{Tu}, \beta_{Tu})$. In the following, when it is possible, we build a coordinate system over R_{Tu} by setting the x-axis (the y-axis) as the coordinate rings that is parallel to the smallest (resp., greatest) side of $R_{T,*}$ and by orienting both axis so that the coordinates of u are positive.

The main idea of Phase Exploration is the following: both robots that are not part of the tower collaborate together in order to explore the whole torus. They alternate between two roles: *Explorer* and *Leader*. Leader $\mathcal{L}$ allows to build a coordinate system $S^{\mathcal{L}}$ over $R_{T\mathcal{L}}$. The explorer is in charge of deterministically exploring the torus over $S^{\mathcal{L}}$. The exploration works in three phases, executed in sequence:

Phase 1: Fig. 10 illustrates that phase. Robot $*$ (*i.e.*, the farthest robot of T) plays the Leader role. Starting from the configuration built by Phase Tower, Robot $*$ first built a $(1, 2)$-rectangle with T by moving in the opposite direction to o, refer to Move #1 in Fig. 10. R_{T*} allows to build a coordinate system S^*, where Robot $*$ occupies Node $(1, 2)$ *w.r.t.* S^*. Then, Robot o initiates a spiral-shaped exploration. It visits the nodes that form the first surrounding square around T and stops at node $(-1, -1)$—Move #2. Next, Robot $*$ moves to node $(2, 3)$ passing through node $(1, 3)$—Moves #3′ and #3″ in in

Fig. 10. Then, Robot o visits the nodes that form the second surrounding square around T and stops at $(-2,-2)$—Move #4. Finally, Robot $*$ moves back to $(1,3)$, followed by Robot o that moves back to $(-2,-1)$—Moves #5 and #6 in Fig. 10.

Note that our method requires that Robot $*$ must be able to move at least three lines away from the tower. Furthermore, Robot o must be able to visit the two squares centered on the tower and the orientation built by Robot $*$ must be unambiguous. These three conditions constrain the torus to be of size at least 7×7.

Phase 2: In this phase, Robot o is the leader. $R_{\mathtt{T}o}$ provides a coordinate system S°, where Robot o is located at $(1,2)$. Robot $*$ now proceeds to the spiral exploration by visiting surrounding squares around T one after another, see Figs. 11 and 12. Robot $*$ first explores the third surrounding square around T, then the fourth, and so forth, until it visits the $(\lfloor\frac{\ell}{2}\rfloor - 1)$-th square. Then, there are two cases depending on the parity of ℓ: If ℓ is odd, then Robot $*$ visits the whole $\lfloor\frac{\ell}{2}\rfloor$-th square and finish at the negative ($w.r.t$ S°) corner of the square, see Fig. 11. Otherwise (ℓ is even), Robot $*$ visits half of the $\lfloor\frac{\ell}{2}\rfloor$-th square only and stops at the positive corner ($w.r.t.$ S°) of the square, see Fig. 11. In both cases, if $\ell = L$, then the exploration is done.

Phase 3: This last phase is performed only if $\ell \neq L$. In that case, Robot $*$ terminates the exploration by going alternatively from the left to the right and from the right to the left among the nodes forming the remaining of the

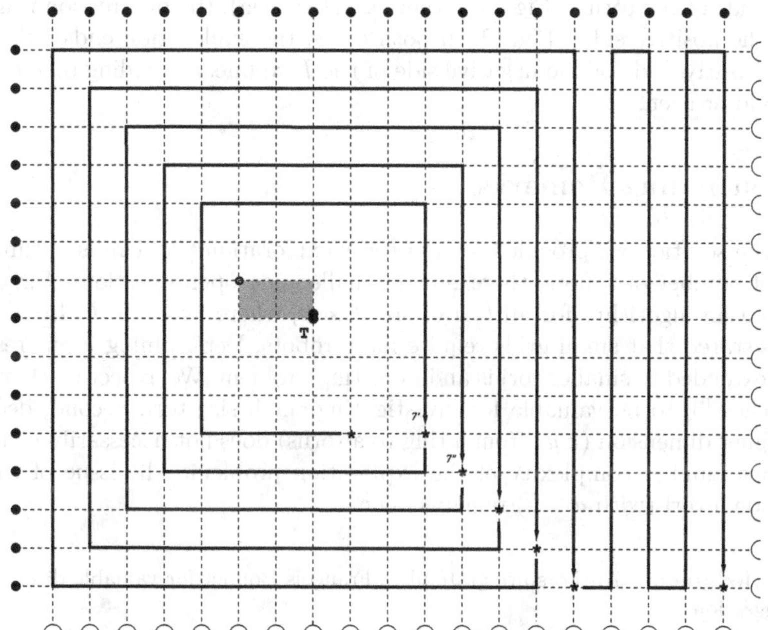

Fig. 11. Second and third phase, odd case.

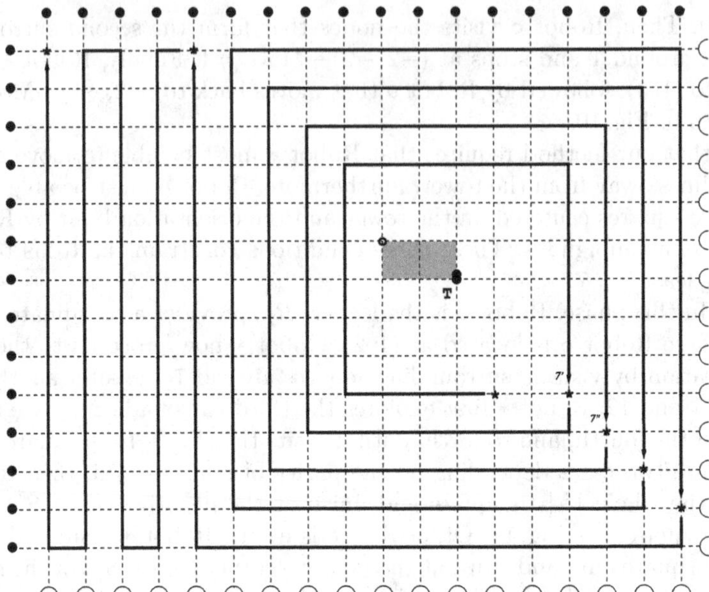

Fig. 12. Second and third phase, even case.

rectangle. If ℓ is odd, then Robot $*$ progresses towards the negative (*w.r.t.* S°) side of the torus—Fig. 11. Otherwise (ℓ is even), the progression is made on the positive side—Fig. 12. In both cases, the exploration ends either on the positive side or the negative side of the L-th line, depending on either L is odd or even.

5 Concluding Remarks

While the solution we provided for the torus exploration problem is optimal in terms of number of robots, there remain challenging open questions. First, we presented an algorithm for all tori of size $\ell \times L$, where $7 \leq \ell \leq L$. In [7], the authors stated that small grids require more robots. Determining if our results can be extended to smaller tori is an interesting problem. We expect mechanized approaches [3] to be valuable for investigating small size tori. Second, dealing with higher dimension (*e.g.*, from a ring to a torus) does not necessarily increase the robot number complexity of the exploration problem. The issue of the d-dimensional tori (with $d > 2$) remains open.

Acknowledgment. Authors are grateful to François Bonnet for valuable discussions and suggestions.

References

1. Baldoni, R., Bonnet, F., Milani, A., Raynal, M.: Anonymous graph exploration without collision by mobile robots. Inf. Process. Lett. **109**(2), 98–103 (2008)
2. Baldoni, R., Bonnet, F., Milani, A., Raynal, M.: On the solvability of anonymous partial grids exploration by mobile robots. In: Baker, T.P., Bui, A., Tixeuil, S. (eds.) OPODIS 2008. LNCS, vol. 5401, pp. 428–445. Springer, Heidelberg (2008)
3. cois Bonnet, F., Défago, X., Petit, F., Potop-Butucaru, M., Tixeuil, S.: Discovering and assessing fine-grained metrics in robot networks protocols. In: 33rd IEEE SRDS Workshops, Workshop on Self-organization in Swarm of Robots, pp. 50–59 (2014)
4. Chalopin, J., Flocchini, P., Mans, B., Santoro, N.: Network exploration by silent and oblivious robots. In: WG, pp. 208–219 (2010)
5. D'Angelo, G., Di Stefano, G., Navarra, A., Nisse, N., Suchan, K.: A unified approach for different tasks on rings in robot-based computing systems. In: IPDPS Workshops, pp. 667–676 (2013)
6. D'Angelo, G., Navarra, A., Nisse, N.: Gathering and exclusive searching on rings under minimal assumptions. In: Chatterjee, M., Cao, J., Kothapalli, K., Rajsbaum, S. (eds.) ICDCN 2014. LNCS, vol. 8314, pp. 149–164. Springer, Heidelberg (2014)
7. Devismes, S., Lamani, A., Petit, F., Raymond, P., Tixeuil, S.: Optimal grid exploration by asynchronous oblivious robots. In: Richa, A.W., Scheideler, C. (eds.) SSS 2012. LNCS, vol. 7596, pp. 64–76. Springer, Heidelberg (2012)
8. Devismes, S., Petit, F., Tixeuil, S.: Optimal probabilistic ring exploration by semi-synchronous oblivious robots. Theor. Comput. Sci. **498**, 10–27 (2013)
9. Flocchini, P., Ilcinkas, D., Pelc, A., Santoro, N.: Remembering without memory: tree exploration by asynchronous oblivious robots. Theor. Comput. Sci. **411**(14–15), 1583–1598 (2010)
10. Flocchini, P., Ilcinkas, D., Pelc, A., Santoro, N.: Computing without communicating: Ring exploration by asynchronous oblivious robots. Algorithmica **65**(3), 562–583 (2013)
11. Flocchini, P., Prencipe, G., Santoro, N.: Distributed Computing by Oblivious Mobile Robots. Synthesis Lectures on Distributed Computing Theory. Morgan & Claypool Publishers (2012)
12. Haba, K., Izumi, T., Katayama, Y., Inuzuka, N., Wada, K.: On gathering problem in a ring for 2n autonomous mobile robots. In: SSS, p. Poster (2008)
13. Klasing, R., Kosowski, A., Navarra, A.: Taking advantage of symmetries: gathering of many asynchronous oblivious robots on a ring. Theor. Comput. Sci. **411**(34–36), 3235–3246 (2010)
14. Lamani, A., Potop-Butucaru, M.G., Tixeuil, S.: Optimal deterministic ring exploration with oblivious asynchronous robots. In: Patt-Shamir, B., Ekim, T. (eds.) SIROCCO 2010. LNCS, vol. 6058, pp. 183–196. Springer, Heidelberg (2010)

Source Routing in Time-Varing Lossy Networks

Dacfey Dzung[2], Rachid Guerraoui[1], David Kozhaya[1](✉), and Yvonne-Anne Pignolet[2]

[1] EPFL IC IIF LPD, INR 315 (Bâtiment INR), Station 14, 1015 Lausanne, Switzerland
{rachid.guerraoui,david.kozhaya}@epfl.ch,
[2] ABB Corporate Research, Raleigh, Switzerland
{dacfey.dzung,yvonne-anne.pignolet}@ch.abb.com

Abstract. This paper addresses the path selection problem arising in multi-hop sensor networks, e.g., Smart Grids. A set of multi-hop paths, of varying transmission quality, connect source and destination nodes. The source must select one path for each message to send without knowing the state of the hops. It can however use information deduced from earlier transmissions to decide on a good path for the current message. The goal is to maximize the discounted number of successfully delivered messages. We prove that the myopic routing policy, arguably the most appealing known way to tackle this problem, can permanently ignore good paths. We also generalize an empirically proven good approach, the Whittle index, and show its intractability for the problem at hand. We propose a new tractable metric, *Harmonic Discounted Index* (HDI), as a measure of attractiveness of transmitting over a path. We evaluate the performance of our HDI metric in a variety of simulation scenarios revealing a superior performance compared to all alternative index policies.

Keywords: Source routing · partially observable Markov decision process · Time-varying lossy channels

1 Introduction

Large sensor networks, as for example needed for smart grids, comprise a wide range of devices, e.g. sensors and actuators, interconnected by communication links of which some might be very unreliable [19]. Unreliability arises as a consequence of the utilized communication technologies, namely power line and wireless [3,6,8,14]. In both, wireless and power line, the link quality can vary a lot, even within short intervals. Due to the transmission ranges and the topologies of these networks, there are typically several multi-hop paths to select from when disseminating information.

This paper addresses the path selection problem arising in source routing for multi-hop sensor networks. Some examples of existing source routing protocols

A. Bouajjani and H. Fauconnier (Eds.): NETYS 2015, LNCS 9466, pp. 200–215, 2015.
DOI: 10.1007/978-3-319-26850-7_14

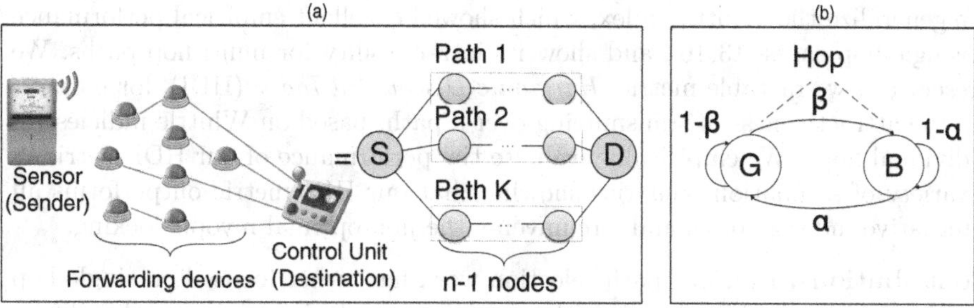

Fig. 1. (a) A network for automated metering connecting a source S to a destination D, by $\mathcal{K}$ independent n-hop paths. (b) Gilbert-Elliot model of a communication hop.

for such networks are RPL non-storing mode [23] and Dynamic Source Routing (DSR) [5]. To keep the network load low and avoid collisions, the goal is to minimize the number of retransmissions through "smart" routing decisions at the source, under constrained knowledge of the states of the underlying lossy hops. We consider a network where a sender has access to multiple independent multi-hop paths (see Fig. 1-(a)), but is restricted to transmitting on one of them at any given point in time to avoid interference. We study how a sender can intelligently utilize past observations and the knowledge of the stochastic properties of individual hops to make routing decisions that maximize the number of successfully delivered messages favoring low message latency.

We consider individual hops to be lossy time-varying communication links. In most routing studies, the time-varying behavior of hops is not explicitly modeled. In this paper however, each hop is modeled as a 2-state discrete Markov chain, known as the *Gilbert-Elliot* model (GE) [9,10] (Fig. 1-(b)). The GE channel is a simple way to capture time-varying channel behavior which is widely used [8,18]. The reliable state, noted G, corresponds to a probability p of successful transmission such that $p = 1$. The unreliable state, noted B, corresponds to a transmission success probability $p = 0$. The transition probabilities between the reliable and the unreliable state can accommodate for the relatively slow processes affecting power line communication quality such as switching of the power grid and activation of electrical equipment, hence state transitions typically occur only every few hours [17,20]. In contrast, typical wireless time-varying behavior occurs due to occasional shadowing, but these effects are typically measured in seconds or minutes, i.e., the wireless transition probabilities are different from power line. In practice, these transition probabilities can be well approximated [12].

We model the path selection problem as a sequential decision task, where a successful message delivery is associated with a unit reward. The performance of a routing policy, can be thus evaluated from the accumulated rewards. We first prove that the myopic routing policy, arguably the most appealing known way to tackle path selection, is optimal under *memory-less* hops. However, under positively correlated hops, we uncover, for the first time, an intriguing locking behavior where good paths can be permanently overlooked for transmission.

We generalize the Whittle index, which showed excellent empirical performance in single-hop cases [13,16], and show its intractability for multi-hop paths. We present a new tractable metric, *Harmonic Discounted Index* (HDI), for measuring the attractiveness of transmitting over a path, based on Whittle indicies[1] of individual hops. We empirically evaluate the performance of our HDI metric in a variety of simulation scenarios showing that our HDI metric outperforms all alternative index policies and circumvents the non-optimal myopic locking.

Contributions. Previous path selection work has either focused on single-hop decisions or simpler hop models with constant transmission success probabilities. Our main contributions can be thus summarized as:

- A first mathematical definition of the path selection problem in a multi-hop and a partially observable Markov decision process (POMDP) setting.
- An optimality and tractability analysis of myopic and whittle routing metrics (indices) for the path selection problem respectively.
- An establishment of a tractable routing metric (HDI) and a relative performance evaluation showing a performance beating alternative routing indices.

Road map. The rest of the paper is organized as follows: Sect. 2 discusses the related work. Section 3 defines the system model. Section 4 presents a mathematical definition of multi-hop path selection. Section 5 shows optimality and tractability analyses of myopic and whittle index policies respectively. Section 6 presents our new HDI metric. Section 7 details performance evaluations in various network scenarios. Finally Sect. 8 concludes the paper. Due to space limitations, proofs and derivations are deferred to a technical report [7].

2 Related Work

Various POMDP formulations and game theory techniques have been broadly applied to several domains [1,11,13,24]. Multichannel opportunistic access, a closely related domain, has been studied under different assumptions. In general, the multichannel opportunistic access problem considers a sender who has to sense and transmit on one of multiple accessible channels, where each evolves independently, regardless of being sensed or not. In comparison with the path selection problem considered in this paper, the sender in our case has access to n-hop paths, where each hop along a path is an independent Markov process that evolves at all times whether it was used for transmission or not. The work in [1] studied the mutlichannel access problem with channels that are independent and identically distributed (i.i.d.) Markov processes. In fact [1] showed that (a) the myopic policy under these assumptions admits a simple universal structure, and (b) guarantees optimality when channels are assumed to be positively correlated,

[1] Despite its wide use in the single hop case, the known theoretical guarantees [21] for the Whittle index are very weak and theoretical analysis remains elusive and challenging, mainly because of its highly-coupled and complex dynamics [11].

i.e. $1 - \beta > \alpha$ (Sect. 3). The authors in [11] studied the same problem however without requiring channels to be i.i.d. They formulated the problem as a special case of POMDP known as the restless bandit problem. The authors studied the average expected reward and proposed an approximation algorithm with a performance guarantee of 2. The work in [13] studied a similar formulation of this problem for non-identically distributed channnels. The authors obtained Whittle index in closed form for both discounted and average reward criteria and showed its optimality under certain conditions when the channels are i.i.d.

3 Problem Model

We consider a network where a source node (sender) is connected to a destination by $\mathcal{K}$ independent n-hop paths (Fig. 1), but is restricted to choose only one of them for transmission. For analytical tractability, we focus on simple non-trivial networks, i.e., paths are assumed independent and the underlying hops are modeled as independent Markov chains with only two states. We assume a global discrete clock represented by $t = \{0, 1, 2, 3, \ldots, \infty\}$. Every communication hop in the system is assumed to conform to an independent Gilbert-Elliot (GE) model (Fig. 1-(b)). At every time unit in t, and only then, every hop may transition to the other state according to its transition probabilities α and β (assumed to be known by the source[2]). If a hop is currently in the reliable state (G), it will remain at the next time unit in this reliable state with probability $(1-\beta)$ or will shift with probability β to the unreliable state (B) (analogously the next state is determined by α if it currently is in the unreliable state). The state of a hop remains fixed in the time interval between consecutive time units in t.

We assume that the source sends a message (be it new or a retransmission) every n time units. This assumption is solely considered for clearer mathematical derivations avoiding notation complexity. So in this paper, the decision times to send, denoted by $T = \{T_0, T_1, T_2, \ldots T_\infty\}$, are deterministic and occurr at $t = \{0, n, 2n, 3n, \ldots, \infty\}$. When sending a message m, none of the current hop states is known and the source decides on a single path for transmission. Once a decision is made, m is transmitted along the selected path, going sequentially through each of the underlying path hops in 1 unit of time, as long as they are reliable. If m traverses an unreliable hop, it is entirely dropped and all consecutive hops will not be traversed. In case a message is dropped, a *packet-drop detection mechanism* informs the source (before the source decides on a new message) about the hop which led to the message loss[3]. This assumption ensures that in case of message loss the source can rightfully guess state information about the hops from the source up to and including the lossy hop. Alternatively, the source knows that m successfully reached the destination, if nothing is heard from this detection mechanism after n time units of sending m.

[2] In practice these probabilities can change and can be well approximated [15].

[3] The exact nature of the packet-drop detection mechanism is not of interest in this work, which is only a first step towards a solution of the general problem. Delayed and incorrect packet-drop detection are beyond the scope of this work.

The objective of the source is to maximize the *discounted* expected number of successfully delivered messages, since low message latency are favored [4,13].

Generalizing Our Model. We illustrate the generality of our work, in a companion technical report [7] showing how our formulation can naturally extend to some relaxations. We particularly examine: (1) model $\mathcal{A}$: when a message is lost, the source does not have to wait but can start a new message transmission directly in the following time step and (2) model $\mathcal{B}$: the available paths have different number of hops. Our theoretical results (Sect. 5) about myopic locking and Whittle intractability extend as well to both models.

4 Path Selection: A Mathematical Definition

We denote by $S(t) = [S_1(t),\ S_2(t), \ldots,\ S_{\mathcal{K}}(t)]$ the set of states of the $\mathcal{K}$ available n-hop paths where: $S_k(t) = \{s_{k,1}(t),\ s_{k,2}(t), \ldots,\ s_{k,n}(t)\}$ such that $s_{k,i}(t) \in \{G, B\}$ is the state of ith hop along path k. Let $a(T_j) = [a_1(T_j),\ a_2(T_j), \ldots,$ $a_{\mathcal{K}}(T_j)] \in [0,1]^{\mathcal{K}}$ be the vector of actions taken at decision time T_j, where $a_k(T_j) = 1$ ($a_k(T_j) = 0$) means transmitting (not transmitting resp.) over the kth path at decision time T_j. Thus, $a_k(T_j) = 1$ implies $a_{k,i}(t)|_{t=j\cdot n+i-1} = 1\ \forall i \in [1,n]$ subject to $\sum_{i=1}^{n} a_{k,i}(t)|_{t=t} = 1$. In other words, when path k is selected for transmission at decision time T_j, every hop along path k is used only once in the time interval $[j \cdot n, (j+1) \cdot n - 1]$, such that the first hop along path k is used first, then the second hop, etc. Whereas $a_k(T_j) = 0$ implies $a_{k,i'}(t)|_{t=j\cdot n+i-1} = 0\ \forall i', i \in [1,n]$, which means that when path k is not selected for transmission at decision time T_j, none of its hops are used in the time interval $[j \cdot n, (j+1) \cdot n - 1]$. The action vector $a(T_j)$ corresponds to the routing decision taken at decision time T_j.

Since the source operates under partial information of the state the hops are in, and since not all states can be observed, this problem can be transformed into a partially observable Markov decision process (POMDP) with all past and current state information contained in a sufficient statistic known as the belief [2]. This hop belief is the conditional probability over the hop state space. In our problem, we assume independent paths, with stochastically independent hops. Accordingly, we maintain independently for each hop, a belief, $w_{k,i}(t)\ \forall k \in [1, \mathcal{K}], i \in [1,n]$ where $w_{k,i}(t)$ is the conditional probability that the relative hop is in the reliable state, given all previous feedback obtained for that hop. Initially, the hop belief is set to the stationary probability, $w_{k,i}(t)|_{t=0} = \frac{\alpha_{k,i}}{\alpha_{k,i}+\beta_{k,i}}$ Afterwards, and at every time unit, each belief is updated independently:

$$w_{k,i}(t+1) = \begin{cases} 1 - \beta_{k,i} & \text{if } a_{k,i}(t) = 1, s_{k,i}(t) = G, \\ \alpha_{k,i} & \text{if } a_{k,i}(t) = 1, s_{k,i}(t) = B, \\ \tau(w_{k,i}(t)) & \text{if } a_{k,i}(t) = 0 \end{cases}$$

where $\tau(w_{k,i}(t)) = (1 - \beta_{k,i})w_{k,i}(t) + \alpha_{k,i}(1 - w_{k,i}(t))$. The source is the sole place deciding which path to use for transmission. It should thus account for the states of the hops relative to the time that the message might reach them. We represent this information by a belief vector Ω_k:

$$\Omega_k(t) = [w_{k,1}(t),\ w_{k,2}(t+1), \ldots, w_{k,n}(t+n-1)] = [w_{k,1}(t),\ \tau(w_{k,2}(t)), \ldots, \tau^{n-1}(w_{k,n}(t))] \tag{1}$$

where $\tau^x(w_{k,i}(t)) = \underbrace{\tau(\tau(\ldots\tau(w_{k,i}(t))))}_{x \text{ times}}$, $\tau^0(w_{k,i}(t)) = w_{k,i}(t)$. The recursive call in τ is done relative to the position of the hop along that path, as a message needs 1 time unit to traverse a hop. The source node thus keeps belief vectors of all $\mathcal{K}$ paths, denoted by $P(t) = [\Omega_1(t),\ \Omega_2(t), \ldots,\ \Omega_{\mathcal{K}}(t)]$.

We assume that a reward of 1 corresponds to a single successful message delivery. Our objective is thus represented by the expected discounted reward which averages the accumulated rewards over time, with a higher coefficient (discount) for earlier rewards. Denote by π, the routing policy, the set of all action vectors, i.e., $a(T)\ \forall T$. Let $R_{a(T_j)}$ be the reward obtained relative to the action vector $a(T_j)$ at decision time T_j. The expected discounted reward over infinite decision times, given an initial belief vector P is thus expressed by:

$$E_\pi\left[\sum_{T_j \in T} \gamma^{\ t} R_{a(T_j)} | P\right] \tag{2}$$

subject to $\sum_{k=1}^{\mathcal{K}} a_k(T_j) = 1$, where $\gamma : 0 < \gamma < 1$ is the discounted factor. $\sum_{k=1}^{\mathcal{K}} a_k(T_j) = 1$ means that, at any decision time, exactly one path is used for transmission. Denote by $V_\gamma(P)$ the value function, i.e. the maximum expected total discounted reward obtained by the optimal policy under the set of initial belief vectors P. Then $V_\gamma(P) = \max_{k\in\mathcal{K}}\{V_\gamma(P; a_k = 1)\}$ where $V_\gamma(P; a_k = 1)$ denotes the total expected discounted reward from selecting path k for transmission at first followed by the optimal policy in future decision times.

The expression of $V_\gamma(P; a_k = 1)$ can be obtained according to Bellman's equation [8]. To illustrate the underlying idea, we develop this expression for the case of $\mathcal{K} = 2$ and $n = 2$, where $P = [\Omega_1, \Omega_2]$ is the set of belief vectors such that $\Omega_k = [w_{k,0}, \tau(w_{k,1})]$ (derivations of (3) and (4) can be found in [7]).

$$\begin{aligned} V_\gamma(P(t); a_1 = 1) = {} & w_{1,1}\tau(w_{1,2}) + \gamma[w_{1,1}\tau(w_{1,2})V_\gamma(\tau(1-\beta_{1,1}), \tau(1-\beta_{1,2}), \\ & \tau^2(w_{2,1}), \tau^3(w_{2,2})) + w_{1,1}(1-\tau(w_{1,2}))V_\gamma(\tau(1-\beta_{1,1}), \tau(\alpha_{1,2}), \tau^2(w_{2,1}), \\ & \tau^3(w_{2,2})) + (1-w_{1,1})V_\gamma(\tau(\alpha_{1,1}), \tau^3(w_{1,2}), \tau^2(w_{2,1}), \tau^3(w_{2,2}))] \end{aligned} \tag{3}$$

$$\begin{aligned} V_\gamma(P(t); a_2 = 1) = {} & w_{2,1}\tau(w_{2,2}) + \gamma[w_{2,1}\tau(w_{2,2})V_\gamma(\tau^2(w_{1,1}), \\ & \tau^3(w_{1,2}), \tau(1-\beta_{2,1}), \tau(1-\beta_{2,2})) + w_{2,1}(1-\tau(w_{2,2}))V_\gamma(\tau^2(w_{1,1}), \tau^3(w_{1,2}), \\ & \tau(1-\beta_{2,1}), \tau(\alpha_{2,2})) + (1-w_{2,1})V_\gamma(\tau^2(w_{1,1}), \tau^3(w_{1,2}), \tau(\alpha_{2,1}), \tau^3(w_{2,2}))] \end{aligned} \tag{4}$$

$V_\gamma(P; a_k = 1)$ can be split into two main components: one which represents the expected immediate reward relative to selecting path k and a second representing the discounted future reward resulting from to choosing path k at the first decision. $V_\gamma(P; a_k = 1) = \underbrace{w_{k,1}\tau(w_{k,2})}_{\text{immediate expected reward}} + \underbrace{\gamma[\ldots]}_{\text{discounted future reward}}$.

Each term, in the future reward, is a function of a joint set of beliefs each spanning the set of real values in the interval $[0, 1]$. The dimensions of these terms grow with $n\mathcal{K}$ and thus the required computations increase immensely as $\mathcal{K}$ and n increase. Solving the Bellman equation pertaining to problem (2), and hence obtaining the optimal policy, becomes rapidly intractable [16]. Therefore, efficient near-optimal solution methods are sought.

5 Index-Based Policies: Formulation and Analysis

Index policies are selection protocols that assign an *index*, to each state of the $\mathcal{K}$ paths and select the path with the highest index for transmission. This index evaluates how rewarding it is to select a path under a particular state. Some path indices are strongly decomposable, i.e. can be computed separately for each path, without regard of the states of other paths. This reduces the complexity of the problem as compared to a full POMDP solution. We examine two such index policies for multi-hop paths: (i) Myopic policy and (ii) Whittle index.

5.1 Myopic Performance

The myopic policy is an index-based policy which assigns the immediate expected reward of selecting a path as an index. It significantly reduces the computation complexity by disregarding any possible effect of the future discounted reward on decision making. It has been shown for stochastically identical single hops (channels), Sect. 2, that such a myopic strategy guarantees an optimal solution [1]. However, to the best of our knowledge, not much has been said about this policy for non-identical hops with equal rewards or for multi-hop paths.

Entirely Memory-less Hops. We first show a scenario of multi-hop paths where future rewards do not contribute to decision making: in this case the myopic policy is optimal. A communication hop (Fig. 1-(b)) becomes entirely memory-less when $1 - \beta_{k,j} = \alpha_{k,j}$. The belief, as a result, remains constant at all times $w_{k,j} = 1 - \beta_{k,j} = \alpha_{k,j} = \tau(w_{k,j})$.

Lemma 1. *In a set of $\mathcal{K}$ independent paths each consisting of n entirely memory-less hops, the myopic policy is optimal.*

Furthermore, the optimal policy may, in this case, transmit over one path only at all decision times, since all hop beliefs remain constant. Due to space limitations proofs can be found in companion technical report [7].

Positively Correlated Hops. We now study a general case of positively correlated hops, i.e. $1 - \beta_{k,i} > \alpha_{k,i}$ $\forall k \in \mathcal{K}$. We show that the optimality of the myopic decisions is not guaranteed. We namely identify a condition under which the myopic policy gets locked, i.e., permanently stops selecting certain paths regardless of how reliable they could be. For presentation simplicity, we first consider one transmission hop per path (the hop notation will be omitted). The results are generalized later in this section to include n-hop paths. The belief of a single hop has two important characteristics [13]: (i) $\alpha_k < \tau(w_k) < 1 - \beta_k$ and (ii) $\tau^t(w_k)$ monotonically converges to $w_0^k = \frac{\alpha_k}{\alpha_k + \beta_k}$ as $t \to \infty$.

Theorem 1. *If a single hop path, k, exists such that for any other path $k' \in \mathcal{K}$, $w_0^k < \alpha_{k'}$, then the myopic policy will never select path k for transmission after the first time k is observed in the unreliable state.*

Corollary 1. *If the beliefs are initialized to their stationary probabilities*[4], *then path k will never be selected by the myopic policy for transmission.*

IMPORTANT: Theorem 1, on its own, does not necessarily indicate that the myopic performance is not good. In fact, Theorem 1 also applies to the entirely memory-less case (Sect. 5.1) where the myopic policy is indeed optimal. The significance of Theorem 1 on the quality of the myopic routing decisions is determined by the stochastic properties of the neglected paths. A simple example of two single hop paths, illustrates the effects. Consider a source with two paths: $Path_1$: $\alpha_1 = 0.6$; $1 - \beta_1 = 0.65$ (frequently switching resembling wireless hops) and $Path_2$: $\alpha_2 = 0.1$; $1 - \beta_2 = 0.93$ (slow switching resembling power line hops). A source selecting paths myopically, will never transmit on $Path_2$ after it observes $Path_2$ in a unreliable state for the first time. Therefore it does not make use of the fact that $Path_2$ can return to the reliable state at a later time. Transmitting forever on $Path_1$ which switches more frequently might be less rewarding than transmitting on $Path_2$ when it is in the reliable state. We simulate in Sect. 5 such examples, proving the non-optimality of myopic decisions.

We generalize our result to n-hop paths (proofs can be found in [7]).

Theorem 2. *If an n-hop path k exists such that for any path $k' \in \mathcal{K}$:*

$$w_0^{k,f} \prod_{h=1}^{f-1} \tau^{n-1}(1 - \beta_{k,h}) \prod_{l=f+1}^{n} \tau^{n+l-1}(1 - \beta_{k,l}) < \prod_{r=1}^{n} \tau^{r-1}(\alpha_{k',r})$$

for any $f \in [1, n]$, then path k will never be played by the myopic policy after the first time its fth hop is observed in an unreliable state.

Theorem 2 establishes conditions where myopic routing decisions can be non-optimal. The significance of the performance gap between the myopic and optimal solution is determined by the stochastic properties of the available paths.

5.2 Whittle Index: A Path Formulation

In this section, we generalize *Whittle* index [22] for multi-hop paths. The Whittle path index depends merely on the properties of that particular path and not of

[4] This initialization is assumed in most of the previous literature [1,13,16].

other paths. So, it is enough to consider a single n-hop path. Given a single n-hop path, at each decision time the source can make one of two possible actions (i) use that path for transmission or idle that path. An optimal selection policy would partition the path state space into a passive and an active set where it is optimal to idle or use the path for transmission respectively. The Whittle index measures the attractiveness of transmitting over a path under a subsidy, λ. For this end, we consider a single multi-hop path identical to the multi-hop path just described except that a constant subsidy[5], λ, is obtained whenever the path is idled. Clearly this subsidy λ affects how the state space is optimally partitioned between the active and the passive set and states which remain active under a larger subsidy are thus more attractive to the source. Based on this intuition, the minimum subsidy required to move a given state from the active set to the passive set constitutes a measure of how attractive that state is [13].

More precisely, we denote by $V_{\gamma,\lambda}(P)$ the value function corresponding to the maximum expected total discounted reward that can be obtained from a single path with subsidy λ and belief vector P (we drop the path index from the notation). Denote by $V_{\gamma,\lambda}(P;a)$ the total expected discounted reward from taking action a at the first decision time followed by the optimal policy in the future. Thus $V_{\gamma,\lambda}(P) = \max\{V_{\gamma,\lambda}(P;a=0), V_{\gamma,\lambda}(P;a=1)\}$. As in Sect. 5.1, we derive the value functions assuming a 2-hop path under subsidy λ.

$$\begin{aligned} &V_{\gamma,\lambda}(P;a=1) = w_1\tau(w_2) + \gamma\left[w_1\tau(w_2)V_{\gamma,\lambda}(\tau(1-\beta_1),\tau(1-\beta_2))\right. \\ &\left.+w_1(1-\tau(w_2))V_{\gamma,\lambda}(\tau(1-\beta_1),\tau(\alpha_2)) + (1-w_1)V_{\gamma,\lambda}(\tau(\alpha_1),\tau^3(w_2))\right]. \\ &V_{\gamma,\lambda}(P;a=0) = \lambda + \gamma V_{\gamma,\lambda}(\tau^2(w_1),\tau^3(w_2)). \end{aligned} \quad (5)$$

Definition 1. *The passive set $\mathcal{P}(\lambda)$ is the set of path states for which it is optimal to make the path passive under subsidy λ.*

We define the passive set for the 2-hop path as $\mathcal{P}(\lambda) = \{[w_1, \tau(w_2] : V_{\gamma,\lambda}(P;a=0) \geq V_{\gamma,\lambda}(P;a=1)\}$ and generalize it for an n-hop path as:

$$\mathcal{P}(\lambda) = \{[w_1, \tau(w_2), \ldots, \tau^{n-1}(w_n)] : V_{\gamma,\lambda}(P;a=0) \geq V_{\gamma,\lambda}(P;a=1)\}. \quad (6)$$

A meaningful Whittle index definition for a path, requires that a path made passive under subsidy λ should also be made passive under a subsidy $\lambda' > \lambda$. We thus define the indexability of a path:

Definition 2. *A path is said to be indexable if its passive set $\mathcal{P}(\lambda)$ increases from $\emptyset$ to the whole state space of $[0,1]^n$ as λ increases from $-\infty$ to $+\infty$. If the path is indexable, the Whittle index is the infimum subsidy λ which makes the passive and active actions equally rewarding:*

$$W(P) = \inf_{\lambda}\{\lambda : V_{\gamma,\lambda}(P;a=0) = V_{\gamma,\lambda}(P;a=1)\}.$$

[5] The subsidy, λ, can be thought of as a counter reward for idling the path.

From Definition 2, a larger index indicates that the path is more attractive, in the sense that it requires a higher subsidy to be made passive. A source can choose at every decision time the path with the highest Whittle index for transmission. It is important to notice though, that the dimensions of $V_{\gamma,\lambda}$ in (5) grow with the number of hops n and the state space hence expands to $[0,1]^n$. Consequently solving for Whittle index, as n increases becomes intractable. This implies that computing the Whittle index efficiently for an n-hop path is not feasible.

6 Harmonic Discounted Index (HDI)

Given the non-optimality of myopic decisions and the intractability of the Whittle index for multi-hop paths, we seek to design an implementable routing path metric. We advocate the intuition behind our path metric, after which we formally present it. A hop can be correlated with a simple conducting wire. A poorly conducting wire, which renders a propagating signal undetectable by a receiver, is equivalent to an unreliable hop which leads to the loss of the message being transmitted. The attractiveness of a hop can thus be directly correlated with a conductance measure. Since we assume independent communication hops, every hop would constitute an independent wire with its own conductance. A multi-hop path, as a result, becomes a sequence of multiple conducting wires connected in series. The metric embodying the attractiveness of transmitting over the path hence translates to the equivalent conductance of the series combination.

6.1 Hop Conductance

We define the hop conductance to be the measure of the attractiveness of transmitting on a communication hop along a path. This conductance is composed of two factors, which we next explain in details.

Attractiveness of Hop Transmission Medium. We consider each hop on its own. This effectively transforms a single n-hop path to n separate 1-hop paths. We assume that the source can transmit on these hops independently, hence reducing the set of decision times T to $t = \{0, 1, 2, \ldots, \infty\}$. The set of belief vectors of an n-hop path $\Omega = [w_1, \tau(w_2), \ldots, \tau^{n-1}(w_n)]$ transforms under this decomposition to $[\Omega_1, \Omega_2, \ldots, \Omega_n]$ where $\Omega_i = w_i \; \forall i \in [1, n]$ since every path now has only 1 hop. Given this decomposition, we consider next a single hop under the subsidy concept and drop the index i from the notation. We measure the attractiveness of transmitting on this hop by calculating its corresponding Whittle index. The maximum expected total discounted reward that can be obtained from a hop with subsidy λ is $V_{\gamma,\lambda}(w) = \max\{V_{\gamma,\lambda}(w; a = 0), V_{\gamma,\lambda}(w; a = 1)\}$, where $V_{\gamma,\lambda}(w; a = 1) = w + \gamma[wV_{\gamma,\lambda}(1-\beta) + (1-w)V_{\gamma,\lambda}(\alpha)]$, and $V_{\gamma,\lambda}(w; a = 0) = \lambda + \gamma[V_{\gamma,\lambda}(\tau(w))]$. The passive set $\mathcal{P}(\lambda)$ for a 1-hop path reduces to $\mathcal{P}(\lambda) = \{w : V_{\gamma,\lambda}(w_i; a = 0) \geq V_{\gamma,\lambda}(w_i; a = 1)\}$. In comparison with the passive set in (6) which describes a property for a whole n-hop path, the passive set here is a per-hop description. In other words, the passive set here is a decomposition of (6) that follows naturally from the decomposition of the belief vector Ω of the

n-hop path. A hop is said to be indexable if $\mathcal{P}(\lambda)$ increases from $\emptyset$ to the state space of $[0,1]$ as λ increases from $-\infty$ to $+\infty$. If a hop is indexable, then its corresponding Whittle index is $W(P) = \inf_{\lambda}\{\lambda : V_{\gamma,\lambda}(w; a=0) = V_{\gamma,\lambda}(w; a=1)\}$. The Whittle index for single hops admits an efficient way of being computed. In fact, a closed form expression of the Whittle index for single hops is established in [13,16]. Thus, we obtain n measures of attractiveness W_i $\forall i \in [1,n]$ for each of the n mediums constituting the individual hops with negligible overhead.

Attractiveness of Hop Feedback. The amount of information that the source has about the states of hops, affects the source's later decisions. When transmitting over some path, losing a message at any of its underlying hops will yield the same result of no immediate reward. However the amount of information revealed to the source, which affects the future rewards, is not the same. Information about the states of the hops on a path are obtained up to the hop leading to message loss (inclusive), refer to Sect. 3. The amount of information revealed to the source, hence increases as a message traverses more hops of a path even if it is destined to failure. Although this information is useless for the current reward, it may be of fundamental value affecting the future rewards (since the obtained information affects later decisions). Consider an example of two 3-hop paths, each decomposed into three 1-hop paths with the following indices: (i) $Path_1$: $W_1 = 0.2$, $W_2 = 0.6$, $W_3 = 0.94$ and (ii) $Path_2$: $W_1 = 0.94$, $W_2 = 0.6$, $W_3 = 0.2$. Despite the fact that $Path_1$ and $Path_2$ consist of 1-hop paths with similar indices, the fact that these 1-hop paths correspond to different hops makes $Path_1$ and $Path_2$ not equivalent. In fact, the amount of information revealed to the source is expected to be higher if $Path_2$ is favored over $Path_1$ especially that we wait n time slots regardless of the destiny of the transmission[6].

The probability of obtaining feedback (hence the attractiveness of feedback) relative to a given hop gradually decreases as this hop becomes further from the source (since it is conditioned on the success probability of all previous hops). We adapt the W_i measures, to embed the feedback attractiveness independently from other hops. This adaptation accounts for the decreasing feedback attractiveness of more distant hops through discounted attractiveness index:

Definition 3. *The hop conductance index of the ith hop of an n-hop path is $DI_i = \delta^{i-1} W_i$, where W_i is the Whittle index of the ith hop and* $0 < \delta < 1$.

We evaluate the impact of δ, in a companion technical report [7], showing a performance gain of about 5 % compared to a hop conductance (DI) without δ.

6.2 Path Conductance

Given an n-hop path associated n independent hop conductances, the metric measuring the attractiveness of transmitting over a path reduces to the overall path conductance. The path conductance in an n-hop path is the equivalent conductance of a series combination of hop conductances.

[6] The only inefficiency of selecting $Path_2$ over $Path_1$ may be the extra transmission energy; however energy is not a focus in this work as devices can be main-powered.

Definition 4. *The path conductance is equivalent to $\frac{1}{n}^{th}$ of the harmonic mean of the n individual hop conductances (DI_i) associated with underlying hops.*

The harmonic mean of a set of values tends strongly toward the smallest values in that set. It has a tendency to increase the impact of small values and alleviate the influence of large outliers. In paths, the smaller the individual hop conductances ($DI_i(s)$) are, the less attractive they are for transmission. Therefore the harmonic mean of these individual measures is most influenced by the least attractive hops along a path. This can be fairly justified by the fact that a single unreliable hop across the whole path is enough to make the whole path bad (yielding no reward) regardless of all other hops. We formally define the path metric:

Theorem 3. *The* Harmonic Discounted Index[7] *(HDI) is a measure of attractiveness for transmitting over a path that circumvents the non-optimal myopic locking and can be computed in* $\mathrm{O}(\mathcal{K}n)$.

$$HDI = \left[\sum_{i=1}^{n}\left(\frac{1}{DI_i}\right)\right]^{-1} \tag{7}$$

7 Experimental Evaluation

This section describes the experimental setup and illustrates performance evaluations of our HDI metric when embedded within an index policy in a variety of simulation scenarios. We evaluate an index policy where we vary the index between different alternatives such as the myopic index, HDI index and other indices based on different ways of combining hop conductances, namely: **Mnlog index**: $\frac{1}{n}\sum_{i=1}^{n}\log(DI_i)$, **Min**: $\min_{i\in[1,n]} DI_i$, **Sum**: $\sum_{i=1}^{n} DI_i$ and **Prod**: $\prod_{i=1}^{n} W_i$. In all simulations, the transition probabilities of hops are generated uniformly at random within given bounds (specified per case). The discounted factors, γ and δ, are fixed to the values $\gamma = 0.95$ and $\delta = 0.95$. For every set of randomly generated paths, 10^4 runs are repeated, where in each run the discounted reward representing the successful message transmissions is accumulated for a horizon of 10^4 decision times. The reported reward is the mean value of the accumulated discounted rewards over all runs, scaled by $1-\gamma$.

Exploring the Transition Space of Hops. We first compare our HDI metric against flooding, i.e., transmitting every message on all available paths. Flooding clearly is an upper bound on the optimal solution. We divide the search space $[0,1]$ of the transition probabilities into eight categories $L1$ through $H4$, ranging from hops that slowly switch between the reliable and unreliable state to those that switch very frequently. Our Results, Fig. 2(a), (b), (c) and (d), show that the performance of our HDI metric is close to that of flooding for the ranges $L1$ through $L4$, (indicating a close to optimal performance). For ranges $H1$ through $H4$, the performance gap grows bigger since hops in these ranges tend to switch

[7] We provide in [7] the routing algorithm which runs at the source node.

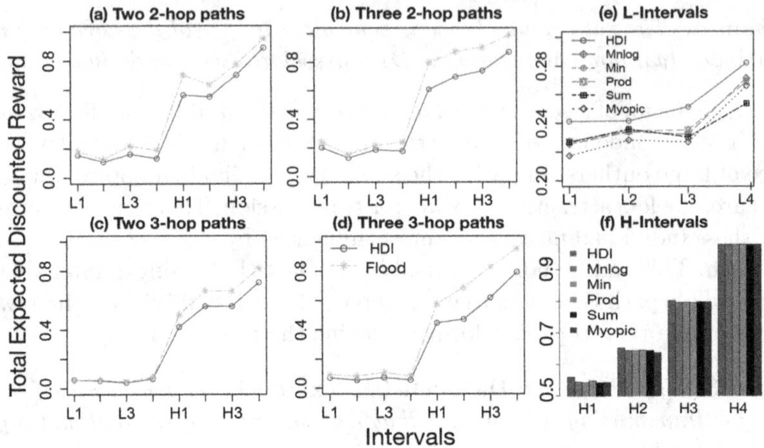

Fig. 2. Performance of HDI index policy over L and H-Intervals.

rapidly between states, spending more time in the reliable state. In these cases decisions are prone to more randomness. Flooding, in comparison with a policy which selects one path only, explores all other potentials, who in this case, have a high probability of being good. We also evaluate the performance of HDI versus the alternative policies given three available 2-hop paths. We separate the results between L and H intervals, relative to the hops constituting the paths. It can be seen (Fig. 2(e,f)) that HDI outperforms all alternatives over all ranges. This improvement decreases as hops go higher in the H interval (discussed in [7]).

	L1	L2	L3	L4		H1	H2	H3	H4
α	$[0, \beta]$	$[0.1, \beta]$	$[0.2, \beta]$	$[0.3, \beta]$	α	$[0, 1-\beta]$	$[0.2, 1-\beta]$	$[0.3, 1-\beta]$	$[0.4, 1-\beta]$
β	$[0.1, 0.2[$	$[0.2, 0.3[$	$[0.3, 0.4[$	$[0.4, 0.5[$	$1-\beta$	$[0.6, 1[$	$[0.7, 1[$	$[0.8, 1[$	$[0.9, 1[$

Typical Smart Grid Sensor Network. Typical smart grid sensory networks contain heterogeneous hops of wireless and power line communication hops [3,6,8]. We simulate such typical smart grid scenario by combining frequent and slow switching hops [8,17,20]. We consider a network having $\mathcal{K}$ independent 2-hop paths available for transmission. Hops along a path are generated uniformly at random as either slow switching (L1 range) or fast switching (ranges H3 and H4). We illustrate the performance measures for different number of available paths varying between $\mathcal{K} = \{2, 3, 4, \ldots, 10\}$. Our results, Fig. 3(I)-(a), show that the HDI selection policy outperforms the myopic policy for all numbers of available paths. We further strengthen the significance of the improvement obtained by our HDI metric by limiting the number of available paths to 2 and comparing all performances with that of flooding for a number of hops per path, spanning $n = \{2, 3, 4\}$. Our results, Fig. 3(I)-(b), show that despite the narrow margin for improvement, our HDI metric succeeds in showing a positive improvement over the myopic policy, revealing a close-to-optimal performance.

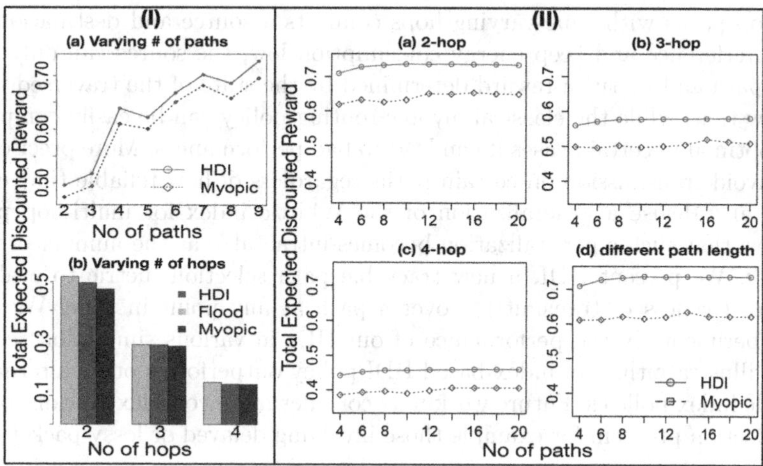

Fig. 3. (I) Performance in typical smart grid networks (II) Performance under locking.

Myopic Performance Under Locking. In this section we confirm (i) the deterioration of myopic performance under locking and (ii) the ability of the HDI metric to circumvent this performance deterioration. We generate a first set of $\mathcal{K}$ independent n-hop paths where hops are randomly generated satisfying $0.7 < 1 - \beta < 0.85$ and $0.6 < \alpha < 1 - \beta$. Such hops switch frequently between states, representing a behavior similar to that of wireless channels. A second set of $\mathcal{K}'$ n-hop paths (of the same size as $\mathcal{K}$) are also created. Every path in $\mathcal{K}'$ satisfies Theorem 2 with some path $k \in \mathcal{K}$, i.e. these paths will be neglected by the myopic policy. Paths in set $\mathcal{K}'$ are chosen to be slow switching, similar to the behavior of power line communication hops [8]. A source can transmit on any path within these two sets. Simulations are carried for $(|\mathcal{K}|+|\mathcal{K}'|) = \{4, 6, 8, \dots, 20\}$ available paths and for $n = \{1, 2, 3, 4\}$ hops/path. Results in Fig. 3(II)(a), (b) and (c) show a noticeable deterioration in the myopic performance where our HDI metric manages to reach an improvement of $\sim 20\,\%$ over myopic.

We slightly modify our simulation to allow paths with different numbers of hops. In particular, every path is generated with a size of $n = \{2, 3, 4\}$, chosen uniformly at random. Our results, Fig. 3(II)(d), show that the myopic deterioration extends to such cases where our HDI metric benefits from any available "short" good paths and maintains $\sim 20\,\%$ improvement over myopic. We also evaluate our HDI index against a per-hop myopic (greedy) index. Results show that a per-hop technique performs worse that source routing myopic (this is expected as per-hop neglects the impact of hops further down a path).

8 Conclusion

This paper studied the path selection problem arising in multi-hop sensor networks. In such scenarios, a communication system consisting of multiple multi-hop paths with time-varying hops connects a source and destination. To avoid interference and keep energy consumption low, the source can only send on one path and accrue a reward determined by the state of the traversed hops. We show that, while the classical myopic routing policy can be easily computed and is optimal in certain cases it can lead to bad performances. More precisely, it might avoid transmission on certain paths regardless of how reliable they could be. We also devise a generalization of the Whittle index for multi-hop paths and show that such a generalization becomes intractable as the number of hops increases. We present HDI, a new tractable path selection metric to evaluate the attractiveness of transmitting over a path at any point in time. We evaluate experimentally the performance of our HDI in various simulation scenarios. We illustrate that an index-based HDI policy outperforms other alternative tractable index policies. Future work may consider more complex versions of the path selection problem for example those involving delayed or lossy packet-drop mechanisms.

References

1. Ahmad, S., Liu, M., Javidi, T., Zhao, Q., Krishnamachari, B.: Optimality of myopic sensing in multichannel opportunistic access. IEEE Trans. Inf. Theor. **55**(9), 4040–4050 (2009)
2. Bertsekas, D.P.: Dynamic Programming and Optimal Control, 2nd edn. Athena Scientific, Belmont (2000)
3. Bumiller, G., Lampe, L., Hrasnica, H.: Power line communication networks for large-scale control and automation systems. IEEE Commun. Mag. **48**(4), 106–113 (2010)
4. Chatterjee, K., Majumdar, R.: Discounting and averaging in games across time scales. Int. J. Found. Comput. Sci. **23**(3), 609–625 (2012)
5. Johnson, D.M.D., Hu, Y.: The dynamic source routing protocol (DSR) for mobile Ad hoc networks for IPv4. Technical report, IETF (2007). http://tools.ietf.org/html/rfc4728
6. DLC+VIT4IP. Scenarios and requirements specification. Technical report, 1010. http://www.dlc-vit4ip.org/wb/media/Downloads
7. Dzung, D., Guerraoui, R., Kozhaya, D., Pignolet, Y.-A.: Dynamic path selection in source routing for time-varying lossy networks. Technical report, Extended version (2014). http://infoscience.epfl.ch/record/206986
8. Dzung, D., Pignolet, Y.-A.: Dynamic selection of wireless/powerline links using Markov decision processes. In: IEEE SmartGridComm (2013)
9. Elliott, E.O.: Estimates of error rates for codes on burst-noise channels. Bell Syst. Tech. J **42**, 1977–1997 (1963)
10. Gilbert, E.N., et al.: Capacity of a burst-noise channel. Bell Syst. Tech. J **39**(9), 1253–1265 (1960)
11. Guha, S., Munagala, K., Shi, P.: Approximation algorithms for restless bandit problems. J. ACM **58**(1), 1–50 (2010)
12. Hasslinger, G., Hohlfeld, O.: The gilbert-elliott model for packet loss in real time services on the internet. In: MMB, pp. 1–15, March 2008
13. Liu, K., Zhao, Q.: Indexability of restless bandit problems and optimality of whittle index for dynamic multichannel access. IEEE Trans. Inf. Theor. **56**(10), 5547–5567 (2010)

14. Mitton, N., Sericola, B., Tixeuil, S., Fleury, E., Lassous, I.G.: Self-stabilization in self-organized wireless multihop networks? Ad Hoc Sens. Wireless Netw. **11**(1–2), 1–34 (2011)
15. Nayyar, N., Gai, Y., Krishnamachari, B.: On a restless multi-armed bandit problem with non-identical arms. In: Allerton, pp. 369–376 (2011)
16. Ny, J., Dahleh, M., Feron, E.: Multi-uav dynamic routing with partial observations using restless bandit allocation indices. In: American Control Conference, pp. 4220–4225 (2008)
17. Rao, R., Akella, S., Guley, G.: Power line carrier (PLC) signal analysis of smart meters for outlier detection. In: IEEE SmartGridComm, pp. 291–296 (2011)
18. Tang, C., McKinley, P.K.: Modeling multicast packet losses in wireless lans. In: MSWIM 2003, pp. 130–133. ACM, New York (2003)
19. Vasseur, J.: Terminology in low power and lossy networks. Technical report, Cisco Systems Inc. (2013)
20. Vasseur, J.-P., Dunkels, A.: Interconnecting smart objects with IP: the next internet. Morgan Kaufmann Publishers, Inc. (2010)
21. Weber, R.R., Weiss, G.: On an index policy for restless bandits. Journal of Applied Probability, pp. 637–648 (1990)
22. Whittle, P.: Restless bandits: activity allocation in a changing world. J. Appl. Probab. **25**, 287–298 (1988)
23. Winter, T., Thubert, P., Brandt, A., Hui, J., Kelsey, R., Levis, P., Pister, K., Struik, R., Vasseur, J., Alexander, R.: RPL: IPv6 routing protocol for low-power and lossy networks. Technical report, IETF (2012). http://tools.ietf.org/html/rfc6550
24. Zayen, B., Hayar, A., Noubir, G.: Game theory-based resource management strategy for cognitive radio networks. Multimedia Tools Appl. **70**(3), 2063–2083 (2014)

A Fully Distributed Learning Algorithm for Power Allocation in Heterogeneous Networks

Hajar Elhammouti[1(✉)], Loubna Echabbi[1], and Rachid Elazouzi[2]

[1] Department of Telecommunications Systems, Networks and Services, STRS, National Institute of Posts and Telecommunications, Rabat, Morocco
{elhammouti,echabbi}@inpt.ac.ma

[2] Department Laboratory of Informatique of Avignon, LIA, University of Avignon, Avignon, France
rachid.elazouzi@univ-avignon.fr

Abstract. In this work, we present a Fully distributed Learning Algorithm for Power allocation in HetNetS, referred to as FLAPH algorithm, that reaches to the global optimum given by the total social welfare. Using a mix of macro and femto base stations, we discuss opportunities to maximize users global throughput. We prove the convergence of our algorithm and compare its performances with the well-established Gibbs algorithm which ensures convergence to the global optimum.

Keywords: Distributed algorithms · HetNets · Nash equilibrium · Global optimum

1 Introduction

One of the reasons to consider heterogeneous networks is that they present better performance for high data traffic in wireless communications. Indeed, to improve the network capacity, one should increase node density. When only macro base stations are deployed, cell splitting by adding other base stations can help to increase the network efficiency. However, not any node can be deployed, only those who would not add much interferences and costs could be added. This can be realized by base stations with lower transmit power. Their transmit power ranges depend on the category they belong to. They are either pico, femto or relay nodes and they are intended for outdoor and indoor deployments [1].

LTE Release 10 supports heterogeneous deployment where picocells, femtocells and relays coexist with macrocells [3]. In a heterogeneous framework, smart resource coordination among base stations and optimization of implicit interactions can improve the aggregate throughput of the network. Thus, distributed approaches are crucial to increase the network performances and allow more autonomy to the base stations.

The present paper formulates the problem of power allocation for multi-user downlinks in heterogeneous networks (HetNets). It is important to see that from an optimization standpoint, optimizing resource allocation is an NP-hard

A. Bouajjani and H. Fauconnier (Eds.): NETYS 2015, LNCS 9466, pp. 216–229, 2015.
DOI: 10.1007/978-3-319-26850-7_15

problem [2]. In this work, we present a Fully distributed Learning Algorithm for Power allocation in HETNETS, referred to as FLAPH algorithm, that reaches to the global optimum given by the total social welfare. We show its qualitative properties and compare it with the well-established Gibbs algorithm in term of convergence and computational costs.

2 Related Work

Optimization of power allocation is an active area of research that has been investigated by many studies. Some researchers were interested in distributed algorithms [10–12]. Yet, these algorithms present a major limit which is the need of a network controller to share information with the nodes.

B. Kauffmann et al. in [5] introduced the Gibbs Sampler algorithm for optimal channel selection and user association in 802.11 wireless access networks. In their work, B. Kauffmann et al. aimed to minimize a specific objective function which is the aggregated transmission delay. Soon after, F. Baccelli et al. in [6] implemented the same algorithm to optimize the aggregate delay subject to the transmitted power and users assignment in homogeneous networks. The Gibbs sampler algorithms, as they were proposed by B. Kauffmann et al. and F. Baccelli et al., are restricted to a specific utility function which is the aggregate delay, and cannot be applied to arbitrary utility functions. Recently, Sem borst et al. in [15] tackled this problem. They developed the Gibbs sampler algorithm for a more generic notion of utility functions and applied it to distributed optimization of power allocation and user assignment in OFDMA homogeneous networks. To accommodate to arbitrary utility functions, they based their algorithm on Markov Random Fields/Gibbs Measures and apply it to a modified graph where the global objective function is equal to the sum of potential energies of the cliques in the new graph. Hence they prove that it is sufficient to optimize local potential energies on the cliques which are, in fact, related to neighborhoods. In that sense, only local information is needed and can be exchanged between neighbors, yet leading to a global optimum.

The Gibbs sampler algorithm is rather called the annealing Gibbs sampler algorithm since it uses combinatorial approximation technique 'the simulated annealing' [4,9] to achieve convergence to optimality. The convergence is achieved for a specific cooling schedule $\{T_t \propto 1/log(t), t \geq 2\}$, where T_t is called the temperature of the algorithm. This cooling schedule has an extremely slow rate which can be inappropriate for practical purposes.

In works presented above, authors are interested in optimizing the social welfare. Thus, agents coordinate to reach optimality. In the literature, other works involve agents utilities. They consider problems where each agent is selfish and wants to maximize its own utility's value. In game theory, this problem has a well know solution concept called the Nash equilibrium (NE). Actually, Nash equilibrium is a situation where no player has the incentive to move unilaterally. Many distributed algorithms that converge to the NE have been proposed in the literature and have been applied to different kinds of problems: pricing [19], routing [17], bandwidth sharing [14]...

Our approach goes in the same line with [8,20] where authors use a learning algorithm to reach the Nash Equilibrium, respectively, for a pricing and a power allocation problem. We rely on an updated version of the algorithm, that, unlike in [8], drives the whole system to a steady state corresponding to the Nash Equilibrium of a specific game which is, at the same time, the global optimum.

The rest of the paper is organized as follows. The next section presents the problem formulation. In Sect. 4 we give an overview on the annealing Gibbs sampler and describe in details the proposed FLAPH algorithm. Section 5 contains numerical results that compare both algorithms in term of convergence and computational costs. Finally, in the last section, we make some concluding remarks and discuss various extensions to this work.

3 Problem Formulation

3.1 Main Notations

We consider a network where coexist two classes of base stations (BSs): femtocell and macrocell. This cellular system consists of a macro base station that typically transmits at high power level, overlaid with several femto base stations which transmit at lower power levels.

We consider N users randomly dispersed in space that are supposed fixed (mobility in not considered in this work). Each user is assigned to one BS, but can receive signal from other BSs. Each BS decides which power to use.

We denote by P_b the amount of power transmitted by cell b. We suppose that the power is discretized such that $P_b \in P_{femto} = \{\delta P_f, 2\delta P_f, 3\delta P_f, .., n\delta P_f\}$ if b is a femtocell and for the macro $P_M \in P_{macro} = \{\delta P, 2\delta P, 3\delta P, .., n\delta P\}$. Each user i has a channel gain with respect to BS b. In this work, we will focus only on the downlink problem (Tables 1, 2).

In the table below, we summarize these notations:

Table 1. Main notations

Notation	Meaning
$\boldsymbol{B}$	Set of base stations, finite
M	The macro-cell
$\mathcal{U}$	The set of users
N	Number of users
K	Number of cells including the macrocell
G	Gain matrix of $N * K$ dimension, G_{ib} is the channel gain from BS b to user i
P	Power vector of K dimension where P_b is the amount of power transmitted by BS b
q	Assignment matrix, such that $q_{ib} = 1$ iff user i is assigned to BS b

3.2 Game Formulation

We formulate the problem as a non-cooperative game $\boldsymbol{G}$ where the players are the base stations and strategies are their possible powers. The major goal of this game is to maximize the social welfare that we define as the general throughput of the network, subject to power allocation constraints:

$$\begin{array}{ll} \text{maximize} & F(P) = \sum_{b \in B} R_b(P) \\ \text{subject to} & \forall b \text{ femto } P_b \in P_{femto}, P_M \in P_{macro} \end{array} \tag{1}$$

We define each BS's utility as the sum of its users throughput which could be given by the C. Shannon theorem [7]:

$$R_b(P) \propto \sum_{i \in M} log_2(1 + S_{i,b}(P)) \tag{2}$$

Where $S_{i,b}(P)$ is the SINR (Signal to Interference and Noise Ratio) of user i with respect to the node b that we formulate as: $S_{i,b}(P) = \frac{G_{ib} P_b}{\eta + \sum_{b' \neq b} G_{ib'} P_{b'}}$. η describes the thermal noise.

So let us denote $U^b_{\boldsymbol{G}}(P) = \sum_{i \in \mathscr{U}} q_{ib} R_{i,b}(P)$ the utility of a player b. Thus:

$$F(P) = \sum_{b \in B} U^b_{\boldsymbol{G}}(P) \tag{3}$$

$U^b_{\boldsymbol{G}}(P)$ can also be seen as the individual utility of each BS.

In the rest of the paper, we will use, in some equations, this notation $U^b_{\boldsymbol{G}}(P_b, P_{-b})$ instead of $U^b_{\boldsymbol{G}}(P)$, where P_b is b^{th} component of vector P which refer to the power state of BS b and P_{-b} is the state of the other BSs.

It is easy to see that a pure Nash Equilibrium is reached when all BSs set their powers to the maximum. Actually, suppose that all BSs choose their maximum of power, if a given BS b decides to reduce its power, then its utility will decrease since the throughput is an increasing function with respect to the power of this BS. We can use the same reasoning to prove that this NE is unique. Indeed, regardless of the initial power vector, faced with a fixed power of its opponents, each BTS will always have incentive to increase its power and thus maximize its utility.

Let us denote the price of anarchy PoA which is measured as follows:

$$PoA = \frac{F(P^{NE})}{F(P^{*})} \tag{4}$$

where $F(P^{NE})$ (resp. $F(P^{*})$) is the social welfare at the NE (resp. global optimum). In Sect. 5, we will consider the optimal social welfare and compare it with the performance achieved at the Nash Equilibrium by using the price of anarchy. We will see that this ratio may be very important in some scenarios and thus in distributed learning BSs cannot set their powers independently, they need additional information from their neighbors in order to coordinate their actions and thus reach the global optimum.

4 Distributed Optimization

4.1 Annealing Gibbs Sampler Algorithm

Distributed methods and learning algorithms aim to have more autonomy in the networks and improve its performances. Gibbs algorithm is a powerful approach based on the update of local utilities which achieves convergence to the global optimum [13,16]. In this subsection, we will present the basic notions related to the annealing Gibbs sampler algorithm.

As it was explained above, this algorithm is based on two main algorithms that are 'the Gibbs Sampler' for sampling resources and 'the simulated annealing' technique as a local search meta-heuristic yet ensuring convergence to the global optimum. The Gibbs sampler can be replaced by Metropolis-Hastings sampler whose behavior is very similar to the Gibbs one [18].

As a stochastic algorithm, the annealing Gibbs sampler, updates randomly its states following a Gibbs measure. Actually, each time the agent randomly chooses an action from the action space based on the Gibbs distribution which is given by:

$$P(x_b = y|x_{-(b,a_b)}) = \frac{exp[\sum_{c \in N_b^+} U_c(y, x_{-(b,a_b)})/T]}{\sum_{x \in S(x_{(b,a_b)})} \exp[\sum_{c \in N_b^+} U_c(y, x_{-(b,a_b)})/T]} \tag{5}$$

with

- x_b the state of node b
- y is the possible value of power that node b may choose.
- $x_{-(b,a_b)}$ the state of nodes other than b
- $S(x_{-(b,a_b)})$ the set of the states of the other nodes than node b
- $S(x_{(b,a_b)})$ the set of the possible states of node b. In our case it defines the state of powers.
- N_b the set of neighbors of node b
- N_b^+ the set of neighbors of node b including b
- U_c is the utility of node c
- T the temperature of the algorithm.

The Gibbs algorithm can be structured in 4 main parts:

1. **Computing probabilities**
   Computing Gibbs probability of each possible state of power, for each BS.
2. **Sampling powers**
   Using the computed probabilities, each BS decides whether to keep its power or to change it.
3. **Updating utilities using the chosen powers**
   Depending on the state the BS has chosen, its individual utility is updated in order to calculate the global utility which is the social welfare of the network.

4. **Computing global energy**
   The global energy, or the global objective function is the sum of the BSs' utilities at each temperature T.

The convergence of Gibbs algorithm is deduced from the well known 'simulated annealing' that ensures convergence to the optimized solution when T decreases slowly to 0 following a specific function $1/log(t), t \geq 2$ [4,9]. This cooling schedule may take a very long time before convergence which makes the annealing Gibbs sampler algorithm not suited for some practical purposes.

4.2 A New Model Description

Let us consider a new game ***G'*** where utilities are modified such that, for each BS b:

$$U^b_{G'}(P) = U^b_G(P) + \sum_{c \in N_b} U^c_G(P) \tag{6}$$

Where N_b is the set of BSs neighbors of b. Two BSs are called 'neighbors' if there is at least one user assigned to one of them and covered by the other:

$$N_b = \{c \in \mathtt{B}, \exists i \in \boldsymbol{U}, q_{ib}P_cG_{ic} \succ 0 \text{ or } q_{ic}P_bG_{ib} \succ 0\} \tag{7}$$

Note that, the macrocell is neighbor of all femtocells since it has a high power which is received by all users.

Therefore, N_b will determine a neighborhood structure. We can represent the heterogeneous network by an undirected graph $\mathscr{G} = (\nu, \epsilon)$, where ν is the set of nodes and ϵ the set of edges. We assume that nodes are BSs and edges are set between all neighbors. $U^b_{G'}(P)$ can also be seen as a local utility of BS b driven by its power state P_b and those of its opponents P_{-b}.

The distributed nature of the FLAPH algorithm we will be studying comes from the notion of local information. Indeed, each agent needs only to know its individual utility and the individual utility of its neighbors to reach optimality. As a result, the exchanged information in the network is limited. We will bring more clarifications about the information needed to the convergence in the next subsection.

4.3 The FLAPH Algorithm

The learning algorithm we propose is the one described in [8]. It is shown in [8] that the distributed algorithm drives the whole system to a steady state corresponding to the Nash Equilibrium of a non-cooperative game. In the new problem formulation, the proposed FLAPH algorithm will converge to the pure Nash Equilbrium of the new game G' which is exactly the global optimum of the social welfare.

Theorem 1. *Let **G'** be the game defined by the utilities $U_{\boldsymbol{G'}}$. Let P^* be the vector of power strategies which represents the global optimum of the social welfare. P^* is a Nash equilibrium of the game **G'**.*

Proof. Let us set some helpful notations:

- Let I_b be the set of users covered by BS b:

$$I_b = \{i \in \mathscr{U}, P_b G_{ib} \succ 0\} \tag{8}$$

- Let I_{cb} be the set of users covered by BSs c and b at the same time:

$$I_{cb} = \{i \in \mathscr{U}, q_{ic} P_b G_{ib} \succ 0 \text{ and } q_{ib} P_c G_{ic} \succ 0\} \tag{9}$$

- Let $I_{b\backslash c}$ be the set of users covered by b and not covered by c:

$$I_{b\backslash c} = \{i \in \mathscr{U}, P_b G_{ib} \succ 0 \text{ and } P_c G_{ic} = 0\} \tag{10}$$

Suppose that players are at the global optimum. Notice that the utility of the Macro base station M in the new game G' is equal to the social welfare of the network (because M covers all the users and then it is neighbor of all femto base stations). Thus, we have:

$$U^M_{G'}(P) = F(P) \tag{11}$$

It is easy to see that at the global optimum P^*, M cannot improve its utility. Suppose that a femtocell b can improve its utility $U^b_{G'}(P^*_b, P^*_{-b})$ by choosing the strategy $\tilde{P}_b$. We have:

$$\begin{aligned}
U^b_{G'}(\tilde{P}_b, P^*_{-b}) &= U^b_G(\tilde{P}_b, P^*_{-b}) + \sum_{c\in N_b} U^c_G(\tilde{P}_b, P^*_{-b}) \\
&= \sum_{i\in\cup_{c\in N_b} I_{b\backslash c}} R_{i,b}(\tilde{P}_b, P^*_{-b}) + \sum_{i\in\cup_{c\in N_b} I_{bc}} q_{ib} R_{i,b}(\tilde{P}_b, P^*_{-b}) \\
&+ \sum_{i\in\cup_{c\in N_b} I_{c\backslash b}} R_{i,c}(\tilde{P}_b, P^*_{-b}) + \sum_{i\in\cup_{c\in N_b} I_{bc}} q_{ic} R_{i,c}(\tilde{P}_b, P^*_{-b}) \\
&= \sum_{i\in\cup_{c\in N_b} I_{b\backslash c}} R_{i,b}(\tilde{P}_b, P^*_{-b}) + \sum_{i\in\cup_{c\in N_b} I_{bc}} (q_{ib} R_{i,b}(\tilde{P}_b, P^*_{-b}) \\
&+ q_{ic} R_{i,c}(\tilde{P}_b, P^*_{-b})) + \sum_{i\in\cup_{c\in N_b} I_{c\backslash b}} R_{i,c}(\tilde{P}_b, P^*_{-b})
\end{aligned} \tag{12}$$

$\sum_{i\in\cup_{c\in N_b} I_{b\backslash c}} R_{i,b}(\tilde{P}_b, P^*_{-b})$ is the sum of the throughput of users who are assigned to b and not covered by any other BS, $\sum_{i\in\cup_{c\in N_b} I_{bc}} (q_{ib} R_{i,b}(\tilde{P}_b, P^*_{-b}) + q_{ic} R_{i,c}(\tilde{P}_b, P^*_{-b}))$ is the sum of the throughput of users in common between b and one of its neighbors c and who are assigned whether to b or c, and $\sum_{i\in\cup_{c\in N_b} I_{c\backslash b}} R_{i,c}(\tilde{P}_b, P^*_{-b})$ is the sum of the throughput of users who are assigned to each c neighbor of b and not covered by b. Let $Urelated_b$ be the set of users related to b as their throughput is counted in utility of b:

$$Urelated_b = (\cup_{c\in I_{bc}} I_{b\backslash c}) \cup (\cup_{c\in N_b} I_{bc}) \cup (\cup_{c\in N_b} I_{c\backslash b}) \tag{13}$$

We consider the complementary of $Urelated_b$ in $\mathscr{U}$ that we denote $Uunrelated_b = (Urelated_b)^C$. The utility of the macrocell M could be written as follows:

$$U_{G'}^{M}(\tilde{P}_b, P^*_{-b}) = \underbrace{U_{G'}^{b}(\tilde{P}_b, P^*_{-b})}_{increased} + \underbrace{\sum_{c \in B} \sum_{i \in Uunrelated_b} q_{ic} R_{i,c}(\tilde{P}_b, P^*_{-b})}_{unchanged} \tag{14}$$

- $U_{G'}^{b}(\tilde{P}_b, P^*_{-b})$ has increased according to our first hypothesis.
- $\sum_{c \in B} \sum_{i \in Uunrelated_b} q_{ic} R_{i,c}(\tilde{P}_b, P^*_{-b}) = \sum_{c \in B} \sum_{i \in Uunrelated_b} q_{ic} R_{i,c}(P^*_b, P^*_{-b})$ because no throughput in the sum will be impacted by the change of the power of BS b since the users are not related to b.

Consequently, $U_{G'}^{M}(\tilde{P}_b, P^*_{-b}) \succ U_{G'}^{M}(P^*_b, P^*_{-b})$ which is absurd. As a conclusion, the Nash equilirium of the new game coincides with the global optimum.

If not unique the N.E will either hold the same social welfare or be dominated by the optimum one. We are just going to state here that the learning algorithm will find a dominant N.E which will correspond to a global optimum. Due to symmetry there may exist other state that yields the same social welfare but they will be equivalent.

Now let us describe how this algorithm works. Since it is a stochastic learning algorithm, nodes should update their strategies following a probability distribution in order to learn the global optimum. Stochastic strategies, utilities and power strategies will be suffixed by t to refer to their values at time step t. We denote s_{bk} the probability that node b chooses the power P_k. These probabilities are calculated as follows:

$$s_{bk}^{t+1} = \begin{cases} s_{bk}^{t} - l U_b^t s_{ij}^{t} & \text{if } P_k \neq P_b^t \\ s_{bk}^{t} + l U_b^t \sum_{k' \neq k} s_{bk'}^{t} & \text{otherwise} \end{cases} \tag{15}$$

Where: U_i^t is the normalized local utility at the time t, such that:

$$U_b^t = \frac{U_{G'}^{b}(P^t)}{\max_{t' \leq t}(U_{G'}^{b}(P^{t'}))} \tag{16}$$

And l a parameter in $[0, 1]$, it is the step size of the probability updating rule. The results of the algorithm are more accurate when l is close to zero (see [8]).

Notice that the probabilities are updated in function of the response of the environment (in function of the local normalized utility U_i^t). Thus the successive choice of the power depends on the environment response, which is a property of a learning algorithm.

The proposed FLAPH algorithm achieves many performances. It is, firstly, a fully distributed algorithm. It can also be implemented on board of each device in an asynchronous way where each agent updates its state depending on its own clock. Finally, it requires limited computational efforts compared to Gibbs algorithm as we will see in Sect. 5.

To measure the local utility of a given BS b, the base station should receive the amount $P_c G_{ic}$ from all its neighbors with respect to its users i in order to measure the interference and calculate the sum of its throughput. And each neighboring BS c should calculate its individual utility in the same way and send it to b in order to compute its local utility. It is then easy to see that information is shared only between neighbors and the neighbors of the neighbors.

```
for each iteration iter do
    for each BS b do
        if the timer of b is activated then
            Randomely choose a power level using current probabilities;
            Compute interference and measure the throughput of assigned
            users;
            Update individual utility;
            Request update from neighbors;
            Hold;
        end
        if reception of an update request from a neighbor then
            Compute interference and Measure the throughput of assigned
            users;
            Update individual utility;
            Send update to the requester;
        end
        if reception of an update response from a neighbor then
            Accumulate the received individual utility;
            if response are still missing from remaining neighbors
            then
                Hold;
            else
                % all neighbors has already responded;
                Update stochastic strategies;
                Reset the timer;
            end
        end
    end
end
```

Algorithm 1. The FLAPH algorithm

5 Numerical Results

5.1 The FLAPH Algorithm Versus Anarchy

In this section, we present a selection of the most representative numerical experiments that we have conducted in order to validate our approach and show the performance of our FLAPH algorithm. First, we focus on 4 experiments with different sizes of BSs' number K users' number N. We use a regular hexagonal pattern for the location of the cells.

We deduce the matrix gain G using the COST-231-Hata-Model (which is a radio propagation model for urban areas, other propagation models can also be used to generate the channel matrix). We suppose $P_{femto} = \{250\,mW, 500\,mW\}$, and $P_{Macro} = \{20000\,mW, 40000\,mW\}$. The thermal background noise is supposed equal to $4.0039e - 12\,mW$. We assume that BSs update their power state in an asynchronous way using an exponential timer with parameter $\lambda = 2$ and we take the step size of the probability updating rule $l = 0.008$. The Figs. 1 and 2 show the overall throughput and indicate the real number of iterations needed for each case before convergence. Note that the number of iterations shown in the horizontal axis is equal to the number of real iterations times the number of

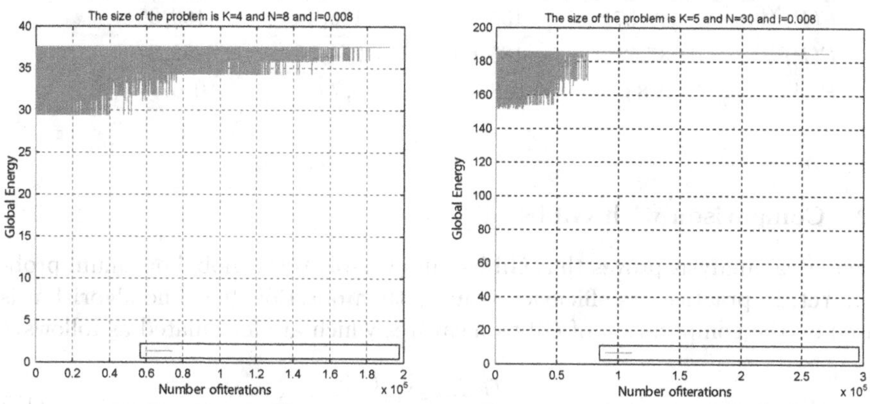

Fig. 1. The FLAPH convergence for $K = 4$ and $N = 8$, and $K = 5$ and $N = 30$.

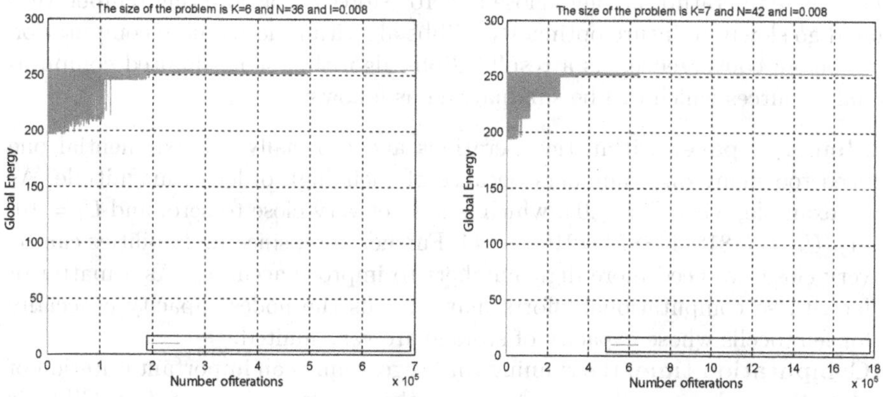

Fig. 2. The FLAPH convergence for $K = 6$ and $N = 36$, and $K = 7$ and $N = 42$.

BSs. Actually, the curves show all the states that system gets through, which is exactly $iter * N$.

We consider the optimal social welfare as reached by the FLAPH algorithm and compare it with the performance achieved at Nash Equilibrium of the uncoordinated game $\boldsymbol{G}$ where BSs set their powers independently (Table 2).

The table below presents the experiments results:

We emphasize that the price of anarchy worsens with increasing size of the problem. In a distributed setting BSs cannot just set their powers independently, they need additional information from their neighbors in order to coordinate their actions and thus reach the global optimum.

Table 2. The price of anarchy's values

Size of problem	$K = 4\ N = 8$	$K = 5\ N = 30$	$K = 6\ N = 36$	$N = 7\ K = 42$
$F(P)^{NE}$	$33,07$	$155,27$	$186,46$	$169,30$
$F(P)^{OP}$	37.52	$185,60$	$254,56$	$252,37$
PoA	$0,88$	$0,83$	$0,73$	$0,67$

5.2 Comparison with Gibbs

Theoretical analysis proves that Gibbs sampler solves the global optimum problem. Yet, in practice, its efficiency is more than questionable. The algorithm is based on the computation of Gibbs measures which are formulated as follows:

$$P(x_b = y|x_{-(b,a_b)}) = \frac{exp[\sum_{c\in N_b^+} U_c(y, x_{-(b,a_b)})/T]}{\sum_{x\in S(x_{(b,a_b)})} exp[\sum_{c\in N_b^+} U_c(y, x_{-(b,a_b)})/T]} \tag{17}$$

The used exponential functions reach very high orders of magnitude especially when the temperature T comes close to zero. Moreover, as lowering temperature should go slowly to insure optimality, Gibbs algorithm needs more computation time before convergence. As a result, Gibbs algorithm shows limited computational resources which can be summarized as follows:

- **Memory space:** arithmetic operations and especially the exponential one need too many digit numbers because of their high order of magnitude. As an example, when $T = 0.03$, which is not yet very close to zero, and $U_i = 10$, $exp(U_i) = 5.818717881447216e + 144$. Furthermore, since probabilities can be very close, we need more digit numbers to improve accuracy. As a matter of fact, these computational efforts may exceeds the nodes capacity especially for femtocells whose capacity of storage are very limited.
- **Computation time:** the running time algorithm is an important criterion of algorithms efficiency. The number of arithmetic operations used by Gibbs is greater than the learning algorithm we proposed. Actually, at each iteration, Gibbs needs to compute the utility of the BS for each state of power to have

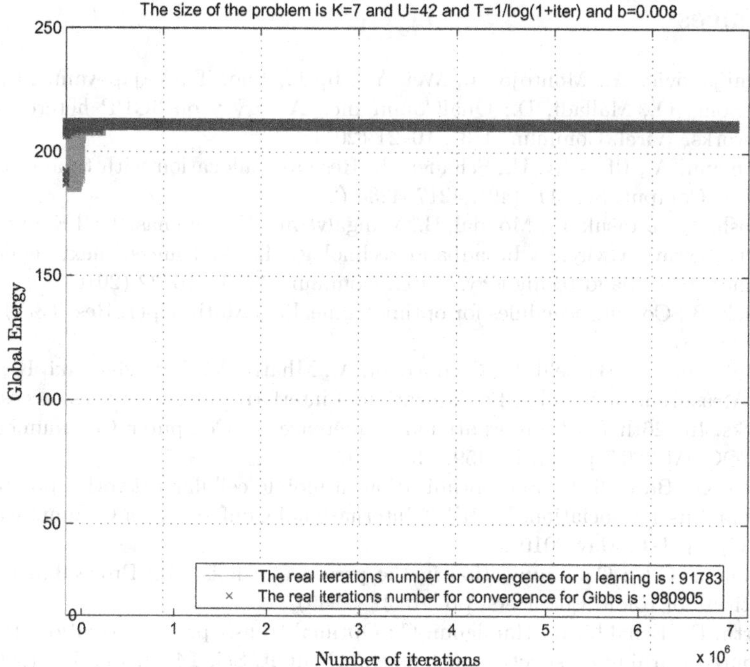

Fig. 3. The FLAPH Vs Gibbs.

the value of $\sum_{x \in S(x_{(b,a_b)})} exp[\sum_{c \in N_b^+} U_c(y, x_{-(b,a_b)})/T]$, which is not the case for the FLAPH algorithm. Therefore, the number of arithmetic operations used in Gibbs equals the number of arithmetic operations used in our learning algorithm times the size of the powers' state. Furthermore, the time needed for convergence in Gibbs is longer when it comes to use slow cooling schedules of the temperature as it is shown in the example of the Fig. 3.

6 Conclusion

In this work, we developed a fully distributed algorithm for power allocation in heterogeneous networks. The algorithm drives the whole system to a steady state corresponding to the global optimum of the social welfare. The algorithm is based in only on local exchanges between the nodes and needs limited computational efforts compared with the annealing Gibbs sampler.

In an ongoing work we investigate better performance of our algorithm by considering a two level optimisation problem where the Macro as a leader fixes its power and then other BSs follow by adjusting their power using the same FLAPH algorithm. The advantage of this version is to exclude The Macro from FLAPH algorithm reducing drastically message exchanges as this latter belongs to all neighborhoods.

References

1. Damnjanovic, A., Montojo, J., Wei, Y., Ji, T., Luo, T., Vajapeyam, M., Yoo, T., Song, O., Malladi, D.: QualComm Inc.: A survey on 3GPP heterogeneous networks. Wirel. Commun. **1**(3), 10–21 (2011)
2. Darmann, A., Pferschy, U., Schauer, J.: Resource allocation with time intervals. Theor. Comput. Sci. **411**(49), 4217–4234 (2010)
3. Ghosh, A., Ratasuk, R., Mondal, B., Mangalvedhe, N., Thomas, T.: TE-advanced: next-generation wireless broadband technology, LTE-advanced: next-generation wireless broadband technology. Wirel. Commun. **17**(3), 10–22 (2010)
4. Hajek, B.: Cooling schedules for optimal annealing. Math. Oper. Res. **13**(2), 311–329 (1988)
5. Kauffmann, B., Baccelli, F., Chaintreau, A., Mhatre, V., Papagiannaki, K., Diot, C.: Measurement-based self organization of interfering 802.11 wireless access networks. In: 26th IEEE International Conference on Computer Communications INFOCOM 2007, pp 1451–1459, May 2007
6. Chen, C., Baccelli, F.: Self-optimization in mobile cellular networks: power control and user association. In: IEEE International Conference on Communications (ICC), pp 1–6, May 2010
7. Shannon, C.E.: Communication in the presence of noise. In: Proceedings of the Institute of Radio Engineers, pp. 10–21 (1949)
8. Barth, D., Echabbi, L., Hamlaoui, C.: Optimal transit price negotiation: the distributed learning perspective. J. Univers. Comput. Sci. **14**(5), 745–765 (2008)
9. Bertsimas, D., Tsitsiklis, J.: Simulated annealing. Stat. Sci. **8**(1), 10–15 (1993)
10. Adeane, J., Rodrigues, M.R.D., Wassell, I.J.: Centralized and distributed power allocation algorithms in cooperative networks. In: 6th Workshop on Signal Processing Advances in Wireless Communications, pp. 333–337. IEEE (2005)
11. Li, J., Svensson, T., Botella, C., Eriksson, T., Xu, X., Chen, X.: Joint scheduling and power control in coordinated multi-point clusters. In: IEEE Vehicular Technology Conference (VTC Fall) 2012, pp. 1–5, November 2012
12. Li, J., Chen, X., Botella, C., Svensson, T., Eriksson, T.: Resource allocation for OFDMA systems with multi-cell joint transmission. In: IEEE 13th International Workshop on Signal Processing Advances in Wireless Communications (SPAWC) 2012, pp. 179–183, June 2012
13. Ahmed Khan, M., Tembine, H., Vasilakos, A.V.: Game dynamics and cost of learning in heterogeneous 4G networks. IEEE J. Sel. Areas Commun. **30**(1), 198–213 (2012)
14. Tuffin, B., Maillé, P.: How many parallel TCP sessions to open: a pricing perspective. In: Stiller, B., Reichl, P., Tuffin, B. (eds.) ICQT 2006. LNCS, vol. 4033, pp. 2–12. Springer, Heidelberg (2006)
15. Borst, S., Markakis, M., Saniee, I.: Distributed power allocation and user assignment in OFDMA cellular networks. In: The Annual Conference on Communication, Control, and Computing (Allerton), pp. 46–64, September 2011
16. Borst, S., Markakis, M., Saniee, I.: Nonconcave utility maximization in locally coupled systems, with applications to wireless and wireline networks. IEEE ACM Trans. Netw. **22**(2), 674–687 (2013)
17. Raghunathan, V., Kumar, P.: On delay-adaptive routing in wireless networks. In: Proceedings of CDC 2004 (2004)
18. Hastings, W.K.: Monte carlo sampling methods msing markov chains and their applications. Biometrika **57**(1), 97–109 (1970)

19. Xing, Y., Maille, P., Tuffin, B., Chandramouli, R.: User strategy learning when pricing a red buffer. Simul. Model. Pract. Theor. **17**, 548–557 (2009)
20. Xing, Y., Chandramouli, R.: Stochastic learning solution for distributed discrete power control game in wireless data networks. IEEE ACM Trans. Netw. **16**(4), 932–944 (2008)

Packet Scheduling over a Wireless Channel: AQT-Based Constrained Jamming

Antonio Fernández Anta[1], Chryssis Georgiou[2], and Elli Zavou[1,3](✉)

[1] IMDEA Networks Institute, Madrid, Spain
elli.zavou@imdea.org
[2] University of Cyprus, Nicosia, Cyprus
[3] Universidad Carlos III de Madrid, Madrid, Spain

Abstract. In this paper we consider a two-node setting with a sender transmitting packets to a receiver over a wireless channel. Unfortunately, the channel can be jammed, thus corrupting the packet that is being transmitted at the time. The sender has a specific amount of data that needs to be sent to the receiver and its objective is to complete the transmission of the data as quickly as possible in the presence of jamming.

We assume that the jamming is controlled by a constrained adversary. In particular, the adversary's power is constrained by two parameters, ρ and σ. Intuitively, ρ represents the rate at which the adversary can jam the channel, and σ the length of the largest bursts of jams it can cause. This definition corresponds to the translation of the Adversarial Queuing Theory (AQT) constrains, typically defined for packet injections in similar settings, to channel jamming.

We propose deterministic scheduling algorithms that decide the lengths of the packets to be sent by the sender in order to minimize the transmission time. We first assume all packets being of the same length (uniform) and characterize the corresponding optimal packet length. Then, we show that if the packet length can be adapted, for specific values of ρ and σ the transmission time can be improved.

Keywords: Packet scheduling · Wireless channel · Unreliable communication · Adversarial jamming · Adversarial Queueing Theory

1 Introduction

1.1 Motivation

The fast transmission of data across wireless channels under different conditions has been an area of investigation for quite some time now [3,6,10,11,14,18, 21–25]. However, it presents several challenges depending on the model and applications it focuses on; especially when considering channel jamming.

This work has been supported in part by the Regional Government of Madrid (CM) grant Cloud4BigData (S2013/ICE-2894, cofunded by FSE & FEDER).
E. Zavou—Partially supported by FPU Grant from MECD.

A. Bouajjani and H. Fauconnier (Eds.): NETYS 2015, LNCS 9466, pp. 230–245, 2015.
DOI: 10.1007/978-3-319-26850-7_16

In our work we look at a wireless channel between a single pair of stations (sender and receiver), with the sender's goal to fully transmit a specific amount of data in the most efficient way. As efficiency measures, we look both at the *transmission time* and the *goodput* ratio (successful transmission rate), which are intuitively reversely proportional. Nonetheless, the communication between the sender and the receiver is being "watched" by a malicious entity that sporadically introduces noise in the channel, jamming the packet that happens to be transmitted at that time. More precisely, we model the errors in the channel to be controlled by an adversary with constrained power; defined by parameters ρ and σ. Parameter ρ represents the rate at which the adversary can jam the channel and σ the largest size of a burst of jams that can be caused. A packet that is jammed needs to be retransmitted; hence a feedback mechanism is assumed that informs the sender when a packet was jammed. The sender must transmit data of total size P. Each packet sent contains a *header* of fixed size h and some *payload* whose size, l, is algorithm-depended. Note that this payload counts towards the total size of P to be transmitted. For simplicity and without loss of generality we assume that $h = 1$ and the time to transmit a packet is equal to its length.

The constrained power of the adversary models a jamming entity with limited resource of energy, e.g., military drones [13,17] or malicious mobile devices [1,2]. For the adversarial jammer in our model, we consider having a battery of capacity σ units, where each unit can be used to cause one jam. Furthermore, in every $1/\rho$ time the battery is charged by one unit, e.g. with solar cells. More details on the model we consider are given in Sect. 2.

In a previous work [4], we studied the impact of adversarial errors on packet scheduling, focusing on the long term competitive ratio of throughput, termed *relative throughput*. We explored the effect of feedback delay and proposed algorithms that achieve close to optimal relative throughput under worst-case errors, and adversarial or stochastic packet arrivals. One of the main differences with this work is that the adversary was not constrained. Another difference is the fact that in the current work the packet sizes are to be chosen by the sender in order to send the desired amount of data efficiently. Furthermore, in [4], jammed packets were not retransmitted; the objective was to route packets as fast as possible and not strive to have each packet transmitted. In the current work, the choice of the packet size is precisely the most critical part from the side of the sender. Thus, we focus in devising scheduling algorithms for the decision of packet length to be used and conduct worst-case analysis for the efficiency measures.

1.2 Contributions

First, we introduce an AQT-based adversarial jamming model in wireless networks. To the best of our knowledge, this is the first work that uses such approach to restrict the power of adversarial jamming in such networks. AQT has been widely used for restricting packet arrivals in similar settings (see related work below). However, no research work has considered the possibility of exploring its effects in the intent to "damage" a network. As already mentioned, our approach of constrained adversarial jamming could be used to model battery-operated malicious devices that have bounded battery capacity and specific recharging rate. In Sect. 2 we formalize the constrained adversarial jamming model we consider.

Then, we present the limitations it imposes on the efficiency of scheduling policies, focusing on the *transmission time* Tr and the *goodput* G as our main performance measures. More precisely, in Sect. 3 we show bounds on both measures, by focusing on executions with *uniform packet lengths.* We first compute the quasi optimal payload size l^* and show that the optimal transmission time satisfies $Tr \in [LB^*, LB^* + l^* + 1)$, where $LB^* = \frac{[P+(\sigma-1)l^*](l^*+1)}{l^*(1-\rho(l^*-1))}$ and the optimal goodput is $G \in (\frac{P}{LB^*+l^*+1}, \frac{P}{LB^*}]$. We also show, that for uniform packets, as the total amount of data P grows, G is upper bounded by $(1-\sqrt{\rho})^2$, and in infinity ($P \to \infty$) the goodput grows to optimal $G^* = (1-\sqrt{\rho})^2$ regardless of σ.

From the above, one might wonder whether scheduling uniform packets is in fact the overall best strategy. In Sect. 4 we show that this is not the case. Focusing on $\sigma = 1$ we show that the optimal goodput derived from uniform packet length transmission, G^*, can be exceeded using an *adaptive algorithm*; an algorithm that decides the length of the packet to be sent next, based on the information provided by a feedback mechanism up to that point in time. In particular, we present the adaptive scheduling algorithm ADP-1 that achieves goodput $G = 1 - \frac{\rho}{2}\left(1 + \sqrt{1 + \frac{8}{\rho}}\right)$, which is greater than G^* for $\rho < \frac{1}{2}(7 - 3\sqrt{5})$. Then, using a parameterized version of ADP-1 and performing case analysis we show its superiority over the uniform packet strategy for $1/\rho > 4$. Specifically, for $1/\rho > 4$ the algorithm achieves greater goodput than G^*.

1.3 Related Work

Adversarial queueing has been used in wireless networks as a methodology for studying their stability under worst case scenarios, removing the stochastic assumptions usually made for the generation of traffic. It concerns the arrival process of packets in the system and it has been introduced by Borodin et al. [7] as a well defined theoretical model since 2001. It has been further studied by Andrews et al. [3] who emphasized the notion of universal stability in such adversarial settings. A variety of works has then followed, using AQT in different network settings, such as on multiple access channels [10,11] and routing in communication networks [8,9]. We associate our constrained type of adversarial channel jams with the AQT model for the arrival process of packets in the following way. Classical AQT considers a *window adversary* that accounts packets being injected within a time window w in such a way that they give a total load of at most wr at each edge of the paths they need to follow, where $w \geq 1$ and $r \leq 1$. In our channel jams, for every window of duration $1/\rho$, there is exactly one new error token available for the adversary to use. In a long execution, considering for example a time interval $T > 1/\rho$, there will be up to $T\rho$ new error tokens available to the adversary.

As stated already, several studies have been done on throughput maximization as well as the effects of jamming in wireless channels. For example, Gummandi et al. [16] consider radio frequency interference on 802.11 networks and show that such networks are surprisingly vulnerable. As a method to withstand these vulnerabilities they propose and analyze a channel hopping design. Tsibonis et al. [24] studied the case of scheduling transmissions to multiple users over a wireless channel with time-varying connectivity and proposed an algorithm that focuses on the weighted sum of channel throughputs, considering saturated packet queues. Thuente et al. [23] studied the effects of different jamming techniques in wireless networks and the trade-off with their energy efficiency. Their study includes from trivial/continuous to periodic and intelligent jamming (taking into consideration the size of packets being transmitted). On a different flavor, Awerbuch et al. [5] design a MAC protocol for single-hop wireless networks that is robust against adaptive adversarial jamming and requires only limited knowledge about the adversary (an estimate of the number of nodes, n, and an approximation of a time threshold T). One of the differences with our work is that the adversary they consider is allowed to jam $(1-\varepsilon)$-fraction of the time steps. On a later work [21], Richa et al. explored the design of a robust medium access protocol that takes into consideration the signal to interference plus noise ratio (SINR) at the receiver end. In [22] they extended their work to the case of multiple co-existing networks; they proposed a randomized MAC protocol which guarantees fairness between the different networks and efficient use of the bandwidth. Gilbert et al. [15] worked on a theoretical analysis of the damage that can be introduced by a tiny malicious entity having limited power in the sense that it can only broadcast up to β times. Our model can be viewed as a generalization of this restriction, by allowing recharging. What is more, Pelechrinis et al. [18] present a detailed survey of the Denial of Service attacks in wireless networks. They present the various techniques used to achieve malicious behaviors and describe methodologies for their detection as well as for the network's protection from the jamming attacks. Finally, Dolev et al. [12] present a survey of several existing results in adversarial interference environments in the unlicensed bands of the radio spectrum, discussing their vulnerability. However, none of the models studied considers an AQT modeling of the power of the adversarial entity.

As mentioned in Sect. 1.1, our adversarial jammer has limited sources of energy and can be used to model, for example, military drones or mobile jammers. Drones or *Unmanned Aerial Vehicles (UAV)* are at the peak of their development. As an upcoming technology that is rapidly improving, it has already attracted the colossi of industry, like Google or Amazon, to invest in UAV research and development, creating even commercial models. There have already been a few research works [13,17] but the area is still being studied; the work in [13] focuses on UAV's risk analysis and the work in [17] focuses in analyzing cellular network coverage using UAV's and software defined radio. Regarding mobile jammers, in the recent years, many companies have made available battery-operated 3G/4G, WiFi or GPS mobile jammers (e.g., [1,2]);

this market can only increase, as wireless communication is becoming the dominating communication technology.

2 Model

2.1 Network Setting

We consider a setting of a sending station (sender) that transmits packets to a receiving station (receiver) over an unreliable wireless channel. The sender has some initial data of size P to be transmitted, and follows some *online scheduling* [19,20] in order to decide the lengths of the packets to be sent in the transmission. The decisions need to be made during the course of the execution, taking into consideration (or not) the channel jams. Each packet p consists of a *header* of a fixed predefined size h and a *payload* of length l chosen by the algorithm. The payload represents the useful data to be sent across the channel and is to be chosen by the sender. The total length of the packet is then denoted by $p_{.len} = h + l$. Note that the total payload from all the packets received successfully by the receiver in the execution must sum up to P. For simplicity and without loss of generality we use $h = 1$ throughout our analysis, and hence $p_{.len} = l + 1$. (Note that l needs not be an integer.) Furthermore, we consider constant bit rate for the channel, which means that the transmission time of each packet is proportional to its length (i.e., a packet of size $l + 1$ takes $l + 1$ time units to be transmitted in full).

2.2 Packet Failures

We model the unavailability of the channel to be controlled by the adversary (σ, ρ)-$\mathcal{A}$, which is defined by its two "restrictive" parameters, $\rho \in [0, 1]$ and $\sigma \geq 1$ as follows. The adversary has a token bucket of size σ where it stores "error tokens" and is initially full. From the beginning of the execution and up to a time t, within interval $T = [0, t]$, there will be $\lfloor \rho T \rfloor$ such error tokens created, where ρ is the rate at which they become available to the adversary. In other words, a new error token becomes available at times $1/\rho, 2/\rho, \ldots$. Note that the values of the adversary parameters are given to it (are not chosen by it) and it can only use them in a "smart" way in order to control the packet jams in the channel. If there is at least one token in the bucket, the adversary can introduce an error in the channel and jam the current packet, consuming one token. If the token bucket if full (i.e., there are already σ error tokens in the bucket) and a new token arrives, then one token is lost (this models the fact that a fully charged battery cannot be further charged). As a worst case analysis, we consider that the adversary jams some bit in the header of the packets in order to ensure their destruction. Therefore, adversary (σ, ρ)-$\mathcal{A}$ defines the error pattern as a collection of jamming events on the channel, jamming the packet that is being transmitted in that instant.

2.3 Efficiency Measure

For the efficiency of a scheduling algorithm, we look at the *total transmission time*, Tr; that is the time from the beginning of an execution to the moment that the complete payload P has been successfully received. We also look at the *goodput rate*, G; that is the ratio of the total amount of payload successfully transmitted over time, despite the jams in the channel. Note that the goodput rate will eventually be maximized in the long-run, assuming infinite amount of data P. Note also, that in most of our analysis we avoid using *floors* and *ceilings* in order to keep the readability of our results as simple as possible for the reader. Nonetheless, this does not affect the correctness of our results since when being applied on large enough time intervals and data, the "losses" become negligible.

2.4 Feedback Mechanism

As for the feedback mechanism, instantaneous feedback to the sender about a packet being received is being considered, as in [4]. We also assume that the notification packets cannot be jammed by the errors in the channel because of their relatively small size. In particular, we consider notification/acknowledgement messages sent for every packet that is received successfully. If such a message is not received by the sender, then it considers the packet to be jammed.

3 Uniform Packet Length

In this section we explore the case in which all packets are of the same length. Nonetheless, we first make the following observation, which bounds the error availability rates used, being such that they permit some data transmission (this holds also for non-uniform packet lengths).

Observation 1. *Let c be the smallest packet size used by an algorithm (i.e., $\forall p, p_{.len} \geq c$). For any error rate $\rho \geq 1/c$, no goodput larger than zero can be achieved.*

Proof. If the error rate is $\rho \geq 1/c$, a new error token arrives during the transmission of any packet (recall that packets are of size at least c). Hence, there are error tokens in the bucket at all times for the adversary to corrupt all packets being transmitted. Using an error token every c time, is sufficient to keep the goodput at zero. □

From this observation, it can be derived that algorithms that only use packets of length $p_{.len} \geq 1/\rho$ are not interesting. In particular, since in this section we consider an algorithm that systematically sends packets of the same length, we assume that the packets used satisfy $p_{.len} < 1/\rho$.

The main goal for the algorithms to be designed is to minimize the transmission time needed to successfully transmit the total amount of data P to the receiver. Knowing both adversarial parameters, ρ and σ, and considering uniform packets of size $p_{.len} = l + 1 < 1/\rho$, we can find the quasi optimal value for the length of the payload l in each packet that minimizes the transmission time. For simplicity, we will assume that the total length of the data to be transmitted P is a multiple of the payload length l. (For large values of P the error introduced by this assumption is negligible.) Then, the objective is that P/l packets arrive successfully at the receiver.

Let us now derive a *lower bound* on the transmission time that can be achieved using uniform packets. We denote with $Tr(l)$ the transmission time with packets of uniform payload l. Let r be the number of packets jammed and retransmitted by the sender. Then,

$$Tr(l) = (P/l + r)(l + 1). \tag{1}$$

Observe that the last packet transmitted was correctly received, since otherwise the data would have been completely transmitted by time $Tr(l) - (l + 1)$, which contradicts the fact that $Tr(l)$ is the transmission time. Hence, the number of packets jammed and retransmitted is upper bounded as

$$r \leq \lceil (Tr(l) - (l + 1))\rho \rceil - 1 + \sigma, \tag{2}$$

where we apply the fact that the last error used by the adversary must have been available before time $Tr(l) - (l + 1)$. We claim that the number of packets jammed by the adversary and retransmitted is in fact equal to the bound of Eq. 2. Otherwise, the adversary could have jammed the last packet sent (at time $Tr(l) - (l + 1)$), achieving a longer transmission time. Hence,

$$r = \lceil (Tr(l) - (l + 1))\rho \rceil - 1 + \sigma. \tag{3}$$

Moreover, since the adversary could not jam the last packet sent, it must also hold that $r + 1 \geq Tr(l)\rho + \sigma = (P/l + r)(l + 1)\rho + \sigma$, from which we can bound the value of r as

$$r \geq \frac{P\rho(l + 1) + (\sigma - 1)l}{l - l\rho(l + 1)}. \tag{4}$$

Let us define the lower bound of the transmission time when packets of uniform payload l are used, as function $LB(l)$. Then,

Lemma 1. *Using uniform packets of payload l, the lower bound of the transmission time is*

$$Tr(l) \geq LB(l) = \frac{P + (\sigma - 1)l}{l(1 - \rho(l + 1))}(l + 1).$$

Proof. Replacing the lower bound of r (Eq. 4) in Eq. 1 we have

$$Tr(l) \geq \left(\frac{P}{l} + \frac{P\rho(l + 1) + (\sigma - 1)l}{l - l\rho(l + 1)}\right)(l + 1) = \frac{P + (\sigma - 1)l}{l(1 - \rho(l + 1))}(l + 1),$$

which when combined with the definition of $LB(l)$, completes the proof. □

Using Calculus, we can find the payload length l^* that minimizes $LB(l)$, which yields the following theorem.

Theorem 1. *Using uniform packets the transmission time is lower bounded as*

$$Tr \geq LB(l^*) = \frac{P + (\sigma - 1)l^*}{l^*(1 - \rho(l^* + 1))}(l^* + 1)$$

and the goodput is upper bounded as

$$G \leq \frac{P}{LB(l^*)} = \frac{Pl^*(1 - \rho(l^* + 1))}{(P + (\sigma - 1)l^*)(l^* + 1)},$$

where

$$l^* = \frac{\sqrt{P(P\rho + (\sigma - 1)(1 - \rho))} - P\rho}{P\rho + \sigma - 1}.$$

Obviously, when P tends to ∞, so does the transmission time Tr. However, we can derive in this case an upper bound on the goodput as follows.

Corollary 1. *Using uniform packets, the goodput is upper bounded as* $G \leq (1 - \sqrt{\rho})^2$, *and in the limit as the value of* P *grows,*

$$G^* = \lim_{P \to \infty} G = (1 - \sqrt{\rho})^2$$

Proof. Using Calculus it can be shown that the upper bound of G obtained in Theorem 1 grows with P. Observe that $\lim_{P \to \infty} G = l^*(1 - \rho(l^* + 1))/(l^* + 1)$ and $\lim_{P \to \infty} l^* = (\sqrt{\rho} - \rho)/\rho = 1/\sqrt{\rho} - 1$. Replacing the latter in the former the claims follow. □

We now show a corresponding *upper bound* on the transmission time. We start by combining Eqs. 1 and 3 as follows:

$$\begin{aligned} r &= \lceil (Tr(l) - (l + 1))\rho \rceil - 1 + \sigma \\ &< (Tr(l) - (l + 1))\rho + \sigma \\ &= ((P/l + r)(l + 1) - (l + 1))\rho + \sigma \\ &= (P/l + r)(l + 1)\rho + \sigma - (l + 1)\rho. \end{aligned}$$

This allows us to find an upper bound of r as

$$r < \frac{P\rho(l + 1) + (\sigma - (l + 1)\rho)l}{l - l\rho(l + 1)}. \tag{5}$$

Let us now define the upper bound of the transmission time when packets of payload l are used, as function $UB(l)$. Then,

Lemma 2. *Using uniform packets of payload* l, *the upper bound of the transmission time is*

$$Tr(l) < UB(l) = \frac{P + (\sigma - (l + 1)\rho)l}{l(1 - \rho(l + 1))}(l + 1).$$

Proof. Replacing the upper bound of r (Eq. 5) in Eq. 1 we have

$$Tr(l) < \left(\frac{P}{l} + \frac{P\rho(l+1) + (\sigma - (l+1)\rho)l}{l - l\rho(l+1)}\right)(l+1) = \frac{P + (\sigma - (l+1)\rho)l}{l(1 - \rho(l+1))}(l+1),$$

which when combined with the definition of $UB(l)$, completes the proof. □

From Observation 1, $\rho < 1/(l+1)$ must hold. Then, $(l+1)\rho < 1$ and the bound obtained in the above lemma is strictly bigger than the lower bound presented in Lemma 1, as expected. In fact, the gap between bounds can be obtained as shown in the following lemma.

Lemma 3. *Using uniform packets of payload l, the transmission time satisfies $Tr(l) \in [LB(l), LB(l) + l + 1)$.*

Proof. Recall that the lower bound $LB(l)$ is obtained in Lemma 1. Subtracting this expression from the upper bound $UB(l)$ presented in Lemma 2, we have

$$\begin{aligned} UB(l) - LB(l) &= \frac{P + (\sigma - (l+1)\rho)l}{l(1 - \rho(l+1))}(l+1) - \frac{P + (\sigma - 1)l}{l(1 - \rho(l+1))}(l+1) \\ &= \frac{l(1 - \rho(l+1))}{l(1 - \rho(l+1))}(l+1) = l+1. \end{aligned}$$

From the above and the fact that $Tr(l) < UB(l)$ the claim follows. □

Corollary 2. *Using uniform packets of payload l, $Tr(l)$ is the only multiple of $l+1$ that falls in the interval $[LB(l), LB(l) + l + 1)$.*

Finally, combining Lemma 3 with Theorem 1 we derive the following theorem.

Theorem 2. *Consider l^* as defined in Theorem 1. Then*

- *the transmission time $Tr(l^*)$ observed is less that $l^* + 1$ (one packet) longer that the optimal. I.e., $Tr(l^*) < Tr + l^* + 1$.*
- *the goodput $G(l^*)$ converges to the optimal goodput G as P grows. Additionally, when P goes to infinity the goodput matches the optimal G^*, i.e. $\lim_{P\to\infty} G(l^*) = \lim_{P\to\infty} G = (1 - \sqrt{\rho})^2$.*

Proof. The first claim follow directly from Lemma 3, since the value of l^* is the one that minimizes $LB(l)$. For the second, recall that $G(l^*) = \frac{P}{Tr(l^*)}$. Hence, observing again Lemma 3 we get that

$$G(l^*) > \frac{P}{LB(l^*) + l^* + 1} = \frac{1}{\frac{LB(l^*)}{P} + \frac{l^*+1}{P}}.$$

As P grows $\frac{l^*+1}{P}$ tends to 0, making $G(l^*)$ converge to $P/LB(l^*)$ which is an upper bound on the optimal goodput. Finally, as shown in Corollary 1, when P tends to infinity, $P/LB(l^*)$ tends to $(1 - \sqrt{\rho})^2$, which completes the proof. □

4 Adaptive Packet Length

As we have shown in the previous section, if all packets have the same size, more precisely size $l^* + 1$, then there is an upper bound on the achievable goodput $G^* = (1-\sqrt{\rho})^2$. In this section, *focusing on the case* $\sigma = 1$, we lift the restriction on uniform packet length and consider an algorithm that adapts the packet length it uses as a function of the observed jams. We show that by using this approach it is possible to achieve a goodput greater than $(1-\sqrt{\rho})^2$, under the restriction of $\rho < 1/4$.

We divide the execution into consecutive periods of length $1/\rho$. In particular, the ith period, $i = 1, 2, \ldots$, spans the time interval $I_i = \left[\frac{i-1}{\rho}, \frac{i}{\rho}\right)$. Note that since error tokens arrive at time instants $1/\rho, 2/\rho, \ldots$ and $\sigma = 1$, at most one packet can be jammed by the adversary in each period. For simplicity, and since we focus on periods of fixed length $1/\rho$, we will use the *useful payload* sent in the period as one of the goodness metrics used, denoted UP. Observe that $\text{UP} = G/\rho$ and therefore, the upper bound on the useful payload that can be achieved with uniform packets is $\text{UP}^* = (1-\sqrt{\rho})^2/\rho$.

4.1 Algorithm ADP-1 for $\rho < \frac{1}{2}(7 - 3\sqrt{5})$

We start by proposing the following algorithm, to be used for small values of ρ (and $\sigma = 1$).

Algorithm ADP-1 Description: Each period starts by scheduling packets of decreasing length $p_{i.len} = Z - i$ for $i = 0, 1, 2, 3 \ldots$. If a packet p_j is jammed during the period, this transmission sequence is stopped, and after p_j, a single more packet is scheduled by the algorithm whose length spans the rest of the period.

We will now show that for ρ small enough, we can specify the parameter Z such that the useful payload achieved in each period is at least UP_u.

Theorem 3. *Adaptive algorithm ADP-1, with* $Z = \frac{1}{2}\left(\sqrt{1+\frac{8}{\rho}} - 1\right)$*, achieves goodput* $G = 1 - \frac{\rho}{2}\left(1 + \sqrt{1+\frac{8}{\rho}}\right)$*. This value is larger than the upper bound for the uniform case if* $\rho < \frac{1}{2}(7 - 3\sqrt{5}) \approx 0.1459$*.*

Proof. There are two cases to be considered in a period:

(a) If the adversary jams a packet p_j, the useless data sent in the period adds to $Z + 1$. This number comes from the j headers of the packets sent before p_j, plus the length $p_{j.len} = Z - j$ of the packet jammed, plus the header of the last packet sent in the period (which cannot be jammed). Hence, in this case, the useful payload of the period is $1/\rho - (Z + 1)$.

Otherwise, (b) if no packet is jammed, the useless data sent in the period correspond only to the headers of the packets sent. Then, if the last packet sent in the interval is p_k, the useless data is $k+1$, and the corresponding useful payload is $1/\rho-(k+1)$. The value Z is chosen so that the total length of the packets sent in this case is equal the length of the interval. From this property, $\sum_{i=0}^{k} p_{i.len} = \frac{1}{\rho}$, the value of Z must satisfy $Z(k+1) - \frac{k(k+1)}{2} = \frac{1}{\rho}$ and hence

$$Z = \frac{k}{2} + \frac{1}{\rho(k+1)}. \tag{6}$$

In a given period the choice of whether case (a) or (b) occurs is up to the adversary, since she can decide which packet to jam, if any. This means that the useful payload achieved will be the minimum of the two cases, $\mathrm{UP} = \min\{1/\rho - (Z+1), 1/\rho - (k+1)\}$. Observe from this Eq. 6 that the length Z of the initial packet increases if the number of packets k decreases. Additionally, it must hold that $Z \geq k$ and therefore UP is maximized when $Z = k$. Hence, the optimal k is the suitable solution of the equation $k = \frac{k}{2} + \frac{1}{\rho(k+1)}$, which is $k = \frac{1}{2}\left(\sqrt{1+\frac{8}{\rho}} - 1\right) = Z$.

The useful payload achieved is then $\mathrm{UP} = \frac{1}{\rho} - \left(\frac{1}{2}\sqrt{1+\frac{8}{\rho}} - \frac{1}{2} + 1\right) = \frac{1}{\rho} - \frac{1}{2}\left(\sqrt{1+\frac{8}{\rho}} + 1\right)$, which is more that $\mathrm{UP}^* = (1-\sqrt{\rho})^2/\rho$ for $\rho < \frac{1}{2}(7-3\sqrt{5}) \approx 0.1459$. The corresponding goodput is $G = \frac{\mathrm{UP}}{1/\rho} = 1 - \frac{\rho}{2}\left(\sqrt{1+\frac{8}{\rho}} + 1\right)$. □

Corollary 3. *Adaptive algorithm ADP-1, with* $Z = \frac{1}{2}\left(\sqrt{1+\frac{8}{\rho}} - 1\right)$ *achieves transmission time* $Tr = \frac{2P}{2-\rho-\sqrt{\rho(\rho+8)}}$.

4.2 Exhaustive Case Study for $\rho \geq \frac{1}{2}(7-3\sqrt{5})$

From the above results, we see that in the case of $\sigma = 1$, instead of using packets of uniform length l^*+1, it is better to use an adaptive algorithm. More precisely, we have shown that for $\rho < \frac{1}{2}(7-3\sqrt{5})$, ADP-1 achieves a better useful payload and goodput rate than the optimal uniform packet algorithm (the one that uses packet length $p_{.len} = l^* + 1$). We now explore the case of $\rho \geq \frac{1}{2}(7-3\sqrt{5})$. As before, we look at periods of length $1/\rho$, which means that the length of the period is at most $\frac{2}{7-3\sqrt{5}} \approx 6.85 < 7$. Hence, we consider only periods of such lengths.

In general, we are going to deal with subintervals of the period of length $1/\rho$. We will denote with $T = [t, t')$ an interval in the execution (subinterval of the period) such that t is an instant at which the adversary has one error token in the error bucket, and t' the time instant at which the next error token becomes available. Hence, the adversary has one error token (and only one) to be used in T. We use $|T|$ to denote the length of the interval, and UP_T to denote the useful payload that has been sent and correctly received by the receiver during T.

Let us first make the following observation.

Observation 2. *If there is at most one packet p of length $p_{.len} > 1$ sent in an interval T, then* $\text{UP}_T = 0$.

Proof. Since the adversary has one error token at the beginning of the interval, it uses it to jam packet p. The rest of packets (if any) have length 1 and carry no payload. □

We consider now different cases depending on the length of the interval, $|T|$, to be explored. We use the following algorithm for any interval T.

> *Algorithm ADP-1$_T$ Description:* As a base case, if $|T| < 2$ then ADP-1$_T$ simply sends a packet that spans the whole interval. Otherwise, let i the integer such that $|T| \in [i, i+1)$. Then ADP-1$_T$ sends a packet p whose length depends on i. If p is jammed, it sends a packet p' that spans the rest of the interval T. Otherwise, it applies recursively algorithm ADP-1$_{T'}$ to the interval $T' = [t + p_{.len}, t')$. Observe that $|T'| < i$.

Lemma 4. *If $|T| < 2$, then $UP_T = 0$.*

Proof. For any packet sent, the header requires 1 unit of length. Since $|T| < 2$, it means that only one packet can be sent within T. Hence, $UP_T = 0$ from Observation 2. □

Lemma 5. *If $|T| \in [2, 3)$, Algorithm ADP-1$_T$ uses uniform packets with $p_{.len} = |T|/2$ and achieves useful payload $UP_T = \frac{|T|}{2} - 1$. The packets used in such interval are uniform.*

Proof. First observe that the algorithm essentially sends two packets of length $|T|/2$. This in fact achieves useful payload $\text{UP}_T = \frac{|T|}{2} - 1$, since the adversary has only one error token to be used in T, and it jams only one packet. No matter which one is jammed, the payload of the unjammed packet, whose length is $\frac{|T|}{2} - 1$, is received correctly.

We show now that this is in fact the best possible useful payload that ADP-1$_T$ can achieve for period T. Since $|T| < 3$ and the header has length one, the algorithm cannot send more than 2 packets. Consider an algorithm ALG that:

- First sends a packet p of length larger than $|T|/2$. Then, the adversary jams p. Since the length of the rest of the interval is $|T| - p_{.len} < |T|/2$, the useful payload $\text{UP}_T < \frac{|T|}{2} - 1$.
- First sends a packet p of length smaller than $|T|/2$ (but at least 1). Then, the adversary does not jam p. After sending p, until the end of T there is a subinterval T' of length $|T'| = |T| - p_{.len} < 2$. From Lemma 4, the useful payload of T' is $\text{UP}_{T'} = 0$. Then, the useful payload of T is $\text{UP}_T = p_{.len} - 1 < \frac{|T|}{2} - 1$.

In both cases the useful payload of ALG is smaller than the one achieved by the algorithm proposed. Hence, the algorithm proposed gives the best possible useful payload for an interval T, where $|T| \in [2, 3)$. □

Lemma 6. *If* $|T| \in [3,4)$*, Algorithm ADP-*1_T *uses uniform packets with* $p_{.len} = |T|/2$ *and achieves useful payload* $UP_T = \frac{|T|}{2} - 1$*. The packets used in such interval are uniform.*

Proof. The proof is similar to that of the previous lemma, with a small difference. In the case that algorithm ALG sends a packet with length $p_{.len} < |T|/2$, the adversary does not jam p and after it is received, there is a subinterval T' of length $|T'| = |T| - p_{.len} < 3$ until the end of T. From Lemmas 4 and 5, the useful payload of T' is upper bounded as $\text{UP}_{T'} \leq \frac{|T'|}{2} - 1 = \frac{|T|-p_{.len}}{2} - 1$. Then, the useful payload of T is $\text{UP}_T \leq p_{.len} - 1 + \frac{|T|-p_{.len}}{2} - 1 = \frac{|T|+p_{.len}}{2} - 2 < \frac{|T|+|T|/2}{2} - 2$, which is smaller than $\frac{|T|}{2} - 1$ for $|T| < 4$. Hence, the algorithm proposed gives the best possible useful payload for an interval T, where $|T| \in [3,4)$. □

Lemma 7. *If* $|T| \in [4,5)$*, Algorithm ADP-*1_T *with* $p_{.len} = (|T|+2)/3$ *achieves useful payload* $\text{UP}_T = \frac{2|T|-5}{3}$*. The packets used in the whole interval are not uniform in this case.*

Proof. Let Algorithm ADP-1_T send first packet p with $p_{.len} = (|T|+2)/3$. If it is jammed, a packet p' of length $|T| - (|T|+2)/3$ is sent successfully. Then, in this case the useful payload is $\text{UP}_T = |T| - (|T|+2)/3 - 1 = \frac{2|T|-5}{3}$. Otherwise, observe that $|T'| = |T| - p_{.len} \in [2,4)$. Then, form Lemmas 5 and 6 the $\text{UP}_{T'} = \frac{|T'|}{2} - 1 = \frac{|T|-p_{.len}}{2} - 1$. Hence, $\text{UP}_T = p_{.len} - 1 + \frac{|T|-p_{.len}}{2} - 1 = \frac{2|T|-5}{3}$.

To prove that this is the best approach for the choice of the packet length, consider an algorithm ALG that

- First sends a packet p of length larger than $(|T|+2)/3$. Then, the adversary jams p. Since the length of the rest of the interval is $|T| - p_{.len} < |T| - (|T|+2)/3$, the useful payload $\text{UP}_T < |T| - (|T|+2)/3 = \frac{2|T|-5}{3}$.
- First sends a packet p of length smaller than $(|T|+2)/3$, but at least 1. Then, the adversary does not jam p. After p there is a subinterval T' of length $|T'| = |T| - p_{.len} < 4$. Then, from Lemmas 4, 5, and 6, the useful payload of T' is upper bounded as $\text{UP}_{T'} \leq \frac{|T'|}{2} - 1 = \frac{|T|-p_{.len}}{2} - 1$. Then, the useful payload of T is $\text{UP}_T = p_{.len} - 1 + \frac{|T|-p_{.len}}{2} - 1 < \frac{2|T|-5}{3}$.

In both cases the useful payload is smaller than the ones achieved by the algorithm proposed. Hence, the algorithm proposed with the packet length chosen, gives the best possible useful payload in an interval T, where $|T| \in [4,5)$. □

Lemma 8. *If* $|T| \in [5,6)$*, Algorithm ADP-*1_T *with* $p_{.len} = (|T|+2)/3$ *achieves useful payload* $UP_T = \frac{2|T|-5}{3}$*. The packets used in the whole interval are not uniform in this case.*

Proof. The proof is similar to that of Lemma 7, with some small differences. The main difference is in the case that algorithm ALG sends a packet with length $p_{.len} < (|T|+2)/3$. As above, the adversary will not jam p and after sending it successfully, there will be a subinterval T' of length $|T'| = |T| - p_{.len} < 5$ until the end of T. Then, from Lemmas 4 to 7, the useful payload of T' is upper bounded as $UP_{T'} \leq \frac{2|T'|-5}{3} = \frac{2(|T|-p.len)-5}{3}$. Hence, the useful payload of T becomes $UP_T \leq p.len - 1 + \frac{2(|T|-p.len)-5}{3}$ which is smaller than $\frac{2|T|-5}{3}$ for $p.len < 3$. The latter holds, since $p.len < (|T|+2)/3$ and $|T| < 6$. Hence again, the algorithm proposed with the packet length chosen, gives the best possible useful payload in an interval T, where $|T| \in [5, 6)$. □

Lemma 9. *If $|T| \in [6, 7)$, Algorithm ADP-1_T with $p.len = (|T|+2)/3$ achieves useful payload $UP_T = \frac{2|T|-5}{3}$. The packets used in the whole interval are not uniform in this case either.*

Proof. The proof follows the same exact logic as Lemmas 7 and 8. The only difference is in the case that algorithm ALG sends a packet with length $p.len < (|T|+2)/3$. As above, the adversary will not jam p and after sending it successfully, the subinterval T' that remains is of length $|T'| = |T| - p.len < 6$. Then, from Lemmas 4 to 8, the useful payload of T' is upper bounded as $UP_{T'} \leq \frac{2|T'|-5}{3} = \frac{2(|T|-p.len)-5}{3}$. Hence, the useful payload of T becomes $UP_T \leq p.len - 1 + \frac{2(|T|-p.len)-5}{3}$ which is smaller than $\frac{2|T|-5}{3}$ for $p.len < 3$. The latter holds, since $p.len < (|T|+2)/3$ and $|T| < 7$. Hence, the algorithm proposed with the packet length chosen, gives the best possible useful payload in an interval T, where $|T| \in [6, 7)$. □

Putting all these results together, and fixing $|T| = 1/\rho$, we get the following theorem.

Theorem 4. *For $\sigma = 1$, $\rho \geq \frac{1}{2}(7 - 3\sqrt{5})$ and $1/\rho \in [4, 7)$, adaptive algorithm ADP-1_T has goodput $G = \frac{2-5\rho}{3}$. This is achieved using first packet p with length $p.len = \frac{1}{3\rho} + \frac{2}{3}$; the packets used are not of uniform length.*

Note that for $1/\rho > 4$, the goodput achieved is bigger than the upper bound of the uniform packet approach, $G > G^*$, and for $1/\rho = 4$ it is equal to the upper bound, $G = G^*$.

5 Conclusions

In this paper we have applied Adversarial Queuing Theory (AQT), a well known theoretical modeling tool, for the first time to restrict adversarial packet jamming on wireless networks. We have chosen to study a constrained adversarial entity, considering a bounded error-token capacity σ and an error-token availability rate ρ. This model could be applied in various battery-operated malicious devices such as drones or mobile jammers. We have first shown upper and lower bounds on transmission time and goodput by exploring the case of uniform packet lengths. Then, focusing on $\sigma = 1$, we have shown that an adaptive algorithm that changes the packet length based on feedback received for jammed packets, can achieve better goodput and transmission time. What might seem surprising is that even for the "simple" case of $\sigma = 1$, the analysis of the adaptive algorithm is nontrivial, and imposes constraints also on ρ.

An intriguing open question is whether it is still possible to obtain better efficiency than the uniform packet lengths "policy" for adaptive algorithms with $\sigma > 1$. Considering for example $\sigma = 2$ seems to already be a challenging task. Another interesting future direction is to investigate the case where one or both parameters ρ and σ are not known; here one will need to monitor the history of the observed jams in an attempt to estimate these parameters. On the other hand, the adversary will try to "hide" the true value of these parameters, yielding an interesting gameplay between the adversary and an algorithm. Another direction to follow would be to consider in addition the channel errors due to congestion and transmission rate.

Acknowledgments. The authors would like to thank Dariusz Kowalski and Joerg Widmer for many fruitful discussions. We would also like to thank the anonymous reviewers for their constructive comments and suggestions that helped us improve the presentation of our work.

References

1. http://alljammer.com/. Accessed 8 April 2015
2. http://www.jammer-store.com/. Accessed 8 April 2015
3. Andrews, M., Awerbuch, B., Fernández, A., Leighton, T., Liu, Z., Kleinberg, J.: Universal-stability results and performance bounds for greedy contention-resolution protocols. J. ACM (JACM) **48**(1), 39–69 (2001)
4. Fernández Anta, A., Georgiou, C., Kowalski, D.R., Widmer, J., Zavou, E.: Measuring the impact of adversarial errors on packet scheduling strategies. In: Moscibroda, T., Rescigno, A.A. (eds.) SIROCCO 2013. LNCS, vol. 8179, pp. 261–273. Springer, Heidelberg (2013)
5. Awerbuch, B., Richa, A., Scheideler, C.: A jamming-resistant mac protocol for single-hop wireless networks. In: Proceedings of the Twenty-Seventh ACM Symposium on Principles of Distributed Computing, PODC 2008, pp. 45–54. ACM, New York (2008)
6. Bhagwat, P., Bhattacharya, P., Krishna, A., Tripathi, S.K.: Enhancing throughput over wireless lans using channel state dependent packet scheduling. In: Proceedings of IEEE Fifteenth Annual Joint Conference of the IEEE Computer Societies. Networking the Next Generation, INFOCOM 1996, vol. 3, pp. 1133–1140. IEEE (1996)
7. Borodin, A., Kleinberg, J., Raghavan, P., Sudan, M., Williamson, D.P.: Adversarial queuing theory. J. ACM (JACM) **48**(1), 13–38 (2001)
8. Chlebus, B.S., Cholvi, V., Kowalski, D.R.: Stability of adversarial routing with feedback. In: Gramoli, V., Guerraoui, R. (eds.) NETYS 2013. LNCS, vol. 7853, pp. 206–220. Springer, Heidelberg (2013)
9. Chlebus, B.S., Cholvi, V., Kowalski, D.R.: Universal routing in multi hop radio networks. In: Proceedings of the 10th ACM International Workshop on Foundations of Mobile Computing, pp. 19–28. ACM (2014)

10. Chlebus, B.S., Kowalski, D.R., Rokicki, M.A.: Adversarial queuing on the multiple-access channel. In: Proceedings of the Twenty-Fifth Annual ACM Symposium on Principles of Distributed Computing, pp. 92–101. ACM (2006)
11. Chlebus, B.S., Kowalski, D.R., Rokicki, M.A.: Stability of the multiple-access channel under maximum broadcast loads. In: Masuzawa, T., Tixeuil, S. (eds.) SSS 2007. LNCS, vol. 4838, pp. 124–138. Springer, Heidelberg (2007)
12. Dolev, S., Gilbert, S., Guerraoui, R., Kowalski, D.R., Newport, C., Kohn, F., Lynch, N.: Reliable distributed computing on unreliable radio channels. In: Proceedings of the 2009 MobiHoc S 3 Workshop on MobiHoc S 3, pp. 1–4. ACM (2009)
13. Faughnan, M.S., Hourican, B.J., MacDonald, G.C., Srivastava, M., Wright, J.A., Haimes, Y.Y., Andrijcic, E., Guo, Z., White, J.C.: Risk analysis of unmanned aerial vehicle hijacking and methods of its detection. In: 2013 IEEE Systems and Information Engineering Design Symposium (SIEDS), pp. 145–150. IEEE (2013)
14. Fu, Z., Zerfos, P., Luo, H., Lu, S., Zhang, L., Gerla, M.: The impact of multihop wireless channel on TCP throughput and loss. In: Twenty-Second Annual Joint Conference of the IEEE Computer and Communications, INFOCOM 2003, IEEE Societies, vol. 3, pp. 1744–1753. IEEE (2003)
15. Gilbert, S., Guerraoui, R., Newport, C.: Of malicious motes and suspicious sensors: on the efficiency of malicious interference in wireless networks. Theor. Comput. Sci. **410**(6), 546–569 (2009)
16. Gummadi, R., Wetherall, D., Greenstein, B., Seshan, S.: Understanding and mitigating the impact of RF Interference on 802.11 networks. ACM SIGCOMM Comput. Commun. Rev. **37**(4), 385–396 (2007)
17. Jakubiak, M.: Cellular network coverage analysis using UAV and SDR. Master's thesis, Tampere University of Technology (2014)
18. Pelechrinis, K., Iliofotou, M., Krishnamurthy, S.V.: Denial of service attacks in wireless networks: the case of jammers. IEEE Commun. Surv. Tutorials **13**(2), 245–257 (2011)
19. Pruhs, K.: Competitive online scheduling for server systems. ACM SIGMETRICS Perform. Eval. Rev. **34**(4), 52–58 (2007)
20. Pruhs, K., Sgall, J., Torng, E.: Online scheduling. In: Handbook of Scheduling: Algorithms, Models, and Performance Analysis, p. 15-1 (2004)
21. Richa, A., Scheideler, C., Schmid, S., Zhang, J.: Towards jamming-resistant and competitive medium access in the SINR model. In: Proceedings of the 3rd ACM Workshop on Wireless of the Students, by the Students, for the Students, pp. 33–36. ACM (2011)
22. Richa, A., Scheideler, C., Schmid, S., Zhang, J.: Competitive and fair throughput for co-existing networks under adversarial interference. In: Proceedings of the 2012 ACM Symposium on Principles of Distributed Computing, pp. 291–300. ACM (2012)
23. Thuente, D., Acharya, M.: Intelligent jamming in wireless networks with applications to 802.11 b and other networks. In: Proceedings of MILCOM, vol. 6 (2006)
24. Tsibonis, V., Georgiadis, L., Tassiulas, L.: Exploiting wireless channel state information for throughput maximization. IEEE Trans. Inf. Theory **50**(11), 2566–2582 (2004)
25. Uysal-Biyikoglu, E., Prabhakar, B., El Gamal, A.: Energy-efficient packet transmission over a wireless link. IEEE/ACM Trans. Netw. **10**(4), 487–499 (2002)

Fisheye Consistency: Keeping Data in Synch in a Georeplicated World

Roy Friedman[1], Michel Raynal[2,3], and Francois Taïani[3(✉)]

[1] The Technion Haifa, Haifa, Israel
[2] Institut Universitaire de France, Paris, France
[3] IRISA, Université de Rennes 1, Campus de Beaulieu, 35042 Rennes Cedex, France
francois.taiani@irisa.fr

Abstract. Over the last thirty years, numerous consistency conditions for replicated data have been proposed and implemented. Popular examples include linearizability (or atomicity), sequential consistency, causal consistency, and eventual consistency. These conditions are usually defined independently from the computing entities (nodes) that manipulate the replicated data; i.e., they do not take into account how computing entities might be linked to one another, or geographically distributed. To address this lack, as a first contribution, this paper introduces the notion of *proximity graph* between computing nodes. If two nodes are connected in this graph, their operations must satisfy a strong consistency condition, while the operations invoked by other nodes are allowed to satisfy a weaker condition. The second contribution exploits this graph to provide a generic approach to the hybridization of data consistency conditions within the same system. We illustrate this approach on sequential consistency and causal consistency, and present a model in which all data operations are causally consistent, while operations by neighboring processes in the proximity graph are sequentially consistent. The third contribution of the paper is the design and the proof of a distributed algorithm based on this proximity graph, which combines sequential consistency and causal consistency (the resulting condition is called *fisheye consistency*). In doing so the paper provides a generic provably correct solution of direct relevance to modern georeplicated systems.

Keywords: Asynchronous message-passing systems · Broadcast · Causal consistency · Data replication · Georeplication · Linearizability · Sequential consistency

1 Introduction

As distributed computer systems continue to grow in size, they make it increasingly difficult to provide strong consistency guarantees (e.g., linearizability [20]), prompting the rise of weaker guarantees (e.g., causal consistency [2] or eventual consistency [39]). These weaker consistency conditions strike a compromise

A. Bouajjani and H. Fauconnier (Eds.): NETYS 2015, LNCS 9466, pp. 246–262, 2015.
DOI: 10.1007/978-3-319-26850-7_17

between consistency, performance, and availability [5,7,10,13,40]. They try in general to minimize the violations of strong consistency, as these create anomalies for programmers and users, and emphasize the low probability of such violations in their real deployments [15].

Recent Related Works. For brevity, we cannot name all the many weak consistency conditions that have been proposed in the past. We focus instead on the most recent works in this area. One of the main hurdles in building systems and applications based on weak consistency models is how to generate an eventually consistent and meaningful image of the shared memory or storage [39]. In particular, a paramount sticking point is how to handle conflicting concurrent write (or update) operations and merge their result in a way that suits the target application. To that end, various conditions that enables custom conflict resolution and a host of corresponding data-types have been proposed and implemented [3,4,9,14,26,30,35,36].

Another form of hybrid consistency conditions can be found in the seminal works on *release consistency* [18,21] and *hybrid consistency* [6,16], which distinguish between strong and weak operations such that strong operations enjoy stronger consistency guarantees than weak operations. This line of work has given rise to a number of contributions in the context of large scale and geo-replicated data centers [38,40].

Motivation and Problem Statement. In spite of their benefits, the above consistency conditions generally ignore the relative "distance" between nodes in the underlying "infrastructure", where the notions of "distance" and "infrastructure" may be logical or physical, depending on the application. This is unfortunate as distributed systems must scale out and geo-replication is becoming more common. In a geo-replicated system, the network latency and bandwidth connecting nearby servers is usually at least an order of magnitude better than what is obtained between remote servers. This means that the cost of maintaining strong consistency among nearby nodes becomes affordable compared to the overall network costs and latencies in the system.

Some production-grade systems acknowledge the importance of distance when enforcing consistency, and do propose consistency mechanisms based on node locations (e.g. whether nodes are located in the same or in different data-centers). Unfortunately these production-grade systems usually do not distinguish between semantics and implementation. Rather, their consistency model is defined in operational terms, whose full implications can be difficult to grasp. In Cassandra [22], for instance, the application can specify for each operation a consistency guarantee that is dependent on the location of replicas. More precisely, the constraints LOCAL_QUORUM requires a quorum of replicas in the local data center, while EACH_QUORUM requires a quorum in each data center. Yet, although these constraints take distance into account, they do not provide the programmer with a precise image of the consistency they deliver.

The need to consider "distance" when defining consistency models, and the current lack of any formal underpinning to do so are exactly what motivates the hybridization of consistency conditions that we propose in this paper (which we call *fisheye consistency*). Fisheye consistency conditions provide strong guarantees only for operations issued at nearby servers. In particular, there are many applications where one can expect that concurrent operations on the same objects are likely to be generated by geographically nearby nodes, e.g., due to business hours in different time zones, or because these objects represent localized information, etc. In such situations, a fisheye consistency condition would in fact provide global strong consistency at the cost of maintaining only locally strong consistency.

Consider for instance a node A that is "close" to a node B, but "far" from a node C, a causally consistent read/write register will offer the same (weak) guarantees to A on the operations of B, as on the operations of C. This may be suboptimal, as many applications could benefit from varying levels of consistency conditioned on "how far" nodes are from each other. Stated differently: a node can accept that "remote" changes only reach it with weak guarantees (e.g., because information takes time to travel), but it wants changes "close" to it to come with strong guarantees (as "local" changes might impact it more directly).

In this work, we propose to address this problem by integrating a notion of *node proximity* in the definition of *data consistency*. To that end, we formally define a new family of hybrid consistency models that links the strength of data consistency with the proximity of the participating nodes. In our approach, a particular hybrid model takes as input a proximity graph, and two consistency conditions (a weaker one and a stronger one), taken from a set of totally ordered consistency conditions (e.g. linearizability, sequential consistency, causal consistency, and PRAM-consistency [25]).

The philosophy we advocate is related to that of Parallel Snapshot Isolation (PSI) proposed in [37]. PSI combines strong consistency (Snapshot Isolation) for transactions started at nodes in the same site of a geo-replicated system, but only ensures causality among transactions started at different sites.

Although PSI and our work operate at different granularities (fisheye-consistency is expressed on individual operations, each accessing a single object, while PSI addresses general transactions), they both show the interest of consistency conditions in which nearby nodes enjoy stronger semantics than remote ones. In spite of this similitude, however, the family of consistency conditions we propose distinguishes itself from PSI in a number of key dimensions. First, PSI is a specific condition while fisheye-consistency offers a general framework for defining multiple such conditions. PSI only distinguishes between nodes at the same physical site and remote nodes, whereas fisheye-consistency accepts arbitrary proximity graphs, which can be physical or logical. Finally, the definition of PSI is given in [37] by a reference implementation, whereas fisheye-consistency is defined in functional terms as restrictions on the ordering of operations that can be seen by applications, independently of the implementation we propose. As a result, we believe that our formalism makes it easier for users to express and understand the semantics of a given consistency condition and to prove the correctness of a program written w.r.t. such a condition.

Roadmap. The next section introduces the system model and the classical sequential consistency (SC) [24] and causal consistency (CC) [2]. Then, Sect. 3 defines the notion of *proximity graph* and the associated fisheye consistency condition, which considers SC as its strong condition and CC as its weak condition. Section 4 presents a broadcast abstraction, and Sect. 5 proposes an algorithm based on this broadcast abstraction that implements the fisheye consistency condition that combines SC and CC. These algorithms are generic, where the genericity parameter is the proximity graph. Interestingly, their two extreme instantiations provide natural implementations of SC and CC. Section 6 concludes.

2 System Model and Basic Consistency Conditions

The system consists of n processes denoted $\Pi = \{p_1, \ldots, p_n\}$. Each process is sequential and asynchronous. "Asynchronous" means that each process proceeds at its own speed, which is arbitrary, may vary with time, and remains always unknown to the other processes.

Processes communicate by passing messages through bi-directional channels. Channels are reliable (no loss, duplication, creation, or corruption), and asynchronous (transit times are arbitrary but finite, and remain unknown to the processes).

2.1 Basic Notions and Definitions Underpinning Consistency Conditions

This section is a short reminder of the fundamental notions typically used to define the consistency guarantees of distributed objects [8,19,27,31].

Concurrent Objects with Sequential Specification. A concurrent object is an object that can be simultaneously accessed by different processes. At the application level the processes interact through concurrent objects [19,31]. Each object is defined by a sequential specification, which is a set including all the correct sequences of operations and their results that can be applied to and obtained from the object. These sequences are called *legal* sequences.

Execution History. The execution of a set of processes interacting through objects is captured by a *history* $\widehat{H} = (H, \rightarrow_H)$, where $\rightarrow_H$ is a partial order on the set H of the object operations invoked by the processes.

Concurrency and Sequential History. If two operations are not ordered in a history, they are said to be *concurrent*. A history is said to be *sequential* if it does not include any concurrent operations. In this case, the partial order $\rightarrow_H$ is a total order.

Equivalent History. Let $\widehat{H}|p$ represent the projection of $\widehat{H}$ onto the process p, i.e., the restriction of $\widehat{H}$ to operations occurring at process p. Two histories $\widehat{H}_1$ and $\widehat{H}_2$ are *equivalent* if no process can distinguish them, i.e., $\forall p \in \Pi : \widehat{H}_1|p = \widehat{H}_2|p$.

Legal History. $\widehat{H}$ being a sequential history, let $\widehat{H}|X$ represent the projection of $\widehat{H}$ onto the object X. A history $\widehat{H}$ is *legal* if, for any object X, the sequence $\widehat{H}|X$ belongs to the specification of X.

Process Order. Notice that since we assumed that processes are sequential, we restrict the discussion in this paper to execution histories $\widehat{H}$ for which for every process p, $\widehat{H}|p$ is sequential. This total order is also called the *process order* for p.

2.2 Sequential Consistency

Intuitively, an execution is sequentially consistent if it could have been produced by executing (with the help of a scheduler) the processes on a monoprocessor. Formally, a history $\widehat{H}$ is *sequentially consistent* (SC) if there exists a history $\widehat{S}$ such that:

- $\widehat{S}$ is sequential,
- $\widehat{S}$ is legal (the specification of each object is respected),
- $\widehat{H}$ and $\widehat{S}$ are equivalent (no process can distinguish $\widehat{H}$—what occurred—and $\widehat{S}$—what we would like to see, to be able to reason about).

One can notice that SC does not demand that the sequence $\widehat{S}$ respects the real-time occurrence order on the operations. This is the fundamental difference between linearizability and SC.

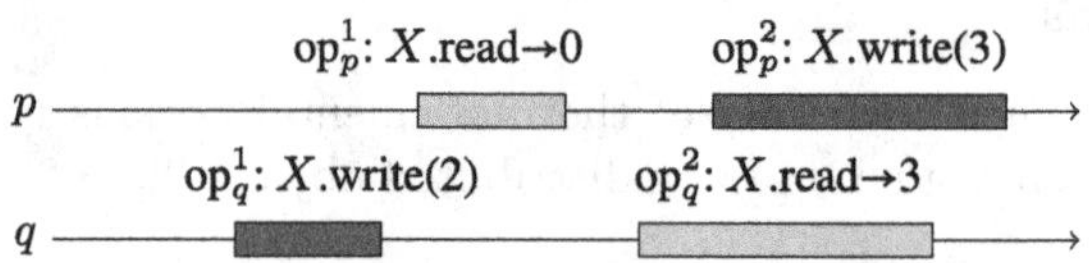

Fig. 1. A sequentially consistent execution

Figure 1 shows an history $\widehat{H}$ that is sequentially consistent. Let us observe that, although op_q^1 occurs before op_p^1 in physical time, op_p^1 does not see the effect of the write operation op_q^1, and still returns 0. A legal sequential history $\widehat{S}$, equivalent to $\widehat{H}$, can be easily built, namely, $X.read \rightarrow 0$, $X.write(2)$, $X.write(3)$, $X.read \rightarrow 3$.

2.3 Causal Consistency

In a sequentially consistent execution, all processes perceive all operations in the same order, which is captured by the existence of a sequential and legal history $\widehat{S}$. Causal consistency [2] relaxes this constraint for read-write registers, and allows different processes to perceive different orders of operations, as long as causality is preserved.

Formally, a history $\widehat{H}$ in which processes interact through concurrent read/write registers is causally consistent (CC) if:

- There is a causal order $\leadsto_H$ on the operations of $\widehat{H}$, i.e., a partial order that links each read to at most one latest write (or otherwise to an initial value $\perp$), so that the value returned by the read is the one written by this latest write and $\leadsto_H$ respects the process order of all processes.
- For each process p_i, there is a sequential and legal history $\widehat{S}_i$ that
  - is equivalent to $\widehat{H}|(p_i + W)$, where $\widehat{H}|(p_i + W)$ is the sub-history of $\widehat{H}$ that contains all operations of p_i, plus the writes of all the other processes,
  - respects $\leadsto_H$ (i.e., $\leadsto_H \subseteq \rightarrow_{S_i}$).

Intuitively, this definition means that all processes see causally related writes in the same order, but can see writes that are not causally related in different orders.

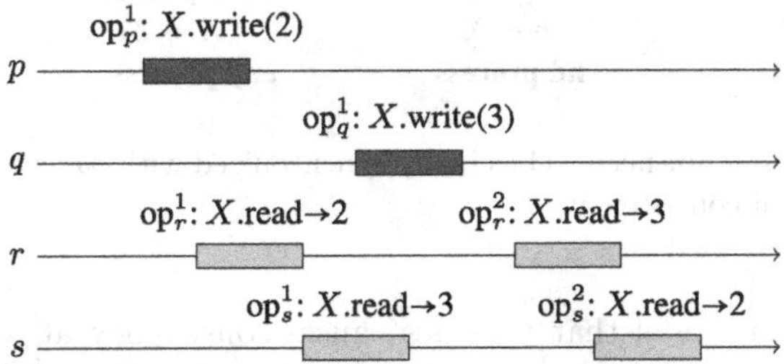

Fig. 2. An execution that is causally consistent (but not sequentially consistent)

An example of causally consistent execution is given in Fig. 2. The processes r and s observe the write operations on X by p (op_p^1) and q (op_q^1) in two different orders. This is acceptable in a causally consistent history because op_p^1 and op_q^1 are not causally related. This would not be acceptable in a sequentially consistent history, where the same total order on operations must be observed by all the processes.

3 The Family of Fisheye Consistency Conditions

This section introduces a hybrid consistency model based on (a) two consistency conditions and (b) the notion of a proximity graph defined on the computing nodes (processes). The two consistency conditions must be totally ordered in the sense that any execution satisfying the stronger one also satisfies the weaker one.

3.1 The Notion of a Proximity Graph

Let us assume that for physical or logical reasons linked to the application, each process (node) can be considered either close to or remote from other processes. This notion of "closeness" can be captured trough a *proximity graph* denoted $\mathcal{G} = (\Pi, E_{\mathcal{G}} \subseteq \Pi \times \Pi)$, whose vertices are the n processes of the system (Π). The edges are undirected. $N_{\mathcal{G}}(p_i)$ denotes the neighbors of p_i in $\mathcal{G}$. $\mathcal{G}$ captures the level of consistency imposed on processes: processes connected in $\mathcal{G}$ must respect a stronger data consistency than unconnected processes.

Example. To illustrate the semantic of $\mathcal{G}$, we extend the original scenario that Ahamad, Niger *et al.* use to motivate causal consistency in [2]. Consider the three processes of Fig. 3, *paris*, *berlin*, and *new-york*. Processes *paris* and *berlin* interact closely with one another and behave symmetrically : they concurrently write the shared variable X, then set the flags R and S respectively to 1, and finally read X. By contrast, process *new-york* behaves sequentially w.r.t. *paris* and *berlin*: *new-york* waits for *paris* and *berlin* to write on X, using the flags R and S, and then writes X.

```
process paris is
    X ← 1
    R ← 1
    a ← X
end process
```

```
process berlin is
    X ← 2
    S ← 1
    b ← X
end process
```

```
process new-york is
    repeat c ← R until c = 1
    repeat d ← S until d = 1
    X ← 3
end process
```

Fig. 3. *new-york* does not need to be closely synchronized with *paris* and *berlin*, calling for a hybrid form of consistency

If we assume a model that provides causal consistency at a minimum, the write of X by *new-york* is guaranteed to be seen after the writes of *paris* and *berlin* by all processes (because *new-york* waits on R and S to be set to 1). Causal consistency however does not impose any consistent order on the writes of *paris* and *berlin* on X. In the execution shown on Fig. 4, this means that although *paris* reads 2 in X (and thus sees the write of *berlin* after its own write), *berlin* might still read 1 in b (thus perceiving 'X.write(1)' and 'X.write(2)' in the opposite order to that of *paris*).

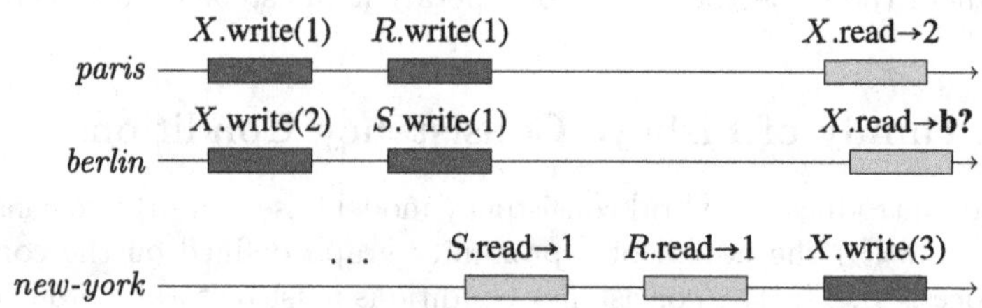

Fig. 4. Executing the program of Fig. 3.

Sequential consistency removes this ambiguity: in this case, in Fig. 4, *berlin* can only read 2 (the value it wrote) or 3 (written by *new-york*), but not 1. Sequential consistency is however too strong here: because the write operation of *new-york* is already causally ordered with those of *paris* and *berlin*, this operation does not need any additional synchronization effort. This situation can be seen as an extension of the *write concurrency freedom* condition introduced in [2]: *new-york* is here free of concurrent write w.r.t. *paris* and *berlin*, making causal consistency equivalent to sequential consistency for *new-york*. *paris* and *berlin* however write to X concurrently, in which case causal consistency is not enough to ensure strongly consistent results.

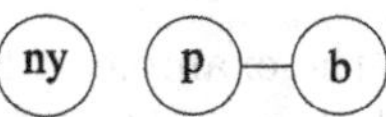

Fig. 5. Capturing the synchronization needs of Fig. 3 with a proximity graph $\mathcal{G}$

If we assume *paris* and *berlin* execute in the same data center, while *new-york* is located on a distant site, this example illustrates a more general case in which, because of a program's logic or activity patterns, no operations at one site ever conflict with those at another. In such a situation, rather than enforce a strong (and costly) consistency in the whole system, we propose a form of consistency that is strong for processes within the same site (here *paris* and *berlin*), but weak between sites (here between *paris*, *berlin* on one hand and *new-york* on the other).

In our model, the synchronization needs of individual processes are captured by the *proximity graph* $\mathcal{G}$ introduced at the start of this section and shown in Fig. 5: *paris* and *berlin* are connected, meaning the operations they execute should be perceived as strongly consistent w.r.t. one another; *new-york* is neither connected to *paris* nor *berlin*, meaning a weaker consistency is allowed between the operations executed at *new-york* and those of *paris* and *berlin*.

3.2 Fisheye Consistency for the Pair (Sequential Consistency, Causal Consistency)

When applied to the scenario of Fig. 4, fisheye consistency combines two consistency conditions (a weak and a stronger one, here causal and sequential consistency) and a proximity graph to form an hybrid distance-based consistency condition, which we call *$\mathcal{G}$-fisheye (SC, CC)-consistency.*

The intuition in combining SC and CC is to require that write operations be observed in the same order by all processes if:

- They are causally related (as in causal consistency),
- Or they occur on "close" nodes (as defined by $\mathcal{G}$).

Formal Definition. Formally, we say that a history $\widehat{H}$ is $\mathcal{G}$-fisheye (SC,CC)-consistent if:

- There is a causal order $\rightsquigarrow_H$ induced by $\widehat{H}$ (as in causal consistency); and
- $\rightsquigarrow_H$ can be extended to a subsuming order $\overset{\star}{\rightsquigarrow}_{H,\mathcal{G}}$ (i.e. $\rightsquigarrow_H \subseteq \overset{\star}{\rightsquigarrow}_{H,\mathcal{G}}$) so that

$$\forall (p,q) \in E_{\mathcal{G}} : (\overset{\star}{\rightsquigarrow}_{H,\mathcal{G}})|(\{p,q\} \cap W) \text{ is a total order}$$

where $(\overset{\star}{\rightsquigarrow}_{H,\mathcal{G}})|(\{p,q\} \cap W)$ is the restriction of $\overset{\star}{\rightsquigarrow}_{H,\mathcal{G}}$ to the write operations of p and q; and

- for each process p_i there is a history $\widehat{S}_i$ that
  - (a) is sequential and legal;
  - (b) is equivalent to $\widehat{H}|(p_i + W)$; and
  - (c) respects $\overset{\star}{\rightsquigarrow}_{H,\mathcal{G}}$, i.e., $(\overset{\star}{\rightsquigarrow}_{H,\mathcal{G}})|(p_i + W) \subseteq (\rightarrow_{S_i})$.

If we apply this definition to the example of Fig. 4 with the proximity graph proposed in Fig. 5 we obtain the following: because *paris* and *berlin* are connected in $\mathcal{G}$, X.write(1) by *paris* and X.write(2) by *berlin* must be totally ordered in $\overset{\star}{\rightsquigarrow}_{H,\mathcal{G}}$ (and hence in any sequential history $\widehat{S}_i$ perceived by any process p_i). X.write(3) by *new-york* must be ordered after the writes on X by *paris* and *berlin* because of the causality imposed by $\rightsquigarrow_H$. As a result, if the system is $\mathcal{G}$-fisheye (SC,CC)-consistent, **b?** can be equal to 2 or 3, but not to 1. This set of possible values is as in sequential consistency, with the difference that $\mathcal{G}$-fisheye (SC,CC)-consistency does not impose any total order on the operation of *new-york*.

Given a system of n processes, let $\varnothing_\Pi = (\Pi, \varnothing)$ denote the graph with no edges, and K_Π denote the complete graph $(\Pi, \Pi \times \Pi)$. It is easy to see that CC is $\varnothing_\Pi$-fisheye (SC,CC)-consistency. Similarly SC is K_Π-fisheye (SC,CC)-consistency.

A Larger Example. Figure 6 and Table 1 illustrate the semantic of $\mathcal{G}$-fisheye (SC,CC) consistency on a second, larger, example. In this example, the processes p and q on one hand, and r and s on the other hand, are neighbors in the proximity graph $\mathcal{G}$ (shown on the left). There are two pairs of write operations: op_p^1 and op_q^1 on the register X, and op_p^2 and op_r^3 on the register Y. In a sequentially consistency history, both pairs of writes must be seen in the same order by all processes. As a consequence, if r sees the value 2 and then 3 for X, s must do the same, and only 3 can be returned by **x?**. For the same reason, only 3 can be returned by **y?**, as shown in the first line of Table 1.

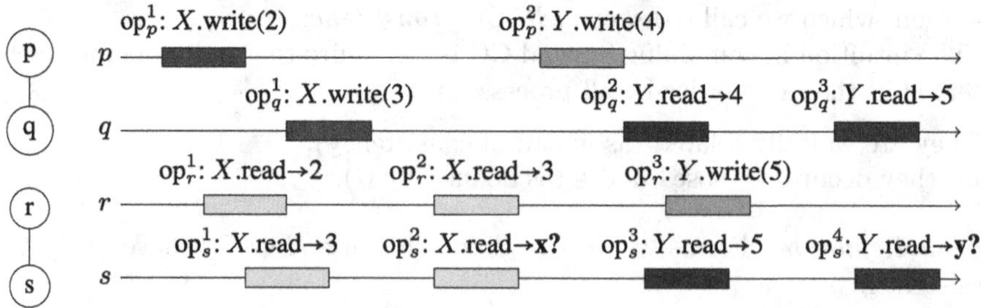

Fig. 6. Illustrating $\mathcal{G}$-fisheye (SC,CC)-consistency

In a causally consistent history, however, both pairs of writes ($\{\text{op}_p^1, \text{op}_q^1\}$ and $\{\text{op}_p^2, \text{op}_r^3\}$) are causally independent. As a result, any two processes can see

Table 1. Possible executions for the history of Fig. 6

Consistency	x?	y?
Sequential Consistency	3	5
Causal Consistency	{2,3}	{4,5}
$\mathcal{G}$-fisheye (SC,CC)-consistency	3	{4,5}

each pair in different orders. **x?** may return 2 or 3, and **y?** 4 or 5 (second line of Table 1).

$\mathcal{G}$-fisheye (SC,CC)-consistency provides intermediate guarantees: because p and q are neighbors in $\mathcal{G}$, op_p^1 and op_q^1 must be observed in the same order by all processes. **x?** must return 3, as in a sequentially consistent history. However, because p and r are not connected in $\mathcal{G}$, op_p^2 and op_r^3 may be seen in different orders by different processes (as in a causally consistent history), and **y?** may return 4 or 5 (last line of Table 1).

4 Construction of an Underlying (SC,CC)-Broadcast Operation

Our implementation of $\mathcal{G}$-fisheye (SC,CC)-consistency uses a broadcast operation with hybrid ordering guarantees. We present here this hybrid broadcast, before moving on to the actual implementation of of $\mathcal{G}$-fisheye (SC,CC)-consistency in Sect. 5.

4.1 $\mathcal{G}$-fisheye (SC,CC)-Broadcast: Definition

The hybrid broadcast we proposed, denoted $\mathcal{G}$-(SC,CC)-broadcast, is parametrized by a proximity graph $\mathcal{G}$ which determines which kind of delivery order should be applied to which messages, according to the position of the sender in the graph $\mathcal{G}$. Messages (SC,CC)-broadcast by neighbors in $\mathcal{G}$ must be delivered in the same order at all the processes, while the delivery of the other messages only need to respect causal order.

The (SC,CC)-broadcast abstraction provides the processes with two operations, denoted TOCO_broadcast() and TOCO_deliver(). We say that messages are toco-broadcast and toco-delivered.

Causal Message Order. Let M be the set of messages that are toco-broadcast. The causal message delivery order, denoted $\rightsquigarrow_M$, is defined as follows [11,34]. Let $m_1, m_2 \in M$; $m_1 \rightsquigarrow_M m_2$, iff one of the following conditions holds:

- m_1 and m_2 have been toco-broadcast by the same process, with m_1 first;
- m_1 was toco-delivered by a process p_i before this process toco-broadcast m_2;
- There exists a message m such that $(m_1 \rightsquigarrow_M m) \wedge (m \rightsquigarrow_M m_2)$.

Definition of the $\mathcal{G}$-fisheye (SC, CC)-broadcast. The (SC,CC)-broadcast abstraction is defined by the following properties.

Validity. If a process toco-delivers a message m, this message was toco-broadcast by some process. (No spurious message.)
Integrity. A message is toco-delivered at most once. (No duplication.)
$\mathcal{G}$-delivery order. For all the processes p and q such that (p, q) is an edge of $\mathcal{G}$, and for all the messages m_p and m_q such that m_p was toco-broadcast by p and m_q was toco-broadcast by q, if a process toco-delivers m_p before m_q, no process toco-delivers m_q before m_p.
Causal order. If $m_1 \rightsquigarrow_M m_2$, no process toco-delivers m_2 before m_1.
Termination. If a process toco-broadcasts a message m, this message is toco-delivered by all processes.

It is easy to see that if $\mathcal{G}$ has no edges, this definition boils down to causal delivery, and if $\mathcal{G}$ is fully connected (clique), this definition specifies total order delivery respecting causal order. Finally, if $\mathcal{G}$ is fully connected and we suppress the "causal order" property, the definition boils down to total order delivery.

4.2 $\mathcal{G}$-fisheye (SC,CC)-Broadcast: Algorithm

Local Variables. To implement the $\mathcal{G}$-fisheye (SC,CC)-broadcast abstraction, each process p_i manages three local variables.

- $causal_i[1..n]$ is a local vector clock used to ensure a causal delivery order of the messages; $causal_i[j]$ is the sequence number of the next message that p_i will toco-deliver from p_j.
- $total_i[1..n]$ is a vector of logical clocks such that $total_i[i]$ is the local logical clock of p_i (Lamport's clock), and $total_i[j]$ is the value of $total_j[j]$ as known by p_i.
- $pending_i$ is a set of messages received but not yet toco-delivered by p_i.

Description of the Algorithm. Let us remind that for simplicity, we assume that the channels are FIFO. Algorithm 1 describes the behavior of a process p_i. This behavior is decomposed into four parts.

The first part (lines 1–6) is the code of the operation TOCO_broadcast(m). Process p_i first increases its local clock $total_i[i]$ and sends the protocol message TOCOBC($m, \langle causal_i[\cdot], total_i[i], i\rangle$) to each other process. In addition to the application message m, this protocol message carries the control information needed to ensure the correct toco-delivery of m, namely, the local causality vector ($causal_i[1..n]$), and the value of the local clock ($total_i[i]$). Then, this protocol message is added to the set $pending_i$ and $causal_i[i]$ is increased by 1 (this captures the fact that the future application messages toco-broadcast by p_i will causally depend on m).

The second part (lines 7–14) is the code executed by p_i when it receives a protocol message TOCOBC($m, \langle s\_caus_j^m[\cdot], s\_tot_j^m, j\rangle$) from p_j. When this occurs

Algorithm 1. The $\mathcal{G}$-fisheye (SC,CC)-broadcast algorithm executed by p_i

1: **operation** TOCO_broadcast(m)
2: $total_i[i] \leftarrow total_i[i] + 1$
3: **for all** $p_j \in \Pi \setminus \{p_i\}$ **do** send TOCOBC($m, \langle causal_i[\cdot], total_i[i], i\rangle$) to p_j
4: $pending_i \leftarrow pending_i \cup \langle m, \langle causal_i[\cdot], total_i[i], i\rangle\rangle$
5: $causal_i[i] \leftarrow causal_i[i] + 1$
6: **end operation**
7: **on receiving** TOCOBC($m, \langle s\_caus_j^m[\cdot], s\_tot_j^m, j\rangle$)
8: $pending_i \leftarrow pending_i \cup \langle m, \langle s\_caus_j^m[\cdot], s\_tot_j^m, j\rangle\rangle$
9: $total_i[j] \leftarrow s\_tot_j^m$ ▷ Last message from p_j had timestamp $s\_tot_j^m$
10: **if** $total_i[i] \le s\_tot_j^m$ **then**
11: $total_i[i] \leftarrow s\_tot_j^m + 1$ ▷ Ensuring global logical clocks
12: **for all** $p_k \in \Pi \setminus \{p_i\}$ **do** send CATCH_UP($total_i[i], i$) to p_k
13: **end if**
14: **end on receiving**
15: **on receiving** CATCH_UP($last\_date_j, j$)
16: $total_i[j] \leftarrow last\_date_j$
17: **end on receiving**
18: **background task** T **is**
19: **loop forever**
20: **wait until** $C \neq \varnothing$ **where**
21: $C \equiv \left\{\langle m, \langle s\_caus_j^m[\cdot], s\_tot_j^m, j\rangle\rangle \in pending_i \;\middle|\; s\_caus_j^m[\cdot] \le causal_i[\cdot]\right\}$
22: **wait until** $T_1 \neq \varnothing$ **where**
23: $T_1 \equiv \left\{\langle m, \langle s\_caus_j^m[\cdot], s\_tot_j^m, j\rangle\rangle \in C \;\middle|\; \forall p_k \in N_{\mathcal{G}}(p_j) : \langle total_i[k], k\rangle > \langle s\_tot_j^m, j\rangle\right\}$
24: **wait until** $T_2 \neq \varnothing$ **where**
25: $T_2 \equiv \left\{\langle m, \langle s\_caus_j^m[\cdot], s\_tot_j^m, j\rangle\rangle \in T_1 \;\middle|\; \begin{array}{r} \forall p_k \in N_{\mathcal{G}}(p_j), \\ \forall \langle m_k, \langle s\_caus_k^{m_k}[\cdot], s\_tot_k^{m_k}, k\rangle\rangle \\ \in pending_i : \\ \langle s\_tot_k^{m_k}, k\rangle > \langle s\_tot_j^m, j\rangle \end{array}\right\}$
26: $\langle m_0, \langle s\_caus_{j_0}^{m_0}[\cdot], s\_tot_{j_0}^{m_0}, j_0\rangle\rangle \leftarrow \underset{\langle m, \langle s\_caus_j^m[\cdot], s\_tot_j^m, j\rangle\rangle \in T_2}{\arg\min} \{\langle s\_tot_j^m, j\rangle\}$
27: $pending_i \leftarrow pending_i \setminus \langle m_0, \langle s\_caus_{j_0}^{m_0}[\cdot], s\_tot_j^m, j_0\rangle\rangle$
28: TOCO_deliver(m_0) to application layer
29: **if** $j_0 \neq i$ **then** $causal_i[j_0] \leftarrow causal_i[j_0] + 1$ **end if** ▷ for $causal_i[i]$ see line 5
30: **end loop forever**
31: **end background task**

p_i adds first this protocol message to $pending_i$, and updates its view of the local clock of p_j ($total_i[j]$) to the sending date of the protocol message (namely, $s\_tot_j^m$). Then, if the local clock of p_i is late ($total_i[i] \le s\_tot_j^m$), p_i catches up (line 11), and informs the other processes of it (line 12).

The third part (lines 15–17) is the processing of a catch up message from a process p_j. In this case, p_i updates its view of p_j's local clock to the date carried by the catch up message. Let us notice that, as channels are FIFO, a view $stotal_i[j]$ can only increase.

The final part (lines 18–31) is a background task executed by p_i, where the application messages are toco-delivered. The set C contains the protocol messages that were received, have not yet been toco-delivered, and are "minimal" with respect to the causality relation $\rightsquigarrow_M$. This minimality is determined from the vector clock $s\_caus_j^m[1..n]$, and the current value of p_i's vector clock

($causal_i[1..n]$). If only causal consistency was considered, the messages in C could be delivered.

Then, p_i extracts from C the messages that can be toco-delivered. Those are usually called *stable* messages. The notion of stability refers here to the delivery constraint imposed by the proximity graph $\mathcal{G}$. More precisely, a set T_1 is first computed, which contains the messages of C that (thanks to the FIFO channels and the catch up messages) cannot be made unstable (with respect to the total delivery order defined by $\mathcal{G}$) by messages that p_i will receive in the future. Then the set T_2 is computed, which is the subset of T_1 such that no message received, and not yet toco-delivered, could make incorrect – w.r.t. $\mathcal{G}$ – the toco-delivery of a message of T_2.

Once a non-empty set T_2 has been computed, p_i extracts the message m whose timestamp $\langle s\_tot_j^m[j], j\rangle$ is "minimal" with respect to the timestamp-based total order (p_j is the sender of m). This message is then removed from $pending_i$ and toco-delivered. Finally, if $j \neq i$, $causal_i[j]$ is increased to take into account this toco-delivery (all the messages m' toco-broadcast by p_i in the future will be such that $m \rightsquigarrow m'$, and this is encoded in $causal_i[j]$). If $j = i$, this causality update was done at line 5.

Theorem 1. *Algorithm 1 implements a $\mathcal{G}$-fisheye (SC,CC)-broadcast.*

The proof relies on the monotonicity of the clocks $causal_i[1..n]$ and $total_i[1..n]$, and the reliability and FIFO properties of the underlying communication channels [7,12,23,34].

5 An Algorithm Implementing $\mathcal{G}$-Fisheye (SC,CC)-Consistency

5.1 The High Level Object Operations Read and Write

Algorithm 2 uses the $\mathcal{G}$-fisheye (SC,CC)-broadcast we have just presented to realize $\mathcal{G}$-fisheye (SC,CC)-consistency using a fast-read strategy. This algorithm is derived from the fast-read algorithm for sequential consistency proposed by Attiya and Welch [7], in which the total order broadcast has been replaced by our $\mathcal{G}$-fisheye (SC,CC)-broadcast.

The write(X, v) operation uses the $\mathcal{G}$-fisheye (SC,CC)-broadcast to propagate the new value of the variable X. To insure any other write operations that must be seen *before* write(X, v) by p_i are properly processed, p_i enters a waiting loop (line 4), which ends after the message WRITE(X, v, i) that has been toco-broadcast at line 2 is toco-delivered at line 11.

The read(X) operation simply returns the local copy v_x of X. These local copies are updated in the background when WRITE(X, v, j) messages are toco-delivered.

Theorem 2. *Algorithm 2 implements $\mathcal{G}$-fisheye (SC,CC)-consistency.*

The proof uses the causal order on messages $\rightsquigarrow_M$ provided by the $\mathcal{G}$-fisheye (SC,CC)-broadcast to construct the causal order on operations $\rightsquigarrow_H$. It then gradually extends $\rightsquigarrow_H$ to obtain $\stackrel{\star}{\rightsquigarrow}_{H,\mathcal{G}}$ by adapting the technique used in [28,32].

Algorithm 2. Implementing $\mathcal{G}$-fisheye (SC,CC)-consistency, executed by p_i

```
operation X.write(v)
    TOCO_broadcast(WRITE(X, v, i))
    delivered_i ← false ;
    wait until delivered_i = true
end operation
operation X.read()
    return v_x
end operation
on toco_deliver WRITE(X, v, j)
    v_x ← v ;
    if (i = j) then delivered_i ← true endif
end on toco_deliver
```

6 Conclusion

This work was motivated by the increasing popularity of geographically distributed systems. We have presented a framework that enables to formally define and reason about mixed consistency conditions in which the operations invoked by nearby processes obey stronger consistency requirements than operations invoked by remote ones. The framework is based on the concept of a proximity graph, which captures the "closeness" relationship between processes. As an example, we have formally defined $\mathcal{G}$-fisheye (SC,CC)-consistency, which combines sequential consistency for operations by close processes with causal consistency among all operations. We have also provided a formally proven protocol for implementing $\mathcal{G}$-fisheye (SC,CC)-consistency.

Another natural example that has been omitted from this paper for brevity is $\mathcal{G}$-fisheye (LIN,SC)-consistency, which combines linearizability for operations by nearby nodes with an overall sequential consistency guarantee.

The significance of our approach is that the definitions of consistency conditions are functional rather than operational. That is, they are independent of a specific implementation, and provide a clear rigorous understanding of the provided semantics. This formal underpinning comes with improved complexity and performance, as illustrated in our implementation of $\mathcal{G}$-fisheye (SC,CC)-consistency, in which operations can terminate without waiting to synchronize with remote parts of the system.

More generally, we expect the general philosophy we have presented to extend to Convergent Replicated Datatypes (CRDT) in which not all operations are commutative [29]. These CRDTs usually require at a minimum causal communications to implement eventual consistency. The hybridization we have proposed opens up the path of CRDTs which are globally eventually consistent, and locally sequentially consistent, a route we plan to explore in future work.

Acknowledgments. This work was partially funded by the French ANR project SocioPlug (ANR-13-INFR-0003), and by the DeSceNt project (Labex CominLabs excellence laboratory ANR-10-LABX-07-01).

References

1. Adve, S., Gharachorloo, K.: Shared memory consistency models: a tutorial. IEEE Comp. Mag. **29**(12), 66–76 (1996)
2. Ahamad, M., Niger, G., Burns, J.E., Hutto, P.W., Kohl, P.: Causal memory: definitions, implementation and programming. Dist. Comput. **9**, 37–49 (1995)
3. Almeida, S., Leitaõ, J., Rodrigues, L.: ChainReaction: a causal+ consistent datastore based on chain replication. In: 8th ACM European Conference on Computer Systems (EuroSys 2013), pp. 85–98 (2013)
4. Alvaro, P., Bailis, P., Conway, N., Hellerstein, J.M.: Consistency without borders. In: 4th ACM Symposium on Cloud Computing (SOCC 2013), p. 23 (2013)
5. Attiya, H., Friedman, R.: A correctness condition for high-performance multiprocessors. SIAM J. Comput. **27**(6), 1637–1670 (1998)
6. Attiya, H., Friedman, R.: Limitations of fast consistency conditions for distributed shared memories. Inf. Process. Lett. **57**(5), 243–248 (1996)
7. Attiya, H., Welch, J.L.: Sequential consistency versus linearizability. ACM Trans. Comp. Sys. **12**(2), 91–122 (1994)
8. Attiya, H., Welch, J.L.: Distributed computing: fundamentals, simulations and advanced topics, 2nd edn., 414 pages. Wiley-Interscience (2004). ISBN 0-471-45324-2
9. Bailis, P., Ghodsi, A., Hellerstein, J.M., Stoica, I.: Bolt-on causal consistency. In: 2013 ACM SIGMOD International Conference on Management of Data (SIGMOD 2013), pp. 761–772 (2013)
10. Birman, K.P., Friedman, R.: Trading Consistency for Availability in Distributed Systems. Technical report #TR96-1579, Computer Science Department, Cornell University, April 2016
11. Birman, K.P., Joseph, T.A.: Reliable communication in presence of failures. ACM Trans. Comp. Sys. **5**(1), 47–76 (1987)
12. Birman, K., Schiper, A., Stephenson, P.: Lightweight causal and atomic group multicast. ACM Trans. Comput. Syst. **9**, 272–314 (1991)
13. Brewer, E.: Towards robust towards robust distributed systems. In: 19th ACM Symposium on Principles of Distributed Computing (PODC), Invited talk (2000)
14. Burckhardt, S., Gotsman, A., Yang, H., Zawirski, M.: Replicated data types: specification, verification, optimality. In: 41st ACM Symposium on Principles of Programming Languages (POPL), pp. 271–284 (2014)
15. DeCandia, G., Hastorun, D., Jampani, M., Kakulapati, G., Lakshman, A., Pilchin, A., Sivasubramanian, S., Vosshall, P., Vogels, W.: Dynamo: amazon's highly available key-value store. In: 21st ACM Symposium on Operating Systems Principles (SOSP 2007), pp. 205–220 (2007)
16. Friedman, R.: Implementing hybrid consistency with high-level synchronization operations. Distrib. Comput. **9**(3), 119–129 (1995)
17. Garg, V.K., Raynal, M.: Normality: a consistency condition for concurrent objects. Parallel Process. Lett. **9**(1), 123–134 (1999)

18. Gharachorloo, K., Lenoski, D., Laudon, J., Gibbons, P., Gupta, A., Hennessy, J.: Memory consistency and event ordering in scalable shared-memory multiprocessors. In: 17th ACM Annual International Symposium on Computer Architecture (ISCA), pp. 15–26 (1990)
19. Herlihy, M., Shavit, N.: The Art of Multiprocessor Programming, 508 pages. Morgan Kaufmann Publishers Inc. (2008). ISBN 978-0-12-370591-4
20. Herlihy, M., Wing, J.: Linearizability: a correctness condition for concurrent objects. ACM Trans. Program. Lang. Syst. **12**(3), 463–492 (1990)
21. Keleher, P., Cox, A.L., Zwaenepoel, W.: Lazy release consistency for software distributed shared memory. In: Proceedings of the 19th ACM International Symposium on Computer Architecture (ISCA 1992), pp. 13–21 (1992)
22. Lakshman, A., Malik, P.: Cassandra: a decentralized structured storage system. SIGOPS Oper. Syst. Rev. **44**, 35–40 (2010)
23. Lamport, L.: Time, Clocks and the ordering of events in a distributed system. Comm. ACM **21**, 558–565 (1978)
24. Lamport, L.: How to make a multiprocessor computer that correctly executes multiprocess programs. IEEE Trans. Comp. **C28**(9), 690–691 (1979)
25. PRAM: A Scalable Shared Memory. Technical Report CS-TR-180-88, Princeton University, September 1988
26. Lloyd, W., Freedman, M.J., Kaminsky, M., Andersen, D.G.: Don't settle for eventual: scalable causal consistency for wide-area storage with COPS. In: 23rd ACM Symposium on Operating Systems Principles, pp. 401–416 (2011)
27. Lynch, N.A.: Distributed Algorithms, 872 pages. Morgan Kaufman, San Francisco (1996)
28. Mizuno, M., Raynal, M., Zhou, J.Z.: Sequential consistency in distributed systems. In: Birman, K.P., Mattern, F., Schiper, A. (eds.) Theory and Practice in Distributed Systems. LNCS, vol. 938, pp. 224–241. Springer, Heidelberg (1995)
29. Oster, G., Urso, P., Molli, P., Imine, A.: Data consistency for P2P collaborative editing. In: 20th Anniversary Conference on Computer Supported Cooperative Work, pp. 259–268. ACM (2006)
30. Preguiça, N.M., Marquès, J.M., Shapiro, M., Letia, M.: A commutative replicated data type for cooperative editing. In: Proceedings of the 29th IEEE International Conference on Distributed Computing Systems (ICDCS 2009), pp. 395–403 (2009)
31. Raynal, M.: Concurrent Programming: Algorithms, Principles, and Foundations, 515 pages. Springer, Heidelberg (2013). ISBN 978-3-642-32026-2
32. Raynal, M.: Distributed Algorirhms for Message-Passing Systems, 500 pages. Springer (2013). ISBN 978-3-642-38122-5
33. Raynal, M., Schiper, A.: A suite of formal definitions for consistency criteria in distributed shared memories. In: 9th International IEEE Conference on Parallel and Distributed Computing Systems (PDCS 1996), pp. 125–131 (1996)
34. Raynal, M., Schiper, A., Toueg, S.: The causal ordering abstraction and a simple way to implement. Inf. Process. Lett. **39**(6), 343–350 (1991)
35. Saito, Y., Shapiro, M.: Optimistic replication. ACM Comput. Surv. **37**(1), 42–81 (2005)
36. Shapiro, M., Preguiça, N.M., Baquero, C., Zawirski, M.: Convergent and commutative replicated data types. Bull. EATCS **104**, 67–88 (2011)
37. Sovran, Y., Power, R., Aguilera, M.K., Li, J.: Transactional storage for georeplicated systems. In: 23rd ACM Symposium on Operating Systems Principles (SOSP), pp. 385–400 (2011)

38. Terry D.B., Prabhakaran, V., Kotla, R., Balakrishnan, M., Aguilera, M.K., Abu-Libdeh, H.: Consistency-based service level agreements for cloud storage. In: 24th ACM Symposium on Operating Systems Principles (SOSP 2013), pp. 309–324 (2013)
39. Terry, D.B., Theimer, M.M., Petersen, K., Demers, A.J., Spreitzer, M.J., Hauser, C.H.: Managing update conflicts in bayou, a weakly connected replicated storage system. In: 15th ACM Symposium on Operating Systems Principles (SOSP 1995), pp. 172–182 (1995)
40. Xie, C., Su, C., Kapritsos, M., Wang, Y., Yaghmazadeh, N., Alvisi, L., Mahajan, P.: SALT: combining ACID and BASE in a distributed database. In: USENIX Operating Systems Design & Implementation (OSDI) (2014)

Peer-to-Peer Full-Text Keyword Search of the Web

Sonia Gaied Fantar[1](✉) and Habib Youssef[2]

[1] ISIM Gabes, University of Gabes, Gabès, Tunisia
soniagaied3@gmail.com
[2] Research Unit Prince, ISITC Hammam Sousse, University of Sousse, Sousse, Tunisia
habib.youssef@fsm.rnu.tn

Abstract. Full-text keywords search of the Web over structured peer-to-peer networks shows promise to become an alternative to the state-of-the-art search engines since P2P overlays propose means for decentralized search across widely-distributed document collections. However, a disadvantage of structured P2P systems is that they consider only the problem of searching for keys, and thus cannot perform content-based retrieval. To deal with this problem, in this paper we consider a full-text retrieval problem in structured P2P networks. Our keyword searching engine *BI-Chord* is build on top of DHT-based P2P systems, entirely distributed, uses bloom filters and inverted index and therefore scales well with the size of the network. Experimental results show that our mechanism is efficient, scalable and provides high quality of search results, i.e. the precision and recall metrics.

1 Introduction

In latest years, a main driver of innovation has been the World Wide Web, letting publication at the scale of tens of millions of content authors. This explosion of published information would be moot if the information could not be found, annotated, and analyzed so that each user can quickly locate information that is both relevant and comprehensive for their needs. While centralized search engines work well, peer-to-peer Web search is worth studying. In fact, Contemporary Web search engines are in essence centralized and require a central coordination service, which, even when replicated, has been identified as a major system bottleneck. Whereas, Web search over P2P overlay networks has the potential to become an alternative to current Web search engines due to its decentralized nature and favorable scalability properties.

Peer-to-peer systems supply good platforms for resource sharing. Among the shared resource, the shared text documents, including scientific papers, legal documents, inventory patents and etc., are important sources of knowledge. With more and more documents being shared, we have to solve the problem: how to locate the documents related to a multi keyword query in P2P systems.

A. Bouajjani and H. Fauconnier (Eds.): NETYS 2015, LNCS 9466, pp. 263–277, 2015.
DOI: 10.1007/978-3-319-26850-7_18

There are two classes of solutions currently proposed for decentralized peer-to-peer web retrieval. With full-text retrieval in unstructured P2P networks [7], queries are processed based on flooding. Unstructured P2P are commonly believed to be the best candidate for supporting full-text retrieval because the query evaluation operations can be handled at the nodes that store the relevant documents. However, search recall is not guaranteed with acceptable communication cost using a flooding-based scheme.

Another class of protocols based on the Distributed Hash Table (DHT) abstraction (CAN [21], Chord [24], Pastry [3], and Tapestry [28]) have been proposed to address scalability. In these protocols, peers organize into a well defined structure called overlay that is used for routing queries. Although DHTs are elegant and scalable, their performance under the dynamic conditions common for peer-to-peer systems is unknown as DHT-based searching engines are based on distributed indexes that partition a logically global inverted index in a physically distributed manner. Due to the exact match problem of DHTs, such schemes provide poor full-text search capacity. To deal with this problem, in this paper, we are led to build a full-text retrieval engine in structured P2P networks based on inverted index to accelerate query processing. The full-text retrieval performance in structured P2P networks engine can be further enhanced using bloom filter to improve search performance and resources availability. Our Peer-to-Peer Information Retrieval approach called BI-Chord is built on top of Chord structured P2P network. To reduce query processing costs in our approach, we focus on using the inverted index that will be distributed to peers. Thereby, partitioning scheme is required. There are two straightforward partitioning schemes for distributing the index: term also known as global partitioning and document or local partitioning. The strategy chosen in BI-Chord is the document partitioning.

More specifically, in this paper, we propose an efficient DHT-based keyword searching engine, which use Bloom Filter encoding besides of inverted index strategy.

We describe both techniques in more detail in Sect. 3. We showed that these two properties guarantee effectiveness and efficiency, essentially.

In addition, our experimental results prove that the retrieval quality is effective to improve the retrieval performance in P2P systems and remains comparable to state-of-the-art centralized search engines.

The remainder of the paper is organized as follows: In Sect. 2 we present the related work. Section 3 describes our peer-to-peer keyword searching engine BI-Chord in detail. In Sect. 5 we present our performance evaluation and Sect. 6 concludes the paper.

2 Related Work

Peer-to-peer information retrieval has been an active research area for about a decade. In this section we reveal the main solutions for P2P information retrieval proposed in the literature over the years.

Publish/subscribe systems are an alternative to query-based systems in cases where the same information is asked for over and over, and where clients want to get updated answers for the same query over a period of time. Recent publish/subscribe systems proposed by Kermarrec et al. in [16] have investigated this paradigm in the P2P context. These systems are successfully used to decouple distributed applications. However, their efficiency is closely tied to the topology of the underlying network, the design of which has been neglected. Peer-to-peer network topologies can offer inherently bounded delivery depth, load sharing, and self-organisation.

Li et al. in [17] describe a system that hash each term into an Identifier and store indices in a DHT using term Identifier as the key. These systems need to intersect the inverted lists of terms to find documents that contain multiple query terms. This cost grows proportionally with corpus size. Moreover, the above systems use simple keyword matching, ignoring the advanced relevance ranking algorithms devised by the IR community.

PlanetP [10] is a publish-subscribe service for P2P communities, supporting content ranking search. PlanetP uses a Bloom filter to summarize contents on each node and floods the summaries to the entire system. The system appears to be limited to a few thousand peers.

Recent work in [7] propose a replication strategy to support efficient and effective full-text retrieval. Authors use replicating the optimal number of Bloom Filters instead of the raw documents. The problem of their replication strategies is that items are replicated regardless of the popularity of the related queries. For full-text search, documents and queries are both replicated to some randomly selected nodes, raising possibly unacceptable storage and communication costs. Chen et al. [6] designed and optimized Bloom Filter settings in a peer-to-peer multikeyword searching technique which requires intersection operations across Wide Area Networks (WANs). Another technical challenge in this regard is sustainable network connectivity. The mobility of such recommender systems requires efficient, effective and reliable network technologies for sustainability [26].

Other way to reduce the bandwidth cost is effective intersection order optimization strategy in Bloom Filter, implemented in [15]. This method can reduce the search cost but the major drawback of this approach is, global keyword information is gathered by using a push-synopsis gossip algorithm.

To deal with bandwidth cost, authors use precomputing the term-set-based index, implemented in [8]. This proposition can significantly reduce the cost and is efficient for multi keyword searching. However the disadvantage of this approach is, exponentially growing index size. Podnar et al. [19] proposed to index only highly discriminative keyword (HDK) to reduce such index size. But if those keywords may rarely or never used in queries, causing high consumption of bandwidth and storage.

Work in [12] shows that content-based query resolution is feasible in DHT systems if these are using Rendezvous Points (RP). More specifically the framework proposes the registration of the content (i.e. attribute-value pairs that describe the content) at RPs. Queries might then be routed, using Chord, to a predefined set of RPs which consequently resolve the query.

Freenet [9] is another distributed information storage and retrieval system that uses instead an intelligent Depth-First-Search (DFS) mechanism to locate the object keys in the system. The advantage of DFS search is that a small set of peers can be queried quickly and efficiently; however by its nature it can take a long time if we want to find all the results to a query.

Luu et al. introduce the ALVIS Peers system [18] a distributed global index approach, with several innovations. During final result fusion each peer that generated an index entry is contacted and asked to recompute the document score based on global and local statistics, thereby generating globally comparable scores. Instead of storing postings for individual terms, the authors use highly discriminative keys. This introduces the problem of having to store many more keys than in a conventional term-peer index. To mitigate this, in later work Skobeltsyn et al. [22,23] they combine their approach with query-driven indexing storing only popular keys in the index and apply top k result storing.

To solve the above problems, in this paper, we propose an efficient DHT-based keyword searching engine, which use Bloom Filter encoding besides of inverted index strategy.

3 Peer-to-peer Keyword Retrieval of the Web

Bloom Filter plays an important role in reducing network traffic in terms of multi keyword search. It is an efficient data structure to represent a set S, which can handle well queries such as "is the element x in set S". By sending a bloom filter i.e., an encoded document set, rather than raw document sets among each participating peers helps in reducing the communication cost effectively. In this section, we explain the theory behind Bloom filters. In Sect. 4, we present our peer-to-peer keyword searching engine BI-Chord and focus on how to optimize the communication cost of P2P multi-keyword search using Bloom Filter over and above inverted index.

3.1 Bloom Filter

Consider an example which shows a simple network with peers P_A and P_B. The peer P_A contains the set of documents A for a given keyword k_A, and peer P_B contains the set of documents B for another keyword k_B. $A \cap B$ is the set of all documents containing both k_A and k_B. A Bloom filter is a hash-based data structure that summarizes membership in a set. By sending a Bloom filter based on A instead of sending A itself, we reduce the amount of communication required for P_B to determine $A \cap B$. The membership test returns false positives with a tunable, predictable probability and never returns false negatives. Thus, the intersection calculated by P_B will contain all of the true intersection, as well as a few hits that contain only k_B and not k_A. The number of false positives falls exponentially as the size of the Bloom filter increases.

The Bloom filter is an efficient, lossy way of describing sets. It is a data structure used for representing a set of elements succinctly. A Bloom filter is a bit-vector V of length m with a family of independent hash functions, each of which maps from elements of the represented set to an integer in $[0, m)$. To create a representation of a set, each set element is hashed, and the bits in the vector associated with the hash functions' results are set. To verify whether the set represented by a Bloom filter contains a given element, that element is hashed and the corresponding bits in the filter are examined. If any of the bits are not set, the represented set definitely does not contain the object. If all of the bits are set, then, the set may contain the object; there is a non-zero probability that it does not, however. This case is called a false positive, and the false positive rate of a Bloom filter is a well-defined, linear function of its width, the number of hash functions and the cardinality of the represented set [5].

Precisely, a filter is first encoded with each element in a set, and then queried to determine the membership of a particular element. In the following, we briefly summarize the working flow of the basic Bloom filter.

A Bloom filter includes a m-bit vector V and a group of hash functions. For a set of n elements, for example $X = x_1, x_2, \ldots, x_n$, the typical operations of a basic Bloom filter are inserting the elements to the Bloom filter and querying the Bloom filter for element membership. k hash functions, $h_1(x), h_2(x), \ldots, h_k(x)$, are used to complete both operations.

We continue by describing algorithms explanations.

(1) Inserting an element to a basic Bloom filter.
   (i) Initialization the Bloom filter: set V to zero.
   (ii) For $\forall x \in X$, compute the hash values of x_i by $h_1(x_i), h_2(x_i), \ldots, h_k(x_i)$.
   (iii) Set the corresponding bits in V to "1", that is, $V[h_1(x_i)] = V[h_2(x_i)] = \ldots = V[h_k(x_i)] = 1$.
(2) Element membership query
   (i) For an element y, compute the hash values of it $by h_1(y), h_2(y), \ldots, h_k(y)$.
   (ii) Check the corresponding bits in array V. Rules for confirmation of element membership of y in X are as follows.

If $V[h_1(y)]\&V[h_2(y)]\&\ldots\&V[h_k(y)] = 1$, the membership of y in X is confirmed.

Else, y is considered being not included in X.

In an element membership query, a positive false may happen when the membership of y in X is confirmed while it doesnot belong to X [13,27].

4 Peer-to-Peer Keyword Searching Engine

There are basically two ways to organize a text index incited by inverted index structure in a distributed environment, in particular local (also called document) index organization and global (or term) index organization. We focus on the case of a local index organization, and consider a Bloom Filter encoding besides of replication strategies. In this section, we first address a general review of our DHT-based keyword searching engine BI-Chord. We then describe in Sect. 4.2 our approach to performing peer-to-peer searches efficiently.

4.1 System Design

Fundamentally, full-text keyword search is the task of associating keywords with document identifiers and later retrieving document identifiers that match combinations of keywords. To do this, our searching systems called BI-Chord use inverted indices, which map each word found in any document to a list of the documents in which the word appears. As mentioned above, an inverted index is a mapping between words and document location sets. It's main purpose is to locate documents that contain a specific word. With a word-based location service available, it is possible to do contents search on shared documents.

In our design BI-Chord, we propose a combination of the distributed lookup protocol Chord [24] which can efficiently locate the node that stores a particular data item, and a Bloom Filter used for efficient exact match searches. A fundamental problem that confronts structured peer-to-peer applications is to efficiently locate the node that stores a particular data item. The distributed lookup protocol Chord, employed in our proposition, addresses this problem. Chord provides support for just one operation: given a key, it maps the key onto a node. Data location can be easily implemented on top of Chord by associating a key with each data item, and storing the key/data item pair at the node to which the key maps. Chord adapts efficiently as nodes join and leave the system, and can answer queries even if the system is continuously changing.
Each document is identified by a unique document identifier, assigned through Chord protocol.

The Chord protocol uses SHA-1 as consistent hash function to assign an m-bit identifier to each peer and each document (each document has a key that can be a title or abstract).

An inverted index consists of many inverted lists, where each inverted list contains the identifiers of all documents in the collection that contain the word w, sorted by document identifier. Likewise, each query consists of a set of words (query terms). The ranking is achieved by comparing the words found in the document and in the query. More precisely, a ranking function assigns a score to each document regarding the current query, based on the frequency of each query word in the page and in the overall collection.

4.2 Inverted Index

For efficient query processing, our searching engine BI-Chord rely on indexing, typically on a variation of the inverted index technique. The inverted index maintains a vocabulary. Specifically, a list of all terms found in the document collection, and a number of posting lists for all terms from the vocabulary. An inverted (or posting) list of a term t stores the references to all documents that contain t together with some auxiliary information. In our case, we opted that the auxiliary information will be the term frequency. we assign to each term in a document a weight for that term, that depends on the number of occurrences of the term in the document. We would like to compute a score between a query term t and a document d, based on the weight of t in d. The simplest approach is to assign the weight to be equal to the number of occurrences of term t in document d.

The query in our DHT-based keyword searching engine can then be processed by intersecting the inverted lists of all query terms, computing the scores of the documents in the intersection and returning k documents with the highest scores.

To reduce query processing costs in BI-Chord, the inverted index will be distributed. Thereby, partitioning scheme is required. There are two straightforward partitioning schemes for distributing the index: Term also known global partitioning and document or local partitioning. The first partitioning scheme called term partitioning assigns terms to peers such that each peer maintains complete posting lists for certain terms. To process a query only the peers responsible for the query terms have to be contacted.

However indexing is costly and it is hard to balance the load as the term frequency distribution follows a power law. Intersecting posting lists that are stored on different servers can be time and bandwidth consuming. Thus, we have favored document partitioning. The main reason for choosing document partitioning is that in large P2P networks it is important to restrict the query processing to a small number of peers instead of broadcasting each query to all peers as in the case of document partitioning. Also the put/get interface of Chord can be easily extended to support such a term partitioned index. An example of our Chord-based keyword searching engine with a local index organization is shown in Fig. 1. we split the document collection in several sub-collections and each sub-collection is indexed locally and independently on a different peer. A query is processed by all peers in parallel and the final result is aggregated from the top-k local answers supplied by each peer [11]. Important advantages of document partitioning are the simplicity of the indexing procedure and nearly even load balancing between the peers. On the other hand, each query has to be processed by each peer which increases the processing costs.

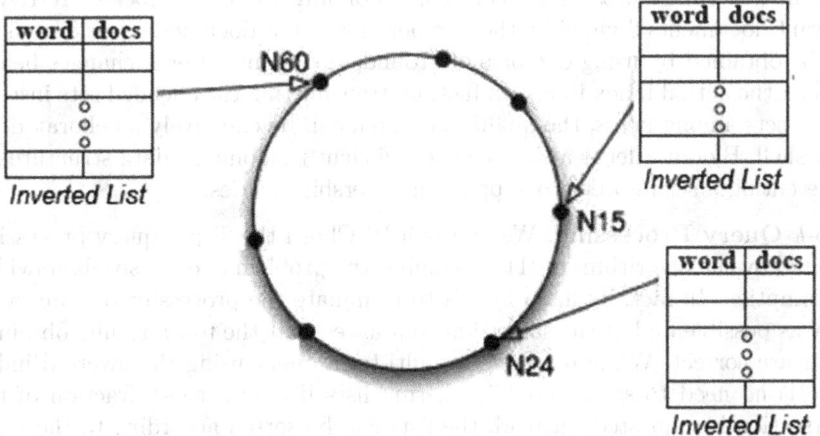

Fig. 1. Distributing an inverted index across the Chord network

An inverted index is a mapping between words and document location sets. It's main purpose is to locate documents that contain a specific word. With a word-based location service available, it is possible to do contents search on shared documents. We assume that a search is performed on some global shared index. Since the system cannot have any centralized structure, this index would have to be distributed evenly across the peers. To build such an index, each peer is required to announce its contents, in the form $(word, location)$. The location points to a document stored on the peer that contains the given word. The inverted index is made by collecting all the announcements. Searching for a word on the index returns the list of all document locations that match that word.

Bloom Filter. In BI-Chord, the data structure Bloom Filter will represent the set of documents and supports membership test queries. The advantage of a Bloom Filter is that it uses significantly less space than a dictionary or hash table of the elements in the set. In contrast, there is a small false-positive rate that can be traded off against space (i.e., some elements may be reported as being in the set when they are not), and a Bloom Filter cannot retrieve a list of the elements in the represented set (we can only test if a given element is in the set). Bloom Filters are used to efficiently compute the intersection between two sets stored on different peers. We note that our search engine only return results that contain all of the query terms. This means that significant savings can be obtained during query execution under a global index organization, by first sending a Bloom Filter of the document identifiers in the shortest inverted list, rather than the complete list, to the next node. In fact, by transmitting the encoded sets instead of raw sets among peers, the communication cost can be effectively saved, and therefore network traffic will be conserved. Many of the document identifiers in the shortest list will not find a match in the other lists, and thus we only have to send a small subset of the items in the shortest inverted list in a second round-trip, at which point any false positives can be detected. As shown later in experiments, a high recall, corresponding to the number of retrieved relevant documents divided by the number of relevant documents (see Sect. 5.2), can be obtained by using one or more rounds of Bloom Filter exchanges before sending the actual index items. In fact, by transmitting the encoded sets instead of raw sets among peers, the quality of search can be effectively ameliorated. In a nutshell, Bloom Filer is a simple space-efficient randomized data structure for representing a set in order to support membership queries.

Top-*k* Query Processing. We apply in BI-Chord the Top-k query processing inspired by the algorithms of [11] to combat the problem of extensive bandwidth consumption. In fact, its main idea is to terminate the processing of a query as early as possible and at the same time guarantee that the top-k results obtained so far are correct. While resolving a multi-term query using the inverted index there is no need to scan complete posting lists if only a top-k fraction of the intersection is requested. Instead, the lists can be sorted according to the score values and it is likely that the top-k query results can be found by probing the documents found in the top-portions of the posting lists only.

Replication Strategy. Structured Peer-to-Peer networks can be a successful mechanism for full-text keyword search of the Web. However, current P2P protocols have long worst case query latencies which prevents them from being used for real time applications. An obvious solution is to employ replication strategies in order to reduce search and data-access latencies, since it should be efficient and meanwhile facilitates efficient full-text keyword search.

Many replication methods are proposed for structured P2P networks, with a specific main goal to achieve. In this paper we present a full-text keyword search of the Web over structured peer-to-peer networks, that optimally shares sets of distributed objects in dynamic large scale infrastructures. BI-Chord is based on the implementation of a DHT (distributed hash table) in which the neighbor replication method is used.

In the neighbor replication method, each peer maintains a list of neighbors such as successor-lists and predecessor-lists in Chord or leaf-sets in pastry. In neighbor replication, the data objects are stored not only in root peer but also on its successor, or on its predecessor, or on its leaf-sets and or on the nodes belonging to the same group as it. The root is node that stores the object location information and it can be different to the owner which is the node that stores the master copy of the object. Chord employs successors-lists replication. Pastry and Kademlia DHTs employ leafsets replication [20].

For each data replication algorithm, there is a special maintenance protocol. The idea is that the maintenance protocols must maintain k copies of each data objects, stored on the root-peer neighbors, without violating the initial placement strategy.

5 BI-Chord Performance

In this section, we provide an experimental evaluation of our peer-to-peer keyword searching engine BI-Chord presented above.

5.1 Simulation Setup

To evaluate the performance of BI-Chord, we implemented it using OverSim [2,4], the P2P Overlay Simulation Framework for OMNeT++ [1], and the Discrete Event Simulator based on the INET Framework for OMNet++ [25]. We implemented Chord complete set of functionalities, including the protocols necessary for information retrieval including bloom filters.

We simulate BI-Chord to support a local inverted index. We split the document collection in several sub-collections and each sub-collection is indexed locally and independently on a different peer.

A query is processed by all peers in parallel and the final result is aggregated from the $top - k$ local answers supplied by each peer. For the experiments we produce several lookup scenarios.

We conduct some experiments to see its performance on two standard document collections where queries and relevance judgments were available

Table 1. Document collections used in the experiments and their characteristics

	CACM	MED
Number of documents	3204	1033
Number of single terms	3029	4315
Average number of words per document	18.4	46.6
Queries number	64	30
Average number of terms per query	9.3	9.5
Average number of relevant documents per query	15.3	23.2

(CACM and MED). The collections used experimentally are characterized by the statistics of Table 1. To measure BI-Chord recall and precision on the above collections, we first distribute documents across a set of peers and then runs and evaluates different search and retrieval algorithms.

5.2 Simulation Results

The two most frequent and basic measures for information retrieval effectiveness are recall and precision.

- The recall is a main metric used to quantify the quality of search results, and is defined as the number of retrieved relevant documents divided by the number of relevant documents.
- The precision is another metric used to quantify the quality of search results, and is defined as the number of retrieved relevant documents divided by the number of retrieved documents.

Recall. In this experiment, we evaluate the recall that is the fraction of relevant documents that are retrieved using the Eq. 1.

$$Recall = \frac{\sharp(relevant - items - retrieved)}{\sharp(relevant - items)} = P(retrieved|relevant) \quad (1)$$

We first assess the performance of BI-Chord by representing its achieved recall. Thus, we assume that when posting a query, the user also provides the parameter k, which is the maximum number of documents that he is willing to accept in answer to a query. Figure 2(a) and (b) plots Chord-LSI average precision over all provided queries as functions of for the MED and CACM collections.

Figure 2(a) and (b) report recall for both the CACM and the MED collections, with respect to the number of documents that should be returned in response to a query. These recalls are the mean of the recalls obtained after each k relevant documents retrieved. In the simulation we vary the parameter k from 10 to 50. We find that when the setting of k varies, the recall of the BI-Chord

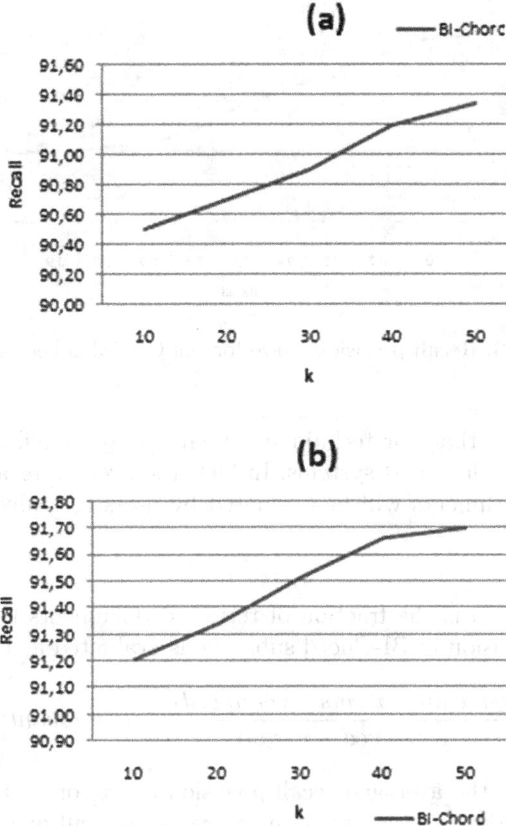

Fig. 2. (a) Recall for the CACM collection with k increased and (b) recall for the MED collection with k increased. k: upper limit on the number of documents that should be returned in response to a query.

increases for both the CACM and the MED collections. When k is increased to the value of 50, the recall reaches the maximum value which is 91.7 % for CACM collections and reaches the maximum value 91.34 % for the MED collections.

The observation drawn from these figures is that our proposition recall grows steadily when the maximum number of documents that peer is willing to accept in answer to a query, increases. This is because more relevant documents are retrieved. Hence, the result confirms that our peer-to-peer keyword searching engine can reduce the computation time.

Results show that BI-Chord achieves an average query recall of 91 %. Basically, the recall in BI-Chord is relatively high, because all inverted lists are sorted by Page rank and the answer set of each query is defined as the top-k results. However, BI-Chord sets a stop condition for the Bloom filter, if too many false-positive results occur, BI-Chord may not be able to retrieve k results, thus the recall have not reached 100 %. Overall, BI-Chord provided a high recall.

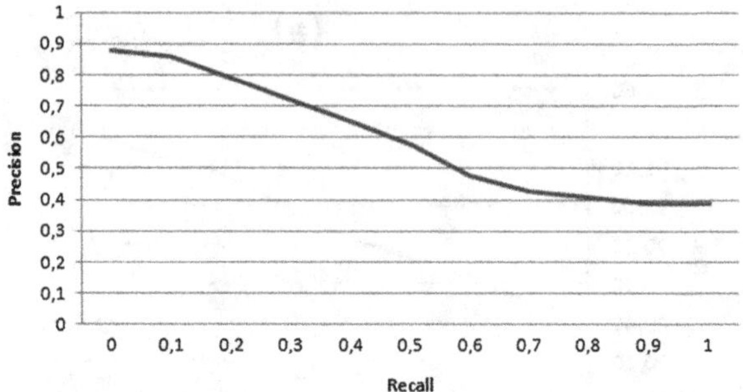

Fig. 3. Recall-precision curve for the CACM collection.

The Fig. 2 shows that our technique is relatively quite efficient if compared quantitatively with classic IR systems. In fact, the average recall is about 91 % of the returned documents will be evaluated by users as really relevant to the query in BI-Chord.

Precision. Precision is the fraction of retrieved documents that are relevant. Therefore, the precision in BI-Chord subspace is evaluated as Eq. 2.

$$Precision = \frac{\sharp(relevant - items - retrieved)}{\sharp(retrieved - items)} = P(relevant|retrieved) \quad (2)$$

Figure 3 depicts the averaged recall-precision curve for all the 64 queries of the CACM collection, i.e., the precision (averaged over all queries) for different recall levels. The main observation that can be drawn from this figure, is that precision is quite good at low recall.

We can observe that a 25 % of the relevant services can be retrieved with precision higher than 80 %, whereas for retrieving more than 60 % of the relevant services the precision drops below 50 %.

The results reveal that the quality of the search results and the efficiency of the system are quite acceptable. However, due to the false positives of Bloom Filters, the returned results may contain undesired documents with very low probability. This may lead to a slight decrease of the precision of the final results. Nevertheless, it is fully comparable to the one obtained with a state-of-the-art centralized query engine.

5.3 Performance Comparison

More related to BI-Chord information retrieval goals, PlanetP [10] and SWMS [14] address the problems of Full-text keywords search of the Web.

The PlanetP system explores the construction of a content addressable publish/subscribe service using gossiping between peers of an unstructured peer-to-peer community, while authors of [14] propose a Sliding Window improved

Multi-keyword Searching method (SWMS) to index and search full-text for short queries on DHT.

We assess BI-Chord's performance by comparing its achieved recall and precision against these latter.

We use two collections of documents (and associated queries and human relevance ranking) to measure BI-Chord's performance. Table 1 presents the main characteristics of these collections. These are among collections that were previously used to evaluate PlanetP and SWMS. Table 2 shows average "Top-k" having k = 10 (see Sect. 4.2) performance for both collections : We make several observations. First, our proposition BI-Chord tracks the performance of SWMS closely, with an recall almost equal to 95 % for MED collection (respectively 93 % for MED collection). To each collection the difference is no more than 2 %. Further, BI-Chord's performance is independent of collection, achieving nearly the same performance for MED and CACM. For CACM collection, BI-Chord's recall (respectively precision) is higher 3 % (respectively 4 %) of PlanetP's. BI-Chord get the best result. These small differences demonstrate that BI-Chord provides high quality of search results and remains comparable to state-of-the-art search engines.

Table 2. "Top-10" precision and recall for CACM and MED collections

		BI-Chord
CACM	Recall	91 %
	Precision	54 %
MED	Recall	91 %
	Precision	59 %

6 Conclusion

DHT based peer-to-peer networks are well-suited for exact match lookups using unique identifiers, but do not directly support text search. In this paper, a multi-keyword searching mechanism based on bloom filter and inverted index for structured P2P networks is proposed. Our main contribution lies in conducting a feasibility analysis for P2P Web search. Simulation results show that our design outperforms existing work. In the future work, we will try to examine the performance of more solutions by using larger scale data collections.

References

1. Omnet++ community site. http://www.omnetpp.org. Accessed January 2015
2. The oversim p2p simulator. http://www.oversim.org/. Accessed January 2015

3. Rowstron, A., Druschel, P.: Pastry: scalable, decentralized object location and routing for large-scale p2p systems. In: IFIP/ACM Middleware (2001)
4. Baumgart, I., Heep, B., Krause, S.: Oversim: a flexible overlay network simulation framework. In: Proceedings of 10th IEEE Global Internet Symposium in Conjunction with IEEE INFOCOM, Anchorage, AK, USA (2007)
5. Bloom, B.H.: Space/time trade-offs in hash coding with allowable errors. Commun. ACM **13**(7), 422–426 (1970)
6. Chen, H., Jin, H., Chen, L., Liu, Y., Ni, L.M.: Optimizing bloom filter settings in peer-to-peer multikeyword searching. IEEE Trans. Knowl. Data Eng. **24**(4), 692–706 (2012)
7. Chen, H., Jin, H., Luo, X., Liu, Y., Gu, T., Chen, K., Ni, L.M.: Bloomcast: efficient and effective full-text retrieval in unstructured p2p networks. IEEE Trans. Parallel Distrib. Syst. **23**, 232–241 (2012)
8. Chen, H., Yan, J., Jin, H., Liu, Y., Ni, L.M.: Tss: efficient term set search in large peer-to-peer textual collections. IEEE Trans. Comput. **59**, 969–980 (2010)
9. Clarke, I., Sandberg, O., Wiley, B., Hong, T.W.: Freenet: a distributed anonymous information storage and retrieval system. In: Federrath, H. (ed.) Designing Privacy Enhancing Technologies. LNCS, vol. 2009, p. 46. Springer, Heidelberg (2001)
10. Cuenca-Acuna, F.M., Nguyen, T.D.: Text-based content search and retrieval in ad hoc p2p communities. In: Gregori, E., Cherkasova, L., Cugola, G., Panzieri, F., Picco, G.P. (eds.) Web Engineering and Peer-to-Peer Computing. LNCS, vol. 2736, pp. 220–234. Springer, Heidelberg (2002)
11. Fagin, R., Lotem, A., Naor, M.: Optimal aggregation algorithms for middleware. J. Comput. Syst. Sci. **66**(4), 614–656 (2003)
12. Gao, J., Steenkiste, P.: Design and evaluation of a distributed scalable content discovery system. IEEE J. Sel. Areas Commun. **22**, 54–66 (2004)
13. Guo, D., Liu, Y., Li, X., Yang, P.: False negative problem of counting bloom filter. IEEE Trans. Knowl. Data Eng. **22**(5), 651–664 (2010)
14. Huang, S., Xue, G.-R., Zhu, X., Ge, Y.-F., Yu, Y.: DHT based searching improved by sliding window. In: Li, Q., Wang, G., Feng, L. (eds.) WAIM 2004. LNCS, vol. 3129, pp. 208–217. Springer, Heidelberg (2004)
15. Jayalakshmi, G., Vijayalakshmi, M.: Effective multi keyword search over p2p network using optimized bloom filter settings. Int. J. Emerg. Technol. Adv. Eng. **3**(1), 85–93 (2013). Special Issue
16. Kermarrec, A.-M., Triantafillou, P.: Xl peer-to-peer pub/sub systems. ACM Comput. Surv. **46**(2), 16:1–16:45 (2013)
17. Li, J., Loo, B.T., Hellerstein, J.M., Kaashoek, M.F., Karger, D.R., Morris, R.: On the feasibility of peer-to-peer web indexing and search. In: Kaashoek, M.F., Stoica, I. (eds.) IPTPS 2003. LNCS, vol. 2735, pp. 207–215. Springer, Heidelberg (2003)
18. Luu, T., Klemm, F., Podnar, I., Rajman, M., Aberer, K.: Alvis peers: a scalable full-text peer-to-peer retrieval engine. In: Workshop on Information Retrieval in Peer-to-Peer Networks P2P-IR at CIKM 2006 (2006)
19. Podnar, I., Rajman, M., Luu, T., Klemm, F., Aberer, K.: Scalable peer-to-peer web retrieval with highly discriminative keys. In: Proceedings of the 23rd International Conference on Data Engineering, ICDE, Istanbul, Turkey, 15–20 April, pp. 1096–1105 (2007)
20. Rahmani, M., Benchaïba, M.: A comparative study of replication schemes for structured p2p networks. In: The Ninth International Conference on Internet and Web Applications and Services, ICIW 2014, pp. 147–158 (2014)
21. Ratnasamy, S., Francis, P., Handley, M., Karp, R., Shenker, S.: A scalable content addressable network. In: ACM SIGCOMM, August 2001

22. Skobeltsyn, G., Luu, T., Podnar Zarko, I., Rajman, M., Aberer, K.: Query-driven indexing for peer-to-peer text retrieval. In: 16th International World Wide Web Conference (WWW 2007). ACM, New York (2007)
23. Skobeltsyn, G., Luu, T., Podnar Zarko, I., Rajman, M., Aberer, K.: Query-driven indexing for scalable peer-to-peer text retrieval. Future Generat. Comput. Syst. **25**, 89–99 (2009)
24. Stoica, I., Morris, R., Karger, D., Kaashoek, M.F., Balakrishnan, H.: Chord: a scalable peer-to-peer lookup service for internet applications. In: ACM SIGCOMM, pp. 149–160 (2001)
25. Varga, A.: The omnet++ discrete event simulation system. In: European Simulation Multiconference (ESM 2001), hal-00250235, version 2, 25 February 2008, June 2001
26. Xia, F., Asabere, N.Y., Ahmed, A.M., Li, J., Kong, X.: Mobile multimedia recommendation in smart communities: a survey. IEEE access, CoRR abs/1312.6565 (2013)
27. Xie, K., Wen, J., Zhang, D., Xie, G.: Bloom filter query algorithm. J. Softw. **20**(1), 96–108 (2009)
28. Zhao, B., Huang, L., Stribling, J., Rhea, S., Kubiatowicz, J.: Tapestry: a global-scale overlay for rapid service deployment. IEEE J-SAC **22**(1), 41–53 (2004)

Profiling Transactional Applications

Vincent Gramoli[1,2(✉)], Rachid Guerraoui[3], and Anne-Marie Kermarrec[4]

[1] NICTA, Sydney, Australia
vincent.gramoli@sydney.edu.au
[2] University of Sydney, Sydney, Australia
[3] EPFL, Lausanne, Switzerland
rachid.guerraoui@epfl.ch
[4] INRIA, Rennes, France
anne-marie.kermarrec@inria.fr

Abstract. What does it mean for two transactional applications to be similar? We address this question in this paper by highlighting four distinctive features of transactional applications: (1) the transaction size, i.e., the average number of memory accesses of the transactions; (2) the read-write ratio, i.e., the ratio between the number of accesses that modify the data and those that do not; (3) the contention, i.e., the number of concurrent accesses to the same shared data, such that at least one of these accesses is a write; (4) the uniformity, i.e., the extend to which transactions access distinct objects. We show that the similarity between an application A and an application A' can be derived from these features and can be used to determine which concurrency control implementation works best for A based on having tested which worked best for A'. We convey the accuracy of the profiling and predictions based on a study with six workloads and ten concurrency control mechanisms.

Keywords: Recommendation system · Performance · Collaborative filtering · Concurrency control

1 Introduction

Profiling applications a priori is key to their effective deployment. The idea is very simple: given some characteristics of an application computed a priori, one can choose the best deployment scheme for the application without having to go through exhaustive testing schemes that might sometimes not even be possible. Profiling is particularly appealing for concurrent applications. In this case, deployment includes, among other things, the choice of the underlying concurrency control mechanism to ensure consistency despite concurrent accesses to shared data. Adopting the wrong mechanism can hamper scalability and impact performance by several orders of magnitude [13]. In addition, there are multiple ways of combining existing mechanisms and going through exhaustive testing may simply be impossible. Hence the need for profiling.

Yet, profiling concurrent applications is very challenging. This difficulty stems from the inherent nondeterminism of concurrent applications as well as from the

A. Bouajjani and H. Fauconnier (Eds.): NETYS 2015, LNCS 9466, pp. 278–292, 2015.
DOI: 10.1007/978-3-319-26850-7_19

layout of the architecture where these programs run [8]. Furthermore, manufactured hardware evolves rapidly by, for example, adopting different cache coherence protocols [20] or multiplying the number of cores.

In this paper, we focus on transactional applications. We highlight four distinctive features: (1) the transaction size, i.e., the average number of memory accesses of the transactions; (2) the read-write ratio, i.e., the ratio between the number of accesses that modify the data and those that do not; (3) the contention, i.e., the number of concurrent accesses to the same shared data, such that at least one of these accesses is a write; and (4) the uniformity, i.e., the extent to which transactions access distinct objects. We show that these features can be computed for an application A and are sufficient to determine its distance from an application A'. In turn, this distance can help predict which concurrency control mechanisms would best fit A based on results obtained on A'.

In some sense, this is like highlighting distinctive features of a person P that would help compute similarities with another person P' and help predict which movies P would like most based on those that P' enjoyed most. In our context, we show for instance that if a new application is similar to others, then the concurrency control mechanism that is known to benefit these latter applications could intuitively benefit the new one as well. Or we can filter out inappropriate concurrency controls based on the observed similarities between applications and their individual performance.

This collaborative filtering technique was initially used to compute the similarities between documents [26] and was more recently applied to measure similarities in large data sets [27]. The key idea is to filter information based on the collaboration of multiple participants or data sources. This technique is popular for its effectiveness in recommendation systems: by collecting tastes and preferences of many users regarding multiple items, the system can recommend an item that one user is likely to prefer. Although similar, the problem we tackle is not to recommend items based on their similarities but rather to suggest concurrency control to applications based on application similarities. The benefit of our approach is that the profile of an application is sufficient to select its most suitable concurrency control, simply by comparing this profile against profiles of existing applications that were previously tested. In particular, it is not necessary to test the new application to identify the concurrency control.

Using Synchrobench [13], we show experimentally that our approach is beneficial to even a small set of applications by precisely identifying the discriminating criteria. In particular, we show that the size of operations, the ratio of shared write accesses over shared read accesses, the contention and the uniformity of memory regions these applications access are effective criteria to compute similarities between applications and to suggest concurrency controls that boost performance. We evaluate our solution on 6 benchmarks for which workloads exhibit a wide range of behaviors with respect to these criteria.

In addition, we applied our approach to 10 concurrency control mechanisms. These mechanisms include various transactional algorithmic designs that are known to affect performance [11]: concurrency control mechanisms that acquire locks eagerly (encounter-time locking), lazily (commit-time locking), that use invisible writes, or visible (in-place) writes. These mechanisms are further refined using different policies similar to existing contention managers [16,17,24,25]. These policies include "kill-attacker" that always aborts the transaction that causes the conflict, the exponential backoff strategy that forces every restarting transaction to wait a period that increases exponentially with its number of restarts and a delaying contention manager that consists in restarting a transaction, which aborted due to an unsuccessful attempt to acquire a lock, only after the lock has been released.

Our experimental evaluation compares the performance in terms of throughput and abort rates of all benchmarks and compute their distance using the *cosine similarity* [26] of workloads based on the aforementioned criteria. Our conclusion is fourfold. First, our results confirm that for a given benchmark and depending on the concurrency control mechanism used in the benchmark, the performance significantly varies for the same update ratios, hence motivating the need for our solution. Second, our results indicate for instance that for data structures that share similar criteria, like red-black trees and skip lists, the same concurrency controls can benefit or penalize both corresponding benchmarks. Third, for benchmarks that have notably different profiles a concurrency control mechanism benefiting one may be substantially detrimental to the other. Finally, seemingly identical benchmarks may have different profiles due to the way they were tuned, performing differently with the same concurrency control.

Section 2 introduces the criteria to draw the profile of each concurrent workload, hence allowing us to compute similarities between them. Section 3 describes the transaction algorithms and contention management mechanisms resulting in the 10 concurrency control mechanisms we present. Section 4 depicts the performance results of our benchmarks as the throughput and abort rates when using each of the proposed mechanisms. Section 5 discusses how to extend our solution to implement a fully automated framework that refines application similarities based on previous runs of the applications. Section 6 presents the related work and finally Sect. 7 concludes the paper.

2 Workload Profiles

We define the *profile* of each workload as a set of four values, each representing its characteristic according to a distinct attribute or *dimension*.

- **Transaction Size:** the transaction size captures the number of memory accesses executed as part of the same transaction between its last (re-)start and its commit.
- **Write/Read Ratio:** the mean ratio of the number of transactional write accesses over the number of transactional read accesses executed by a single transaction between its last (re-)start and its commit.
- **Contention:** the chance of conflicts inherent to this workload. Note that the contention is not related to the write/read ratio as two transactions executing mostly writes on disjoint data may not contend.

- **Uniformity:** the level of uniformity in the distribution of transactional accesses over memory locations. A lower value indicates skewness so that the same few locations are more likely accessed by any transaction than other locations. Note that the same workload can be skewed and not contended.

As we explain below, these four dimensions allow us to compare statically different workloads based on the distance between the vectors of their profile.

2.1 Workloads

To compare concurrency control, we evaluate six workloads freely available with Synchrobench [13], a micro-benchmark suite for synchronization techniques. The first workload is a hash table that maps a key to a value in constant size buckets implemented as linked lists and where n threads execute the three operations similarly to the list-based set workload. It features simple transactional operations `put`, `delete`, `contains`, that consists of adding, removing an element from a set and checking for the presence of an element in the set, respectively. The workload consists of spawning n threads that repeatedly execute randomly these transactional operations with a proportion of `put` and `delete` over `contains` specified with an update ratio u. These operations execute on a hash table initialized with a given number of elements (indicated by parameter i), each operation takes a value uniformly at random in a range of r possible values. Other workloads include a linked list, a red-black (RB) tree, an AVL speculation-friendly (AVL SF) tree [5] and a skip list where n threads execute operations with the same distribution. The last workload is a double-ended queue that consists of an array where values are always `enqueued` at the head and `dequeued` from the tail, hence implementing a queue abstraction (the update ratio is thus always 100 %).

2.2 Profile-Based Comparisons

To identify the profile of each of these applications, we ran experiments using Synchrobench [13] and observed the size of transactions, compared the size of the *read-set* or the number of shared read accesses within the same committing transaction to the size of the *write-set* of the number of shared write accesses per committing transactions. The profile of each workload namely the hash table, the list-based set, the red-black tree, the speculation-friendly tree, the skip list and the double-ended queue are depicted in Table 1. Given this profile, we can measure the distance between two workloads depending on the offset between their coordinates. We deduce the profile of each workload by observing the length of transactions, the proportion of write vs. read accesses to the shared memory, the frequencies at which two transactions access same shared locations and the distribution of accessed locations.

Linked list transactions are larger than others as the number of accesses per transaction is linear in the number of elements and the list contains as many elements as other structures. Empirically, we observed for 2^{16}-sized data structures

Table 1. Profile of the workloads depending on the transaction size, the proportion of write over read and the amount of conflicts

Workload	Hash table	Linked list	RB tree	AVL SF tree	Skip list	Deque
Tx size	−	++	+	+	+	−
Write/read	+	−	−	−	−	++
Contention	−	−	+	−	+	++
Uniformity	++	+	−	−	+	−

that the average linked list transaction size was $66K$. We also confirmed that transactions were very small on constant access time data structures: we observed 5 shared accesses per transactions on hash tables and queues. Finally, we found slightly varying transaction size on logarithmic access time data structures: 61 for the skip list, 40 for the red-black tree and 23 for the speculation-friendly tree. These differences are reported in the row 'Tx size' of Table 1.

No operation in any workload has a number of write accesses linear in the number of elements, this number is either constant in the linked list, queue, hash table sizes and is typically logarithmic in the skip list size and it may be logarithmic in the tree size when restructuring is involved. Experimentally, we observed that the linked list has a ratio of write over read shared accesses of $\frac{1}{32K}$ whereas the hash table experience a ratio that varies from $\frac{1}{6}$ with a load factor of 10 to $\frac{4}{5}$ with a load factor of 1. The deque ratio is $\frac{2}{3}$, the skip list ratio is $\frac{1}{30}$, the AVL SF tree ratio is $\frac{1}{20}$ and the RB tree ratio is $\frac{1}{7}$.

The contention is induced by the probability for two operations to access the same shared location so that at least one of these accesses is a write. This is very likely for the deque as all operations write to the same 3 (on average) locations located either at the head or the tail of the queue (depending whether they enqueue or deque). Finally, the uniformity indicates the skewness in the distribution of access locations among all locations. The deque as well as trees are highly skewed as their head, tail and root are the most accessed locations. The hash table experiences the highest uniformity because the hash function tends to balance the accesses among all buckets.

Non-discriminating Criteria. If we represent the six workloads as three-dimensional vectors by ignoring the fourth criterion (uniformity) $(x, y, z) = (1,2,1), (3,1,1), (2,1,2), (2,1,1), (2,1,2), (1,3,3)$ in the column order in which they are listed in Table 1 then the Euclidean distance

$$\sqrt{(x_1 - x_2)^2 + (y_1 - y_2)^2 + (z_1 - z_2)^2}$$

is 0 between skip list and red-black tree, the distance between each of these two and the AVL SF tree is 1. The linked list is closer to the AVL SF tree (with distance 4) than the skip list or red-black tree (5), the hash table is at distance 3 from the skip list or red-black tree, and at distance 2 from the AVL SF tree and the two furthest workloads are AVL SF tree and deque with a distance of 9.

Table 2. Similarities between workloads in term of the cosine similarity of their profile

	Hash table	Linked list	RB tree	AVL SF tree	Skip list	Deque
Hash table	1	0	-0.41	0	0	-0.29
Linked list	0	1	0.4	0.67	0.58	-0.87
RB tree	-0.41	0.4	1	0.81	0.7	0
AVL SF tree	0	0.67	0.81	1	0.58	-0.5
Skip list	0	0.58	0.7	0.58	1	-0.5
Deque	-0.29	-0.87	0	-0.5	-0.5	1

This selection of three criteria does not help differentiating the skip list and the red-black tree. Note that this observation holds regardless of the distance metric we choose because the skip list and the red-black tree would share exactly the same profile. To refine our profiles and differentiate these two workloads we have to take into account the fourth criterion, namely uniformity.

Discriminating Criteria. Picking only three criteria may not be discriminating enough. If we refine our profiles using the four criteria, we can represent the six workloads with four-dimensional vectors

$$\begin{pmatrix} w \\ x \\ y \\ z \end{pmatrix} \text{ as } \begin{pmatrix} -1 \\ 0 \\ -1 \\ 1 \end{pmatrix}, \begin{pmatrix} 1 \\ -1 \\ -1 \\ 0 \end{pmatrix}, \begin{pmatrix} 0 \\ -1 \\ 0 \\ -1 \end{pmatrix}, \begin{pmatrix} 0 \\ -1 \\ -1 \\ -1 \end{pmatrix}, \begin{pmatrix} 0 \\ -1 \\ 0 \\ 0 \end{pmatrix} \text{ and } \begin{pmatrix} -1 \\ 1 \\ 1 \\ -1 \end{pmatrix}.$$

Cosine Similarity. Given the fourth criteria, we can now refine our notion of distance by taking the cosine similarity to compare the direction of these vectors. Note that the cosine similarity is more effective to distinguish between profiles that do not share a majority of coordinates than existing alternatives like the Euclidean distance, the Pearson Correlation Coefficient or the Tanimoto Coefficient [27].

The cosine similarity between two vectors $v_1 = (w_1, x_1, y_1, z_1)$ and $v_2 = (w_2, x_2, y_2, z_2)$ is:

$$\frac{v_1 \cdot v_2}{||v_1|| \times ||v_2||} = \frac{w_1 \times w_2 + x_1 \times x_2 + y_1 \times y_2 + z_1 \times z_2}{\sqrt{w_1^2 + x_1^2 + y_1^2 + z_1^2} \times \sqrt{w_2^2 + x_2^2 + y_2^2 + z_2^2}}.$$

The cosine similarities between each pair of profiles is depicted in the symmetric Table 2.

3 Algorithms for Concurrency Control

To identify whether a specific concurrency control algorithm can benefit a particular workload, we choose four different transactional memory (TM) algorithms and four different contention managers algorithms (CM). The three TM algorithms are the following:

- **EagerAcq:** eager acquirement is a technique that consists of acquiring a lock on some shared variable immediately. To allow for read sharing, our transactions simply acquire a lock on the variables they attempt to update. With eager acquirement, the transaction acquires the lock before deciding to commit or abort.
- **InvWrite:** invisible write is the technique of deferring the write to the commit time of the transaction. With this approach a transaction that writes some shared variables lets concurrent transactions access the same variables between the time it "speculatively" writes them and the time it commits. This is the technique used in TL2 [9], it shortens the average protection duration of transactions by postponing all lock-acquirements to the commit phase.
- **WriteInPlace:** as opposed to invisible writes, writing in place consists of effectively updating the memory before reaching the commit. If the transaction aborts, then some compensating actions must be executed to roll-back the unsuccessful updates.

We also choose three different contention manager (CM) algorithms:

- **KillAttacker:** this strategy consists simply of choosing to abort the transaction that detects the conflict (the attacker) rather than the other conflicting transaction (the victim). A transaction is restarted immediately after it aborts.
- **ExpBackoff:** this strategy forces an aborting transaction to wait a duration that increases exponentially with the number of aborts before restarting. Once a transaction at some process commits, the next transaction executed by the same process starts without any delay.
- **Delay:** this strategy uses the same KillAttacker strategy without restarting a transaction immediately after it aborts. If a transaction aborts while trying to access a locked variable, the transaction waits until the lock is released before restarting.
- **Adaptive:** this strategy maintains multiple metadata like the number of restarts and a priority for each transaction to allow for a more elaborate CM implementation, upon conflict resolution the transaction with the lowest priority is aborted and after 4 restarts a transaction increases its priority to increase its chance of committing.

4 Performance Results

In this section, we show that the similarity between workload profiles helps choose a concurrency control that boosts performance and discard one that lowers performance.

4.1 Experimental Settings

The machine is a 32-way x86-64 Intel Xeon E5-2450 machine with 2 sockets of 8 hyperthreaded cores each running at 2.1 GHz Ubuntu 12.04.4 LTS and gcc 4.6.3.

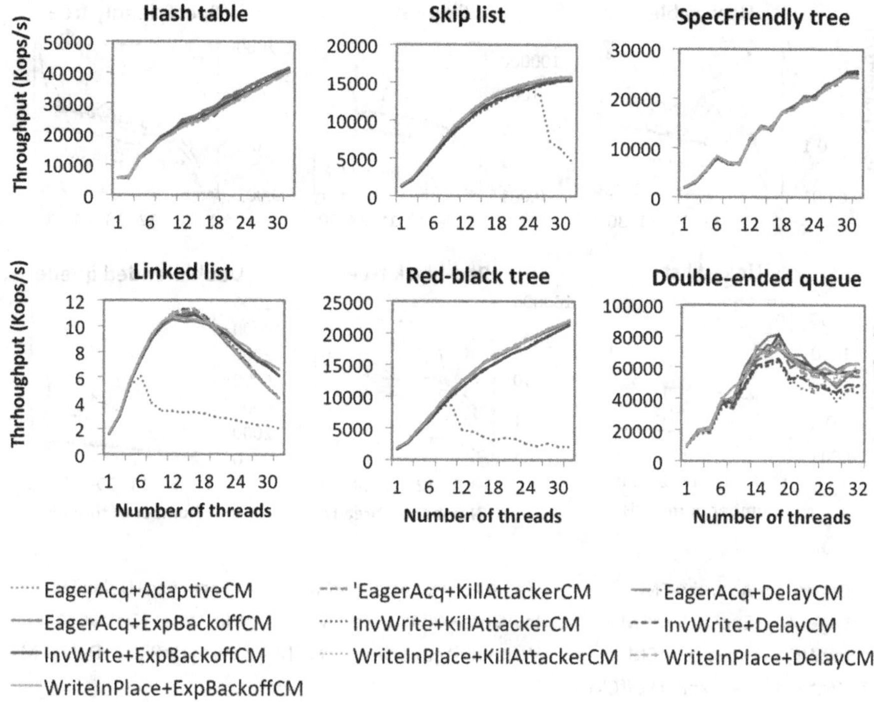

Fig. 1. The throughput of each concurrency control on various workloads when update rate is 10 %

In all our experiments, we used TinySTM v1.0B [11] and Synchrobench v1.1.0-alpha [13] to average the value over 5 runs of 2 s each for each individual point with 1, 2, 4, 8, 12, 16, 18, 20, 22, 24, 26, 28, 30 and 32 threads and update ratios 10 % and 50 % effective (except for the double-ended queue whose operations are only updates). All data structures have expected size of 2^{16} during the experiments. The reason of our choices is that TinySTM offers contention management and conflict resolution policies that are common to most TM algorithms and Synchrobench is the most comprehensive benchmark-suite for evaluating synchronization techniques. The transactional memory (TM) algorithms include invisible write with eager acquirement or lazy acquirement and visible write with eager acquirement. The contention manager (CM) algorithms include the delay contention manager that waits until a lock is released before restarting the transaction that aborted due to its acquirement attempt, the strategy of killing the (attacker) transaction that detects the conflicts with another (also called suicide), and the exponential back-off strategy that consists of waiting before restarting for a duration that increases exponentially each time the same transaction aborts.

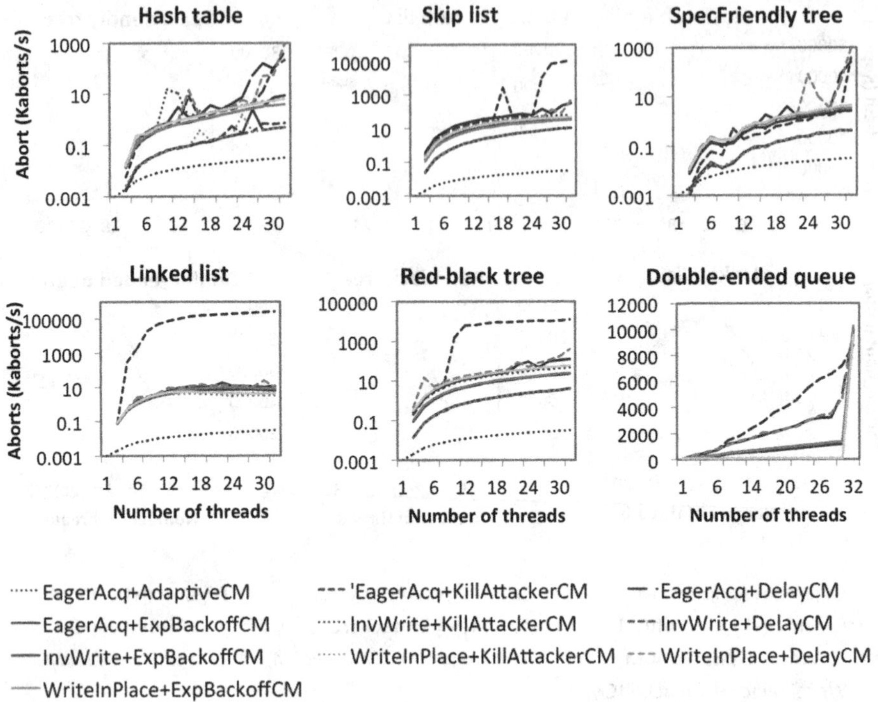

Fig. 2. The abort rate of each concurrency control on various workloads when update rate is 10 %

4.2 Similar Profiles

Figure 1 gives the throughput as thousands of operations per second for each workload with 10 % effective updates, meaning that 90 % of the operations never modify the structure. The two workloads with the closest (most similar) profiles are the red-black tree and the speculation-friendly AVL tree as they have the same structure, however, the transactions execute differently on one or the other because rebalancing is not executed as frequently. The speculation-friendly tree has also shorter transactions and separate local rotation transactions that involve a constant number of nodes whereas the global red-black tree rotation is one unique transaction [5]. Due to this difference, the red-black tree throughput suffers dramatically more from the use of EagerAcq and adaptive CM than the speculation-friendly tree. Figure 2 gives thousands of aborted transactions per second in log scale for each workload with 10 % of updates: the speculation-friendly tree does not abort as often as the red-black tree but we can see that WriteInPlace+Delay and EagerAcq+KillAttacker are combinations that trigger lots of abort on both structures.

Figures 3 and 4 give respectively the throughput and abort rate of each workload with 50 % of updates. The skip list and the red-black tree, which have very

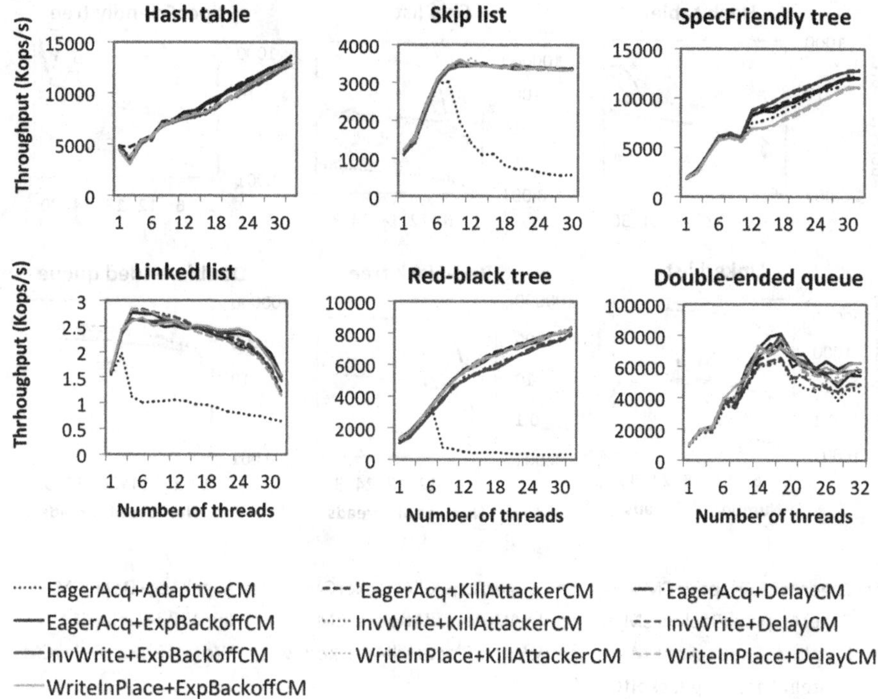

Fig. 3. The throughput of each concurrency control on various workloads when update rate is 50 %

close profile as well, experience very bad performance in the same scenario with a TM with eager acquirement and an adaptive CM. This phenomenon is exacerbated under higher contention as depicted in Fig. 3. Actually, such a concurrency control prevents the red-black tree from scaling up to 12 threads (resp. 8 threads) at 10 % updates (resp. 50 % updates) while it prevents the skip list from scaling to 26 threads (resp. 10 threads) at 10 % updates (resp. 80 % updates). Note that this is not necessarily the case for other workloads, as the speculation-friendly AVL and hash table experience reasonable performance with such a combination of algorithms. Interestingly, the deque and the linked list experience bad performance with the same combination, but it is clear that the drop in performance is relatively more significant in the case of the red-black tree and the skip list than the other workloads.

We also observe that the best combination for the skip list and the red-black tree are similar: they tend to be boosted by the write-in-place and the invisible write transactional strategies almost irrespective of the contention manager used in combination. Moreover, besides the EagerAcq+AdaptiveCM combination we can clearly see that any of the remaining combinations leads to performance that are close to the peak performance of each of these two workloads, hence

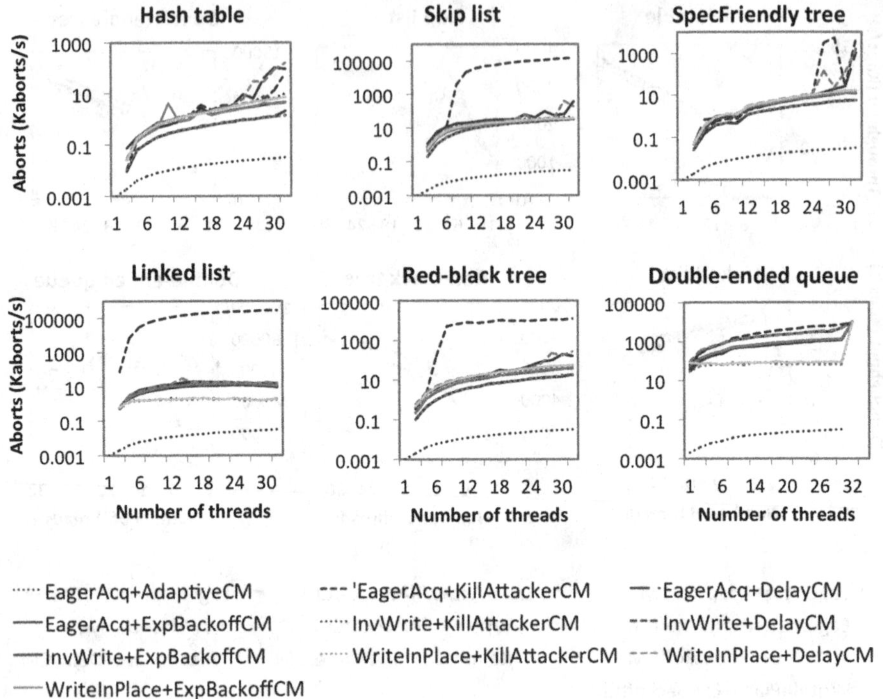

Fig. 4. The abort rate of each concurrency control on various workloads when update rate is 50 %

indicating that all could be chosen with negligible impact on the performance of these two workloads.

4.3 Different Profiles

The two workloads with the most different profiles, namely the linked list and the double-ended queue, experience very different performance results, which confirms the matching to their profile dissimilarities. An important remark is that our transactional algorithms are workload-oblivious, which is the reason why the linked list performance does not scale (we left the evaluation of more appropriate transactional algorithms, like Elastic [12] and Polymorphic transactions [15], to future work).

The first observation is that the overall performance of the linked list and double-ended queue (deque) is very different: the deque reaches the best peak performance while the linked list reaches the lowest performance of all workloads, which translates into a performance difference of up to 4 orders of magnitude between these two extremes. Note that the linked list implements a set whose operations may be read-only whereas the deque does not have read-only operations but the constant complexity of the deque pays off compared to the linear

Table 3. Empirical evaluation of the best and worst TM and CM algorithms for each workload

Workload	Hash table	Linked list	RB tree	AVL SF tree	Skip list	Deque
Best TM	EagerAcq	WriteInPlace	Inv. write	none	WrInPlace	WrInPlace
Worst TM	WriteInPlace	EagerAcq	EagerAcq	none	EagerAcq	InWrite
Best CM	ExpBackoff	KillAtt	Delay	ExpBackoff	KillAtt	ExpBackoff
Worst CM	Delay	Adaptive	Adaptive	Delay	Adaptive	KillAtt

complexity of the linked list. Second, these two workloads do not maximize their performance with the same algorithm, in particular, the best performance of the linked list is reached when using the "Kill Attacker" contention manager, which is actually the one that minimizes the performance of the deque, as summarized in Table 3. Third, the linked list shows very distinct performance results depending on the algorithm used whereas the performance of the deque may perform reasonably well with any concurrency control combination.

Interestingly, the same algorithm (EagerAcq+AdaptiveCM) minimizes the performance of the linked list, the red-black tree and the skip list workloads, which are all reasonably close. We can conclude that the workloads with similar profiles tend to show similar performance when synchronized with the same concurrency control while it is generally not the case for workloads of substantially different profiles.

5 Discussion

Our preliminary results rely on static profiles that are computed prior to performance evaluation and allow us to classify the best and worst concurrency controls as summarized in Table 3. For this technique to be widely adopted, it is necessary to feed this profile database at runtime with new workloads that run for some time with randomly chosen concurrency controls. Once the profile of the application is refined, the concurrency control that benefits workloads with similar profiles is chosen to run the given workload. This process is restarted as the database of profile is fed with new workloads.

A dynamic profiling at runtime can help progressively picking the right concurrency control as the system learns about a growing amount of applications. While there exist complex applications where a pattern evolves during the application execution, we also notice that many applications use a recurrent workload pattern (e.g., the STAMP vacation application [2] would exclusively use the red-black tree structure).

An interesting direction to explore is thus to fully integrate our solution within the applications so that each application could dynamically switch between concurrency controls depending on its current execution pattern. Our previous work on transaction polymorphism already proposes compatible concurrency controls within a single transactional memory system [14,15]. This compatibility guarantees that transactions that abort can safely restart using a more appropriate concurrency control mechanism while others are concurrently running with the old concurrency control. This integration will facilitate the learning phase where information regarding performance and workload profile criteria would be collected. Finally, it would be ideal for our solution to automatically adjusts itself by adapting the weight of criteria based on past tests and observed performance results.

6 Related Work

Wang et al. exploited machine learning techniques to choose the best algorithms to execute a particular transactional workload [21]. They characterize the profiles of various workloads, including three data structure workloads, by approximating the length of transactional and non-transactional executions in clock ticks. Here we study six different data structures and we focus on transactional code, hence using shared accesses rather than clock ticks to measure an execution length.

Castro et al. used machine learning for binding threads to cores to optimize transactional applications but not to select the most suitable concurrency control algorithms [4]. Interestingly, they extended their work to adapt thread affinity at runtime and identified two workload characteristics in common with ours—transaction size and contention—but to identify the best affinity, not the best concurrency control algorithm [3].

Rughetti et al. implemented a technique to select the level of concurrency that maximizes the performance of various applications including STAMP ones [22,23]. Didona et al. [10] determine dynamically the optimal level of parallelism by exploiting online exploration in shared memory transactional applications and machine learning in distributed transactional applications. One could benefit from our technique to select the ideal concurrency control before using theirs to select the ideal level of concurrency.

Existing transactional memory algorithms feature various transaction algorithms one can select statically, including TinySTM [11], RSTM [19], $\mathcal{E}$-STM [12] to name a few. Our work is motivated by the well-known observation that transactional workloads are known to be highly dependent on the concurrency control used [2].

Collaborative filtering was initially used to compute the similarity between documents by Singhal [26] and was then applied to the context of data mining to compute the similarity within the same cluster by Tan et al. [27] while Boutet et al. [1] recently applied it to distributed recommendation systems. Lucia and Ceze similarly exploited statistics in the Aviso framework [18] to predict the possibilities of bugs and to avoid appropriately the failures in future executions of the applications. Based on statistical inference Aviso schedules applications differently. The technique exploits collaboration among applications similarly to our approach but the goal of avoiding bugs differs from ours. As far we know, our work is the first to exploit recommendation systems in the context of concurrent applications.

7 Conclusion

Based on the similarities between transactional applications, we built a recommendation system to choose a concurrency control that maximizes performance depending on application similarities. Using 10 concurrency control mechanisms, our experiments show that the cosine similarity of 6 transactional workloads can be used to determine suitable concurrency controls. The similarities between a skip list and a red-black tree make their performance vulnerable to the same concurrency control algorithms. Finally, seemingly identical tree structures may have different profiles depending on their "speculation-friendliness", leading potentially to different performance with the same concurrency control.

Future work includes generalizing collaborative filtering on structures that use different synchronization primitives, including an efficient lock-based binary search tree [6] and CAS-based skip list [7]. The challenge here will be to propose the adequate synchronization techniques (e.g., lock, CAS and transaction) for an application based on its profile and the performance results observed with other applications.

References

1. Boutet, A., Frey, D., Guerraoui, R., Jégou, A., Kermarrec, A.-M.: WhatsUp decentralized instant news recommender. In: IPDPS (2013)
2. Minh, C.C., Chung, J.W., Kozyrakis, C., Olukotun, K.: STAMP: stanford transactional applications for multi-processing. In: IISWC (2008)
3. Castro, M., Góes, L.F.W., Fernandes, L.G., Méhaut, J.-F.: Dynamic thread mapping based on machine learning for transactional memory applications. In: Kaklamanis, C., Papatheodorou, T., Spirakis, P.G. (eds.) Euro-Par 2012. LNCS, vol. 7484, pp. 465–476. Springer, Heidelberg (2012)
4. Castro, M., Goes, L.F.W., Ribeiro, C.P., Cole, M., Cintra, M., Mehaut, J.-.F.: A machine learning-based approach for thread mapping on transactional memory applications. In: HIPC 2011, pp. 1–10 (2011)
5. Crain, T., Gramoli, V., Raynal, M.: A speculation-friendly binary search tree. In: PPoPP, pp. 161–170 (2012)
6. Crain, T., Gramoli, V., Raynal, M.: A contention-friendly binary search tree. In: Wolf, F., Mohr, B., an Mey, D. (eds.) Euro-Par 2013. LNCS, vol. 8097, pp. 229–240. Springer, Heidelberg (2013)
7. Crain, T., Gramoli, V., Raynal, M.: No hot spot non-blocking skip list. In: ICDCS, July 2013
8. David, T., Guerraoui, R., Trigonakis, V.: Everything you always wanted to know about synchronization but were afraid to ask. In: SOSP, pp. 33–48 (2013)
9. Dice, D., Shalev, O., Shavit, N.N.: Transactional locking II. In: Dolev, S. (ed.) DISC 2006. LNCS, vol. 4167, pp. 194–208. Springer, Heidelberg (2006)
10. Didona, D., Felber, P., Harmanci, D., Romano, P., Schenker, J.: Identifying the optimal level of parallelism in transactional memory applications. In: Gramoli, V., Guerraoui, R. (eds.) NETYS 2013. LNCS, vol. 7853, pp. 233–247. Springer, Heidelberg (2013)
11. Felber, P., Fetzer, C., Riegel, T.: Dynamic performance tuning of word-based software transactional memory. In: PPoPP, pp. 237–246 (2008)

12. Felber, P., Gramoli, V., Guerraoui, R.: Elastic transactions. In: Keidar, I. (ed.) DISC 2009. LNCS, vol. 5805, pp. 93–107. Springer, Heidelberg (2009)
13. Gramoli, V.: More than you ever wanted to know about synchronization: synchrobench, measuring the impact of the synchronization on concurrent algorithms. In: PPoPP, pp. 1–10 (2015)
14. Gramoli, V., Guerraoui, R.: Democratizing transactional programming. Commun. ACM **57**(1), 86–93 (2014)
15. Gramoli, V., Guerraoui, R.: Reusable concurrent data types. In: Jones, R. (ed.) ECOOP 2014. LNCS, vol. 8586, pp. 182–206. Springer, Heidelberg (2014)
16. Guerraoui, R., Herlihy, M., Pochon, B.: Toward a theory of transactional contention managers. In: PODC, pp. 258–264 (2005)
17. Herlihy, M., Luchangco, V., Moir, M., Scherer III, W.N.: Software transactional memory for dynamic-sized data structures. In: PODC, pp. 92–101 (2003)
18. Lucia, B., Ceze, L.: Cooperative empirical failure avoidance for multithreaded programs. In: ASPLOS, pp. 39–50 (2013)
19. Marathe, V.J., Spear, M.F., Heriot, C., Acharya, A., Eisenstat, D., Scherer III, W.N., Scott, M.L.: Lowering the overhead of software transactional memory. Technical report 893, University of Rochester, March 2006
20. Martin, M.M.K., Hill, M.D., Sorin, D.J.: Why on-chip cache coherence is here to stay. Commun. ACM **55**(7), 78–89 (2012)
21. Wang, Q., Kulkarni, S., Cavazos, J., Spear, M.: A transactional memory with automatic performance tuning. ACM Trans. Archit. Code Optim. **8**(4), 1–23 (2012)
22. Rughetti, D.: Autonomic concurrency regulation in software transactional memories. Ph.D. thesis, Sapienza University of Rome (2014)
23. Rughetti, D., Di Sanzo, P., Ciciani, B., Quaglia, F.: Machine learning-based self-adjusting concurrency in software transactional memory systems. In: IEEE MASCOTS, pp. 278–285 (2012)
24. Scherer III, W.N., Scott, M.L.: Advanced contention management for dynamic software transactional memory. In: PODC, pp. 240–248 (2005)
25. Scherer III, W.N., Scott, M.L.: Contention management in dynamic software transactional memory. In: Proceedings of the ACM PODC Workshop on Concurrency and Synchronization in Java Programs, July 2004
26. Singhal, A.: Modern information retrieval: a brief overview. Bull. IEEE Comput. Soc. Tech. Committee on Data Eng. **24**(4), 35–42 (2001)
27. Tan, P.-N., Steinbach, M., Kumar, V.: Introduction to Data Mining. Pearson Addison Wesley, Boston (2006)

Disaster-Tolerant Storage with SDN

Vincent Gramoli[1,2](✉), Guillaume Jourjon[1], and Olivier Mehani[1]

[1] NICTA, Sydney, Australia
vincent.gramoli@sydney.edu.au,
{guillaume.jourjon,olivier.mehani}@nicta.com.au
[2] University of Sydney, Sydney, Australia

Abstract. Cloud services are becoming centralized at several geo-replicated datacentres. These services replicate data within a single datacentre to tolerate isolated failures. Unfortunately, the effects of a disaster cannot be avoided, as existing approaches migrate a copy of data to backup datacentres *only after* data have been stored at a primary datacentre. Upon disaster, all data not yet migrated can be lost.

In this paper, we propose and implement *SDN-KVS*, a disaster-tolerant key-value store, which provides strong disaster resilience by replicating data *before* storing. To this end, SDN-KVS features a novel communication primitive, SDN-cast, that leverages Software Defined Network (SDN) in two ways: it offers an SDN-multicast primitive to replicate critical update request flows and an SDN-anycast primitive to redirect request flows to the closest available datacentre. Our performance evaluation indicates that SDN-KVS ensures no data loss and that traffic gets redirected across long distance key-value store replicas within 30 s after a datacentre outage.

1 Introduction

With the advent of cloud services, the computation needed by individuals is progressively becoming geo-centralised in datacentres. While effective in terms of management and costs, this centralisation puts services at risk in the face of disasters, such as earthquakes or nuclear power plant explosions, which can affect large geographical regions. Few years ago, these risks motivated Wall Street financial institutions to build datacentres outside the blast radius of a nuclear attack on New York City, creating a ring of land in New Jersey called the "Doughnut",[1] illustrated in Fig. 1. Located within a range of 30 to 70 km from the city centre, these backup datacentres aim to maintain rapid data transfer with the CBD to mitigate disasters.

Making services tolerant to disasters can be particularly challenging. Consider a fault-tolerant key-value store, which serves `get` and `put` requests from

NICTA is funded by the Australian Government through the Department of Communications and the Australian Research Council through the ICT Centre of Excellence Program.

[1] http://www.datacentreknowledge.com/archives/2008/03/10/new-york-donut-boosts-nj-data-centers/.

A. Bouajjani and H. Fauconnier (Eds.): NETYS 2015, LNCS 9466, pp. 293–307, 2015.
DOI: 10.1007/978-3-319-26850-7_20

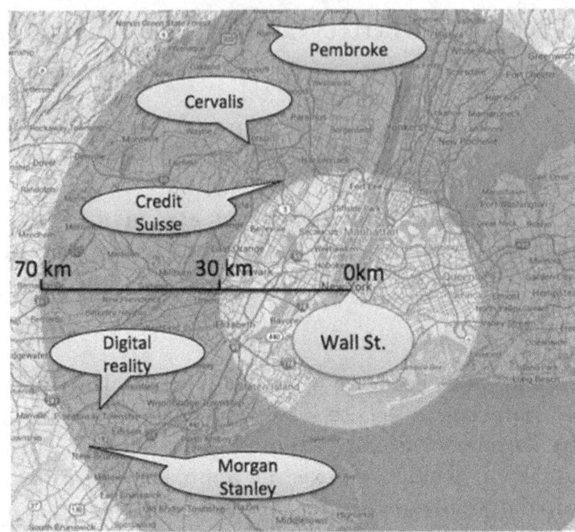

Fig. 1. The New York doughnut represents the locations where financial companies replicate their datacentres

clients; various possible implementations (*e.g.*, MongoDB, IBM's Spinnaker, Amazon's SimpleDB) are offered by cloud service providers. Despite their simplicity, these applications tolerate isolated failures but not disasters by instantly replicating the effect of an update, say a successful `put` request, to multiple servers in one (not multiple) datacentre. Existing alternatives can mitigate disaster effects with mirroring, replication and logging techniques across datacentres of distant geographical locations [15,16,19]. Typically, these solutions store the client data at one of these replicated datacentres before starting the migration to another datacentre as depicted in Fig. 2a. The challenge is then to minimise the migration delay as this may translate into some amount of data that can be lost during a disaster, also known as non-nil *Recovery Point Objective (RPO)* [17]. In this scenario, data are vulnerable to disasters between the time they are stored at the first datacentre and the time they are fully copied or logged at remote places. If a disaster affects the first datacentre, data stored but not migrated become unavailable until recovery or can even be definitely lost.

In this paper, we propose *SDN-KVS*, a consistent SDN-based Key-Value Store that adopts the opposite approach of *replicating before storing*. To this end, we leverage Software Defined Networks (SDN), namely the decoupling of control functions from the data processing and forwarding functions remotely controllable. In particular, we replicate the network flows even before data are actually stored at any datacentre as illustrated in Fig. 2b (this is the multicast feature of SDN-cast). Once the client issues a request to a particular datacentre, an SDN-enabled switch located at the edge of the network (outside any datacentre), duplicates the critical request flow and forwards a copy to two identical versions of the Key-Value Store service running at the targeted datacentre and

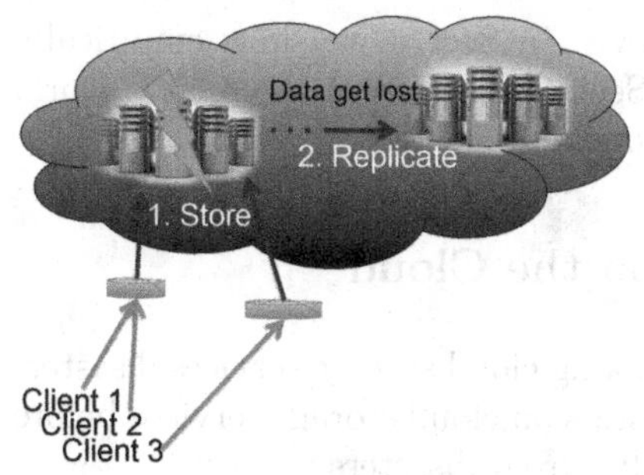

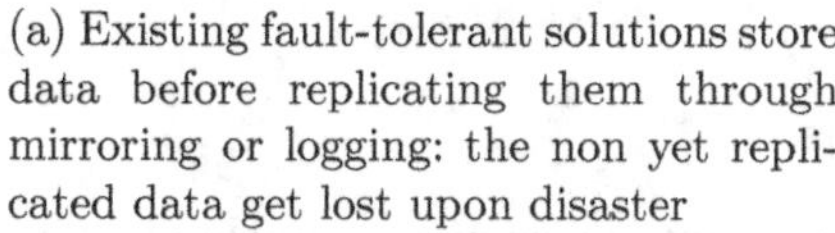

(a) Existing fault-tolerant solutions store data before replicating them through mirroring or logging: the non yet replicated data get lost upon disaster

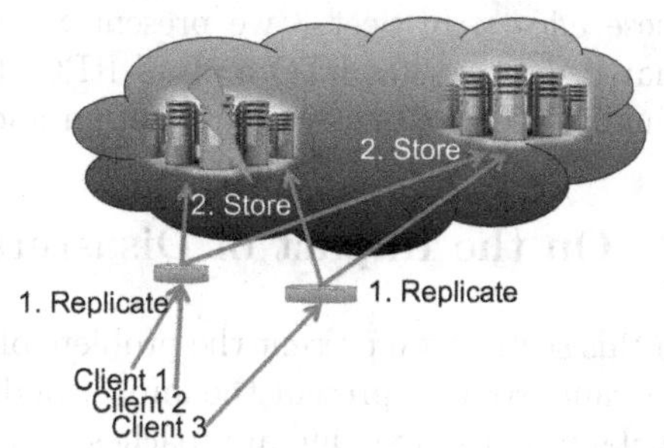

(b) SDN-cast replicates data before storing them: the network duplicates the critical traffic to remote datacentres

Fig. 2. SDN-cast proactively ensures data persistence as opposed to approaches that use a best effort recovery of data after disasters

at the backup datacentre. By duplicating the traffic at the network level, the storage application guarantees that the data is already replicated before it is stored. This is in contrast with previous solutions that require to first receive data before the mirroring, the replication or the remote logging of data can start.

Another consequence of disasters is the network outage that prevents remote clients from accessing the running backup service during a period of time, referred to as the *Recovery Time Objective (RTO)* [17]. More specifically, if a backup server starts rapidly operating using a different IP address, it may not be instantaneously accessible as refreshing DNS caches at the edge of the network could take hours or even days. The main problem is that the network itself takes a long time to recover from a disaster, hence delaying the application recovery. Our solution detects effectively outage at the network level to minimize RTO. The key to rapidly redirect the traffic to a backup datacentre is to distribute the network control that is usually centralized in the network core—typically in the datacentre network—to the network edge (this redirection is handled by the anycast feature of SDN-cast).

We evaluate SDN-KVS on top of an emulated wide area network connecting a client to two geo-replicated datacentres in Australia and Ireland, each running a copy of our key-value store application. Although not guaranteed to share the same state, our key-value store instances are strongly consistent and tolerate isolated failures by exploiting intra-datacentre replication but relies on our SDN-cast solution to cope with disasters. In this evaluation we demonstrate how SDN-multicast duplicates the flows between multiple datacentres while SDN-anycast detects edge failures in Sydney to redirect the traffic to the backup datacentre in Dublin. Results show that SDN-cast can achieve a nil RPO and a 30 s RTO, meeting higher disaster recovery objectives than any technique we are aware of.

The remainder of the paper is organised as follows. In Sect. 2, we evaluate the effects of disasters on data and explain how existing solutions aim at mitigating these effects. In Sect. 3 we present SDN-KVS. In Sect. 4 we show empirically that it ensures 30 s RTO and nil RPO. In Sect. 5, we present the related work. Finally, Sect. 6 discusses our solution and concludes.

2 On the Impact of Disasters on the Cloud

In this section, we present the problem of making cloud storage services disaster-tolerant. We first present the impact of disasters on cloud storage services before explaining why existing approaches may suffer from disasters.

2.1 The Case of Amazon Datacentres

Even common natural disasters can have important consequences on cloud computing services. On June 14th 2012, Amazon's datacentre in West Virginia (also known as its US-east-1 region) experienced a power outage of only half an hour. While the cause may seem negligible (severe storms), the consequences of this outage were dramatic for all the companies that relied on the Amazon Web Services running in West Virginia datacentre at that time. More precisely, the outage affected companies, like Pinterest and Instagram during up to 15 h[2], because the power outage induced a cascade of problems affecting the whole service infrastructure of these companies. Larger disasters, as the extreme heat that led to the 2012 India blackout whose power outage affected 9 % of the world population, could potentially have more important consequences.

In fact, datacentre service outages represent a key challenge of cloud computing. A recent survey indicates that the cumulative datacentre outage in the US in 2010 was 134 min, translating into a cost of $680,000. Three years later the datacentre service downtime reduced to 119 min, however, the related cost increased to $901,500. This cost increase reflects that more critical services are outsourced to the cloud environment making the financial loss more important in case of failures.[3]

Read-only cloud services, like web services, are easy to make tolerant to disasters. As long as the service does not store client-generated content, the service can simply be copied across geo-replicated datacentres to achieve disaster tolerance. In the Amazon US-east-1 region outage scenario, Netflix, which offers video-on-demand services, minimized service outage by simply redirecting the traffic towards a secondary Amazon datacentre.[4] The problem is more complex for services that store client-generated content: their customer may request updates at any time but require their requests to be safely stored in real-time. One popular example of such storage service is the key-value store service.

---

[2] https://gigaom.com/2012/06/29/some-of-amazon-web-services-are-down-again/.
[3] http://www.datacentreknowledge.com/archives/2013/12/03/study-cost-data-center-downtime-rising/.
[4] http://www.nytimes.com/2011/04/23/technology/23cloud.html.

2.2 Recovering a Storage Service After a Disaster

Key-value stores are cloud services popularized by the NoSQL movement that favoured simplicity over expressivity of data access. They offer a simple interface to manipulate key-value pairs, which exports `get`, `put` and `update` functions that respectively retrieve, insert and modify a pair of key and value. A key-value store achieves fault-tolerance by making sure that the effects of an update request (`put` and `update`) on a specific key-value pair get replicated at multiple servers.

While appealing, the replication needed for fault-tolerance also raises problems related to the consistency of data, as communication must occur between servers to ensure that the new value updated by a client is propagated to multiple servers. There are various forms of consistency provided by key-value stores ranging essentially from eventual consistency to strong consistency. To ensure the uniqueness of the value of a data, two concurrent updates of the same key, say `put(k,v)` and `put(k,v')` requests, should be consistently ordered by all servers. This can be achieved using timestamps computed based on the unique IP address of some server and a local counter that together "tag" the version of a value, indicating for example that `v'` is more up-to-date than `v`. This is similar to the technique used by multi-writer atomic register implementations in the message passing model [12].

Another consistency requirement is that a second update, issued after a first one on the same key has completed, should always have a value tagged with a later version. This requires that each request, whether it be a read-only, like a `get`, or an update, like a `put`, starts by requesting the current highest version to a *quorum* (*i.e.*, a mutually intersecting set) of servers before proceeding with propagating the most up-to-date value with the largest version. One example, employed by Dynamo [4] is to propagate any write request on a key to a quorum of two replicas of this key to guarantee fault tolerance of the data propagated. Using a quorum system, the read/write requests are strongly consistent. Note that a quorum system within a datacentre can be reconfigured to tolerate an unbounded number of isolated failures [3] but cannot tolerate disaster.

3 SDN-KVS: Disaster-Tolerant Key-Value Store

To tolerate failures and disasters our approach is twofold. As for fault-tolerance, we replicate all data within a datacentre where communication cost is low. This guarantees that the data persist despite isolated failures. We also replicate critical traffic (*e.g.*, `put` requests) to a datacentre towards a second datacentre located in a different region, similar to the backup datacentre in New Jersey. It is the responsibility of the client to distinguish normal from critical traffic (*e.g.*, by establishing separate connections), as cross-regions critical traffic experiences significant delays compared to non-critical traffic within a local region.

3.1 Correctness and Resilience Across Regions

Our key-value store guarantees the strongest form of consistency we know of, called linearizability [7]. Within the same datacentre this is ensured using quorum systems and global timestamp as previously discussed: fetching a key-value pair (resp. the highest version of the storage) requires to contact a set of servers that includes at least one of the servers where the last update of the corresponding pair (resp. the highest version of the storage) was replicated.

To globally guarantee strong consistency, we need additional requirements. Provided that remote datacentres share a common initial state, say as given by some common virtual machine image, replicating critical traffic across datacentres guarantees that critical data is not lost upon geo-localized disaster, even if an entire datacentre goes down. It is also important to guarantee that the key-value store services respond identically to write requests despite possible reordering of requests at distant locations. Our implementation actually acknowledges identically a put and an update even though the corresponding request does not succeed in updating the store. This ensures that when two distant servers receive two update requests in different order, the corresponding response is identical (simply acknowledged). Note that these requests necessarily come from distinct clients as our new SDN-cast primitive uses exclusively TCP as we describe below.

While linearizable, both datacentres may have distinct states because of distinct ordering of concurrent updates. As each client directly connects to the closest datacenter before or after a disaster, the only problem arises when a disaster occurs: the same client may read twice the same data item and observe a different results at the first datacentre right before the disaster and at the backup datacentre right after the disaster. In this case, we require that the client synchronises with the newly contacted datacentre before issuing requests (this is made possible as the application receives a RST packet in case of disaster as we describe later).

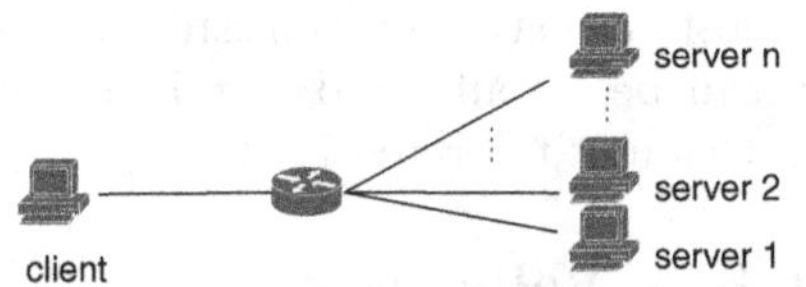

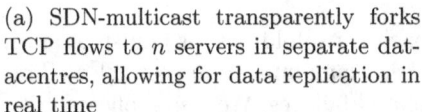

(a) SDN-multicast transparently forks TCP flows to n servers in separate datacentres, allowing for data replication in real time

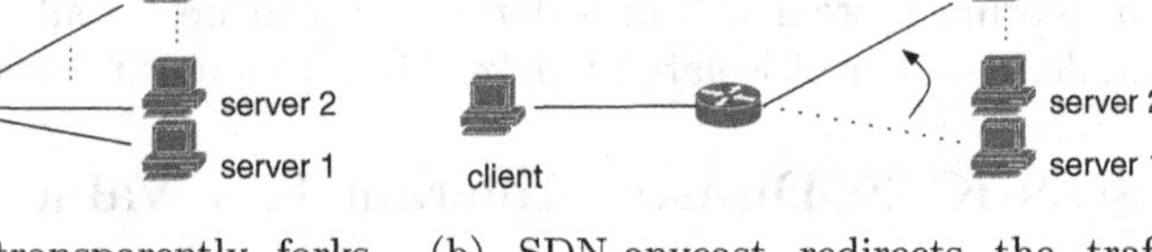

(b) SDN-anycast redirects the traffic from one server in the primary datacentre to the server of a remote available datacentre upon network outage detection

Fig. 3. SDN-cast (a) duplicates critical traffic to two datacentres before disasters and (b) redirects the traffic to the backup datacentre upon disaster

The two components of SDN-cast, namely SDN-multicast and SDN-anycast, are depicted in Fig. 3. When the client sends a critical (`put`) request to a datacentre, SDN-multicast forks the TCP connection to multiple datacentres, thereby replicating the information before storing it (see Sect. 3.2). This is transparent to the client: when it receives an acknowledgement, it has already been safely replicated at different geographical locations. This guarantees that the sent data will persist despite a disaster. SDN-multicast hence achieves a nil RPO for all successful critical requests.

Upon detection of a network disaster, SDN-anycast redirects the traffic to backup datacentres, thereby guaranteeing that the data can still be accessed. This is used both for access to the critical data, which was geo-replicated by SDN-multicast, and to redirect all traffic to the surviving datacentres. As opposed to other approaches, SDN-anycast uses network-level failure detection to achieve a RTO of about 30 s (see Sect. 3.3).

The control plane is located at the edge to cope with region-wide disasters. (Note that the case of a disaster occurring at the network edge is of limited interest as the client would be affected by the disaster even if the datacentres were not.)

3.2 SDN-Based Multicast for a Nil RPO

The forking mechanism can be placed anywhere on the path between clients and servers. When traffic destined to any server under its jurisdiction is received, it replicates the packets to the whole set of live servers. From the client's perspective, the forking mechanism maintains the end-to-end reliability semantics of TCP: data is acknowledged only when all live servers have acknowledged it. This mechanism is illustrated in Fig. 4 in the case of two servers.

In order not to break the TCP session on any side (client or servers) of the connection, special care must be taken when replicating the packets. The client sends data from its own sequence space, and so does each server. Sequence and acknowledgement numbers therefore need to be adjusted depending on the server before packets are sent. To do so the TCP forking mechanism records the initial sequence number on the first (SYN) return packet it sees (*dc1_seq* in Fig. 4). It then computes and stores an offset from the initial sequence number of each of the other servers ($Offset_2 = dc2\_seq - dc1\_seq$ in the figure). This offset is added to the sequence number of return packets, and subtracted from the acknowledgement number on replicated forward packets. This allows to map the client's view of the server's sequence space to the actual range used by each server.

Once the connection is properly open at the client and servers, the former can send any data, such as `put` instructions for the key–value store. The switch transparently duplicates the TCP stream to all live servers, and an acknowledgement is sent back to the client only once successfully received by all servers. This assumes that all servers to which the traffic is replicated reply with exactly the same message. This is not unreasonable, as all servers are identical, varying only in their location, and expected to handle the data they receive in the same way. The connection can finally be closed in a similar fashion, with FINs and ACKs being transparently replicated (and their sequence/ack numbers adjusted), until the slowest server closes its side, letting the client finalise its.

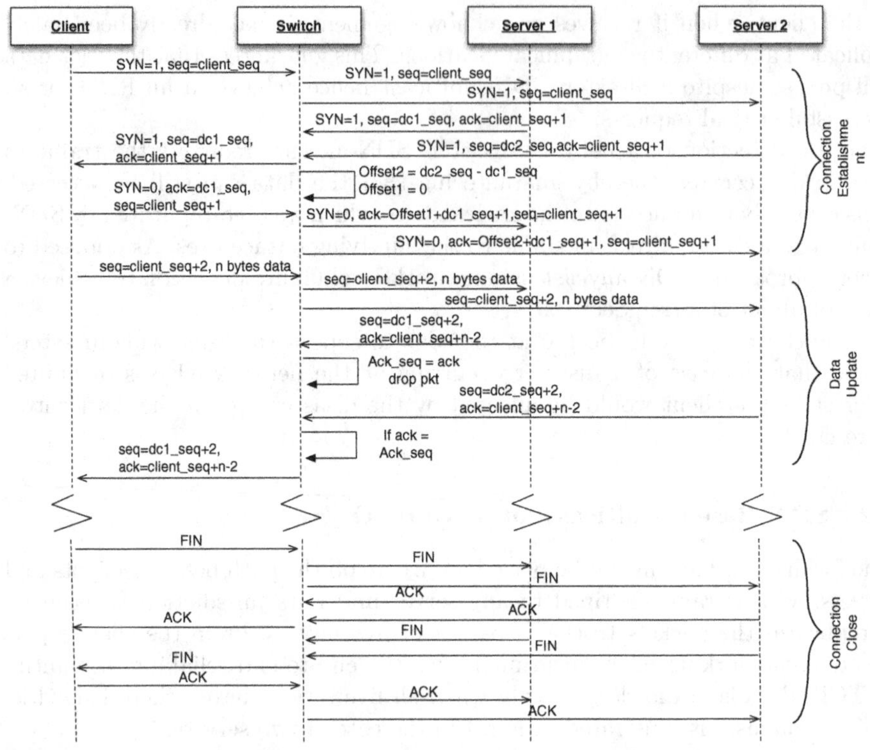

Fig. 4. Mechanism for forking a TCP connection: the client establishes a normal connection to Server 1; the Switch replicates the traffic to Server 2; return traffic from the servers is only forwarded to the client when both servers have replied; sequence numbers and acknowledgements are adjusted by recording and applying offsets between servers's sequence numbers as needed

It is important to note that only a few fields are manipulated in the switch. Sequence, or acknowledgement numbers—depending on the direction of the traffic—have a static offset applied. SACK options are left untouched, but forcefully disabled during the initial handshake to force a fallback to cumulative ACKs. Beyond these changes, the TCP packet is left untouched. This allows to leverage the TCP stacks of the endpoints (client and servers) to take care of rate adaptation and loss recovery. As the end-to-end semantics and control of TCP is preserved, the client and servers will however exchange packets as allowed by the slowest link.

3.3 SDN-Based Anycast for Minimum RTO

SDN-anycast uses SDN-enabled switches connected to controllers located at the edge of the network to redirect flows upon network outage. In order to decide when to start the redirection, we propose a mechanism inside the edge controller. As SDN-anycast can detect network outage using lower level protocols (*e.g.*, LLDP, ICMP or transport timeouts, as used in Algorithm 1), it can responsively redirect the traffic with minimum delays. This detection algorithm takes information from the various edge switches while the decision is centrally taken by the SDN controller responsible for these switches. This centralised algorithm, presented in Algorithm 1, aims to minimise the RTO depending on the number of services currently deployed.

```
Data: Client flow to service
Result: Possible detection of failure
detection;
if duplicate packet from client then
    possibleFailure ++ ;
    if possibleFailure ≥ Threshold then
        add action to rewrite packets for Service to alternative server ;
        for every connections affected by failure do
            send RST packet ;
        end
    end
else
    if packet from Service then
        possibleFailure = 0;
    end
end
```

Algorithm 1. Detection of server failure through TCP timeouts, and mitigation by forcing a new connection

4 Experimental Evaluation

In this section, we show empirically that SDN-anycast recovers the throughput and latency of the key-value store service within RTO $\leq$ 30 s and that SDN-multicast increases the cumulated goodput by forking TCP connections between a single client and multiple geo-replicated datacentres to achieve nil RPO with no client or inter-datacentre overhead. We used Mininet [6] and the Python-based POX controller to evaluate the performance of our geo-replicated key-value store in the face of disaster.

4.1 Recovering Storage Service with SDN-Anycast

To evaluate the Recovery Time Objective (RTO) SDN-cast achieves, we deployed our solution over a topology comprising a local datacentre in Sydney, Australia, and a remote one of in Dublin, Ireland (see Fig. 5). These are the current respective locations of Amazon's existing AP-southeast-2 and EU-west-1 regions. Note that this represents one of the greatest distance between datacentres worldwide (~17,200 km) whereas most backup datacentres are located within only 30–70 km from the primary datacentre, as we illustrated in Fig. 1. Both datacentres run the same image of the service in the same initial empty state replicated on a distributed system of 9 machines with quorums of size 5.

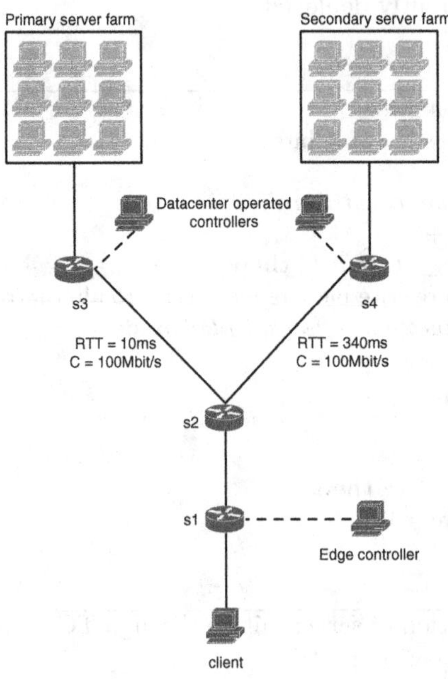

Fig. 5. Experimental topology deployed in Mininet to represent a client accessing a local datacentre in Sydney (left) and a remote datacentre in Dublin, Ireland (right)

The link from switches s_2 to s_3 has a one-way delay of 5 ms and a capacity of 100 Mbit/s whereas the link from s_2 to s_4 has a delay of 170 ms and a capacity of 100 Mbit/s (the RTT between the Sydney and Ireland Amazon EC2 datacentres is about 340 ms). Inside each datacentre, we have configured a key–value store over a quorum system of nine servers, meaning that a server receiving `put`, `update` or `get` requests exchanges messages with 8 or 9 other replicas before acknowledging the client of the success of its request, hence guaranteeing a high level of intra-datacentre fault tolerance. Both switches s_3 and s_4 act as load balancers inside each datacentre.

Our experiment scenario is as follows. At time $t = 0$, one of the client starts reading from the local datacentre as fast as possible, filling the pipe between s_2 and s_3. At time $t = 200$, we emulate a disaster by cutting the link between s_2 and s_3. Once the connection is cut, the TCP client starts retransmitting unacknowledged packets. The controller can therefore learn that a possible disaster has occurred in the network. As we fixed the detection threshold described

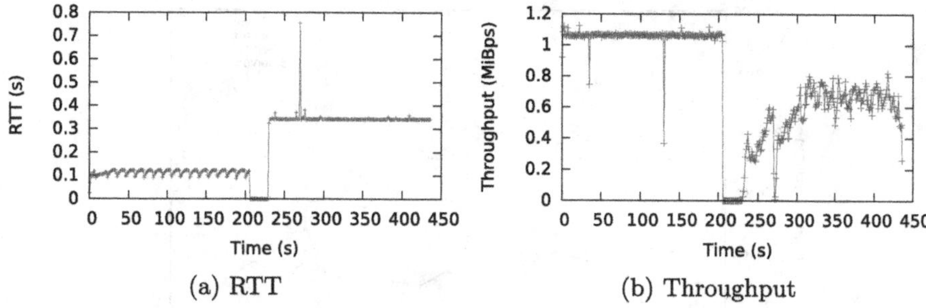

(a) RTT (b) Throughput

Fig. 6. SDN-anycast allows to achieve fast service recovery (*i.e.*, RTO $\leq$ 30 s) and no data loss (*i.e.*, nil RPO) across the globe

in Algorithm 1 to 5 packets, the waiting period varies from 15 to 25 s. After this inactive period, the controller instructs the switch to redirect traffic to the secondary datacentre, and to terminate the connections with the now-defunct primary datacentre. The client then reconnects to the service with the same IP address but traffic is directed to the second datacentre.

In Fig. 6, we present RTT and throughput measurements extracted from the captured trace at the client side. Figure 6a shows the RTT computed by the TCP sender. In particular, we can see that during the first 200 s the flow experienced an RTT of around 100 ms. During the second 200 s period, the flow experiences a minimum RTT of 340 ms necessary to reach the remote datacentre. Figure 6b presents the throughput achieved by the TCP flow. As expected, when the delay is short, the TCP connection is able to fill the pipe when accessing the local datacentre. With a larger RTT it however becomes impossible for TCP to fully utilise the pipe. Nonetheless, the connection was successfully switched over to the Irish datacentre when the Sydney one failed. Using this technique, we empirically observed an RTO lower than 30 s.

4.2 Service Goodput of SDN-Multicast

The benefit of SDN-multicast in our scenario is to avoid the need of application-level replication, as it directly integrates the same service within the network. This reduces the number of communication between members of a group.

More specifically, a client process sends a message to a group of server processes by initiating a single TCP connection through which it sends multiple messages. All messages are reliably delivered in-order to all servers. The TCP acknowledgements are simply collected at the switch level. Once all servers have acknowledged a specific sequence, the switch forwards the acknowledgement to the client.

In order to illustrate this use-case, we deployed our forking solution over a simple topology similar to the one presented in Fig. 3b where we varied the number of servers from 1 to 6. In this series of experiments we set identical RTTs between the set of servers and the client, and links capacity to 100 Mbit/s.

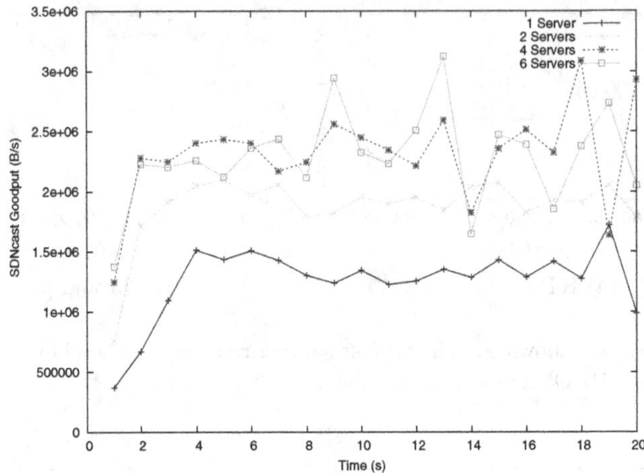

Fig. 7. Performance evaluation of SDN-multicast to up to 6 datacenters concurrently

Figure 7 presents the service goodput, defined as the number of bytes transmitted and acknowledged by all servers, as a function of time. As OpenFlow ≤1.3 does not currently offer actions to rewrite TCP sequence or acknowledgement fields, we had to let the switches forward all packets to the controller, hence creating a significant overhead and loss of performances: ideally, we would have expected a linear relation between the number of servers and the gain in goodput. Nevertheless, we can observe that our solution increases the service goodput. We envision this increase to become even more significant when OpenFlow switches support the necessary actions.

5 Related Work

Synchronous Replication. Data persistence in case of disasters was explored in the context of databases [5] and gained momentum recently with the geo-centralization of data in cloud datacentres. While asynchronous replication [10,16] was shown in practice to be effective to limit bandwidth consumption, synchronous replication is needed to prevent data losses [15,19]. Synchronous replication requires first to store the data then to replicate the data somewhere else before acknowledging the client, a lengthy process generally suited for relatively short distances. Our approach is the opposite: first to replicate the traffic to store data at multiple locations concurrently before acknowledging the client.

Manipulation of Network Flows. Many solutions have been proposed, over the last fifteen years, to extend network functionalities. They generally vary in terms of the layer at which they are implemented and the location (*e.g.*, end-host, edge or core) of their deployment. Table 1 compares the features of various proposals, presented below, to SDN-cast, in terms of multicast capabilities, geo-localized disaster recovery and transparency to the client.

Table 1. Feature comparison of SDN-cast with related work

	NAT	TCP Splice [13]	Flow Aggregation [2]	MPTCP [1] SCTP	Any-cast [18]	Dr. Multi-cast	SDN-Cast
Multicast	×	×	×	×	×	✓	✓
Recovery	×	×	×	✓	✓	×	✓
Transparency	✓	×	×	×	✓	×	✓

Similar to our proposal, solutions based on middle-boxes have been widely adopted in today's Internet. In particular, Network Address Translation (NAT) offers transparent static redirection services to end-user applications, and are generally deployed at the edge of the networks. TCPSplice [13] is a kernel-land TCP proxy allowing to intercept and redirect TCP sessions. Unlike application proxies, it offers near router speed performance. To mitigate the problems introduced by wireless communication, and use the links more efficiently, a flow aggregator inside a TCP proxy was proposed to allow to adapt the protocol to better use GSM links [2]. thoroughly studied [8,14]. Although they provide many advantages, it is well-known that they introduce limitations for the evolution of end-to-end protocol such as TCP [8]. Nonetheless, as compared to our in-network layer-4 switch proposal, none of these solutions support both dynamic redirection of traffic and flow replication to multiple destinations.

Transport protocols supporting multiple paths such as MPTCP [1] or SCTP allows the use multiple paths within the same transport session. This is instrumental in supporting network fail-over by switching from one interface to another without connection disruption. However, switching conditions are hard-coded in the transport, and cannot be adjusted depending on arbitrary parameters. Unlike SDN-multicast, however, each end-to-end sessions can only be established to a single host, and cannot be failed-over to different, or multicasted to several, servers. Moreover, both protocols require support at both end-hosts to be used.

Dr. Multicast [18] provides multicast functionalities by coping with the limited scalability of IP multicast within one datacentre, however, it is not transparent as it requires the client to catch system calls and converts IP multicast addresses.

Software Defined Network (SDN). SDN offers inherent fault tolerance capabilities by allowing a controller to use lower layer signals such as LLDP to detect link failures in a timely fashion, and to adjust the behaviour of the switches it controls. This technique has therefore been suggested to reconfigure networks upon failures, especially in the context of datacentre networking [9]. SDN was recently used to mitigate the effects of disasters [20], similarly to our SDN-anycast feature. The goal was however to use alternative network paths in case of path failures, and this solution does not cope with the problem of data loss that SDN-multicast addresses: it only mitigates the effects of disasters rather than avoiding them. The use of multiple controllers was already shown effective in reducing the fault-tolerance of a particular SDN using NOX controllers and the Mininet virtualised environment [11]. In SDN-multicast, we leverage these capabilities to implement layer-4 switching mechanisms to improve RTOs and RPOs.

6 Discussion and Conclusion

We proposed SDN-KVS, a disaster-tolerant storage that exploits a novel SDN-cast communication paradigm to avoid losses of critical data. Even at extreme distances (Australia to Ireland), SDN-KVS achieves a 30 s RTO and guarantees that storage requests survive region-wide disasters.

As our solution is deployed at the end of the common path towards all servers (*e.g.*, leaf network edge or local ISP), the forking mechanism saves resources along that path by removing the need for multiple connection carrying the same traffic. We envision that as a side effect, it could potentially reduce bufferbloat issues by only using one TCP stream instead of one per server for the same data.

Our solution allows multicasting of TCP streams transparently to the client side. Due to its layer 4 orientation, it ignores any payload. While this is desirable for performance reasons in most cases, this is problematic if some application parameters need to be negotiated between client and server. This is particularly the case for SSL sessions, as each servers would try to negotiate a different session with the client. To provide similar levels of security, IPSec would be a better candidate for use with our forking mechanism.

The current version of OpenFlow (v.1.4) limits the capabilities of SDN-multicast. In particular, we were limited, in the forking experiment by the lack of support for manipulation of the acknowledgement and sequence number fields in the TCP header. It is also unclear whether arithmetic operations such as additions or subtractions of offsets are readily available. We believe that such actions should be considered for addition in future OpenFlow specifications.

For our solution to be widely-adopted, the SDN-anycast information should be made accessible to ISPs to reconfigure efficiently the network. By proactively redirecting traffic to live servers upon disaster, our SDN-anycast could simplify the task of edge ISP forensic departments as it would prevent a large number of connection establishments failures due to downstream disasters that would have triggered DDoS investigation procedures.

References

1. Barré, S., Bonaventure, O., Raiciu, O., Handley, M.: Experimenting with multipath TCP. In: SIGCOMM, pp. 443–444 (2010)
2. Chakravorty, R., Katti, S., Crowcroft, J., Pratt, I.: Flow aggregation for enhanced TCP over wide-area wireless. In: INFOCOM (2003)
3. Chockler, G., Gilbert, S., Gramoli, V., Musial, P.M., Shvartsman, A.A.: Reconfigurable distributed storage for dynamic networks. J. Parallel Distrib. Comput. **69**(1), 100–116 (2009)

4. DeCandia, G., Hastorun, D., Jampani, M., Kakulapati, G., Lakshman, A., Pilchin, A., Sivasubramanian, S., Vosshall, P., Vogels, W.: Dynamo: amazon's highly available key-value store. In: SOSP, pp. 205–220 (2007)
5. Garcia-Molina, H., Polyzois, C.A., Hagmann, R.B.: Two epoch algorithms for disaster recovery. In: VLDB, pp. 222–230 (1990)
6. Handigol, N., Heller, B., Jeyakumar, V., Lantz, B., McKeown, N.: Reproducible network experiments using container-based emulation. In: CoNEXT, pp. 253–264 (2012)
7. Herlihy, M., Wing, J.: Linearizability: a correctness condition for concurrent objects. ACM Trans. Program. Lang. Syst. **12**(3), 463–492 (1990)
8. Honda, M., Nishida, Y., Raiciu, C., Greenhalgh, A., Handley, M., Tokuda, H.: Is it still possible to extend TCP? In: IMC (2011)
9. Jain, S., Kumar, A., Mandal, S., Ong, J., Poutievski, L., Singh, A., Venkata, S., Wanderer, J., Zhou, J., Zhu, M., Zolla, J., Hölzle, U., Stuart, S., Vahdat, A.: B4: experience with a globally-deployed software defined WAN. In: SIGCOMM, pp. 3–14 (2013)
10. Ji, M., Veitch, A.C., Wilkes, J.: Seneca: remote mirroring done write. In: ATC, pp. 253–268 (2003)
11. Kim, J., Santos, J.R., Turner, Y., Schlansker, M., Tourrilhes, J., Feamster, N.: CORONET: fault tolerance for software defined networks. In: ICNP (2012)
12. Lynch, N., Shvartsman, A.: Robust emulation of shared memory using dynamic quorum-acknowledged broadcasts. In: FTCS, pp. 272–281 (1997)
13. Maltz, D., Bhagwat, P.: TCP splicing for application layer proxy performance, RC 21139. IBM, March 1998
14. Medina, A., Allman, M., Floyd, S.: Measuring interaction between transport protocols and middleboxes. In: IMC, pp. 336–341 (2004)
15. Oracle: Oracle optimized solution for disaster recovery on oracle supercluster (2013)
16. Patterson, R.H., Manley, S., Federwisch, M., Hitz, D., Kleiman, S., Owara, S.: SnapMirror: file-system-based asynchronous mirroring for disaster recovery. In: FAST, pp. 117–129 (2002)
17. Verma, A., Voruganti, K., Routray, R., Jain, R.: SWEEPER: an efficient disaster recovery point identification mechanism. In: FAST, pp. 297–312 (2008)
18. Vigfusson, Y., Abu-Libdeh, H., Balakrishnan, M., Birman, K., Burgess, R., Chockler, G., Li, H., Tock, Y.: Dr. multicast: Rx for data center communication scalability. In: EuroSys, pp. 349–362 (2010)
19. Wood, T., Lagar-Cavilla, H.A., Ramakrishnan, K.K., Shenoy, P., Van der Merwe, J.: PipeCloud: using causality to overcome speed-of-light delays in cloud-based disaster recovery. In: SoCC, pp. 17:1–17:13 (2011)
20. Xie, A., Wang, X., Wang, W., Lu, S.: Designing a disaster-resilient network with software defined networking. In: IWQoS, pp. 135–140, May 2014

On the Complexity of Linearizability

Jad Hamza(✉)

LIAFA, Université Paris Diderot, Paris, France
jhamza@liafa.univ-paris-diderot.fr

Abstract. It was shown in Alur et al. [1] that the problem of verifying finite concurrent systems through Linearizability is in EXPSPACE. However, there was still a complexity gap between the easy to obtain PSPACE lower bound and the EXPSPACE upper bound. We show in this paper that Linearizability is EXPSPACE-complete.

1 Introduction

Linearizability [8] is the standard consistency criterion for concurrent data-structures. Filipovic et al. [5] proved that checking that a library L is linearizable with respect to a specification S is equivalent to observational refinement. Formally, as long as linearizability holds, any multi-threaded program using the specification S as a library can safely replace it by L, without adding any unwanted behaviors.

Many practical tools [3,4,11–13] for checking linearizability or detecting linearizability violations exist, and here is a short summary of the work done on the complexity.

Checking that a single execution is linearizable is already an NP-complete problem [7]. Moreover, Alur et al. [1] showed that the problem of checking Linearizability for finite concurrent libraries used by a finite number of threads is in EXPSPACE when the specification is a regular language. The best known lower bound is PSPACE-hardness, obtained from a simple reduction of the reachability problem for finite concurrent programs [1], leaving a large complexity gap.

This result was refined in Bouajjani et al. [2] where it was shown that a simpler variant of Linearizability – called Static Linearizability, or Linearizability with fixed linearization points – is PSPACE-complete for the same class of libraries.

Furthermore, Linearizability is undecidable when the number of threads is unbounded [2]. Tools used for detecting linearizability violations often start by underapproximating the set of executions by bounding the number of threads. It is thus necessary to develop a better understanding of Linearizability for a bounded number of threads.

We prove that Linearizability is EXPSPACE-complete, showing that there is an inherent difficulty to the problem. We introduce for this a new problem on regular languages, called Letter Insertion. This problem can be reduced in polynomial time to Linearizability.

A. Bouajjani and H. Fauconnier (Eds.): NETYS 2015, LNCS 9466, pp. 308–321, 2015.
DOI: 10.1007/978-3-319-26850-7_21

We then show that Letter Insertion is EXPSPACE-hard, closing the complexity gap for Linearizability. Our proof is similar to the proofs of EXPSPACE- hardness for the problems of inclusion of extended regular expressions with intersection operator, or interleaving operator, given in Hunt [9], Fürer [6] and Mayer and Stockmeyer [10]. They all use a similar encoding of runs of Turing machines as words, and using the problem at hand, Letter Insertion in this case, to recognize erroneous runs.

To summarize, our two contributions are:

- finding the Letter Insertion problem, a problem equivalent to Linearizability, but which has a very simple formulation in terms of regular automata,
- using this problem to show EXPSPACE-hardess of Linearizability.

We recall in Sect. 2 the definition of Linearizability, and we introduce the Letter Insertion problem. We show in Sect. 3 that Letter Insertion can be reduced in polynomial time to Linearizability. And finally, we show in Sect. 4, that Letter Insertion is EXPSPACE-hard, which is the most technical part of the paper. When combined, Sects. 3 and 4 show that Linearizability is EXPSPACE-hard.

2 Definitions

2.1 Libraries

In the usual sense, a *library* is a collection of *methods* that can be called by other programs. We start by giving our formalism for methods, and define libraries as sets of methods.

In order to simplify the presentation, and since they do not affect our EXPSPACE-hardness reduction, we will use a number of restrictions on the methods. First, we will define the methods without return values and parameters. Second, each instruction of a method can either read or write to the shared memory, but we don't formalize atomic compare and set operations. Finally, we limit ourselves to a unique *shared variable*.

Let $\mathbb{D}$ be a finite set used as the *domain* for the shared variable and let $d_0 \in \mathbb{D}$ be a special value considered as initial.

A *method* is a tuple (Q, δ, q_0, q_f) where

- Q is the set of states,
- $\delta \subseteq Q \times \{\mathsf{read}, \mathsf{write}\} \times \mathbb{D} \times Q$
- $q_0 \in Q$ is the initial state (in which the method is called)
- $q_f \in Q$ is the final state (in which the method can return)

One point which might be considered unusual in our formalism is that a read instruction *guesses* the value that it is going to read. In usual programming languages, this can be understood as first reading a variable, and then having an assume statement to constrain the value of the read variable. This formalism choice is a presentation choice, and has no effect on the complexity of the problem.

As hinted previously, a *library* $Lib = \{M_1, \ldots, M_m\}$ is a set of methods. For every $j \in \{1, \ldots, m\}$, let $(Q^j, \delta^j, q_0^j, q_f^j)$ be the tuple corresponding to M_j. We define Q to be the (disjoint) union of all Q^j.

Let k be an integer representing the number of *threads* using *Lib*. Threads run concurrently and call the methods of *Lib* arbitrarily. The system composed of k threads calling arbitrarily the methods of *Lib* is called Lib^k.

Formally, a *configuration* of Lib^k is a pair $\gamma = (d, \mu)$ where $d \in \mathbb{D}$ is the current value of the shared variable and μ is a map from $\{1, \ldots, k\}$ to $Q \uplus \{\bot\}$, specifying, for each thread i, the state in which the method called by thread i is. The symbol $\bot$ is used for threads which are *idle* (not calling any method at the moment).

A *step* from a configuration $\gamma = (d, \mu)$ to $\gamma' = (d', \mu')$ can be:

- thread i calling method j, denoted by $\gamma \xrightarrow{\texttt{call}(i, M_j)} \gamma'$, with $\mu(i) = \bot$, $\mu' = \mu[i \leftarrow q_0^j]$, and $d' = d$,
- thread i returning from method j, denoted by $\gamma \xrightarrow{\texttt{ret}(i)} \gamma'$, with $\mu(i) = q_f^j$, $\mu' = \mu[i \leftarrow \bot]$, and $d' = d$,
- thread i doing a read in method j, denoted by $\gamma \rightarrow \gamma'$ (no label) with $\mu(i) = q \in M_j$, $\mu' = \mu[i \leftarrow q']$, $(q, \mathsf{read}, d, q') \in \delta^j$, and $d' = d$,
- thread i doing a write in method j, denoted by $\gamma \rightarrow \gamma'$ (no label) with $\mu(i) = q \in M_j$, $\mu' = \mu[i \leftarrow q']$, $(q, \mathsf{write}, d', q') \in \delta^j$.

An *execution* of Lib^k is a sequence of steps $\gamma_0 \rightarrow \gamma_1 \ldots \rightarrow \gamma_l$ where $\gamma_0 = (d_0, \mu_0)$, with $\mu_0(i) = \bot$ for all i, is the initial configuration.

The *trace* h of an execution is the sequence of labels (call's and return's) of its steps. The set of traces of Lib^k is denoted by $Traces(Lib^k)$. Note that in a trace, a call event may be without a corresponding return event (if the method has not returned yet). In which case, the call event is said to be *open*. A trace with no open calls in called *complete*.

Given a complete trace h, we define for each pair of matching call and return events a *method event*. We say that a method event e_1 *happens before* another method event e_2 if the return event of e_1 is before the call event of e_2 in h; this defines a *happen-before* relation on the method events. The *label* of a method event is the method name corresponding to its call event.

2.2 Linearizability

Let h be a trace of $Traces(Lib^k)$ for some library *Lib* and integer k. A complete trace h' is said to be a *completion* of h if we can remove some (possibly zero) open calls from h, as well as close some others open calls (possibly zero) by adding return events at the end of h in order to obtain h'.

A *specification* for a library $Lib = \{M_1, \ldots, M_m\}$ is a language of finite words S over the alphabet $\{M_1, \ldots, M_m\}$.

Definition 1 (Linearizability). *A complete trace h is said to be* linearizable *with respect to a specification S if there exists a total order on the method events,* *respecting the happen-before order, such that the corresponding sequence of labels is a word in S. A trace h is said to be* linearizable *with respect to S if it has a completion which is linearizable (with respect to S).*

Problem 1 (Linearizability). Input: A library $Lib = \{M_1, \ldots, M_m\}$, a non-deterministic finite automaton (NFA) S representing the specification, and an integer k given in unary.

Question: Are all the traces of $Traces(Lib^k)$ linearizable w.r.t. S?

Note: the size of the input is the size of all the automata appearing in the input (number of states + number of transitions + size of the alphabet) to which we add k.

We give in Figs. 1, 2, and 3 some examples to illustrate Linearizability. To represent executions, we draw a method event as an interval, where the left end of the interval corresponds to the call event of the method event, and the right end corresponds to the return event. This way, when two method events overlap, they can be ordered arbitrarily, but when a method event e_1 is completely before a method event e_2, e_1 has to be ordered before e_2.

Above an interval, we write the name of the method corresponding to the method event, and below, we write the (unique) name of the method event.

These executions can be seen as being produced by concrete libraries whose goal is to implement the *atomic* specification: $S = (M_A M_B)^*$. Figure 1 represents an execution which is linearizable, since its method events can be ordered as the sequence $e_1e_2e_3e_4$, whose corresponding sequence of labels is $M_A M_B M_A M_B$. Figure 2 represents an execution which is linearizable, since its method events can be ordered as the sequence $e_1e_2e_3e_4e_5e_6$, whose corresponding sequence of labels is $M_A M_B M_A M_B M_A M_B$. Figure 3 represents an execution which is similar to Fig. 1 but is not linearizable. A library producing the execution in Fig. 3 would thus not be linearizable with respect to S.

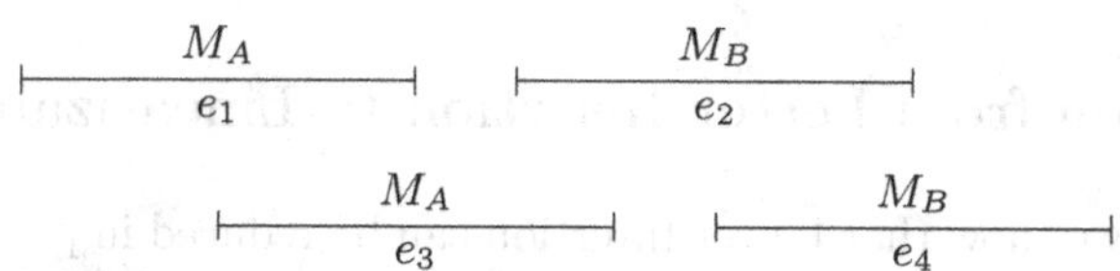

Fig. 1. A linearizable execution, which can be ordered as $e_1e_2e_3e_4$

2.3 Letter Insertion

We were able to define a new problem, *Letter Insertion*, which: (1) can be reduced to Linearizability, (2) is very easy to state (compared to Linearizability), (3) is still complex enough to capture the difficult part of Linearizability as we'll show it is EXPSPACE-hard.

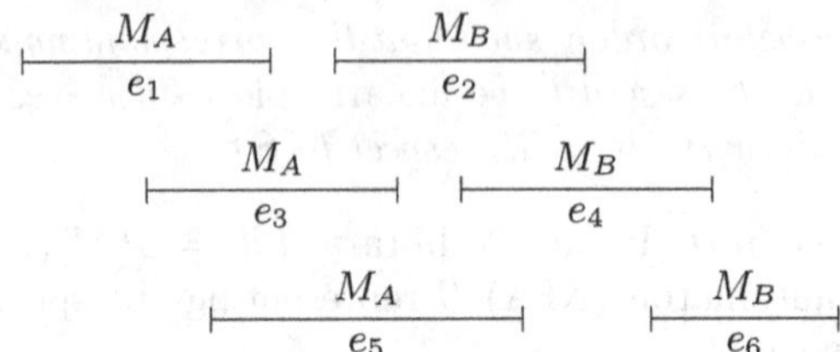

Fig. 2. A linearizable execution, which can be ordered as $e_1e_2e_3e_4e_5e_6$

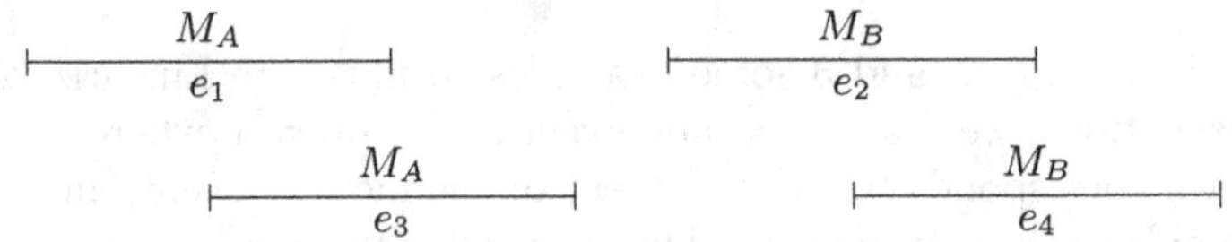

Fig. 3. A non-linearizable execution

Problem 2 (Letter Insertion). Input: A set of *insertable* letters $A = \{a_1, \ldots, a_l\}$. An NFA N over an alphabet $\Gamma \uplus A$.

Question: For all words $w \in \Gamma^*$, does there exist a decomposition $w = w_0 \cdots w_l$, and a permutation p of $\{1, \ldots, l\}$, such that $w_0 a_{p[1]} w_1 \ldots a_{p[l]} w_l$ is accepted by N?

Said differently, for any word of Γ^*, can we insert the letters $\{a_1, \ldots, a_l\}$ (each of them exactly once, in any order, anywhere in the word) to obtain a word accepted by N?

Note: the size of the input is the size of N, to which we add l.

3 Reduction from Letter Insertion to Linearizability

In this section, we show that Letter Insertion can be reduced in polynomial time to Linearizability. When we later show that Letter Insertion is EXPSPACE-hard, we will get that Linearizability is EXPSPACE-hard as well.

Intuitively, the letters $A = \{a_1, \ldots, a_l\}$ of Letter Insertion represent methods which are all overlapping with every other method, and the word w represents methods which are in sequence. Letter Insertion asks whether we can insert the letters in w in order to obtain a sequence of N while linearizability asks whether there is a way to order all the letters, while preserving the order of w, to obtain a sequence of N, which is equivalent.

Lemma 1. *Letter Insertion can be reduced in polynomial time to Linearizability.*

Proof. Let $A = \{a_1, \ldots, a_l\}$ and N an NFA over some alphabet $A \uplus \Gamma$.

Define k, the number of threads, to be $l+2$.

We will define a library *Lib* composed of

- methods $M_1, \ldots, M_l$, one for each letter of A
- methods M_γ, one for each letter of Γ
- a method M_{Tick}.

and a specification S_N, such that (A, N) is a valid instance of Letter Insertion if and only if Lib^k is linearizable with respect to S_N.

For the domain of the shared variable, we only need three values: $\mathbb{D} = \{\mathsf{Begin}, \mathsf{Run}, \mathsf{End}\}$ with Begin being the initial value.

The methods M_γ are all identical. They just read the value Run from the shared variable (see Fig. 4).

The methods $M_1, \ldots, M_l$ all read Begin, and then read End (see Fig. 5).

The method M_{Tick} writes Run, and then End (see Fig. 6).

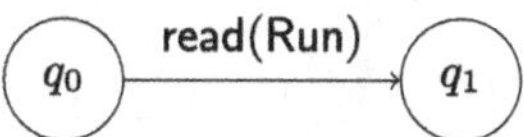

Fig. 4. Description of M_γ, $\gamma \in \Gamma$

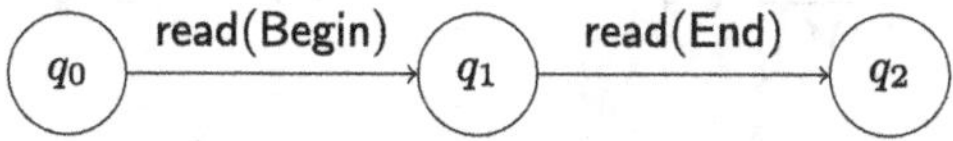

Fig. 5. Description of $M_1, \ldots, M_l$

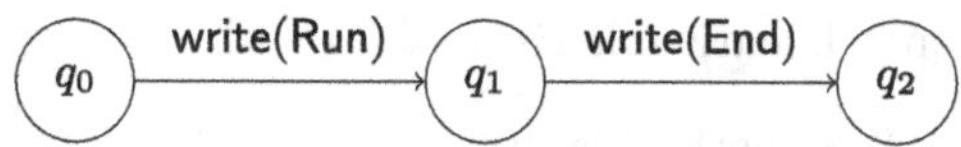

Fig. 6. Description of M_{Tick}

The specification S_N is defined as the set of words w over the alphabet $\{M_1, \ldots, M_l\} \cup \{M_{\mathsf{Tick}}\} \cup \{M_\gamma | \gamma \in \Gamma\}$ such that one the following condition holds:

- w contains 0 letter M_{Tick}, or more than 1, or
- for a letter M_i, $i \in \{1, \ldots, l\}$, w contains 0 such letter, or more than 1, or
- when projecting over the letters M_γ, $\gamma \in \Gamma$ and M_i, $i \in \{1, \ldots, l\}$, w is in N_M, where N_M is N where each letter γ is replaced by the letter M_γ, and where each letter a_i is replaced by the letter M_i.

Since N is an NFA, S_N is also an NFA. Moreover, its size is polynomial in the size of N. We can now show the following equivalence:

1. there exists a word w in Γ^*, such that there is no way to insert the letters from A in order to obtain a word accepted by N
2. there exists an execution of *Lib* with k threads which is not linearizable w.r.t. S_N

(1) $\implies$ (2). Let $w \in \Gamma^*$ such that there is no way to insert the letters A in order to obtain a word accepted by N. We construct an execution of *Lib* following Fig. 7, which is indeed a valid execution.

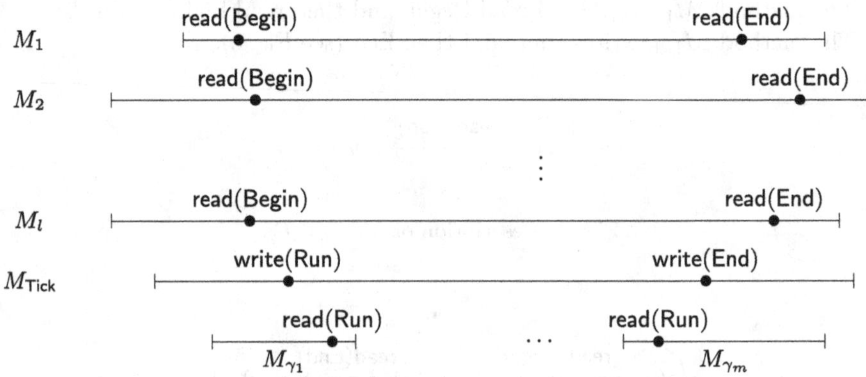

Fig. 7. Non-linearizable execution corresponding to a word $\gamma_1 \ldots \gamma_m$ in which we cannot insert the letters from $A = \{a_1, \ldots, a_l\}$ to make it accepted by N. The points represent steps in the automata.

This execution is not linearizable since

- it has exactly one M_{Tick} method, and
- for each $i \in \{1, \ldots, l\}$, it has exactly one M_i method, and
- no linearization of this execution can be in N_M, since there is no way to insert the letters A into w to be accepted by N.

Note: The value of the shared variable is initialized to Begin, allowing the methods M_i ($i \in \{1, \ldots, l\}$) to make their first transition. M_{Tick} then sets the value to Run, thus allowing the methods $M_\gamma, \gamma \in \Gamma$ to execute. Finally, M_{Tick} sets the value to End, allowing the methods $M_\gamma, \gamma \in \Gamma$ to make their second transition and return. This tight interaction will enable us to show in the second part of the proof that all non-linearizable executions of this library have this very particular form.

(2) $\implies$ (1). Let r be an execution which is not linearizable w.r.t. S_N. We first show that this execution should roughly be of the form shown in Fig. 7.

First, since it is not linearizable w.r.t. S_N, it must have at least one completed M_{Tick} method event. If it only had open M_{Tick} events (or no M_{Tick} events at all), it could be linearized by dropping all the open calls to M_{Tick}. Moreover, it cannot have more than M_{Tick} method event (completed or open), as it could also be linearized, since S_N accepts all words with more than one M_{Tick} letter.

We can show similarly that for each $i \in \{1, \ldots, l\}$, it has exactly one M_i method which is completed (and none open).

Moreover, the methods M_i ($i \in \{1, \ldots, l\}$) can only start when the value of the shared variable is Begin, and they can only return after reading the value End. Since this value can only be changed (once) by the single M_{Tick} method of our executions, this ensures that the methods M_i ($i \in \{1, \ldots, l\}$) (and M_{Tick} itself) all overlap with one another, and with every other completed method.

This implies that the completed methods $M_\gamma, \gamma \in \Gamma$ can only appear in a single thread t (since $M_1, \ldots, M_l, M_{\mathsf{Tick}}$ already occupy $l + 1$ threads amongst the $l + 2$ available). Thus, we define $w \in \Gamma^*$ to be the word corresponding to the completed methods M_γ, $\gamma \in \Gamma$ of the execution in the order in which they appear in thread t.

Since r is not linearizable, we cannot insert M_i ($i \in \{1, \ldots, l\}$) into the completed methods of thread t in order to be accepted by S_N. In particular, this implies that there is no way to insert the letters A in w in order to be accepted by N.

4 Letter Insertion is EXPSPACE-hard

We now reduce, in polynomial time, arbitrary exponentially bounded Turing machines, to the Letter Insertion problem, which shows it is EXPSPACE-hard. We first give a few notations.

A *deterministic Turing machine* $\mathcal{M}$ is a tuple (Q, δ, q_0, q_f) where:

- Q is the set of states,
- $\delta : (Q \times \{0,1\}) \to (Q \times \{0,1\} \times \{\leftarrow, \rightarrow\})$ is the transition function
- q_0, q_f are the initial and final states, respectively.

A computation of $\mathcal{M}$ is said to be *accepting* if it ends in q_f.

For the rest of the paper, we fix a Turing machine $\mathcal{M}$ and a polynomial P such that all runs of $\mathcal{M}$ starting with an input of size n use at most $2^{P(n)}$ cells, and such that the following problem is EXPSPACE-complete.

Problem 3 (Reachability). Input: A finite word t.

Question: Is the computation of $\mathcal{M}$ starting in state q_0, with the tape initialized with t, accepting?

Lemma 2 (Letter Insertion). *Letter Insertion is* EXPSPACE-*hard.*

Note: the Sublemmas 3, 4, 5, 6 and 7 are all part of the proof of Lemma 2.

Proof. We reduce in polynomial time the Reachability problem for EXPSPACE Turing machines to the *negation* of Letter Insertion. This still shows that Letter Insertion is EXPSPACE-hard, as the EXPSPACE complexity class is closed under complement.

Let t be a word of size n. Our goal is to define a set of letters A and an NFA N over an alphabet $\Gamma \uplus A$, such that the following two statements are equivalent:

- the run of $\mathcal{M}$ starting in state q_0 with the tape initialized with t is accepting (which, by definition of $\mathcal{M}$, uses at most $2^{P(n)}$ cells),
- there exists a word w in Γ^*, such that there is no way to insert (see Problem 2) the letters A in order to obtain a word accepted by N.

More specifically, we will encode runs of our Turing machine as words, and the automaton N, with the additional set of insertable letters A, will be used in order to detect words which:

- don't represent *well-formed sequences of configurations* (defined below),
- or represent a sequence of configurations where the initial configuration is not initialized with t and state q_0, or where the final configuration isn't in state q_f,
- or contain an error in the computation, according to the transition rules of $\mathcal{M}$.

A *configuration* of $\mathcal{M}$ is an ordered sequence $(c_0, \ldots, (q, c_i), \ldots, c_{2^{P(n)}-1})$ representing that the content of the tape is $c_0, \ldots, c_{2^{P(n)}-1} \in \{0, 1\}$, the current control state is $q \in Q$, and the head is on cell i.

We denote by $\mathbf{i}$ the binary representation of $0 \leq i < 2^{P(n)}$ using $P(n)$ digits. Given a configuration, we represent cell i by: "$\mathbf{i} : c_i;$" if the head of $\mathcal{M}$ is not on cell i, and by "$\mathbf{i} : qc_i;$" if the head is on cell i and the current state of $\mathcal{M}$ is q. The configuration given above is represented by the word:

$$\$\mathbf{0} : c_0; \mathbf{1} : c_1; \ldots \mathbf{i} : qc_i; \ldots \mathbf{2^{P(n)}} - \mathbf{1} : c_{2^{P(n)}-1}; \hookleftarrow .$$

Words which are of this form for some $c_0, \ldots, c_{2^{P(n)}-1} \in \{0, 1\}$, $q \in Q$, are called *well-formed configurations.* A sequence of configurations is then encoded as $\triangleright \mathsf{cfg}_1 \ldots \mathsf{cfg}_\mathsf{k} \Box$ where each cfg_i is a well-formed configuration. A word of this form is called a *well-formed sequence of configurations.* We now fix Γ to be $\{0, 1, \triangleright, \Box, \$, \hookleftarrow, ;, :\}$.

Lemma 3. *There exists an NFA* N_{notWF} *of size polynomial in* n*, which recognizes words which are not well-formed configurations.*

Proof. A word is not a well-formed configuration if and only if one of the following holds (the + denotes the disjunction or union of regular expressions, and * denotes the Kleene star, 0 or more repetitions):

- it is not of the form $\$((0 + 1)^{P(n)} : (Q + \epsilon)(0 + 1);)^* \hookleftarrow$, or
- it has no symbol from Q, or more than one, or
- it doesn't start with $\$\mathbf{0} :$, or
- it doesn't end with $\mathbf{2^{P(n)}} - \mathbf{1} : (Q + \epsilon)(0 + 1); \hookleftarrow$, or
- it contains a pattern $\mathbf{i} : (Q + \epsilon)(0 + 1); \mathbf{j} :$ where $j \neq i + 1$.

For all violations, we can make an NFA of size polynomial in n recognizing them, and then take their union. The most difficult one is the last, for which there are detailed constructions in Fürer [6] and Mayer and Stockmeyer [10].

We here give a sketch of the construction. Remember that $\mathbf{i}$ and $\mathbf{j}$ are binary representation using $P(n)$ bits. We want an automaton recognizing the fact that $j \neq i + 1$. The automaton guesses the least significant bit b ($P(n)$ possible choices) which makes the equality $i + 1 = j$ fail, as well as the presence or not of a carry (for the addition $i + 1$) at that position. We denote by $\mathbf{i}[b]$ the bit b of $\mathbf{i}$ and likewise for $\mathbf{j}$. Then, the automaton checks that: (1) there is indeed a violation at that position (for instance: no carry, $\mathbf{i}[b] = 0$ and $\mathbf{j}[b] = 1$) and (2) there is carry if and only if all bits less significant than b are set to 1 in $\mathbf{i}$.

Lemma 4. *There exists an NFA $N_{\mathsf{NotSeqCfg}}$ of size polynomial in n, which recognizes words which:*

- *are not a well-formed sequence of configurations, or where*
- *the first configuration is not in state q_0, or*
- *the first configuration is not initialized with t, or*
- *the last configuration is not in state q_f.*

Proof. Non-deterministic union between N_{notWF} and simple automata recognizing the last three conditions.

The problem is now in making an NFA which detects violations in the computation with respect to the transition rules of $\mathcal{M}$. Indeed, in our encoding, the length of one configuration is about $2^{P(n)}$, and thus, violations of the transition rules from one configuration to the next are going to be separated by about $2^{P(n)}$ characters in the word. We conclude that we cannot make directly an automaton of polynomial size which recognizes such violations.

This is where we use the set of insertable letters A. We are going to define and use it here, in order to detect words which encode a sequence of configurations where there is a computation error, according to the transition rules of $\mathcal{M}$.

The set A, containing $2P(n)$ new letters, is defined as $A = \{p_1, \dots, p_{P(n)}, m_1, , \dots, m_{P(n)}\}$.

We want to construct an NFA N_{NotDelta}, such that, for a word w which is a well-formed sequence of configurations, these statements are equivalent:

- w has a computation error according to the transition rules δ of $\mathcal{M}$
- we can insert the letters A in w to obtain a word accepted by N_{NotDelta}.

The idea is to use the letters A in order to identify two places in the word corresponding to the same cell of $\mathcal{M}$, but at two successive configurations of the run.

As an example, say we want to detect a violation of the transition $\delta(q, 0) = (q', 1, \rightarrow)$, that is, which reads a 0, writes a 1, moves the head to the right, and changes the state from q to q'.

Assume that w contains a sub-word of the following form:

$$\mathbf{i} : q0; \ldots \$ \ldots \mathbf{i} : 1; \mathbf{i+1} : q''c_{i+1};$$

where q'' is different than q'

The single \$ symbol in the middle of the sub-word ensures that we are checking violations in successive configurations. Here, with the current state being q, the head read 0 on cell i, wrote 1 successfully, and moved to the right. But the state changed to q'' instead of q'. Since we assumed that $\mathcal{M}$ is deterministic, this is indeed a violation of the transition rules.

We now have all the ingredients in order to construct N_{NotDelta}. It will be built as a non-deterministic choice (or union) of N_t for all possible transitions $t \in \delta$ (with δ seen as a relation).

As an example, we show how to construct the automaton $N^{(1)}_{((q,0),(q',1,\rightarrow))}$, part of N_{NotDelta}, and recognizing violations of $\delta(q,0) = (q',1,\rightarrow)$, where the head was indeed moved to right, but the state was changed to some state q'' instead of q', like above. Other violations may be recognized similarly.

$N^{(1)}_{((q,0),(q',1,\rightarrow))}$ starts by finding a sub-word of the form:

$$(m_1 0 + p_1 1) \ldots (m_{P(n)} 0 + p_{P(n)} 1) : q0; \tag{1}$$

meaning the state is q and the head points to a cell containing 0. After that, it reads arbitrarily many symbols, but exactly one \$ symbol, which ensures that the next letters it reads are from the next configuration. Finally, it looks for a sub-word of the form

$$(p_1 0 + m_1 1) \ldots (p_{P(n)} 0 + m_{P(n)} 1) : (0+1); (0+1)^* : q'' \tag{2}$$

for some $q'' \neq q'$.

We can now show the following.

Lemma 5. *For a well-formed sequence of configurations w, these two statements are equivalent:*

1. *there is a way to insert the letters A into w to be accepted by $N^{(1)}_{((q,0),(q',1,\rightarrow))}$*
2. *in the sequence of configurations encoded by w, there is a configuration where the state was q and the head was pointing to a cell containing 0, and in the next configuration, the head was moved to the right, but the state was not changed to q' (computation error).*

Proof. ($\Leftarrow$). We insert the letters A in front of the binary representation of the cell number where the violation occurs. The violation involves two configurations: in the first, we insert m's in front of 0's, and p's in front of 1's, and in the second, it's the other way around.

This way, we inserted all the letters of A (exactly) once into w, and $N^{(1)}_{((q,0),(q',1,\rightarrow))}$ is now able to recognize the patterns (1) and (2) described above.

($\Rightarrow$). For the other direction, let w be a well-formed sequence of configurations such that there exists a way to insert the letters A into w, in order to obtain a word w_A accepted by $N^{(1)}_{((q,0),(q',1,\rightarrow))}$.

Since each letter of A can be inserted only once, the sub-word matched by $(m_1 0 + p_1 1) \dots (m_{P(n)} 0 + p_{P(n)} 1)$ in pattern (1) in $N^{(1)}_{((q,0),(q',1,\rightarrow))}$ has to be the same as the one matched by $(p_1 0 + m_1 1) \dots (p_{P(n)} 0 + m_{P(n)} 1)$ in pattern (2), up to exchanging m's and p''s.

Moreover, having exactly one \$ symbol in between the two patterns ensures that they correspond to the same cell, but in two successive configurations.

Finally, the facts that q'' is different that q' and that $\mathcal{M}$ is deterministic ensures that the sequence of configurations represented by w indeed contains a computation error according to the rule $\delta(q, 0) = (q', 1, \rightarrow)$.

We thus get the following lemma for the automaton N_{NotDelta}.

Lemma 6. *For a word w which is a well-formed sequence of configurations, these statements are equivalent:*

- *we can insert the letters A in w to obtain a word accepted by N_{NotDelta},*
- *w has a computation error according to the transition rules δ of $\mathcal{M}$.*

Proof. Construct all the N_t for $t \in \delta$ (with δ considered as a relation). Construct similarly an automaton recognizing the violation where a cell changes while the head was not here. Take the union of all these automata, the proof then follows from Lemma 5.

By taking the union $N = N_{\mathsf{NotSeqCfg}} \cup N_{\mathsf{NotDelta}}$, we finally get the intended result, which ends the reduction.

Lemma 7. *The following two statements are equivalent.*

- *the run of $\mathcal{M}$ starting in state q_0 with the tape initialized with t is accepting,*
- *there exists a word w in Γ^*, such that there is no way to insert the letters A in order to obtain a word accepted by N.*

Proof. ($\Rightarrow$) Let w be the well-formed sequence of configurations representing the sequence of configurations of the accepting run in $\mathcal{M}$, with the tape initialized with t. Then by Lemmas 4 and 6, there is no way to insert the letters A in order to obtain a word accepted by $N_{\mathsf{NotSeqCfg}}$ or N_{NotDelta}.

($\Leftarrow$) Let $w \in \Gamma^*$ be a word such that there is no way to insert the letters A in order to obtain a word accepted by N. First, since w is not accepted by $N_{\mathsf{NotSeqCfg}}$, it represents a well-formed sequence of configurations, starting in state q_0 with the tape initialized with t and ending in state q_f (Lemma 4). Moreover, since there is no way to insert the letters to obtain a word from N_{NotDelta}, w has no computation error according to the transition rules δ of $\mathcal{M}$ (Lemma 6).

This ends the proof of Lemma 2.

Since Letter Insertion is EXPSPACE-hard and, Letter Insertion reduces to Linearizability, we get the main result of the paper.

Theorem 1 (Linearizability). *Linearizability is* EXPSPACE*-complete.*

Proof. It was previously shown that Linearizability is in EXPSPACE [1]. EXPSPACE-hardness follows from Lemmas 1 and 2

5 Conclusion

We define a new problem, Letter Insertion, simpler than Linearizability, but still hard enough to capture the main difficulties of Linearizability. We showed that the Letter Insertion problem is EXPSPACE-hard, and could thus deduce that the Linearizability problem is EXPSPACE-hard.

Our result applies even with all the following restrictions: the number of threads is given in unary, there is a unique shared variable whose domain size is 3, the library has a constant number of automata "shapes" (3 in our reduction) using less than 3 states, the methods of the library are deterministic, the methods of the library have no loop, and the instructions within the methods can only read or write, but never do both atomically.

For future work, we plan to show that restricting ourselves to deterministic specifications (using a DFA instead of an NFA in the input of the problem) does not reduce the complexity. Furthermore, it would be interesting to find a large class of specifications including the most common ones (stack, queue, ...) for which our lower-bound does not apply and where we could reduce the complexity.

References

1. Alur, R., McMillan, K.L., Peled, D.: Model-checking of correctness conditions for concurrent objects. Inf. Comput. **160**(1–2), 167–188 (2000)
2. Bouajjani, A., Emmi, M., Enea, C., Hamza, J.: Verifying concurrent programs against sequential specifications. In: Felleisen, M., Gardner, P. (eds.) ESOP 2013. LNCS, vol. 7792, pp. 290–309. Springer, Heidelberg (2013)
3. Burckhardt, S., Dern, C., Musuvathi, M., Tan, R.: Line-up: a complete and automatic linearizability checker. In: Proceedings of the 2010 ACM SIGPLAN Conference on Programming Language Design and Implementation, PLDI 2010, pp. 330–340. ACM, New York (2010). http://doi.acm.org/10.1145/1806596.1806634
4. Elmas, T., Qadeer, S., Sezgin, A., Subasi, O., Tasiran, S.: Simplifying linearizability proofs with reduction and abstraction. In: Esparza, J., Majumdar, R. (eds.) TACAS 2010. LNCS, vol. 6015, pp. 296–311. Springer, Heidelberg (2010)
5. Filipovic, I., O'Hearn, P.W., Rinetzky, N., Yang, H.: Abstraction for concurrent objects. Theor. Comput. Sci. **411**(51–52), 4379–4398 (2010)
6. Fürer, M.: The complexity of the inequivalence problem for regular expressions with intersection. In: de Bakker, J., van Leeuwen, J. (eds.) Automata, Languages and Programming. LNCS, vol. 85, pp. 234–245. Springer, London (1980). http://dl.acm.org/citation.cfm?id=646234.682559
7. Gibbons, P.B., Korach, E.: Testing shared memories. SIAM J. Comput. **26**(4), 1208–1244 (1997)

8. Herlihy, M., Wing, J.M.: Linearizability: a correctness condition for concurrent objects. ACM Trans. Program. Lang. Syst. **12**(3), 463–492 (1990)
9. Hunt, H.: The equivalence problem for regular expressions with intersection is not polynomial in tape. Department of Computer Science: Technical report, Cornell University, Department of Computer Science (1973). http://books.google.fr/books?id=52j6HAAACAAJ
10. Mayer, A.J., Stockmeyer, L.J.: The complexity of word problems - this time with interleaving. Inf. Comput. **115**(2), 293–311 (1994). http://dx.doi.org/10.1006/inco.1994.1098
11. Rajamani, S.K., Walker, D. (eds.): Proceedings of the 42nd Annual ACM SIGPLAN-SIGACT Symposium on Principles of Programming Languages, POPL 2015, Mumbai, India, 15–17 January 2015. ACM, New York (2015). http://dl.acm.org/citation.cfm?id=2676726
12. Vafeiadis, V.: Automatically proving linearizability. In: Touili, T., Cook, B., Jackson, P. (eds.) CAV 2010. LNCS, vol. 6174, pp. 450–464. Springer, Heidelberg (2010)
13. Vechev, M.T., Yahav, E., Yorsh, G.: Experience with model checking linearizability. In: Păsăreanu, C.S. (ed.) SPIN 2009. LNCS, vol. 5578, pp. 261–278. Springer, Heidelberg (2009)

Antichains for the Verification of Recursive Programs

Lukáš Holík[1](✉) and Roland Meyer[2]

[1] Brno University of Technology, Brno, Czech Republic
holik@fit.vutbr.cz
[2] University of Kaiserslautern, Kaiserslautern, Germany
meyer@cs.uni-kl.de

Abstract. Safety verification of while programs is often phrased in terms of inclusions $L(A) \subseteq L(B)$ among regular languages. Antichain-based algorithms have been developed as an efficient method to check such inclusions. In this paper, we generalize the idea of antichain-based verification to verifying safety properties of recursive programs. To be precise, we give an antichain-based algorithm for checking inclusions of the form $L(G) \subseteq L(B)$, where G is a context-free grammar and B is a finite automaton. The idea is to phrase the inclusion as a data flow analysis problem over a relational domain. In a second step, we generalize the approach towards bounded context switching.

1 Introduction

We reconsider a standard task in algorithmic verification: model checking safety properties of recursive programs. To explain our model, assume we are given a recursive program P operating on a finite set of Boolean variables V. For this program, we are asked to check a safety property given by a finite automaton B. The task amounts to checking the inclusion

$$L(G(P)) \cap \bigcap_{v \in V} L(B(v)) \subseteq L(B).$$

Here, $G(P)$ is a context-free grammar whose language is the set of valid paths in the recursive program P. A path is valid if procedures are called and return in a well-nested manner. The context-free grammar only models the flow of control. It does not ensure the correct use of the Boolean variables. Indeed, there could be words in $L(G(P))$ where a write of 1 to variable v is followed by a read of value 0. To take data into account, we intersect the context-free language with a regular language $L(B(v))$ for each variable. The intersection only keeps words from $L(G(P))$ that obey the semantics of operations on the data domain. Such a separation of a program's semantics into the control and the data aspect is standard in verification [16].

The only non-regular part in the above inclusion is the control-flow language $L(G(P))$. We move the intersection with the regular languages to the

A. Bouajjani and H. Fauconnier (Eds.): NETYS 2015, LNCS 9466, pp. 322–336, 2015.
DOI: 10.1007/978-3-319-26850-7_22

right-hand side of the inclusion and obtain an equivalent formulation:

$$L(G(P)) \subseteq L(B) \cup \bigcup_{v \in V} \overline{L(B(v))}.$$

Since regular languages are closed under complement and closed under finite union, the right-hand side of the new inclusion is again a regular language $L(A)$.

The discussion allows us to define the safety verification problem for recursive programs that is the subject of this paper as follows. Given a context-free grammar G and a finite automaton A, check the inclusion

$$L(G) \subseteq L(A).$$

The classical algorithm for checking the inclusion determinizes A with the powerset construction, forms the complement, and computes the product with G. The result is the (context-free) emptiness problem $L(G \times \mathit{compl}(\mathit{det}(A))) = \emptyset$. The main bottleneck of this algorithm is the determinization of A. It may cause an exponential blow-up even in space, and makes the approach impractical. Actually, deciding the inclusion is PSPACE-complete.

For the simpler problem with finite automata on both sides, $L(A_1) \subseteq L(A_2)$, an efficient heuristics has been found. It is based on the so-called antichain principle [7, 25] and prevents the state explosion in many practical cases. The observation is that the states in $A_1 \times \mathit{compl}(\mathit{det}(A_2))$ can be equipped with an ordering. For the emptiness check, it is sufficient to explore transitions from states that are minimal according to this ordering.

Our contribution is a generalization of the antichain principle to the problem $L(G) \subseteq L(A)$. The proposed algorithm computes a finite partitioning of Σ^* such that each partition contains words that are all accepted or all rejected by A. To test the inclusion, it is enough to test that G does not accept a word whose partition is rejected by A. The partitions are represented by sets of relations over states of the automaton A. Every relation encodes one possibility of how a word generated by a certain non-terminal of the grammar can influence the state of the automaton. This is the same concept as the one used in the proof that Büchi automata are closed under complement [3].

We formulate our algorithm via a reduction of $L(G) \subseteq L(A)$ to a data flow analysis problem $\mathit{DFA}(G, A)$. Implementing the antichain principle then amounts to modifying chaotic iteration so that it computes on a lattice of antichains [25] rather than a full powerset lattice. The reduction is theoretically appealing and allows for an elegant formulation of the antichain principle. Moreover, it reveals a close connection between automata theory and data flow analysis that opens up a possibility of using antichain optimizations in data flow analysis.

As a last step, we add parallelism to the picture. For multi-threaded recursive programs, safety verification can be formulated as

$$L(G_1) \sqcup\!\sqcup \ldots \sqcup\!\sqcup L(G_m) \subseteq L(A).$$

The problem is known to be undecidable [21]. For bug hunting, however, under-approximations have proven useful. The most prominent under-approximation is bounded context switching [20]. The observation made in practice is that bugs show up within few interactions among threads. If the threads share the same processor, this means bugs show up after few context switches — hence the name. Recall that a context switch occurs if one thread leaves the processor in order for another thread to be scheduled.

We propose a compositional approach to solving the above context-bounded inclusion. In a first step, we solve m data flow analysis problems $\mathit{DFA}(G_i, A)$, one for each grammar. In a second step, we combine the analysis results. The reduction $\mathit{DFA}(G_i, A)$ generalizes $\mathit{DFA}(G, A)$. We move from (sets of) relations to an analysis on (sets of) words of relations.

To sum up, the contributions of this paper are threefold:

1. The formulation of $L(G) \subseteq L(A)$ as a data flow analysis problem $\mathit{DFA}(G, A)$.
2. The antichain improvement of chaotic iteration for solving $\mathit{DFA}(G, A)$.
3. The generalization to bounded context switching.

Related Work. Antichain algorithms were first proposed in [7] in the context of solving games with imperfect information. The antichain principle was subsequently used to optimize language inclusion and universality checking of finite automata [25]. The basic idea of antichain algorithms, subsumption, is older and was used e.g. already in solving reachability of well-structured systems [1,12]. The antichain algorithms of [25] were further extended and improved in many ways. In our context, the generalization to the Ramsey-based universality and language inclusion checking for Büchi automata [13] is central. It introduces an ordering on what we call relations (in the related literature, the notion is called e.g. (super)graph, transition profile, or box). The problem of deciding language inclusion of nested word automata is closely related to the inclusion of a context-free language in a regular one, and is also similarly motivated. An extension of the Ramsey-based algorithm for nested word automata has been published in [14], and an alternative algorithm based on different principles, but using antichains, appears in [5].

Verification algorithms that use inclusion checking as a central subroutine have been proposed in [9–11]. These works focus on multi-threaded programs without recursion and develop complete algorithms (for inclusion). We tackle recursive programs, instead. In the multi-threaded setting, inclusion checking is undecidable [21] so that we consider an under-approximation of the problem. We show how to generalize the antichain principle to bounded context switching [20]. The approximation of bounded context switching has also been applied to relaxed memory models [2]. In the present work, however, we limit ourselves to Sequential Consistency.

In verification, the relational domain that we make use of is generalized to procedure summaries [22,24]. Summaries characterize the input-output relation of a procedure. They are not limited to tracking the state changes of a finite automaton. The language-theoretic view to verification problems is shared with [4,9–11,15,16,18]. We are not aware of any use of antichains for data flow analysis or of a formulation of regular inclusion as a data flow analysis problem.

The domain for bounded context switching seems to be new. Our compositional analysis is related to the eager approach in [17].

2 Preliminaries

We introduce the three technical concepts used in this paper: regular inclusion, antichain algorithms, and data flow analysis.

2.1 CFG-REG

Given a finite alphabet Σ, we use Σ^* for the set of all finite words over Σ and write ε for the empty word. The concatenation of words $u, v \in \Sigma^*$ yields the word $u \cdot v \in \Sigma^*$. The shuffle of u and v is the set of interleavings of both words, for example $ab \sqcup\!\sqcup\, c = \{cab, acb, abc\} \subseteq \Sigma^*$.

A *context-free grammar* is a tuple $G = (\Sigma, X, x_0, R)$ where Σ is a finite alphabet and X is a finite set of non-terminals with initial symbol $x_0 \in X$. Component $R \subseteq X \times (\Sigma \uplus X)^*$ is the set of production rules. The language of G is defined using the derivation relation $\Rightarrow_G \subseteq (\Sigma \uplus X)^* \times (\Sigma \uplus X)^*$. Consider two words $\alpha, \beta \in (\Sigma \uplus X)^*$. Then $\alpha \Rightarrow_G \beta$ if there are $\alpha_1, \alpha_2 \in (\Sigma \uplus X)^*$, $x \in X$, and $(x, \gamma) \in R$ so that $\alpha = \alpha_1 \cdot x \cdot \alpha_2$ and $\beta = \alpha_1 \cdot \gamma \cdot \alpha_2$. We write $\Rightarrow_G^*$ for the reflexive and transitive closure of $\Rightarrow_G$. Moreover, if G is clear from the context we drop the subscript from $\Rightarrow_G$. The language of a non-terminal $x \in X$ is the set of words derivable from it:

$$L(x) \;:=\; \{\alpha \in \Sigma^* \mid x \Rightarrow^* \alpha\}.$$

The *language of* G is $L(G) := L(x_0)$.

A context-free grammar is called *right-linear* if $R \subseteq X \times (\{\varepsilon\} \uplus (\Sigma \cdot X))$. Right-linear grammars correspond to finite automata where the non-terminals are the states, x_0 is the initial state, and the $x \in X$ with $(x, \varepsilon) \in R$ are the accepting states. This correspondence allows us to use the terminology for finite automata when talking about right-linear grammars. We shall use A, A_1, A_2 for right-linear grammars and G, G_1, G_2 for context-free grammars that are not necessarily right-linear. Throughout the paper, we use $G = (\Sigma, X, x_0, R)$ and $A = (\Sigma, Y, y_0, \rightarrow)$. Moreover, we write $y_1 \xrightarrow{a} y_2$ for $(y_1, a, y_2) \in \rightarrow$. We extend the notation to words: $y_1 \xrightarrow{w} y_2$ means there is a w-labeled path from y_1 to y_2.

Our contribution is an efficient algorithm for solving the following problem that we refer to as CFG-REG:

Given: A context-free grammar G and a right-linear grammar A.
Problem: Does $L(G) \subseteq L(A)$ hold?

As a running example, we consider $L(G_{ex}) \subseteq L(A_{ex})$ where the context-free grammar G_{ex} and the finite automaton A_{ex} are defined as follows:

$$\begin{array}{llllll} G_{ex}: & x_0 \rightarrow a \cdot x_1 & x_0 \rightarrow b \cdot x_1 & A_{ex}: & y_0 \rightarrow a \cdot y_1 & y_0 \rightarrow b \cdot y_2 \\ & x_1 \rightarrow c \cdot x_2 & x_1 \rightarrow d \cdot x_2 & & y_1 \rightarrow c \cdot y_3 & y_2 \rightarrow d \cdot y_4 \\ & x_2 \rightarrow \varepsilon & & & y_3 \rightarrow \varepsilon & y_4 \rightarrow \varepsilon. \end{array}$$

We have $L(G_{ex}) = \{ac, ad, bc, bd\}$ and $L(A_{ex}) = \{ac, bd\}$, so the inclusion fails. An attentive reader may notice that the context-free grammar G_{ex} is right-linear. This is only for the sake of simplicity, the algorithm of course works for any CFG, but G_{ex} allows us to illustrate the main concepts well.

2.2 Antichain Algorithms

To explain the idea behind antichain algorithms, consider a simplified variant of CFG-REG where we check $L(A_1) \subseteq L(A_2)$ for given finite automata A_1 and A_2. The standard approach is to reformulate the inclusion as

$$L(A_1) \cap \overline{L(A_2)} = \emptyset.$$

Checking this emptiness involves determinizing A_2 using the powerset construction, which results in $det(A_2)$, complementing $det(A_2)$ by inverting the final states, giving $compl(det(A_2))$, and computing the product with A_1,

$$A_1 \times compl(det(A_2)).$$

The resulting automaton $A_1 \times compl(det(A_2))$ is then checked for emptiness. Unfortunate in this construction is that $det(A_2)$ may be exponential and that we need another product with the states of A_1.

Antichain algorithms check emptiness of $A_1 \times compl(det(A_2))$ on-the-fly. To explain the concept, we elaborate on the behavior of the product automaton. Let $A_i = (\Sigma, Y_i, y_{0,i}, \rightarrow_i)$ for $i = 1, 2$. States in the product automaton take the shape (y_1, Z_1) where $y_1 \in Y_1$ is a single state of A_1 and $Z_1 \subseteq Y_2$ is a set of states of A_2. We call (y_1, Z_1) a product state and Z_1 a macro state. Transitions in the product state (y_1, Z_1) are derived from transitions in y_1, because the macro state Z_1 in the determinized automaton can react to any input. If we have a transition $y_1 \xrightarrow{a} y_2$, then the product state takes a transition

$$(y_1, Z_1) \xrightarrow{a} (y_2, Z_2).$$

Here, Z_2 is the set of all states $z_2 \in Y_2$ that are reachable from some $z_1 \in Z_1$ with an a-labelled transition, $z_1 \xrightarrow{a} z_2$.

The goal is to disprove emptiness of $A_1 \times compl(det(A_2))$. This amounts to finding a product state (y, Z) where y is accepting in A_1 and Z is rejecting in the sense that it does not contain a final state of A_2. The larger the set Z becomes, the harder it is to avoid the final states of A_2. To disprove emptiness, we should thus only explore states that are minimal according to the following partial order $\leq$ on product states:

$$(y, Z) \leq (y', Z') \quad \text{if} \quad y = y' \text{ and } Z \subseteq Z'.$$

This is the idea of antichain algorithms: only explore states (y, Z) that are minimal according to $\leq$. The name stems from the fact that minimal elements in partial orders are incomparable, and sets of incomparable elements are also called antichains.

It remains to argue that we can safely discard larger states. We already discussed that state y_1 of A_1 determines the transitions of the product state (y_1, Z_1). Macro state Z_1 is guaranteed to have the successor state defined. A larger set Z_1' will not enable or disable a transition. Moreover, the transition relation is monotone in the following sense. If $(y_1, Z_1) \xrightarrow{a} (y_2, Z_2)$ and we have $(y_1, Z_1) \leq (y_1, Z_1')$, then $(y_1, Z_1') \xrightarrow{a} (y_2, Z_2')$ with $(y_2, Z_2) \leq (y_2, Z_2')$. This means a larger state (y_1, Z_1') again leads to a larger state (y_2, Z_2') from which it is harder to accept than from (y_2, Z_2). In short, $(y, Z) \leq (y, Z')$ yields

$$L(y, Z') \subseteq L(y, Z)$$

for the product automaton $A_1 \times compl(det(A_2))$. So if we focus on minimal states, we are guaranteed to explore all behaviors.

2.3 Data Flow Analysis

Our presentation of data flow analysis follows standard textbooks [19,23]. A data flow analysis problem is given as a system of inequalities $\overline{\Delta} \geq Op(\overline{\Delta})$ that is interpreted over a domain of data flow values. The system of inequalities reflects the control flow in the program under scrutiny. For each location $l = 1, \ldots, n$ in the program there is a variable Δ_l. Intuitively, variable Δ_l records the analysis information obtained at location l. For each command c leading to l there is an inequality

$$\Delta_l \geq op_c(\Delta_1, \ldots, \Delta_n).$$

Operation op_c captures the effect that the command has on the already gathered analysis information. The inequality states that this effect should contribute to the analysis information at location l.

The domain that the system is interpreted over defines the actual analysis information being computed. As is common, we assume the domain to be a complete lattice $(D, \leq)$. A complete lattice is a partially ordered set where every subset of elements $D' \subseteq D$ has a least upper bound that we denote by $\bigsqcup D'$. As a second condition, the operations op_c used in the system of inequalities should be monotone, which means for all $d, d' \in D$ with $d \leq d'$ we have $op_c(d) \leq op_c(d')$.

A solution to the data flow analysis problem is a function *sol* that assigns to each variable Δ_l a value $sol(\Delta_l) \in D$ so that the inequalities are satisfied. We are interested in the least solution *lsol* wrt. a component-wise comparison of elements according to $\leq$. A unique least solution is guaranteed to exist by Knaster and Tarski's theorem.

If D is a finite set, the least solution to the system of inequalities can be computed with a Kleene iteration on D^n. This iteration, however, requires us to recompute, in every step, the analysis information for all n program locations — even if the analysis information has not changed. More efficient is the following algorithm, known as *chaotic iteration*. It is the algorithm we improve upon in this article:

$sol(\Delta_1) := \bot; \dots sol(\Delta_n) := \bot;$
while $\exists$ inequality with $sol(\Delta_l) \not\geq op_c(sol(\Delta_1), \dots, sol(\Delta_n))$ **do**
$sol(\Delta_l) := sol(\Delta_l) \sqcup op_c(sol(\Delta_1), \dots, sol(\Delta_n));$

We start with all variables set to the least element in the lattice, denoted by $\bot$. As long as there is a command that can contribute to the value of a variable, we form the join to add the value.

Lemma 1 ([6]). *Consider $\overline{\Delta} \geq Op(\overline{\Delta})$ over a complete lattice $(D, \leq)$ where D is finite. Chaotic iteration terminates and gives the least solution lsol.*

3 From CFG-REG to Data Flow Analysis

We give a reduction of CFG-REG to a data flow analysis problem. It maps instance $L(G) \subseteq L(A)$ to the instance $DFA(G, A)$. Key to the reduction is an appropriate domain of data flow values. The idea is to determine the state changes that a word $w \in L(x)$ derived from a non-terminal $x \in X$ may induce on A. Phrased differently, the analysis considers words equivalent that induce the same state changes. In our running example $L(G_{ex}) \subseteq L(A_{ex})$, rule (x_2, ε) rewrites non-terminal x_2 to the empty word. As data flow information about x_2, we therefore add the relation $\rho(\varepsilon) = id$. Relation $\rho(\varepsilon)$ is indeed the identity as the empty word does not incur a state change. For a letter a, relation $\rho(a)$ contains precisely the pairs of states (y, y') so that y does an a-labeled transition to y'. In the running example, we have $\rho(a) = \{(y_0, y_1)\}$.

For the definition of $DFA(G, A)$, we formalize the mapping from words to relations over states as

$$\begin{aligned} \rho : \ & \Sigma^* \to \mathbb{P}(Y \times Y) \\ & w \mapsto \{(y_1, y_2) \mid y_1 \xrightarrow{w} y_2\}. \end{aligned}$$

Words are equipped with the operation of concatenation. Function ρ behaves homomorphically if we endow $\mathbb{P}(Y \times Y)$ with relational composition as operation. Recall that the relational composition of $\rho_1, \rho_2 \in \mathbb{P}(Y \times Y)$ is defined by

$$\rho_1; \rho_2 \ := \ \{(y_1, y_2) \mid \exists y : (y_1, y) \in \rho_1 \text{ and } (y, y_2) \in \rho_2\}.$$

With a component-wise definition, the operation carries over to sets of relations. The following lemma states that ρ is a homomorphism.

Lemma 2. *For all $w_1, w_2 \in \Sigma^*$, we have $\rho(w_1 \cdot w_2) \ = \ \rho(w_1); \rho(w_2)$.*

With this result, we only have to specify the data flow information for single letters. Relational composition will give us the analysis information for words.

The domain of data flow values is the complete lattice

$$(\mathbb{P}(\mathbb{P}(Y \times Y)), \subseteq).$$

The powerset $\mathbb{P}(\mathbb{P}(Y \times Y))$ contains all sets of relations between states in the given automaton. The domain is a standard powerset lattice with inclusion as ordering. It is complete. We operate on sets of relations to distinguish words that do not induce the same state changes. Consider the rules $(x_0, a \cdot x_1)$ and $(x_0, b \cdot x_1)$ in our running example $L(G_{ex}) \subseteq L(A_{ex})$. In the automaton, we have $(y_0, a \cdot y_1)$ and $(y_0, b \cdot y_2)$. A derivation of letter a induces the single state change $\rho(a) = \{(y_0, y_1)\}$ and similarly $\rho(b) = \{(y_0, y_2)\}$. There is, however, no word that admits a transition from y_0 to y_1 and from y_0 to y_2. Therefore, we cannot form the union of the relations $\rho(a)$ and $\rho(b)$ but have to compute on sets of relations $\{\rho(a), \rho(b)\}$. Indeed, for the running example an analysis based on relations rather than sets of relations gives incorrect results.

In data flow analysis, the current information is modified by operations *op*. In our setting, *op* forms a relational composition. With this in mind, the system of inequalities $DFA(G, A)$ for $L(G) \subseteq L(A)$ is defined as follows. We associate with every non-terminal $x \in X$ a variable Δ_x. Moreover, we use Δ_a for the set that only contains $\rho(a)$. Similarly, we let $\Delta_\varepsilon := \{id\}$. The system of inequalities contains one inequality for every rule in the grammar as follows. Let $(x, w) \in R$ with $w = w_1 \dots w_n \in (\Sigma \cup X)^*$. Then we have

$$\Delta_x \supseteq \Delta_{w_1}; \dots; \Delta_{w_n}.$$

The data flow analysis problem $DFA(G_{ex}, A_{ex})$ for our running example is

$$\begin{array}{ll} \Delta_{x_0} \supseteq \{\{(y_0, y_1)\}\}; \Delta_{x_1} & \Delta_{x_0} \supseteq \{\{(y_0, y_2)\}\}; \Delta_{x_1} \\ \Delta_{x_1} \supseteq \{\{(y_1, y_3)\}\}; \Delta_{x_2} & \Delta_{x_1} \supseteq \{\{(y_2, y_4)\}\}; \Delta_{x_2} \\ \Delta_{x_2} \supseteq \{id\}. & \end{array}$$

The least solution *lsol* to $DFA(G, A)$ has a well-defined meaning. It assigns to Δ_x precisely the relations $\rho(w)$ induced by the words w derivable from x.

Lemma 3. $lsol(\Delta_x) = \rho(L(x))$.

Proof. If $x = \varepsilon$ or $x = a \in \Sigma$ then the lemma trivially holds by the definition of Δ_x. Now consider $x \in X$. Note that x is not qualified further which means we reason simultaneously for all $x \in X$.

$lsol(\Delta_x) \subseteq \rho(L(x))$: Equivalently, for all $\rho \in lsol(\Delta_x)$, there is $w \in L(x)$ with $\rho(w) = \rho$. Assume that relation ρ is added to Δ_x within the k-th step of the Kleene iteration. We will proceed by induction on k. If $k = 0$, then the claim holds trivially since Δ_x is initialised as the empty set. Let the claim hold for $k \geq 0$. To show that it holds for $k + 1$, assume that ρ was added to Δ_x with the $(k + 1)$-st step of the Kleene iteration. It was constructed as $\rho = \rho_1; \dots; \rho_n$ due to an equation $\Delta_x \supseteq \Delta_{y_1}; \dots; \Delta_{y_n}$ where each ρ_i is either i. $\rho(\varepsilon)$ if $y_i = \varepsilon$, or ii. $\rho(a)$ if $y_i = a \in \Sigma$, or iii. is an element of $lsol(\Delta_{y_i})$ if $y_i \in X$. In the case iii., ρ_i was inserted into $lsol(\Delta_{y_i})$ within at most the k-th step of the Kleene iteration. By the induction hypothesis, this means that there is some $w_i \in L(y_i)$ with $\rho(w_i) = \rho_i$. This together with Lemma 2 gives that $\rho = \rho_1; \dots; \rho_n = \rho(w_1 \cdot \ldots \cdot w_n)$. By the definition of the system of equations, there is a rule $(x, y_1 \cdot \ldots \cdot y_n) \in R$ and hence $w_1 \cdot \ldots \cdot w_n \in L(x)$ by the definition of $L(x)$.

$lsol(\Delta_x) \supseteq \rho(L(x))$: Equivalently, for all $w \in L(x)$ we have $\rho(w) \in lsol(\Delta_x)$. We proceed by induction on the length ℓ of a derivation of w. For $\ell = 1$, the derivation uses only one rule, (x, ε) or (x, a) for some $a \in \Sigma$. Depending on the case, we have $\rho(w) = id$, or $\rho(w) = \rho(a)$. Due to the existence of the used rule, Δ_x will obtain $\rho(w)$ at the first step of the Kleene iteration. Assume the claim holds for the length of a derivation $\ell > 1$. Let the first rule used be $(x, y_1 \cdots y_n)$ where $y_1, \ldots, y_n \in \Sigma \cup X$. Then w must be of the form $w_1 \cdot \ldots \cdot w_n$ where each $w_i \in \Sigma^*$ is i. the empty word, ii. a terminal, or iii. is obtained from y_i by a derivation of length at most ℓ. In case iii., $\rho(w_i) \in lsol(\Delta_{y_i})$ by the induction hypothesis. Because of this and the definitions of the system of inequalities and the composition of sets of relations, $lsol(\Delta_x)$ contains the composition $\rho(w_1); \ldots; \rho(w_n)$. By Lemma 2, $\rho(\Delta_x)$ contains $\rho(w_1 \cdot \ldots \cdot w_n) = \rho(w)$. □

A relation $\rho \subseteq Y \times Y$ is said to be *rejecting* if there is no pair $(y_0, y) \in \rho$ so that y is accepting. With Lemma 3, there is no accepting run of A on the words that induced the relation. Hence, the words belong to the complement of the automaton's language.

Theorem 1. *$L(G) \subseteq L(A)$ holds if and only if $lsol(\Delta_{x_0})$ does not contain a rejecting relation.*

4 Chaotic Iteration with Antichains

The previous section associates with each instance $L(G) \subseteq L(A)$ of CFG-REG a data flow analysis problem $DFA(G, A)$. Chaotic iteration as presented in the preliminaries computes a solution to such an analysis problem. We now improve upon chaotic iteration using the antichain principle.

When solving $DFA(G, A)$, chaotic iteration computes on sets of relations. Antichain algorithms compute on sets of incomparable elements. Together, this means we should replace the powerset domain $(\mathbb{P}(\mathbb{P}(Y \times Y)), \subseteq)$ used in our data flow analysis by a reduced domain of incomparable relations.

We construct the reduced domain in two steps. First, we note that relations $\rho_1, \rho_2 \in \mathbb{P}(Y \times Y)$ are partially ordered wrt. inclusion $\rho_1 \subseteq \rho_2$. The goal of chaotic iteration is to find a rejecting relation. To this end, it will be beneficial to focus on $\subseteq$-minimal elements. We therefore define the reduced domain to consist of all antichains of relations — sets of relations that are pairwise $\subseteq$-incomparable:

$$\mathbb{A}(\mathbb{P}(Y \times Y)) := \{\Delta \subseteq \mathbb{P}(Y \times Y) \mid \forall \rho_1, \rho_2 \in \Delta : \rho_1 \not\subseteq \rho_2\}.$$

In a second step, we lift the partial ordering $\subseteq$ on the set of relations to a partial ordering $\preceq$ on the set of antichains $\mathbb{A}(\mathbb{P}(Y \times Y))$ as follows:

$$\Delta_1 \preceq \Delta_2, \quad \text{if} \quad \forall \rho_1 \in \Delta_1 \, \exists \rho_2 \in \Delta_2 : \rho_1 \supseteq \rho_2.$$

For every relation $\rho_1 \in \Delta_1$ there is a $\subseteq$-smaller relation $\rho_2 \in \Delta_2$. Intuitively, this means Δ_2 is more likely to lead to a rejecting relation. We refer to the resulting partially ordered set as *antichain lattice*, similar to [25]. The following lemma justifies the name.

Lemma 4. $(\mathbb{A}(\mathbb{P}(Y \times Y)), \preceq)$ *is a complete lattice.*

Since the underlying set is finite, it is sufficient to show that joins exist. Let $\Delta_1, \Delta_2 \in \mathbb{A}(\mathbb{P}(Y \times Y))$. The least upper bound is

$$\Delta_1 \sqcup \Delta_2 := min(\Delta_1 \cup \Delta_2).$$

The main result states that chaotic iteration remains complete when we use the antichain lattice.

Theorem 2. *Chaotic iteration on DFA(G, A) is sound and complete when using the antichain lattice.*

When we restrict chaotic iteration to antichains, we consider a smaller domain of sets of relations. If we find a rejecting relation in this smalller domain, we find the rejecting relation in the larger domain. In this sense, our analysis is sound.

It remains to show completeness. If there is no rejecting relation with a chaotic iteration on antichains, then there is none when we iterate on the full powerset lattice. The following lemma is the key to proving completeness. It states that $\subseteq$-minimal relations are sufficient for proving rejection and that inclusion is compatible with composition.

Lemma 5. *Consider* $\rho_1 \subseteq \rho_2$. *(1) If* ρ_2 *is rejecting, then* ρ_1 *is rejecting (2) For all* $\rho \in \mathbb{P}(Y \times Y)$ *we have* $\rho_1;\rho \subseteq \rho_2;\rho$.

To give an idea of why completeness holds, consider an arbitrary set of relations $\Delta \subseteq \mathbb{P}(Y \times Y)$ that may contain comparable elements. To obtain an antichain, we prune the set to the $\subseteq$-minimal relations. If there are rejecting relations in Δ, by Lemma 5(1) there is a minimal one. Moreover, with Lemma 5(2) continuing chaotic iteration on the minimal elements does not impair completeness.

5 Bounded Context Switching

We generalize our verification approach to multi-threaded recursive programs. In this setting, safety verification problems can be formulated as

$$L(G_1) \sqcup\!\sqcup \ldots \sqcup\!\sqcup L(G_m) \subseteq L(A).$$

Every context-free grammar $G_i = (\Sigma_i, X_i, x_{0,i}, R_i)$ represents (cf. Sect. 1) the valid control paths of a single thread in the multi-threaded program of interest. We can assume the threads to use different commands, which translates to disjointness of the alphabets, $\Sigma_i \cap \Sigma_j = \emptyset$ for all $i \neq j$. The shuffle operator $\sqcup\!\sqcup$ models the interleaving of computations from different threads. The task is to check whether every interleaving is valid wrt. the specification $A = (\Sigma, Y, y_0, \rightarrow)$ where $\Sigma = \biguplus \Sigma_i$. When modelling programs, specification A contains all feasible paths satisfying the verified property as well as all infeasible paths, where a read from a Boolean variable follows a write of the opposite value, like in Sect. 1.

The inclusion above, and hence safety verification of multi-threaded recursive programs, is undecidable [21]. A current trend in the verification community is to consider under-approximations of the problem that explore only a subset of the space of all computations. Under-approximations are good for bug hunting. If a bug is found in the restricted set of computations, it will remain present in the full semantics of the multi-threaded program. If the under-approximation is bug-free, however, we cannot conclude correctness of the program.

A prominent approach to under-approximation is *bounded context switching*. To explain the idea, assume the threads modeled by G_1 to G_m share the same processor. In this setting, a computation $w \in L(G_1) \sqcup\!\sqcup \ldots \sqcup\!\sqcup L(G_m)$ of the multi-threaded program may contain several context switches (a context switch occurs if one thread leaves the processor and another thread is scheduled). Phrased differently, the computation consists of several phases, $w = w_1 \cdot \ldots \cdot w_n$. In each phase, only one thread has the processor, without being preempted by another thread. Bounded context switching now only considers computations where each thread has at most k phases, for a given $k \in \mathbb{N}$. Note that the resulting set of computations is still infinite and even searches an infinite state space. What is limited is the number of interactions among threads. Indeed, the actions of one thread become visible to the other threads only at a context switch.

In the language-theoretic formulation, a context switch corresponds to an alphabet change. A phase is thus a maximal subword from a same alphabet. More formally, we say a word $w \in L(G_1) \sqcup\!\sqcup \ldots \sqcup\!\sqcup L(G_m)$ is *k-bounded*, $k \in \mathbb{N}$, if there are subwords $w = w_1 \cdot \ldots \cdot w_n$ so that

(1) for each w_i there is an alphabet $\Sigma_{\varphi(i)}$ with $w_i \in \Sigma^*_{\varphi(i)}$,
(2) $\Sigma_{\varphi(i)} \neq \Sigma_{\varphi(i+1)}$ for all $i \in [1, n-1]$,
(3) there are at most k subwords from each $\Sigma^*_{\varphi(i)}$.

We use $L_k(G_1, \ldots, G_m)$ to denote the set of all k-bounded words in the shuffle. The problem BCS-REG that is the subject of this section is defined as follows:

Given: Context-free grammars $G_1, \ldots, G_m$, a right-linear grammar A, and a number $k \in \mathbb{N}$.
Problem: Does $L_k(G_1, \ldots, G_m) \subseteq L(A)$ hold?

We propose a compositional approach to solving BCS-REG. We first approach the problem from the point of view of each single thread. Then we combine the obtained partial solutions into a solution for the overall multi-threaded program. A computation of the i-th thread is divided into k phases by context switches, which corresponds to a split of a word from $L(G_i)$ into k subwords. During each phase, the state of A is changed by the computation of the i-th thread. Between the phases, the environment, i.e., the other threads, change the state of A regardless of the i-th thread. We first, for every thread, compute a k-tuple of relations representing how the state of A can change during each of the k phases, assuming an arbitrary environment. The k-tuples will be obtained as a solution to the data flow analysis problem $DFA(G_i, A)$ in Sect. 3 that is now interpreted over a different domain.

To represent the behavior of the whole multi-threaded program, we shuffle the k-tuples of relations computed for the different threads. Such a shuffle represents an interleaving of the corresponding phases. From the point of view of a single thread, the shuffle concretizes a state change caused by *an arbitrary environment* to a state change caused by *a feasible computation of the other threads.* Finally, by composing the state changes caused by subsequent phases in the interleaving, we obtain a state change that is the overall effect of a computation of the whole multi-threaded program.

To better explain the idea and illustrate the technical development, consider the inclusion $L_2(G_1, G_2) \subseteq L(A)$ with

$$\begin{array}{llllll} G_1 : x_{0,1} \to a_1 \cdot x_{1,1} & G_2 : x_{0,2} \to a_2 \cdot x_{1,2} & A : y_0 \to a_1 \cdot y_1 & y_1 \to a_2 \cdot y_2 \\ \quad x_{1,1} \to b_1 & \quad x_{1,2} \to b_2 & \quad y_2 \to b_1 \cdot y_3 & y_3 \to b_2 \cdot y_4 \\ & & & y_4 \to \varepsilon. \end{array}$$

Consider the word $a_1 \cdot a_2 \cdot b_1 \cdot b_2 \in L_2(G_1, G_2)$. It contains the phases a_1 and b_1 from $L(G_1)$. Phase a_1 induces the state change $\{(y_0, y_1)\}$ on the automaton A. Phase b_1 leads to $\{(y_2, y_3)\}$. Since we have to keep the state changes for each phase, the data flow analysis $DFA(G_1, A)$ determines (amongst others) the word of relations $\{(y_0, y_1)\} \cdot \{(y_2, y_3)\} \in lsol(\Delta_{x_0})$.

Technically, a *word of relations* is a word $\sigma = \rho_1 \cdot \ldots \cdot \rho_n$ whose letters are relations from $\mathbb{P}(Y \times Y)$. We use $\mathbb{P}(Y \times Y)^{\leq k}$ for the set of all such words of length up to $k \in \mathbb{N}$. We again construct a powerset lattice over this domain

$$(\mathbb{P}(\mathbb{P}(Y \times Y)^{\leq k}), \subseteq).$$

To re-use the system of inequalities from Sect. 3, we have to generalize the operation of relational composition to words of relations, $\sigma_1; \sigma_2$. The idea is to take a choice. Either we concatenate the words σ_1 and σ_2 or we compose the last relation in σ_1 with the first relation in σ_2. The former case reflects a context switch, the latter case occurs if there is no context switch (between the subwords inducing the last relation of σ_1 and the first relation of σ_2, respectively).

For the definition of this relational composition operator, consider the words of relations $\sigma_1 = \rho_{1,1} \cdot \ldots \cdot \rho_{1,k_1}$ and $\sigma_2 = \rho_{2,1} \cdot \ldots \cdot \rho_{2,k_2}$ in $\mathbb{P}(Y \times Y)^{\leq k}$. The operation of concatenation $\sigma_1 \cdot \sigma_2$ is defined as σ_1 and σ_2 are words. The composition of the last relation in σ_1 with the first relation in σ_2 is

$$\sigma_1 \circ \sigma_2 := \rho_{1,1} \cdot \ldots \cdot \rho_{1,k_1-1} \cdot (\rho_{1,k_1}; \rho_{2,1}) \cdot \rho_{2,2} \cdot \ldots \cdot \rho_{2,k_2}.$$

The relational composition $\sigma_1; \sigma_2$ yields the set of words (of relations) containing both $\sigma_1 \cdot \sigma_2$ and $\sigma_1 \circ \sigma_2$, provided the length constraint is met:

$$\sigma_1; \sigma_2 := \{\sigma_1 \cdot \sigma_2, \sigma_1 \circ \sigma_2\} \cap \mathbb{P}(Y \times Y)^{\leq k}.$$

With a component-wise definition, we lift the relational composition to sets of words of relations.

In the example, $\{ \{(y_0, y_1)\} \}$ and $\{ \{(y_2, y_3)\} \}$ are two sets each containing one word consisting of a single relation. Relational composition yields

$$\begin{aligned} lsol(\Delta_{x_{0,1}}) &= \{ \{(y_0, y_1)\} \}; \{ \{(y_2, y_3)\} \} \\ &= \{ \{(y_0, y_1)\} \cdot \{(y_2, y_3)\}, \{(y_0, y_1)\} \circ \{(y_2, y_3)\} \} \\ &= \{ \{(y_0, y_1)\} \cdot \{(y_2, y_3)\}, \emptyset \}. \end{aligned}$$

The empty set indicates that $a_1 \cdot b_1$ is not executable on the automaton A.

We use $DFA(G_i, A)$ for the data flow analysis problem that is derived from G_i and A using the above powerset lattice and the above relational composition. The following is the analogue of Lemma 3

Lemma 6. *$lsol(\Delta_x)$ contains precisely the words of relations induced by $L(x)$.*

Since words σ_1, σ_2 of relations are ordinary words over a special alphabet, also the shuffle operation $\sigma_1 \sqcup\!\sqcup \sigma_2$ is defined. With reference to the above reduction,

$$lsol(\Delta_{x_{0,1}}) \sqcup\!\sqcup \ldots \sqcup\!\sqcup lsol(\Delta_{x_{0,m}})$$

yields precisely the words of relations that correspond to the k-bounded interleavings among words derivable in the different grammars.

For the desired inclusion $L_k(G_1, \ldots, G_m) \subseteq L(A)$, we check whether a word in the shuffle $lsol(\Delta_{x_{0,1}}) \sqcup\!\sqcup \ldots \sqcup\!\sqcup lsol(\Delta_{x_{0,m}})$ corresponds to a rejecting relation. To this end, we compose the relations in the word. The idea is that each word of relations in the shuffle corresponds to contiguous words in $L_k(G_1, \ldots, G_m)$. Therefore, we no longer have to deal with subwords. We define

$$eval(\rho_1 \cdot \ldots \cdot \rho_n) \;:=\; \rho_1; \ldots; \rho_n.$$

Theorem 3. *Inclusion $L_k(G_1, \ldots, G_m) \subseteq L(A)$ holds if and only if there is no rejecting relation in $eval(lsol(\Delta_{x_{0,1}}) \sqcup\!\sqcup \ldots \sqcup\!\sqcup lsol(\Delta_{x_{0,m}}))$.*

To conclude the example, note that $lsol(\Delta_{x_{0,2}}) = \{ \{(y_1, y_2)\} \cdot \{(y_3, y_4)\}, \emptyset \}$. Among other words, we have

$$\sigma := \{(y_0, y_1)\} \cdot \{(y_1, y_2)\} \cdot \{(y_2, y_3)\} \cdot \{(y_3, y_4)\} \in lsol(\Delta_{x_{0,1}}) \sqcup\!\sqcup lsol(\Delta_{x_{0,2}}).$$

The evaluation yields $eval(\sigma) = \{(y_0, y_4)\}$. Still, the inclusion fails since we find the rejecting relation $eval(\emptyset \cdot \emptyset) = \emptyset \in eval(lsol(\Delta_{x_{0,1}}) \sqcup\!\sqcup lsol(\Delta_{x_{0,2}}))$.

6 Conclusions and Future Work

We developed algorithms for the safety verification of recursive programs. This verification task is often phrased as an inclusion $L(G) \subseteq L(A)$ of a context-free language modeling the program of interest in a regular language representing the safety property. Our first contribution is a reformulation of the inclusion $L(G) \subseteq L(A)$ as a data flow analysis problem $DFA(G, A)$. The data flow analysis determines the state changes that the words derived in the grammar induce on the given automaton. This means the underlying domain of data flow values consists of sets of relations among states.

The data flow analysis problem $DFA(G, A)$ can be solved by a standard algorithm called chaotic iteration. Our second contribution is an improvement of chaotic iteration. We show that the computation can be restricted to antichains of relations — while preserving completeness. Antichains are sets of relations that are pairwise incomparable. Phrased differently, our result reduces the powerset lattice used in $DFA(G, A)$ to a lattice of antichains [25].

As a last contribution, we show how to generalize the approach to programs that are multi-threaded and recursive. While in this setting safety verification is known to be undecidable in general [21], an under-approximate variant of the problem remains decidable: Restricted to a bounded number of context switches, we can still check an inclusion $L(G_1) \sqcup\!\sqcup \ldots \sqcup\!\sqcup L(G_m) \subseteq L(A)$. Our approach is compositional in that it combines results from independent data flow analyses $DFA(G_i, A)$. The reduction generalizes $DFA(G, A)$ from (sets of) relations to (sets of) words of relations.

As an immediate task for future work, we will implement our antichain-based chaotic iteration and conduct an experimental evaluation. On the theoretical side, we plan to check whether a variant of the antichain principle can be used in related data flow analyses. One can also imagine importing algorithms to speed up the solution of $DFA(G, A)$. An interesting candidate seems to be Newton iteration as presented in [8].

Acknowledgement. This work was supported by the DFG project R2M2: Robustness against Relaxed Memory Models, the Czech Science Foundation (projects 14-11384S and 202/13/37876P), the BUT FIT project FIT-S-14-2486, and the EU/Czech IT4Innovations Centre of Excellence project CZ.1.05/1.1.00/02.0070.

References

1. Abdulla, P.A., Cerans, K., Jonsson, B., Tsay, Y.-K.: General decidability theorems for infinite-state systems. In: LICS, pp. 313–321. IEEE (1996)
2. Atig, M.F., Bouajjani, A., Parlato, G.: Getting rid of store-buffers in TSO analysis. In: Gopalakrishnan, G., Qadeer, S. (eds.) CAV 2011. LNCS, vol. 6806, pp. 99–115. Springer, Heidelberg (2011)
3. Büchi, J.R.: On a decision method in restricted second order arithmetic. In: Lane, S.M., Siefkes, D. (eds.) The Collected Works of J. Richard Büchi. Springer, New York (1990)
4. Bouajjani, A., Esparza, J., Touili, T.: A generic approach to the static analysis of concurrent programs with procedures. In: POPL, pp. 62–73. ACM (2003)
5. Bruyère, V., Ducobu, M., Gauwin, O.: Visibly pushdown automata: universality and inclusion via antichains. In: Dediu, A.-H., Martín-Vide, C., Truthe, B. (eds.) LATA 2013. LNCS, vol. 7810, pp. 190–201. Springer, Heidelberg (2013)
6. Cousot, P., Cousot, R.: Automatic synthesis of optimal invariant assertions: mathematical foundations. In: Artificial Intelligence and Programming Languages, pp. 1–12. ACM (1977)

7. De Wulf, M., Doyen, L., Raskin, J.-F.: A lattice theory for solving games of imperfect information. In: Hespanha, J.P., Tiwari, A. (eds.) HSCC 2006. LNCS, vol. 3927, pp. 153–168. Springer, Heidelberg (2006)
8. Esparza, J., Kiefer, S., Luttenberger, M.: Newtonian program analysis. JACM **57**(6), 33:1–33:47 (2010)
9. Farzan, A., Kincaid, Z., Podelski, A.: Inductive data flow graphs. In: POPL, pp. 129–142. ACM (2013)
10. Farzan, A., Kincaid, Z., Podelski, A.: Proofs that count. In: POPL, pp. 151–164. ACM (2014)
11. Farzan, A., Kincaid, Z., Podelski, A.: Proof spaces for unbounded parallelism. In: POPL, pp. 407–420. ACM (2015)
12. Finkel, A., Schnoebelen, P.: Well-structured transition systems everywhere!. Theor. Comput. Sci. **256**(1–2), 63–92 (2001)
13. Fogarty, S., Vardi, M.Y.: Efficient Büchi universality checking. In: Esparza, J., Majumdar, R. (eds.) TACAS 2010. LNCS, vol. 6015, pp. 205–220. Springer, Heidelberg (2010)
14. Friedmann, O., Klaedtke, F., Lange, M.: Ramsey goes visibly pushdown. In: Fomin, F.V., Freivalds, R., Kwiatkowska, M., Peleg, D. (eds.) ICALP 2013, Part II. LNCS, vol. 7966, pp. 224–237. Springer, Heidelberg (2013)
15. Heizmann, M., Hoenicke, J., Podelski, A.: Nested interpolants. In: POPL, pp. 471–482. ACM (2010)
16. Heizmann, M., Hoenicke, J., Podelski, A.: Software model checking for people who love automata. In: Sharygina, N., Veith, H. (eds.) CAV 2013. LNCS, vol. 8044, pp. 36–52. Springer, Heidelberg (2013)
17. Lal, A., Touili, T., Kidd, N., Reps, T.: Interprocedural analysis of concurrent programs under a context bound. In: Ramakrishnan, C.R., Rehof, J. (eds.) TACAS 2008. LNCS, vol. 4963, pp. 282–298. Springer, Heidelberg (2008)
18. Long, Z., Calin, G., Majumdar, R., Meyer, R.: Language-theoretic abstraction refinement. In: de Lara, J., Zisman, A. (eds.) FASE 2012. LNCS, vol. 7212, pp. 362–376. Springer, Heidelberg (2012)
19. Nielson, F., Nielson, H.R., Hankin, C.: Principles of Program Analysis. Springer, Heidelberg (1999)
20. Qadeer, S., Rehof, J.: Context-bounded model checking of concurrent software. In: Halbwachs, N., Zuck, L.D. (eds.) TACAS 2005. LNCS, vol. 3440, pp. 93–107. Springer, Heidelberg (2005)
21. Ramalingam, G.: Context-sensitive synchronization-sensitive analysis is undecidable. ACM Trans. Program. Lang. Syst. **22**(2), 416–430 (2000)
22. Reps, T., Horwitz, S., Sagiv, M.: Precise interprocedural dataflow analysis via graph reachability. In: POPL, pp. 49–61. ACM (1995)
23. Seidl, H., Wilhelm, R., Hack, S.: Compiler Design - Analysis and Transformation. Springer, Heidelberg (2012)
24. Sharir, M., Pnueli, A.: Two approaches to interprocedural data flow analysis. Technical report 2, New York University (1978)
25. De Wulf, M., Doyen, L., Henzinger, T.A., Raskin, J.-F.: Antichains: a new algorithm for checking universality of finite automata. In: Ball, T., Jones, R.B. (eds.) CAV 2006. LNCS, vol. 4144, pp. 17–30. Springer, Heidelberg (2006)

BAPU: Efficient and Practical Bunching of Access Point Uplinks

Tao Jin[1], Triet D. Vo-Huu[2](✉), Erik-Oliver Blass[3], and Guevara Noubir[2]

[1] Qualcomm Corporate Research and Development, San Diego, CA, USA
[2] Northeastern University, Boston, MA, USA
vohuudtr@ccs.neu.edu
[3] Airbus Group Innovations, 81663 Munich, Germany

Abstract. Today's throttled uplink of residential broadband renders a broad class of popular applications such as HD video uploading and large file transfer impractical. Aggregation of WiFi APs is one way to bypass this limitation. Motivated by this problem, we present BAPU (**B**unching of **A**ccess **P**oint **U**plinks) to achieve two major goals: (1) support commodity clients by refraining from client modifications, (2) support both UDP and TCP based applications. We justify the need for client transparency and generic transport layer support and present new challenges. In particular, a naive multiplexing of a single TCP session through multiple paths results in a significant performance degradation. We describe BAPU's mechanisms and design. We developed a prototype of BAPU with commodity hardware, and our extensive experiments show that BAPU aggregates up to 95 % of the total uplink capacity for UDP and 88 % for TCP.

1 Introduction

Today, mobile devices are equipped with high-resolution cameras and are quickly becoming the primary device to generate personal multimedia content. Such fast growth of User Generated Content (UGC) naturally leads to an ever increasing demand of instant sharing of UGC through online services, e.g., YouTube and Dailymotion, or in an end-to-end manner. In addition, there is a trend of instantly backing up personal files in "Cloud Storage" like Dropbox or iCloud. All these services require sufficient uplink bandwidth for fast data transfer. While today's ISPs offer high-speed downlink, uplink bandwidth is usually throttled. As a result, instant sharing of HD content or fast data backup in the "Cloud" is still impractical in today's residential broadband. Consequently, there is a need to scale backhaul uplinks.

1.1 Aggregating AP to Bypass Broadband Limitations

Given that WiFi capacity typically exceeds the broadband uplink capacity by at least one order of magnitude, a single client WiFi can communicate with multiple

A. Bouajjani and H. Fauconnier (Eds.): NETYS 2015, LNCS 9466, pp. 337–353, 2015.
DOI: 10.1007/978-3-319-26850-7_23

APs in range and aggregate the idle bandwidth behind them. Several AP aggregation solutions (e.g., FatVAP [17] and THEMIS [12]) have been proposed in the past few years. Their rationale is to route TCP/UDP sessions through different APs such that the traffic load splits across multiple broadband links, thereby achieving a higher aggregated throughput. Yet, a single TCP/UDP connection is assigned to a single AP, in which case the connection throughput cannot exceed the single broadband link capacity. Since most uplink hogging applications such as iCloud establish single transport layer connections for data transfer, current AP aggregation solutions are not suitable for single session uplink scaling, unless the application is redesigned to adapt to the AP aggregation technology. Recently, Link-Alike [15] multiplexes single UDP flow across multiple APs. However, Link-Alike's design is specific to UDP file transfer, resulting pieces of files to arrive in out-of-order sequence, which prohibits TCP based applications (e.g., HD video streaming) that require a strictly in-order delivery and deadline meeting. Besides, multiplexing single TCP sessions through multiple paths is a challenging problem (and will be discussed later). Moreover, client modifications are required to support TCP. In this work, we require a new AP aggregation solution offering complete transparency on the client with generic support for either TCP or applications.

1.2 Feasibility of AP Aggregation

While WiFi aggregation allows bypassing broadband limitations, it is yet unclear whether aggregation is practical in reality. We now present our recent study on urban WiFi and broadband resources, revealing several interesting insights regarding the feasibility of AP aggregation in residential broadband.

Mostly Idle Broadband Uplinks: Since Feb. 2011, we have developed and deployed a WiFi testbed in Boston's urban area, aiming to monitor the usage pattern of residential broadband. This testbed consists of 30 home WiFi APs running customized OpenWRT firmware with two major broadband ISPs, Comcast and RCN. During a 18 month period, we have collected over 70 million records. Figure 1 shows the uplink bandwidth usage during a 24 h time window. Throughout the day, there is at least 50 % chance that uplink is completely idle. Even during peak hours, there is over 90 % chance that the uplink bandwidth usage is below 100 Kbps. Consequently, there exists a considerable amount of idle uplink bandwidth, making AP aggregation a viable approach.

WiFi Densely Deployed in Residential Area: Our recently conducted Wardriving measurements in 4 residential areas in Boston identify 22000 APs, 14.2 % of which are unencrypted. As shown in Fig. 2, there are on average 17 APs available at each location, with an average 7 to 12 APs on each channel. This enormous presence of WiFi justifies the feasibility of AP aggregation in urban area.

WiFi Becoming Open and Social: Driven by the increasing demand of ubiquitous Internet access, there is a new trend that broadband users share their

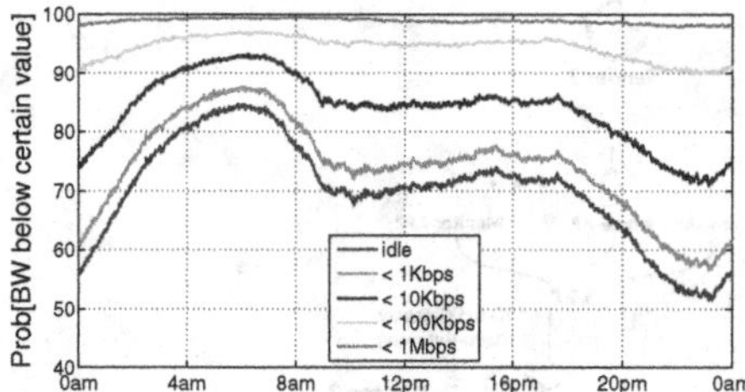

Fig. 1. Residential uplink bandwidth usage.

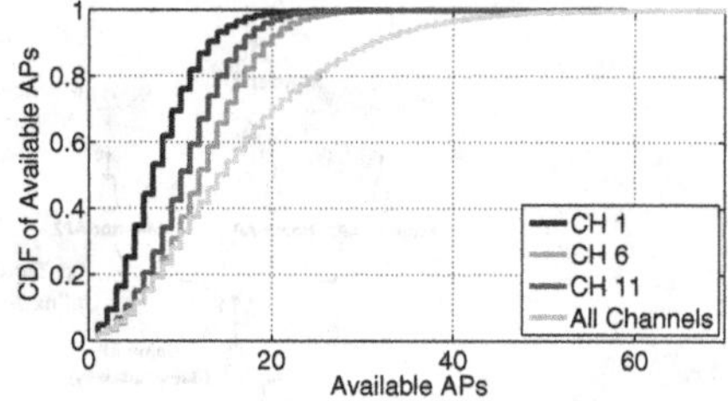

Fig. 2. Available APs in Wardriving.

bandwidth as public WiFi signal to mobile users. Mainstream home WiFi APs, e.g., LinkSys and D-Link, already offer a standard feature which hosts two SSIDs, one encrypted for private use, the other unencrypted for public sharing. FON [9], a leading company in this area, claims to have over 7 million social hotspots worldwide. Given this trend of WiFi becoming social and cloud-powered, a software solution on APs allows much easier progressive adoption of AP aggregation technologies compared to a few years ago.

Based on this discussion, we present BAPU, a complete software solution for WiFi APs allowing broadband uplink aggregation. BAPU features complete transparency to client devices and high aggregated throughput for both TCP and UDP, even in lossy wireless environment. Our major contributions are summarized as follows:

Transparency to Client: BAPU does not require any modification to clients. The client device conducts regular 802.11 communications with its home AP while AP aggregation happens in a "transparent" way. Also, all legacy network applications benefit from such transparency and seamlessly utilize BAPU.

Efficient Aggregation for Both TCP and UDP: Multiplexing a single TCP flow through multiple paths raises many technical challenges, making efficient aggregation non-trivial. We propose a novel mechanism called *Proactive-ACK*. Through an in-depth analysis of TCP stack behavior, we show how *Proactive-ACK* performs efficient TCP multiplexing. BAPU achieves high aggregated throughput for *both* TCP and UDP.

Prototype with Commodity Hardware: We have prototyped our complete BAPU system on commodity 802.11n WiFi APs with OpenWRT firmware.

Evaluation: We conduct an extensive set of experiments to evaluate BAPU in various realistic network settings. Our results show that BAPU efficiently achieves over 95 % and 88 % of total uplink bandwidth for UDP and TCP transmissions, respectively.

2 System Overview

For ease of understanding, we first introduce two typical application scenarios that benefit from BAPU – see Fig. 3.

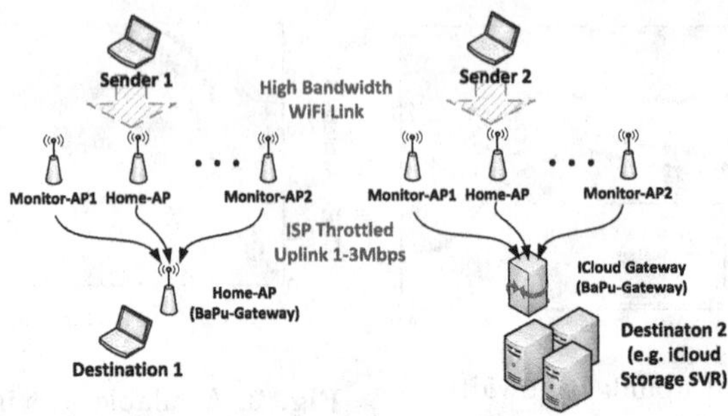

Fig. 3. BAPU system architecture and example application scenarios. Scenario 1 (left): Sender 1 shares an HD video with a remote end user. Scenario 2 (right): Sender 2 backs up a large file to iCloud. The uplink aggregation is enabled via BAPU-enabled Home-AP and Monitor-APs.

Scenario 1. Instant Sharing of HD Video: In order to retain the control of personal content, Sender 1 streams his HD video in real time directly from his hard drive to Destination 1. Both users are connected to their own Home-APs. Sender 1's uplink is throttled by his ISP to 1 $\sim$ 3Mbps, preventing him to handle the 8 Mbps HD video in real time. However with BAPU, the idle uplink of the neighboring Monitor-APs are exploited to boost uplink throughput. BAPU-*Gateway*, the Home-AP of Destination 1, aggregates and forwards multiplexed traffic to Destination 1.

Scenario 2. Instant Backup of Large File: Sender 2 wishes to backup his HD video clip to some cloud storage service such as iCloud. With the 3 Mbps uplink rate, it takes over an hour to upload a 30 min HD video. With BAPU, uploadingss time is greatly reduced by deloying a BAPU-*Gateway* in front (or part) of the cloud storage servers for handling parallel uploads from Home-AP and neighboring Monitor-APs.

BAPU Protocol Description. In BAPU, *Sender* is associated with its *Home-AP*, and the uploading of data is aggregated via unencrypted wireless link. The data, however, is protected with some end-to-end security mechanism (e.g., SSL/TLS). *Home-AP* and *Monitor-AP* are configured to run in *both* WiFi AP mode and WiFi monitor mode[1]. The WiFi link between the *Sender* and its *Home-AP* generally provides high bandwidth, up to hundreds of Mbps with 802.11n. The link between a BAPU-*AP* and the *Destination*, however, is throttled by the ISP. At the remote end, we place a BAPU-*Gateway* immediately before the *Destination*. The connection between the BAPU-*Gateway* and the *Destination* is either wired or wireless high-speed link. Note that being in proximity, unicasts between *Sender* and *Home-AP* (AP mode) can be overheard by (some of) the *Monitor-AP*s (monitor mode). At a high level, BAPU is a central-

[1] Modern WiFi drivers (e.g., ath9k) support multiple modes for one physical WiFi interface.

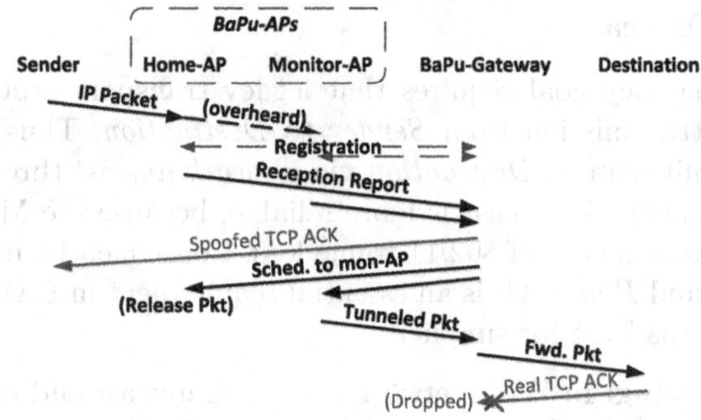

Fig. 4. BAPU Protocol Traffic Flow. The ACKs (red color) are managed for TCP only (Color figure online).

ized system with the controller residing at BAPU-*Gateway*, providing an uplink aggregation carried out as follows (Fig. 4).

1. *Sender* starts a TCP/UDP upload to *Destination* through its *Home-AP* via WiFi.
2. *Home-AP* and *Monitor-AP* overhear WiFi packets and identify "BAPU" session by checking the destination IP and port.
3. BAPU-*AP*s register themselves to BAPU-*Gateway*.
4. *Home-AP* and *Monitor-AP* capture *Sender*'s packets in monitor mode, and collaborate to upload data for *Sender*, following a schedule determined by BAPU-*Gateway*.
5. *Home-AP* and *Monitor-AP* send reports to BAPU-*Gateway* for each packet.
6. In an *UDP* session, BAPU-*Gateway* determines which BAPU-*AP* will forward the captured packet, and broadcast a scheduling message to all BAPU-*AP*s.
7. A *TCP* session is much more challenging to support than UDP. To properly multiplex *Sender*'s single TCP flow through multiple paths, we devise a new mechanism called *Proactive-ACK*: BAPU-*Gateway* sends spoofed TCP ACKs to *Sender* as BAPU session goes on. *Proactive-ACK* is designed to make BAPU work efficiently with legacy TCP congestion control.
8. The scheduled AP forwards packets to *Destination* tunnelled through BAPU-*Gateway*.

3 Uplink Aggregation

In this section, we discuss technical challenges and describe our solutions for BAPU system to achieve an efficient and practical aggregation system. We remark that BAPU shares some similarities in the high-level architecture with previous work (e.g., Link-alike [15], FatVAP [17]). However, from pure practicality aspects, the applicability of those systems is severely limited due to heavy modification of client devices or support for only specific applications (e.g., large file transfer, UDP). Contrary, BAPU targets *transparency* and *high-throughput* transmissions for *both* UDP and TCP applications.

3.1 Network Unicast

First, the transparency goal requires that legacy transport protocols must be usable for data transmission from *Sender* to *Destination*. Thus, *Sender* must be able to transmit data to *Destination* via *network unicast* through its *Home-AP*. Second, the network unicast is more reliable, because the MAC layer handles retransmissions in case of 802.11 frame loss. Consequently, network unicast between *Sender* and *Home-AP* is an essential requirement in BAPU, while prior work [15] chose broadcast for simplicity.

Packet Overhearing: In WiFi networks, network unicast and broadcast differ in the next-hop physical address in the MAC layer. This complicates the packet overhearing capability at *Monitor-AP*s, since the *Sender* uses its *Home-AP*'s physical address as the next-hop address in the 802.11 header, while *Monitor-AP*s automatically discard the packet due to a mismatched physical address. To allow *Monitor-AP*s to capture overheard packets, BAPU's solution is to configure BAPU-*AP*s to operate simultaneously in two modes: *AP mode* and *monitor mode*. The former mode is used for serving clients in the AP's own WLAN, whereas the latter is used for overhearing packets in raw format.

Packet Identification: Each packet sent from the *Sender* (BAPU protocol's step 1) contains the session information in the packet's IP header such as the protocol, the source and destination IP addresses and ports. With this information, *Home-AP* can uniquely identify the *Sender* (step 2). In contrast, *Monitor-AP*s may have ambiguity in identifying the *Sender*, as *Sender*s from different WLANs may (legally) use the same IP address. To resolve such conflict, we create a frame parser for the packet's MAC header to obtain the `BSSID` that identifies the WLAN the session belongs to. Therefore, any session in BAPU is now uniquely determined by the following 6-tuple $< \texttt{BSSID}, \texttt{proto}, \texttt{srcIP}, \texttt{dstIP}, \texttt{srcPort}, \texttt{dstPort} >$.

Duplicate Elimination: Unicasting a packet may involve a number of (MAC-layer) retransmissions due to wireless loss between the *Sender* and its *Home-AP*. This increases the transmission reliability. Nevertheless, it is possible that a nearby *Monitor-AP* can overhear more than one (re)transmission of the same packet and eventually forward unnecessary duplicates to *Destination*, flooding *Monitor-AP*'s uplink. To identify the duplicate packets, we keep records of `IPID` field of each overheard IP packet. Since `IPID` remains the same value for each MAC-layer retransmission, it allows *Monitor-AP*s to identify and discard the same packet. It is worth noting that in TCP transmission, the TCP sequence number (SEQ) is not a good indicator to identify the duplicate packets, as it is unique for TCP retransmission, but not for MAC-layer retransmissions.

3.2 Tunnel Forwarding

The transparency goals requires that the high-level application be unaware of the aggregation protocol in BAPU. A seemingly straightforward solution is that *Home-AP* and *Monitor-AP*s forward the *Sender*'s packets with spoofed IP addresses. It is, however, impractical for two reasons: (1) many ISPs block spoofed

IP packets; (2) forwarded packets by *Monitor-AP*s are unreliable, because they are raw packets overheard from the air. Our approach is that each BAPU-*AP* conveys the *Sender*'s data via a separate TCP tunnel. Since we support a transparency for aggregation over multiple paths, the techniques for tunnelling and address resolving in each single path require a careful design at both BAPU-*AP*s and BAPU-*Gateway*.

Tunnel Connection: Once a BAPU-*AP* identifies a new *Sender-Destination* session (step 2) based on the 6-tuple, it establishes a tunnel connection to BAPU-*Gateway*. Regardless of the session protocol, a tunnel connection between the BAPU-*AP* and BAPU-*Gateway* is always a TCP connection. The choice of TCP tunnel is partially motivated by the *TCP-friendliness.* We desire to aggregate the idle bandwidth of BAPU-*AP*s without overloading the ISP networks. Besides, since TCP tunnel can provide a reliable channel, it helps keep a simple logic for handling a reliable aggregated transmission.

Forwarding: In the registration (step 3) to BAPU-*Gateway*, the BAPU-*AP* receives an `APID` as its "contributor" identifier for the new session. The `APID` is used in all messages in the protocol. Both control messages (registration, report, scheduling) and data messages are exchanged via the reliable TCP tunnel. On reception of a scheduling message with matching `APID`, the *Monitor-AP* encapsulates the corresponding *Sender*'s packet in a BAPU data message and sends it to BAPU-*Gateway* (step 8), which then extracts the original data packet, delivers to the *Destination*. In BAPU, short control messages only introduce small overhead in the backhaul.

NAT: In WLAN, the *Sender* is behind the *Home-AP*, typically a NAT box. In BAPU, the *Sender*'s data are conveyed to the *Destination* via separate tunnels from each participating BAPU-*AP*, which carries out NAT translation with NAT mapping records obtained from BAPU-*Gateway* in step 3. Besides, since the downlink capacity is enormous, we allow all reverse (downlink) traffic from *Destination* to *Sender* to traverse along the *default downlink path.* In addition, as there might be multiple tiers of NAT boxes in the middle, we must ensure that the NAT mapping for a session is properly installed on all NAT boxes along the path, and the first few packets of a new session are not tunnelled.

3.3 Scheduling

The bandwidth aggregation performance depends on the efficiency of multiplexing data among BAPU-*AP*s to best utilize the idle uplink bandwidth. In BAPU, we adopt a *centralized scheduler* at BAPU-*Gateway*. There are two main factors to select this design. *First,* it does not only simplify the implementation, but also allows easy extension of the design with extra logic to further optimize the scheduling strategy. *Second*, a scheduler usually requires complex processing and memory capability, which might overload the BAPU-*AP*s with much lower capability if scheduling decisions are distributedly performed by BAPU-*AP*s. Our scheduling strategy is based on received reports in steps 6 and 7 of the protocol. Each report from a BAPU-*AP* contains a sending buffer size obtained from the Linux kernel (via `ioctl`). This value specifies how much a BAPU-*AP* can contribute to the aggregation. Based on reports, BAPU-*Gateway* applies First-Come-First-Served strategy to select a forwarder among BAPU-*AP*s who have captured the same packet. The rationale for choosing this approach are (1) *Fairness:* Sharing bandwidth takes into account the available bandwidth of participating BAPU-*AP*s because AP owners have different subscription plans. (2) *Protocol independence:* Scheduling decision is made based on the BAPU-*AP*s' sharing capability, not on the particular transport protocol.

4 TCP with Proactive-ACK

4.1 TCP Issues with Aggregation

Brief Overview on TCP: TCP ensures successful and in-order data delivery between *Sender* and *Destination*. The *Sender* maintains a CWND (congestion window) during the on-going session, which determines the TCP throughput. The *Sender*'s CWND size is affected by acknowledgements from the *Destination*. First, the growth rate of CWND depends on the rate of receiving acknowledgements, i.e., the link latency. Second, missing acknowledgement within a RTO (retransmission timeout) causes the *Sender* to issue a *retransmission*. On reception of out-of-order sequences, the *Destination* sends a DUPACK (duplicate acknowledgement) to inform the *Sender* of missing packets. By default [3], the *Sender* will issue a *fast retransmission* upon receiving 3 consecutive DUPACKs. Both retransmission and fast retransmission cause the *Sender* to cut off the CWND accordingly to adapt to the congested network or slow receiver.

Performance Issues with Aggregation: TCP was designed based on the fact that the out-of-order sequence is generally a good indicator of lost packets or congested network. However, such assumption no longer holds in BAPU.

Out-of-order Packets: In BAPU, packets belonging to the same TCP session are *intentionally* routed through multiple BAPU-*AP*s via diverse backhaul connections in terms of capacity, latency, traffic load, etc. This results in *serious* out-of-order sequence at BAPU-*Gateway*, which eventually injects the out-of-order packets to the *Destination*.

Double RTT: Also, due to the aggregation protocol, data packets in BAPU are delivered to the *Destination* with a double round-trip-time (RTT) compared to a regular link. This causes the *Sender*'s CWND to grow more slowly and peak at lower values. Consequently, with an *unplanned* aggregation method, the TCP congestion control mechanism is *falsely* triggered, resulting in considerably low throughput. As we show later in Sect. 5, a simplified prototype of BAPU, which share similarities with the system in [15], gives poor TCP throughput.

Simple Solution (SIMPLEBUFFER) Does not Work: To address the TCP performance issue, we investigate a simple approach: data packets forwarded by BAPU-*AP*s are buffered at BAPU-*Gateway* until a continuous sequence is received or a predefined buffering timeout is reached before delivering it to the *Destination*.

This solution, however, encounters the following issues: (1) *Optimality:* Due to the difference in capacity, latency, loss rate among backhaul uplinks, it is unclear how to determine the optimal buffer size and timeout. (2) *Suboptimal RTT:* The buffering mechanism results in *double RTT* issue. (3) *Performance:* We implemented the buffering mechanism at BAPU-*Gateway*, and verified that it *does not* help improving the TCP throughput (Sect. 5.2).

4.2 BAPU's Solution

We introduce a novel mechanism called *Proactive-ACK* (step 7) to support TCP with uplink aggregation. The principle is to actively control the exchange of acknowledgements instead of relying on the default behaviour of the end-to-end session. By Proactive-ACK, we solve both *out-of-order packet* and *double RTT* issues. In the following paragraphs, we call acknowledgements actively sent by BAPU-*Gateway spoofed*, while the ones sent by the *Destination* are *real* acknowledgements.

Spoofing Proactive-ACK: In BAPU, most of out-of-order packets are caused by the aggregation mechanism via multiple BAPU-*AP*s. To avoid delivering out-of-order packets to the *Destination* and the resulting cut-off of the CWND at the *Sender*, we maintain a sequence map at BAPU-*Gateway*, indicating **reported**, **delivered** or **pending** sequence numbers. Once BAPU-*Gateway* collects a continuous range of reported sequence numbers, BAPU-*Gateway* sends a *spoofed* ACK back to the *Sender*. The intuition is that all the packets that are reported by some BAPU-*AP*s are currently stored in their buffer. Due to the reliability of the TCP tunnel, the reported packets will be eventually forwarded to BAPU-*Gateway* in reliable manner. Therefore, immediately sending a *spoofed* Proactive-ACK back to the *Sender* avoids false DUPACKs and helps maintain a healthy CWND growth at the *Sender*. Also, the RTT is not doubled.

Eliminating DUPACKs: Since *spoofed* ACKs keep the *Sender*'s CWND continuously grow, BAPU-*Gateway* can take time and buffer all out-of-order data packets forwarded from BAPU-*AP*s, and deliver *only* in-order packets to the *Destination*. Therefore, in BAPU, out-of-order packets and associated DUPACKs are eliminated from *Destination*.

Spoofing DUPACKs: It is possible that some packets are actually lost in the air between the *Sender* and BAPU-*AP*s. Concretely, if the report for an expected TCP sequence number is not received within a certain time, it is implied to be lost on all participating BAPU-*AP*s. Now that BAPU-*Gateway* sends a spoofed DUPACK back to the *Sender* in order to mimic the TCP fast retransmission mechanism for fast recovery.

Managing Real ACKs and TCP Semantics: Since BAPU-*Gateway* sends spoofed ACKs to the *Sender*, on reception of real ACKs from the *Destination*, BAPU-*Gateway* discards the real ACKs. However, BAPU-*Gateway* does save the TCP header fields in the real ACKs, such as advertised receiver window and

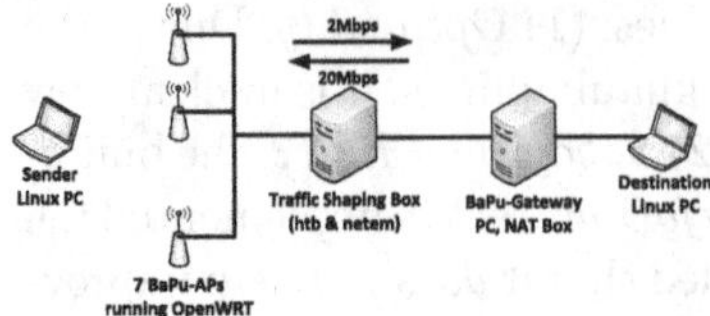

Fig. 5. BAPU experiment setup.

Table 1. Distance vs. Network RTT.

Regional: 500 - 1,000 mi	32 ms [2]
Cross-continent: ∼ 3,000 mi	96 ms [2]
Multi-continent: ∼ 6,000 mi	192 ms [2]
Inter-AP in greater Boston	20 ms ∼ 80 ms

Inter-AP RTT are measured by our Open Infrastructure WiFi testbed [1] in greater Boston, covering Comcast, RCN, and Verizon.

timestamp, which maintains the TCP semantics and the state of the TCP connection. While BAPU-*Gateway* generates the *spoofed* ACKs, it uses the latest header field values extracted from *real* ACKs to prepare the acknowledge segment.

We have one important remark on TCP semantics. If an AP which has been scheduled to forward a selected packet is suddenly offline, such packet lost would *not* be recognized by *Sender* because it has received spoofed ACK. In this case, we resort to *Home-AP* which carries out unicast between itself and *Sender* and should have a backup copy. Despite the slight difference in TCP semantics, we verify that Proactive-ACK gives a significantly improved TCP throughput. We present these results in Sect. 5.

5 Evaluation

In this section, we evaluate the performance of BAPU for UDP and TCP in various system settings. Our experiment setup is shown in Fig. 5. Our testbed consists of a *Sender*, 7 BAPU-*APs*, a BAPU-*Gateway*, a *Destination* and a traffic shaping box. All APs are Buffalo WZR-HP-G300NH 802.11n wireless routers. This model has a 400MHz CPU with 32 MB RAM. We reflashed the APs with OpenWRT firmware, running Linux kernel 2.6.32 and `ath9k` WiFi driver. In our experiments, we select one BAPU-*AP* as a *Home-AP* which the *Sender* is always associated to, the other 6 BAPU-*APs* act as *Monitor-APs* to capture the traffic in monitor mode. The BAPU-*Gateway* runs on a Linux PC, and the *Destination* runs behind the BAPU-*Gateway*. The *Sender* and the *Destination* are both laptops with 802.11n WiFi card, running the standard Linux TCP/IP stack. To emulate traffic shaping as with residential broadband, we use the traffic shaping box between the BAPU-*APs* and BAPU-*Gateway*. We use Linux' `iptables` and `tc` with the `htb` module to shape the downlink bandwidth to 20 Mbps and the uplink to 2 Mbps. Also, to emulate network latency between BAPU-*APs* and BAPU-*Gateway*, we use `netem` to shape the RTT with different values. The bandwidth and latency parameter are selected to represent the typical bandwidth capacity and latency in residential cable broadband measured in Boston's urban area (Table 1).

In our experiments, we issue long-lived 30 min `iperf` flows (both TCP and UDP) from *Sender* to *Destination*. We choose 1350 Byte as TCP/UDP payload size to make sure that the whole client IP packet can be encapsulated in one IP packet while an BAPU-*AP* sends it through its TCP tunnel. All throughput values reported in

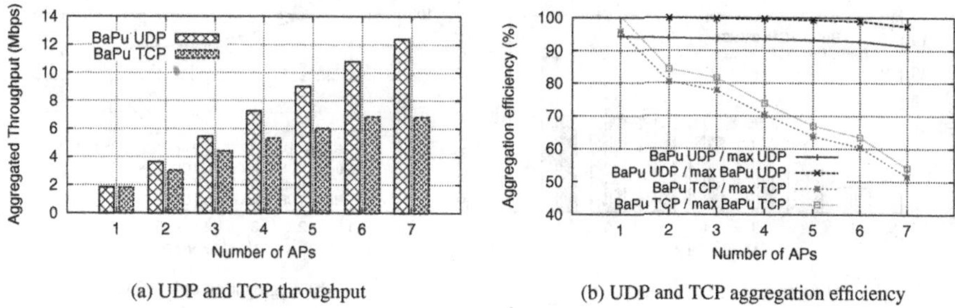

(a) UDP and TCP throughput

(b) UDP and TCP aggregation efficiency

Fig. 6. BAPU aggregation for UDP and TCP with 2 Mbps 32 ms RTT uplinks.

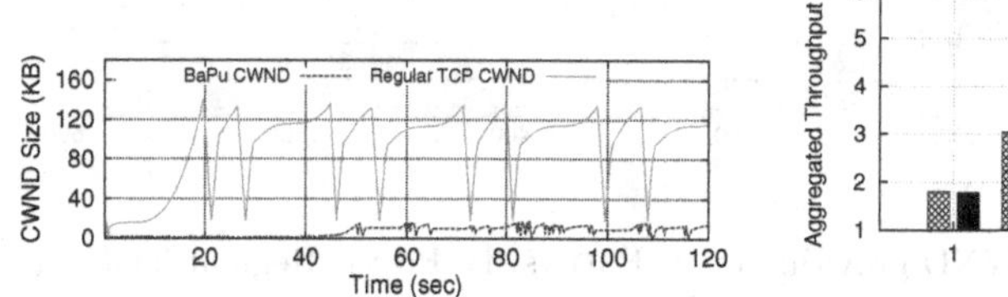

Fig. 7. Sender's TCP CWND growth: BAPU vs. Regular TCP.

Fig. 8. BAPU vs. SIMPLEBUFFER.

our experiment are the `iperf` throughput, which is the *goodput*. In the evaluation, we compare throughput of UDP and TCP in a variety of scenarios: A. BAPU – BAPU system without any buffering or Proactive-ACK mechanism; B. SIMPLE-BUFFER – BAPU system without Proactive-ACK, but enhanced by buffering at BAPU-*Gateway*; C. BAPU-PRO – this is the full BAPU system.

5.1 BAPU: Efficient UDP, Poor TCP

System Efficiency with UDP Throughput: We now first measure BAPU's efficiency by the throughput with UDP, as it provides a light-weight end-to-end transmission between *Sender* and *Destination*. Figure 6a shows the achieved aggregated UDP throughput with numbers of participating BAPU-*AP*s increasing from 1 to 7. We observe that the aggregated UDP throughput increases proportionally with the number of BAPU-*AP*s, and achieves 12.4 Mbps with 7 BAPU-*AP*s. To put this figure into perspective, note that related work by Jakubczak et al. [15] achieves similar UDP throughput but *without* support for TCP or client transparency.

Low TCP Throughput: We conduct the same experiments also for TCP transmission. Figure 6a shows that the aggregated TCP throughput does not benefit much when the number of BAPU-*AP*s increases. The TCP aggregated throughput is always lower than the UDP's in the same setup, and the gap between UDP and TCP performance increases along with the number of BAPU-*AP*s.

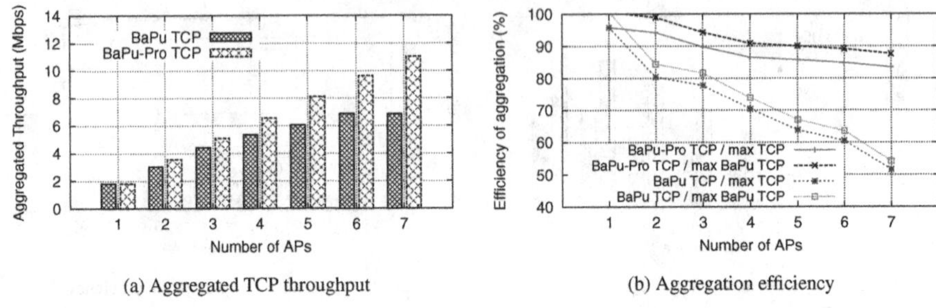

(a) Aggregated TCP throughput

(b) Aggregation efficiency

Fig. 9. BAPU-PRO vs. BAPU: comparison with 2 Mbps 32 ms RTT uplinks.

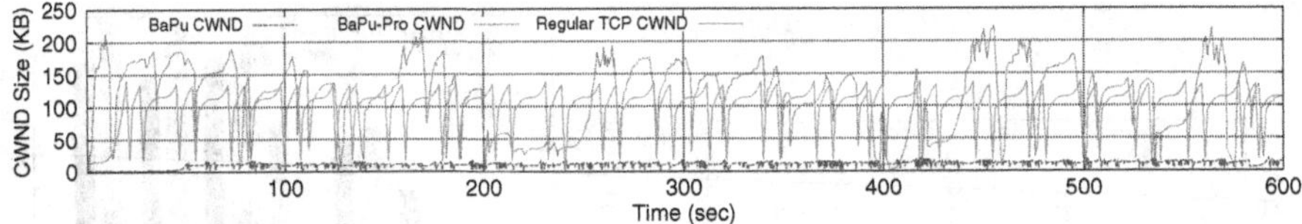

Fig. 10. Sender's TCP CWND growth: BAPU-PRO vs. BAPU vs. Regular TCP.

Aggregation Efficiency: In addition to measuring aggregated throughput, we evaluate our system based on another metric, *aggregation efficiency*. We define *aggregation efficiency* as the ratio between practical throughput over the maximum theoretical goodput. Due to the TCP/IP header and BAPU protocol overhead, the actual goodput is less than the uplink capacity. With all protocol header overhead accounted, we derive the maximum theoretical goodput as the given backhaul capacity of 2 Mbps. As shown in Fig. 6b, BAPU UDP can harness close to 100 % idle bandwidth. Even if we consider the extra overhead incurred by BAPU protocol messages, UDP aggregation efficiency is still over 90 % in all cases. In contrast, the aggregation efficiency for TCP degrades quickly as more BAPU-*AP*s join the cooperation. With 7 BAPU-*AP*s, BAPU transforms only 50 % of idle bandwidth to effective throughput.

Discussion on BAPU's Poor TCP Performance: We can observe several factors in Sect. 4 that decrease the aggregated TCP throughput. In this section, we carry out an analysis on the *Sender*'s CWND size in BAPU. To justify our analysis, we inspect the TCP behavior by examining the Linux kernel TCP stack variables. We call `getsockopt()` to query the `TCP_INFO` data structure containing the system time stamp, *Sender*'s CWND, number of retransmissions, etc. We also modified the `iperf` code to log `TCP_INFO` for each call to send application data. Figure 7 shows the CWND growth in a 120 s `iperf` test with 7 BAPU-*AP*s (theoretical throughput is 2Mbps $\times$ 7 = 14Mbps) in comparison with standard TCP through a single AP with 14 Mbps uplink capacity. The *Sender*'s CWND remains at a very low level. Our captured packet trace at the *Sender* shows that lots of DUPACK packets and RTO incur a lot of retransmissions, resulting in low TCP throughput.

5.2 Does SIMPLEBUFFER help TCP performance?

As discussed in Sect. 4, a simple *buffering* mechanism does *not* solve the TCP performance issue due to difference in BAPU-*AP* uplink characteristics (latency, packet loss). In this section, we experimentally show that a buffering mechanism cannot help in improving the TCP throughput. Figure 8 depicts the throughput comparison between BAPU and SIMPLEBUFFER. Surprisingly, the throughput is even degraded with SIMPLEBUFFER. Our trace inspection shows a lot of TCP Timeout Retransmissions due to the packets being buffered at BAPU-*Gateway* for too long.

5.3 BAPU-PRO Performance

We now conduct a comprehensive set of experiments to evaluate the performance of BAPU-PRO. First, we validate our Proactive-ACK mechanism by comparing BAPU-PRO against BAPU. Second, we measure the performance of BAPU-PRO under a variety of network settings (network latency, wireless link quality, etc.). Finally, we demonstrate that BAPU-PRO is feasible for both, streaming and large file transfer applications.

TCP Throughput – BAPU-PRO vs. BAPU: We carry out the same `iperf` test as described in Sect. 5.1 with BAPU-PRO. As shown in Fig. 9a, the aggregated TCP throughput of BAPU-PRO significantly outperforms the one of BAPU. With 7 BAPU-*AP*s, BAPU-PRO achieves 11.04 Mbps, i.e., 62 % improvement over BAPU. Furthermore, Fig. 9b shows that BAPU-PRO achieves at least 88 % aggregation efficiency in our setup, and it achieves at least 83 % of the upper limit of standard TCP throughput. These results demonstrate that BAPU-PRO can achieve high aggregated throughput with high aggregation efficiency for TCP in practical settings.

Proactive-ACK Benefit: To justify our Proactive-ACK mechanism, we adopt the same method as in Sect. 5.1 to examine the TCP CWND growth. Figure 10 shows that BAPU-PRO allows the CWND to grow to very high values, contributing to the high throughput. For convenience, we also run a regular TCP session with a throttled bandwidth 11 Mbps (similar to the BAPU-PRO's resulted throughput). The CWND growth for BAPU-PRO and regular TCP shares a similar pattern, which implies that our design and implementation can efficiently and transparently aggregate multiple slow uplinks.

Impact of Network Latency: For TCP transmissions, RTT is an important factor that has impact on the throughput. We measure the performance of BAPU with different network latency settings listed in Table 1. Besides fixed latency values for each typical setting, we also assign to each BAPU-*AP* a random RTT value between 20 ms and 80 ms. We carry out this test for 10 runs and report the average throughput. As shown in Fig. 11a, BAPU-PRO throughput slightly declines as network latency increases. In random latency setting, the resulted throughput shows no significant difference.

Impact of Lossy Wireless Links: The wireless links in a real neighbourhood can be very lossy for a variety of reasons, such as cross channel interference and

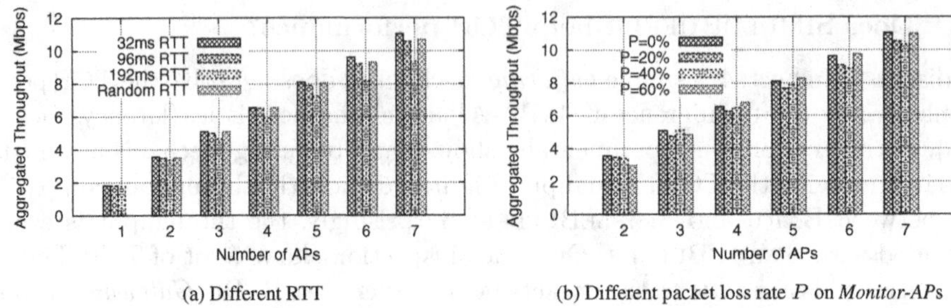

(a) Different RTT

(b) Different packet loss rate P on *Monitor-APs*

Fig. 11. BAPU-PRO TCP throughput.

distant neighboring APs. Besides, since *Monitor-APs* switch between transmit and receive mode, they cannot overhear all transmitted packets. To estimate the potential of BAPU highly lossy wireless environments, we emulate packet loss at *Monitor-APs* by dropping received packets with a probability P. No losses were inflicted on *Home-AP*, because *Sender* carries out unicast to *Home-AP*, and 802.11 MAC already handles packet loss and retransmissions automatically. We conduct the experiment with 3 values of P: 20 %, 40 %, and 60 %. As indicated in Fig. 11b, the throughput reduction on lossy wireless links is very limited in all cases. The good performance can be explained by the link diversity combined with the centralized scheduling mechanisms. The probability of some packet not overheard by *at least one Monitor-AP* is negligible small, especially in case of high number of participating APs. This also explains why 7 BAPU-*APs* achieve higher throughput with $P = 60\,\%$ than with $P = 20\,\%$.

Streaming vs. Large File Transfer: One important goal in BAPU's design is to support instant sharing of high-bitrate HD videos directly between users using streaming. The motivation behind is that today the major online streaming services (e.g., Netflix) run on TCP based streaming technologies, such as HTTP based Adaptive Bitrate Streaming. Real time streaming generally requires *stable* instantaneous throughput. In this experiment, we study the potential of BAPU as a solution to high-bitrate real-time streaming. To emulate HD streaming, we use `nuttcp` to issue a TCP flow with a fixed 11 Mbps sending rate. As shown in Fig. 12, `nuttcp` achieves a reasonably stable instantaneous throughput during a 100 second session. It implies that BAPU can sustain high-bitrate streaming through aggregated uplinks. In comparison, the `iperf` flow with unlimited sending rate shows much higher fluctuation.

6 Related Work

While BAPU is inspired by design principles of previous work, it addresses unique constraints and goals and presents a set of novel techniques that achieve high efficiency. Previous research has addressed TCP performance improvements over wireless links by using intermediate nodes that assist in the recovery of lost packets,

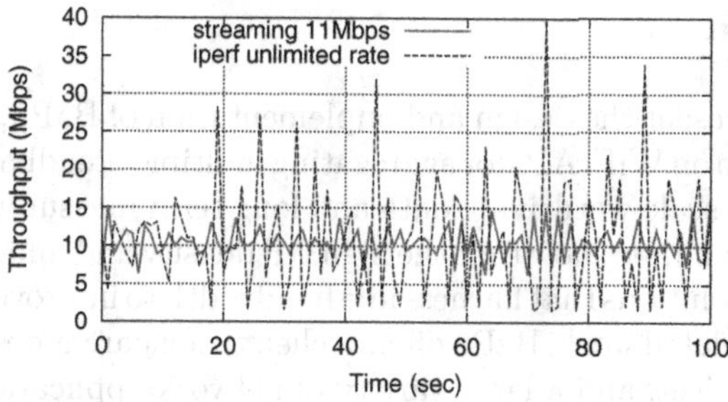

Fig. 12. Instantaneously received throughput: 11 Mbps Streaming vs. Unlimited rate.

e.g., Snoop TCP [5], and Split TCP [18]. Multiple radio links for improving throughput have also been explored from several perspectives including traffic aggregation [17], multipath forwarding [15], and mitigation of wireless losses [21,22]. In addition to systems that rely on multiple radio interfaces [4], other solutions and algorithms have been proposed for a single client radio interface that switches across multiple access points while providing upper layers of the network stack with a transparent access [8,17,20,28]. Solutions to overcome limited APs backhaul through aggregation using such a virtualized radio interfaces include the initial Virtual-WiFi [20] system where two TCP connection are serviced by two different APs, FatVAP [17] and ARBOR [28] that achieve fast switching by smart AP selection, and Fair WLAN [12] for fairness. These systems require techniques for fast switching across access points to reduce impact on TCP performance, e.g., delay and packet loss as discussed in Juggler [16] and WiSwitcher [11]. An analytical model [25] is proposed to optimize concurrent AP connections for highly mobile clients. They also implement Spider, a multi-AP driver using optimal AP and channel scheduling to improve the aggregated throughput. *Unlike* BAPU, these papers do not focus on aggregating the throughput for single transport layer connection, which is critical for *client transparency.* Divert [22] and ViFi [6] reduce path-dependent downlink loss from an AP to a client. However, rather than improving the wireless link quality, BAPU targets aggregation of the wired capacity behind APs. In BAPU, the sender regularly communicates with its home AP. As discussed, BAPU borrows ideas from Link-alike [15] where access points coordinate to opportunistically schedule the traffic over backhaul links. Contrary to Link-alike, BAPU does not require client devices to use broadcast. Moreover, BAPU transparently supports protocols like TCP. Being completely transparent to the clients and constraining each link AP-Destination flow to be TCP-friendly makes efficient multipath transport a key component of our system. We stress that, in contrast to BAPU, the large body of related work on multipath transport, cf. [7,10,13,14,19,23,24,26, 27], does not support transparent, unmodified client devices and TCP/IP stacks while efficiently aggregating AP backhaul.

7 Conclusion

In this work, we present the design and implementation of BaPu, a complete software based solution on WiFi APs for aggregating multiple broadband uplinks. First, based on our large scale wardriving data and long term measurement in Boston's residential broadband, we show that the high AP density and under utilized broadband uplinks suit solutions that harness idle bandwidth to improve uplink throughput. Contrary to related work, BaPu offers a client transparent design, generic support for legacy devices, and a large variety of network applications. To this end, BaPu employs a novel mechanism (Proactive-ACK) to address the challenges of multiplexing single TCP sessions through multiple paths without degrading performance. To analyze the benefits of BaPu, we have carried out an extensive set of experiments for both UDP and TCP in a variety of realistic network settings. BaPu achieves over 95 % aggregation efficiency for UDP and over 88 % for TCP – even in lossy wireless environment. As a future work, it would be interesting to reproduce and compare the results in different neighborhoods and different countries. Also, incentive mechanisms and support from AP manufacturers and subscription providers need to be developed in order for BaPu to be useful for both AP owners and users.

References

1. Open infrastructure: A wireless network research framework for residential networks. http://www.ccs.neu.edu/home/noubir/projects/openinfrastructure/
2. Akamai. Akamai HD Network. Technical report (2011). http://bit.ly/1xN2NNB
3. Allman, M., Paxson, V., Blanton, E.: Tcp congestion control (2009)
4. Bahl, P., Adya, A., Padhye, J., Walman, A.: Reconsidering wireless systems with multiple radios. SIGCOMM Compututer Communication Review 34, 39–46 (2004). ISSN 0146-4833
5. Balakrishnan, H., Seshan, S., Amir, E., Katz, R.H.: Improving TCP/IP performance over wireless networks. In: Proceedings of MobiCom (1995)
6. Balasubramanian, A., Mahajan, R., Venkataramani, A., Levine, B.N., Zahorjan, J.: Interactive wifi connectivity for moving vehicles. In: Proceedings of SigComm (2008)
7. Barré, S., Paasch, C., Bonaventure, O.: MultiPath TCP: from theory to practice. In: Domingo-Pascual, J., Manzoni, P., Palazzo, S., Pont, A., Scoglio, C. (eds.) NETWORKING 2011, Part I. LNCS, vol. 6640, pp. 444–457. Springer, Heidelberg (2011)
8. Chandra, R., Bahl, P.: Multinet: connecting to multiple IEEE 802.11 networks using a single wireless card. In: Proceedings of INFOCOM (2004)
9. FON. FON (2012). http://corp.fon.com/us/
10. Ford, A., Raiciu, C., Handley, M., Bonaventure, O.: TCP Extensions for Multipath Operation with Multiple Addresses. Internet-Draft (2012)
11. Giustiniano, D., Goma, E. , Lopez, A., Rodriguez. P.: Wiswitcher: an efficient client for managing multiple aps. In: Proceedings of PRESTO (2009)
12. Giustiniano, D., Goma, E., Toledo, A.L., Dangerfield, I., Morillo, J., Rodriguez, P.: Fair WLAN backhaul aggregation. In: MobiCom (2010)

13. Hsieh, H.-Y., Sivakumar, R.: A transport layer approach for achieving aggregate bandwidths on multi-homed mobile hosts. In: Proceedings of MobiCom (2002)
14. Hsieh, H.-Y., Kim, K.-H., Zhu, Y., Sivakumar, R.: A receiver-centric transport protocol for mobile hosts with heterogeneous wireless interfaces. In: Proceedings of MobiCom (2003)
15. Jakubczak, S., Andersen, D.G., Kaminsky, M., Papagiannaki, K., Seshan, S.: Link-alike: using wireless to share network resources in a neighborhood. SIGMOBILE Mobile Computing Communications Review (2008)
16. Anthony, J.N., Scott, W., Noble, B.D.: Juggler: virtual networks for fun and profit. IEEE Trans. Mob. Comput. **9**, 31–43 (2010)
17. Kandula, S., Lin, K.C., Badirkhanli, T., Katabi, D.: FatVAP: aggregating AP backhaul capacity to maximize throughput. In: Proceedings of NSDI (2008)
18. Kopparty, S., Krishnamurthy, S.V., Faloutsos, M., Tripathi, S.K.: Split tcp for mobile ad hoc networks. In: GLOBECOM (2002)
19. Magalhaes, L., Kravets, R.H.: Transport level mechanisms for bandwidth aggregation on mobile hosts. In: Proceedings of Conference on Network Protocols (2001)
20. Microsoft Research. Virtual wifi (2012). http://bit.ly/1IjD4iw
21. Miu, A., Balakrishnan, H., Koksal, C.E.: Improving loss resilience with multi-radio diversity in wireless networks. In: MobiCom, pp. 16–30 (2005)
22. Miu, A.K., Tan, G., Balakrishnan, H., Apostolopoulos, J.: Divert: fine-grained path selection for wireless lans. In: Proceedings of MobiSys (2004)
23. Radunović, B., Gkantsidis, C., Gunawardena, D., Key, P.: Horizon: balancing TCP over multiple paths in wireless mesh network. In: MobiCom (2008)
24. Raiciu, C., Barre, S., Pluntke, C., Greenhalgh, A., Wischik, D., Handley, M.: Improving datacenter performance and robustness with multipath TCP. In: SIGCOMM 2011 (2011)
25. Soroush, H., Gilbert, P. , Banerjee, N., Levine, B.N., Corner, M., Cox, L.: Concurrent Wi-Fi for mobile users: analysis and measurements. In: CoNEXT (2011)
26. Steward, R.: Stream control transmission protocol. IETF RFC 4960 (2007)
27. Wischik, D., Raiciu, C., Greenhalgh, A., Handley, M.: Design, implementation and evaluation of congestion control for multipath TCP. In: Proceedings of NSDI (2011)
28. Xing, X., Mishra, S., Liu, X.: ARBOR: hang together rather than hang separately in 802.11 wifi networks. In: Proceedings of INFOCOM (2010)

Memory Efficient Self-stabilizing Distance-k Independent Dominating Set Construction

Colette Johnen(✉)

University Bordeaux, LaBRI, UMR 5800, 33400 Talence, France
johnen@labri.fr

Abstract. We propose a memory efficient self-stabilizing protocol building distance-k independent dominating sets. A distance-k independent dominating set is a distance-k independent set and a distance-k dominating set(The protocol $\mathcal{SID}$ was presented in a brief announcement at SSS'13.).

Our algorithm, named $\mathcal{SID}$, is silent; it converges under the unfair distributed scheduler (the weakest scheduling assumption).

The protocol $\mathcal{SID}$ is memory efficient : it requires only $log(2((n+1)(k+1))^2)$ bits per node.

The correctness and the termination of the protocol $\mathcal{SID}$ is proven.

The computation of the convergence time of the protocol $\mathcal{SID}$ is an opened question.

Keywords: Distributed algorithm · Fault tolerance · Self-stabilization · Distance-k dominating set · Distance-k independent set · Distance-k independent dominating set · Memory efficient

1 Introduction

The clustering of networks consists of partitioning network nodes into non-overlapping groups called clusters. Each cluster has a single head, called leader, that acts as local coordinator of the cluster, and eventually a set of standard nodes. leader. Clustering is found very attractive in infrastructure-less networks, like ad-hoc networks, since it limits the responsibility of network management only to leaders, and it allows the use of hierarchical routing.

Silent self-stabilizing protocols building k-hops clustering set are proposed [1–4]. In k-hop clusters, the distance between a standard node and its leader is at most k; the set of cluster heads can be not a distance-k independent set. The protocol of [1] is designed for $k = 2$. Routing tables are maintained by the cluster heads to store routing information to nodes both within and outside the cluster. The goal of the protocol in [2] is to build bounded size clusters (each cluster has at most $Cluster\_Max$ nodes). The protocol of [3] is designed for weighted edges

Partially supported by the ANR project DISPLEXITY (ANR-11-BS02-014). This study has been carried out in the frame of "the Investments for the future" Programme IdEx Bordeaux CPU (ANR-10-IDEX-03-02).

A. Bouajjani and H. Fauconnier (Eds.): NETYS 2015, LNCS 9466, pp. 354–366, 2015.
DOI: 10.1007/978-3-319-26850-7_24

networks; it requires $O(log(k^4.\Delta^2.D^2.n^6))$ bits per node, where Δ is a bound on node degree and D is the network diameter. The protocol of [4] requires at least $log(2.k.n^2.n^{k+1}))$ bits per node.

In [5,6], Larsson and Tsigas propose self-stabilizing (l,k)-clustering protocols under various assumptions. These protocols ensure, if possible, that each node has l cluster-heads at distance at most k.

In [7], a silent self-stabilizing protocol extracting a minimal distance-k dominating set from any distance-k dominating set is proposed. A minimal distance-k dominating set has no proper subset which also a distance-k dominating set. The protocol requires at least $O(log(n^k))$ bits per node.

The paper [8] presents a silent self-stabilizing protocol building a small distance-k dominating set : the obtained dominating set contains at most $\lceil n/(k+1)\rceil$ nodes. The protocol of [8] requires $log(2.n^2.(n/k)^k)$ bits per node. The protocol of [9] builds competitive distance-k dominating sets : the obtained dominating set contains at most $1 + \lfloor (n-1)/(k+1)\rfloor$ nodes. The protocol of [9] requires $O(log(2.k.(\Delta+1)^3.n^3))$ bits per node.

Contribution. In this paper, we consider the problem of computing a distance-k independent dominating set in a self-stabilizing manner in case where $k > 1$. A nodes set is distance-k independent dominating set (also called maximal distance-k independent set) if and only if this set is a distance-k independent set and a distance-k dominating set. A set of nodes, I is distance-k independent if the distance between any pair of I's nodes is at least $k+1$. A set of nodes D is distance-k dominating if every node is within distance k of a node of D.

The protocol $\mathcal{SID}$ is simple : no use of the hierachical collateral composition, no need of leader election process, neither the building of spanning tree. It converges under the unfair distributed scheduler (the weakest scheduling assumption); and it is silent.

According to our knowledge, [10] is the only previous work proposing a silent self-stabilizing protocol building a maximal distance-k independent set assuming that $k > 1$. The protocol of [10] converges in $4n + k$ rounds; the computation of the convergence time of the protocol $\mathcal{SID}$ is an open question. The protocol in [10], requires $log((n+1)^{k+1})$ bits per node. The protocol $\mathcal{SID}$, requires less memory space - only $log(2.((n+1).(k+1))^2)$ bits per node. To achieve this result, the technique uses is quite different and new; for instance two distincts total order relations on the same objects are used.

2 Specification of Problem and Computation Model

A distributed system S is an undirected graph $G = (V, E)$ where the vertex set, V, is the set of nodes and the edge set, E, is the set of communication links. A link $(u, v) \in E$ if and only if u and v can directly communicate (links are bidirectional); so, the node u and v are neighbors. N_v denotes the set of v's neighbors: $N_v = \{u \in V \mid (u, v) \in E\}$. The distance between the nodes u and v is denoted by $dist(u, v)$. The set of nodes at distance at most k to a node v is denoted by $\mathtt{k-neigborhood(v)} = \{u \in V \mid dist(u, v) \in [1, k]\}$.

Definition 1 ***(distance-k independent dominating set).*** *Let D be a subset of V; D is a* ***distance-k dominating set*** *if and only if $\forall v \in V/D$ we have* $\mathtt{k-neigborhood(v)} \cap D \neq \emptyset$.

Let I be a subset of V; I is a ***distance-k independent set*** *if and only if $\forall u \in I$ we have* $\mathtt{k-neigborhood(u)} \cap I = \emptyset$.

A subset of V is a distance-k independent dominating set if this subset is a distance-k dominating set and a distance-k independent set.

At every node v in the network is assigned an identifier, denoted by id_v. Two distinct nodes have different identifier. It is possible to order the identifier values.

Each node maintains a set of shared variables. A node can read its own variables and those of its neighbors, but it can modify only its variables. The *state* of a node is defined by the values of its local variables. The cartesian product of states of all nodes determines the *configuration* of the system. Let var be a shared variable, $\mathtt{var}(v)_c$ denotes the value of var for the node v in the configuration c. The *program* of each node is a set of *rules.* Each rule has the form: $Rule_i :< Guard_i > \longrightarrow < Action_i >$. The *guard* of a v's rule is a boolean expression involving the state of the node v, and those of its neighbors. The *action* of a v's rule updates v's state. A rule can be executed by a node v only if it is *enabled,* i.e., its guard is satisfied by the node v. A node is said to be enabled if at least one of its rules is enabled. A configuration is *terminal* if and only if no node can execute a rule.

During a *computation step* from a configuration one or more enabled nodes simultaneously perform an action to reach another configuration. A *computation* e is a sequence of configurations $e = c_0, c_1, ..., c_i, ...$, where c_{i+1} is reached from c_i by a single computation step, $\forall i \geqslant 0$. A computation e is *maximal* if it is infinite, or if it reaches a terminal configuration.

Definition 2 ***(Silent Self-stabilization).*** *Let $\mathcal{L}$ be a predicate on the configuration. A distributed system S is a silent self-stabilizing system to $\mathcal{L}$ if and only if (1) all terminal configurations satisfy $\mathcal{L}$; (2) all computations reach a terminal configuration.*

3 The Protocol $\mathcal{SID}$

In the following subsection, we gives the notation used by the protocol $\mathcal{SID}$.

3.1 *k*-augmentedID Type

Definition 3. ***k-augmentedID type*** *An k-augmentedID value, a, is $\perp$ or an n-tuple (d, x) such that d is integer with $0 \leq d \leq k$, and x is a node identifier. Let $a = (d, x)$ be k-augmentedID value. We use the following notation $a.dist = d$ and $a.id = x$.*

Let v be a node of V, id_v^+ is the following k-augmentedID value: $(0, id_v)$.

Definition 4. ***The total order relation*** *dom* ***on*** *k-augmentedID*

- $dom(a, b) = a$ *if* $b = \perp$, $a.id < b.id$ *or* $a.id = b.id \wedge a.dist < b.dist$, *otherwise* $dom(a, b) = b$.
- *The k-augmentedID value* $a1$ *dominates the k-augmentedID value* $a2$ *if and only if* $dom(a1, a2) = a1$.
- *Let* X *be a finite set of k-augmentedID values.* $dom(X)$ *is the k-augmentedID value, denoted* dX, *belonging to* X *such that any value of* X *is dominated by* dX *(i.e.* $\forall y \in X$ *we have* $dom(dX, y) = dX$*).*

Definition 5. ***The total order relation*** *min* ***on*** *k-augmentedID*

- $min(a, b) = a$ *if* $b = \perp$, $a.dist < b.dist$ *or* $a.dist = b.dist \wedge a.id < b.id$ *otherwise* $min(a, b) = b$.
- *The k-augmentedID value* $a1$ *is larger than the k-augmentedID value* $a2$ *if and only if* $min(a1, a2) = a2$.
- *Let* X *be a finite set of k-augmentedID values.* $min(X)$ *is the k-augmentedID value, denoted* mX, *belonging to* X *such that any value of* X *is larger than* mX *(i.e.* $\forall y \in X$ *we have* $min(mX, y) = mX$*).*

The node $u1$ is *closer* to the node v than the node $u2$ iff $d1 = dist(u1, v)) < dist(u2, v) = d2$ or $id_{u1} < id_{u2}$. Notice that $(d2, id_{u2}))$ is larger than $min((d1, id_{u1})$.

Definition 6. ***The operation +1*** *on k-augmentedID is defined as follow:* $a + 1 = a$ *if* $a = \perp$ *or if* $a.dist = k$ *otherwise* $a + 1 = (a.dist + 1, a.id)$

3.2 Code of the Protocol $\mathcal{SID}$

The variables, the function and procedure specifications, the predicates and the rules of $\mathcal{SID}$ are presented in protocol 1. By lack of space, the code of the functions and the procedures are omitted in the paper, they can found in the technical report of LaBRI [11]).

The variable `firstH`(v) contains the identifier of the closest head to v (with its distance to v).

The variable `secondH`(v) contains the identifier of the second closest head to v (with its distance to v) inside its `k − neighborhood`. If a node v does not have two heads in its `k − neighborhood` then `secondH`(v) is set to $\perp$.

A node v is said to be a head if `firstH`$(v) = id_v^+ = (0, id_v)$; otherwise v is an ordinary node. We will prove that in any terminal configuration the Head set built by the protocol $\mathcal{SID}$ is a distance-k independent dominating set. We will also establish that all computations are finite.

In the Fig. 1 is presented a terminal configuration of $\mathcal{SID}$ in the case where $k = 4$. In each node, it is indicated the value of `firstH`, denoted by fH, and the value of `secondH` denoted by sH. The legitimate configuration has three heads. On the same network with the same value for k, is presented another terminal configuration having a single head in the Fig. 2.

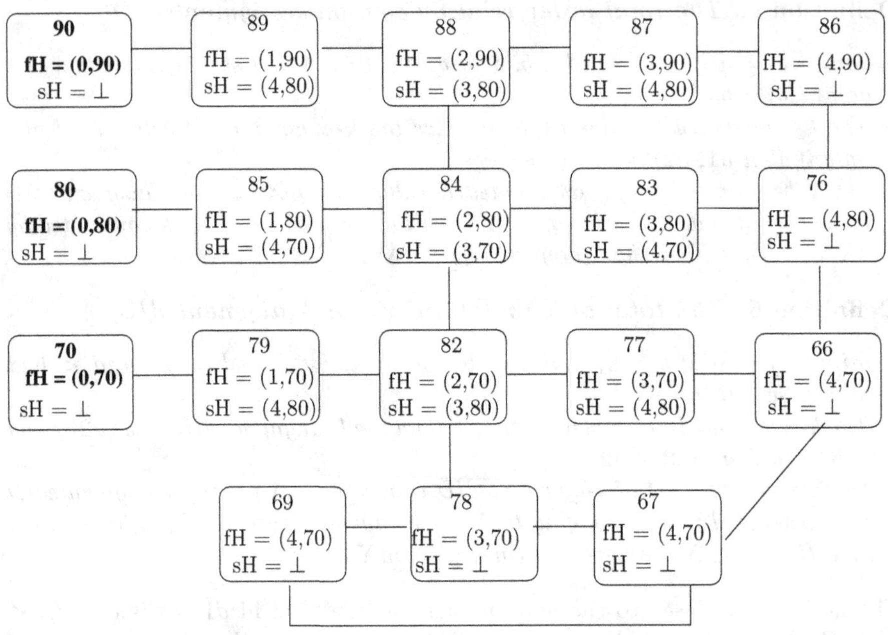

Fig. 1. A legitimate configuration of $\mathcal{SID}$ with $k = 4$

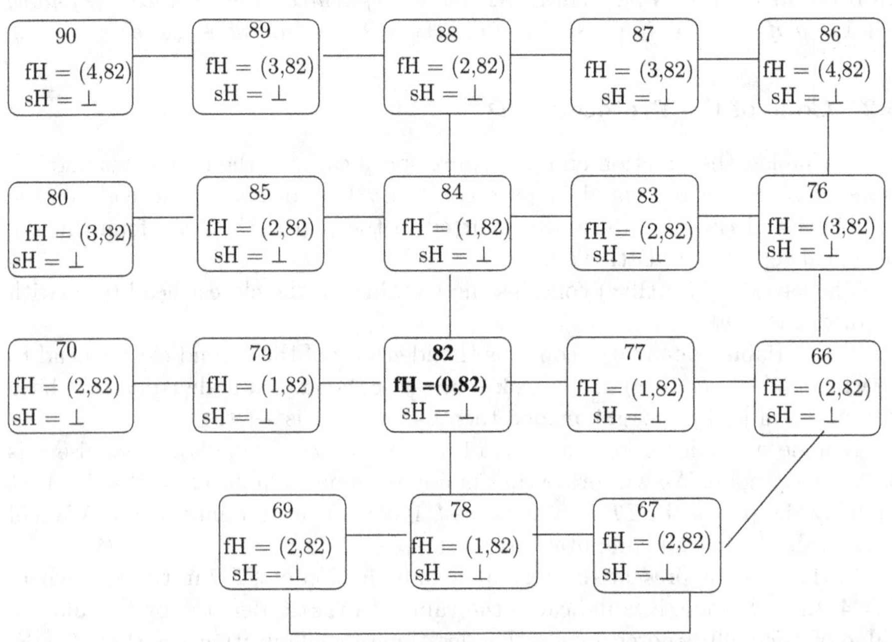

Fig. 2. A terminal configuration of $\mathcal{SID}$ having a single head

Algorithm 1. code of $\mathcal{SID}$ on the node v

Shared variables

- `firstH`(v) and `secondH`(v). They take value in k-augmentedID.

Internal variable

- *beReal* is a boolean variable used by some funtions.

Notation

- `FirstS`(v) = $\{a + 1 \in k\text{-augmentedID} \mid a = \texttt{firstH}(u) \lor a = \texttt{secondH}(u)$ $\textit{with } u \in N_v \land a.dist < k \land a.id \neq id_v\}$
- `secondS`(v) = $\{a \in \texttt{FirstS} \mid a.id \neq \texttt{firstH}(v).id\}$

Boolean function specifications

- `isDefended`(v) returns true iff `FirstS`(v) $\neq \emptyset$.
- `isDominated`(v) returns true iff $id_v^+ \neq dom(\texttt{FirstS}(v) \cup id_v^+)$.
- `correctFirstH`(v) returns true iff `firstH`(v) = min(`FirstS`(v)).
- `correctSecondH`(v) returns true iff `secondH`(v) = min(`secondS`(v)$\cup \perp$).

Procedure specifications

- `computingFirstH`(v) sets `firstH`(v) to min(`FirstS`(v)).
- `computingsSecondH`(v) sets `secondH`(v) to min(`secondS`(v) $\cup \perp$).

Predicates

- `Head`(v) $\equiv$ `firstH`(v) = $(0, id_v)$
- `toResign`(v) $\equiv$ `isDominated`(v)
- `toElect`(v) $\equiv \neg$`isDefended`(v)
- `headToUpdate`(v) $\equiv$ `secondH`(v) $\neq \perp$
- `ordinaryToUpdate`(v) $\equiv \neg$`correctFirstH`(v) $\lor\ \neg$`correctSecondH`(v)

Rules

RE(v) : $\neg$`Head`(v) $\land$ `toElect`(v) $\longrightarrow$ `firstH`(v) := $(0, id_v)$; `secondH`(v) :=$\perp$
RU(v) : $\neg$`Head`(v) $\land\ \neg$`toElect`(v) $\land$ `ordinaryToUpdate`(v) $\longrightarrow$
`computingFirstH`(v); `computingSecondH`(v)
RR(v) : `Head`(v) $\land$ `toResign`(v) $\longrightarrow$
`computingFirstH`(v); `computingSecondH`(v)
RC(v) : `Head`(v) $\land\ \neg$`toResign`(v) $\land$ `headToUpdate`(v) $\longrightarrow$ `secondH`(v) :=$\perp$

The function `isDefended`(v) returns true if the set `FirstS`(v) is not empty otherwise the function returns false.

The function `isDominated`(v) returns true if a value x of `FirstS`(v) dominates the value $id_v^+ = (0, id_v)$; otherwise the function returns false.

The function correctFirstH(v) returns true if the value of firstH(v) is min(FirstS(v)); otherwise or if the set FirstS(v) is empty then the function returns false.

The procedure computingFirstH(v) sets firstH(v) to min(FirstS(v)) if the set FirstS(v) is not empty; otherwise the value of firstH(v) is $\perp$. In the latter case, v verifies the predicate toElect(v) and it does not verify the predicate toResign(v). So the procedure computingFirstH(v) is never preformed when set FirstS(v) is empty.

The function correctSecondH(v) returns true if the value of secondH(v) is min(secondS(v) $\cup \perp$); otherwise the function returns false. The procedure computingSecondH(v) sets secondH(v) to min(secondS(v)$\cup \perp$).

Once the system is stabilized, the set FirstS(v) contains some heads in **k − neighborhood** of v. More precisely, this set contains the closest and second closest head to v if there are at least one Head in the **k − neighborhood** of v.

If the k's neighborhood of a node v does not contain any head then the set FirstS(v)) is empty. So the predicate toElect(v) is verified. If v is an ordinary node then v is enabled (the rule **RE** is enabled). Therefore, the heads set is a distance-k dominating set, in a terminal configuration.

If one or several Heads have in their k-neighborhood another Head then at least one of these Heads is enabled. Let us name, v, the Head having the largest identifier among the Heads that have Heads in their k-neighborhood. Once the system is stabilized, the FirstS(v) contains a value (d, id_u) such that $id_v > id_u$ and $d < k$. The node v is enabled : it verifies the predicate toResign. So, the set of heads is a distance-k independent set, in any terminal configuration.

3.3 Illustration of $\mathcal{SID}$ Behavior

In the Fig. 3, an execution with $k = 2$ under the synchronous schedule is presented. During the first computation step, the node having the identifier 8 detectes that its neighbor having the identifier 7 is a Head, so it becomes ordinary by executing the rule **RE** (it sets its firstH variable to $(1, 7)$)). Also during the first step, the node at distance 1 of the Head 4 updates its shared variables (i.e. it executes the rule **RU**). During the 2th step (starting at the configuration b), two Heads detect that there are at distance 2 of the Head 4, as their identifier are larger than 4, they execute the rule **RR** (i.e. they become ordinary). During the 3rd step (starting at the configuration c), two ordinary nodes (the node of identifier 8 and the node of identifier 9) detect that they have no Head in their 2-neighborhood so they become Head (i.e. they execute the rule **RE**). During the 5th step, the node 9 detects that it is at distance 2 of the Head 8; so it resigns. during the last computations step, the only rule executed is **RU** to update the variable secondH. So, no node will change its status (i.e. to become a Head or Ordinary). The configuration g is terminal and also legitimate.

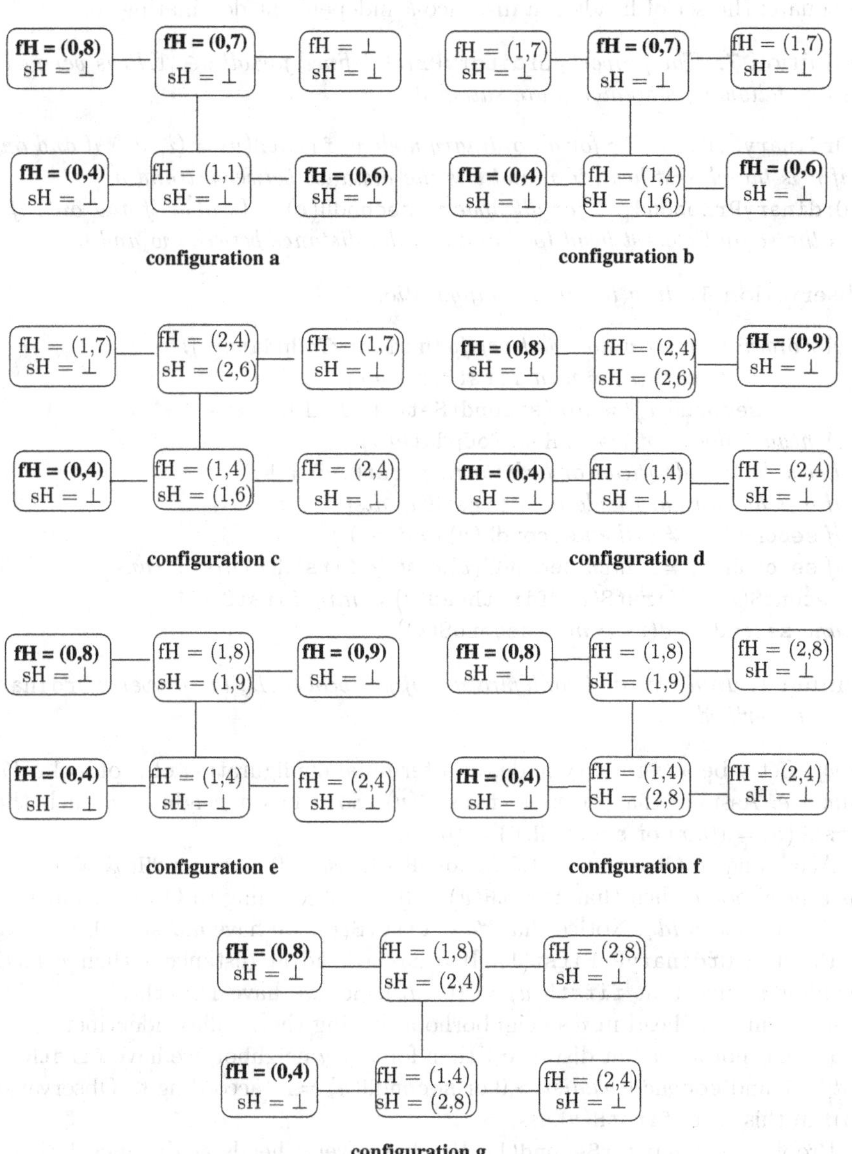

Fig. 3. An execution of $\mathcal{SID}$ with $k = 2$

4 Correctness of the Protocol $\mathcal{SID}$

In this section, we prove that all terminal configurations of $\mathcal{SID}$ protocol are legitimate: the set of heads is a distance-k independent dominating set.

Definition 7. *The property* `OrdinaryPr`*(i) defined for all* $i \in [1, k]$ *is verified if the two following statements are satisfied:*

- `OrdinaryPrFirst`*(i): for all ordinary node* v, `firstH`$(v) = (i, id_u)$ *if and only if* u *is the closest head to* v *and* i *is the distance between* u *and* v.
- `OrdinaryPrSecond`*(i): for all node* v, `secondH`$(v) = (i, id_w)$ *if and only if* w *is the second closest head to* v *and* i *is the distance between* w *and* v.

Observation 1. *In a terminal configuration,*

1. *An ordinary node* v *does not verify* `OrdinaryToUpdate`(v)*;*
   so `firstH`$(v) = min($`firstS`$(v))$ *and*
   `secondH`$(v) = min($`secondtSet`$(v) \cup \perp)$.
2. *A head* u *does not verify* `HeadToUpdate`(u)*;*
3. *Let* w *be a node (head or ordinary),* `firstH`$(w) \neq \perp$*;*
4. *if* v *is an ordinary node then* `firstH`$(v).dist > 0$ *;*
5. *if* `secondH`$(v) \neq \perp$ *then* `secondH`$(v).dist > 0$ *;*
6. *if* `secondH`$(v) \neq \perp$ *then* `secondH`$(v).dist \geq$ `firstH`$(v).dist$ *because* `secondS`$(v) \subset$ `firstS`(v), `firsthead`$(v) = min($`firstS`$(v))$ *and* `secondhead`$(v) = min($`secondS`$(v))$

Lemma 1. *In a terminal configuration of protocol $\mathcal{SID}$, the property* `Ordinary Pr(1)` *is verified.*

Proof. Let v be an ordinary node, in a terminal configuration of protocol $\mathcal{SID}$, named c. Assume that $(1, x) \in$ `firstS`(v). So v has a neighbor u such that `firstH`$(u) = (0, x)$ or `secondH`$(u) = (0, x)$.

According to Observation 1.5 `secondH`$(u).dist > 0$ or `secondH`$(u) = \perp$. So v has a neighbor u such that `firstH`$(u) = (0, x)$. According to Observation 1.4 u is a head; so $x = id_u$. Notice that $\forall a \in$ `firstS`(v), we have $a.dist > 0$, in c.

Proof of `OrdinaryPrFirst`(1). If v has a head at distance 1 then v has a neighbor u such that `firstH`$(u) = (0, id_u)$. So, we have `firstH`$(v) = (1, id_u)$ with u being the head in v's neighborhood having the smallest identifier.

If v has not a head at distance 1 then for any u neighbor, we have `firstH`(u). $dist > 0$. and `secondH`$(u).dist > 0$ or `secondH`$(u) = \perp$ (according to Observation 1.5). In this case, `firstH`$(v).dist > 1$.

Proof of `OrdinaryPrSecond`(1). If v has several heads at distance 1 then v has a neighbor w such that `firstH`$(w) = (0, id_w)$ with $id_w \neq$ `firstH`$(v).id$. So, `secondH`$(v) = (1, id_w)$ with w being the head in v's neighborhood having the second smallest identifier.

If v has at most one head at distance 1 then v has not a neighbor w such that `firstH`$(w) = (0, id_w)$ with $id_w \neq$ `firstH`$(v).id$. In this case, `secondH`$(v).dist$ is larger than 1 or `secondH`$(v) = \perp$. □

Lemma 2. *Let i be a positive integer smaller than k. In a terminal configuration of protocol $\mathcal{SID}$, if the properties* `OrdinaryPr(j)` *are verified for all $j \in [1, i]$ then the property* `OrdinaryPr`$(i+1)$ *is verified.*

Proof. Let us assume that the properties `OrdinaryPr(j)` are verified for all $j \in [1, i]$ in any terminal configuration of protocol $\mathcal{SID}$.

In a terminal configuration c, $(j, x) \in$ `firstS`(v) iff v has a neighbor u such that `firstH`$(u) = (j-1, x)$, or `secondH`$(u) = (j-1, x)$. If $j = 1$ then u is a head in c, according to Observation 1. If $1 < j \leq i+1$ then x is the identifier of a head in c at distance $j-1$ of u, according to the property `OrdinaryPr`$(j-1)$. So x is the identifier of a head at distance at most j of v, in c.

Proof of `OrdinaryPrFirst`(i+1). Let v' be the closest head to v and d' the distance from v' to v in the terminal configuration c. Assume that $0 < d' \leq i+1$. v has a neighbor u at distance $d'-1$ to v'. In c, the node v' is the closest head of u; so `firstH`$(u) = (d'-1, id_{v'})$, according to the properties `OrdinaryPr`$(d'-1)$. According to the properties `OrdinaryPr`(j) $\forall j \in [1, i]$, in c, we have the following properties,

- if $(l, id) \in$ `firstS`(v) then $l \geq d'$; and
- if $(d', id) \in$ `firstS`(v) then $id \geq id_{v'}$. In c,

We conclude that `firstH`$(v) = (d', id_{v'})$, in c.

Proof of `OrdinaryPrSecond`(i+1). Assume that the network has several heads. Let v" be the second closest head to v and d" the distance from v" to v, in a terminal configuration c. v has a neighbor u at distance d" -1 to v" in c. (we have d" > 0). v" is the first or second closest head to u, in c. Assume that d" $\leq i+1$. According to the property `OrdinaryPr`$(d$" $-1)$, `firstH`$(u) = (d''-1, id_{v''}) \vee$ `secondH`$(u) = (d''-1, id_{v''})$, in c. According to the properties `OrdinaryPr`(j) $\forall j \in [1, i)$, in c, we have the following properties,

- if $(l, id) \in$ `secondS`(v) then $l \geq d''$;
- if $(d'', id) \in$ `secondS`(v) then $id \geq id_{v''}$.

We conclude that `secondH`$(v) = (d'', id_{v''})$. □

The following corollary is a direct result of lemmas 1 and 2. It establishes that the set of heads is a distance-k dominating set.

Corollary 1. *Let v be a ordinary node, in a terminal configuration of protocol $\mathcal{SID}$.* `firstH`(v)*.id is the closest head to v; their distance is* `firstH`(v)*.dist* $\leq k$. *If* `secondH`$(v) = \perp$ *then v has a single head in its k-neigborhood; otherwise* `secondH`(v)*.id is the second closest head to v; their distance is* `secondH`(v)*.dist.*

The following theorem establishes that the set of heads is a distance-k independent set in any terminal configuration.

Theorem 1. *Let v be a head, in a terminal configuration of protocol $\mathcal{SID}$. v has not head in its k-neigborhood.*

Proof. We will prove that if a head has another head in its k-neigborhood then the configuration c is not terminal.

Let *wrongHeadSet* the set of heads having one or several heads in their k-neigborhood. Assume that *wrongHeadSet* is not empty. We denote by $v1$ the node of *wrongHeadSet* having the largest identifier. We denote by $v2$, the closest head to $v1$ and by d the distance between $v1$ and $v2$. We have $0 < d \leq k$ and $id_{v2} < id_{v1}$.

The node $v1$ has a neighbor u at distance $d-1$ of $v2$. The node $v2$ is the first or the second closest head to u. According to corollary 1, $(d-1, id_{v2}) = \texttt{firstH}(u)$ or $(d-1, id_{v2}) = \texttt{secondH}(u)$. $v1$ is enabled because $v1$ satisfied the predicate $\texttt{toResign}(v1)$. □

5 Termination of the Protocol $\mathcal{SID}$

In this section, we prove that all maximal computations of protocol $\mathcal{SID}$ under any unfair distributed scheduler are finite by *reductio ad absurdam* arguments.

Lemma 3. *Let e be a maximal computation.*

The values taken by `firstH` *and* `seconHead` *along e by any node belong to the same set containing $3nk$ k-augmentedID values.*

Proof. Let e be a maximal computation starting from a configuration, named $c0$. In a configuration c reached by e, for any node v, $\texttt{firstH}(v)_c.\ id$ is either the identifier of an node or this value appears in the initial configuration (i.e. there is a node u, such that $\texttt{firstH}(v)_c.id = \texttt{firstH}(u)_{c0}.id \vee \texttt{firstH}(v)_c.id = \texttt{secondH}(u)_{c0}.id$). So, the value taken by a variable `firstH` in e belongs to a set having $3nk$ values. Similary we prove that the value taken by a variable `secondH` along e belongs to the same bounded set. □

Observation 2. *Along any computation, a node performs at most one time the rule* **RC**.

Lemma 4. *Let e be a maximal computation. e has a suffix in which the only rule performed is* **RU**.

Proof. Assume that a or several nodes perform infinitely often the action **RE** or the action **RR** along e. Between two consecutive actions **RE** by a node u, this node has performed on time the action **RR**. So a node u that infinitely often performs the action **RE** or the action **RR** changes its status infinitely often. We name u^+ the node having the smallest identifier among the nodes that change their status infinitely often. e has a suffix $e1$ where only nodes having a identifier larger than id_{u^+} changes their status (i.e. they perform the action **RE** or the action **RR**).

As the set of value taken by $\texttt{firstH}(u^+)$ is bounded (Lemma 3) along $e1$, infinitely often after the action $\textbf{RR}(u^+)$, $\texttt{firstH}(u^+)$ has the same value, denoted by $(l+1, id)$. Notice that $id < id_{u^+}$ and $0 < l < k$. So u^+ has a neighbor u_l such that, infinitely often before the action $\mathbf{RR}(u^+)$, u_l verifies $\texttt{firstH}(u_l) = (l, id)$ or $\texttt{secondH}(u_l) = (l, id)$.

At time, where u^+ becomes head, we have $\texttt{firstS}(u^+) = \emptyset$. So, the values of u_l variables are infinitely often larger than (l, id). Thus, u_l gives infinitely often to one of its variables the value (l, id), but also gives a larger value to the same variable.

Assume that $l > 0$. At time where u_l gives the value (l, id) to one of its variable : u_l has a neigbor u_{l-1}, having the value $(l - 1, id)$. At time where u_l gives a larger value than (l, id) to the same variable : u_{l-1} has a larger value than $(l - 1, id)$. We conclude that there is a series of $l + 1$ nodes : $u_l, u_{l-1}, ..u_0$ such that u_i has infinitely often has the value (i, id) and infinitely often does not have this value along $e1$.

Along $e1$, u_0 performs infinitely often the action **RR** and the action **RE**. We have $id = id_{u_0} < id_{u^+}$: there is a contradiction. □

Lemma 5. *Let e be a maximal computation. e has a suffix in which no rule is performed.*

Proof. According to Lemma 4, e has a suffix, named $e2$, in which the only rule performed is **RU**. Assume that a node or several nodes changing infinitely often their value `firstH` or their value `secondH` along $e2$. We named min^+ the smallest value infinitely often allocated to the variable `firstH` or to the variable `secondH` of one of these nodes. Let $e3$ be the suffix of $e2$ in which no variable `firstH` and no variable `secondH` gets a value smaller than min^+. Along $e3$, infinitely often, a node, named u^+, performs **RU** action to set the value min^+ to its variable `firstH` or its variable `secondH`; and infinitely often, u^+ performs **RU** action to set to the same variable a value larger than min^+.

Let $c \rightarrow c'$ be a computation step of $e3$ where u^+ performs **RU** action to set a value larger than min^+ to its variable `firstH` or to its variable `secondH`. In c, min^+ is smaller than $min(\texttt{firstS}(u^+))$ or min^+ is smaller than $min(\texttt{secondS}(u^+))$. This property stays verified after this computation step along $e3$. So u^+ never sets the value min^+ to its variable `firstH` (resp. to its variable `secondH`). There is a contradiction. □

As no computation can be infinite, any maximal computation reaches a terminal configuration.

Corollary 2. *under the unfair distribued scheduler, Any maximal computation reaches a terminal configuration.*

6 Conclusion

A simple and silent self-stabilizing protocol building distance-k independent dominating sets is presented. The protocol converges under the unfair distributed scheduler (the weakest scheduling assumption). The computation of the convergence time of the protocol is an open question. In [10], we establish that any distance-k independent sets contain at most $\lfloor(2n)/(k+2)\rfloor$ nodes, n being the network size. So the protocol of [10] and the presented protocol have the same upper bound on the size of built k independent dominating sets : $\lfloor(2n)/(k+2)\rfloor$ nodes.

The protocol $\mathcal{SID}$ is memory efficient : it requires only $log(2.((n+1).(k+1))^2)$ bits per node.

References

1. Bein, D., Datta, A.K., Jagganagari, C.R., Villain, V.: A self-stabilizing link-cluster algorithm in mobile Ad Hoc networks. In: International Symposium on Parallel Architectures, Algorithms and Networks (ISPAN 2005), pp. 436–441 (2005)
2. Bui, A., Clavière, S., Datta, A.K., Larmore, L.L., Sohier, D.: Self-stabilizing hierarchical construction of bounded size clusters. In: Kosowski, A., Yamashita, M. (eds.) SIROCCO 2011. LNCS, vol. 6796, pp. 54–65. Springer, Heidelberg (2011)
3. Caron, E., Datta, A.K., Depardon, B., Larmore, L.L.: Self-stabilizing k-clustering algorithm for weighted graphs. J. Parallel Distrib. Comput. **70**, 1159–1173 (2010)
4. Datta, A.K., Larmore, L.L., Vemula, P.: A self-stabilizing O(k)-time k-clustering algorithm. Comput. J. **53**(3), 342–350 (2010)
5. Larsson, A., Tsigas, P.: A self-stabilizing (k, r)-clustering algorithm with multiple paths for wireless Ad-hoc networks. In: IEEE 31th International Conference on Distributed Computing Systems, (ICDCS 2011), pp. 353–362. IEEE Computer Society (2011)
6. Larsson, A., Tsigas, P.: Self-stabilizing (k,r)-clustering in clock rate-limited systems. In: Even, G., Halldórsson, M.M. (eds.) SIROCCO 2012. LNCS, vol. 7355, pp. 219–230. Springer, Heidelberg (2012)
7. Datta, A., Devismes, S., Larmore, L.: A self-stabilizing $o(n)$-round k-clustering algorithm. In: 28th IEEE Symposium on Reliable Distributed Systems (SRDS 2009), pp. 147–155 (2009)
8. Datta, A.K., Larmore, L.L., Devismes, S., Heurtefeux, K., Rivierre, Y.: Self-stabilizing small k-dominating sets. Int. J. Networking Comput. **3**(1), 116–136 (2013)
9. Datta, A.K., Larmore, L.L., Devismes, S., Heurtefeux, K., Rivierre, Y.: Competitive self-stabilizing k-clustering. In: IEEE 32th International Conference on Distributed Computing (ICDCS 2012), pp. 476–485 (2012)
10. Johnen, C.: Fast, silent self-stabilizing distance-k independent dominating set construction. Inf. Process. Lett. **114**(10), 551–555 (2014)
11. Johnen, C.: Memory efficient self-stabilizing k-independent dominating set construction. Technical report RR-1473-13, Univ. Bordeaux, LaBRI, UMR 3800, F-33400 Talence, France, June 2013

Optimizing Diffusion Time of the Content Through the Social Networks: Stochastic Learning Game

Soufiana Mekouar[1(✉)], Sihame El-Hammani[1], Khalil Ibrahimi[2], and El-Houssine Bouyakhf[1]

[1] LIMIARF, FSR, Mohammed-V Agdal University, Rabat, Morocco
{soufiana.mekouar,elhammani.sihame}@gmail.com, bouyakhf@mtds.com
[2] LARIT, FSK, IBN-Tofail University, Kenitra, Morocco
khalil.ibrahimi@gmail.com

Abstract. Both customers and companies have a great interest to optimize the diffusion time. The contents generators always try to disseminate their information in the minimum time in order to benefit the most of the received reward. In our paper, we suppose that each node in the social network is interested to diffuse its content with the goal of optimizing its delivery time and selling its information to the receivers. Each content generator must target its adapted neighbors, who will play the role of relay and will allow the arrival of the information to its destination before the expiry of its time. The objective of our work is to disseminate the content through neighbors characterized by a high connectivity and a high quality of relationships in terms of being interested to share the same type of information. We model our problem as a stochastic learning game, where each player tries to maximize its utility function by selecting the optimal action depending on the state of the system and on the action taken by the competitor.

1 Introduction

The social network is a gathering of individuals of the same interest in a small group that allows to be connected to the rest of the world by sharing ideas, experiences, photos and exchange of various contents. It allowed users to produce, create and consume contents. It gives a wide access to information and plays an important role in the diffusion of ideas and information between users. It has become a way of life for the majority of users. Each node tries to share the most its content in the social network, to gain more profit. This attracted the scientific community to study the maximization of the content diffusion through the social network [1,2,9]. We consider in this paper, the competition between two sources (i.e. seller of contents) that create the content and wish to disseminate it in a limited time to the receiver (i.e. buyer of content). Each source has its neighbors, and it is required to find the most appropriate of them that will play the role of relay and will permit to disseminate the information within a certain delay. The target neighbors are those who have a high degree and a good sharing

A. Bouajjani and H. Fauconnier (Eds.): NETYS 2015, LNCS 9466, pp. 367–381, 2015.
DOI: 10.1007/978-3-319-26850-7_25

quality. We suppose that a source can accelerate the diffusion of its content just by increasing the sharing probability of the information between its neighbors. Also, we assume that once the interested user receives the information, he will be satisfied and will not require any other content. We formulate the problem as a two player zero-sum stochastic game. We use the minimax Q-Learning to calculate the equilibrium by employing the linear programming, where each player tries to maximize its utility and to minimize the one of the competitor. The principal contributions in this paper are:

- Target the source's neighbors who have a high connectivity that gives them an attractive personality, more experience and better reputation of good content's diffusion.
- Target neighbors with a good quality of relationship in terms of sharing the same content type as the source. This will increase the arrival probability of the information to its destination.
- Suppose that each content has a time constraint which determines the validity of the content. If this time is expired, it is no need to diffuse the content.

2 Related Work

The selection of influential nodes is widely studied in literature. Authors in [1,4,5] treated the problem of selection of k nodes to maximize this influence. Our model differs of these works in the selection of the best neighbors, by which we disseminate the content to reach the destination.

In [6], the authors facilitated access to streaming content by caching service of popular content. With the same manner, in [7], the author accelerated the content diffusion by using some services, such as caching, and recommendation system by the content distributor that gives a preferential treatment to individuals who pay for advertising. He formulated the competition problem between several contents generators; each one has a level of popularity (diffusion rate) by a stochastic game. The solution shows the advertising strategy. This is similar to our work, but in our model we assume that the message received by the recipient has a delay defined as a validity time. If this deadline is expired, the node must not disseminate the information.

Several studies have focused on the selection of the most influential nodes [3,4,8], with the attention to target these ones, to maximize the diffusion. They showed that finding these influential nodes sets are NP-hard. They used an analysis based on sub-modular functions, and they employ heuristic analysis of social networks such as the centrality to maximize the diffusion.

In [10], the model focuses on the decision taken by individual who creates content and competes through consumers and their interactions. This, offer to content generator the opportunity of advertises proposed by the owner of the social network or other ones to accelerate the diffusion. In [8], they attempted to trace the propagation path of the content, since the observation of node that influences another is difficult, based on the infection node time. They identify the network that show the time of infection node by formalizing the problem and developing an evolutionary algorithm that infers the network of influence and diffusion. In the same direction, in [3], they defined the problem of maximizing the dissemination that seeks to add k connections per user such that the propagation probability of the content is maximized. The goal is to compute the set of pertinent recommendation as the diffusion is maximized. And, in [9], they formulated the problem of maximizing the dissemination with a probabilistic voter model where its behavior depends on the initial assignment of f_0 that must be equal to 1 in order to maximize diffusion. The heuristic used is to select the node with high degree.

For [11], the authors proposed the time-critical influence maximization problem, in which a user wants to maximize influence spread within a given deadline. They design two heuristic algorithms; the first one is based on a dynamic programming procedure. The second converts the problem to the original IC model and then applies existing fast heuristics to it. They show that time-critical influence maximization under the time-delayed IC model maintains desired properties such as sub-modularity. Also, in [12] the authors considered a game-based model, where each individual makes a selfish rational choice in terms of its payoff in adopting the new innovation. They study how diffusion effect can be maximized by seeding a subset of individual. They design polynomial-time approximation algorithms for three representative classes, Erdos-Rényi, planted partition and geometrically structured graph models.

In this paper, we try to combine between the *connectivity* and the *high sharing quality* to spread the content to its receiver in an appropriate time in a competitive environment.

3 Formulation Model

We consider n nodes in the social network as illustrated in Fig. 1. We have two sources (S1 and S2) from these nodes that generate the same type of contents. This content can be a commercial service (as example the diffusion of the information about the popular tourist spots in a city, hotel categories, promotion in a market, or travel times). At each step, the node who has the information (either the source, or a neighbor) tries to disseminate it through one of its best neighbor, in order that the content can be available to the receiver in the appropriate time.

The sources and receivers are separated by intermediates nodes, represented by the source's neighbors, neighbors of neighbors and so on. Each neighbor has a degree (e.g. x_3 its degree is 3) and a sharing probability of the same type of content (e.g. x_3 has two probabilities noted by $p_{3,8}$ and $p_{3,9}$).

Each node must choose the neighbor having the highest degree and the highest sharing probability of the same type of the source's content. To realize this, the node is based on its own information that is the fraction of connections and the quality of relationships of its neighbors. In the following subsection, we attempt to give a computational model for computing the fraction of interested

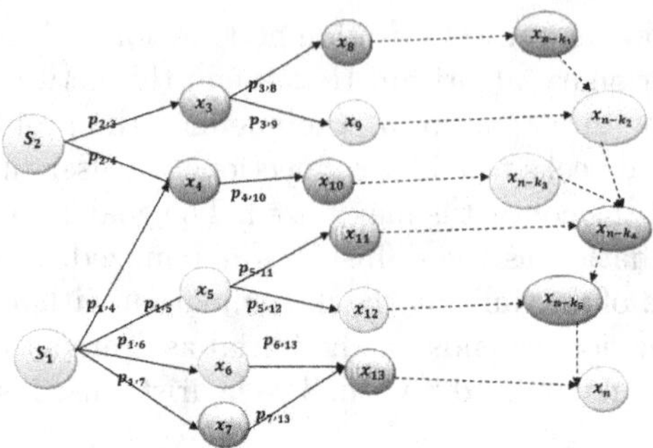

Fig. 1. Competition between two sources (S_1 and S_2) to deliver the content to the receiver on time. The receivers are colored by orange, the neighbors are colored by cyan and finally the sources are colored by green. The source S_1 compares the connectivity of each one of its neighbors (x_4, x_5, x_6 and x_7) to choose the highest. For the relationships quality it compares the sharing probability ($p_{4,10}$,$p_{5,11}$, $p_{5,12}$,...) at each edge, then it chooses the neighbor with the highest probability (Color figure online).

users by the sources' contents, the fraction of node's neighbor and the sharing probability of the same content's type.

The Fraction of Users Interested in the Contents: We consider that we have n nodes in the social network. We suppose having two sources from these nodes that can be passive or active by participating in generating and sharing the content. We define R as the fraction of the population that just might be interested in the two sources contents, we take $R = n - 2$. And we denote M as the fraction of the population that is really interested in getting one of the contents generated by the two sources, this fraction can be written as follows:

$$M^{'}(t) = \beta M(t)(R - M(t)) \tag{1}$$

Let β be the sharing rate of the content, that can be defined as: $\beta = \frac{m}{n}$, where m is the number of nodes that share the same type of content, $m \leq n - 1$. The solution of the differential equation with the initial condition $M(0) = \epsilon$, where $0 < \epsilon \leq R$, is given by:

$$M(t) = \frac{R\,\epsilon\; exp(\beta Rt)}{R - \epsilon + \epsilon\; exp(\beta Rt)} \tag{2}$$

The Fraction of Node Neighbors: Each node i in the social network has a fraction of its neighbors noted by $x_i(t)$, which can be calculated by the equation:

$$x_i^{'}(t) = \beta x_i(t)(M(t) - x_i(t)), \tag{3}$$

The solution of the Eq. (3) gives the neighbors fraction of a node i, where the initial condition is $x(0) = \gamma$, and $0 \leq \gamma \leq R$.

$$x_i(t) = \frac{(R - \epsilon + \epsilon\, exp(\beta Rt)\, R\, \gamma)}{R^2 - \gamma\, \epsilon + \beta\, R\, \gamma((R - \epsilon)t + \frac{\epsilon}{\beta R}\, exp(\beta Rt))} \tag{4}$$

We can distinguish two particular cases:

- $\epsilon = 0$ equivalent to that the source has no neighbor at the instant $t = 0$.
- $\epsilon = R$ equivalent to that all nodes that may be interested in the contents of the source are neighbors of the latter.

Sharing Quality of a Neighboring Node: The sources generate the content and diffuse it through their neighbors. When the information arrives at a node, this latter has the decision to share it or not. Let $p_i(t)$ be the probability of sharing the content by the node i.

$$p_i^{'}(t) = \beta x_i(t)(1 - p_i(t)). \tag{5}$$

We take the initial condition $p_i(0) = 0$, (at time t = 0, the probability that a neighbor shares the same type of content diffused by the source is zero). Then, the solution of the Eq. (5), using the Eq. (4) is:

$$p_i(t) = 1 - \frac{R^2}{R^2 - \gamma\, \epsilon + \beta\, R\, \gamma((n - \epsilon)t + \frac{\epsilon}{\beta\, R}\, exp(\beta Rt))}. \tag{6}$$

3.1 Diffusion Policy

We consider that we have n nodes in the social network and two sources from these nodes that can be passive or active by participating in generating or sharing the content. We assume that m of these nodes share the same kind of content as the source. So, the probability that all these shared contents will arrive with success to the receivers is given by:

$$p_m = \binom{n-1}{m} p^m q^{n-m-1} \tag{7}$$

With some abuse of notation, from Eq. (6), and by ignoring the index i, we define p as the sharing probability of the same content type like the source.

3.2 Formulation of Two Sources Zero-Sum Stochastic Game

We consider in this paper, a two player zero-sum stochastic game. The sources are the players that try to spread their contents and put it available to the recipients. Therefore, they choose one of the available actions to ensure that their contents arrive on time to the destinations.

In this paper, we formulate the optimization problem of the content delivery time by a zero-sum stochastic game. We consider the source (the competitor) and the neighboring nodes that help it to disseminate the information on time as only one player (as another player). The game is set in pairs between the source and a neighbor and after between two neighbors till the information arrives to its destination.

Each player tries to maximize its utility function, with the choice of the optimal action, basing on the history of states and actions performed previously. We describe below the components of the stochastic game, which is supposed to be observable by all nodes:

States: At each time t, each source i knows its neighbors x_i and knows the quality of relationships maintained with its neighbors in terms of sharing the same content type. We define the state of a node i by $s_i = (nC_i, qr_i)$. Where nC_i denotes the proportion of neighbors of the source i, $nC_i = \begin{cases} 0, \text{ low degree.} \\ 1, \text{ high degree.} \end{cases}$, and qr_i is the relations quality with those neighbors of i, $qr_i = \begin{cases} 0, \text{ not share the same content type.} \\ 1, \text{ share the same content type.} \end{cases}$
The state s_i of each source/player is defined by one of these main states: $s1 = (0,1), s2 = (0,0), s3 = (1,1), s4 = (1,0)$.

Action: Each user has the choice between diffuse or not the content with certain intensity. This choice depends on several parameters as the competitor action, the current and past system state, the validity time of the information and the number of interested users by the content. In this paper, we argue that each user has the choice between actions according to the content validity time. Then, we mention the action of the users as follows:

A = $\{a_{k_0}(\textit{not diffuse}), a_{k_1}(\textit{diffuse with low intensity}), a_{k_2}(\textit{diffuse with high intensity})\}$

Where, D_m is the time limit of the content. And $j, k \in \{k_0, k_1, k_2\}$,
$k_0 \in [\frac{5D_{th}}{6}, D_{th}], k_1 \in]\frac{D_{th}}{2}, \frac{5\,D_{th}}{6}[, k_2 \in [0, \frac{D_{th}}{2}], a_n \in A, n \in \{1, ..., D_m\}$.

Reward: Each player attempts to maximize the content diffusion with neighbors characterized by high connectivity and good sharing quality, in order that the information arrives to its destination before the expiry of its validity time. Once this content has reached the interested, the transmitter receives a reward from the recipient. So, the immediate reward of the source is given by:

$$R_i(s, a_k, b_j) = u_s(a_k, b_j)\,(\vec{v_1}\, g_i(D) + \vec{v_2}\, M(t)), \tag{8}$$

Where:

- $u_s(a_{k_1}, b_j)$: is the reward received by the source when it chooses the action a_{k_1} and the competitor chooses the action b_j at state s, where $s \in S = \{s1, s2, s3$ and $s4\}$,
- $\vec{v_1}$: is the reward vector of diffusing a content, that decreases with the validity time,
- $\vec{v_2}$: is the reward vector of diffusing a content, that increases with the fraction of interested users by this content,

- $g(D)$: is a decreasing function with the delay time D. The delay time D is initialized to 1 and increases at each step of time by 1,

$$g_i(D) = \frac{1}{D+1}.$$

- $M(t)$: is obtained from Eq. (2). So, we can write Eq. (17) as:

$$R_i(s, a_k, b_j) = u_s(a_k, b_j)\,(\vec{v_1}\,\frac{1}{D+1} + \vec{v_2}\,M(t)). \tag{9}$$

Transition Probability: The change of state of a player depends on its intensity of sharing the information with another node.

So, we define δ as the accelerate rate of diffusion with low intensity and σ as the accelerate rate of diffusion with high intensity. And we consider that the system is modeled by a Markov chain in discrete time on the state space $S = \{s_1, s_2, ..., s_n\}$, where $s_i = (nC_i, qr_i)$.

Consequently, a player switches from the state $s \in S$ to $s' \in S$ after choosing the action a, based on the current state of the system, and the estimated action b taken by the competitor. Then, the transition probability is given by:

$$P(S^{'}|S, a_k, b_j) = \prod_{i=1}^{n} P(s_i^{'}|s_i, a_k, b_j).$$

This transition probability for our two players zero-sum stochastic game can be written as:

$$P(s^{'}|s, a_k, b_j) = \begin{cases} \sigma p_m, & \text{for } S1 \text{ and } a = a_{k_2}, b \neq a_{k_2}, \\ 1 - \sigma p_m, & \text{for } S2 \text{ and } a \neq a_{k_1}, b = a_{k_2}, \\ \delta p_m, & \text{for } S3 \text{ and } a = a_{k_1}, b = a_{k_2}, \\ 1 - \delta p_m, & \text{for } S4 \text{ and } a = a_{k_0}, b \neq a_{k_0}. \end{cases}$$

Where, $S1 = \{s^{'} = s3, s = s1 \text{ or } s^{'} = s3, s = s2\}$, $S2 = \{s^{'} = s1, s = s2 \text{ or } s^{'} = s2, s = s1\}$, $S3 = \{s^{'} = s_1, s = s_3 \text{ or } s^{'} = s1, s = s4\}$ and $S4 = \{s^{'} = s2, s = s3 \text{ or } s^{'} = s2, s = s4\}$.

4 Optimal Policy of Our Stochastic Game

Each source tries to maximize its utility by spreading the content to one of its best neighbors, according to certain criteria, with the aim that its content arrives to the recipient in the opportune time. We are led to consider a two players zero-sum stochastic game, where the source targets to extract the optimal policy that maximizes its discount utility. Thus, we express the expected utility as:

$$U_i(s, a_k, b_j) = \mathbb{E}\Big[\sum_{t=0}^{\infty} \gamma_t R_i^{\pi}(s, a_k, b_j)\Big]. \tag{10}$$

Where $\gamma_t \in [0,1]$ is the discount factor and $R_i^{\pi}(s, a_k, b_j)$ is the estimated reward of player i at state s with effectuating the strategy/policy π.

The policy in our game for a player is defined as the distribution probability over the space of actions A depending on the state of the player, like $\pi_i : S \longrightarrow P(A)$. As example, for $a \in A$ and $s \in S$, we have the policy for a source $\overrightarrow{\pi_1}(s, a_k) = [\pi_1(s, a_0), \pi_1(s, a_1), \pi_1(s, a_2), ..., \pi_1(s, a_{D_m})]$, such that $\pi_1(s, a_0) + \pi_1(s, a_1) + \pi_1(s, a_2) + ... + \pi_1(s, a_{D_m}) = 1$. Same for the competitor that has its proper policy over the space of actions A, so we have: $\overrightarrow{\pi_2}(s, b_j) = [\pi_2(s, a_0), \pi_2(s, a_1), \pi_2(s, a_2), ..., \pi_2(s, a_{D_m})]$, such that $\pi_2(s, a_0) + \pi_2(s, a_1) + \pi_2(s, a_2) + ... + \pi_2(s, a_{D_m}) = 1$.

Shapley [13], shows that it exists for the both players, always an optimal stationary Markov strategy, that depends only on the current state. The strategy/policy is stationary if it is independent of time, i.e., $\pi_{t+1} = \pi_t$. So, we have to find this optimal strategy.

Since the game is non-cooperative between the two sources, we deduce that there is an unique equilibrium for each player. To find it, we begin by defining the value function that gives us the maximum of the expected utility.

$$V(s, D) = \max_{\overrightarrow{\pi_1}(s,a_k)} \min_{\overrightarrow{\pi_2}(s,b_j)} \sum_{a_k \in A} Q_{s,D}(a_k, b_j)\overrightarrow{\pi_1}(s, a_k). \tag{11}$$

Where $\overrightarrow{\pi_1}(s, a_k)$ is the probability to choose the action a_k at the state s. $Q_{s,D}(a_k, b_j)$ is the action-value function, that represents the estimated utility, described as the reward of the game between the two sources in competition. The value of $Q_{s,D}(a_k, b_j)$ proves that in a state the selected action is the best. This is a simple way for an agent to learn how to react with an optimum manner [14]. The update of the action-value function is given by:

$$Q_{s,D}(a_k, b_j) = R_i(s, a_k, b_j) + \gamma \sum_{s' \in S} P(s' | s, a_k, b_j) V(s', D). \tag{12}$$

The source improves its action-value function from its experience in updating its Q-function [15] as follows:

$$Q_{s,D}(a_k, b_j) = (1 - \alpha) Q_{s,D}(a_k, b_j) + \alpha U, \tag{13}$$

Where,

$$U = R_i(s, a_k, b_j) + \gamma V(s', D). \tag{14}$$

α is the learning factor and $V(s', D)$ is obtained by Eq. (11). As a result, both players find the equilibrium using the minimax-Q Learning [15,16]. In Eq. (13) the value at state s', $V(s', D)$, is used as the estimated future rewards, and its value increases with iterations. It is proved in [17] that the learning minimax-Q converges to the limit of the correct Q and V values. The aim of minimax-Q learning [16,18] for a source is to obtain the optimal policy that maximizes its reward and minimizes the one of the competitor. So, this allows us to define the matrix noted by $Q_{s,D}(a_k, b_j)$. The rows of this matrix are formed by the source strategies $\pi_1(s,a_k), \forall a \in A$ and the columns are formed by the competitor strategies $\pi_2(s,b_j), \forall b_j \in A$. Thus, the value of the game is given as:

$$\max_{\overrightarrow{\pi_1}(s,a_k)} \min_{\overrightarrow{\pi_2}(s,b_j)} (\overrightarrow{\pi_2}(s,b_j))^t Q_{s,D}(a_k,b_j)\overrightarrow{\pi_1}(s,a_k), \tag{15}$$

We fix the strategy of the source $\overrightarrow{\pi_1}(s,a_k)$, So, Eq. (15) becomes:

$$\min_{\overrightarrow{\pi_2}(s,b_j)} (\overrightarrow{\pi_2}(s,b_j))^t Q_{s,D}(a_k,b_j)\overrightarrow{\pi_1}(s,a_k) \tag{16}$$

Where $Q_{s,D}(a_k,b_j)\overrightarrow{\pi_1}(s,a_k)$ is a vector and $\overrightarrow{\pi_2}(s,b_j)$ is a distribution probability for the action chosen by the competitor.

Let's note ku as the index of columns elements in the payoff game matrix $Q_{s,D}(a_k,b_j)$. Where $ku = [\pi_2(s,b_0)\pi_2(s,b_1)\pi_2(s,b_2),...,\pi_2(s,b_{D_m})]$. The goal is to find the minimal elements of $Q_{s,D}(a_k,b_j)\overrightarrow{\pi_1}(s,a_k)$.Then, the solution of (16) is to find the $\min_{ku}[Q_{s,D}(a_k,b_j)\overrightarrow{\pi_1}(s,a_k)]_k$. So, Eq. (15) becomes:

$$\max_{\overrightarrow{\pi_1}(s,a_k)} \min_{ku}[Q_{s,D}(a_k,b_j)\overrightarrow{\pi_1}(s,a_k)]_{ku} \tag{17}$$

We note $F = \min_{ku}[Q_{s,D}(a_k,b_j)\overrightarrow{\pi_1}(s,a_k)]_{ku}$

So, $[Q_{s,D}(a_k,b_j)\overrightarrow{\pi_1}(s,a_k)]_{ku} \geq \min_{\overrightarrow{\pi_2}(s,b_j)} [Q_{s,D}(a_k,b_j)\overrightarrow{\pi_1}(s,a_k)]_{ku} = F$.

Then, the problem in (15) becomes:

$$\max_{\overrightarrow{\pi_1}} F \tag{18}$$

S.t

$$[Q_{s,D}(a_k,b_j)\overrightarrow{\pi_1}(s,a_k)]_{ku} \geq F$$

$$\sum_{a_k \in A} \pi_1(s,a_k) = 1$$

$$\overrightarrow{\pi_1}(s,a_k) \geq 0$$

$\overrightarrow{\pi_1}(s,a_k) \geq 0$ means that each element of the probability vector $\overrightarrow{\pi_1}(s,a_k)$ is non-negative.

The problem described in (18) can be written as:

$$\max_{v} e_1 v \tag{19}$$

S.t

$$Q' v \leq 0$$

$$e_2 v = 1$$

$$\overrightarrow{\pi_1}(s,a_k) \geq 0$$

Where $v = \begin{pmatrix} \overrightarrow{\pi_1}(s,a) \\ F \end{pmatrix}$, $e_1 = [0,1], e_2 = [1,0], Q' = [1, -Q_{s,D}(a,b)]$.

So, the source can easily calculate the optimal strategy by solving the linear program (19).

4.1 Minimax Q-learning Algorithm

In this subsection we give the Minimax Q-learning Algorithm of our game.

Algorithm 1. Minimax Q-learning algorithm for a two-players zero-sum stochastic game.

$D = 1, 2, \ldots\ldots\ldots, D_m$,

Initialization:

$a_k, b_j \in$ A X A such as $A = \{a_1, a_2, \ldots, a_{D_m}\}$,

$s = (nC_i, qr_i)$, $nC_i = \{0, 1\}$, $qr_i = \{0, 1\}$,

$V(s, D) = 1$, $Q_{s,D}(a_k, b_j) = 1$.

Action choice:

Each source/player (competitor) chooses an action $a_k \in A$ ($b_j \in A$) according to its distribution probability over the space of action A depending on the state of the player.

Learn:

The source receives the reward $R_i(s, a_k, b_j)$, when it chooses the action a_k at state s and the competitor takes the action b_j.

The source updates its function $Q_{s,D}(a_k, b_j)$ according to (13)

The update of the optimal strategy is given by:

$$\pi_1^*(s, a_k) = \arg \max_{\vec{\pi_1}(s,a_k)} \min_{\vec{\pi_2}(s,b_j)} Q_{s,D}(a_k, b_j).$$

The update of $V(s, D)$ is calculated by:

$$V(s, D) = \max_{\vec{\pi_1}(s,a_k)} \min_{\vec{\pi_2}(s,b_j)} \sum_{a_k \in A} \vec{\pi_1}(s, a_k) Q_{s,D}(a_k, b_j).$$

The Learning factor decay with rate d is computed as: $\alpha = \alpha\, d$, $0 < d < 1$

Stop if $D = D_{th}$, D_{th} is obtained via the Proposition 5.

Proposition 5. *Our stochastic game has a time threshold D_{th}. If $D \geq D_{th}$ the source should not diffuse the content $a = a_0$. This threshold is given by: $D_{th} = \min\{D_{th1}, D_{th2}\}$, where*

$$D_{th1} \leq \frac{(3u_s(a_{k_0}, b_j) - u_s(a_{k_1}, b_j))\,\vec{v_1}}{3\,(u_s(a_{k_1}, b_j)\,M(t)\,\vec{v_2} + P(s', s, a_{k_1}, b_j)\,V(s, 3(D_{th}+1)) - P(s', s, a_{k0}, b_j)\,V(s, D_{th}+1)) - M(t)\,\vec{v_2}\,u_s(a_{k_0}, b_j))} - 1$$

$$D_{th2} \leq \frac{(u_s(a_{k_0}, b_j) - u_s(a_{k_2}, b_j))\,\vec{v_1}}{u_s(a_{k2}, bj)\vec{v_2}\,M(t) + P(s', s, a_{k_2}, b_j)\,V(s, D_{th}+1) - P(s', s, a_{k_0}, b_j)\,V(s, D_{th})\check{}\,u_s(a_{k_0}, b_j)\vec{v_2}M(t)} - 1$$

Proof 1. *When the time reaches a threshold $D = D_{th}$, it is better to not diffuse the content, which means:*

The user has to not diffuse rather than diffuse with low intensity which give us:

$$Q_{a_{k_0}}, b_j(s, D_{th}) \geq Q_{a_{k_1}}, b_j(s, 3\,(D_{th}+1))$$

This gives:

$$u_s(a_{k_0}, b_j)\,(\vec{v_2}\,M(t) + \vec{v_1}\,(1/D_{th})) + P(s^{'}, s, a_{k_0}, b_j)\,V(s, D_{th}) \geq u_s(a_{k_1}, b_j)\,(\vec{v_2}\,M(t) + \vec{v_1}\,(1/3(1+D_{th})) + P(s^{'}, s, a_{k_0}, b_j)\,V(s, 3(D_{th}+1))$$

$$D_{th1} \leq \frac{(3u_s(a_{k_0}, b_j) - u_s(a_{k_1}, b_j))\,\vec{v_1}}{3\,(u_s(a_{k_1}, b_j)\,M(t)\,\vec{v_2} + P(s^{'}, s, a_{k_1}, b_j)\,V(s, 3(D_{th}+1)) - P(s^{'}, s, a_{k0}, b_j)\,V(s, D_{th}+1)) - M(t)\,\vec{v_2}\,u_s(a_{k_0}, b_j))} - 1$$

The user has to not diffuse rather than diffuse with high intensity when the time validity reach the threshold, which means:

$$Q_{a_{k_0}}, b_j(s, D_{th}) \geq Q_{a_{k_2}}, b_j(s, D_{th})$$

This gives:

$$u_s(a_{k_0}, b_j)\,(\vec{v_2}\,M(t) + \vec{v_1}\,(1/D_{th})) + P(s^{'}, s, a_{k_0}, b_j)\,V(s, D_{th}) \geq u_s(a_{k_1}, b_j)\,(\vec{v_2}\,M(t) + \vec{v_1}\,(1/1+D_{th}) + P(s^{'}, s, a_{k_0}, b_j)\,V(s, D_{th}+1)$$

$$D_{th2} \leq \frac{(u_s(a_{k_0}, b_j) - u_s(a_{k_2}, b_j))\,\vec{v_1}}{u_s(a_{k2}, bj)\vec{v_2}\,M(t) + P(s^{'}, s, a_{k_2}, b_j)\,V(s, D_{th}+1) - P(s^{'}, s, a_{k_0}, b_j)\,V(s, D_{th})?u_s(a_{k_0}, b_j)\vec{v_2}M(t)} - 1$$

D_{th} is the minimum of the two threshold D_{th1} and D_{th2}

5 Numerical Results

We consider in this paper n equals to 100 nodes and we suppose that we have a source and a competitor from these nodes. The source and competitor can be for example two telecommunication operators, which advertise the same contents type. This information can be for instance a list of the available hotels in a city, destined to the tourists that are equipped with smart phones, and wish reserved. In this case, the information must arrive on time to the receivers (tourists) before certain hotels become full. Once the tourist gets the information he will be satisfied and will not look for other content. We take for the fraction of interested users $\epsilon = 0.25$, the rate of diffusion with high intensity is $\sigma = 6$ and the rate of diffusion with low intensity is $\delta = 2$. The validity of the content vary between 1 and 24 h. The sharing rate of the content is $\beta = 0.3$ and the fraction of the source neighbors is $\gamma = 0.15$. We recall that the action space of the source and the competitor is the same.

In state s_1, the user has a low degree and a high sharing quality of the same content type as the source. So, from Fig. 2, we observe in s_1 that most appropriate action is when the user chooses to diffuse with low intensity and the competitor with high intensity, because in this case the source gets the higher value of its utility function. Also, we notice that the user choice to diffuse with high or low intensity or not diffuse the content has almost the same effect. All curves have the same behavior compared to the validity time of the content. At the beginning

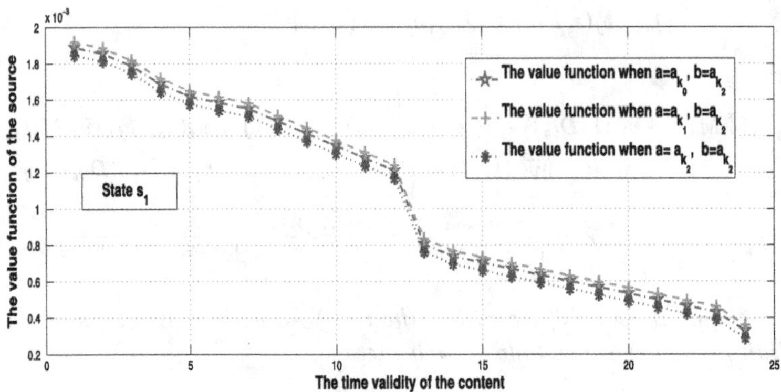

Fig. 2. The value-function of the source versus content validity time at state s_1.

the three curves have a high utility, after 12 h, the utility becomes less important and decreases with the time validity. This result is due to the fact that during the first life time of the content, the user gets a better utility thanks to the increasing number of interested user by the information and the fact that the validity time does not achieve the threshold D_{th}.

From this figure, we can also infer that the source try to target its best neighbors, but it does not get enough utility. This is due to its low degree of sharing that does not allow it to find many neighbors. But, thanks to the method adopted in our paper, the source has managed to disseminate its information before it expires.

In state s_2, the user has a low degree and a bad sharing quality of the same content type as the source. Then, from Fig. 3, we notice that the utility of the user when it chooses to not diffuse and the competitor to diffuse with high intensity is the highest.

We can explain this result by the fact that the source does not try to make an effort to find the right neighbor. It doesn't have many neighbors and in addition it has a bad sharing quality with them, in term of sharing the same content type. Therefore, and because of this system state that doesn't allow to disseminate the source information on time, it can be concluded that the best utility corresponds to the choice of the action a_{k0} (not diffuse).

In state s3, the user has a high degree and a good sharing quality of the same content type as the source. Thus, we perceive from Fig. 4 that when both user and competitor choose the action diffuse, the utility received is more important than any other case. This performance is the result of the effort of both user and its competitor to diffuse with high intensity and good sharing quality, so, the gain is better. Since, the two sources are in competition to disseminate their information on time, which makes the information viral due to the effect "word of mouth".

We conclude also from this figure, that at state s3, it is better to diffuse with high intensity when the competitor diffuse on the same rate and not diffuse when

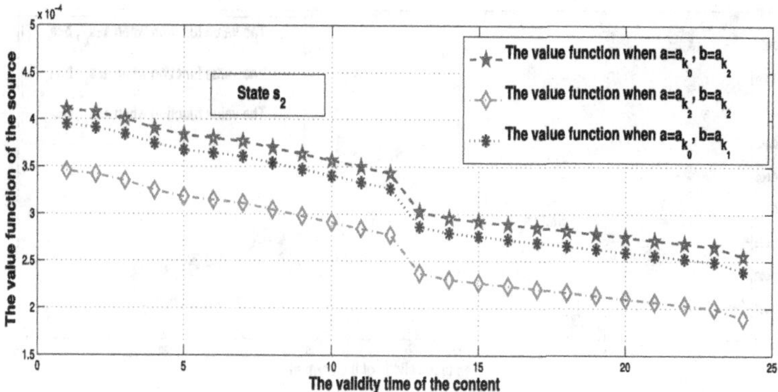

Fig. 3. The value-function of the source versus content validity time at state s_2.

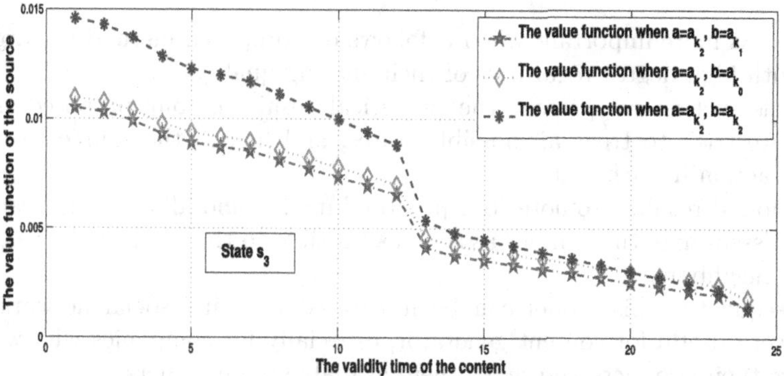

Fig. 4. The value-function of the source versus content validity time at state s_3.

the competitor diffuse with low intensity. This result can be explained by the fact that the shared information is not enough popular and there is not much destination that ask for it.

Indeed, we can infer also from Fig. 4, that the source succeed to put the information available to the receiver on time and to target the adequate neighbors that have the high degree and the high sharing quality. This is thanks to our adopted methodology that guarantees the best utility in such state.

In state s_4, the user has a high degree and a bad sharing quality of the same content type as the source. So, in this state, from Fig. 5 we detect that the most suitable action of the source is to diffuse with low intensity when the competitor diffuses with high intensity. Doubtlessly, the user that has the high degree despite of its bad sharing quality can disseminate the information on its appropriate time, with a good utility, but, the diffusion must be performed with low intensity.

This demonstrates that neighbors with high degree have a crucial power on the diffusion and the influence dissemination. Accordingly, the utility gained by

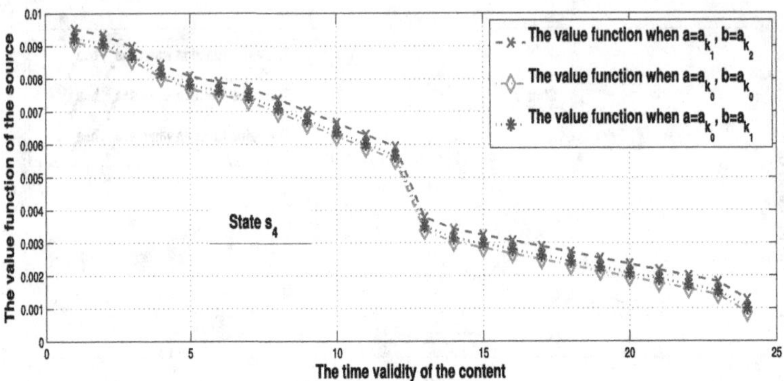

Fig. 5. The value-function of the source versus content validity time at state s_4.

the source is more important when it follows our proposed method by targeting nodes with high degree regardless of their sharing quality.

In this section we present the numerical results of our proposed model. Where, we tried to treat all possible states, and helped the source to choose the best action in each state.

The found results promotes our proposed model, and allows us to reach our goal to disseminate the content as soon as possible to the receivers by targeting the best neighbors.

Consequently, this model can be integrated into any social network, and can be very useful for content generator, especially for companies who want to advertise their products and make them available to customers.

6 Conclusion

In this paper, we studied the information diffusion problem within a certain delay. Where, the generator of content must target neighbors with a high connectivity and a good behavior towards its content type. These neighbors act as relays and help in transferring the source information on time to its destination. Thereafter we studied the competition between two sources generating the same type of content, where each of them maximizes its utility and minimizes that of the other. We used the minimax Q-learning to find the equilibrium and we defined a threshold limit of the contents. If the time reaches this threshold, the sources stop the diffusion process of their contents, because the information will not going to have any more utility to arrive at its destination. In future work, we propose to study the multi-player stochastic game on the dissemination of content including the popularity of the information.

References

1. Kempe, D., Kleinberg, J.M., Tardos, E.: Maximizing the spread of influence through a social network. In: Proceedings of the Ninth ACM SIGKDD International Conference on Knowledge Discovery and Data Mining, KDD, pp. 137–146. ACM (2003)
2. Kempe, D., Kleinberg, J.M., Tardos, E.: Influential nodes in a diffusion model for social networks. In: Caires, L., Italiano, G.F., Monteiro, L., Palamidessi, C., Yung, M. (eds.) ICALP 2005. LNCS, vol. 3580, pp. 1127–1138. Springer, Heidelberg (2005)
3. Even-Dar, E., Shapira, A.: A note on maximizing the spread of influence in social networks. In: Deng, X., Graham, F.C. (eds.) WINE 2007. LNCS, vol. 4858, pp. 281–286. Springer, Heidelberg (2007)
4. Kim, H., Yoneki, E.: Influential neighbours selection for information diffusion in online social networks. In: 21st International Conference on Computer Communications and Networks (ICCCN), Munich, Germany, pp. 1–7 (2012)
5. Jung, K., Heo, W., Chen, W.: Irie: scalable and robust influence maximization in social networks. In: Proceedings of 12th International Conference on Data Mining (ICDM 2012), pp. 918–923. IEEE Computer Society, Washington, DC (2012)
6. Haddad, M., Altman, E.: The interplay between caching and popularity. In: NetGCOOP: International Conference on NETwork Games, COntrol and OPtimization, pp. 1–4. IEEE (2011)
7. Altman, E.: A stochastic game approach for competition over popularity in social networks. Dynamic Games and Applications, Online publication, September 2012
8. Rodriguez, M.G., Leskovec, J., Krause, A.: Inferring networks of diffusion and influence. In: Proceedings of the 16th ACM SIGKDD International Conference on Knowledge Discovery and Data Mining, KDD 2010, pp. 1019–1028. ACM, New York (2010)
9. Even-Dar, E., Shapira, A.: A note on maximizing the spread of influence in social networks. Inf. Process. Lett. **111**(4), 184–187 (2011)
10. Altman, E.: A semi-dynamic model for competition over popularity and over advertisement space in social networks. In: VALUETOOLS, pp. 273–279. IEEE (2012)
11. Chen, W., Lu, W., Zhang, N.: Time-critical influence maximization in social networks with time-delayed diffusion process. arXiv preprint arXiv:1204.3074 (2012)
12. Ok, J., Jin, Y., Shin, J., Yi, Y.: On maximizing diffusion speed in social networks: impact of random seeding and clustering. In: The 2014 ACM International Conference on Measurement and Modeling of Computer Systems, SIGMETRICS 2014, pp. 301–313. ACM, New York (2014)
13. Shapley, L.S.: Stochastic games. Proc. Nat. Acad. Sci. U.S.A. **39**(10), 1095 (1953)
14. Watkins, C.J.: Learning from Delayed Rewards. Diss. University of Cambridge (1989)
15. Bowling, M., Veloso, M.: Rational and convergent learning in stochastic games. In: Proceedings of the 17th International Joint Conference on Artificial Intelligence - IJCAI 2001, vol. 2, pp. 1021–1026. Morgan Kaufmann Publishers Inc., San Francisco (2001)
16. Littman, M.L.: Markov games as a framework for multi-agent reinforcement learning. In: ICML 1994, pp. 157–163 (1994)
17. Littman, M.L., Szepesvári, C., Littman, M.L.: A generalized reinforcement-learning model: convergence and applications. In: ICML, pp. 310–318 (1996)
18. Bowling, M., Veloso, M.: An analysis of stochastic game theory for multiagent reinforcement learning. No. CMU-CS-00-165. Carnegie-Mellon Univ. Pittsburgh PA School of Computer Science (2000)

Tracking Causal Dependencies in Web Services Orchestrations Defined in ORC

Matthieu Perrin, Claude Jard(✉), and Achour Mostéfaoui

LINA, Université de Nantes, 2 rue de la Houssinière, 44322 Nantes, France
{matthieu.perrin,claude.jard,achour.mostefaoui}@univ-nantes.fr

Abstract. This article shows how the operational semantics of a language like ORC can be instrumented so that the execution of a program produces information on the causal dependencies between events. The concurrent semantics we obtain is based on asymmetric labeled event structures. The approach is illustrated using a Web service orchestration instance and the detection of race conditions.

1 Introduction

Several languages have been proposed to program applications based on Web service orchestrations (BPEL [1] is probably one of the best known). The present work is based on Orc [2,3], an orchestration language whose definition is based on a mathematical semantics, which is needed to define precisely the notion of causality. Orc is designed over the notion of *sites*, a generalization of functions that can encapsulate any kind of externally defined web sites or services as well as Orc expressions. As usual for languages, the operational semantics of Orc was defined as a labeled transition system. Such semantics produces naturally sets of sequential traces, which explicitly represent the observable behaviors of an Orc program [4].

Finding the causal dependencies in a program is very useful for error detection. In a non-deterministic concurrent context, this analysis cannot be based solely on the static structure of the program and requires execution. Dependencies are also very difficult to extract from a sequential record without additional information to unravel the interleaving of events. This is especially true for the analysis of QoS or of non functional properties, like timing constraints derived from the critical path of dependencies [5]. We consider any Orc program, which has been already parsed and expanded into its Orc calculus intermediate form. In this program, we distinguish the actions, which are the site calls, and the publications (return values of expressions). An event is the occurrence of an

This work has been partially supported by a French government support granted to the CominLabs excellence laboratory (Project *DeSceNt:Plug-based Decentralized Social Network*) and managed by the French National Agency for Research (ANR) in the "Investing for the Future" program under reference Nb. ANR-10-LABX-07-01. It was also partially funded by the French ANR project SocioPlug (ANR-13-INFR-0003).

A. Bouajjani and H. Fauconnier (Eds.): NETYS 2015, LNCS 9466, pp. 382–396, 2015.
DOI: 10.1007/978-3-319-26850-7_26

action during the execution of the Orc program. The events are linked by causal dependencies, that force the events to be executed in a certain order. We can distinguish three kinds of dependencies:

- the dependencies that are imposed by the control flow of the program defined by the semantics of the Orc combinators and imposed by the binding mechanism of Orc variables;
- the dependencies that are provided by the server executing the site calls. These external dependencies are not part of the Orc description, but could be returned by the site. We will consider at least that the possible return of a site call is directly caused by this call;
- the dependencies induced by preemption (the pruning operator of Orc).

The method used in this article is to extend the standard structural operational semantics (SOS [6]) to rewrite extended expressions, in which additional information has been added to compute causal and weakly-causal dependencies. This information is also made visible by extending the labeling of transitions. Concurrency is just the complement of the weak-causal relation, and conflicts are defined by cycles in this relation. Capturing causality and concurrency by instrumenting the semantics rules is a difficult job. This is mainly due to the fact that these relationships are global and therefore difficult to locate on the syntactic forms. The solution is to keep information about the causal past in a context associated with each rule. We build the necessary links between different contexts during the execution of rules. The aim is that such instrumented semantics reproduces the standard behavior of the program while calculating the additional information needed to track concurrency, causality and conflicts between the events produced by the execution.

After this introduction, the article presents the contribution compared to the existing works. Section 3 presents the Orc language from the perspective of its core calculus and its operational semantics, illustrated using an example of orchestration of Web services. Section 4 presents our proposed instrumented semantics based on the construction of event structures, giving the concurrent semantics of Orc. This section sets out the formal correctness of the approach stating that this new semantics produces the same executions as the standard semantics. Before concluding the paper, Sect. 5 reuses the example of Sect. 3 to show the causal structure obtained from its execution in the instrumented semantics and how this can be used to find errors.

2 Related Work

The need to dynamically trace the causal dependencies during the execution of the a program in order to monitor, detect errors or analyze performances is well recognized for concurrent applications. Causality, seen as a partial order [7], can be tracked in different ways. Some works are based on an instrumentation of either the underlying operating system or the source code. For example, vector clocks have been widely used by the distributed algorithms community in the context of message-passing systems [8]. The context of Web service orchestrations is more complex as a language like Orc can generate unbounded concurrency patterns. To our knowledge, the only instrumentation made on programs is [9], based on Java byte-code. However, in the considered model, the only source of causality comes from variable accesses. The second approach is to change the semantics so that it produces causal information which leads to a *concurrent semantics.* The challenge is then to maintain a good form of equivalence with the original semantics. Several debugging techniques rely on this principle, especially for performing replay ([10] is a good example for a fragment of the Oz language). The most successful works in concurrent semantics were conducted on process algebra (e.g. pi-calculus [11]). Our contribution is in the same vein, but for the Orc language, in the complex context of wide-area computing. Other attempts of concurrent semantics for Orc based on event structures have already been published [12,13]. They use an ad hoc connection of Petri net diagrams or Join calculus. It is not clear how this semantics can be implemented in practice at compile-time that transforms the source code into a concurrent model. An instrumented semantics solves this problem and allows to catch causal dependencies at runtime.

3 The Orc Programming Language

3.1 Core Calculus

Orc is a full programming language, that looks like a functional language with many non-functional aspects to handle concurrency. The interested reader can refer to [14] concerning the ability of Orc to design large-scale distributed applications. The Orc programming language is designed over a process calculus: the Orc core calculus. All the conveniences offered in the full Orc language are derived from very few central concepts present in the calculus: sites and operators. Values such as booleans, numbers and strings, arithmetic and logic operators, as well as complex data types such as shared registers, are just external sites. Even choices are implemented through the use of sites `ift` and `iff`, that publish a signal if their argument is true or false respectively. Besides sites, four operators are provided by the calculus to orchestrate the execution. These operators describe the sequencing of actions ("$f >x> g$"), the launching of parallel threads ("$f|g$"), an original preemption operator ("pruning: $f <x< g$") and an alternative in case of no response ("otherwise: $f; g$"). The full syntax of the calculus is specified by the grammar given in Fig. 1. From now on, we denote by Orc_s the set of the expressions allowed by this syntax. The expressions of the calculus that correspond to real Orc programs, denoted by the set *Orc*, are those that do not contain $?k$ and $\bot$ expressions. The rules of the operational semantics are given in Fig. 2.

There are two kinds of sites in Orc: the external ones, denoted V in the syntax, and the internal ones defined as an Orc expression with the syntax **def** $y(x) = f\#g$ where f is the body of the site and g is the remaining of the program in which y can be used as any site. For the sake of clarity, we

$f, g, h \in$ Expression	$::=$	$p \| p(p) \| ?k \| f \vert g \| f >x> g \| f <x< g \| f ; g \| D\#f \| \perp$
$D \in$ Definition	$::=$	$\textbf{def } y(x) = f$
$v \in$ Orc Value	$::=$	$V \| D$
$p \in$ Parameter	$::=$	$v \| \textbf{stop} \| x$
$w \in$ Response	$::=$	$NT(v) \| T(v) \| Neg$
$n \in$ Hidden Label	$::=$	$?V_k(v) \| ?D \| h(\omega) \| h(!v)$
$l \in$ Label	$::=$	$!v \| n \| \omega$

Fig. 1. The syntax of the Orc core calculus.

consider in this work that the sites are curryfied, so they have exactly one argument. Site definitions are recursive, which allows the same expressivity as any functional language. Calls to external sites are strict, i.e. their arguments have to be bound before the site can be called, while an internal site can be called immediately, and its arguments are evaluated lazily. When an external site is called, it sends its responses to a placeholder $?k$. A response can be either a non-terminating value $NT(v)$ if further responses are expected, or a terminating value $T(v)$ if this is the last publication of the site, or Neg if the site terminates without publishing any value. In $f|g$, the parallel composition expresses pure concurrency; f and g are run in parallel, their events are interleaved and the expression stops when both f and g have terminated. Sequentiality can be expressed by the sequential operator, like in $f >x> g$, where the variable x can be used in g. Here, f is started first, and then a new instance of $g[v/x]$, where x is bound to v, is launched as a consequence of each publication of v. In $f <x< g$, the pruning operator is used to express preemption. The variable x can be used in f. Both f and g are started, but f is paused when it needs to evaluate x. When g publishes a value, it is bound to x in f, and g is stopped. Other events that could have been produced by g are preempted by the publication. For example, if g is supposed to publish two values a and b, only one will be selected and published in each execution. We say that these two events are in conflict. The pruning operator is left-associative: in $f <x< g <y< h$, f, g and h are started in parallel, the first publication of g is bound to x and the first publication of h is bound to y. The otherwise operator is used in $f; g$. In this expression, f is first started alone and g is started if and only if f stops without publishing any value. Finally, the **stop** symbol can be used by the programmer exactly like a site or a variable to denote a terminated program. **stop** still produces an event ω to notify its parent expression that it has terminated. It then evolves into $\perp$, the inert final expression. $?k$ and $\perp$ cannot be used directly.

3.2 Illustration

We now illustrate the use of Orc in Fig. 3. This program defines the internal site `find_best(agencies, destination)` that computes the best offers proposed by the agencies listed in `agencies` for the destination given as a parameter. It publishes a unique value that is a pair composed of the best offer augmented with

$$(\textsc{Publish})\ \frac{}{v \xrightarrow{!v} \mathbf{stop}}\ v \text{ closed}$$

$$(\textsc{Stop})\ \frac{}{\mathbf{stop} \xrightarrow{\omega} \bot}$$

$$(\textsc{StopCall})\ \frac{}{\mathbf{stop}(p) \xrightarrow{\omega} \bot}$$

$$(\textsc{ExtStop})\ \frac{}{V(\mathbf{stop}) \xrightarrow{\omega} \bot}$$

$$(\textsc{ExtCall})\ \frac{}{V(v) \xrightarrow{?V_k(v)} ?k}\ k \text{ fresh}$$

$$(\textsc{DefDeclare})\ \frac{[D/y]f \xrightarrow{l} f'}{D\#f \xrightarrow{l} f'}\ D \text{ is } \mathbf{def}\ y(x) = g$$

$$(\textsc{IntCall})\ \frac{}{D(p) \xrightarrow{?D} [D/y][p/x]g}\ D \text{ is } \mathbf{def}\ y(x) = g$$

$$(\textsc{ParLeft})\ \frac{f \xrightarrow{l} f'}{f|g \xrightarrow{l} f'|g}\ l \neq \omega$$

$$(\textsc{ResT})\ \frac{?k \text{ receives } T(v)}{?k \xrightarrow{!v} \mathbf{stop}}$$

$$(\textsc{ParRight})\ \frac{g \xrightarrow{l} g'}{f|g \xrightarrow{l} f|g'}\ l \neq \omega$$

$$(\textsc{ResNt})\ \frac{?k \text{ receives } NT(v)}{?k \xrightarrow{!v} ?k}$$

$$(\textsc{ParStop})\ \frac{f \xrightarrow{\omega} \bot \quad g \xrightarrow{\omega} \bot}{f|g \xrightarrow{\omega} \bot}$$

$$(\textsc{ResNeg})\ \frac{?k \text{ receives } Neg}{?k \xrightarrow{\omega} \bot}$$

$$(\textsc{OtherV})\ \frac{f \xrightarrow{!v} f'}{f;g \xrightarrow{!v} f'}$$

$$(\textsc{SeqV})\ \frac{f \xrightarrow{!v} f'}{f >x> g \xrightarrow{h(!v)} (f' >x> g)|[v/x]g}$$

$$(\textsc{OtherN})\ \frac{f \xrightarrow{n} f'}{f;g \xrightarrow{n} f';g}$$

$$(\textsc{SeqN})\ \frac{f \xrightarrow{n} f'}{f >x> g \xrightarrow{n} f' >x> g}$$

$$(\textsc{OtherStop})\ \frac{f \xrightarrow{\omega} \bot}{f;g \xrightarrow{h(\omega)} g}$$

$$(\textsc{SeqStop})\ \frac{f \xrightarrow{\omega} \bot}{f >x> g \xrightarrow{\omega} \bot}$$

$$(\textsc{PruneV})\ \frac{g \xrightarrow{!v} g'}{f <x< g \xrightarrow{h(!v)} [v/x]f}$$

$$(\textsc{PruneLeft})\ \frac{f \xrightarrow{l} f'}{f <x< g \xrightarrow{l} f' <x< g}\ l \neq \omega$$

$$(\textsc{PruneN})\ \frac{g \xrightarrow{n} g'}{f <x< g \xrightarrow{n} f <x< g'}$$

$$(\textsc{PruneStop})\ \frac{g \xrightarrow{\omega} \bot}{f <x< g \xrightarrow{h(\omega)} [\mathbf{stop}/x]f}$$

Fig. 2. The rules of the operational semantics.

additional information and the list of other offers sorted by price. The program is composed of three internal sites. It uses three shared objects, that are created in lines 15 to 17: the stack `offers` and the registers `best_offer` and `best_agency`. At line 16, a new register is created through a call to the site `Register()` and is bound to the variable `r`. It is then initialized to a default value: `r.write(null)` that can be seen as a shortcut for `r("write")>w>w(null)`, so the shared register is a site that can publish its accessors when it is called. As writing in a register does not publish any value, the otherwise operator is finally used to bound the value to `best_offer`. At line 11, the site `find_offers` can be started before the variables are created (left hand side of pruning operators). `each` publishes in parallel all the sites contained into the stack `agencies`, so all known agencies have to publish their offers. Each time a new offer is found, it is added into `offer` and its price is compared to the current best known offer. The test is

```
1 def find_best(agencies, destination) =
2   def find_offers() =
3     each(agencies) > agency > agency(destination) > offer >
4     (offers.add((offer, agency)) |
5     (best_offer.read() > o > compare(o, offer) > b >
6     ift(b) > x > (best_agency.write(agency) | best_offer.write(offer))))       #
7   def extend_best() =
8     best_agency.read() > ba > best_offer.read() > bo > ba.exists(bo) > b >
9     (ift(b) > x > ba.get_info(bo) | iff(b) > x > alarm("inconsistent"))       #
10  def sort_offers(offers, best_offer) =
11    offers.sort(); best_offer.read() = offers.first() >b>
12    (ift(b) > x > offers | iff(b) > x > alarm("not best"))                     #
13  ((t <t< (find_offers() | timer(2000))) > t >
14  ((e_b, s_o) <e_b< extend_best() <s_o< sort_offers()))
15  <offers< Stack()
16  <best_offer< (Register() >r> r.write(null); r)
17  <best_agency< Register()                                                     #
```

Fig. 3. Identification of the best offers for a destination proposed by a pool of agencies.

first evaluated and passed as an argument to `ift`. If true, the program publishes a signal and the registers can be updated. `find_offers` does not publish any value. In parallel with its call, we start a timer that publishes after 2 s a signal. The signal will halt this part of the program thanks to the pruning operator, and starts the line 14, thanks to the sequential operator. Line 14 calls both `extend_best` and `sort_offers` and publishes the result when both sites have published. The two sites call an external site either to sort the offers or to get extra information about the best offer, and they perform a test that raises an alarm if something wrong is detected (Fig. 3).

Figure 4 shows a possible trace of the program of Fig. 3. In this example, both alarms are due to inconsistencies in the shared registers. To avoid the alarm "inconsistent", it is necessary to write into `best_offer` and `best_agency` atomically, and to avoid the other alarm, the comparison with the current value of `best_offer` and its edition should be atomic. The event `best_offer.write(01)` is a cause for both alarms, but it is impossible to detect it in the sequential trace without any information about causality.

4 Instrumented Semantics

4.1 Method

SOS specifications take the form of a set of inference rules that define the valid transitions of a composite piece of syntax in terms of the transitions of its components. Rewriting transforms terms by executing a rule (it may be a non-deterministic transition in case of multiple alternatives). The successive transitions represent the program behavior. This may produce a sequence of values,

1. each([A1, A2])
2. timer(2000)
3. new_register()
4. new_register()
5. A1(D)
6. r.write(null)
7. best_offer.read()
8. new_stack()
9. offers.add(O1)
10. A2(D)
11. offers.add(O2)
12. compare(null, 01)
13. best_offer.read()
14. compare(null, 02)
15. ift(true)
16. ift(true)
17. best_offer.write(O2)
18. best_offer.write(O1)
19. best_agency.write(A1)
20. best_agency.write(A2)
21. best_agency.read()
22. best_offer.read()
23. A2.exists(O1)
24. iff(false)
25. ift(false)
26. alarm("inconsistent")
27. offers.sort()
28. best_offer.read()
29. offers.first()
30. =(O1, O2)
31. iff(false)
32. ift(false)
33. alarm("not best")

Fig. 4. A possible execution for the program in Fig. 3 where agencies = $[A1, A2]$ and destination = D. Each agency publishes an offer $O1$ and $O2$ respectively. For the sake of space and clarity, we only show site calls in this execution.

that can be brought by the labeling of rules. Our approach is based on an instrumentation of the rules, that appends additional information to the labels in order to track the partial order of events. Actually, a label in the instrumented semantics is a tuple $e = (e_k, e_l, e_c, e_a)$, where e_k is an identifier taken in a countable set K, that is unique for the execution, e_l is a label similar to those of the standard semantics and e_c and e_a contain the finite sets of the identifiers of the causes and the weak causes of the event, respectively. Informally, an event e is a cause of e' if e always happens before e', regardless of the scheduling chosen by the system. Similarly, e is a weak cause of e' if e' can never happen after e, either because e is one of its causes or because e' preempts e.

In order to record the information concerning the past of an expression, we enrich the language with a new syntactic construction: $\langle f, c, a\rangle_L$ means that c and a are the causes of the Orc instrumented expression f. Thus, if f has c and a as causes and if it can evolve into f', this transition should also have c and a as causes. The index L expresses the kind of events that can activate the rule: $!v$ matches any publication, l stands for any label and ω means that c and a are only the causes of the termination of the program. We also consider that the external sites track causality themselves, as an internally-defined function would do. It makes sense as some sites (e.g. +) handle their calls independently, while others (e.g. shared registers, management library) induce more complex causality patterns between the calls. Hence, the responses we get include this additional information. The verification of these responses is not the subject here, and we suppose them to be correct by hypothesis.

Apart from the introduction of the instrumentation construction and the new information in the responses, the syntax of the instrumented expressions (Fig. 5) is very similar to the regular one. The set of all the expressions allowed by this extended syntax is Orc_i. We can notice that every valid Orc program is also a valid instrumented expression, which means that the instrumented semantics can be applied without program transformation.

$$
\begin{array}{lll}
f, g, h \in \text{Expression} & ::= & p \| p(p) \| ?k \| f|g \\
& & \| f > x > g \| f < x < g \| f ; g \\
& & \| D\#f \| \bot \| \langle f, K, K \rangle_L \\
D \in \text{Definition} & ::= & \mathbf{def}\ y(x) = f \\
v \in \text{Orc Value} & ::= & V \| D \\
p \in \text{Parameter} & ::= & v \| \mathbf{stop} \| x \| \langle p, K, K \rangle_L \\
w \in \text{Response} & ::= & NT(v, K, K) \| T(v, K, K) \\
& & \| Neg(K, K) \\
n \in \text{Hidden Label} & ::= & ?V_k(v) \| ?D \| h(\omega) \| h(!v) \\
l \in \text{Label} & ::= & !v \| n \| \omega
\end{array}
$$

Fig. 5. The extended syntax of the instrumented semantics.

4.2 Labeled Asymmetric Event Structure

Labeled asymmetric event structures (LAES) [15] are natural objects to represent concurrent executions in a compact way.

Definition 1 (Labelled Asymmetric Event Structure). *A* labelled asymmetric event structure *(LAES) is a tuple* $(E, L, \leq, \nearrow, \Lambda)$.

- E *is a set of* events,
- L *is a set of* labels,
- $\leq$, causality *is a partial order on* E,
- $\nearrow$, weak causality *is a binary relation on* E,
- $\Lambda : E \mapsto L$ *is the* labelling function,
- *each* $e \in E$ *has a finite* causal history $[e] = \{e' \in E | e' \leq e\}$,
- *for all events* $e < e' \in E, e \nearrow e'$, *where* $<$ *is the irreflexive restriction of* $\leq$,
- *for all* $e \in E$, $\nearrow \cap [e] \times [e]$, *the restriction of weak causality to the causal history of* e, *is acyclic.*

We also define an induced *conflict* relation $\#_a$ as the smallest set of finite parts of E such that: for $E' \subset E$ and $e_0, e_1, ..., e_n \in E$,

- if $e_0 \nearrow e_1 \nearrow \cdots \nearrow e_n \nearrow e_0$ then $\{e_0, e_1, \cdots, e_n\} \in \#_a$,
- if $E' \cup \{e_0\} \in \#_a$ and $e_0 \leq e_1$ then $E' \cup \{e_1\} \in \#_a$.

Informally, two events are in conflict if they cannot occur together in the same execution.

A LAES can be seen as a structure that encodes concisely several sequential executions; each of them being a linearization of the LAES.

Definition 2 (Linearization). *Let* $\mathcal{E} = (E, L, \leq, \nearrow, \Lambda)$ *be a LAES. A* finite linearization *of* $\mathcal{E}$ *is a word* $w = \Lambda(e_0) \ldots \Lambda(e_n)$ *where the different* $e_i \in E$ *are distinct and such that:*

- *it is left-closed for causality:*

$$\forall e \in E, \forall e' \in \{e_0, \ldots, e_n\}, e \leq e' \Rightarrow e \in \{e_0, \ldots, e_n\},$$

$$(\textsc{CauseYes})\frac{f \xrightarrow{k,l,c,a}_i f'}{\langle f, c', a'\rangle_L \xrightarrow{k,l,c\cup c',a\cup a'\cup c'}_i \langle f', c', a'\rangle_L}\ l \in L$$

$$(\textsc{CauseNo})\frac{f \xrightarrow{k,l,c,a}_i f'}{\langle f, c', a'\rangle_L \xrightarrow{k,l,c,a}_i \langle f', c', a'\rangle_L}\ l \notin L$$

Fig. 6. The semantics of the new operator $\langle f, c, a\rangle_L$ is defined by two additional rules.

- *the weak causality is respected:*

$$\forall i, j \in \{0, \ldots, n\}, e_i \nearrow e_j \Rightarrow i < j.$$

We denote $Lin(\mathcal{E})$ as the set of all finite linearizations of $\mathcal{E}$.

Let $(E, L, \leq, \nearrow, \Lambda)$ be an asymmetric event structure and $e, e' \in E$ two events. We say that:

- e is a *cause* of e', if e happens before e' in all executions;
- e is a *weak cause* of e', if there is no execution in which e happens after e';
- e and e' are *concurrent*, denoted $e||e'$, if they can occur in either order. Formally, $e||e'$ if neither $e \nearrow e'$ nor $e' \nearrow e$.
- e is *preempted* by e', denoted $e \rightsquigarrow e'$, if e' can occur independently from e, but after that, e cannot occur anymore. Formally, $e \rightsquigarrow e'$ if $e \nearrow e'$ and $e \not\leq e'$.

4.3 Rules

Essentially, the instrumented semantics presented in Fig. 7 decorates the rules of standard semantics, except that two rules are added (see Fig. 6). The transition system defined by this instrumented semantics is denoted $\rightarrow_i$ and the sequential executions starting from a program f are contained in the set $[\![f]\!]_i$.

Informally, the expression $\langle f, c, a\rangle_L$ evolves exactly like f, but some causes and weak causes may be added to the event. For example, if $L = !v$ and f produces an internal event, that is not a publication, only the rule CauseNo can be applied, so the instrumentation will have no effect. On the other hand, if f publishes a value, the rule CauseYes applies and c and a are added to the causes and weak causes of the publication. Note that c is also added to the weak causes. This is to ensure that causality is always a special case of weak causality.

Let us now comment the most relevant instrumentations of the other rules. Let us consider rule SeqV. When a value is published, a new instance of the right hand side expression is created. All the events produced by this new expression need the former publication to *have occurred before* them, i.e. they are consequences of this publication. This is why the new expression is instrumented. Even if PruneV and SeqV are syntaxically very similar in their standard forms, the fact that both hand sides of the pruning operator are run in parallel makes them very different in terms of causality. In the expression $(1|x) < x < 2$, the

$$(\textsc{Publish})\ \frac{}{v \xrightarrow{k,!v,\emptyset,\emptyset}_i \langle \textbf{stop}, \{k\}, \emptyset\rangle_l}\ \begin{array}{l} v \text{ closed}\\ k \text{ fresh}\end{array}$$

$$(\textsc{Stop})\ \frac{}{\textbf{stop} \xrightarrow{k,\omega,\emptyset,\emptyset}_i \bot}\ k \text{ fresh} \qquad (\textsc{StopCall})\ \frac{P \xrightarrow{k,\omega,c,a}_i \bot}{P(p) \xrightarrow{k,\omega,c,a}_i \bot}$$

$$(\textsc{ExtStop})\ \frac{P \xrightarrow{k,!V,c,a}_i P' \quad p \xrightarrow{k',\omega,c',a'}_i p'}{P(p) \xrightarrow{k,\omega,c\cup c',a\cup a'}_i \bot}$$

$$(\textsc{ExtCall})\ \frac{P \xrightarrow{k,!V,c,a}_i P' \quad p \xrightarrow{k',!v,c',a'}_i p'}{P(p) \xrightarrow{k,?V_k(v),c\cup c',a\cup a'}_i \langle ?k, c \cup c' \cup \{k\}, a \cup a'\rangle_l}$$

$$(\textsc{DefDeclare})\ \frac{[D/y]f \xrightarrow{k,l,c,a}_i f'}{D\#f \xrightarrow{k,l,c,a}_i f'}\ D \text{ is } \textbf{def } y(x) = g$$

$$(\textsc{IntCall})\ \frac{P \xrightarrow{k,!D,c,a}_i P'}{P(p) \xrightarrow{k,?D,c,a}_i \langle [D/y][p/x]g, c \cup \{k\}, a\rangle_l}\ D \text{ is } \textbf{def } y(x) = g$$

$$(\textsc{ResT})\ \frac{?k \text{ receives } T(v,c,a)}{?k \xrightarrow{j,!v,c,a\cup c}_i \langle \textbf{stop}, c \cup \{j\}, a\rangle_\omega}\ j \text{ fresh}$$

$$(\textsc{ParLeft})\ \frac{f \xrightarrow{k,l,c,a}_i f'}{f|g \xrightarrow{k,l,c,a}_i f'|g}\ l \neq \omega \qquad (\textsc{ResNt})\ \frac{?k \text{ receives } NT(v,c,a)}{?k \xrightarrow{j,!v,c,a\cup c}_i ?k}\ j \text{ fresh}$$

$$(\textsc{ParRight})\ \frac{g \xrightarrow{k,l,c,a}_i g'}{f|g \xrightarrow{k,l,c,a}_i f|g'}\ l \neq \omega \qquad (\textsc{ResNeg})\ \frac{?k \text{ receives } Neg(c,a)}{?k \xrightarrow{j,\omega,c,a\cup c}_i \bot}\ j \text{ fresh}$$

$$(\textsc{ParStop})\ \frac{f \xrightarrow{k,\omega,c,a}_i f' \quad g \xrightarrow{k',\omega,c',a'}_i g'}{f|g \xrightarrow{k,\omega,c\cup c',a\cup a'}_i \bot}$$

$$(\textsc{SeqV})\ \frac{f \xrightarrow{k,!v,c,a}_i f'}{f >x> g \xrightarrow{k,h(!v),c,a}_i (f' >x> g)|\langle [v/x]g, c \cup \{k\}, a\rangle_l}$$

$$(\textsc{OtherV})\ \frac{f \xrightarrow{k,!v,c,a}_i f'}{f;g \xrightarrow{k,!v,c,a}_i f'} \qquad (\textsc{SeqN})\ \frac{f \xrightarrow{k,n,c,a}_i f'}{f >x> g \xrightarrow{k,n,c,a}_i f' >x> g}$$

$$(\textsc{OtherN})\ \frac{f \xrightarrow{k,n,c,a}_i f'}{f;g \xrightarrow{k,n,c,a}_i f';g} \qquad (\textsc{SeqStop})\ \frac{f \xrightarrow{k,\omega,c,a}_i \bot}{f >x> g \xrightarrow{k,\omega,c,a}_i \bot}$$

$$(\textsc{OtherStop})\ \frac{f \xrightarrow{k,\omega,c,a}_i \bot}{f;g \xrightarrow{k,h(\omega),c,a}_i \langle g, c \cup \{k\}, a\rangle_l}$$

$$(\textsc{PruneV})\ \frac{g \xrightarrow{k,!v,c,a}_i g'}{f <x< g \xrightarrow{k,h(!v),c,a}_i \langle [\langle v, c \cup \{k\}, a\rangle_l/x]f, c \cup \{k\}, a\rangle_\omega}$$

$$(\textsc{PruneN})\ \frac{g \xrightarrow{k,n,c,a}_i g'}{f <x< g \xrightarrow{k,n,c,a}_i f <x< \langle g', \emptyset, \{k\}\rangle_{!v}}$$

$$(\textsc{PruneLeft})\ \frac{f \xrightarrow{k,l,c,a}_i f'}{f <x< g \xrightarrow{k,l,c,a}_i f' <x< g}\ l \neq \omega$$

$$(\textsc{PruneStop})\ \frac{g \xrightarrow{k,\omega,c,a}_i \bot}{f <x< g \xrightarrow{k,h(\omega),c,a}_i \langle [\langle \textbf{stop}, c \cup \{k\}, a\rangle_l/x]f, c \cup \{k\}, a\rangle_\omega}$$

Fig. 7. The instrumented version of the rules of the operational semantics.

second publication of 2 is a consequence of the first one, but not the publication of 1. This is why the instrumentation covers the occurrences of the newly bound variable. However, this is not sufficient. Consider the program (**stop** $<x<$ 2); 3. The publication of 3 must wait the end of the left hand side (i.e. the publication of 2). However, this publication is useless, in the sense that no variable x can be bound to its value. To handle this case, we add an instrumentation to the whole expression that is only triggered when the expression stops. Finally, the rule PRUNEN is also interesting as it generates weak causality. Indeed, in the program $x <s< ((1+1)|3)$, the left hand side can call site + and then publish 3, or publish 3 directly, but can never publish 3 and then call site +, because a publication preempts any other event. Of course, it could also wait for the answer of the site and then publish 2, which would preempt the publication of 3. This preemption relation is operated by an instrumentation that contains k as weak causes and that is triggered only in case of publication.

4.4 Concurrent Executions

The equivalent of traces in the instrumented semantics are the *concurrent executions*, represented by LAES.

Definition 3 (Concurrent Execution). *Let* $\sigma = \sigma^1 \dots \sigma^n \in [\![f_0]\!]_i$*, where for all* i, $\sigma^i = (\sigma^i_k, \sigma^i_l, \sigma^i_c, \sigma^i_a)$*. We define the* concurrent execution *of* σ *as the LAES:*

$$\overline{\overline{\sigma}} = (\{\sigma^1_k, \dots, \sigma^n_k\}, \{\sigma^1_l, \dots, \sigma^n_l\}, \leq, \nearrow, \Lambda)$$

where for all $i, j \in \{1, \dots, n\}$*:*

- $\sigma^i_k \leq \sigma^j_k$ *if* $\sigma^i_k \in \sigma^j_c$ *or* $i = j$,
- $\sigma^i_k \nearrow \sigma^j_k$ *if* $\sigma^i_k \in \sigma^j_a$,
- $\Lambda(\sigma^i_k) = \sigma^i_l$.

As the fields σ^i_c and σ^i_a only contain events that happened before σ^i in the sequential execution, both $\leq$ and $\nearrow$ are order relations and every event has a finite causal history. For the same reason, $\nearrow$ is acyclic. Moreover, it is easy to check that weak causality is more general than causality, so this definition actually corresponds to a real LAES.

We now state the main result: the behavior of a program is preserved by the instrumented semantics. It is established through two properties. The first one justifies the name of the instrumented semantics and the second one proves that the instrumentation is correct, i.e. that it does not define incorrect behaviors. Note that we do not give a complete proof of the two propositions for lack of space, but it can be found in [16].

Proposition 1 (Instrumentation). *The projections of the executions produced by the instrumented semantics on their labels correspond exactly to the executions of the standard semantics:*

$$\forall f \in Orc, \{\sigma^1_l ... \sigma^n_l | \sigma \in [\![f]\!]_i\} = [\![f]\!].$$

In other words, it is always possible to instrument a standard execution to get a concurrent execution, and conversely we can get a standard execution from an instrumented execution by a simple projection.

The proof of this property is straightforward since both semantics contain similar rules. The only difficulty comes from the applications of CAUSEYES and CAUSENO, that slightly modifie the structure of the derivation trees. All in all, both executions are similar.

Proposition 2 (Correctness). *The linearizations that can be inferred from an execution in the instrumented semantics are correct with respect to the standard semantics:*

$$\forall f \in Orc, \forall \sigma \in [\![f]\!]_i, Lin(\overline{\overline{\sigma}}) \subset [\![f]\!].$$

This proof is much more complicated. Let us consider a linearization $L \in Lin(\overline{\overline{\sigma}})$. To prove that $L \in [\![f]\!]$, we show that it is possible to progressively transform $\sigma_l^1 ... \sigma_l^n$ into L by applying a series of small steps that correspond either to the inversion of two consecutive concurrent events, to the preemption of an event by its successor or to a prefixation of the sequence. As $\sigma_l^1 ... \sigma_l^n \in [\![f]\!]$ and each step preserves this property, we get that $L \in [\![f]\!]$. The main difficulty concerns the proof of the correctness of the two first steps, as it requires a proof for all pairs of possible consecutive rules.

By introducing concurrency and preemption between events that were arbitrarily ordered by the standard semantics, the instrumented semantics gathers many sequential executions into one concurrent execution, which hugely reduces the number of different executions. However, all the events contained in a concurrent execution are also contained into a single sequential execution. Therefore, no instrumentation is able to capture conflict, as two conflictual events would never occur together. This is why completeness cannot be achieved with this approach.

5 Application

Let us reuse the example presented in Sect. 3 and the execution of Fig. 4. Figure 8 shows the trace augmented with the causal information gained by the instrumented semantics.

Figure 9 shows the LAES in its graphical form. Events taht correspond to site calls are represented in circles and connected by three kinds of arrows. Direct causality is figured by solid and dashed arrows. Solid arrows represent program causality, that is specified by the instrumented semantics, while dashed arrows represent data causes, that are managed by the sites themselves. A *call* to a write on a site is a cause of the *publications* of the next read on this site, so the write is a cause of all the consequences of the read. Moreover, preemption is figured by dotted arrows. The call to `each()` — and all its consequences — is preempted by the publication made by `timer(2000)` — and all its consequences.

$(1, l_1, \emptyset, \emptyset)$
$(2, l_2, \emptyset, \emptyset)$
$(3, l_3, \emptyset, \emptyset)$
$(4, l_4, \emptyset, \emptyset)$
$(5, l_5, \{1\}, \{1\})$
$(6, l_6, \{4\}, \{4\})$
$(7, l_7, \{1,4\text{-}6\}, \{1,4\text{-}6\})$
$(8, l_8, \emptyset, \emptyset)$
$(9, l_9, \{1,5,8\}, \{1,5,8\})$
$(10, l_{10}, \{1\}, \{1\})$
$(11, l_{11}, \{1,8,10\}, \{1,8,10\})$
$(12, l_{12}, \{1,4\text{-}7\}, \{1,4\text{-}7\})$
$(13, l_{13}, \{1,4,6,10\}, \{1,4,6,10\})$
$(14, l_{14}, \{1,4,6,10,13\}, \{1,4,6,10,13\})$
$(15, l_{15}, \{1,4\text{-}7,12\}, \{1,4\text{-}7,12\})$
$(16, l_{16}, \{1,4,6,10,13,14\}, \{1,4,6,10,13,14\})$
$(17, l_{17}, \{1,4,6,10,13,14,16\}, \{1,4,6,10,13,14,16\})$
$(18, l_{18}, \{1,4\text{-}7,12,15\}, \{1,4\text{-}7,12,15\})$
$(19, l_{19}, \{1,3\text{-}7,12,15\}, \{1,3\text{-}7,12,15\})$
$(20, l_{20}, \{1,3,4,6,10,13,14,16\}, \{1,3,4,6,10,13,14,16\})$
$(21, l_{21}, \{2\}, \{2, 1\})$
$(22, l_{22}, \{1\text{-}7,10,12\text{-}16,19\text{-}21\}, \{1\text{-}7,10,12\text{-}16,19\text{-}21\})$
$(23, l_{23}, \{1\text{-}7,10,12\text{-}19,22\}, \{1\text{-}7,10,12\text{-}19,22\})$
$(24, l_{24}, \{1\text{-}7,10,12\text{-}19,22,23\}, \{1\text{-}7,10,12\text{-}19,22,23\})$
$(25, l_{25}, \{1\text{-}7,10,12\text{-}19,22,23\}, \{1\text{-}7,10,12\text{-}19,22,23\})$
$(26, l_{26}, \{1\text{-}7,10,12\text{-}19,22\text{-}24\}, \{1\text{-}7,10,12\text{-}19,22\text{-}24\})$
$(27, l_{27}, \{2\}, \{2, 1\})$
$(28, l_{28}, \{1,2,5,9\text{-}11,27\}, \{1,2,5,9\text{-}11,27\})$
$(29, l_{29}, \{1,2,5,9\text{-}11,27\}, \{1,2,5,9\text{-}11,27\})$
$(30, l_{30}, \{1,2,4\text{-}7,9\text{-}18,27\text{-}29\}, \{1,2,4\text{-}7,9\text{-}18,27\text{-}29\})$
$(31, l_{31}, \{1,2,4\text{-}7,9\text{-}18,27\text{-}30\}, \{1,2,4\text{-}7,9\text{-}18,27\text{-}30\})$
$(32, l_{32}, \{1,2,4\text{-}7,9\text{-}18,27\text{-}30\}, \{1,2,4\text{-}7,9\text{-}18,27\text{-}30\})$
$(33, l_{33}, \{1,2,4\text{-}7,9\text{-}18,27\text{-}31\}, \{1,2,4\text{-}7,9\text{-}18,27\text{-}31\})$

Fig. 8. An execution augmented with causal information. Numbers refer to the events of Fig. 4.

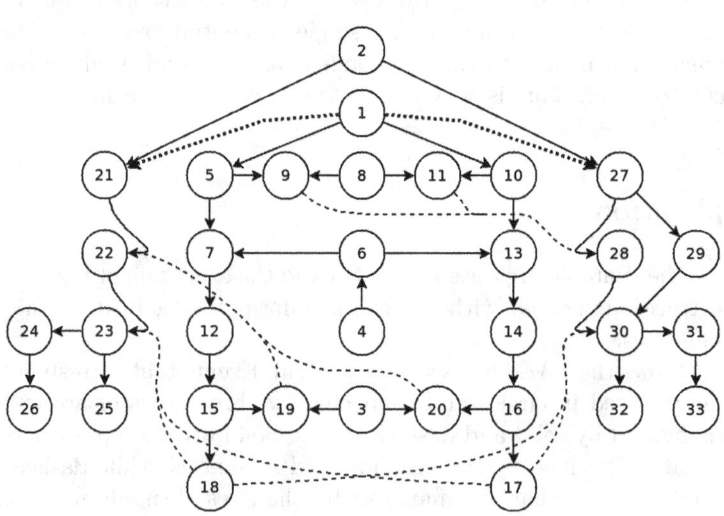

Fig. 9. Corresponding LAES in a graphical form.

Root Causes Analysis. This execution concurrently raises two alarms. Let us consider their last common causes, i.e. the events that are causes of both alarms, and that are not causes of another such event. The alarms have two last common causes: `timer(2000)` and `best_offer.write(01)`. The timer is not to blame here, as it has no causes and is just used as a starter for the program. Indeed, `best_offer.write(01)` is the root cause for these two alarms. If this event did not exist, the value published by `best_offer.read()` would be `02` for both calls, `A2.exists(02)` and `=(02, 02)` would be true and no alarm would be raised.

Detection of Race Conditions. We can see that the events `best_offer.write(01)` and `best_offer.write(02)` are concurrent, as well as `best_agency.write(01)` and `best_agency.write(02)`. In this context, these events can interleave so that `best_offer` and `best_agency` get inconsistent values.

6 Conclusion

We based our work on the Orc core calculus, as it is expressive enough to easily generate many situations found in distributed systems, such as causality, concurrency and preemption, and remains simple enough to be tractable in a formal work. Our contribution consists of an instrumentation of the standard structural operational semantics of Orc that tracks causality and weak causality at run-time to build LAES, well suited to represent concurrent executions. We think LAES are an interesting tool to access important properties of orchestrations. We illustrate this point on two questions: root cause analysis and detection of race conditions. Beyond the Orc language, we think that the article presents a general approach that can be used for other non-deterministic languages with concurrency operators. Based on this work, we think it is possible to produce the same information using a source to source transformation. Such a technique would be easier to implement, as it does not require to modify the execution engine of the language.

References

1. Andrews, T., Curbera, F., Dholakia, H., Goland, Y., Klein, J., Leymann, F., Liu, K., Roller, D., Smith, D., Thatte, S., Trickovic, I., Weerawarana, S.: Business Process Execution Language for Web Services. Version 1.1, 5 May 2003. http://download.boulder.ibm.com/ibmdl/pub/software/dw/specs/ws-bpel/ws-bpel.pdf
2. Kitchin, D., Quark, A., Cook, W., Misra, J.: ORC language. http://orc.csres.utexas.edu
3. Kitchin, D., Quark, A., Cook, W., Misra, J.: The orc programming language. In: Lee, D., Lopes, A., Poetzsch-Heffter, A. (eds.) FMOODS 2009. LNCS, vol. 5522, pp. 1–25. Springer, Heidelberg (2009)
4. Kitchin, D.E., Cook, W.R., Misra, J.: A language for task orchestration and its semantic properties. In: Baier, C., Hermanns, H. (eds.) CONCUR 2006. LNCS, vol. 4137, pp. 477–491. Springer, Heidelberg (2006)

5. Rosario, S., Benveniste, A., Haar, S., Jard, C.: Foundations for web services orchestrations: functional and QoS aspects. In: ISOLA 2006, 2nd International Symposium on Leveraging Applications of Formal Methods, Verification and Validation, Cyprus, 15–19 November 2006 (2006)
6. Plotkin, G.D.: The origins of structural operational semantics. J. Log. Algebr. Program. **60–61**, 3–15 (2004)
7. Lamport, L.: Time, clocks, and the ordering of events in a distributed system. Commun. ACM **21**(7), 558–565 (1978)
8. Fidge, C.J.: Timestamps in message-passing systems that preserve the partial ordering. In: Proceedings of the 11th Australian Computer Science Conference (ACSC 1988), pp. 56–66, February 1988
9. Roşu, G., Sen, K.: An instrumentation technique for online analysis of multithreaded programs. Concurrency Comput. Pract. Experience **19**, 311–325 (2007). Wiley Online Library
10. Giachino, E., Lanese, I., Mezzina, C.A.: Causal-consistent reversible debugging. In: Gnesi, S., Rensink, A. (eds.) FASE 2014 (ETAPS). LNCS, vol. 8411, pp. 370–384. Springer, Heidelberg (2014)
11. Boreale, M., Sangiorgi, D.: A fully abstract semantics for causality in the π-calculus. Acta Informaticae **35**(5), 353–400 (1998)
12. Rosario, S., Kitchin, D.E., Benveniste, A., Cook, W., Haar, S., Jard, C.: Event Structure semantics of orc. In: Dumas, M., Heckel, R. (eds.) WS-FM 2007. LNCS, vol. 4937, pp. 154–168. Springer, Heidelberg (2008)
13. Bruni, R., Melgratti, H., Tuosto, E.: Translating orc features into petri nets and the join calculus. In: Bravetti, M., Núñez, M., Zavattaro, G. (eds.) WS-FM 2006. LNCS, vol. 4184, pp. 123–137. Springer, Heidelberg (2006)
14. Misra, J., Cook, W.: Computation orchestration: a basis for wide-area computing. J. Softw. Syst. Model. **6**(1), 83–110 (2007)
15. Winskel, G.: Event structures. In: Brauer, W., Reisig, W., Rozenberg, G. (eds.) Advances in Petri Nets 1986, Part II. LNCS, vol. 255, pp. 325–392. Springer, Heidelberg (1987)
16. Perrin, M., Jard, C., Mostéfaoui, A.: Building a concurrent operational semantics for the ORC language. Technical report, LINA, Université de Nantes (2014). https://hal.archives-ouvertes.fr/hal-01101340v2

Web Services Trust Assessment Based on Probabilistic Databases

Zohra Saoud [1(✉)], Noura Faci[1], Zakaria Maamar[2], and Djamal Benslimane[1]

[1] Université Lyon 1, Villeurbanne, France
zohra.saoud@univ-lyon1.fr
[2] Zayed University, Dubai, UAE

Abstract. This paper discusses the assessment of Web services trust. This assessment is undermined by the uncertainty that raises due to end-users' ratings that can be questioned and variations in Web services performance at run-time. To tackle the first uncertainty a fuzzy-based credibility model is suggested so that the gap between end-users (known as *strict*) and the current majority is reduced. To deal with the second uncertainty we propose a probabilistic trust approach. A series of experiments are carried out to validate the probabilistic approach built upon probabilistic databases and a fuzzy-based credibility model. The results show that the probabilistic approach improves significantly trust quality. Future work consists of incorporating several credibility models into one probabilistic trust model.

Keywords: Web service · Trust · Probability · Credibility · Fuzzy clustering

1 Introduction

It is largely accepted that current Web Services (WSs) selection approaches rely on non-functional properties (*aka* Quality of Service (QoS)) that providers announce publicly or on collecting qualitative/quantitative values that end-users provide with respect to past experiences of using these Web services. Qualitative/quantitative values permit to establish feedback/ratings that refer to the satisfaction of end-users with the overall performance of WSs. However a complete reliance on both providers and end-users raises trustworthiness concerns among future end-users due to biases such as beefing-up a WS's QoS and/or undermining a WS performance both done purposely. To address these biases two types of trust models are reported in the literature. The first uses end-users' feedback/ratings to compute a trust value (e.g., [13]). The second observes the behaviors of WSs over a period of time to compute a trust value (e.g., [23]). We are particularly interested in the first trust model. Indeed end-users with either limited or non-existent experience of using WSs cannot provide proper trust values. When establishing trust these end-users "wrestle" with two kinds of *uncertainty*: *(i)* Uncertainty ($\mathtt{U}_1$) over feedback/rating. $\mathtt{U}_1$ arises from the lack

A. Bouajjani and H. Fauconnier (Eds.): NETYS 2015, LNCS 9466, pp. 397–410, 2015.
DOI: 10.1007/978-3-319-26850-7_27

of consistent ratings that end-users provide over time. Credibility should help tackle $\mathtt{U}_1$ when aggregating end-users' feedback/ratings into a common trust value (e.g., [13,15]). *(ii)* Uncertainty ($\mathtt{U}_2$) over the capacity of a WS in fulfilling the QoS that its provider announces and thus, satisfying end-users' requests. $\mathtt{U}_2$ arises from the inconsistency of the assessed QoS values due to a WS's dynamic nature and/or malicious behavior. Trust should help tackle $\mathtt{U}_2$ (e.g., [10]).

Feedback/ratings concurrently reduce and introduce uncertainty. Uncertainty arises due to end-user subjectivity, experience mismatch with a particular context, and provider's reliability. We should assess trust despite these factors.

Credibility-based trust approaches such as RateWeb [13] and Cloud Armor [15] assume that end-users have good expertise and/or are untrustworthy. When end-users disagree on a certain feedback/rating for a WS these approaches use the majority opinion to reach consensus. End-users' ratings close to the majority opinion are more credible than those with distant ratings. However these approaches neglect end-users with both good expertise and trustworthy that we refer to as *strictexperts*. They usually do not have any interest in aligning themselves with the majority. For the sake of achieving consensus fuzzy clustering technique would reduce the gap between *strict experts*' feedback/ratings and the current majority opinion.

Feedback/rating inconsistencies lead to disagreement amongst end-users' opinions. Troffaes shows that probabilities can address this disagreement [22]. As stated earlier end-user's credibility helps tackle uncertainty over feedback/ ratings ($\mathtt{U}_1$). Therefore we associate credibility with probabilities. Let assume three end-users, u_1, u_2, and u_3 who have experienced WS_j and let the following statement $\mathcal{S}$: u_i **`has correctly observed that`** WS_j **`satisfies his requests`**. The uncertainty here reflects the probability that $\mathcal{S}$ happens. This probability can be estimated by computing u_i's Credibility (Cr_i). Let e_1, e_2, and e_3 denote respectively, the events that u_1, u_2, and u_3 state each that WS_j satisfies their requests. Combining e_1, e_2, and e_3 when computing trust raises issues like what is the probability that u_1, u_2, and u_3 **jointly** state that WS_j satisfies their requests, and what is the probability that u_1 and u_2 **only** state that WS_j satisfies their requests? Probabilistic databases permit to represent these kinds of events by associating an occurrence (or existence) probability with each statement [4]. These databases can also support develop complex queries that combine various selection criteria (e.g., only end-users who provide at least n ratings).

Our contributions include: (i) modeling *end-user's credibility* based on a fuzzy clustering technique so that *strict end-users*' ratings are taken into account; (ii) assessing trust under uncertainty using probabilistic databases; *(iii)* building a distributed trust assessment framework based on a proposed credibility model; and (vi) developing a system that measures the quality of trust.

The remainder of this paper is organized as follows. Section 2 presents our literature review. Section 3 describes how end-user's credibility is modeled. Section 4 presents the proposed probabilistic model for trust assessment. Section 5 gives details on the proposed trust assessment framework and discusses experiments. Finally, concluding remarks and future work are reported in Sect. 6.

2 Related Work

Uncertainty like those (i.e., U_1 and U_2) reported in Sect. 1 impacts the way of establishing WS trust. In the following we discuss two research streams for tackling U_1 and U_2, respectively: credibility-based and probabilistic.

In [13] Malik and Bouguettaya discuss trust for WSs selection and composition. They propose several decentralized trust assessment techniques to ensure a better accuracy of the feedback collected over time. They advocate that feedback of highly credible consumers are most trusted than those with low credibility. To this end, Malik and Bouguettaya examine the feedback based on the distance from the majority opinion using $\mathcal{K}$-means clustering and group similar feedback into clusters. The highly populated cluster is the majority cluster whose centroid represents the majority feedback. Along with the majority principle, the authors' trust model takes into account other social metrics such as consumers' feedback history, consumers' preferences, and temporal sensitivity.

In [15] Noor et al. propose a credibility model that distinguishes credible from misleading feedback in a cloud context. This model uses factors such as majority consensus and feedback density. To measure how close a cloud consumer's feedback is to the majority's feedback, Noor et al. use the slandered (i.e., root-mean-square) deviation. Feedback density overcomes the problem of misleading feedback from consumers. These latter give multiple feedback to a certain cloud service in a short period of time.

TRAVOS is a trust model used in open Agent systems [21]. An agent trusts a peer based on previous direct interactions. Interactions' outcomes are expressed using a binary rating for successful/unsuccessful interaction. The obtained binary ratings are then used to form the probability-density function that models the probability of a successful interaction with an agent. If there is a lack of direct experiences the model uses other agents' experiences to compute the trust value. The model determines the credibility of agents to filter feedback/ratings provided by agents that are inaccurate due to their limited knowledge or malicious behaviors.

In [25] Yu and Singh propose a probabilistic trust management scheme that relies on Dempster-Shaker theory [11]. This theory combines evidence from different sources in order to reach a degree of belief that takes into account all the available evidences. This scheme extends the probability theory so that uncertainty is modeled. There is no direct relationship between a possible outcome and its negation. Since the sum of the possible outcomes' probabilities is not necessarily equal to 1, the remaining probability is interpreted as a state of uncertainty.

The above probabilistic approaches overlook uncertainty over feedback/ ratings (U_1) and/or uncertainty over the capacity of WSs (U_2) and hence, trust computation becomes irrelevant and inaccurate. Peers' feedback/ratings reduce uncertainty, but also introduce additional uncertainty. We address this overlook in our probabilistic trust approach.

3 The Credibility Model

This section discusses the appropriateness of using fuzzy clustering for establishing and formalizing end-users' credibility. Then, it presents how to assess this credibility.

3.1 Basics

Credibility has two components [2]: expertise and trustworthiness. In this work we recall that we target *strict end-users* who are known for their *strong* expertise and trustworthiness in a certain community. These end-users stick to their ratings regardless of the majority for reasons listed in [17] including veracity– they tell the truth, objectivity– their ratings are based on evidences, and accuracy– they estimate their ratings well. Several studies in social psychology (e.g., [12,19]) evaluate the impact of source credibility on belief and attitude changes. These studies demonstrate that credible sources are persuasive and can affect existing beliefs (e.g., ratings) and attitudes more than non-credible sources. Therefore, *strict end-users* can "push" the majority to question (even review) their ratings. To study how this happens we rely on Yager's *participatory learning* paradigm [24]. It represents situations where the current ratings are correct, but not necessarily accurate (resp., wrong) and only require a *limited* (resp. *significant*) tuning by the majority members. Our proposal is to reduce the gap between *strict end-users*' ratings and the current majority's rating so that a consensus is reached in a "reasonable" time frame. As *strict end-users* can be in several groups they can affect groups' beliefs in different manners (e.g., strongly and weakly).

3.2 Credibility Assessment

Strong and *weak* membership terms are fuzzy because they are not well-defined (i.e., uncertain) and/or their semantics are dependent on domains and/or user preferences. To deal with uncertainty in group membership and derive overlapping groups we adopt fuzzy clustering. Consensus clustering algorithms like $\mathcal{K}$-means [9] and fuzzy $\mathcal{C}$-means [1] generate robust clusters, detect "unusual" ones, and handle noise and outliers [14]. Existing credibility-based trust approaches such as [13,15] rely on $\mathcal{K}$-means to compute the Majority ($\mathcal{M}_K$) consensus as a centroid of the most populated cluster. We use Bezdek's Algorithm discussed in [1] to reduce the gap between *strict end-users*' (u_i) ratings and $\mathcal{M}_K$ consensus. Each u_i provides a set of ratings ($\mathcal{X}_i$) on a set of common WSs.

The algorithm takes as input $\mathcal{ME}=\{\mathcal{ME}_{i,j}\}$ a membership matrix where $\mathcal{ME}_{i,j}$ represents the membership degree of $\mathcal{X}_{i=1,n}$ in the Cluster $\mathcal{C}_j$ and generates as output a number of clusters ($Nb_{cluster}$) with fuzzy boundaries. A new *Majority Cluster* ($\mathcal{C}_{Maj}$) needs to be identified taking into account that *each end-user's rating has a degree of membership per cluster.* We use three strategies to decide on $\mathcal{C}_{Maj}$ that rely on qualitative values of membership degree in a fuzzy cluster: weak, moderate, and strong. Once $\mathcal{C}_{Maj}^{strategy \in \{weak, moderate, strong\}}$ is established with a specific strategy, the next step is to compute the credibility of end-users in this cluster. Equation 1 identifies u_i's credibility as a distance from his rating to the majority opinion represented by the centroid of $\mathcal{C}_{Maj}$. This credibility is computed using the normalized euclidean distance $\|*\|_{\mathcal{N}}$ as the similarity measure:

$$\mathcal{CR}_i^j = 1 - \left\| \mathcal{X}_i - centroid(\mathcal{C}_{Maj}^{strategy}) \right\|_{\mathcal{N}}, \quad (1)$$
$$strategy \in \{weak, moderate, strong\}$$

The next step in our approach is to assess WSs' trust according to end-users' credibility values.

4 Trust Model

In this section, we provide a probabilistic database-based trust model. The proposed model consolidates end-users' ratings taking into account end-user credibility. To keep the paper self-contained we firstly briefly review probabilistic databases. Readers are referred to [3] for more details. Furthermore, we discuss how our probabilistic database is structured by using a tuple-independent uncertainty-model and how trust is assessed based on query evaluation.

4.1 Probabilistic Databases in Brief

Formally, $\mathcal{P}ro$babilistic $\mathcal{D}$ata$\mathcal{B}$ase $\mathcal{P}rob\mathcal{DB}$ = ($\mathcal{S}$, $\mathcal{T}$, *prob*) is a triple consisting of a database $\mathcal{S}$chema ($\mathcal{S}$), a finite set of $\mathcal{T}$uples ($\mathcal{T}$), and a function *prob* that assigns a probability value to each tuple $t \in \mathcal{T}$. $\mathcal{S}$ defines $\mathcal{P}ro$babilistic $\mathcal{R}$elations $\mathcal{P}rob\mathcal{R}$ represented as $\mathcal{P}rob\mathcal{R}(A_1, \ldots, A_m, p)$ where $A_1, \ldots, A_m$ denote a finite set of Attributes and p denotes the probability value attached to t in a relation instance of $\mathcal{P}rob\mathcal{R}$. $prob(t)$ represents the confidence that the tuple exists in the database, i.e., a higher value of $prob(t)$ means a higher confidence that t is valid. The $\mathcal{S}em$antics ($\mathcal{S}em$) of $\mathcal{P}rob\mathcal{DB}$ is defined through the *possible worlds model* [4]. In [3] Cavallo and Pittarelli define $\mathcal{S}em(\mathcal{P}rob\mathcal{DB})$ as a discrete probability space over a finite number (n) of database instances. They refer to the various alternative states of $\mathcal{P}rob\mathcal{DB}$ as "possible worlds" (pwd_k). $\mathcal{P}rob\mathcal{DB}$ with n tuples can include 2^n possible worlds, i.e., one for each subset of tuples. Possible worlds express the following uncertainty: "*one of the possible worlds is true, but we do not know which one, and the probabilities represent degrees of belief in the various possible worlds*" [6]. Formally, $\mathcal{S}em(\mathcal{P}rob\mathcal{DB})$=($\mathcal{PWD}$,$\mathcal{P}$) where $\mathcal{PWD} = \{pwd_1, \ldots, pwd_n\}$ and $\mathcal{P} : \mathcal{PWD} \rightarrow [0, 1]$ such that $\sum_{j=1,n} \mathcal{P}_j = 1$.

Different data models exist to handle uncertainty in databases. For instance, tuple-level uncertainty models (e.g., [5,16]) associate existence probabilities with tuples. These models are attractive in data integration for multiple reasons [18]: they typically result in first-normal form relations; they provide simple and intuitive querying semantics; and they are easier to store and manipulate compared to attribute-level uncertainty-models. The independent tuple-level uncertainty-model like the one in [4] is commonly used for data integration and information extraction in probabilistic data management. In this model, $\mathcal{P}rob\mathcal{DB}$ is an ordinary relational database where each tuple is associated with a probability of being true regardless of any other tuple.

4.2 Our Probabilistic Data-Model

Our trust approach aims at designing $\mathcal{P}rob\mathcal{DB}$ in order to assess trust. Let us consider the following tuple t: u_i `has correctly observed that` WS_j `satisfies his requests`. The uncertainty here reflects the probability ($prob(t)$) that t occurs. Therefore, $prob$(t) means the extent to which this observation is true. When $prob$(t) is equal to 1 (resp. 0) t is valid (resp. is not) in all cases. A probability $prob(\mathrm{t}) \in]0,1[$ means that t can occur in some cases, only. We model this uncertainty by $\mathcal{CR}_i$.

To design $\mathcal{P}rob\mathcal{DB}$ we first pre-process a traditional relational database ($\mathcal{DB}$) that contains on top of collected ratings additional information on service providers and evaluation periods. To obtain $\mathcal{P}rob\mathcal{DB}$ we extract from $\mathcal{DB}$ relevant views for trust assessment and add extra details such as credibility values obtained by the credibility model in Sect. 3 to these views. Thus, $\mathcal{DB}$ is built upon an extended schema compared to $\mathcal{P}rob\mathcal{DB}$.

For illustration purposes let assume a database that contains one probabilistic relation $\mathcal{P}rob\mathcal{R}(service, end\text{-}user, rating, p)$ where *service*, *end-user*, *rating* denote service's identifier, end-user's name, and satisfaction degree of end-user in this service (Fig. 1a). $\mathcal{P}rob\mathcal{R}$ consists of three tuples t_1, t_2, and t_3 with probabilities 0.12, 0.84, and 0.88, respectively. These latter correspond to credibility values computed by using our credibility model on a random dataset.

Figure 1b shows the possible worlds pwd_k for $\mathcal{P}rob\mathcal{DB}$ and their associated probabilities ($\mathcal{P}_k$). Each pwd_k contains a subset of the tuples present in $\mathcal{P}rob\mathcal{DB}$. $\mathcal{P}_k$ is calculated using the independence assumption (multiply together the existence probabilities of tuples present in pwd_k and non-existence probabilities of tuples not present in pwd_k). For example, $\mathcal{P}_2$ for $pwd_2 = \{\mathrm{t}_1, \mathrm{t}_2\}$ is computed as $0.12{*}0.84{*}(1-0.88) = 0.01$.

Possible world interpretation is highly intuitive and offers a concise semantics for query evaluation over probabilistic databases. Let $\Phi_{service=s_1}$ be a query that looks for s_1 in certain tuples in $\mathcal{P}rob\mathcal{DB}$. This query is evaluated against each pwd_k separately ($\Phi(pwd_k)$). The probability associated with $\Phi(pwd_k)$ corresponds to $\mathcal{P}_k$. The result is in $\cup_{k=1,8}\,\Phi(pwd_k)$ that contains a set of tuples t'. Equation 2 assesses $\mathcal{P}rob(t')$:

$$\mathcal{P}rob(t') = \sum_{k,\ t' \in \Phi(pwd_k)} \mathcal{P}_k \tag{2}$$

Fig. 2a shows the results of executing $\Phi_{service=s_1}$ on $pwd_{k=1,8}$. $\Phi(pwd_6)$ and $\Phi(pwd_8)$ result in an empty set but with non-zero probabilities. Although the set is empty, it could be relevant for an end-user. Indeed this indicates that

service	end-user	rating	...
s_1	u_1	0.2	
s_2	u_1	0.76	
s_1	u_3	0.97	

⟶

	service	end-user	rating	p
t1	s_1	u_1	0.2	0.12
t2	s_2	u_1	0.76	0.84
t3	s_1	u_3	0.97	0.88

(a) $\mathcal{DB}$ *versus* $\mathcal{ProbDB}$

service	end-user	rating
s_1	u_1	0.2
s_2	u_1	0.76
s_1	u_3	0.97

$pwd_1, P_1 = 0.09$

service	end-user	rating
s_1	u_1	0.2
s_2	u_1	0.76

$pwd_2, P_2 = 0.01$

service	end-user	rating
s_1	u_1	0.2
s_1	u_3	0.97

$pwd_3, P_3 = 0.02$

service	end-user	rating
s_2	u_1	0.76
s_1	u_3	0.97

$pwd_4, P_4 = 0.65$

service	end-user	rating
s_1	u_1	0.2

$pwd_5, P_5 = 0.01$

service	end-user	rating
s_2	u_1	0.76

$pwd_6, P_6 = 0.09$

service	end-user	rating
s_1	u_3	0.97

$pwd_7, P_7 = 0.12$

service	end-user	rating

$pwd_8, P_8 = 0.12$

(b) $\mathcal{ProbDB}$'s possible worlds

Fig. 1. Probabilistic database illustration

service	end-user	rating
s_1	u_1	0.2
s_1	u_3	0.97

$\Phi(pwd_1), P_1 = 0.09$

service	end-user	rating
s_1	u_1	0.2

$\Phi(pwd_2), P_2 = 0.01$

service	end-user	rating
s_1	u_1	0.2
s_1	u_3	0.97

$\Phi(pwd_3), P_3 = 0.02$

service	end-user	rating
s_1	u_3	0.97

$\Phi(pwd_4), P_4 = 0.65$

service	end-user	rating
s_1	u_1	0.2

$\Phi(pwd_5), P_5 = 0.01$

service	end-user	rating

$\Phi(pwd_6), P_6 = 0.09$

service	end-user	rating
s_1	u_3	0.97

$\Phi(pwd_7), P_7 = 0.12$

service	end-user	rating

$\Phi(pwd_8), P_8 = 0.12$

(a) Resulting possible worlds

service	end-user	rating	Probability
s_1	u_1	0.2	$P_1+P_2+P_3+P_5=0.13$
s_1	u_3	0.97	$P_1+P_3+P_4+P_7=0.88$
			$P_6+P_8=0.21$

(b) Query result

Fig. 2. Query evaluation in $\mathcal{ProbDB}$

the existing data are not sufficient to infer relevant answers for the end-user. Figure 2b also shows the final probability computation. Data inaccuracy leads to a large number of answers with low probabilities and thus, low precision. End-users would appreciate receiving answers with high probabilities.

We note that $\mathcal{ProbR}$ contains tuples linked to end-users who provide ratings for different services. These end-users can be constant (i.e., always credible or not) or inconsistent (i.e., swing from credible to uncredible and *vice versa*) in their evaluations. Indeed some end-users are more credible than others and provide correct ratings, while others are less credible and do the opposite.

Let consider two tuples t_1 and t_2 related to u_1. If t_1 is false, then it is false because u_1 is wrong. t_2 is likely to be false, too. Thus, if one tuple is false, the probability that the other tuple is false increases as well. Therefore, the proposed probabilistic data-model does not comply with the independent tuple model (e.g., [4]); each tuple is associated with a probability that needs to be independent from the rest of tuples.

It is worth noticing that it is not straightforward to represent probabilistic databases when all tuples represent independent events. However, more complex probabilistic databases can sometimes be decomposed into tuple independent relations and then be "normalized" [20].

Figure 3 shows how we normalize $\mathcal{ProbDB}$ ($\mathcal{ProbDB}^{\mathcal{N}}$) into two tuple-independent probabilistic relations $\mathcal{PEER}$ and $\mathcal{ProbR}_1$. $\mathcal{PEER}$ stores all end-users and their respective credibility values. Since $\mathcal{PEER}$ should often be updated we consider it as a view instead of a table. u_i is credible about WS_j if his ratings are consistent. Equation 3 assesses u_i's credibility ($\mathcal{CR}_i$) over the ratings he provided in the past.

$$\mathcal{CR}_i = \prod_j \mathcal{CR}_i^j \tag{3}$$

From $\mathcal{ProbR}$ we compute $\mathcal{CR}_1$ as $0.12 * 0.84 = 0.1$. As u_3 provides only one rating, $\mathcal{CR}_3$ remains the same in $\mathcal{PEER}$. $\mathcal{ProbR}_1$ stores all tuples that now are independent subject to the end-user credibility.

$\mathcal{PEER}$

end-user	p
u_1	0.1
u_3	0.88

$\mathcal{ProbR}_1$

service	end-user	rating	p
s_1	u_1	0.2	0.12
s_2	u_1	0.76	0.84
s_1	u_3	0.97	0.88

Fig. 3. $\mathcal{ProbDB}$ normalization

4.3 Trust Assessment as a Query Evaluation

To establish WS's trust from $\mathcal{ProbDB}^{\mathcal{N}}$ we develop specific queries. An end-user trusts WS_j if it has successfully satisfied a large number of end-users' requests. As mentioned earlier WS's trust establishment consists of aggregating end-users' ratings into one probabilistic value. This can be expressed using a like SQL query *SELECT AVG* to obtain the *rating* average value from $\mathcal{ProbR}_1$. Intuitively, applying this query on pwd_k means that end-users in pwd_k **jointly** observe that WS_j satisfies their requests with probability $\mathcal{P}_k$. Let $\mathcal{F}_{AVG(rating)}(\sigma_{service=WS_1})$ be the following SQL query:

SELECT AVG(*rating*) **FROM** $\mathcal{ProbDB}^{\mathcal{N}}$
WHERE $service = WS_1$;

$\mathcal{ProbDB}^{\mathcal{N}}$ is interpreted as $2^5 = 32$ pwd_k. Figure 4a shows pwd_1's content. Figure 4b shows that $\mathcal{F}_{AVG(rating)}(\sigma_{service=WS_1})$'s evaluation returns four possible answers for trust value 0.585, 0.2, 0.97 and empty set ordered by existence

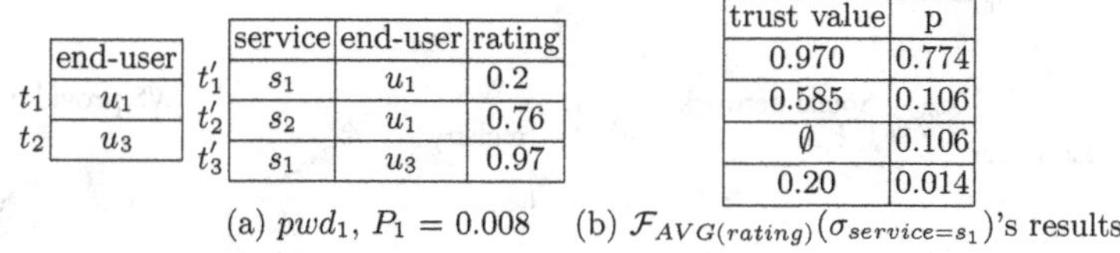

	end-user
t_1	u_1
t_2	u_3

	service	end-user	rating
t'_1	s_1	u_1	0.2
t'_2	s_2	u_1	0.76
t'_3	s_1	u_3	0.97

(a) pwd_1, $P_1 = 0.008$

trust value	p
0.970	0.774
0.585	0.106
$\emptyset$	0.106
0.20	0.014

(b) $\mathcal{F}_{AVG(rating)}(\sigma_{service=s_1})$'s results

Fig. 4. Query evaluation on $\mathcal{ProbDB}^{\mathcal{N}}$

probability. In [8] Jayram et al. represents $\mathcal{F}_{AVG()}(\sigma)$'s result over probabilistic databases as a weighted average of possible answers for the trust value.

Despite the simplicity of possible worlds semantics it raises some challenging computational concerns even for simple query operations like in [4]. Many studies have shown that the query evaluation problem is ♯P-hard. Several algorithms (e.g., [4,8]) are provided to handle complex queries over massive data streams.

5 The Trust Assessment Framework

Our credibility model relies on fuzzy clustering technique to assess end-user's credibility. A probabilistic database-based trust model is discussed. In this section we present the design and development of a trust assessment framework for WSs built upon these credibility and trust models. We also discuss performance and robustness studies of this framework so that the quality of trust is established.

5.1 Framework Design

Our framework includes three main components that are *feedback collector*, *credibility evaluator*, and *trust evaluator*. For performance purposes we suggest hosting these components on the client-side. Figure 5 illustrates a Web service-based environment that supports our distributed trust assessment framework.

Upon subscription to the framework *trust managers* are deployed on end-users' platforms. After each transaction the end-user sends his *trust manager* feedback/ratings about the experience with the Web service. These feedback/ ratings are stored in the feedback database. A prospective end-user requests his *trust manager* for some specific WS. Upon receipt of the request the *feedback collector* collects a set of feedback/ratings either from end-users in the same community that stems from different social networks or from other *trust managers*. Then, the *credibility evaluator* computes each end-user's credibility based on Eq. 1. The end-users' credibility values are then used to generate the *probabilistic feedback database*. The *trust evaluator* evaluates trust upon the end-user's request based on the feedback/ratings that end-users have shared. Trust is assessed as a query executed over the feedback probabilistic database built using end-users feedback/ratings and their associated credibility values generated by the *Credibility evaluator*. Finally, the *trust manager* sends the end-user the most trusted service. In the rest of this section these components are explained.

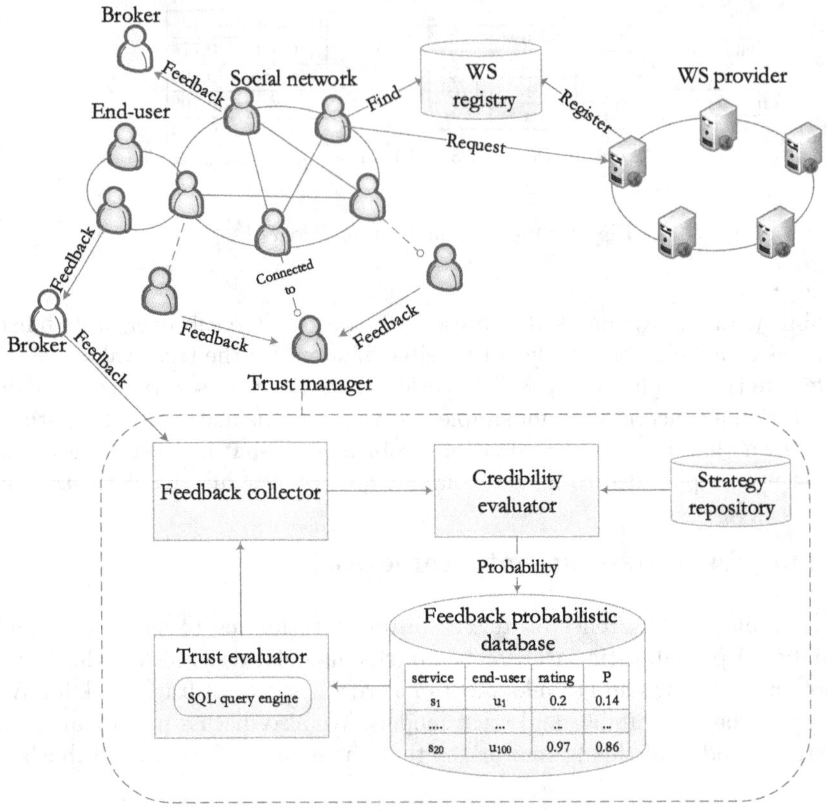

Fig. 5. Trust assessment framework

Feedback collector supports queries from prospective end-users about trust values in a given context. Brokers are deployed over different social networks to make these collected information available when needed. These brokers update dynamically feedback/ratings after each transaction completion. Therefore an end-user receives the response from the *trust manager* more quickly compared to other approaches like [13,15] where feedback/ratings are collected upon request. Moreover, the end-user is informed about any transaction and/or trust request involving a certain Web service.

Credibility evaluator checks if all feedback/ratings that are communicated by either end-users without *trust managers* or *other trust managers* are currently valid. To this end the *credibility evaluator* screens the feedback repository to look for feedback/ratings from peers with social links like friendship and supervision with the prospective end-user. As per Sect. 3.2 three strategies establish the majority based on fuzzy clusters' characteristics like the number of end-users with "low" and/or "high" membership degrees. Therefore, an end-user should specify his own "low" and "high" fuzzy values as membership functions according to the Web service's context of use that could be critical.

Trust evaluator is an "editor" that allows end-users to execute trust queries over the *probabilistic feedback database.* Certain queries require that the *trust evaluator* evaluates trust with constraints such as over some specific evaluation periods.

5.2 Prototype and Experiments

We implemented the trust assessment framework in JAVA using Eclipse IDE and PostgreSQL for feedback/ratings and trust storage. First, we developed different graphical user interfaces to cater for end-users' requirements like trust level. The experiments analyze the quality of trust in terms of the framework's robustness and performance. Robustness is an important quality attribute when end-users heavily rely on the framework for executing critical applications. It is defined by the IEEE standard glossary of software engineering terminology as: "*The degree to which a system or component can function correctly in the presence of invalid inputs or stressful environmental conditions*" [7]. To destabilize the framework we inject invalid feedback/ratings from malicious end-users.

Nowadays there is a lack of publicly available real datasets of feedback/ratings on Web services. Therefore we looked for a dataset that encompasses similar information and could be suitable for Web services evaluation. MovieLens[1] seems to be a good dataset for our work. This latter contains 100,000 feedback/ratings from 943 users on 1682 movies (or items). Ratings represent the overall amount of satisfaction and range from 1 to 5. Each user rates at least 20 items. We consider an item as a Web service and normalize the items' rating values. We also use the open-source library *Apache Mahout* for the fuzzy $\mathcal{C}$-means algorithm (Sect. 3.2). We fix the number of clusters c and termination criterion ϵ to 3 and 0.05, respectively.

Parameter Setting. The first stage of the experiments consists of altering a variable ratio of existing end-users' feedback/ratings in the dataset and preserving feedback/ratings of the remaining end-users known as normal. The former become either malicious or strict. Table 1 shows an example of mapping between rating categories for normal end-users and those for malicious *versus* strict end-users. As malicious end-users tell the opposite of what they initially perceive their satisfaction is reversed. Strict end-users usually expect more from Web services. This restricts the rating categories upon which Web services are rated. This permits to disturb the framework for analyzing how it behaves in presence of altered end-users.

Experimental Results. We provide several experiments that compute trust values based on two parameters: (i) ratio of altered end-users in the dataset; and (ii) choice of a credibility model ($\mathcal{M}_i$)(iii) choice of a pre-defined trust model ($\mathcal{TM}_j$). We use two credibility models: $\mathcal{M}_1$ $\mathcal{K}$-means clustering-based

[1] http://www.movielens.org.

Table 1. Actual *versus* false/strict rating categories

Actual	False	Strict
1	5	1
2	5	1
3	1	2
4	1	3
5	1	4

credibility model, $\mathcal{M}_2$ $\mathcal{C}$-means clustering-based credibility model. We define a deterministic trust model ($\mathcal{TM}_1$) as follows:
Let $\mathcal{L}_i$ be the set of end-users (u_k) who send $u_{i \neq k}$ ratings ($\mathcal{X}_k^j$) about WS_j performance. u_i estimates a WS_j's trust ($\mathcal{T}_{\mathcal{X}^j_{\mathcal{L}_i}}$) according to both $\mathcal{X}_k^j$ and $\mathcal{CR}_k$. Equation 4 establishes $\mathcal{T}_{\mathcal{X}^j_{\mathcal{L}_i}}$ as a weighted average of $\mathcal{X}_k^j$.

$$\mathcal{T}_{\mathcal{X}^j_{\mathcal{L}_i}} = \frac{1}{\sum\limits_{k \in \mathcal{L}_i} \mathcal{CR}_k} \times \sum_{k \in \mathcal{L}_i} (\mathcal{CR}_k \times \mathcal{X}_k^j) \tag{4}$$

$\mathcal{TM}_2$ refers to our proposed trust model as per Sect. 4. Trust is assessed as a query evaluated on the probabilistic database $\mathcal{ProbDB}^{\mathcal{N}}$. Database tuples' probabilities are assessed using the chosen credibility model.

In the following $\mathcal{TM}_j\mathcal{M}_i$ indicates that $\mathcal{TM}_j$ uses $\mathcal{M}_i$.

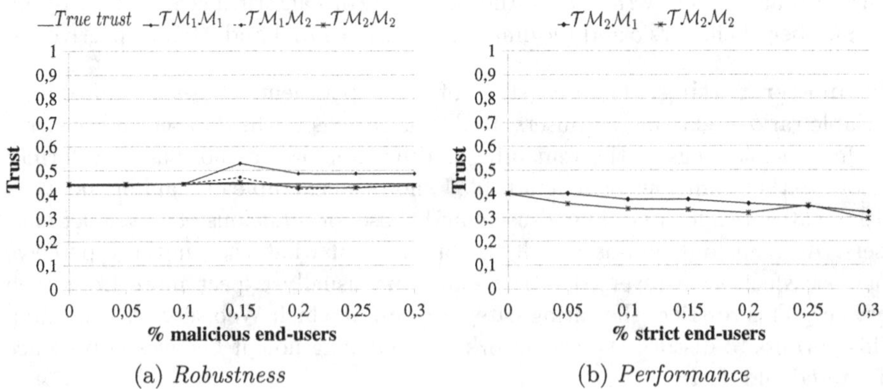

(a) *Robustness* (b) *Performance*

Fig. 6. Quality of trust

The first experiment analyzes the performance of the probabilistic model $\mathcal{TM}_2\mathcal{M}_2$ in achieving realistic trust values compared to the deterministic trust models $\mathcal{TM}_1\mathcal{M}_1$ and $\mathcal{TM}_1\mathcal{M}_2$ in the presence of malicious end-users. We compare the value of trust computed before and after introducing malicious end-users. Figure 6(a) shows that $\mathcal{TM}_2\mathcal{M}_2$ returns more accurate trust values (i.e., closer to the actual one) than the other models. Therefore, $\mathcal{TM}_2\mathcal{M}_2$ helps in improving the framework's robustness. The second experiment compares trust values obtained with the probabilistic trust models $\mathcal{TM}_2\mathcal{M}_1$ and $\mathcal{TM}_2\mathcal{M}_2$ in the presence of strict end-users. Figure 6(b) shows that the trust values obtained with $\mathcal{TM}_2\mathcal{M}_2$ are always lower than those given with $\mathcal{TM}_2\mathcal{M}_1$. This shows that strict end-users' ratings are well considered using $\mathcal{TM}_2\mathcal{M}_2$. This also demonstrates that the $\mathcal{C}$-means clustering-based credibility model maintains high levels of performance in the probabilistic approach.

6 Conclusion

In this paper we proposed a new probabilistic database-based model for assessing Web service trust. In this model the focus is on strict end-users who have no interest in aligning themselves with the majority opinion. Fuzzy clustering was used to determine an end-user's credibility. A probabilistic trust approach is introduced for assessing WSs' trust under uncertainty that raises from the lack of consistent ratings that end-users provide over time and the inconsistency of the assessed QoS values. The probabilistic trust approach relies on probabilistic databases that stem from probability theory coupled with possible worlds semantics. Our probabilistic database is structured around the tuple-independent uncertainty model. Trust is assessed by using specific queries applied on the probabilistic database. A trust assessment framework implements the proposed probabilistic approach. Finally, several experiments have been conducted to evaluate the trust results obtained with the probabilistic approach compared to other credibility-based trust approaches. The experiments demonstrated that trust quality is substantially improved. As future work we will explore the possibility to incorporate several credibility models into one trust model using block-independent uncertainty model to structure our probabilistic database.

References

1. Bezdek, J.: Pattern Recognition with Fuzzy Objective Function Algorithms. Kluwer Academic Publishers, New York (1981)
2. Bordens, K., Horowitz, I.: Social Psychology. Psychology Press, Mahwah (2001)
3. Cavallo, R., Pittarelli, M.: The theory of probabilistic databases. In: Very Large Data Bases Conferences. Brighton, England (1987)
4. Dalvi, N., Suciu, D.: Efficient query evaluation on probabilistic databases. VLDB J. **16**(4), 523–544 (2007)
5. Fuhr, N., Rölleke, T.: A probabilistic relational algebra for the integration of information retrieval and database systems. ACM Trans. Inf. Syst. (TOIS) **15**(1), 32–66 (1997)
6. Huang, J., Antova, L., Koch, C., Olteanu, D.: Maybms: a probabilistic database management system. In: SIGMOD Conference, New York, USA (2009)
7. IEEE: Standard glossary of software engineering terminology. Technical report. IEEE Computer Society Press (1990)

8. Jayram, T.S., Kale, S., Vee, E.: Efficient aggregation algorithms for probabilistic data. In: Annual ACM-SIAM Symposium on Discrete Algorithms, New Orleans, USA (2007)
9. Kanungo, T., Mount, D., Netanyahu, N., Piatko, C., Silverman, R., Wu, A.: An efficient k-means clustering algorithm: analysis and implementation. IEEE Trans. Pattern Anal. Mach. Intell. **24**(7), 881–892 (2002)
10. Kim, Y., Kim, D.: A study of online transaction self-efficacy, consumer trust, and uncertainty reduction in electronic commerce transaction. In: Proceedings of the Annual Hawaii International Conference on System Sciences (HICSS), Hawaii, USA (2005)
11. Kyburg, H.E.: Bayesian and non-bayesian evidential updating. Artif. Intell. **3**(1), 271–294 (1987)
12. Lesko, W.: Readings in Social Psychology: General, Classic and Contemporary Selections. Allyn & Bacon, Boston (1997)
13. Malik, Z., Bouguettaya, A.: Rateweb: reputation assessment for trust establishment among web services. Very Large Data Bases (VLDB) J. **18**(4), 885–911 (2009)
14. Nguyen, N., Caruana, R.: Consensus clusterings. In: International Conference on Data Mining, Omaha, USA (2007)
15. Noor, T., Sheng, Q., Ngu, A., Alfazi, A., Law, J.: Cloud armor: a platform for credibility-based trust management of cloud services. In: The ACM Conference on Information and Knowledge Management (CIKM) (2013)
16. Sarma, A., Benjelloun, O., Halevy, A., Widom, J.: Working models for uncertain data. In: International Conference on Data Engineering (ICDE), Atlanta, USA (2006)
17. Schum, D., Morris, J.: Assessing the competence and credibility of human sources of intelligence evidence: contributions from law and probability. Law Probab. Risk **6**(1), 247–274 (2007)
18. Sen, P., Deshpande, A.: Representing and querying correlated tuples in probabilistic databases. In: International Conference on Data Engineering (ICDE), Istanbul, Turkey (2007)
19. Sternthal, B., Phillips, L., Dholakia, R.: The persuasive effect of source credibility: a situational analysis. Pub. Opin. Q. **42**(3), 285–314 (1978)
20. Suciu, D., Olteanu, D., Koch, C.: Probabilistic Databases. Synthesis digital library of engineering and computer science (2011)
21. Teacy, W.T., Patel, J., Jennings, N.R., Luck, M.: Travos: trust and reputation in the context of inaccurate information sources. Auton. Agents Multi-Agent Syst. **12**(2), 183–198 (2006)
22. Troffaes, M.: Generalizing the conjunction rule for aggregating conflicting expert opinions. Int. J. Intell. Syst. **21**(3), 361–380 (2006)
23. Wang, Y., Singh, M.: Formal trust model for multiagent systems. In: Proceedings of the International Joint Conference on Artifical Intelligence, Hyderabad, India (2007)
24. Yager, R.R.: Participatory learning: a paradigm for building better digital and human agents. Law Probab. Risk **3**(1), 133–145 (2004)
25. Yu, B., Singh, M.P.: An evidential model of distributed reputation management. In: International Joint Conference on Autonomous Agents and Multi-Agent Systems, Bologna, Italy (2002)

Virtual and Consistent Hyperbolic Tree: A New Structure for Distributed Database Management

Telesphore Tiendrebeogo[1] and Damien Magoni[2(✉)]

[1] Polytechnic University of Bobo-Dioulasso, Bobo-Dioulasso, Burkina Faso
tetiendreb@gmail.com

[2] LaBRI, University of Bordeaux, Talence, France
magoni@labri.fr

Abstract. We describe a new structure called Virtual and Consistent Hyperbolic tree (VCH-tree) for implementing a distributed database system. This structure is based on the hyperbolic geometry and can support queries over large spatial data sets, distributed over interconnected servers. The VCH-tree is comparable to the well-known R-tree structure, but it leverages the hyperbolic geometry properties of the Poincaré disk model. It maintains a balanced Q-degree spatial tree that scales with insertions of data objects into a large number of servers, reachable through hyperbolic coordinates. A user application manipulates the structure from a client node. The client can connect to the system through one of the servers that is already in the VCH-tree. Messages are then routed towards the proper server by a greedy algorithm which uses the hyperbolic coordinates attributed to each server. We have performed simulations to assess the efficiency and reliability of the VCH-tree. Results show that our VCH-tree exhibits expected performances for being used by distributed database applications.

1 Introduction

In order to build spatial databases, we promote a distributed indexing system relying on the hyperbolic geometry [1]. We aim at indexing large data sets of spatial objects, each uniquely identified by an object identifier (OID) and stored in a scalable and reliable index called a VCH-tree, that generalizes the R-tree structure commonly used as a distributed data structure [16]. A VCH-tree allows the redundancy of object references, like the R-tree [5] or the R*-tree [9]. The fundamental principle of our system is to map a large OID space onto a set of servers in a deterministic and distributed way. Roughly, given an object key, the system is able to obtain the location of several servers where are stored the corresponding values.

To be able to route queries in other systems, each server usually maintains the status of its connections to all the other servers, which increases drastically the number of messages exchanged, and this may constitute a severe scaling limitation. The same applies to the number of routing hops that must not grow too fast with the number of servers in the system [7]. Moreover, most distributed

A. Bouajjani and H. Fauconnier (Eds.): NETYS 2015, LNCS 9466, pp. 411–425, 2015.
DOI: 10.1007/978-3-319-26850-7_28

database systems suffer from a lack of flexibility concerning storage queries (i.e., where the values are stored) involving consequently a heavy lookup traffic load on the paths of the underlying servers.

Our VCH-tree can address all the aforementioned issues while maintaining a good trade-off between robustness, efficiency and system complexity. In this paper, we make the following contributions:

- We define a new structure for indexation in a distributed database system without any constraints. The database servers can connect arbitrarily to each other, the data objects can be inserted, updated or deleted without the cost of maintaining any global knowledge of the servers' topology.
- We define a method for mapping database OIDs to the addresses of the servers in the hyperbolic plane. This mapping enables OIDs to be forwarded to their storing server by using a greedy routing algorithm. Values are stored in order to avoid overloading a particular zone of the distributed system. Furthermore, storing and retrieving queries can be solved within $O(logN)$ hops.
- To improve database object availability and access performance, our system embeds a redundancy and caching mechanism that can be adjusted to obtain a good trade-off between reliability and storage consumption.
- We have carried out simulations to evaluate the performances of the VCH-tree and have shown that they match the theoretical properties.

The VCH-tree structure presented in this paper, derives from our Distributed Hash Table (DHT) system defined in our previous work [17]. The key difference is that data objects which are spatially close, are attributed nearby hyperbolic addresses in a VCH-tree.

The remainder of this paper is organized as follows. Section 2 gives a brief overview of the related previous work. Section 3 highlights some properties of the hyperbolic plane when represented by the Poincaré disk model. Section 4 defines the local addressing and greedy routing algorithms of the VCH-tree. Section 5 defines the binding algorithm of the VCH-tree. Section 6 presents the results of our evaluation obtained by simulations and we conclude in Sect. 7.

2 Related Work

Until recently, most of the spatial indexing design efforts have been devoted to centralized systems [4] although, for non-spatial data, research devoted to an efficient distribution of large data sets is well-established [2,3]. Many Scalable Distributed Data Structure (SDDS) schemes are hash-based, e.g., variants of LH* [8], or use a Distributed Hash Table [2,13]. Some SDDSs are range partitioned, from RP* based systems [10] up to BATON [4] most recently.

There were also proposals for k-d partitioning, e.g., k-RP [14] using distributed kd-trees for data points, or hQT* [10] using quad-trees for the same purpose. Hambrusch and Khokhar [6] present a distributed data structure based on orthogonal bisection trees (2-d KD trees). Kriakov et al. [12] describe an adaptive index method which offers dynamic load balancing of servers and distributed collaboration. The structure requires a coordinator which maintains the load of each server.

3 Hyperbolic Geometry

The model that we use in our system to represent the hyperbolic plane is called the Poincaré disk model. In the Poincaré disk model, the hyperbolic plane is represented by the open unit disk of radius 1 centered at the origin. In this specific model:

- Points are represented by points within this open unit disk.
- Lines are represented by arcs of circles intersecting the disk and meeting its boundaries at right angles.

In this model, we refer to points by using complex coordinates.

An important property is that we can tile the hyperbolic plane with polygons of any sizes, called p-gons. Each tessellation is represented by a notation of the form $\{p, q\}$ where each polygon has p sides with q of them at each vertex. There exists a hyperbolic tessellation $\{p, q\}$ for every couple $\{p, q\}$ obeying $(p-2)*(q-2) > 4$. In a tiling, p is the number of sides of the polygons of the *primal* (the black edges and green vertices in Fig. 1) and q is the number of sides of the polygons of the *dual* (the red triangles in Fig. 1).

Our purpose is to partition the plane and address each node uniquely. We set p to infinity, thus transforming the primal into a regular tree of degree q. The dual is then tessellated with an infinite number of q-gons. This particular tiling splits the hyperbolic plane in distinct spaces and constructs an embedded tree that we use to assign unique addresses to the nodes. An example of such a hyperbolic tree with $q = 3$ is shown in Fig. 1.

In the Poincaré disk model, the distances between any two points z and w are given by curves minimizing the distance between these two points and are called geodesics of the hyperbolic plane. To compute the length of a geodesic between two points z and w and thus obtain their hyperbolic distance $d_{\mathbb{H}}$, we use the Poincaré metric which is an isometric invariant given by the formula:

$$d_{\mathbb{H}}(z, w) = \operatorname{arcosh}\left(1 + 2 \times \frac{|z-w|^2}{(1-|z|^2)(1-|w|^2)}\right) \quad (1)$$

This formula is used by the greedy routing algorithm shown in the next section.

4 Topology of the Servers

We now explain in this section how we create the hyperbolic addressing tree for database servers interconnections and how queries can be routed in our distributed database system. The first step in the creation of a VCH-tree of servers

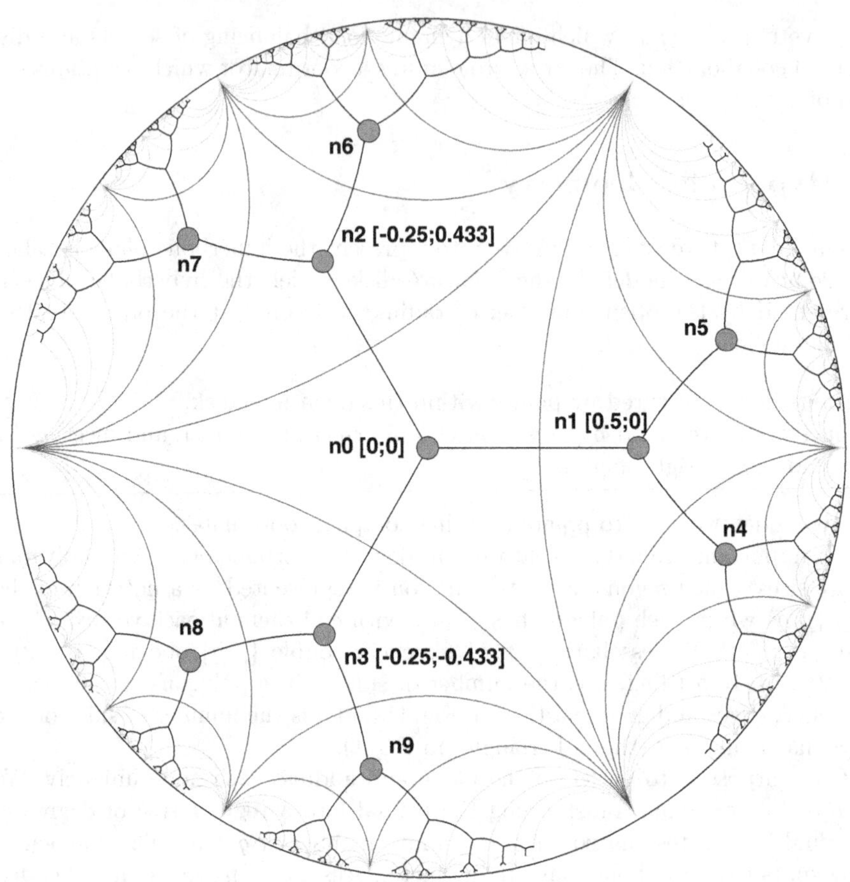

Fig. 1. 3-regular tree in the hyperbolic plane

nodes is to start the first database server and to choose the degree of the addressing tree.

We recall that the hyperbolic coordinates (i.e., a complex number) of a server node of the addressing tree are used as the address of the corresponding database server in the distributed data base system. A server node of the tree can give the addresses corresponding to its children in the VCH-tree. The degree determines how many addresses each database server will be able to give for news nodes servers connections. The degree of the VCH-tree is defined at the beginning for all the lifetime of the distributed database system. The distributed database system is then built incrementally, with each new data server joining one or more existing data servers. Over time, the data servers will leave the overlay until there is no server left which is the end of the distributed database system. So, for every data object that must be stored in the system, an OID is associated with him and map then in key-value pair. The key will allow to determine in which data servers the object will be stored (as explained in the following section). Furthermore when a data object is deleted, the system must be able to update this operation in all the system by forwarding query. This method is scalable because unlike Kleinberg [11], we do not have to make a two-pass algorithm over the whole distributed system to find its highest degree. Also in our system, a server can connect to any other server at any time in order to obtain an address.

The first step is thus to define the degree of the tree because it allows building the *dual*, namely the regular $q - gon$. We nail the root of the tree at the origin of the *primal* and we begin the tiling at the origin of the disk in function of q. Each splitting of the space in order to create disjoint subspaces is ensured once the half spaces are tangent; hence the *primal* is an infinite q-regular tree. We use the theoretical infinite q-regular tree to construct the greedy embedding of our q-regular tree. So, the regular degree of the tree is the number of sides of the polygon used to build the *dual* (see Fig. 1). In other words, the space is allocated for q child database servers. Each database server repeats the computation for its own half space. In half space, the space is again allocated for $q - 1$ children. Each child can distribute its addresses in its half space. Algorithm 1 shows how to compute the addresses that can be given to the children of a database server. The first database server takes the hyperbolic address (0;0) and is the root of the tree. The root can assign q addresses.

Algorithm 1. Calculating the Coordinates of a Server's Children

procedure CALCCHILDRENCOORDS(*server*, *q*)
    $step \leftarrow \text{arcosh}\left(\frac{1}{\sin\left(\frac{\pi}{q}\right)}\right)$
    $angle \leftarrow \frac{2\pi}{q}$
    $childCoords \leftarrow server.Coords$
    for $i \leftarrow 1, q$ **do**
        $ChildCoords.rotationLeft(angle)$
        $ChildCoords.translation(step)$
        $ChildCoords.rotationRight(\pi)$
        if $ChildCoords \neq server.ParentCoords$ **then**
            STORECHILDCOORDS(*ChildCoords*)
        end if
    end for
end procedure

This distributed algorithm ensures that the database servers are contained in distinct spaces and have unique coordinates. All the steps of the presented algorithm are suitable for distributed and asynchronous computation. This algorithm allows the assignment of addresses as coordinates in dynamic topologies. As the global knowledge of the distributed database system is not necessary, a new server can obtain coordinates simply by asking an existing server to be its parent and to give it an address for itself. If the asked server has already given all its addresses, the new server must ask an address to another existing database server. When a new server obtains an address, it computes the addresses (i.e., hyperbolic coordinates) of its addresses that will be given to its potential children. Those are new database servers that will connect to the distributed database system. The addressing VCH-tree is thus incrementally built at the same time than the distributed database system.

When a new database server has connected to database servers already inside the distributed database system and has obtained an address from one of those database servers, it can start sending requests to store or lookup database object in the distributed database system. The routing process is done on each database server on the path (starting from the sender) by using Algorithm 2, a greedy algorithm based on the hyperbolic distances between the servers. When a query is received by a database server, the database server computes the distance from each of its neighbors to the destination and forwards the query to its neighbor which is the closest to the destination (destination database server computing is given in Sect. 5).

Algorithm 2. Routing a Query in the Distributed Database System

function GETNEXTHOP(*server*, *query*) **return** server
  $w = query.destinationServerCoords$
  $m = server.Coords$
  $d_{min} = \text{arcosh}\left(1 + 2 \times \frac{|m-w|^2}{(1-|m|^2)(1-|w|^2)}\right)$
  $p_{min} = server$
  for all $neighbor \in server.Neighbors$ **do**
    $n = neighbor.Coords$
    $d = \text{arcosh}\left(1 + 2 \times \frac{|n-w|^2}{(1-|n|^2)(1-|w|^2)}\right)$
    if $d < d_{min}$ **then**
      $d_{min} = d$
      $p_{min} = neighbor$
    end if
  end for
  return p_{min}
end function

In a real network environment, link and server failures are expected to happen often. If the addressing VCH-tree is broken by the failure of a database server or link, we flush the addresses attributed to the servers beyond the failed server or link and reassign new addresses to those servers (some servers may have first to reconnect to other servers in order to restore connectivity). But this solution is not developed in this paper.

5 Storage and Retrieval of Data Objects

In this section we explain how our distributed database system computes the destination database servers addresses for storing and retrieving queries. Indeed, the first server contacted by a client (prime server) for sending a query in the system consider the latter as a data object that can be stored or looked up. Thus this server generates an OID associated to the data object and the latter is mapped onto hyperbolic addresses corresponding to destination database servers' addresses in the VCH-tree.

On startup, each new client query is associated with the data object with OID corresponding to the name of the query and that identifies the query it runs on. This name will be kept by data object during all the lifetime of the distributed database system.

When the prime database server computes some specific addresses of database servers, when it is about a storage query, it stores the name (OID) and value of query in these specific addresses of distributed database servers, thus the data object in the DHT, when it is about a retrieving query, it contacts database servers which addresses has been computed. In our distributed system, the name is used as a key by a mathematical transformation. If the same name is already stored in the distributed database system, an error message is sent back to the prime server (Server by whom the client is directly bound) in order to generate another name. Thus the distributed database system structure itself ensures that OIDs are unique.

An (OID, value) pair, with the OID acting as a key is called a *binding*. Figure 2 shows how and where a given binding is stored in the distributed database system. A binder is any database server that stores these pairs. The depth of a server in the addressing VCH-tree is defined as the number of parent servers to go through for reaching the root of the VCH-tree (including the root itself). When the distributed database system is created, a maximum depth for the potential binders is chosen. This value is defined as the *binding VCH-tree depth*. To ensure a load balancing of the system, the depth d is chosen such that d minimizes the inequality 2, where d is the depth, q is the degree and N is the number of servers:

$$1 + q \times \left(\frac{1 - (q-1)^d}{2 - q} \right) \geq N \tag{2}$$

When a new database server joins the distributed database system by connecting to other servers, it obtains an address from one of these servers. Next, the server stores its own binding in the system. So, during his life, each database server tries to join others by sending a join query. Each server cannot accept that a limited number of join queries independently of the degree of the VCH-tree. The new connections serve as shortcuts during the phases of storage and retrieving of data objects. We call these connections, shortcut links as indicated in Fig. 2.

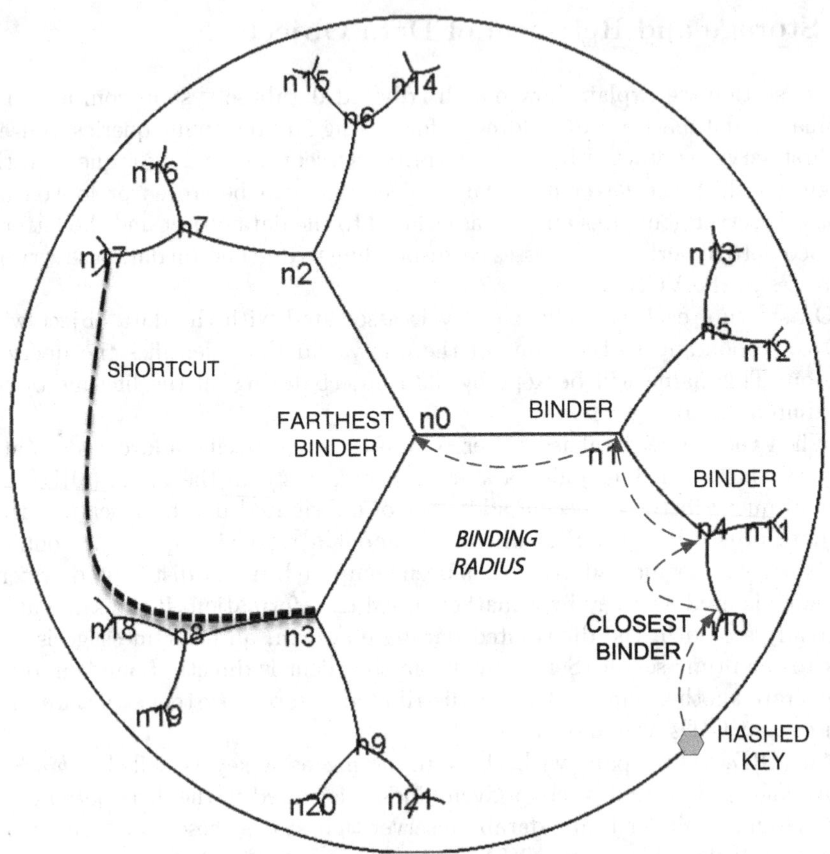

Fig. 2. Storage in the VCH-tree

5.1 Storage Query Processing

When a client wants to send a storage query (i.e., insertion), the first server with whom it is connected consider a query as an object (thus generating an OID) and creates a key by hashing its name with the SHA-512 algorithm. It divides the 512-bit key into 16 equally sized 32-bit subkeys (for redundant storage). The server selects the first subkey and maps it to an angle by a linear transformation.

The angle is given by:

$$\alpha = 2\pi \times \frac{\texttt{32-bit subkey}}{\texttt{0xFFFFFFFF}} \tag{3}$$

The database server then computes a virtual point v on the unit circle by using this angle:

$$v(x, y) \text{ with} \begin{cases} x = cos(\alpha) \\ y = sin(\alpha) \end{cases} \tag{4}$$

Next the database server determines the coordinates of the closest binder to the computed virtual point above by using the given *binding tree depth*.

In the figure we set the *binding VCH-tree depth* to three to avoid cluttering the figure. It's important to note that this closest binder may not really exist if no database server is currently owning this address. The database server then sends a storage query to this closest database server. This query is routed inside the distributed database system by using the greedy algorithm of Sect. 4. If the query fails because the binder does not exist or because of database server/link failures, it is redirected to the next closest binder which is the father of the computed binder.

The path from the computed closest binder to the farthest binder is defined as the binding radius. This process ensures that the queries are always stored first in the binders closer to the unit circle and last in the binders closer to the disk center. However to avoid overloading the farthest binder particularly and to ensure load balancing, we limit the number of stored pairs S as shown by the inequality 5, where N is equal to the number of servers and q is equal to the degree of the VCH-tree:

$$S \leq \left\lfloor \frac{1}{2} \times \frac{log(N)}{log(q)} \right\rfloor \tag{5}$$

Furthermore the previous solution, any binder will be able to set a maximum number of stored queries and any new database server to store will be refused and the query redirected as above. Besides, to provide redundancy and so ensure the availability and reduce the latency period in the lookup process, the database server does the storage process described above for each of the other 15 subkeys. Thus 16 different binding radii will be used at the most and this will improve the even distribution of the pairs (key-value).

In addition to this and still for redundancy purposes, a pair key-value of the data object may be stored in more than one database server of the binding radius. A binder could store a data object and still redirect its query for storage it in other ancestor binders. The number of stored copies of a key-value pair along the binding radius may be an arbitrary value set at the distributed system creation. Similarly the division of the key in 16 subkeys is arbitrary and could be increased or reduced depending on the redundancy needed. To conclude we can define two redundancy mechanisms for storage copies of a given binding:

1. We can use more than one binding radius by creating several uniformly distributed subkeys.
2. We can store the data object key-value pair in more than one binder in the same binding radius.

These mechanisms enable our distributed database system to cope with a non-uniform growth of the database servers and they ensure that a data object will be stored in a redundant way that will maximize the success rate of its retrieval. The numbers of subkeys and the numbers of copies in a radius are parameters that can be set at the creation of the distributed database system. Increasing them leads to a tradeoff between improved reliability and lost storage space in binders. Besides our solution has the property of consistent hashing: if one database server fails, only its keys are lost but the other binders are not impacted and the whole system remains coherent. Algorithm 3 illustrates the previous mechanism.

Algorithm 3. Storage Algorithm

```
function STORE(Query)
    OID ← Query.GetOID()
    Key ← Hash(OID)
    for all red ∈ R_Circular do
        depth ← P_Max
        i ← 1
        while i ≤ ⌊1/2 × log(N)/log(q)⌋ && depth ≥ 0 do
            SubKey[red][depth] ← ComputeSubkey(Key)[red][depth]
            TargetServerAddr[red][depth] ← ComputeAddr(SubKey[red][depth])
            TargetServer ← GetTarget(TargetServerAddr[red][depth])
            if route(Query, TargetServer) then
                i++
                put(OID, Query)
            end if
            depth −−
        end while
    end for
end function
```

5.2 Lookup Query Processing

Now, if the client wants to lookup a data object in the distributed database system, a prime server is contacted and generates an OID for the client query. Here again, the OID is mapped into a key by the SHA-512 algorithm, thus the 512 bits key is divided into 16 subkeys. Each subkey, by the process described in Sect. 5.1, will be transformed into an address that represents the address of the database server where the data object is stored. The latter is contacted by the prime database server for updating, deleting or retrieving the associated value. When the redundancy mechanism has been used to store the data object, the lookup repeats the latter process of lookup for any subkey, thus the operation will be performed on all database servers that contain the data object. Our distributed system ensures the coherence of data objects of the distributed database. This mechanism is illustrated by Algorithm 4.

6 Evaluation

We performed experiments for evaluating the behavior of a VCH-tree over large datasets. Furthermore, we consider that the system is static so there are no

Algorithm 4. Lookup and Update Algorithm

```
function LOOKUP(Query) return Value
    QueryOID ← Target.GetQueryOID()
    Key ← Hash(QueryOID)
    for all red ∈ R_Circular do
        depth ← P_Max
        i ← 1
        while i ≤ ⌊1/2 × log(N)/log(q)⌋ && depth ≥ 0 do
            TargetServerAddr[red][depth] ← GetValue(Key)
            Value ← GetValue(TargetServerAddr[red][depth], QueryOID)
            if Value ! = null then
                if Query == delete then
                    delete(OID)
                end if
                if (Query == update) then
                    update(OID)
                end if
                if Query == select then
                    return Value
                end if
                i + +
            end if
            depth − −
        end while
    end for
end function
```

join or leave of database servers during the simulation. We use the Peersim [15] simulator for running event-driven simulations. The study involved the following parameters of the VCH-tree:

- The number of database servers connected and used to store the data objects. Here we have considered 10000 database servers;
- Each run lasts 2 h of simulated time;
- We try to store 6 millions of data objects in our distributed database system following an exponential distribution with a median equal to 10 min;
- The maximum capacity for each server is set to 6000 objects.

We studied the behavior of our structure for both data objects' storage and retrieval in the system. We are interested in observing the scalability of our system, the shape of the hyperbolic tree, the storage load balancing and the length of the paths of the queries.

6.1 Spatial Shape of the VCH-tree

Figure 3 shows an experimental distribution of points corresponding to the scatter plot of the distribution of the database servers in our system. We can see

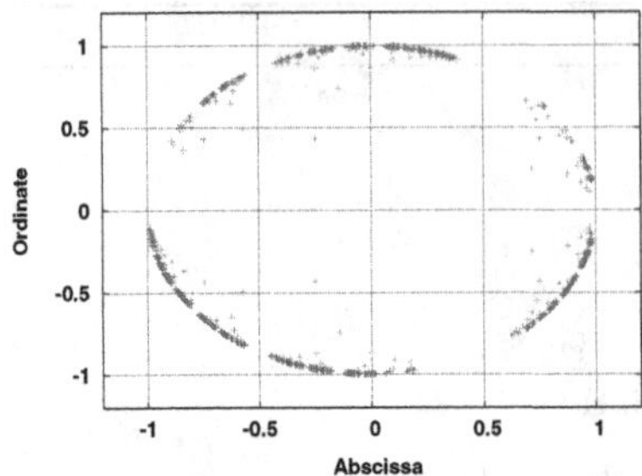

Fig. 3. Scatter plot of the spatial positions of the database servers.

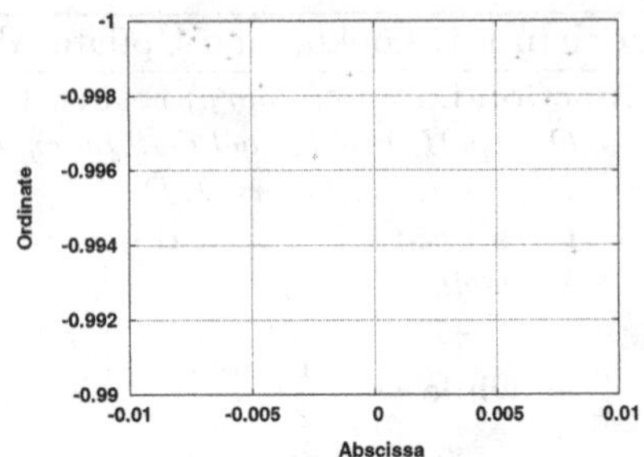

Fig. 4. Scatter plot of the positions of the servers in the neighborhood of the unit circle.

that our VCH-tree is balanced. Indeed, we can notice by part and others around the unit circle which we have database servers. This has an almost uniform distribution around the root, which implies that our system builds a well-balanced tree that will more easily allow to reach a proper load balancing for the storage.

Figure 4 shows correspondingly Poincaré disk model that no address of database server belongs on the edge of the unit circle. Indeed, the addresses of database server were obtained by projection of the tree of the hyperbolic plane in a circle of the Euclidian plane of radius 1 and of center with coordinates (0; 0).

This result shows that our distributed database system can grow towards infinity in theory. In practice, other parameters such as real number precision do bring limitations.

6.2 Load Balancing in the VCH-tree

Figure 5 shows a plot of the average number of objects stored by the database servers over time. So this figure shows a regular growth of this number of data objects stored in function of time. Indeed, 293.27 data objects on average are stored by database server after 10 min vs 620.4 after 2 h. It is interesting to notice that the standard deviation remains low, approximately at 10 % of the average. This indicates a low dispersal of the number of objects stored on the servers during the simulation.

Indeed, if we use our results to build the confidence interval, we can say that after 10 min of simulation, 68.2 % of the database servers store between 263.69 and 322.71 data objects and 95 % store between 234.18 and 352.22 against 68.2 % of the database servers which store between 560.18 and 681.58 data objects after 2 h and 95 % of the database servers who store between 497.95 and 742.84 data objects after 2 h. In view of these results, we can say that our system maintains a proper load balancing between database servers which ensures the stability of our distributed database system.

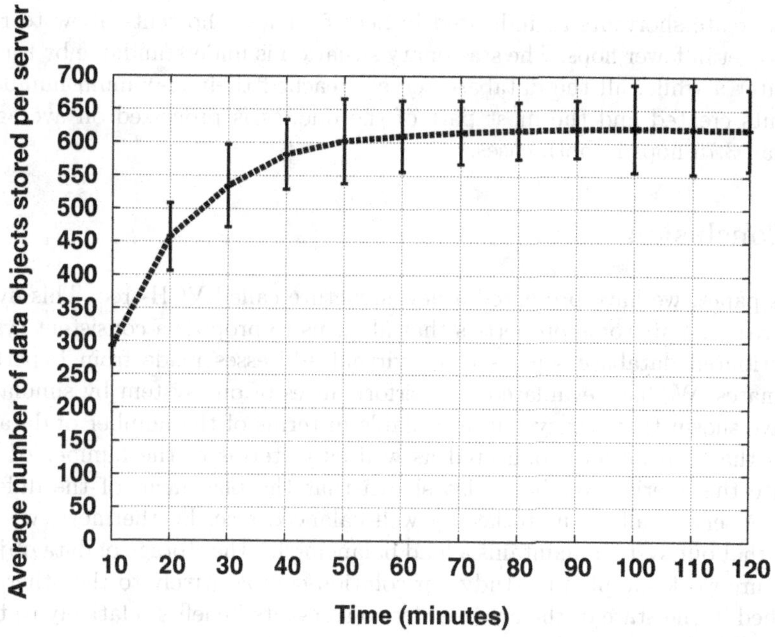

Fig. 5. Average load on the database servers over time

6.3 Storage and Retrieval Efficiency in the VCH-tree

Figures 6 and 7 show that during the simulation, queries in both cases can be answered within O(log N) where N is equal to the number of database servers in the system. As the standard deviation is very low (less than 5 % of the average for storage and retrieval), we did not represent it on the figures. In the worst case, queries need to travel less than 4 database servers in the system for either storing, or retrieving a data object. Besides, what is also interesting to note is that the plot decreases slowly to become stationary after around 100 min in both cases. It can be explained because during the simulation, the database

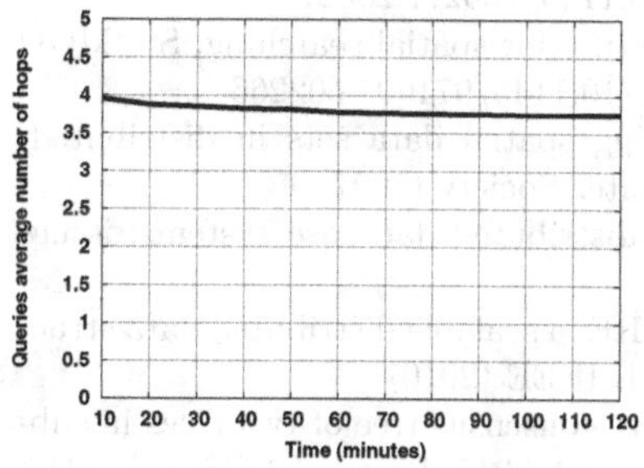

Fig. 6. Path length of storage queries

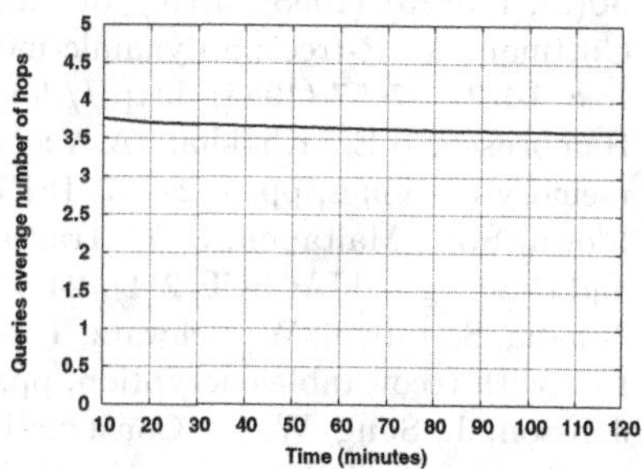

Fig. 7. Path length of retrieval queries

servers create shortcuts as indicated in Sect. 5. These shortcuts allow to reach their target in fewer hops. The stationary situation is understandable by the fact that after a while, all the database servers reached their maximum number of shortcuts created and the most part of the queries is processed on average in less than 3.75 hops in both cases.

7 Conclusion

In this paper, we have presented a new structure called VCH-tree. This hyperbolic tree presents some properties that allow us to propose a consistent system of distributed database servers using virtual addresses made from hyperbolic coordinates. We have evaluated the performances of our system by simulation. We have shown that our system is scalable in terms of the number of database servers that can be interconnected as well as in terms of the number of hops to route the queries. We have also shown that the placement of the different database servers allows us to keep a well-balanced tree. Furthermore, we have shown that our system maintains a load balancing for the storage of data objects. For future work, we plan to study our solution comparatively to the other ones described in the state of the art in order to assess its benefits relatively to those existing solutions.

References

1. Anderson, J.W.: Hyperbolic Geometry. Springer undergraduate mathematics series, 2nd edn. Springer, Berlin (2005)
2. Crainiceanu, A., Linga, P., Gehrke, J., Shanmugasundaram, J.: Querying peer-to-peer networks using p-trees. In: Proceedings of the 7th International Workshop on the Web and Databases: Colocated with ACM SIGMOD/PODS 2004, WebDB 2004, pp. 25–30. ACM, New York (2004). http://doi.acm.org/10.1145/1017074.1017082
3. Devine, R.: Design and implementation of DDH: a distributed dynamic hashing algorithm. In: Lomet, D.B. (ed.) FODO 1993, vol. 730, pp. 101–114. Springer, Heidelberg (1993)
4. Gaede, V., Günther, O.: Multidimensional access methods. ACM Comput. Surv. **30**(2), 170–231 (1998). http://doi.acm.org/10.1145/280277.280279
5. Guttman, A.: R-trees: a dynamic index structure for spatial searching. SIGMOD Rec. **14**(2), 47–57 (1984). http://doi.acm.org/10.1145/971697.602266
6. Hambrusch, S.E., Khokhar, A.A.: Maintaining spatial data sets in distributed-memory machines, pp. 702–707. IEEE Computer Society (1997)
7. Idowu, S.A., Maitanmi, S.O.: Transactions- distributed database systems: issues and challenges. IJACSCE **2**(1), 24–26 (2014)
8. Jajodia, S., Litwin, W., Schwarz, T.J.E.: LH*RE: a scalable distributed data structure with recoverable encryption, pp. 354–361. IEEE (2010)
9. Jansson, J., Sung, W.-K.: Constructing the R* consensus tree of two trees in sub-cubic time. In: de Berg, M., Meyer, U. (eds.) ESA 2010, Part I. LNCS, vol. 6346, pp. 573–584. Springer, Heidelberg (2010)

10. Karlsson, J.S.: hQT*: a scalable distributed data structure for high-performance spatial accesses, pp. 37–46 (1998)
11. Kleinberg, R.: Geographic routing using hyperbolic space. In: 26th IEEE International Conference on Computer Communications, INFOCOM 2007, pp. 1902–1909. IEEE, May 2007
12. Kriakov, V., Delis, A., Kollios, G.: Management of highly dynamic multidimensional data in a cluster of workstations. In: Bertino, E., Christodoulakis, S., Plexousakis, D., Christophides, V., Koubarakis, M., Böhm, K. (eds.) EDBT 2004. LNCS, vol. 2992, pp. 748–764. Springer, Heidelberg (2004)
13. Lakshman, A., Malik, P.: Cassandra: a decentralized structured storage system. SIGOPS Oper. Syst. Rev. **44**(2), 35–40 (2010). http://doi.acm.org/10.1145/1773912.1773922
14. Litwin, W., Neimat, M.A.: k-RP*s: a scalable distributed data structure for high-performance multi-attribute access, pp. 120–131. IEEE Computer Society (1996)
15. Montresor, A., Jelasity, M.: PeerSim: a scalable P2P simulator. In: Proceedings of the 9th International Conference on Peer-to-Peer (P2P 2009), pp. 99–100, Seattle, WA (2009)
16. Silberschatz, A., Korth, H., Sudarshan, S.: Database Systems Concepts, 5th edn. McGraw-Hill, Inc., New York (2006)
17. Tiendrebeogo, T., Ahmat, D., Magoni, D.: Reliable and scalable distributed hash tables harnessing hyperbolic coordinates. In: 2012 5th International Conference on New Technologies, Mobility and Security (NTMS), pp. 1–6, May 2012

EPiC: Efficient Privacy-Preserving Counting for MapReduce

Triet D. Vo-Huu[1(✉)], Erik-Oliver Blass[2], and Guevara Noubir[1]

[1] Northeastern University, Boston, MA 02115, USA
vohuudtr@ccs.neu.edu
[2] Airbus Group Innovations, 81663 Munich, Germany

Abstract. In the face of an untrusted cloud infrastructure, outsourced data needs to be protected. We present EPiC, a practical protocol for the privacy-preserving evaluation of a fundamental operation on data sets: frequency counting. We show how a general pattern, defined by a Boolean formula, is arithmetized into a multivariate polynomial and used in EPiC. To increase the performance of the system, we introduce a new efficient privacy-preserving encoding with "somewhat homomorphic" properties based on previous work on the Hidden Modular Group assumption. Besides a formal analysis where we prove EPiC's privacy, we also present implementation and evaluation results. We specifically target Google's prominent MapReduce paradigm as offered by major cloud providers. Our evaluation performed both locally and in Amazon's public cloud with up to 1 TB data sets shows only a modest overhead of 20 % compared to non-private counting, attesting to EPiC's efficiency.

1 Introduction

Cloud computing is a promising technology for large enterprises and even governmental organizations. Major cloud computing providers such as Amazon and Google offer users to outsource their data and computation. While the idea of moving data and computation to a (public) cloud for cost savings is appealing, trusting the cloud to store and protect data against *adversaries* is a serious concern for users. The encryption of data is a viable privacy protection mechanism, but it renders subsequent operations on encrypted data a challenging problem. To address this problem, *Fully Homomorphic Encryption* (FHE) techniques have been investigated, cf. Gentry [8] or see Vaikuntanathan [15] for an overview. FHE guarantees that the cloud neither learns details about the stored data nor about the results. However, today's FHE schemes are still overly inefficient [5,9,16], and a deployment in a real-world cloud would outweigh any cost advantage offered by the cloud. Moreover, any solution for a real-world cloud needs to be tailored to the specifics of the cloud computing paradigm, e.g., MapReduce [6].

This paper presents EPiC – Efficient PrIvacy-preserving Counting for MapReduce, an efficient, practical, yet privacy-preserving protocol for a fundamental data analysis primitive in MapReduce: *counting occurrences* of patterns. In an outsourced data set comprising a large number of encrypted data

A. Bouajjani and H. Fauconnier (Eds.): NETYS 2015, LNCS 9466, pp. 426–443, 2015.
DOI: 10.1007/978-3-319-26850-7_29

records, EPiC allows the cloud user to specify a pattern, and the cloud will count the number of occurrences of this pattern (and therefore histograms) in the stored ciphertexts without revealing the pattern and how often it occurs. A pattern is expressed as a Boolean formula on countable fields of data records and can specify a specific field value, a value comparison, a range of field values, and more complex forms of conjunctions/disjunctions among sub-patterns. For example, in an outsourced data set of patient health records, a pattern could be $age \in [50, 70]$ *and* $(diabetes = 1$ *or* $hypertension = 1)$. The main idea of EPiC is to transform the problem of privacy-preserving pattern counting into a summation of polynomial evaluations. Our work is inspired by Lauter et al. [11] to use *somewhat homomorphic* encryption to address specific privacy-preserving operations. In EPiC, we extend a previous work on cPIR protocols [14] to design a new "encoding" mechanism that exhibits somewhat homomorphic properties. While we call our encoding encryption in the rest of this paper, we stress that our encryption does not provide traditional IND-CPA security, but only weaker properties suited to the context we target in this paper, i.e., the summation of polynomial evaluations. In return, our "encryption" is particularly efficient in this context. We also show how a general pattern, defined by a Boolean formula, is arithmetized into a multivariate polynomial over $GF(2)$, optimizing for efficiency. In conclusion, the contributions of this paper are:

- EPiC, a new protocol to enable privacy-preserving pattern counting in MapReduce clouds. EPiC reduces the problem of counting occurrences of a Boolean pattern to the summation of a multivariate polynomial evaluated on encrypted data.
- A new, practical "somewhat homomorphic" encoding/encryption scheme specifically addressing secure counting in a highly efficient manner.
- An implementation of EPiC and its encryption mechanism together with an extensive evaluation in a realistic setting. The source code is available for download [17].

2 Problem Statement

Overview: We will use an example application to motivate our work. Imagine a hospital scenario where patient records are managed electronically. To reduce cost and grant access to, e.g., other hospitals and external doctors, the hospital refrains from investing into an own, local data center, but plans to outsource patient records to a public cloud. Regulatory matters require the privacy-protection of sensitive medical information, so outsourced data has to be encrypted. However, besides uploading, retrieving or editing patient records performed by multiple entities (hospitals, doctors etc.), one entity eventually wants to collect some statistics on the outsourced patient records without the necessity of downloading all of them.

2.1 Cloud Counting

More specifically, we assume that each patient record R includes one or more countable fields $R.c$ containing some patterns. A user (e.g., doctor) $\mathcal{U}$ wants to extract the frequency of occurrence of pattern χ, e.g., how many patients have $R.disease = \chi$. Due to the large amount of data, downloading each patient record is prohibitive, and the counting should be performed by the cloud. While encryption of data, access control, and key management in a multi-user cloud environment are clearly important topics, we focus on the problem of a-posteriori extracting information out of the outsourced data in a privacy-preserving manner. The cloud must neither learn details about the stored data, nor any information about the counting, what is counted, the count itself, etc. Instead, the cloud processes $\mathcal{U}$'s counting queries "obliviously". We will now first specify the general setup of counting schemes for public clouds and then formally define privacy requirements. Note that throughout this paper, we will assume the countable fields to be non-negative integer fields. Besides, records may contain non-countable data, e.g., pictures or doctors' notes, that can be IND-CPA (AES-CBC) encrypted – Therewith, it is of no importance for privacy defined below.

Definition 1 (Cloud Counting). *Let $\mathcal{R}$ denote a sequence of records $\mathcal{R} := \{R_1, \ldots, R_n\}$. Besides some non-countable data, each record R_i contains m different countable fields. The k-th countable field of the i-th record, denoted as $R_{i,k}, 1 \leq k \leq m$, can take values $R_{i,k} \in \mathcal{D}_k = \{0, 1, \ldots, |\mathcal{D}_k| - 1\}$, where $\mathcal{D}_k$ denotes the domain of the k-th field with size[1] $|\mathcal{D}_k|$. For the "multi-domain" of m countable fields we write $\mathcal{D} = \mathcal{D}_1 \times \cdots \times \mathcal{D}_m$. A privacy-preserving counting scheme comprises the following probabilistic polynomial time algorithms:*

1. KEYGEN(κ): *using a security parameter κ, outputs a secret key $\mathcal{S}$.*
2. ENCRYPT($\mathcal{S}, \mathcal{R}$): *uses secret key $\mathcal{S}$ to encrypt the sequence of records $\mathcal{R}$ to $\mathcal{E} := \{E_{R_1}, \ldots, E_{R_n}\}$, where E_{R_i} denotes the encryption of record R_i.*
3. UPLOAD($\mathcal{E}$): *uploads the sequence of encryptions $\mathcal{E}$ to the cloud.*
4. PREPAREQUERY($\mathcal{S}, \chi$): *generates an encrypted query Q out of secret $\mathcal{S}$ and the multiple-field pattern $\chi \in \mathcal{D}$.*
5. PROCESSQUERY($Q, \mathcal{E}$): *uses an encrypted query Q, the sequence of ciphertexts $\mathcal{E}$, and outputs a result E_Σ. This algorithm performs the actual counting.*
6. DECODE($\mathcal{S}, E_\Sigma$): *takes secret $\mathcal{S}$ and E_Σ to output a final result, the occurrences Σ (the "count") of the specified pattern in $\mathcal{R}$.*

According to this definition, cloud user $\mathcal{U}$ encrypts the sequence of records and uploads them into the cloud. If $\mathcal{U}$ wants to know the number of occurrences of χ in the records, he prepares a query Q, which is – as we will see later – simply a fixed-length sequence of encrypted values. U then sends Q to the cloud, and the cloud processes Q. Finally, the cloud sends a result E_Σ back to U who can decrypt this result and learn the number Σ of occurrences of pattern χ, i.e., the count.

---

[1] Domain size $|\mathcal{D}_k|$ indicates the number of different values a field can take.

2.2 Privacy

In the face of an untrusted cloud infrastructure, cloud user $\mathcal{U}$ wants to perform counting in a privacy-preserving manner. Informally, we demand (1) *storage privacy*, where the cloud does not learn anything about stored data, and (2) *counting privacy*, where the cloud does not learn anything about queries and query results. The cloud, which we now call "adversary" $\mathcal{A}$, should only learn "trivial" privacy properties like the total size of outsourced data, the total number of patient records or the number of counting operations performed for $\mathcal{U}$. We formalize privacy for counting using a game-based setup. In the following, $\epsilon(\kappa)$ denotes a negligible function in the security parameter κ.

Definition 2 (Bit Mapping). *Let $\mathcal{R} = \{R_1, \ldots, R_n\}$ be a set of records, and $R_{i,k} \in \{0,1\}^*$ the k-th field of record R_i. Let $\chi, \Sigma \in \{0,1\}^*$ be bit string representations of a pattern and a count. For $X \in \{R_{i,k}, \chi, \Sigma\}$, $\mathrm{bit}(j, X)$ denotes the j-th bit of X.*

Definition 3 (Storage Privacy). *A challenger generates two same-size same-field-types sets of records $\mathcal{R}, \mathcal{R}'$ and two patterns $\chi, \chi' \in \mathcal{D}$. The challenger then uses* Encrypt *and* PrepareQuery *to compute the encrypted sets of records $\mathcal{E}, \mathcal{E}'$ and two encrypted counting queries Q, Q' corresponding to two patterns χ, χ'. Using* ProcessQuery*, he evaluates $\mathcal{E}$ with Q, and $\mathcal{E}'$ with Q' to get encrypted results E_Σ, E'_Σ. The challenger sends $I := \{\mathcal{E}, \mathcal{E}', Q, Q', E_\Sigma, E'_\Sigma\}$ to adversary $\mathcal{A}$. For any patterns χ, χ', any X, X' such that either $X \in \{\{R_{i,k}\}\}$ and $X' \in \{\{R_{i,k}\}\}$ or $X = \chi$ and $X' = \chi'$ or $X = \Sigma$ and $X' = \Sigma'$, and for any $b = \mathrm{bit}(j, X)$ and $b' = \mathrm{bit}(j', X')$, the adversary $\mathcal{A}$ outputs 1, if she guesses $b = b'$, and 0 otherwise. A protocol preserves storage privacy,* iff *for any probabilistic polynomial time (PPT) algorithm $\mathcal{A}$, the probability of correct output is not higher than a random guess. That is, $\left|\Pr\left[\mathcal{A}(I) = 1 | b = b'\right] - \frac{1}{2}\right| \leq \epsilon(\kappa)$* and *$\left|\Pr\left[\mathcal{A}(I) = 0 | b \neq b'\right] - \frac{1}{2}\right| \leq \epsilon(\kappa)$.*

Definition 4 (Counting Privacy). *A challenger generates two same-size same-field-types sets of records $\mathcal{R}, \mathcal{R}'$, and two patterns χ, χ', uses* Encrypt, PrepareQuery, *and* ProcessQuery, *and sends encrypted $I := \{\mathcal{E}, \mathcal{E}', Q, Q', E_\Sigma, E'_\Sigma\}$, to $\mathcal{A}$. Now, $\mathcal{A}$ outputs 1, if $\chi = \chi'$, and 0 otherwise. A protocol preserves counting privacy,* iff *for any PPT algorithm $\mathcal{A}$ the probability of correct output is not better than a random guess: $\left|\Pr\left[\mathcal{A}(I) = 1 | \chi = \chi'\right] - \frac{1}{2}\right| \leq \epsilon(\kappa)$ and $\left|\Pr\left[\mathcal{A}(I) = 0 | \chi \neq \chi'\right] - \frac{1}{2}\right| \leq \epsilon(\kappa)$.*

Similar to traditional indistinguishability, *storage privacy* and *counting privacy* captures the intuition that, by storing data and counting, the cloud should not learn anything about the content it stores. In addition, the cloud should not learn anything about the counting performed, such as which pattern is counted, whether a pattern is counted twice or what the resulting count is.

2.3 MapReduce

The efficiency of counting relies on the performance of ProcessQuery which involves processing huge amounts of data in the cloud. Cloud computing usually processes data in parallel via multiple nodes in the cloud data center based on some computation paradigm. For efficiency, PROCESSQUERY has to take the specifics of that computation into account. One of the most widespread, frequently used framework for distributed computation that is offered by major cloud providers today is MapReduce [6]. EPiC's counting "job" runs in two phases. First, in the "mapping" phase, *Mapper* nodes scan data through *Input-Splits* (data pieces split automatically by MapReduce framework) and evaluate the counting's *map* function on the data. These operations are performed by all Mappers in parallel. The outputs of each *map* function are sent to one *Reducer* node, which, in the "reducing" phase, aggregates them and produces a final output that is sent back to the user. This setup takes advantage of the parallel nature of a cloud data center and allows for scalability and elasticity.

3 EPiC Protocol

To motivate the need for a more sophisticated protocol like EPiC, we briefly discuss why possible straightforward solutions do not work in our particular application scenario.

Precomputed Counters: One could imagine that the cloud user, in the purpose of counting a value χ_k in a single countable field $\mathcal{D}_k$, simply stores encrypted counters for each possible value of χ_k in domain $\mathcal{D}_k$ in the cloud. Each time records are added, removed or updated, the cloud user updates the encrypted counters. However, this approach does not scale very well in our scenario where multiple cloud users (different "doctors") perform updates and add or modify records. An expensive user side locking mechanism would be required to ensure consistency of the encrypted counters. Moreover, in the case of complex queries involving multiple fields, all possible combinations of counters need to be updated by users involving a lot of user side computation.

Per-Record Counters ("Voting"): Alternatively and similar to a naive voting scheme, each encrypted record stored in the cloud could be augmented with an encrypted "voting" field containing $|\mathcal{D}_k|$ subsets, each of $\log_2 n$ bits. If a record's countable value in field $\mathcal{D}_k$ matches the value corresponding to a subset, then the according subset is set to 1. To find the count, the cloud sums the encrypted voting fields (using additive homomorphic encryption) for all records. Again, such an approach requires heavy locking mechanism and recomputation of counters for each operation of adding, removing, or modifying a record. In conclusion, these straightforward solutions require heavy user-side computation and do not provide efficient, practical, and flexible solutions for multi-user, multiple field data sets.

3.1 EPiC Overview

For ease of understanding, we *initially* introduce EPiC for the simpler case of counting on only a single countable field $\mathcal{D}_k$ in a multiple countable fields data set where values are in GF(q). Subsequently, we extend EPiC to support counting on Boolean combinations of multiple countable fields $\mathcal{D}_1, \ldots, \mathcal{D}_m$ over GF(q). Finally, for performance improvement, we further optimize our mechanisms by considering conversion of (generic) finite fields GF(q) into binary finite fields GF(2).

EPiC's main rationale is to perform the counting in the cloud by evaluating an *indicator polynomial* $P_\chi(\cdot)$, as query Q, specific to the pattern χ the cloud user $\mathcal{U}$ is interested in. Conceptually, the cloud evaluates $P_\chi(\cdot)$ on the countable fields' values of each record. The outcome of all individual polynomial evaluations is a (large) set of values of either "1" or "0". The cloud now adds these values and sends the sum back to $\mathcal{U}$, who learns the number of occurrences of χ in the investigated set of records.

3.2 Counting on a Single Field

Without loss of generality, we assume a user $\mathcal{U}$ wishes to count occurrences of χ in the first field $\mathcal{D}_1$ in an oblivious manner. The idea is to prepare a univariate indicator polynomial $P_\chi(x)$ such that $P_\chi(x) = \begin{cases} 1, \text{ if } x = \chi \\ 0, \text{otherwise} \end{cases}$, and scan through the data set $\mathcal{R} = \{R_1, \ldots, R_n\}$ of all records to compute the sum $\sum_{i=1}^{n} P_\chi(R_{i,1})$. The result is the number of occurrences of χ in the first field in the data set. The idea for generating $P_\chi(x)$ is to construct the polynomial in the Lagrange interpolation form $P_\chi(x) := \sum_{j=0}^{|\mathcal{D}_1|-1} a_j \cdot x^j := \prod_{\alpha \in \mathcal{D}_1, \alpha \neq \chi} \frac{x-\alpha}{\chi-\alpha}$. The polynomial $P_\chi(x)$ is of degree $|\mathcal{D}_1| - 1$, and its coefficients a_j are uniquely determined.

Encrypted Polynomial: In EPiC, each countable value $R_{i,k}$ is encrypted to $E_{R_{i,k}}$. The above indicator polynomial based counting method for plaintext values can be applied in a similar manner. User $\mathcal{U}$ prepares the indicator polynomial based on plaintext χ, but $\mathcal{U}$ encrypts coefficients a_j to E_{a_j} before sending them to the cloud, which now computes the encrypted sum $E_\Sigma := \sum_{i=1}^{n} P_\chi(E_{R_{i,1}}) = \sum_{i=1}^{n} \sum_{j=0}^{|\mathcal{D}_1|-1} E_{a_j} \cdot (E_{R_{i,1}})^j$. Note that the polynomial *coefficients* are encrypted (and potentially large), but the polynomial *degree* remains $|\mathcal{D}_1| - 1$. In order for the cloud to compute E_Σ and user $\mathcal{U}$ to decrypt it later, additively and multiplicatively homomorphic properties are required for the encryption, which we describe in Sect. 3.5. As a final step, $\mathcal{U}$ simply receives back E_Σ and only decrypts the count $\sigma := \text{DEC}(E_\Sigma) = P_\chi(x)$. This does not require high computational costs at the user, suiting the cloud computing paradigm well.

Cloud Computation Cost: The above technique requires $n \cdot |\mathcal{D}_1|$ additions, $n \cdot |\mathcal{D}_1|$ multiplications, and $n \cdot (|\mathcal{D}_1| - 1)$ exponentiations. We can improve efficiency by rearranging the order of computations: $E_\Sigma := \sum_{i=1}^{n} P_\chi(E_{R_{i,1}}) = \sum_{i=1}^{n} \sum_{j=0}^{|\mathcal{D}_1|-1} E_{a_j} \cdot (E_{R_{i,1}})^j = \sum_{j=0}^{|\mathcal{D}_1|-1} (E_{a_j} \cdot \sum_{i=1}^{n} (E_{R_{i,1}})^j)$. Therewith, the number of multiplications is reduced to $|\mathcal{D}_1|$. We also note that in the case of a binary domain ($|\mathcal{D}_1| = 2$), there are no exponentiations. This observation motivates our optimization described later in Sect. 3.4.

Oblivious Counting: *First*, the query is submitted to the cloud as a sequence of encrypted coefficients of the indicator polynomial; *second*, no matter what query is made, exactly $|\mathcal{D}_1|$ coefficients (including 0-coefficients) are sent, thus preventing the cloud to infer query information based on the query size.

3.3 Counting Patterns Defined by a Boolean Formula

We now extend the indicator polynomial based counting technique towards a general solution for counting patterns defined by any Boolean combination of *multiple* fields in the data set. The key technique for defining an indicator polynomial corresponding to an arbitrary Boolean expression among multiple fields is to transform Boolean operations to arithmetic operations, which is similar to *arithmetization* [3,12].

Conjunctive Counting: Assume cloud user $\mathcal{U}$ is interested in counting the number of records that have their m countable fields set to the pattern $\chi = (\chi_1, \ldots, \chi_m)$. Here, χ_k, $1 \le k \le m$, denotes the queried value in the k-th field. Let $\varphi = (x_1 = \chi_1 \wedge \ldots \wedge x_m = \chi_m)$ be the conjunction among m fields in the data set. User $\mathcal{U}$ can now construct $P_\varphi(\mathbf{x}) = \prod_{k=1}^{m} P_{\chi_k}(x_k)$, where $\mathbf{x} = (x_1, \ldots, x_m)$ denotes the variables in the multivariate polynomial $P_\varphi(\mathbf{x})$, and $P_{\chi_k}(x_k)$ is the univariate indicator polynomial (as defined in Sect. 3.2) for counting χ_k in the k-th field. Therewith, $P_\varphi(\mathbf{x})$ yields 1 only when χ is matched. Note that the size of the multi-domain $\mathcal{D}$ is $|\mathcal{D}| = \prod_{k=1}^{m} |\mathcal{D}_k|$, and the degree of $P_\varphi(\mathbf{x})$ is $\sum_{k=1}^{m} (|\mathcal{D}_k| - 1)$.

Disjunctive Counting: Assume the data set has 2 countable fields, and $\mathcal{U}$'s objective is to count the number of records that have value χ_1 in $\mathcal{D}_1$ or value χ_2 in $\mathcal{D}_2$. The multivariate indicator polynomial for this disjunction is $P_{\chi_1 \vee \chi_2}(\mathbf{x}) = P_{\chi_1}(x_1) + P_{\chi_2}(x_2) - P_{\chi_1 \wedge \chi_2}(\mathbf{x})$, where $P_{\chi_1}(x_1), P_{\chi_2}(x_2)$ are univariate indicator polynomials for $\mathcal{D}_1, \mathcal{D}_2$, respectively, and $P_{\chi_1 \wedge \chi_2}(\mathbf{x})$ is a multivariate indicator polynomial for conjunctive counting between $\mathcal{D}_1$ and $\mathcal{D}_2$. This method can be easily generalized to design counting query for disjunctions of m fields.

Complement Counting: $\mathcal{U}$ can count records that do not satisfy a condition among fields by "flipping" the satisfying indicator polynomial: $P_{\neg\varphi}(\mathbf{x}) = 1 - P_\varphi(\mathbf{x})$.

Integer Range Counting: Assume $\mathcal{U}$ wants to count records having a field $\mathcal{D}_k$ lying in an integer range $[a, b]$, i.e., $\varphi = (x_k = a \vee x_k = a+1 \vee \ldots \vee x_k = b)$. Based on disjunctive constructing method, we have $P_{[a,b]}(x_k) = P_a(x_k) + P_{a+1}(x_k) + \ldots + P_b(x_k) - P_{a \wedge a+1} - \ldots$; Since $(x_k = u)$ and $(x_k = v)$ are exclusive disjunctions for any $u \neq v \in [a, b]$, $P_{[a,b]}(x_k)$ reduces to $P_{[a,b]}(x_k) = \sum_{\chi_k = a}^{b} P_{\chi_k}(x_k)$.

Integer Comparison Counting: Integer comparisons can be constructed based on integer range counting, e.g., $P_{\chi_k \leq a}(x_k) = P_{[0,a]}(x_k)$, or $P_{\chi_k > a}(x_k) = P_{[a+1,|\mathcal{D}_k|-1]}(x_k)$.

Privacy: Although the user-defined queries are different in construction, the encrypted queries Q always have exactly $|\mathcal{D}| = \prod_{k=1}^{m} |\mathcal{D}_k|$ encrypted coefficients as we include zero coefficients also. As mentioned in Sect. 3.2, this prevents the cloud to differentiate queries based on query sizes.

Efficiency: The user-side computation involving constructing the query's coefficients is carried on plain-text before encryption, hence it introduces much lower computation cost compared to the computation burden on the cloud. To improve the user-side performance, one could apply optimizing techniques for reducing complex expressions, but this is out of scope of our work. To improve the cloud's performance, we rearrange the order of computations for the sequence of encrypted fields $E(R_i) = (E_{R_{i,1}}, \ldots, E_{R_{i,m}})$ and coefficients $a_{\mathbf{j}}$, $\mathbf{j} = (j_1, \ldots, j_m) \in \mathcal{D}$ to achieve $E_\Sigma = \sum_{i=1}^{n} P_\chi(E(R_i)) = \sum_{\mathbf{j} \in \mathcal{D}} (E_{a_{\mathbf{j}}} \cdot \sum_{i=1}^{n} \prod_{k=1}^{m} (E_{R_{i,k}})^{j_k})$.

3.4 Optimization Through Arithmetization in $GF(2)$

EPiC's efficiency relies on the computations performed by the cloud. As discussed in Sect. 3.2, there are *no exponentiations* required for counting on a binary field. Consequently, we optimize EPiC by converting generic (non-binary) fields into multiple binary fields, thereby avoiding costly exponentiations. Note that as the conversion preserves Boolean expression output, results shown in Sect. 3.3 still hold, and protocol details discussed later in Sect. 3.6 remain unchanged.

Our idea is to store every generic field $\mathcal{D}_k$ as separate binary fields $\mathcal{D}_{k,1}$, $\mathcal{D}_{k,2}$, ..., $\mathcal{D}_{k,\|\mathcal{D}_k\|}$.[2] Therefore, m generic fields $\mathcal{D}_1, \ldots, \mathcal{D}_m$ become $\sum_{k=1}^{m} \|\mathcal{D}_k\|$ binary fields $\mathcal{D}_{1,1}, \ldots, \mathcal{D}_{1,\|\mathcal{D}_1\|}, \ldots, \mathcal{D}_{m,1}, \ldots, \mathcal{D}_{m,\|\mathcal{D}_m\|}$. The indicator polynomial for counting χ_k in field $\mathcal{D}_k$ becomes $P_{\chi_{k,1} \wedge \ldots \wedge \chi_{k,\|\mathcal{D}_k\|}}(x_{k,1}, \ldots, x_{1,\|\mathcal{D}_k\|}) = \prod_{l=1}^{\|\mathcal{D}_k\|} P_{\chi_{k,l}}(x_{k,l})$, where $x_{k,l}$ represents the l-th bit in the generic field $\mathcal{D}_k$, and $\chi_{k,l}$ denotes the corresponding queried bit value. Applying arithmetization to "transform" from Boolean to multivariate polynomials, Boolean expressions of m generic fields can be converted into equivalent multiple binary fields. For convenience in later sections, we call the conversion to binary fields "GF(2) arithmetized" (shortly "G"), while the original is "Basic" (shortly "B"). We note that although the number of coefficients of the GF(2) arithmetized multivariate indicator polynomial corresponding to each query remains the same as in the generic case, the (multivariate) degree of the GF(2) arithmetized polynomial is much lower at $\deg(P^{(G)}) = \sum_{k=1}^{m} \|\mathcal{D}_k\| = \sum_{k=1}^{m} \lceil \log_2 |\mathcal{D}_k| \rceil \ll \sum_{k=1}^{m} (|\mathcal{D}_k| - 1) = \deg(P^{(B)})$. This implies a significant improvement for computational costs on the cloud. We refer to EPiC's evaluation in Sect. 4 for details.

[2] $\|X\| = \lceil \log_2 |X| \rceil$ denotes size in bits of X.

3.5 Encryption

Since EPiC's indicator polynomial based counting technique involves additions and multiplications on ciphertexts, a homomorphic encryption scheme is needed as a building block. While there already exist various schemes [5,8,11,16], their computational complexities are high, rendering their use in current clouds impractical. Although EPiC can seamlessly integrate related work, we design a new somewhat homomorphic encryption scheme derived from the computational Private Information Retrieval (cPIR) technique of Trostle and Parrish [14]. Our new scheme is a secret key encryption scheme, where the cloud does not have the secret key to decrypt the data, but instead blindly performs operations on outsourced data. As we will see, this scheme does not enjoy the same security properties, i.e., IND-CPA, as related work, but only security with respect to Definitions 3 and 4 as required in the specific context of EPiC. Due to its weaker security properties, our scheme is especially practical in the settings we target.

Key Generation – $\text{KeyGen}(s_1, s_2, n, \mathcal{D})$: Parameters $s_1, s_2 \in \mathbb{N}$ are security parameters, $n \in \mathbb{N}$ is the upper bound for the total number of records in the data set, and $\mathcal{D} = \mathcal{D}_1 \times \ldots \times \mathcal{D}_m$ is the multi-domain of m countable fields. KeyGen computes a random prime q, a random prime p, and a random (maybe non-prime) $b \in \mathbb{Z}_p$. The secret key, the output of KeyGen, is defined as $K := \{p, b\}$.

Encryption – $\text{Enc}(\mathcal{P})$: Selects a random number r, $\|r\| \leq s_2$, and encrypts the plaintext $\mathcal{P}$ to $\mathcal{C} = \text{Enc}(\mathcal{P}) := b \cdot (r \cdot q + \mathcal{P}) \bmod p$.

Decryption – $\text{Dec}(\mathcal{C})$: Decrypts $\mathcal{C}$ to $\mathcal{P} = \text{Dec}(\mathcal{C}) := b^{-1} \cdot \mathcal{C} \bmod p \bmod q$.

Arithmetic: The addition and multiplication operations on ciphertexts take place in the integers. There is no modulo reduction, as the cloud does not know p. One can verify that this scheme provides additively and multiplicatively homomorphic properties.

Selection of p and q: Since ciphertexts increase for every multiplication and addition, this scheme requires a careful selection of q and p in advance such that $q > n$ and $\|p\| \geq s_1 + \|n\| + \|q\| + \sum_{k=1}^{m}(s_2 + \|q\|) \cdot (|\mathcal{D}_k| - 1)$.

Security: The security of our encryption scheme (cf. Sect. 3.7) is based on the Hidden Modular Group Order hardness assumption and the cPIR protocol in [14]. The rationale is that, for appropriate security parameters, more than half of the bits of p are still secret against any PPT adversary; and if a PPT adversary can break the cPIR protocol, the Hidden Group Order p is also revealed, violating the assumption.

3.6 Detailed Protocol Description

With all ingredients ready, we now describe EPiC using the notation of Sect. 2.1.

$\text{KeyGen}(\kappa)$: Based on security parameter κ, cloud user $\mathcal{U}$ chooses s_1, s_2 for the somewhat homomorphic encryption, determines an upper bound n for the total number of records that might be stored and the appropriate multi-domain $\mathcal{D}$ for the countable fields. $\mathcal{U}$ generates a secret key K from the somewhat homomorphic encryption $\text{KeyGen}(s_1, s_2, n, \mathcal{D})$ and a symmetric key K' for a block cipher such as AES used for non-countable data. The secret key $\mathcal{S} := \{K, K'\}$ is used throughout EPiC.

$\text{Encrypt}(\mathcal{S}, \mathcal{R})$: Assume $\mathcal{U}$ wants to store n records $\mathcal{R} = \{R_1, \ldots, R_n\}$. Each record R_i is encrypted separating the countable values $R_{i,k}$ from the rest of the record. $R_{i,k}$ is encrypted using the somewhat homomorphic encryption mechanism, i.e., $E_{R_{i,k}} := \text{Enc}(\{p, b\}, R_{i,k})$. For the rest of the record R_i, a random initialization vector IV is chosen and the record is $\text{AES}_K - \text{CBC}$ encrypted. In conclusion, a record R_i encrypts to $E_{R_i} := \{E_{R_{i,1}}, \ldots, E_{R_{i,m}}, IV, \text{AES}_K - \text{CBC}(R_{i,rest})\}$. The output of Encrypt is the sequence of encrypted records. $\mathcal{E} := \{E_{R_1}, \ldots, E_{R_n}\}$.

$\text{Upload}(\mathcal{E})$: Upload simply sends all records as one large file to the MapReduce cloud where the file is automatically split into *InputSplits*.

$\text{PrepareQuery}(\mathcal{S}, \chi)$: To prepare a query for χ, $\mathcal{U}$ computes the $|\mathcal{D}|$ coefficients $a_{\mathbf{j}}$, $\mathbf{j} \in \mathcal{D}$, of the indicator polynomial $P_\chi(\mathbf{x})$ as described in Sect. 3.3. Coefficients $a_{\mathbf{j}}$ are encrypted and sent to the cloud. The cloud will be using these coefficients to perform the evaluation of $P_\chi(\mathbf{x})$. Consequently in EPiC, the output Q of PrepareQuery sent to the cloud is $Q := \{E_{a_{\mathbf{j}}}, \mathbf{j} \in \mathcal{D}\}$.

$\text{ProcessQuery}(Q, \mathcal{E})$: Based on the data set size and the cloud configuration, the MapReduce framework selects M Mapper nodes and 1 Reducer node. Algorithm 1 depicts the specification of EPiC's *map* and *reduce* functions that will be executed by the cloud. In the mapping phase, for each input record R_i in their locally stored InputSplits, the Mappers compute in parallel all monomials $\prod_{k=1}^{m} (E_{R_{i,k}})^{j_k}$ of the countable fields and add the same-degree monomials together. After the Mappers finish scanning over all records, the sums $s_{\mathbf{j}}$ of monomials are output as key-value pairs. These pairs contain the multi-degree $\mathbf{j}$ as key, and the computed sum $s_{\mathbf{j}}$ as value. In MapReduce, output of the Mappers is then automatically sent ("emitted") to the Reducer. Based on the sums received from all Mappers, the Reducer combines them together to obtain the *global* sums $S_{\mathbf{j}}$, i.e., the sums over all records in the data set. In a last step, the Reducer uses the coefficients $E_{a_{\mathbf{j}}}$ received from $\mathcal{U}$ to evaluate the polynomial by computing the inner product with the global sums. The result E_Σ is sent back to $\mathcal{U}$ and can be decrypted to obtain the count value.

$\text{Decode}(\mathcal{S}, E_\Sigma)$: $\mathcal{U}$ receives E_Σ and computes the counting result $\sigma = \text{Dec}(E_\Sigma)$.

3.7 Privacy Analysis

We now formally prove Storage and Counting privacy for EPiC and its underlying encryption. We stress that, below, we neither target nor prove that our encryption provides traditional IND-CPA security. Instead, we show that, in combination with other details of our protocol, it provides security according to Definitions 3 and 4.

Algorithm 1. PROCESSQUERY

For each Mapper M:

```
init s_j := 0, ∀j ∈ D
forall E_{R_i} in InputSplit(M) do
    read {E_{R_{i,1}}, ..., E_{R_{i,m}}}
    forall j = (j_1, ..., j_k) ∈ D do
        s_j := s_j + ∏_{k=1}^{m} (E_{R_{i,k}})^{j_k}
    end
end
emit {j, s_j}, ∀j ∈ D
```

Reducer R:

```
init E_Σ := 0, S_j := 0, ∀j ∈ D
forall {j, s_j} in MappersOutput do
    S_j := S_j + s_j
end
forall j in D do
    E_Σ := E_Σ + E_{a_j} · S_j
end
write {E_Σ}
```

Lemma 1 (Storage Privacy). *Based on the security of the cPIR scheme by Trostle and Parrish [14], EPiC preserves storage privacy.*

Proof. cPIR-security by Trostle and Parrish [14] can be summarized as follows. With a $u \times u$ bit database, a user wants to retrieve an y-th row and sends an encrypted PIR request to the cloud: $P = \{E_{v_1}, \ldots, E_{v_u}\}$, where $E_{v_k} = \text{ENC}(v_k)$, cf. Section 3.5, and $v_k = 1$, if $k = y$, and $v_k = 0$ otherwise. This cPIR protocol is secure *iff* for all PPT adversaries $\mathcal{A}^*$, the probability of finding y is negligible more than guessing, i.e., $\Pr[\mathcal{A}^*(P) = y] \le 1/u + \epsilon^*(\kappa)$. We now prove our lemma by reduction from cPIR security. We show that, for security parameter κ, any PPT $(t(\kappa), \epsilon(\kappa))$-adversary $\mathcal{A}$ breaking EPiC's storage privacy (Definition 3) in $t(\kappa)$ steps with non-negligible advantage $\epsilon(\kappa)$ can be used to construct a $(t^*(\kappa), \epsilon^*(\kappa))$-adversary $\mathcal{A}^*$ as a subroutine breaking the cPIR protocol in [14]. We construct $\mathcal{A}^*$ based on the *parity* of u.

1. u is Odd. First, $\mathcal{A}^*$ receives as input the PIR request P and splits P into two halves $\mathcal{E} = \{E_{v_1}, \ldots, E_{v_{\lfloor u/2 \rfloor}}\}$, $\mathcal{E}' = \{E_{v_{\lfloor u/2 \rfloor+1}}, \ldots, E_{u-1}\}$, i.e., treating the PIR request as two EPiC data sets of the same size ($\lfloor u/2 \rfloor$ records). Since E_{v_k} are either encryptions of 0 or 1, $\mathcal{E}$ and $\mathcal{E}'$ are now viewed as single-binary-field data sets, where each record contains only 1 countable binary field. $\mathcal{A}^*$ randomly selects $l_1, l_2, l'_1, l'_2 \in [1, u]$ and creates two EPiC counting queries $Q = \{E_{v_{l_1}}, E_{v_{l_2}}\}, Q' = \{E_{v_{l'_1}}, E_{v_{l'_2}}\}$. These are two valid queries, because for single-binary-field data sets $\mathcal{E}, \mathcal{E}'$, any EPiC query contains exactly 2 encrypted coefficients of 0 or 1, cf. Section 3.3. Then $\mathcal{A}^*$ runs PROCESSQUERY on $\mathcal{E}$ with Q, and $\mathcal{E}'$ with Q', thereby obtaining E_Σ and E'_Σ. $\mathcal{A}^*$ forwards $I = \{\mathcal{E}, \mathcal{E}', Q, Q', E_\Sigma, E'_\Sigma\}$ to $\mathcal{A}$. $\mathcal{A}^*$'s output depends on $\mathcal{A}$'s output as follows.

If $\mathcal{A}$ outputs 0, $\mathcal{A}^*$ outputs u. The intuition is that, since $\mathcal{A}$ "believes" the two halves $\mathcal{E}$ and $\mathcal{E}'$ are the same, $\mathcal{A}'$ concludes that the requested element must not belong to either $\mathcal{E}$ or $\mathcal{E}'$, i.e., $v_u = 1$. If $\mathcal{A}$ outputs 1, $\mathcal{A}^*$ randomly selects $k \in [1, u-1]$ and outputs k. The intuition is that "$\mathcal{A}$ outputs 1" indicates the requested row index is between 1 and $u - 1$, and $\mathcal{A}^*$ simply makes a random guess for it. The probability for $\mathcal{A}^*$ to output correctly is $\Pr[\mathcal{A}^*(P) = y] = \Pr[\mathcal{A} = 0 | y = u] \cdot \Pr[y = u] + \Pr[\mathcal{A} = 1, k = y | y < u] \cdot \Pr[y < u] = \left(\frac{1}{2} + \epsilon(\kappa)\right) \cdot$

$\frac{1}{u} + \left(\frac{1}{2} + \epsilon(\kappa)\right) \cdot \frac{1}{u-1} \cdot \frac{u-1}{u} = \frac{1}{u} + \frac{2\epsilon(\kappa)}{u}$. Therewith, $\mathcal{A}^*$ has a non-negligible advantage of $\epsilon^*(\kappa) = 2\epsilon(\kappa)/u$ in finding y.

2. u is Even. $\mathcal{A}^*$ makes a new PIR request P' by removing the last element v_u from P, that is $P' = \{E_{v_1}, \dots, E_{v_{u-1}}\}$. Then $\mathcal{A}^*$ uses the same approach as above for P', i.e., splitting P' into 2 halves, feeding both to $\mathcal{A}$. Now, $\mathcal{A}^*$ outputs $u-1$, if $\mathcal{A}$ outputs 0, or outputs random $k \in [1, u-2]$ otherwise. It can be observed that $\mathcal{A}^*$ can find y with non-negligible probability, only if $y \neq u$, i.e., the requested element is not the last element discarded from P. Otherwise, $\mathcal{A}^*$ cannot find y. More precisely, the probability of correct guess is $\Pr[\mathcal{A}^*(P) = y] = \Pr[\mathcal{A}^*(P') = y | y < u] \cdot \Pr[y < u] + \Pr[\mathcal{A}^*(P') = y | y = u] \cdot \Pr[y = u] = \left(\frac{1}{u-1} + \frac{2\epsilon(\kappa)}{u-1}\right) \cdot \frac{u-1}{u} + 0 \cdot \frac{1}{u} = \frac{1}{u} + \frac{2\epsilon(\kappa)}{u}$. Therefore, $\mathcal{A}^*$ also has a non-negligible advantage of $2\epsilon(\kappa)/u$ in finding y.

Consequently, in both cases, $\mathcal{A}^*$ has a non-negligible advantage $\epsilon^*(\kappa) = 2\epsilon(\kappa)/u$ of breaking the cPIR protocol in $t^*(\kappa) = t(\kappa)$ steps, rendering our reduction tight. □

Lemma 2 (Counting Privacy). *Based on the security of the cPIR scheme by Trostle and Parrish [14], EPiC preserves counting privacy.*

Proof. We prove our lemma by reduction from cPIR security. Recall the cPIR-security definition as in Lemma 1's proof. We assume the existence of a PPT $(t(\kappa), \epsilon(\kappa))$-EPiC-adversary $\mathcal{A}$ breaking EPiC's counting privacy (Definition 4) in $t(\kappa)$ steps with non-negligible advantage $\epsilon(\kappa)$. In the following, we construct a new $(t^*(\kappa), \epsilon^*(\kappa))$-PIR-adversary $\mathcal{A}^*$ that breaks this cPIR security.

$\mathcal{A}^*$ receives as input the PIR request $P = \{E_{v_1}, \dots, E_{v_u}\}$, where $v_y = 1$ and $v_k = 0, \forall k \neq y$. The goal of $\mathcal{A}^*$ is to guess y. First, $\mathcal{A}^*$ sets $\mathcal{E} = \mathcal{E}' = P$ and randomly picks 4 elements $E_{l_1}, E_{l_2}, E_{l'_1}, E_{l'_2}$ from P to make two EPiC queries $Q = \{E_{l_1}, E_{l_2}\}, Q' = \{E_{l'_1}, E_{l'_2}\}$. Note that $\mathcal{E}, \mathcal{E}'$ can be viewed as EPiC's two identical single-binary-field data sets, and Q, Q' are valid queries (corresponding to some patterns χ, χ') for $\mathcal{E}, \mathcal{E}'$. Then $\mathcal{A}^*$ runs ProcessQuery on $\mathcal{E}$ with Q and on $\mathcal{E}'$ with Q' to obtain E_Σ, E'_Σ. Now, $\mathcal{A}^*$ forwards $I = \{\mathcal{E}, \mathcal{E}', Q, Q', E_\Sigma, E'_\Sigma\}$ to $\mathcal{A}$ and observes $\mathcal{A}$'s output.

Let $U = \{1, \dots, u\}, L = \{l_1, l_2, l'_1, l'_2\}$. If $\mathcal{A}$ returns 1, $\mathcal{A}^*$ concludes that the two queries Q and Q' are identical, implying that $E_{v_y} \notin Q \cup Q'$, i.e., $y \notin L$. Therewith, $\mathcal{A}^*$ makes a guess for y by selecting a random $k \in U \setminus L$ and outputs k. Otherwise, if $\mathcal{A}$ returns 0, $\mathcal{A}^*$ concludes that v_y is in either Q or Q', thus $\mathcal{A}^*$ outputs a random $k \in L$. The probability of the correct guess is $\Pr[\mathcal{A}^*(P) = y] = \Pr[\mathcal{A}(I) = 1, k = y | y \in U \setminus L] \cdot \Pr[y \in U \setminus L] + \Pr[\mathcal{A}(I) = 0, k = y | y \in L] \cdot s\Pr[y \in L] = \left(\frac{1}{2} + \epsilon(\kappa)\right) \cdot \frac{1}{u-4} \cdot \frac{u-4}{u} + \left(\frac{1}{2} + \epsilon(\kappa)\right) \cdot \frac{1}{4} \cdot \frac{4}{u} = \frac{1}{u} + \frac{2\epsilon(\kappa)}{u}$. That is A^* has a non-negligible advantage $\epsilon'(\kappa) = 2\epsilon(\kappa)/u$ of breaking the cPIR protocol in $t^*(\kappa) = t(\kappa)$ steps. □

4 Evaluation

To show its real-world applicability, we have implemented EPiC in Hadoop's MapReduce framework v1.0.3 [2], and evaluated it on Amazon's public MapReduce cloud [1]. Our EPiC implementation is written in Java, and all cryptographic operations are *unoptimized*, relying on Java's standard BigInteger data type. Still, exponentiation, e.g. $\mathcal{C}^j$, with $j = 15$ and $|\mathcal{C}| \approx 4000$ takes <2 ms on a 1.8 GHz Intel Core i7 laptop, a single addition is not measurable with <1 μs. Figure 1 shows a benchmark of various operations on the ciphertexts using our encryption scheme. In our evaluation, we use security parameters $s_1 = 400$ bits as suggested by Trostle and Parrish [14] for good security, and $s_2 = |r| = 160$ bits. We have implemented a data generator program to randomly generate patient records with m countable fields with size between 4 and 10 bits.

We have evaluated the performance of EPiC by comparing our "Basic" and "GF(2) arithmetized" solutions with a "non-privacy-preserving" solution. Unless otherwise sta-ted, the single/multi-domain size in both "Basic" and "GF(2) arithmetized" solutions is always set to the same value $|\mathcal{D}|$ for comparison. For brief presentation, we use subscript "B" for Basic, and "G" for GF(2) arithmetized approach, e.g., $\|p_B\|$, $\|p_G\|$ indicate the size in bits of p in Basic, GF(2)

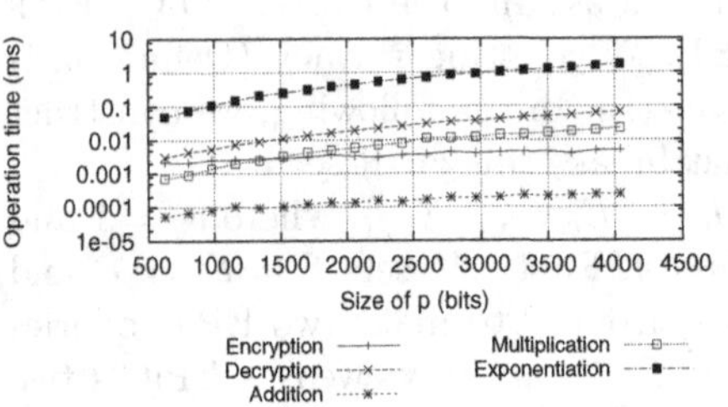

Fig. 1. Computation time on ciphertext.

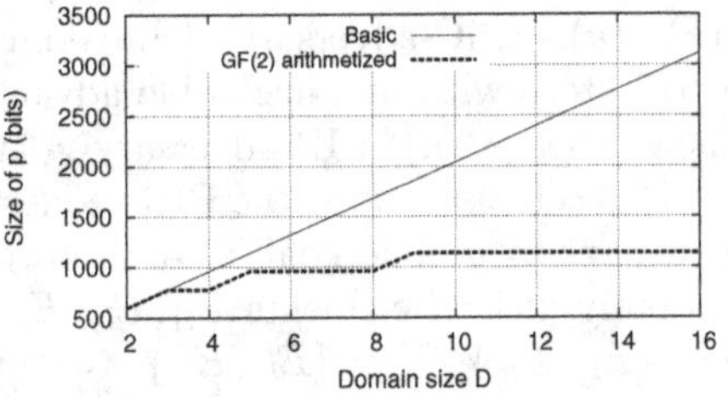

Fig. 2. Size of p depends on size of domain $\mathcal{D}$.

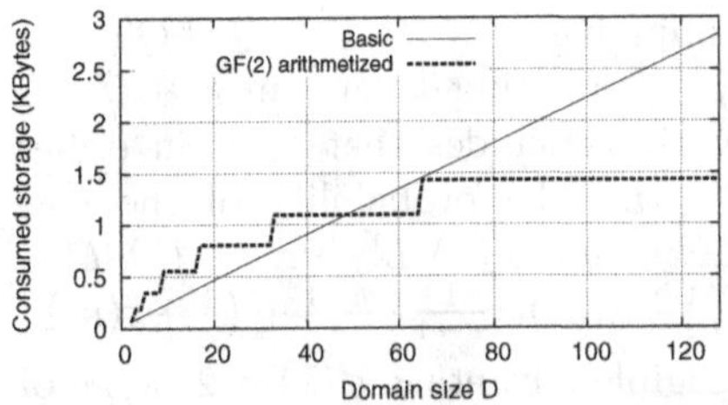

Fig. 3. Consumed storage for each field.

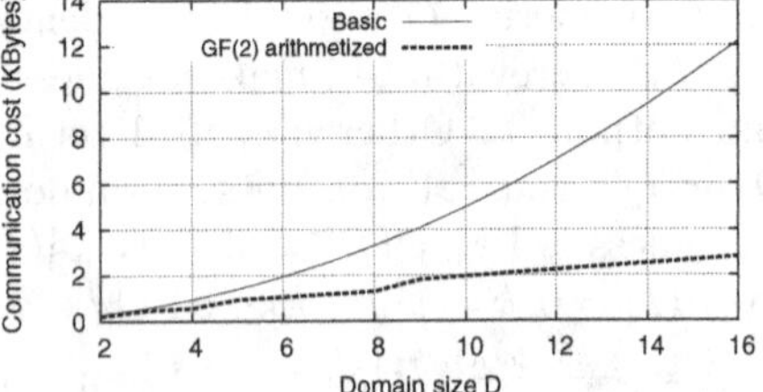

Fig. 4. Communication cost

arithmetized approach respectively. We also set $u = s_1 + \|n\| + \|q\|$, $v = s_2 + \|q\|$ as fixed parameters (with respect to $|\mathcal{D}|$).

Size of Prime p. As discussed in Sect. 3.5, prime q depends only on the number of records n, while prime p also depends on $|\mathcal{D}|$. We show the benefit of the GF(2) arithmetized approach ($m = \|\mathcal{D}\|, |\mathcal{D}_k| = 2$) by demonstrating that a conversion to multiple binary fields reduces $\|p\|$ significantly to $\|p_G\| = u + \|\mathcal{D}\| \cdot v$, while the Basic approach ($m = 1, |\mathcal{D}_1| = |\mathcal{D}|$) requires that $\|p_B\| = u + (|\mathcal{D}| - 1) \cdot v$. Figure 2 shows $\|p\|$'s logarithmic increase with GF(2) arithmetized and linear increase with Basic approach.

Storage Cost. The storage cost depends on the size of the data stored on the cloud, which is determined by the size of p. In Basic approach, a generic field of domain $\mathcal{D}$ requires a storage of $S_B = \|p_B\| = u + (|\mathcal{D}| - 1) \cdot v$ bits. In GF(2) arithmetized approach, the equivalent multiple binary fields requires a storage of $S_G = \|\mathcal{D}\| \cdot \|p_G\| = \|\mathcal{D}\| \cdot (u + \|\mathcal{D}\| \cdot v)$ bits. Again, in Fig. 3, we see a linear increase of storage in Basic, and logarithmic increase in GF(2) arithmetized approach.

User Computation Cost. $\mathcal{U}$ prepares the query in plaintext, which incurs very low computation cost compared to ciphertext operations performed on the cloud. Encrypting one coefficient takes about 1 ms (Fig. 1), resulting in roughly $|\mathcal{D}|$ ms for encrypting all $|\mathcal{D}|$ coefficients of the query, regardless of using Basic or GF(2) arithmetized.

Communication Cost. Due to oblivious counting, user $\mathcal{U}$ prepares and sends all $|\mathcal{D}|$ coefficients corresponding to *all* monomials to the cloud. The total size of the encrypted coefficients is $|\mathcal{D}| \cdot \|p\|$. In Basic approach, the query size is $Q_B = |\mathcal{D}| \cdot \|p_B\| = |\mathcal{D}| \cdot (u + (|\mathcal{D}| - 1) \cdot v)$. In contrast, the GF(2) arithmetized approach reduces to $Q_G = |\mathcal{D}| \cdot \|p_G\| = |\mathcal{D}| \cdot (u + \|\mathcal{D}\| \cdot v)$. For example of a data set containing $n = 10^6$ records with a countable field of domain size $|\mathcal{D}| = 1024$ (i.e., $\|\mathcal{D}\| = 10$), the corresponding query size in each approach is $Q_B = 22.5$ MB, and $Q_G = 280$ KB, respectively.

The answer size (size in bits of the received ciphertext as final sum) depends on the maximum size of the multivariate monomial. The monomial size is determined by the ciphertext size (i.e., $\|p\|$) and the number of performed multiplications, i.e., its multi-degree. Let d denote the maximum multi-degree of monomials, then, $d = |\mathcal{D}|$ in the Basic approach, and $d = \|\mathcal{D}\|$ in the GF(2) arithmetized approach. We have $A_B = |\mathcal{D}| \cdot \|p_B\| = |\mathcal{D}| \cdot (u + (|\mathcal{D}| - 1) \cdot v)$ and $A_G = \|\mathcal{D}\| \cdot \|p_G\| = \|\mathcal{D}\| \cdot (u + \|\mathcal{D}\| \cdot v)$. For example of a data set of $n = 10^6$ records with a countable field of $|\mathcal{D}| = 1024$, the answer size in each approach is $A_B = 22.5$ MB, and $A_G = 2.7$ KB, respectively.

Total transfer cost: The total communication cost, $C = Q + A$, as shown in Fig. 4, is much less in GF(2) arithmetized approach than in Basic approach: $C_B = Q_B + A_B = 2 \cdot |\mathcal{D}| \cdot (u + (|\mathcal{D}| - 1) \cdot v)$, $C_G = Q_G + A_G = (|\mathcal{D}| + \|\mathcal{D}\|) \cdot (u + \|\mathcal{D}\| \cdot v)$.

Cloud Computation. We have evaluated the cloud computation cost for large-scale data sets on Amazon's public cloud. As Amazon imposes an (initial) limit of 20 instances per job, we restrict ourselves to 20 Standard Large On-Demand instances [1]. Each instance comprises 4 2.27 GHz Intel Xeon CPUs and a total of 7.5 GB RAM.

Variable Data Set Size: First, we fix the size of each record to 1 MB. The data set size (x-axis) is varied from 100 GB to 1 TB. We query a countable field of size $|\mathcal{D}| = 16$. Figure 5 shows the average counting time for a MapReduce job on the whole data set of different sizes. The y-axis shows the total time for MapReduce to evaluate the user's query. This is the time that a user has to pay for to Amazon. To put our results into perspective, we not only show the time for both Basic and GF(2) arithmetized approaches, but as well the time a "non-privacy-preserving" counting would take, i.e., the countable field is not encrypted and directly counted. Moreover, we also show the overhead ratio between EPiC's two approaches and non-private counting. The additional overhead introduced by EPiC over non-private counting is less than 20 %. We conjecture that only 20 % overhead/additional cost over non-privacy-preserving counting is acceptable in many real-world situations, rendering EPiC practical.

Variable Record Size: To also evaluate the effect of the size of the records on the general performance, we run the system with a fixed data set size of 50 GB. The record size is changed from 100 KB to 1 MB. Figure 6 shows that, while IO

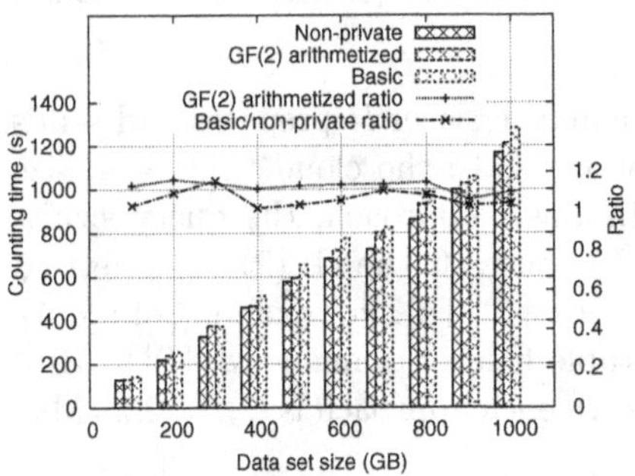

Fig. 5. Counting time vs. data set size. $|\mathcal{D}| = 16$.

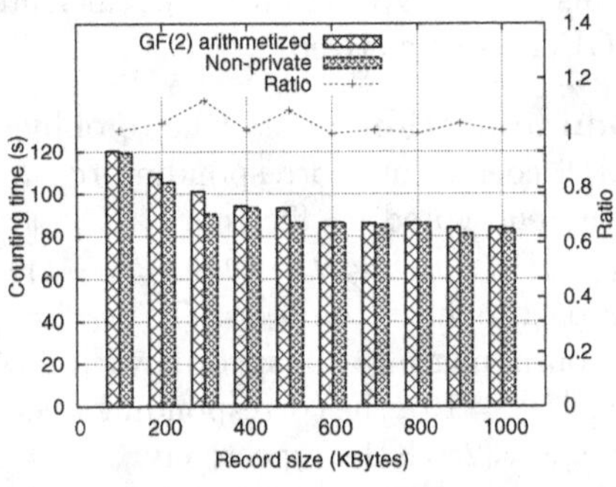

Fig. 6. 50 GB, varying record size. $|\mathcal{D}| = 16$.

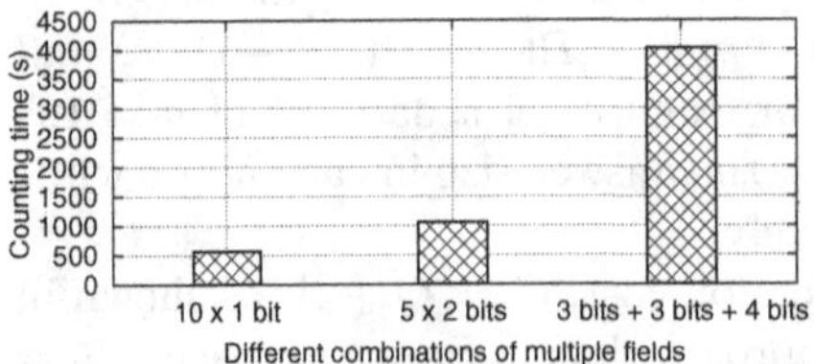

Fig. 7. Effect of different field combinations.

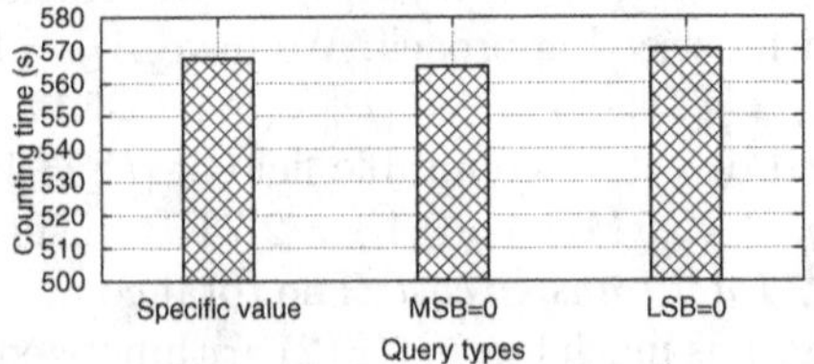

Fig. 8. Different query types on the same data.

time remains unchanged, a higher number of records increases counting time in EPiC. However, the overhead of EPiC is still under 20 % even for small record sizes such as 100 KB compared to non-private counting. That is, EPiC is efficient even for small patient records.

Effect of Multiple Fields: To study the efficiency of transforming a single countable field $\mathcal{D}$ into multiple fields of different size, we conduct an experiment on a data set size of 100 GB. The total domain size is set to $|\mathcal{D}| = 1024$ (10 bits). We compare three cases: (a) transform $\mathcal{D}$ into 10 single binary fields; (b) transform $\mathcal{D}$ into 5 quaternary fields each of 2 bits; (c) transform $\mathcal{D}$ into 3 fields of 3 bits, 3 bits, and 4 bits, respectively. In Fig. 7, we can see that the GF(2) arithmetized approach yields the best performance.

Query Types: Finally, to evaluate the effects of different query types on the performance, we run EPiC with a fixed data set of 100 GB. Total domain size is $|\mathcal{D}| = 1024$. We make 3 different queries: (a) query for a specific value; (b) query for the MSB of the field equal to 0; (c) query for the LSB of the field equal to 0. Figure 8 demonstrates that there is no significant difference in counting time between different queries.

5 Related Work

Protecting privacy of outsourced data and delegated operations in a cloud computing environment is the perfect setting for fully homomorphic encryption. While there is certainly a lot of ongoing research in fully homomorphic encryption (see Vaikuntanathan [15] for an overview), current implementations indicate high storage and computational overhead [9], rendering fully homomorphic encryption impractical for the cloud.

Similar to EPiC, Lauter et al. [11] observe that often weaker "somewhat" homomorphic encryption might be sufficient. Lauter et al. [11]'s scheme is based on a protocol for lattice-based cryptography by Brakerski and Vaikuntanathan [5]. However, for the specific application scenario considered in this paper, EPiC's somewhat homomorphic encryption scheme allows for much faster exponentiation. Superficially, our work bears similarity with the work of Kamara and Raykova [10] that protect polynomial evaluation by randomized reduction techniques. With q being the degree of a polynomial, the user splits each data record into $2 \cdot q + 1$ shares, each of size $2 \cdot q + 1$. Shares are then uploaded and evaluated in parallel, and results are aggregated. However, storage expansion, even for modest values of q, the approach quickly becomes impractical. Also, for different polynomials, the user would need to upload the data multiple times.

Searching on encrypted data has received a lot of attention recently, cf. seminal papers [4,13]. While closely related, it is far from straightforward to adopt these schemes to perform efficient counting in a highly parallel cloud computing, e.g., MapReduce environment. Also notice that, e.g., Boneh et al. [4] rely on the computation of very expensive bilinear pairings for each element of a data set, rendering this approach impractical in a cloud setting. Much research has been done to compute statistics in a privacy-preserving manner using *differential privacy*, see the seminal paper by Dwork [7]. Contrary to the threat model considered in this paper, the adversary in differential privacy research is not the cloud infrastructure, but a curious user querying statistics to learn information about individual entries in a data set. EPiC addresses the opposite problem, where a user does not trust the cloud infrastructure.

6 Conclusion

In this paper, we present EPiC to address a fundamental problem of statistics computation on outsourced data: privacy-preserving pattern counting. EPiC's main idea is to count occurrences of patterns in outsourced data through a privacy-preserving summation of the pattern's indicator-polynomial evaluations over the encrypted dataset records. Using a "somewhat homomorphic" encryption mechanism, the cloud neither learns any information about outsourced data nor about the queries performed. Our implementation and evaluation results for MapReduce running on Amazon's cloud with up to 1 TB of data show only modest overhead compared to non-privacy-preserving counting. This makes EPiC practical in a real-world cloud computing setting today.

Acknowledgement. This work was partially supported by NSF grant 1218197.

References

1. Amazon Elastic MapReduce. http://aws.amazon.com/elasticmapreduce/
2. Apache. Hadoop (2010). http://hadoop.apache.org/
3. Babai, L., Fortnow, L.: Arithmetization: a new method in structural complexity theory. Comput. Complex. **1**(1), 41–66 (1991). ISSN 1016-3328
4. Boneh, D., Di Crescenzo, G., Ostrovsky, R., Persiano, G.: Public key encryption with keyword search. In: Cachin, C., Camenisch, J.L. (eds.) EUROCRYPT 2004. LNCS, vol. 3027, pp. 506–522. Springer, Heidelberg (2004)
5. Brakerski, Z., Vaikuntanathan, V.: Fully homomorphic encryption from Ring-LWE and security for key dependent messages. In: Rogaway, P. (ed.) CRYPTO 2011. LNCS, vol. 6841, pp. 505–524. Springer, Heidelberg (2011)
6. Dean, J., Ghemawat, S.: MapReduce: simplified data processing on large clusters. In: Proceedings of Symposium on Operating System Design and Implementation, San Francisco, USA, pp. 137–150 (2004)
7. Dwork, C.: Differential privacy. In: Bugliesi, M., Preneel, B., Sassone, V., Wegener, I. (eds.) ICALP 2006. LNCS, vol. 4052, pp. 1–12. Springer, Heidelberg (2006)
8. Gentry, C.: Fully homomorphic encryption using ideal lattices. In: STOC 2009, pp. 169–178 (2009)
9. Gentry, C., Halevi, S.: Implementing gentry's fully-homomorphic encryption scheme. In: Paterson, K.G. (ed.) EUROCRYPT 2011. LNCS, vol. 6632, pp. 129–148. Springer, Heidelberg (2011)
10. Kamara, S., Raykova, M.: Parallel homomorphic encryption. In: Adams, A.A., Brenner, M., Smith, M. (eds.) FC 2013. LNCS, vol. 7862, pp. 213–225. Springer, Heidelberg (2013)

11. Lauter, K., Naehrig, N., Vaikuntanathan, V.: Can homomorphic encryption be practical?. In: Proceedings of ACM Workshop on Cloud Computing Security, Chicago, USA (2011)
12. Shamir, A.: IP = PSPACE. J. ACM **39**(4), 869–877 (1992). ISSN 0004-5411
13. Song, D., Wagner, D., Perrig, A.: Practical techniques for searches on encrypted data. In: Proceedings of Symposium on Security and Privacy, Berkeley, USA, pp. 44–55 (2000)
14. Trostle, J., Parrish, A.: Efficient computationally private information retrieval from anonymity or trapdoor groups. In: Burmester, M., Tsudik, G., Magliveras, S., Ilić, I. (eds.) ISC 2010. LNCS, vol. 6531, pp. 114–128. Springer, Heidelberg (2011)
15. Vaikuntanathan, V.: Computing blindfolded: new developments in fully homomorphic encryption. In: FOCS 2011, Washington, DC, USA, pp. 5–16 (2011). ISBN 978-0-7695-4571-4
16. van Dijk, M., Gentry, C., Halevi, S., Vaikuntanathan, V.: Fully homomorphic encryption over the integers. In: Gilbert, H. (ed.) EUROCRYPT 2010. LNCS, vol. 6110, pp. 24–43. Springer, Heidelberg (2010)
17. Vo-Huu, T.D., Blass, E.-O., Noubir, G.: EPiC Source Code. http://www.ccs.neu.edu/home/noubir/projects/epic

A Thrifty Universal Construction

Wang Cheng(✉) and Rachid Guerraoui

École Polytechnique Fédérale de Lausanne, Lausanne, Switzerland
{cheng.wang,rachid.guerraoui}@epfl.ch

Abstract. A universal construction is an algorithm which transforms any sequential implementation of an object into a concurrent implementation of that same object in a linearizable and wait-free manner. Such constructions require underlying low-level universal shared objects such as *compare-and-swap* and *load-linked/store-conditional.*

In this paper, we present the first universal construction that (a) uses exactly one *compare-and-swap* object and (b) has time complexity (number of accesses to low-level shared objects) and memory complexity (size of low-level shared objects) that are both independent of the size of the high-level object to be implemented.

1 Introduction

Algorithms for implementing data structures shared by multi-processes (also called concurrent objects) play a fundamental role in concurrent systems. The traditional approaches to implement shared objects are usually based on locks. However, lock-based techniques have several drawbacks: they induce the possibility of deadlocks and do not tolerate very slow cores.

To address such issues, a number of *non-blocking* implementations have emerged [7,13–15]. In these implementations, the delay of some process could not prevent other processes from making progress. There are mainly two kinds of non-blocking implementations: *lock-free* and *wait-free* [11]. Lock-freedom guarantees system progress: i.e. at least one process can complete any operation in a finite number of steps, while wait-freedom guarantees process progress: i.e. every process can complete any operation in a finite number of steps.

The landmark paper of Herlihy [9] showed a generic mechanism to obtain wait-free objects by introducing the idea of *universal construction*. Specifically, a universal construction can implement any shared object automatically from the corresponding sequential implementation of that very same object. The implementation is expected to be wait-free and *linearizable* [12].

Universal constructions require low-level universal objects to be shared by processes, besides basic read-write atomic objects. Such objects have infinite *consensus number* [9]. The very notation of *consensus number* characterizes the power of a low-level shared object to implement other high-level objects. A shared object is of consensus number n if, together with registers, it could be used to implement any wait-free object in any system of n processes. The strongest type of shared object, called a *universal object*, has infinite consensus

A. Bouajjani and H. Fauconnier (Eds.): NETYS 2015, LNCS 9466, pp. 444–455, 2015.
DOI: 10.1007/978-3-319-26850-7_30

number. It could be used to implement any object in a system of any size. The most common universal objects used in universal algorithms are CAS (*compare-and-swap*) objects and LL/SC (*load-linked/store-conditional*) objects. Although these objects are supported in several systems, it is highly desirable to access them as little as possible for they induce a considerable access time.

Most of existing universal constructions copy the entire state of the high-level object for applying local operations, and update the high-level object with local copies. For large shared objects, copying might be problematic. In this paper we ask whether it is possible to devise a universal construction using a small number of low-level universal objects and without copying the entire state.

We answer this question in the affirmative. We present a thrifty universal construction that (a) uses exactly one *compare-and-swap* object and (b) has time complexity (number of accesses to low-level shared objects) and memory complexity (size of low-level shared objects) that are both independent of the size of the high-level object to be implemented. Our construction maintains a local copy of the high-level object for every process. It exploits the least number (only one CAS) of universal shared objects to synchronize all the processes. We assume practical constraints on the size of shared object, i.e. each underlying shared object could only hold a small amount of information like names of operations, arguments of operations plus a sequential number. The size of underlying low-level objects (registers and one CAS) is independent of the size of the high-level object.

The rest of the paper is organized as follows. After the model section, a lock-free algorithm is presented to illustrate the basic ideas in Sect. 3. Then we present our wait-free construction in Sect. 4 based on the lock-free construction. In Sect. 5, the complexity of our construction is analyzed.

Related Work. Herlihy's original approach in [9,10] copies the entire state of the high-level object. Most universal constructions presented in the past do so: these include GroupUpdate [1], FlatCombining [8], RedBlue [5] and Sim [6]. These algorithms assume that a low-level object is large enough to store an entire object. If we rule out this possibility and let the size of the underlying low-level shared objects be independent of the size of the high-level object, then the shared-access complexity of such algorithm would depend on the size of the high-level object. This is not practical if the size of the high-level object is big.

Anderson and Moir [3] suggest to view the high-level object as a number of blocks. When a process wants to change a block, it only needs to make a local copy of that block instead of the entire state. Barnes [4] presents another approach to handle large objects. In the construction of [4], when a process wants to apply an operation on a high-level object, it only copies the variables it needs to access into its local memory. The complexity of these algorithms improves upon the full copy approach, but still depends on the size of the high-level object. Meanwhile, in order to update blocks and variables linearizably, a universal object for each block and variable is necessary. Therefore, the number of universal objects in these algorithms also depends on the size of the high-level object.

2 Model and Definitions

We consider the standard model of asynchronous shared memory machines of [10]. We consider an asynchronous system of n processes with identifier $\{0, 1, \ldots, n-1\}$ that communicate through accessing shared objects. There are only two primitive shared objects considered in our system: the *atomic* register and the CAS (*compare-and-swap*) object. An atomic register stores a value and supports atomic *read* and *write* operations. Following the convention in programming languages, we use access and assignment to replace *read* and *write* in our pseudo code. A CAS object supports a special atomic operation denoted CAS.*cas* in addition to the atomic *read*. CAS.*cas* takes two value: v_{old} and v_{new}. If the CAS's current value is equal to v_{old}, it is replaced by v_{new}; otherwise is unchanged. The return of the operation CAS.cas($v_{\text{old}}, v_{\text{new}}$) is a boolean value indicating whether the value of the CAS is changed or not.

We constraint the size of the underlying shared objects (registers and CAS) to be independent of the size of the high-level object. Shared objects can only hold a small amount of information like names and arguments of operations along with a sequence number. In addition, every process has a private local memory. We limit the system to have only one CAS object. An implementation of a high-level object from these primitive objects provides an algorithm for each process to simulate every operation of the high-level object. In a universal construction, each process has a function called *Apply(invoc)* to perform an operation on the given data structure modeling the high-level object. We assume that any number of processes may experience *crash failures*, i.e., they may stop running at any unpredictable time.

3 Thrifty Lock-Free Construction

We first present in this section a lock-free algorithm (denoted TLC) using only one CAS. In the algorithm each process has a local copy of the high-level object and applies the same invocations in the same order as the other processes. The details are as follows.

3.1 Algorithm Description

Our implementation, called Thrifty Lock-free Construction (TLC), uses a shared array *History* to synchronize all the processes. *History* represents the sequential order of all the invocations that every process should follow. Initially, each item of *History* is $\perp$ and each item will be updated to a unique invocation in the future. The index of every item in this array is called a *sequential number*. The latest sequential number is the largest index before which all the items of *History* are non-empty. When process p wants to apply an invocation to the high-level object, p tries to insert the invocation into *History* with index equal to the latest sequential number. After this, the invocation could be noticed by other processes. If this insertion into *History* is total-ordered, then linearizability

Algorithm 1. Thrifty Lock-free Construction (TLC)

```
Shared Objects :
    CAS: compare-and-swap object initialized to -1
    History: an array with all items initialized to ⊥. It is used to contain all
    the invocations and the order of items in the array represents the sequential
    order of all invocations
    SubHistory: n arrays with all of the items are initialized to ⊥.
    SubHistory[i] contains the history invocations of process i
end
Local Objects :
    ProcessId: the unique id of the process (among {0, ..., n − 1})
    LocalCopy: local copy of target object
    SeqLocation: an index in History before which all the invocations have
    been executed, initialized to 0
end
                          /* code for process p */
Function apply(invoc)
    while true do
        /* run all recent invocations first                          */
        currentTime = CAS.read()
        round, pid, flag = decode(currentTime)        /* see Algorithm 2 */
        for k ∈ [SeqLocation, round) do
            if History[k] ≠ Null then
                output = LocalCopy.run(History[k])
                if History[k] = invoc then return output
            end
        end
        SeqLocation = round

        if flag = PREPARED then                 /* help pending process */
            History[round] = SubHistory[pid][round]
            CAS.cas(currentTime, currentTime+n)  /* change from PREPARED
            to FINISHED */
        else if flag = FINISHED then              /* race for next round */
            round = round + 1
            nextSeqTime = 2 · round · n + processId
            SubHistory[ProcessId][round] = invoc
            if CAS.cas(currentTime, nextSeqTime) then
                History[round] = SubHistory[ProcessId][round]
                CAS.cas(nextSeqTime, nextSeqTime+n)
            end
        end
    end
end
```

follows naturally. However such total-ordered insertion could not be acquired with only atomic registers. In TLC, we exploit the power of a single CAS to update the items of *History* atomically.

First, the value of the CAS contains the information of the latest sequential number. Each process that intends to apply an invocation first should acquire the next sequential number. This is done by applying a CAS.cas invocation (Line 30). If the CAS.cas returns true, the process succeeds in acquiring the next sequential number and would try to insert its invocation into *History* with respect to the sequential number (Line 31). However this is not enough for a process p to insert its invocation into the *History* linearizably because p may delay between Line 30 and Line 31. To address this problem, a helping mechanism is introduced. Each time p succeeds in acquiring the next sequential number, it not only updates the sequential number information of the CAS, it also puts its identifier inside the CAS so that other processes could know which process to help.

There are two different phases for a process to apply an invocation. The first phase is called *prepare phase*. In this phase, the processes first race for the next sequential number in Line 30. Then the process that has gotten the next sequential number copies its invocation into array *SubHistory* in Line 29 so that other processes could read in the second phase. When this first phase completes, we say that the status of the system is PREPARED. The second phase, denoted as *help phase*, is to copy the invocation of the pending process into array *History*. This phase may be done by the process which originally wants to apply the invocation (Line 31), or it could be done by other processes for helping (Line 24). When this phase completes, we say that the status of the system is FINISHED. When the system is in FINISHED status, a new invocation could be applied.

The value of the CAS has three pieces of information: (1) the latest sequential number, (2) the identifier of the process that owns the sequential number, (3) the status of the system which can be either PREPARED or FINISHED. All of this information is encoded into an integer. Suppose the sequential number is k and the process owning the sequential number is i. If the status is PREPARED, then the encoded value is $2kn+i$. Otherwise if the status is FINISHED, then the encoded value is $(2k+1)n+i$. The decode function is as in Algorithm 2. Note that this encode method and decode function are used in wait-free construction as well.

Algorithm 2. Decode function

```
Function decode(t)
    if t = 2kn + i then
        return (k, i, PREPARED)
    else if t = (2k + 1)n + i then
        return (k, i, FINISHED)
    end
end
```

In TLC, the initial value of CAS is −1, which means the information is encode with a value of sequential number as −1 and FINISHED status. So all the processes start to race for round 0 with sequential number 0 at the beginning. If the sequential number encoded in CAS is k, then we say the system is in *round k*.

3.2 Correctness

We prove that the system proceeds as the sequential number in the CAS increases and there is a unique invocation corresponding to each sequential number.

Lemma 1. *The system proceeds round by round and the sequential number in CAS increases by* 1 *for each round.*

Proof. Suppose the system is in a particular round k, i.e. the sequential number encoded in CAS is k. We show the system will make progress into round $k+1$. First, for this particular round, there must be a process p that gets the corresponding sequential number *round* in Line 30 and tries to assign its value to History[k] in Line 31. This means that the *prepare phase* will complete eventually and the system will turn to the *help phase*. In the *help phase*, every process writes an invocation into History[k] and then update the system to FINISHED status (see Line 24 and its following line). So the *help phase* will complete eventually and system will proceed to the next round with sequential number increased by 1. □

Lemma 2. *The algorithm TLC is lock-free.*

Proof. From the lemma above, the system always makes progress. Hence, it is lock-free. □

Lemma 3. *For each round k, there is one and only one invocation assigned to History[k].*

Proof. Since the system proceeds round by round, for each round k, History[k] must be updated in Line 24. However, every process may write into History[k] in Line 30 possibly due to the delay of p. Suppose History[k] is assigned a value v for the first time for round k. Before this assignment to History[k], SubHistory[p][k] must already be assigned v and is only assigned for once in the whole execution in Line 29. In the following steps, every write into History[k] (by p in line B or other helping processes in line 24) is a copy of SubHistory[p][k]. Since SubHistory[k] is written only once, the lemma is proved. □

Lemma 4. *All the processes run the invocations in the same order as they appear in the array History.*

Proof. For each round, if p does not get the sequential number, p will load invocations one by one from History and apply them. If p gets sequential number in round k, p's invocation will be written into History[k]. All the processes will apply this invocation as the k-th invocation. So all the processes's execution histories are the same as array *History*. □

Lemma 5. *Every invocation is assigned at most once into array History.*

Proof. Suppose p_i has an invocation assigned to array *History*. Then p_i must get the corresponding sequential number in Line 30. However, in the if-block starting from Line 30, p_i executes the invocation and returns the output. After the function returns, p_i will not try to race a sequential number for this invocation any more. So every invocation is assigned at most once into array *History*. □

Lemma 6. *The algorithm TLC is linearizable.*

Proof. By the above lemmas, every process has the same local execution history. Hence, linearizability is immediate and the linearizable point for a invocation is the sequential number acquired for the invocation. □

4 Thrifty Universal Construction

In this section, we present a universal construction based on the previous lock-free implementation. The underlying idea is to help any pending process get a sequential number for its pending invocation, while in the previous section the processes only help pending processes which have already gained sequential numbers to announce the corresponding pending invocations.

4.1 Algorithm Description

This universal algorithm denoted TUC has the same framework as TLC in the previous section. TUC also uses a shared array *History* to synchronize all the processes and the index of *History* is the sequential order of invocations. So in this section we mainly describe the significant ideas in TUC that are different from TLC.

In order to achieve wait-freedom, every process should make progress. When a process p wants to apply an invocation, p first registers its invocation in a shared register (Line 10,11) so that other processes could notice. These registered and incomplete invocations are called *pending invocations*. In each round, every process tries to apply the pending invocations in the same order as the process identifier. More specifically, if in one round the invocation of process with identifier i is executed, then in the next round every process tries to apply the invocation of process with identifier $i+1$, then $i+2$ and so on. Processes search for pending invocations by looping through the invocations pool (array *InvocationList*) for all the processes, which guarantees that every pending invocation could be applied.

Therefore, the array *InvocationList* shared as pending invocations pool is significant to guarantee wait-freedom. In order that other processes could load correct pending invocations from *InvocationList*, each process should maintain an index (*PendingIndex* in the algorithm) that indicates the location of latest invocation in array *InvocationList*. When a process wants to apply an invocation, it first increases its pending index by 1 and then writes its invocation into *invocationList* with the new pending index.

Algorithm 3. Thrifty Universal Construction (TUC)

```
Shared Objects :
    CAS, History, SubHistory: as in the lock-free construction - Algorithm 1
    InvocationList: n arrays each of which stores invocations of one process
    PendingIndex: n items array to store the index of pending invocations in
    InvocationList
end
Local Objects :
    ProcessId, LocalCopy, SeqLocation: as in the lock-free construction - Algorithm 1
end
                                   /* code for process p */
Function apply(invoc)
    PendingIndex[ProcessId] = PendingIndex[ProcessId]+1
    InvocationList[ProcessId][PendingIndex[ProcessId]] = invoc
    while true do
        /* run all recent invocations first                                  */
        currentTime = CAS.read()
        round, pid, flag = decode(currentTime)            /* see Algorithm 2 */
        for k ∈ [SeqLocation, round) do
            if History[k] ≠ Null then
                output = LocalCopy.run(History[k])
                if History[k] = invoc then return output
            end
        end
        SeqLocation = round

        if flag = PREPARED then                     /* help pending process */
            invocationIndex, History[round] = SubHistory[pid][round]
            InvocationList[pid][invocationIndex] = Null
            CAS.cas(currentTime, currentTime+n)   /* change from PREPARED to FINISHED
            */
        else if flag = FINISHED then                 /* race for next round */
            helpId = pid + 1
            while true do                        /* select a process to help */
                helpIndex = PendingIndex[helpId]
                if InvocationList[helpId][helpIndex] ≠ Null then
                    break while
                else
                    helpId = helpId + 1 mod n
                end
            end
            round = round + 1
            nextSeqTime = 2 · round · n + helpId
            SubHistory[helpId][round]= (helpIndex, InvocationList[helpId][helpIndex])
            if CAS.cas(currentTime, nextSeqTime) then
                invocationIndex, History[round] = SubHistory[helpId][round]
                InvocationList[helpId][invocationIndex] = Null
                CAS.cas(currentTime, currentTime+n)        /* change from PREPARED to
                FINISHED */
            end
        end
    end
end
```

4.2 Correctness

The steps of the proofs are similar to those in the previous section. The details of each proof should however be reconsidered because of the more complicated helping mechanism.

Lemma 7. *The system proceeds round by round and the sequential number increases by* 1 *for each round.*

Proof. In the beginning of each round i, the processes try to find a process to help (while loop from Line 29) and assign the latest sequential number to the process (Line 40). Since every pending process has one pending invocation in the pool *InvocationList*, the pool is not empty. There must be a process p that succeeds in finding one pending invocation and getting the current sequential number for it. Then the system enters the *help phase* of round i. In *help phase*, every process writes an invocation into History[round] and sets the corresponding pendingInvocation as empty before the system is updated to FINISHED status (Line 24 and its following two lines). So the *help phase* will complete eventually and system will proceed to the next round with sequential number increased by 1 (Line 40). □

Lemma 8. *For each round k, there is one and only one invocation assigned to History[k].*

Proof. As in Lemma 3, we only need to show that for round k, History[k] is assigned a unique value. History[k] is updated in Line 41 and Line 24 with value from SubHistory[helpId][k]. Thus we only need to show the non-empty value SubHistory[helpId][k] is unique. Again, SubHistory[helpId][k] is determined by (helpIndex, InvocationList[helpId][helpIndex]). In the algorithm, InvocationList[helpId][helpIndex] is only updated to a non-empty value once by process with identifier helpId in Line 11, so it is unique. The lemma follows. □

Lemma 9. *All the processes run the invocations in the same order as they appears in array History.*

Proof. As we can see from the algorithm, processes only execute an invocation in Line 18 and the invocation to apply comes exactly from array *History*. Therefore this lemma follows. □

Lemma 10. *Every invocation is assigned exactly once into array History.*

Proof. As the value of helpId loops among all the processes, every process with pending invocation will be helped in some round. This means that every invocation will be assigned a sequential number by Line 40 and eventually the invocation will be assigned to array History in Line 41 or Line 24. □

Lemma 11. *The algorithm TUC is linearizable and wait-free.*

Proof. Since every process has the same execution history and every invocation is executed exactly once, the algorithm is linearizable and wait-free. □

5 Complexity

It is common to consider the shared-access time complexity of shared object implementations. In the following, we analyze this shared-access time complexity and show that it is independent of the size of the high-level object.

First we introduce an important notation to measure this complexity. Suppose a process p wants to apply an invocation I in TUC. Let us say the last invocation p applied has index k_1 in *History*, and the sequential number in the CAS is k_2 when p writes I into array *InocationList*. The difference between k_1 and k_2 is the delay between p and the system corresponding to I, denoted by d_I, i.e. $d_I = k_2 - k_1$.

Lemma 12. *For any invocation I of process p, the delay d_I is independent of the size of the high-level object.*

Proof. Suppose k_1, k_2 and d_I as above. In our universal construction, all the processes apply the same invocations from the array *History*. Hence the progress of process p depends on how fast p could access these invocations and how many shared objects p needs to copy. Since we do not copy the entire object, the progress of process p does not relate to the size of the high-level object. The number k_1 represents the progress of process p, and the number k_2 depends on how fast p could access the shared memory. Hence both k_1 and k_2 are independent of the size of the high-level object. The lemma follows.

Lemma 13. *Suppose p wants to apply invocation I. The shared-access time complexity of our universal construction is $O(d_I + n)$, where d_I is the delay between p and the system as defined above.*

Proof. Suppose k_1, k_2 and d_I as above. In order to apply invocation I, p first needs to apply all the invocations in *History* with index from k_1 to k_2. This would cost d_I shared-accesses.

In our universal algorithm, every process tries to help other processes in the same order of the identifier of the processes. In every next round the helping process identifier is increased by at least one. Therefore within at most n increments every process will be helped. Suppose I was inserted into *History* with index k_3, then $k_3 - k_2 \leq n$. Take the race in Line 40 into account, p needs another at most $2(k_3 - k_2) \leq 2n$ share-access to apply I locally. Therefore the total share-access is less than $d_I + 2n$, i.e. $O(d_I + n)$. □

The delay for an individual process and system are not the same. Suppose the fastest process for shared-access is p_f. We say a process is fast if its speed of shared-access is only constant time slower than p_f. For a fast process p, there are $O(n)$ invocations from other processes between p's every two successive invocations. So, for every fast process, the shared-access complexity is $O(n)$.

6 Concluding Remarks

6.1 Optimizations

The first optimization is inspired by the following observation: if some processes are faster in performing their local computation and accessing the shared-objects then they could announce their invocation outputs so that other processes could get the outputs even before their own local applications of the invocations. In order to implement this optimization, we only need to add n shared arrays. Each array is a pool to store the outputs of all invocations of a particular process. A slower process could get the output earlier by just checking its corresponding output pool. This checking could be done in parallel with function application. The optimization is wait-free because it is just an extension to the algorithms in Sects. 3 and 4 without any modification of the existing data structure. As this optimization is easy to implement, we omit it in the pseudo code to keep the algorithm simple to demonstrate the main idea.

The second optimization is related to garbage collection. It follows from the following observation. The item of history with small sequential number could be discarded if all of the processes have large sequential numbers. For example, if all processes have executed the invocation with sequential number k then all the items in the arrays *History*, *SubHistory* with indexes less than k are not useful any more. The optimization is to replace arrays with dynamic linked lists in the construction. And each process has a shared register storing its current sequential number and other processes can only read the register. By reading these registers, a process could predict whether an item in array History is read by all processes. If all processes have read one item in *History*, then it is safe to remove that item from the corresponding linked list.

6.2 Lock-Freedom vs Wait-Freedom

In this paper, we present two algorithms: the first one is lock-free whereas the second one is wait-free. The lock-free construction is much simpler than the wait-free one. In fact, the lock-free algorithm was presented not only for pedagogical purposes. It does constitute in itself an appealing practical solution. Recently, Herlihy and Shavit [11] suggested a surprising property of lock-free algorithms: in practice, they often behave as if they are wait-free. Specifically, the impact of worst-case execution is negligible. Later Alistarh, Hillel and Shavit [2] showed that a general class of lock-free algorithms under a stochastic scheduler is wait-free with probability 1. Our lock-free construction falls into the class of algorithms discussed in [2], so it is a wait-free construction with probability 1.

References

1. Afek, Y., Dauber, D., Touitou, D.: Wait-free made fast. In: Proceedings of the Twenty-seventh Annual ACM Symposium on Theory of Computing. pp. 538–547. ACM (1995)

2. Alistarh, D., Censor-Hillel, K., Shavit, N.: Are lock-free concurrent algorithms practically wait-free? In: Proceedings of the 46th Annual ACM Symposium on Theory of Computing. pp. 714–723. ACM (2014)
3. Anderson, J.H., Moir, M.: Universal constructions for large objects. IEEE Trans. Parallel Distrib. Syst. **10**(12), 1317–1332 (1999)
4. Barnes, G.: A method for implementing lock-free shared-data structures. In: Proceedings of the Fifth Annual ACM Symposium on Parallel Algorithms and Architectures. pp. 261–270. ACM (1993)
5. Fatourou, P., Kallimanis, N.D.: The redblue adaptive universal constructions. In: Keidar, I. (ed.) DISC 2009. LNCS, vol. 5805, pp. 127–141. Springer, Heidelberg (2009)
6. Fatourou, P., Kallimanis, N.D.: A highly-efficient wait-free universal construction. In: Proceedings of the Twenty-third Annual ACM Symposium on Parallelism in Algorithms and Architectures. pp. 325–334. ACM (2011)
7. Fraser, K.: Practical lock-freedom. Ph.D. thesis, University of Cambridge (2004)
8. Hendler, D., Incze, I., Shavit, N., Tzafrir, M.: Flat combining and the synchronization-parallelism tradeoff. In: Proceedings of the 22nd ACM Symposium on Parallelism in Algorithms and Architectures. pp. 355–364. ACM (2010)
9. Herlihy, M.: Wait-free synchronization. ACM Trans. Program. Lang. Syst. (TOPLAS) **13**(1), 124–149 (1991)
10. Herlihy, M.: A methodology for implementing highly concurrent data objects. ACM Trans. Program. Lang. Syst. (TOPLAS) **15**(5), 745–770 (1993)
11. Herlihy, M., Shavit, N.: On the nature of progress. In: Fernàndez Anta, A., Lipari, G., Roy, M. (eds.) OPODIS 2011. LNCS, vol. 7109, pp. 313–328. Springer, Heidelberg (2011)
12. Herlihy, M.P., Wing, J.M.: Axioms for concurrent objects. In: Proceedings of the 14th ACM SIGACT-SIGPLAN Symposium on Principles of Programming Languages. pp. 13–26. ACM (1987)
13. Michael, M.M.: High performance dynamic lock-free hash tables and list-based sets. In: Proceedings of the Fourteenth Annual ACM Symposium on Parallel Algorithms and Architectures. pp. 73–82. ACM (2002)
14. Moir, M.: Practical implementations of non-blocking synchronization primitives. In: Proceedings of the Sixteenth Annual ACM Symposium on Principles of Distributed Computing. pp. 219–228. ACM (1997)
15. Valois, J.D.: Lock-free linked lists using compare-and-swap. In: Proceedings of the Fourteenth Annual ACM Symposium on Principles of Distributed Computing. pp. 214–222. ACM (1995)

Knowledgeable Chunking

Bertil Chapuis(✉) and Benoît Garbinato

University of Lausanne, Lausanne, Switzerland
{bertil.chapuis,benoit.garbinato}@unil.ch

Abstract. Chunking algorithms are often used by storage solutions in order to factorize and deduplicate data. Such algorithms make the assumption that the consecutive versions of a file share a lot of similarities. Unfortunately, file formats often use compression algorithms and minor changes have the potential to completely reorganize the internal layout of a file. In consequence, chunking algorithms become less efficient in factorizing data. In this paper, we evaluate content-defined chunking with file formats that use data compression. We show how content-defined chunking algorithms can take the file format into account. Finally, we demonstrate that adding file format knowledge to a popular chunking algorithm significantly improves its performance.

1 Introduction

When synchronizing data, minimizing the amount of transferred information is the main challenge. Similarly, when storing data, reducing the amount of storage is usually the primary objective. If files are versioned, this becomes even more important, because two successive revisions of the same file are often sharing most of their content. For these reasons, content-defined chunking algorithms (CDC) became very popular. Such algorithms split long sequences of bytes into several chunks. Since cryptographic hash functions are assumed to be good enough to avoid collisions, the hash signatures of the chunks act as unique identifiers or access keys. Using these signatures, it becomes straightforward to verify if a chunk has already been stored or transferred in order to reduce storage requirements or network bandwidth. In contrast to common compression algorithms, which make a space time tradeoff, CDC algorithms factorize data without sacrificing too much computing time. For example, the popularity of Dropbox relies on a very basic fixed size chunking algorithm [2]. This chunking algorithm is not making a space-time tradeoff but the fact that chunks are stored only once already brings a factorization benefit similar to compression. This paper starts by reminding the major contributions made in the area of content-defined chunking. Then, we evaluate two well-known algorithms against the consecutive versions of a file whose format uses compression. Finally, we show that inserting file format knowledge in a popular chunking algorithm significantly improves its performances in term of deduplication.

A. Bouajjani and H. Fauconnier (Eds.): NETYS 2015, LNCS 9466, pp. 456–460, 2015.
DOI: 10.1007/978-3-319-26850-7_31

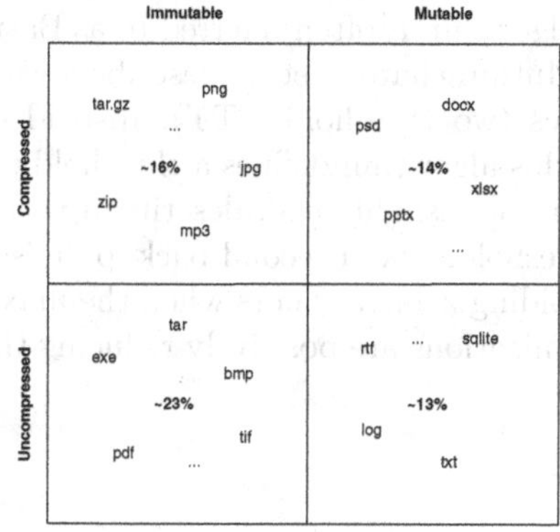

Fig. 1. File format classification

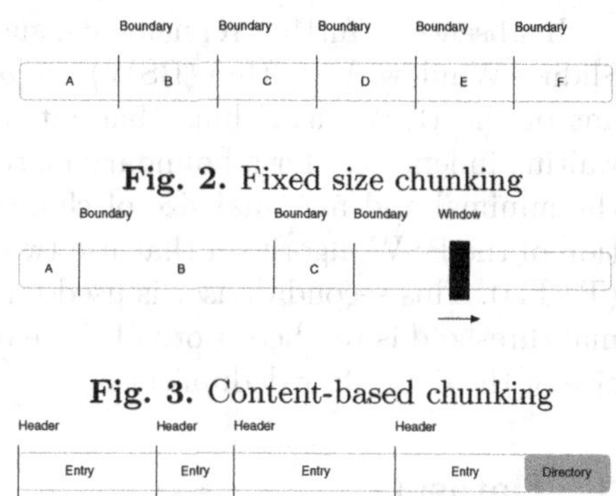

Fig. 2. Fixed size chunking

Fig. 3. Content-based chunking

Fig. 4. Zip entries and headers

2 Related Work

Data deduplication can be considered as a special form of data compression: instead of trading space for time in order to find very fine grained redundancies, deduplication aims at avoiding redundancies at a coarser scale. In the following, we first provide an architectural overview of a typical storage solution that use chunking and then we describe some of the most common chunking algorithms.

A recent study clearly demonstrates the significant effect of deduplication on storage requirements [4]. At the heart of such storage systems, we find chunking algorithms, which split files into sub-parts. A common approach for integrating deduplication in storage systems consists in hashing the content of chunks and using the resulting hash signatures as unique access keys. This simple scheme makes it possible to store and transmit data only once: if the same content is stored elsewhere in the system, it will have the same access key. Venti, from Bell Labs, was one of the first storage solution that use CDC for reducing storage requirements [6]. The RSync algorithm [8] and the Low Bandwidth network File System (LBFS) clearly show the effect of CDC on network bandwidth [5].

Figure 2 illustrates a fixed size chunking (FSC) algorithm that comes with a major drawback: when bytes are added at the beginning of a file, all the following chunk boundaries are shifted. To solve this issue, Content-Defined Chunking (CDC) algorithms heavily rely on rolling hash functions such as Rabin-Karp [7]. As illustrated in Fig. 3, the idea is to create a fixed size sliding window, depicted here by a black box. The window slides on the byte sequence F to be chunked (typically a file), one byte after the other. At each step, the hash signature of the window is computed using the previous sum and the incoming byte. As soon as the hash of the window matches a boundary pattern, a chunk is created. Now, if we repeat the same process on some other byte sequence F', a modified version of F, we understand that unlike FSC, CDC can identify chunk boundaries that resists to modifications anywhere in the byte sequence.

In absence of further refinements, such algorithm is often referred to as Basic Sliding Window Algorithm (BSW). In [5], Muthitacharoen et al. describe a variant of the BSW algorithms that introduces two thresholds (TT). Instead of waiting indefinitely for a boundary match, this algorithm defines a threshold for the minimal and maximal size of chunks. In [3], Eshghi et al. describe a variation of the BSW algorithm that use two thresholds and a second backup divisor (TTTD). This second divisor is used for avoiding arbitrary cuts when the maximal threshold is reached. Both of these optimizations are positively reducing the size of the data after deduplication.

3 Dataset

Today, most studies include a limited number of snapshots of data. In this context, as demonstrated in [4], hashing the content of files can capture a large part of the factorization benefit. However, if snapshots were taken continuously each time a change occurs in the system, the benefits brought by CDC would probably be much greater.

To highlight this fact, Fig. 1 displays statistics about the files stored in the home directories of our faculty. Immutable and compressed files ($\sim$ 16 %) as well as immutable and uncompressed files ($\sim$ 23 %) can efficiently be factorized without chunking algorithms since such content only has few versions. Mutable and uncompressed files ($\sim$ 13 %) are ideally suited for chunking algorithms since their content is mutating and similarities exit between versions. Compressed and mutable files ($\sim$ 14 %) mutate but differ since the compression algorithm affect the internal layout of the file, making chunking less efficient. These statistics were gathered using one snapshot and some files do not have extensions ($\sim$ 6 %) or have extensions we did not categorized ($\sim$ 25 %). Assuming a system that archive all changes that occur on a hard drive, we quickly realize that the mutable data may grow very quickly, well beyond the aforementioned proportions.

For this reason, snapshots of data do not constitute a suitable dataset for our experiment. In consequence, we let a robot, let's call him Andrew, build our experimental dataset on the basis of its memoirs [1]. The robot tells the story paragraph after paragraph and makes a backup of the document after each addition. In order to make the biography more appealing, the robot adds pictures to the document every 50 paragraphs. The versions are saved in the docx file format which is actually a zip archive with deflate compression. The resulting dataset includes 2656 versions of a word document, the latest version containing 77'847 words and 54 jpeg images.

4 Experiment

Since common chunking algorithms loose their efficiency with compressed and mutable files, we target this specific category. Most file formats include a form of object models. As shown in Fig. 4, zip files prefix zip entries, which correspond to archived files, with a specific header. PDF files also prefix text, paragraphs and images with specific headers. Such headers are not recognized by chunking algorithms, but carry interesting information. For example, if the archive contains an image, this data could easily be located making it possible to find immutable data inside mutable documents. Furthermore, in case of minor modifications, the internal layout of a compressed file may be partially preserved. As a consequence, giving file format knowledge to the chunking algorithm may help in finding similarities much more efficiently. To confirm our assumptions, we give file format knowledge to the TTTD algorithms. The resulting algorithm, called KTTTD, defines chunk boundaries by first looking for object model prefixes and then for content-defined boundaries. This approach has a minimal impact on the performances of the algorithm, since files still need to be parsed only once.

5 Results

In order to measure the impact of file format knowledge, we compared KTTTD with TT and TTTD, using two configurations based on the parameters described in [3]. The first configuration generates small chunks with an average size of 2 KB, a minimum threshold of 928 bytes and a maximum threshold of 5'649 bytes. The second configuration generates larger chunks. In this case, they have an average size of 32 KB, a minimum threshold of 14'850 bytes and a maximum threshold of 45'197 bytes. Since the files generated for our experiment remains quite small (the largest of our file is approximately 260 KB), such a configuration gives the opportunity to the standard content-based algorithms to compete with the one that include file format knowledge. A larger average size for chunks would not gives many opportunities for data deduplication.

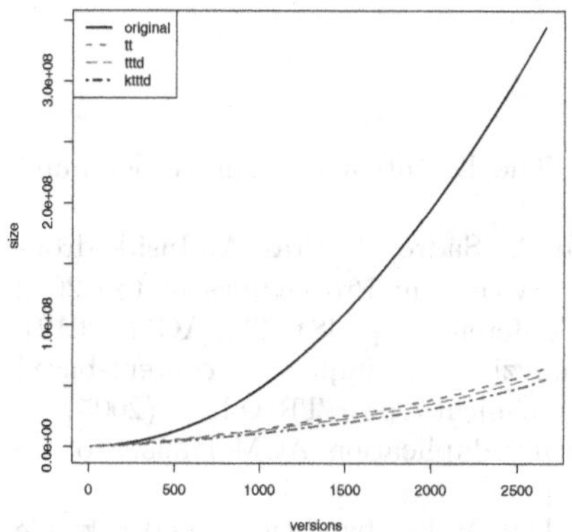

Fig. 5. 2 kb average chunk size

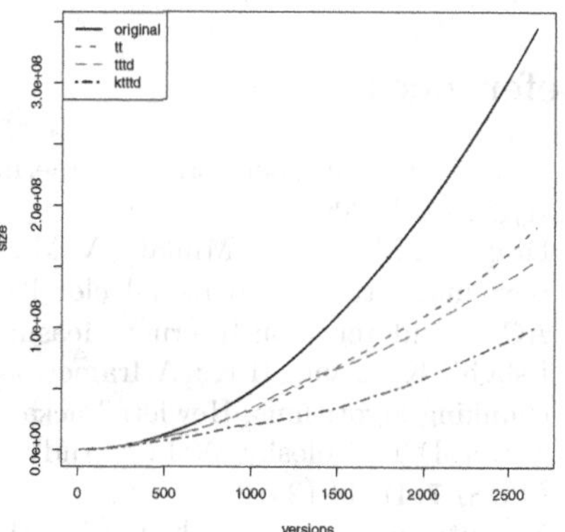

Fig. 6. 32 kb average chunk size

Our setup handles the documents of our dataset incrementally and store the resulting metadata and chunks in a data store. After each addition, we measure the size of the data store in order to highlight how it evolves. Figure 5 shows the results obtained with the first configuration. In this context, the three algorithms have almost similar performances. The deduplication is quite impressive with a resulting chunk store that weights approximately 16 % of the original data. While very thigh, the gain of KTTTD over TTTD is approximately 8 %, which is small but not negligible since it surpasses the gain of TTTD over TT, which is roughly 6 %. Figure 6 presents the results obtained with the second configuration. With bigger chunks, the gain brought by file format knowledge becomes much more impressive. TT and TTTD have similar performances, which is not surprising since the internal layout of the files can potentially changes a lot because of the compression. It tends to confirm the results obtained with random data in [3]. However, KTTTD performs much better and seems to successfully extract immutable data from the docx files. The average gain of KTTTD over TTTD is approximately 35 %, which is far from being negligible.

6 Conclusions

Given that a significant portion of data is mutable and compressed, systematically storing every version of files that use compression have an important cost in term of storage. Unfortunately, content-defined chunking algorithms perform poorly with such data. To address this problem, we proposed a solution that adds file format knowledge to CDC algorithms. We demonstrated the gain brought by this addition in the context of the docx file format, which rely on the zip specification and use compression. Our work will now consist in validating our finding against real world datasets and finding ways to detect the object models introduced by file formats automatically. Some lessons could also be learned from this study that may help in devising better archival formats that takes the requirements of modern storage solutions into account.

References

1. Asimov, I., Silverberg, R., Timmerman, H.: The Bicentennial Man. Millennium, Hyderabad (2000)
2. Drago, I., Mellia, M., Munafo, M.M., Sperotto, A., Sadre, R., Pras, A.: Inside dropbox: understanding personal cloud storage services. In: Proceedings of the 2012 ACM Conference on Internet Measurement Conference, pp. 481–494. ACM (2012)
3. Eshghi, K., Tang, H.K.: A framework for analyzing and improving content-based chunking algorithms. Hewlett-Packard Labs Technical report TR vol. 30 (2005)
4. Meyer, D.T., Bolosky, W.J.: A study of practical deduplication. ACM Trans. Storage (TOS) **7**(4), 14 (2012)
5. Muthitacharoen, A., Chen, B., Mazieres, D.: A low-bandwidth network file system. In: ACM SIGOPS Operating Systems Review, vol. 35, pp. 174–187. ACM (2001)
6. Quinlan, S., Dorward, S.: Venti: a new approach to archival storage. FAST **2**, 89–101 (2002)
7. Rabin, M.O.: Fingerprinting by random polynomials. Center for Research in Computing Techn., Aiken Computation Laboratory, University (1981)
8. Tridgell, A., Mackerras, P. et al.: The rsync algorithm (1996)

Enhancing Readers-Writers Exclusion with Upgrade/Downgrade Primitives

Michael Diamond[1], Prasad Jayanti[2(✉)], and Jake Leichtling[1]

[1] Google, Mountain View, USA
mdiamond@google.com, jake.leichtling@gmail.com
[2] Dartmouth College, Hanover, USA
prasad@cs.dartmouth.edu

Abstract. We design an algorithm for readers-writers exclusion that allows a writer to downgrade to a reader and a reader to attempt to upgrade to a writer. The highlights of our algorithm are: (i) the upgrade and downgrade methods are linearizable and wait-free, and (ii) all properties deemed desirable, such as concurrent entering, FCFS for writers, FIFE for readers, are satisfied, and (iii) RMR complexity is constant.

1 Introduction

1.1 The Readers-Writers Exclusion Problem

In the context of a system of asynchronous processes communicating via atomic shared variables, we study the *readers-writers exclusion* problem [1]. Three types of readers-writers exclusion are commonly studied in the literature — one where readers have priority over writers, another where writers have priority, and a third version where neither class has priority over the other and no process starves. In this paper, we study only the reader-priority and the starvation-free versions of the problem.

Suppose that a process p enters the CS as a writer and, after some reading and writing of the buffer $\mathcal{B}$, finds that it only has some reading left to perform. It would be ideal if p can simply downgrade its status from a writer to a reader, thereby allowing other readers in the try section to also enter the CS. This scenario motivates the need for supporting a "downgrade" primitive, which a writer in the CS can execute to bring down its privilege from writing to reading. If the downgrade primitive were not supported, p would have to quit the CS and reenter the CS as a reader, which not only involves considerable overhead but also leaves opportunity for other writers to modify the buffer between p's writing and reading.

Similarly, suppose that p enters the CS as reader and, after reading parts of the buffer $\mathcal{B}$, finds a need to modify the buffer. Instead of quitting the CS and reentering as a writer, it would be ideal if p can request to upgrade its status from reader to that of writer. Of course, the request cannot always succeed: for instance, if another reader q is also in the CS, p's upgrade request must

A. Bouajjani and H. Fauconnier (Eds.): NETYS 2015, LNCS 9466, pp. 461–467, 2015.
DOI: 10.1007/978-3-319-26850-7_32

fail, since otherwise the exclusion property would be violated. However, under suitable conditions — for example, when all other processes are in the remainder section — p's upgrade will succeed, giving it the license to modify the buffer.

We stipulate that the upgrade and downgrade primitives be atomic because a process in the CS can then switch its status (from writer to reader or vice versa) instantaneously.

We make two contributions. First, we specify upgrade and downgrade in a clean way that integrates seamlessly with standard properties, such as concurrent entering, reader-priority etc., identified in the literature for readers-writers synchronization. Second, we design an algorithm that transforms any readers-writers exclusion algorithm into one that additionally supports upgrade and downgrade primitives as linearizable and wait-free operations. The highlight is that our transformation preserves the type of the original readers-writers algorithm: if the original algorithm satisfies reader priority, so does the new algorithm; and, if the original algorithm satisfies starvation-freedom, so does the new algorithm also. Our transformation also preserves RMR complexity on Cache-Coherent (CC) multiprocessors: if the original algorithm has $O(1)$ RMR complexity, so does the new algorithm, i.e., execution of any of Try, Exit, Upgrade, or Downgrade procedures incurs only a constant number of remote memory references (RMRs), regardless of how many processes are running concurrently.

1.2 Comparison to Previous Work

Upgradeable and Downgradeable reader-writer locks are implemented in the boost C++ libraries [2], .NET [3], and in Java utilities [4]. There are significant differences between what these implementations provide and our lock. While these three implementations are reentrant and interruptible, our lock is not. On the other hand, the lock in java.util.concurrent.locks supports only the downgrade feature, so readers cannot attempt to gain write permission. The .NET and boost implementations are closer to our lock, yet also present significant differences. In these two implementations, a process attempts to acquire one of three tiers of the lock: "reader," "upgradeable reader," or "writer." An upgradeable-reader is a process that is currently a reader, but has the ability to call the upgrade method anytime it wants. No more than one process can be an upgradeable reader at a time, though an upgradeable reader may downgrade to a regular reader without blocking. Thus, at most one reader can call the upgrade method at a time. In contrast, our algorithm allows for any reader to call upgrade at any time. The boost and .net locks offer blocking as well as nonblocking implementations of upgrade. Our lock offers wait-free upgrade with the additional property that, if an upgrade fails, at no point during its execution does the upgrade prevent new readers from entering the CS in a bounded number of steps. The boost lock is starvation-free and the .net lock gives priority to writers. Our lock, on the other hand, can either be starvation-free or give priority to readers. Finally, our lock ensures that properties, such as concurrent entering and FIFE, are satisfied even as processes upgrade or downgrade their status.

2 Problem Specification

The system consists of asynchronous processes communicating via atomic shared variables. Each process' program is a loop that consists of two sections of code: the *Try section*, followed by *Exit section*. We say that a process is in the *Remainder section* if its program counter is at the first statement of the Try section; and we say that a process is in the *Critical section (CS)* if its program counter is at the first statement of the Exit section. Initially, all processes are in their Remainder section.

The Try section, in turn, consists of two code fragments — the *doorway*, followed by the *waiting room* — with the requirement that the doorway is a bounded "straight line" code [5]. Each time a process executes the Try section, it nondeterministically selects at the start of the doorway to be either a reader or a writer. Thus, when it completes the Try section, it enters the CS as either a reader or a writer.

Each process has access to two *atomic* primitives — *Upgrade* and *Downgrade*; Upgrade returns *true* or *false*, and Downgrade always returns *true*. A process can execute *Downgrade* only if it is a writer and is in the CS; and it can execute *Upgrade* only if it is a reader and is in the CS. If a writer in the CS executes the atomic primitive *Downgrade*, it instantaneously changes to a reader. If a reader in the CS executes the atomic primitive *Upgrade* and Upgrade returns true, it instantaneously changes to a writer; if Upgrade returns false, the process remains a reader. A process in the CS may execute Upgrade and Downgrade any number of times.

We now define two properties. The first stipulates that an upgrade attempt must succeed if all other processes are in the remainder section. If we wish to give priority to readers over writers, a reader in the CS should not be able to upgrade (and become a writer) if another reader is waiting. The second property rigorously states this condition.

- Upgradeability: If a reader in the CS executes the atomic primitive *Upgrade* at a time when no other readers are in the Try, Critical, or Exit sections, then *Upgrade* returns *true*.
- Upgrade respects reader priority: If a reader in the CS executes the atomic primitive *Upgrade* at a time when another reader is in the waiting room, *Upgrade* returns *false*.

Because of space constraints, we refer the reader to [6] for the definitions of the other properties generally deemed desirable for readers-writers lock (namely, bounded exit, livelock/starvation freedom [7], concurrent entering [8,9], FCFS for writers, FIFE for readers [10]), and for a reader-priority lock (namely, reader-priority and unstoppable reader properties).

An *algorithm for readers-writers exclusion*, also called a *readers-writers lock*, specifies four procedures — Try section, Exit section, Upgrade, and Downgrade — such that

- Upgrade and Downgrade procedures are linearizable [11] and wait-free [12].

- The following properties are satisfied: exclusion, livelock freedom, bounded exit, concurrent entering, FCFS for writers, and FIFE for readers.
- Reader priority and unstoppable reader properties are satisfied (when implementing a reader-priority lock) and starvation freedom is satisfied (when implementing a starvation-free lock).

3 The Algorithm

We design the algorithm in two steps. In the first and the difficult step, we show how to transform any single-writer lock $\mathcal{L}$ that does not support upgrade and downgrade into a single-writer lock $\mathcal{L}'$ that supports upgrade and downgrade. The highlight of this transformation is that it preserves the type of $\mathcal{L}$: if $\mathcal{L}$ is a starvation-free lock, so is $\mathcal{L}'$; and if $\mathcal{L}$ is a reader-priority lock, so too is $\mathcal{L}'$. In the second (and the easy) step, we transform the single-writer lock into one that supports any number of concurrent writers. Because of space constraints, we present only the algorithm for the first step.

Shared Variables

$RC \in \{0\} \cup \mathbb{Z}^+$, initialized to 0
$US \in \{$UPGRADING, UPGRADED, NULL$\}$, initialized to NULL
Permit $\in \{$TRUE, FALSE$\}$, initialized to TRUE
DowngradingWriter $\in \{$TRUE, FALSE$\}$, initialized to FALSE

Local Variables

original-status $\in \{$R, W$\}$
current-status $\in \{r, w, \dot{w}\}$
status $\equiv$ (*original-status*, *current-status*)

READER-TRY()
F&A(RC, 1)
CAS(US, UPGRADING, NULL)
$\mathcal{L}$.READER-DOORWAY()
$\mathcal{L}$.READER-WAITINGROOM()
if US == UPGRADED
    wait until *Permit* == TRUE
wait until *DowngradingWriter* == FALSE

(R, r)-EXIT()
F&A(RC, −1)
$\mathcal{L}$.READER-EXIT()

(R, r)/(W, r)-UPGRADE()
if $RC \neq 1$ return FALSE
US = UPGRADING
if $RC \neq 1$ return FALSE
Permit = FALSE
return CAS(US, UPGRADING, UPGRADED)

(R, $\dot{w}$)/(W, $\dot{w}$)-RE-DOWNGRADE()
Permit = TRUE

WRITER-TRY()
$\mathcal{L}$.WRITER-TRY()

(W, w)-EXIT()
$\mathcal{L}$.WRITER-EXIT()

(W, w)-DOWNGRADE()
DowngradingWriter = TRUE
F&A(RC, 1)
$\mathcal{L}$.WRITER-EXIT()
DowngradingWriter = FALSE

(W, r)-EXIT()
F&A(RC, −1)

Fig. 1. Algorithm for transforming a single-writer multi-reader lock $\mathcal{L}$ into a single-writer multi-reader lock $\mathcal{L}'$ that supports upgrade and downgrade

3.1 Process Status

For any process p that is not in the Remainder section, its *status* is (X, y), where

- $X \in \{R, W\}$ is p's *original status*: if p entered the Try section as a reader, then $X = R$ and we call p an original reader; if p entered the Try section as a writer, then $X = W$ and we call p an original writer. Note that the original status of a process remains the same from the start of the Try section to the completion of the Exit section.
- $y \in \{r, w, \dot{w}\}$ is p's *current status*: if $y = r$, p is currently a reader; if $y = \dot{w}$, p is currently a writer, having upgraded from being a reader; and if $y = w$, p is currently a writer and has always been a writer.

For example, when an original writer enters the CS, its status is (W, w). If it executes Downgrade, its status becomes (W, r). If it then executes Upgrade and the upgrade succeeds, its status becomes $(W, \dot{w})$.

3.2 Procedure Naming Convention

Our algorithm, which transforms a single-writer lock $\mathcal{L}$ that does not support upgrade and downgrade into a single-writer lock $\mathcal{L}'$ that supports upgrade and downgrade, is presented in Fig. 1, where we use the following convention for naming procedures. Most procedures' names begin with a status value (X, y),

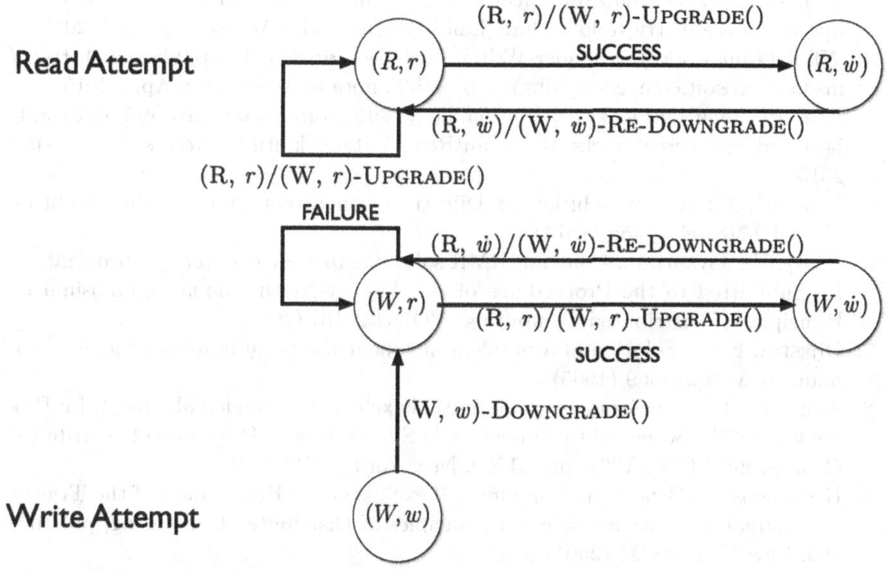

Fig. 2. A diagram illustrating how a process's status changes as it upgrades and downgrades, and what upgrade and downgrade procedures are available to it given its status.

which means that only a process whose status is (X, y) can execute that procedure. For example, the procedure (W, w)-DOWNGRADE can be executed only by processes whose status is (W, w). Similarly, $(R, \dot{w})/(W, \dot{w})$-RE-DOWNGRADE can be executed only by processes whose status is either $(R, \dot{w})$ or $(W, \dot{w})$.

Figure 2 describes how a process' status changes as it upgrades and downgrades, and what upgrade and downgrade procedures are available to it given its status. In the figure, only procedures that potentially change the current status of a process are shown. Note that an attempt to upgrade is not guaranteed to succeed, so, if $(\text{R}, r)/(\text{W}, r)$ – UPGRADE() returns false, the process' current status continues to be r.

Notice that we have not provided an EXIT procedure for a process whose current status is $\dot{w}$. Such a process can exit by first downgrading (to change its current status to r) and then executing an appropriate EXIT procedure.

Acknowledgment. We thank Vibhor Bhatt whose conversations with the second author sparked off this research. We also thank the reviewers for pointing us to the earlier work on upgrade and downgrade.

References

1. Courtois, P.J., Heymans, F., Parnas, D.L.: Concurrent control with "readers" and "writers". Commun. ACM **14**(10), 667–668 (1971)
2. Boost C++ Libraries description. http://www.boost.org/doc/libs/1_5_/doc/html/thread/synchronization.html#thread.synchronization.mutex_concepts.upgrade_lockable.try_unlock_shared_and_lock_upgrade. Accessed: 8 April 2015d
3. .NET Framework 4.5 Reader-Writer Lock Description, howpublished. https://msdn.microsoft.com/en-us/library/bz6sth95 note = Accessed: 8 April 2015
4. java.util.concurrent.locks description. http://docs.oracle.com/javase/7/docs/api/java/util/concurrent/locks/ReentrantReadWriteLock.html. Accessed: 8 April 2015
5. Lamport, L.: A new solution of Dijkstra's concurrent programming problem. CACM **17**(8), 453–455 (1974)
6. Bhatt, V., Jayanti, P.: Constant RMR solutions to reader writer synchronization. In: Submitted to the Proceedings of the Twenty-Ninth Annual Symposium on Principles of Distributed Computing (PODC 2010) (2010)
7. Dijkstra, E.W.: Solution of a problem in concurrent programming control. Commun. ACM **8**(9), 569 (1965)
8. Joung, Y.-J.: Asynchronous group mutual exclusion (extended abstract). In: Proceedings of the Seventeenth Annual ACM Symposium on Principles of Distributed Computing, PODC 1998, pp. 51–60, New York. ACM (1998)
9. Hadzilacos, V.: A note on group mutual exclusion. In: Proceedings of the Twentieth Annual ACM Symposium on Principles of Distributed Computing, pp. 100–106, New York. ACM (2001)

10. Fischer, M.J., Lynch, N.A., Burns, J.E., Borodin, A.: Resource allocation with immunity to limited process failure. In: Proceedings of the 20th Annual Symposium on Foundations of Computer Science, SFCS 1979, pp. 234–254, Washington. IEEE Computer Society (1979)
11. Herlihy, M.P., Wing, J.M.: Linearizability: a correctness condition for concurrent objects. ACM TOPLAS **12**(3), 463–492 (1990)
12. Herlihy, M.P.: Wait-free synchronization. ACM TOPLAS **13**(1), 124–149 (1991)

Context-Based Query Expansion Method for Short Queries Using Latent Semantic Analyses

Btihal El Ghali[1(✉)], Abderrahim El Qadi[2], Mohamed Ouadou[1], and Driss Aboutajdine[1]

[1] LRIT Associated Unit to the CNRST - URAC N°29 Faculty of Science, Mohammed V- University, Rabat, Morocco
{btihal.elghali,ouadou55}@gmail.com, aboutaj@fsr.ac.ma

[2] TIM, High School of Technology Moulay Ismaïl University, Meknes, Morocco
elqadi_a@yahoo.com

Abstract. Short queries are the key difficulty in information retrieval (IR). A plenty of query expansion techniques has been proposed to solve this problem. In this paper, we propose three different models for query suggestion using the cosine similarity (CS), the Language Models (LM) or their fusion. The expansion terms are selected using the Latent Semantic Analyses method based on the result of the three query suggestion methods. The approaches proposed improve the precision of the user query by adding additional context to it. Experimental results show that expanding short queries by our approaches improves the effectiveness of the IR system by 48,1 % using the CS based model, 19,2 % using the LM model, and 13,5 % using the fusion model.

Keywords: Query context · Query suggestion · LM · LSA · Query expansion

1 Introduction

Query suggestion is the fact of proposing queries that are almost similar to the user query, and it can be considered as a method for improving retrieval performance by extracting the context around the user's query. Indeed, the query is only a partial and often ambiguous expression of the user's information needs, and it was observed that users usually submit very short queries [1]. Considering the context, the partial information of the query can be completed and the ambiguity can be resolved to a certain degree [2].

For a correct interpretation of the user's query, it has been demonstrated that it should be placed in its appropriate context [3]. The context is a large notion that includes the user context (his domains of interest, his preferences and his historic of research) and the query context, which means the environment of the query (its relevant documents and its terms…). The first context needs the research to be done using users profiles, but a single profile can group a large variety of domains and interests, that are

A. Bouajjani and H. Fauconnier (Eds.): NETYS 2015, LNCS 9466, pp. 468–473, 2015.
DOI: 10.1007/978-3-319-26850-7_33

not always relevant for a particular query. Thus, the solution is to use the second context as an appropriate context to improve the precision of the query.

The main objective of this work is to provide high-level suggestions for the original user query that we are using later for expanding the query with additional context. We consider the query context that we build using the top-ranked documents of the initial query, the most related queries extracted from a log of past queries and their top-ranked documents. We propose also to apply the Latent Semantic Analyses method to search for the most similar terms to the new user query terms. Then, these similarities are merged together with the expression of cohesion weight presented in [4] to order the candidate terms for expansion according to the whole query to expand.

This paper is structured as follows: The Sect. 2 describes our context-based query expansion method. Section 3 shows the most important experimental results, while Sect. 4 summarizes the main conclusions of this work.

2 The Context-Based Query Expansion Method

In this paper, we propose three query suggestion models. These models classified past queries, which are extracted from a query logs, according to the new user query using the expression of score:

$$\mathrm{Score}(\mathrm{q_N}, \mathrm{q_P}) = \gamma\ \mathrm{Score_T}(\mathrm{q_N}, \mathrm{q_P}) + (1 - \gamma)\ \mathrm{Score_D}(\mathrm{q_N}, \mathrm{q_P}) \qquad (1)$$

With $\gamma \in [0, 1]$ is a parameter that we used for normalization. In a previous work, the experimentations done show that the best value of γ is 0,2. The ScoreT is calculated using vectors that represent the presence or not of a term in a query. While, ScoreD is computed using vectors that represent the presence or not of a document between the clicked document of a query.

The query suggestion models presented are as follows:

- **Model 1:** Technique based on the Query Recommendation Algorithm (TQRA):

$$Score_{M1}(q_N, q_P) = \gamma\ Score_{QRA-T}(q_N, q_P) + (1 - \gamma)\ Score_{QRA-D}(q_N, q_P) \qquad (2)$$

- **Model 2:** Technique based on the Language Models (TLM):

$$\mathrm{Score_{M2}}(\mathrm{q_N}, \mathrm{q_P}) = \gamma\ \mathrm{Score_{LM-T}}(\mathrm{q_N}, \mathrm{q_P}) + (1 - \gamma)\ \mathrm{Score_{LM-D}}(\mathrm{q_N}, \mathrm{q_P}) \qquad (3)$$

- **Model 3:** Method of suggestion based on Language Models (LM) using the terms vectors and QRA using the documents vectors:

$$\mathrm{Score_{M3}}(\mathrm{q_N}, \mathrm{q_P}) = \gamma\ \mathrm{Score_{LM-T}}(\mathrm{q_N}, \mathrm{q_P}) + (1 - \gamma)\ \mathrm{Sim_{QRA-D}}(\mathrm{q_N}, \mathrm{q_P}) \qquad (4)$$

2.1 Query Recommendation Algorithm

In this case, we used the Query Recommendation Algorithm (QRA) presented in [5]. We eliminated the steps 1 and 2 of the algorithm that concern the clustering of the past queries and the identification of the appropriate cluster of a new query when submitted. In order to suggest related past queries to an input query, we represent each query with a term-weight vector and a document-weight vector [6].

2.2 Language Model

In this paper, we used the language models [2, 7, 8], to order the past queries Q_p according to their capacity to generate the new user query Qn. The ranking function that we used is the typical score function defined by KL-divergence [3, 9]:

$$\mathrm{Score_{LM}}(Q_n, Q_p) = \sum\nolimits_{t \in V} P(t|\theta_{Q_P}) \log P(t|\theta_{Q_P}) \approx -\mathrm{KL}(\theta_{Q_n} \| \theta_{Q_P}) \quad (5)$$

Where θ_{Q_n} is the language model of the new query, θ_{Q_p} the language model created for a past query, and V the vocabulary of terms.

$P(t|\theta_Q)$ represent the probability of a term t in the language model of the query and are measured using the Maximum Likehood Estimation (MLE).

To resolve the main problem that occurs for language models, we used the Jelinek-Mercer interpolation smoothing [7] method:

$$P\left(t|\theta'_{Q_p}\right) = (1-\lambda)P\left(t|\theta_{Q_p}\right) + \lambda P(t|\theta_C) \quad (6)$$

Where γ is an interpolation parameter and θ_c the language model of the collection of queries extracted from the search engine log.

2.3 Latent Semantic Analyses for Query Expansion

The Latent Semantic Analyses (LSA) [10] is a technique, which projects queries and documents into a space with "latent" semantic dimensions.

In this work, we propose to apply the LSA as a query expansion method to the results of the query suggestion techniques proposed.

Finally, By using the common measure of similarity cosine *Simc* [11] and combining the similarities of each candidate term t_j for all the new query terms $t_i \in Q$ we can calculate the cohesion weight [4] of a candidate term, which represent the relationship (correlation) between this term and the whole query to expand:

$$CoWeight(Q, t_j) = ln\left(\prod_{t_i \in Q} (Simc(t_i, t_j) + 1)\right) \quad (7)$$

3 Experimental Results

As a collection of test, we used the database CISI from the standard collection SMART. This collection provides 111 queries, 1460 documents.

We used only the short queries (Queries containing less than five terms), and we computed the performance of the IR system using the Un-interpolated Average Precision (UAP) measure. In our experimentations, we searched for relevant documents until the 20th retrieved document.

In Fig. 1, we present the results of UAP for the three models TQRA, TLM and LM-QRA using two suggested queries and five terms of expansion, while varying the number of documents to which the LSA is applied for expanding queries.

We notice in Fig. 1 that the highest values of UAP are given using 9 documents for the model 1 and 2 (0,77 for TQRA and 0,53 for TLM). We propose to continue our experimentations using 9 documents for each used query. The figure shows ups and downs in the value of UAP while adding more documents. We can explain that by the fact that the top-ranked documents used in the expansion can be relevant or not.

Figure 2 describes the value of UAP while varying the number of expansion terms from 1 to 10.

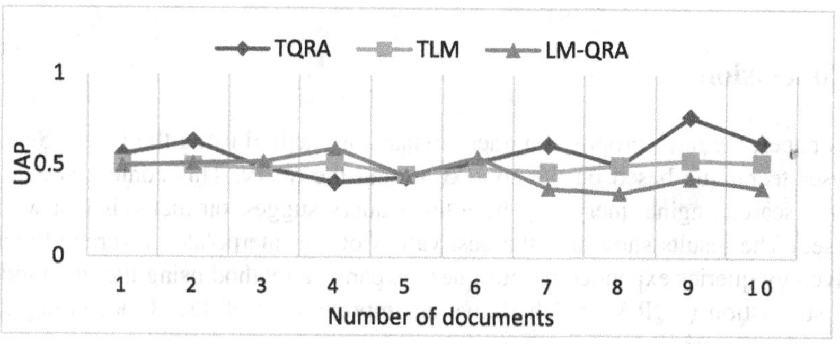

Fig. 1. UAP values using the three suggested models while varying the number of documents.

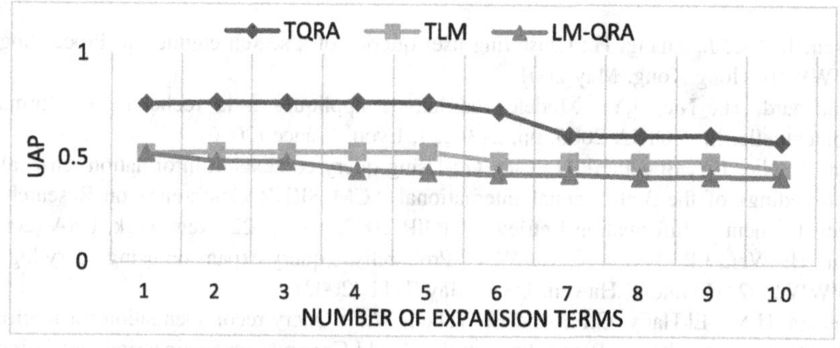

Fig. 2. UAP values using the three proposed models while varying the number of terms.

Figure 2 is showing that while varying the number of terms used for expanding short queries, the value of UAP is decreasing continually when using the model LM-QRA. Thus, the highest value (0,52) is given using one expansion term. Concerning the two other models, they started with high values of UAP (0,75 for TQRA and 0,52 for TLM) and increased slowly until reaching the highest value when adding 4 or 5 terms of expansion (0,77 for TQRA and 0,53 for TLM).

We propose to compare the value of UAP of the initial queries (before expansion) with the best values of each case of expansion using the three suggestion models.

Table 1 shows that the case of expansion based on the model TQRA gives the highest value by improving the UAP of 48,1 %, 19,2 % using the LM model, and 13,5 % using the fusion model compared to the initial user query.

Table 1. Comparison of the best values of each expansion method with the initial queries.

Suggestion method	–	TLM	TQRA	LM-QRA
UAP	0,52	0,62	0,77	0,59

4 Conclusion

In this paper, we have proposed a query expansion method using the Latent Semantic Analyses technique based on the context around the query. This context is extracted from the search engine query logs by a three query suggestion methods that we have proposed. The results show that the best values of Un-interpolated Average Precision are given by queries expanded by our query expansion method using the first model of query suggestion (TQRA) which shows an improvement of 48,1% according to the original short queries.

References

1. Wen, J., Nie, J., Zhang, H.: Clustering user queries of a search engine. In: Proceedings of WWW10, Hong Kong, May 2001
2. Bouchard, H., Nie, J.Y.: Modèles de langue appliqués à la recherche d'information contextuelle. In: CORIA 2006, pp. 213–224, Lyon, France (2006)
3. Bai, J., Nie, J-Y. Bouchard, H., Cao, G.: Using query contexts in information retrieval. In: Proceedings of the 30th Annual International ACM SIGIR Conference on Research and Development in Information Retrieval, SIGIR 2007, pp. 15–22, New York, USA (2007)
4. Cui, H., Wen, J.R., Nie, J.Y., Ma, W.Y.: Probabilistic query expansion using query logs. In: WWW2002, Honolulu, Hawaii, USA, May 7–11 (2002)
5. Zahera, H.M., El Hady, G.F., Abd El-Wahed, W.F.: Query recommendation for improving search engine results. In: Proceedings of the World Congress on Engineering and Computer Science (WCECS 2010), vol. I, San Francisco USA, October (2010)

6. El Ghali, B., El Qadi, A., El Midaoui, O., Ouadou, M., Aboutajdine, D.: Probabilistic query expansion method based on a query recommendation algorithm. Int. J. Web Appl. (IJWA). **5** (1), 1–12 (2013)
7. Cao, G., Nie, J., Bai, J.: Integrating word relationships into language models. In: Proceedings of SIGIR 2005, Salvador Brazil, August 2005
8. Zhai, C.: Statistical language models for information retrieval: a critical review. Found. Trends Inf. Retrieval **2**(3), 137–215 (2008)
9. Asfari, O., Doan, B-L., Bourda, Y., Sansonnet, J-P.: Context-based hybrid method for user query expansion. In: Proceedings of the Fourth International Conference on Advances in Semantic Processing, SEMAPRO 2010, pp. 69–74, Italy Florence (2010)
10. Landauer, T.K., Foltz, P.W., Laham, D.: An introduction to latent semantic analysis. Discourse Process. **25**, 259–284 (1998)
11. Slimani, T., Ben Yaghlane, B., Mellouli, K.: Une extension de mesure de similarité entre les con-cepts d'une ontologie. In: Proceedings of SETIT 2007, 4th International Conference: Sciences of Electronic, Technologies of Information and Tele-Communications, Tunisia, March 2007

Towards a Formal Semantics and Analysis of BPMN Gateways

Outman El Hichami[1](✉), Mohamed Naoum[1], Mohammed Al Achhab[2], Ismail Berrada[3], and Badr Eddine El Mohajir[1]

[1] Faculty of Sciences, UAE, Tetouan, Morocco
el.hichami.outman@taalim.ma, naoum.mohamed@gmail.com, b.elmohajir@ieee.ma
[2] National School of Applied Sciences, UAE, Tetouan, Morocco
alachhab@ieee.ma
[3] Faculty of Sciences and Technology, USMBA, Fez, Morocco
iberrada@univ-lr.fr

Abstract. This paper deals with formal verification of BPMN models. The lack of an unambiguous definition of the BPMN notations, and the mixing of incompatible BPMN patterns may lead to wrong or incomplete semantics, resulting in some behavioral errors such as deadlocks and multiple termination problems. As formal verification requires formal specification models and in order to create a correct business process, most used approaches consider the formalization of either a subclass of BPMN patterns or specific forms of these patterns. In this paper, thanks to Max+ Algebra, we propose to extend existing approaches by including most of BPMN notations.

Keywords: Business process · BPMN · Formal semantics

1 Introduction

The Business Process Modeling Notation (BPMN) [1] is a standard notation for business process modeling. It presents an execution semantics of process instances that defines precisely how models in the BPMN notation should behave.

The BPMN models are composed of a set of activity nodes and a set of control nodes that can be connected by a flow relation. Other notations exist, for which we refer to a subset of BPMN related to control flow modelling in order to define a precise execution semantics of BPMN elements which are the most used in the modelisation of the service-based business processes.

Several approaches have been proposed to the formal validation of BPMN [2–5]. All these approaches are based on the mapping of BPMN to a formal presentation like Petri Nets [6] in order to use the formal analysis tools available for these models.

A variety of techniques define a formal semantics of BPMN [7,8], which use Petri nets as the target formal model. However, Petri nets are limited in the semantics that they can represent. It is difficult to represent the inclusive. Such

A. Bouajjani and H. Fauconnier (Eds.): NETYS 2015, LNCS 9466, pp. 474–478, 2015.
DOI: 10.1007/978-3-319-26850-7_34

concepts can be represented in Max+ Algebra equations. Our work supports this claim by showing that the formalization of this paper is relatively complete.

For illustrative purposes, we develop a complete execution semantics of BPMN patterns associated with control flow in terms of Max+ Algebra equations, which is a useful mathematical tool, to specify and evaluate the performance of interaction and interoperability in the processes composition where conflicts appear.

The remainder of this paper is organized as follows. In Sect. 2, a brief overview of BPMN standard and an abstract syntax of Max+ Algebra system is given. Analysis of execution semantics for BPMN elements related to control flow modelling are presented in Sect. 3. Section 4 concludes the paper and presents some perspectives.

2 Preliminaries

2.1 Business Process Modeling Notation (BPMN)

Before elaborating a formal semantics of BPMN, this section provides a gentle introduction to the BPMN elements related to control flow modelling that define the behavior of the processes and have an impact on the conflict situation. Hence, three types of nodes named event, task, and gateway are considered as well as one type of edges called sequence flow. The main elements of BPMN include the following:

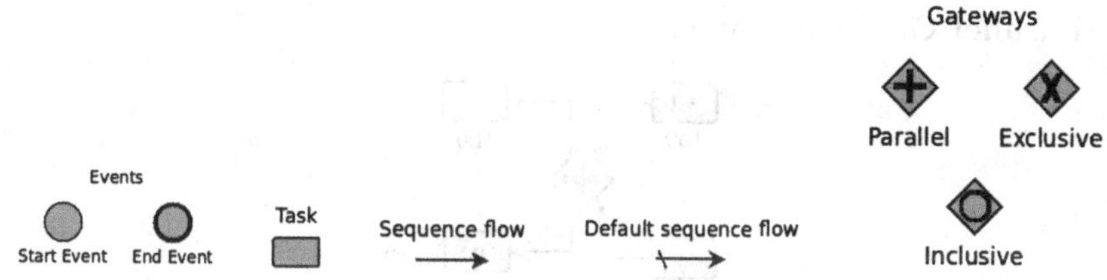

- An event could be a start or an end event.
- A task describes a type of work that has to be completed within a business process.
- A sequence flow links two objects in a process diagram.
- A default sequence flow is taken only if all the other outgoing sequence flows are not valid.
- Gateways are used to control how the sequence flows converge or diverge within a process.

2.2 Max+ Algebra

In Max+ Algebra, we work with the Max+ semi-ring which is the set $\mathbb{R}_{max} = \{-\infty\} \cup \mathbb{R}$. The operations maximum (implied by the max operator $\oplus$) and addition (plus operator $\otimes$), with; $\oplus$ admits a neutral element noted as $\varepsilon = -\infty$ and $\otimes$ admits a neutral element noted as $e = 0$.

3 Formal Models for BPMN Using Max+ Algebra

3.1 Cumulative Application and Firing Condition

Before giving the Max+ Algebra model, let us define:

- The firing of a task occurs after the end of a time t_i associated to this task.
- To calculate the cumulative total at the firing of the task a_i, we define the following cumulative application that represents the date of kth firing of a_i

$$\begin{aligned} a_i : \mathbb{N}^* &\rightarrow \mathbb{R}_{max} \\ k &\rightarrow a_i(k), with \quad : \ i \in \{0, 1, ..., |T|\} \end{aligned} \tag{1}$$

where $|T|$ is the number of all tasks in the BPMN model.

Remark: We note $a_i = 1$, when a task a_i will be executed.

A sequence flow that has an exclusive or inclusive gateway as its source requires a condition to direct the flow. Consequently, we associate to each task a boolean variable that acts as a firing condition. A sequence flow is fired if this condition evaluates to *true*. Formally, we define the following function:

$$\begin{aligned} Cond : T &\rightarrow \{True, False\} \\ a_i &\rightarrow Cond(a_i) \end{aligned} \tag{2}$$

3.2 Parallel Gateway Pattern

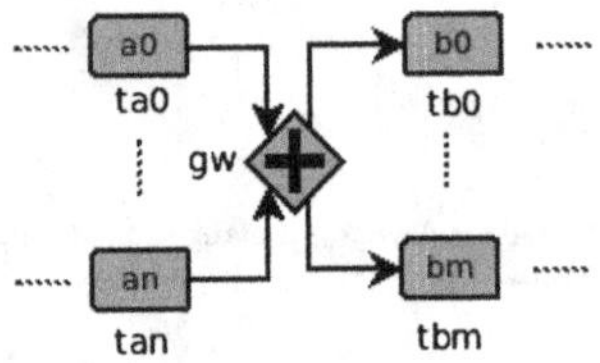

The analytical behavior of this graphical model is given in system (3). $\forall\, k \in \mathbb{N}^*, \forall a_i \in \bullet gw, \forall b_j \in gw\bullet, a_i(k) \neq \varepsilon$,

$$\begin{cases} b_0(k) = t_0 \otimes \left(\bigoplus_{i=0}^{n} a_i(k) \right) \\ \vdots = \vdots \\ b_m(k) = t_m \otimes \left(\bigoplus_{i=0}^{n} a_i(k) \right) \end{cases} \tag{3}$$

Where $gw\bullet$ is the set of all downstream tasks of gw and $\bullet gw$ is the set of all upstream tasks of gw.

3.3 Exclusive Gateway Pattern

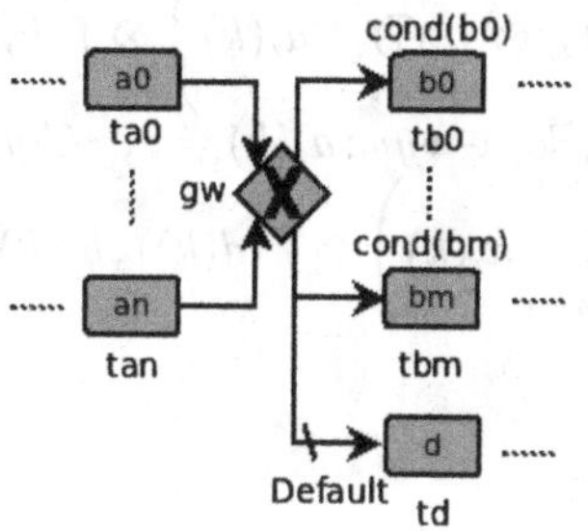

In this pattern, it is not obvious to formally express the firing of the downstream tasks. With the aim to describe this functioning by Max+ Algebra equations and in order to facilitate the mathematical analysis, we associate to each task the following function:

$$\begin{aligned} f : \mathbb{R}_{max} &\rightarrow \{e, \varepsilon\} \\ x &\rightarrow f(x) \end{aligned} \tag{4}$$

When only a task a_i is fired for the kth firing (i.e., $f\big(a_i(k)\big) = e$), all other tasks a_x (with $a_x \neq a_i$) are not fired (i.e., $f\big(a_x(k)\big) = \varepsilon$). The behavior of the modeled exclusive gateway pattern is represented by the system (5): $\forall\ k \in \mathbb{N}^*$,

$$\begin{cases} -\forall a_i \in \bullet gw, \forall b_j \in gw\bullet, \exists! a_i \in \bullet gw, \exists! b_j \in gw\bullet; a_i(k) \neq \varepsilon, f\big(b_j(k)\big) = e \\ \quad \Rightarrow b_{j,Cond(b_j)}(k) = \Big(\big(t_{b_j} \otimes a_i(k)\big) \otimes f\big(b_j(k)\big)\Big), b_{j,\neg Cond(b_j)}(k) = \varepsilon \\ -\forall a_i \in \bullet gw, \forall b_j \in gw\bullet, \exists! a_i \in \bullet gw; a_i(k) \neq \varepsilon, \neg Cond(b_j), f\big(d(k)\big) = e \\ \quad \Rightarrow d(k) = \Big(\big(t_d \otimes a_i(k)\big) \otimes f\big(d(k)\big)\Big), b_j(k) = \varepsilon \end{cases} \tag{5}$$

3.4 Inclusive Gateway Pattern

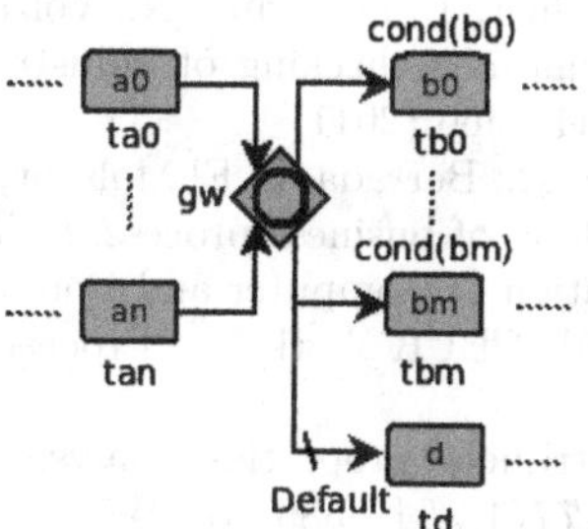

Using a standard formalization, this pattern may be expressed under the following form: $\forall\ k \in \mathbb{N}^*$,

$$\begin{cases} -\forall a_i \in \bullet gw, \forall b_j \in gw\bullet, \exists a_i \in \bullet gw, \exists b_j \in gw\bullet; a_i(k) \neq \varepsilon, f\left(b_j(k)\right) = e \\ \Rightarrow b_{j,Cond(b_j)}(k) = \left(t_{b_j} \otimes \bigoplus_{i=0,a_i=1}^{n} a_i(k) \right) \otimes f\left(b_j(k)\right), b_{j,\neg Cond(b_j)}(k) = \varepsilon \\ -\forall a_i \in \bullet gw, \forall b_j \in gw\bullet, \exists a_i \in \bullet gw; a_i(k) \neq \varepsilon, \neg Cond(b_j), f\left(d(k)\right) = e \\ \Rightarrow d(k) = \left(t_d \otimes \bigoplus_{i=0,a_i=1}^{n} a_i(k) \right) \otimes f\left(d(k)\right), b_j(k) = \varepsilon \end{cases} \tag{6}$$

4 Conclusion

This paper deals with the development of a theory and a generic method to model and analyze business process with conflicts in Max+ Algebra. This method allows to arbitrate these conflicts by given the corresponding linear equations of the chosen BPMN patterns which are the most used in the modelisation of the service-based business processes.

In future work, we plan to adapt the proposed approach with our previous works [2,5] so that to develop a plug-in which can integrate the formal verification techniques of business processes in the design phase.

References

1. OMG.: Business Process Modeling Notation (BPMN) Version 2.0. OMG Final Adopted Specification. Object Management Group (2011)
2. El Hichami, O., Al Achhab, M., Berrada, I., El Mohajir, B.: Short: graphical specification and automatic verification of business process. In: Noubir, G., Raynal, M. (eds.) Networked Systems. LNCS, vol. 8593, pp. 341–346. Springer, Heidelberg (2014)
3. van der Aalst, W.M.P., van Dongen, B.F.: Discovering petri nets from event logs. In: Jensen, K., Aalst, W.M.P., Balbo, G., Koutny, M., Wolf, K. (eds.) Transactions on Petri Nets and Other Models of Concurrency VII. LNCS, vol. 7480, pp. 372–422. Springer, Heidelberg (2013)
4. Fahland, D., Favre, C., Koehler, J., Lohmann, N., Volzer, H., Wolf, K.: Analysis on demand: instantaneous soundness checking of industrial business process models. Data Knowl. Eng. **70**(5), 448–466 (2011)
5. El Hichami, O., Al Achhab, M., Berrada, I., El Mohajir, B.: Visual specification language and automatic checking of business process. In: 8th International Workshop on Verification and Evaluation of Computer and Communication Systems (VECoS 2014), vol. 1256, pp. 93–101. CEUR Workshop Proceedings, Bejaia, Algeria, 29–30 September (2014)
6. Murata, T., Koh, J.Y.: Petri nets: properties, analysis and applications. an invited survey paper. Proc. IEEE **77**(4), 541–580 (1989)
7. Dijkman, R.M., Dumas, M., Ouyang, C.: Formal semantics and analysis of BPMN process models using Petri nets. Technical report 7115, Queensland University of Technology, Brisbane (2007)
8. Dijkman, R.M., Dumas, M., Ouyang, C.: Semantics and analysis of business process models in BPMN. Inf. Softw. Technol **50**(12), 1281–1294 (2008)

A User Centered Design Approach for Transactional Service Adaptation in Context Aware Environment

Widad Ettazi[1(✉)], Hatim Hafiddi[1,2], and Mahmoud Nassar[1]

[1] IMS Team, SIME Laboratory, ENSIAS, Mohammed V University, Rabat, Morocco
widad.ettazi@um5s.net.ma, hatim.hafiddi@gmail.com, nassar@ensias.ma

[2] ISL Team, STRS Laboratory, INPT, Rabat, Morocco

Abstract. Today, information systems are radically marked by considerable progress in the areas of software engineering, telecommunications and ubiquitous computing. This has led to the development of new interaction pattern where the service oriented architecture is the de facto pattern. In this article, we are particularly interested in transactional services. We position our approach in the context of a user-centered model driven engineering (MDE) approach in order to move from one perspective where models were contemplative artifacts to a perspective where they become productive artifacts. For this, we first present our approach for managing context-aware transactional services (CATS). Then, we propose a CATS specification and metamodel. The adaptation mechanism is also detailed in this paper.

Keywords: Context-awareness · Transactional service · Adaptation · Model driven engineering · Transaction model

1 Introduction

Service-oriented architectures have a number of requirements in a transaction-based infrastructure; transactions must be able to adjust to systems that are not necessarily in a perfect environment. These systems will operate in a flexible, dynamic environment, but less reliable and that presents contextual requirements (e.g., connectivity, battery level, user's preferences) that hinder the execution of transactions. Many transactional models and techniques have been proposed [5, 6], but they have limitations, namely, a non-consideration of the context information and the conception of advanced models with transactional properties that differ from one application to another. Several standards specifications have been proposed, including WS-Transaction specification and Business Transaction Protocol. However, they don't take into account the context information. Let's consider, for instance, a simple transaction that books a room in a hotel. Current approaches will simply commit the transaction if the required room is available in the hotel. They do not take into account the context information such as *a room should be booked in a hotel which is located nearby*. Therefore, it is imperative to take into account the context information in the management of CATS.

A. Bouajjani and H. Fauconnier (Eds.): NETYS 2015, LNCS 9466, pp. 479–484, 2015.
DOI: 10.1007/978-3-319-26850-7_35

Our paper is structured as follows. We discuss in the next section some backgrounds. Section 3 highlights our CATS specification and metamodel. Section 4 addresses the adaptation mechanism. Section 5 reviews related research. Finally, we conclude the paper in Sect. 6.

2 Background

2.1 Context-Awareness

Context-awareness refers to systems capable of perceiving a set of conditions of use in order to adjust their behavior in terms of providing information and services. According to Dey et al. [1], "a system is context-aware if it uses context to provide relevant information and services to the user, where relevance depends on the task requested by the user".

2.2 Transactional Service

We use the term *Transactional Service (TS)* to indicate a sequence of activities performed by a user in order to carry out a specific task or fulfill a specific goal by means of a service-oriented platform. In a context-aware transactional service, the execution of operations and the context-awareness are combined. The resulting complexity of CATS requires them to be designed prior to being implemented. Disregarding the context-awareness aspect, during the design process of transactional service, results in systems with low accommodation and inappropriate behaviors.

3 User-Centered Adaptation Approach

3.1 CATS Specification

In our approach, we propose a new model for context-aware transactional service called Context-Aware Transactional Service Model (CATSM). According to CATSM, a transactional service (TS) is hierarchical and is based on the transaction model shown in Fig. 1. The global transaction can be decomposed into a set of sub-transactions TSi. To cope with the context-awareness aspect, we associate to each transaction an environment descriptor (ED), which refers to the state, resources, and conditions of service execution environment (i.e., service, user, device and environment contexts). For more flexibility and resistance to failures, a sub-transaction may be associated to alternative transactions (ATS). We note that according to the environment descriptor EDij of each ATSij, only one alternative will be invoked if the transaction to which it is associated has failed. A compensation mechanism is also invoked by adding to each sub-transaction TSi and each alternative ATSi a compensating transaction CTSi.

In CATSM, we associate with each transaction a behavior type, namely, *replayable*, *replaceable*, *compensatable* and *critical*. A transaction is said to be replaceable if it may be replaced by an alternative transaction which will be invoked depending on the

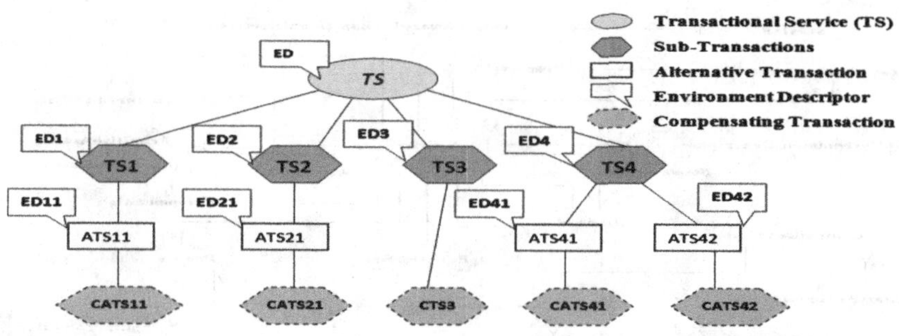

Fig. 1. Structure of CATS

environment descriptor. It is replayable if it can be retried one or more times after its failure. A transaction is defined as compensatable if it provides mechanisms to undo its effects. It is said to be critical if it requires the cancelling of the global transaction after its failure. The commit of the global transaction is associated with one of the following four types of atomicity (Strict, Semantic, Relaxed, Classic) depending on the semantic of the application and its requirements in terms of transactional properties.

3.2 Adaptation Metamodel

Figure 2 illustrates our CATS metamodel. This metamodel is based on the following specification:

- *ContextAwareTransactionalService* aggregates a list of *Activity*. Activities modeled by the transaction model have to be meaningful for the user of the context-aware application. The semantics associated with the existing properties are tuned to be user-centered.
- The *PropertySet* of an *Activity* is the set of transactional properties that this activity supports.
- The *PropertySet* of an *Activity* defines its *ExecutionContract*, which reflects the transaction execution model. Such contracts define additional semantics and constraints.
- The *BehaviorSet* of an *Activity* defines its *Profile*. This set is a sub-set of {*critical, replayable, replaceable, compensatable*}.
- *Activity* may be associated with *Alternative* in case the *Profile* contains the {*replaceable*} parameter.
- *Activity* may be associated with *Compensation* in case the *Profile* contains the {*compensatable*} parameter.
- Each *Activity* is associated with its *EnvironmentDescriptor* which defines the required environment conditions of execution.
- An *EnvironmentDescriptor* aggregates a list of *ContextDescriptor*.
- A *ContextDescriptor* aggregates a list of *ContextParameter*.
- For a given *AdaptationPolicy* and *ContextDescriptor*, a set of *ContextCondition* is deducted.

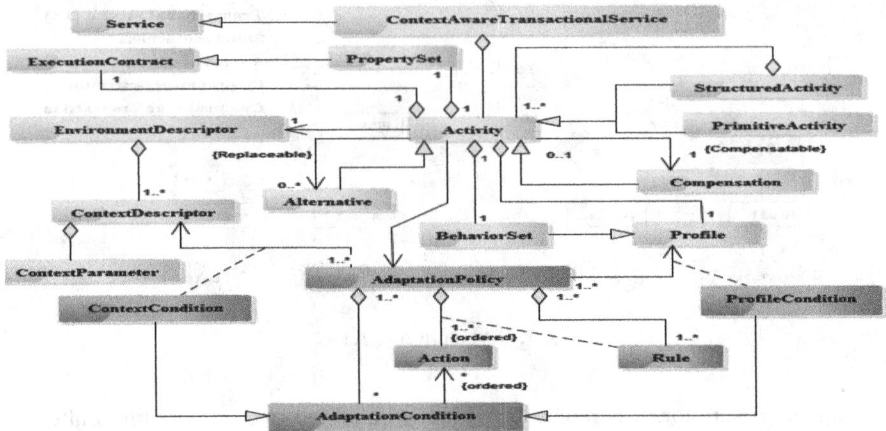

Fig. 2. CATS adaptation metamodel

- For a given *AdaptationPolicy* and *Profile*, a set of *ProfileCondition* is deducted.
- An *AdaptationPolicy* aggregates a set of *AdaptationCondition*, *Action* and *Rule*.

4 Adaptation Mechanism

This section illustrates the adaptation mechanism. Figure 3 sketches the different modules that are involved in the execution of a transaction in the CATSM.

- **Context Manager:** It provides context information and the mechanisms to collect and update data in case of context changes.
- **Adaptation Policy Manager:** Is responsible for inspecting the adaptation policy and converting the policy file into a data format that will be used in the reconfiguration module. The adaptation policy is determined by transactional requirements.

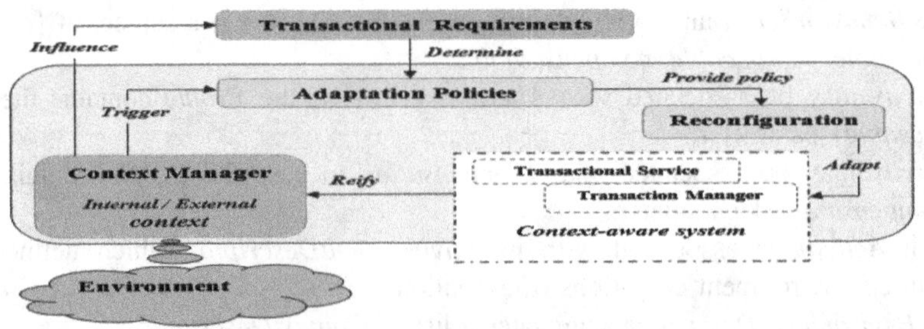

Fig. 3. Adaptation mechanism architecture

- **Reconfiguration Module:** Is responsible for evaluating and interpreting the adaptation policy based on the context state information provided by the context manager and the inspecting result of the policy manager to trigger the execution of the appropriate adaptation.
- **Transaction Manager:** Once the *CATSM* structure is identified by the reconfiguration manager, the transactional service coordinator (*TSC*) handles the processing and the execution of the global transaction. Then, it submits the sub-transactions to the sub-coordinators *TSCi*, which are associated with the different services *TSi*. Each *TSCi* is running its *TSi* and exchanges messages with *TSC*.

5 Related Work

To meet the variables requirements of transactional services, the need to relax ACID properties has been proposed in many researches since the early 90s. There was a great effort on extended transaction models [6]. Reference [4] developed a model for context-aware transactions in the context of mobile systems. This model provides a new set of transactional properties called RACCD. Reference [3] presented an approach to select the most appropriate service for a task in a workflow at runtime. To decide which service is more appropriate, the transactional property of candidate services is used to make the best choice. However, the approach simply leads to a process failure when no suitable service is found. Reference [5] introduced the AMT model which allows programmers to define transactional alternatives for an application task. Reference [2] proposed a MDE approach to achieve the context-aware service. However, this adaptation work has not focused on the transactional aspects of context-aware services.

6 Conclusion

In this paper, we presented a user-centered design approach for the management of context-aware transactional services. The proposed approach is based on the requirements specification in terms of transactional properties which specifies on one hand, the desired degree of atomicity, and allows on the other hand, the choice of an adaptation policy based on the alternative mechanism. In the short term, we intend to design a context-aware transaction commit protocol for the execution of CATS. In the medium term, our goal is to propose a framework allowing CATS development.

References

1. Dey, A., Abowd, G., Salber, D.: A conceptual framework and toolkit for supporting the rapid prototyping of context-aware applications. Hum.-Comput. Inter. **16**(2), 97–166 (2001)
2. Hafiddi, H., Baidouri, H., Nassar, M., ElAsri, B., Kriouile, A.: A context-aware service centric approach for service oriented architectures. In: 13th International Conference on Enterprise Information Systems, ICEIS 2011, vol. 3, pp. 8–11 (2011)

3. El Haddad, J., Manouvrier, M., Ramirez, G., Rukoz, M.: QoS-driven selection of web services for transactional composition. In: IEEE International Conference on Web Services, ICWS 2008, pp. 653–660 (2008)
4. Younas, M., Awan, I.: Mobility management scheme for context aware transactions in pervasive and mobile cyberspace. IEEE Trans. Industr. Electron. **60**(3), 1108–1115 (2013)
5. Serrano-Alvarado, P.: defining an adaptable mobile transaction service. In: Chaudhri, A.B., Unland, R., Djeraba, C., Lindner, W. (eds.) EDBT 2002. LNCS, vol. 2490, pp. 616–626. Springer, Heidelberg (2002)
6. Elmagarmid, A.K.: Database Transaction Models for Advanced Applications. Morgan Kaufmann, San Francisco (1992). ISBN: 1-55860-214-3

A Self-stabilizing PIF Algorithm for Educated Unique Process Selection

Oday Jubran(✉) and Oliver Theel

Carl von Ossietzky Universität Oldenburg, 26111 Oldenburg, Germany
{jubran,theel}@informatik.uni-oldenburg.de

Abstract. Many applications, methods, and models are based on underlying self-stabilizing mutual exclusion algorithms. The efficiency of such applications is correlated to the efficiency of the algorithms, which reflects a quick recovery from failures, and a fast service time. In this work, we focus on a property correlated to this field, namely *Educated Selection*, which indicates that the selection of processes to be granted unique privilege is deterministic and based on evaluating the local states of processes, or the global configuration. We present a self-stabilizing Propagation of Information with Feedback (PIF) algorithm for trees using the shared memory model. The algorithm exploits the PIF technique for achieving fast educated unique process selection.

Keywords: Self-stabilization · Propagation of information with feedback (PIF) · Mutual exclusion · Educated selection

1 Introduction

Self-stabilization [1] ensures that a system's desired behavior is eventually obtained and never voluntarily violated regardless of the system's initial behavior. Self-stabilization was considered in distributed systems using the *shared memory model*, where a process is enabled to execute an action if a condition over the registers, visible to the process, is satisfied. Running an action changes the registers' values, potentially enabling other processes to run actions.

The mutual exclusion problem was considered in self-stabilization, e.g. [2]. Mutual exclusion comprises: (1) a safety property that at most one process is granted a privilege in each state, and (2) a liveness property that each process is privileged infinitely often. The second property is usually referred as *fairness.*

Mutual exclusion does not necessarily require the process selection for granting the privilege to be deterministic. However, for some systems, it is useful if the process selection is based on local or global criteria, e.g. energy measurements or QoS indicators, towards increasing the performance of the systems. We denote such deterministic process selection as an *educated selection.*

This work was partially supported by the German Research Foundation (DFG) as part of the Transregional Collaborative Research Center "Automatic Verification and Analysis of Complex Systems" (SFB/TR 14 AVACS, http://www.avacs.org/).

A. Bouajjani and H. Fauconnier (Eds.): NETYS 2015, LNCS 9466, pp. 485–489, 2015.
DOI: 10.1007/978-3-319-26850-7_36

The *Propagation of Information with Feedback* (PIF) [3] is a useful token-passing approach for educated selection, in which a process sends a wave of tokens, and receives a feedback. In this work, we apply a PIF approach for educated unique process selection by extending an earlier approach [4]. We present a self-stabilizing PIF algorithm for trees using the shared memory model. The algorithm performs reasonably fast educated unique process selection based on local or global criteria in (a)synchronous environments.

Outline. Section 2 gives the basic notation. Section 3 presents our self-stabilizing PIF algorithm. Section 4 draws a conclusion.

2 Notation

We consider a tree topology using the shared memory model. A **tree** $T = (P, E)$ is a set of *processes* P and *edges* $E \subseteq P \times P$. The *parent* of a process p is denoted by θ_p, and the children of p are denoted by C_p. The root is denoted by *root*, and the set of leaves (resp. inner processes) in P is denoted by *Leaves* (resp. *Inner*). The number of all processes is n. Each **process** has variables, constants, and a unique id in $\{0, ..., n-1\}$: A process p of id i is denoted by p_i, and a variable v of p_i is referred by $p_i.v$. A **state** σ is a valuation of the variables of some process p. A **configuration** is a vector $[\sigma_0, ..., \sigma_{n-1}]$ of the states of all processes.

3 Algorithm

We present an algorithm, which is based on an extended scheme of the well-known mutual exclusion algorithm of Dijkstra [2]. Section 3.1 presents the algorithm for educated selection based on local states, and Sect. 3.2 extends the algorithm for educated selection based on global configurations

3.1 Educated Selection Based on Local States

Algorithm 1 shows the algorithm. Each process owns the following variables: (1) $up \in \mathbb{B}$ and $x \in \mathbb{B}$. We assert that $up = \top$ for the root, and $up = \bot$ for each leaf. (2) $\ell \in \{0, ..., n-1\}$: this variable stores a process's id to direct particular tokens to selected processes. We say that a process p *points* to a process p_i when $p.\ell = i$. (3) We abstract the local criteria of each process p_i by a variable $m_i \in \mathbb{R}$, such that p_i is selected only if the value of $p_i.m$ is the maximum among all other processes. We assume that the value of $p_i.m$ is updated by p_i independent of the algorithm, and is returned by the function $update_m()$.

We define the function $choose : 2^P \Rightarrow \{0, ..., n-1\}$ as follows: given a subset $P' \subseteq P$, the function returns the id of a process that has the maximum value of m among P'. A process runs *critSection*(), if it is privileged.

The stable behavior of Algorithm 1 is an infinite repetition of two PIF cycles, where in each cycle, the root propagates a token to all processes, and receives a feedback from all processes, yielding four types of tokens.

Algorithm 1. Algorithm for a Process p in a Topology $T = (P, E)$

Constants: $id \in \{0, ..., n-1\}$

Variables: $x \in \mathbb{B}$, $up \in \mathbb{B}$, $\ell \in \{0, ..., n-1\}$, $m \in \mathbb{R}$

Assertions: $root.up = \top \wedge \forall q \in Leaves \bullet q.up = \bot$

Tokens

$token_1 : \theta_p.x \neq x \wedge \neg x$ % Search Token

$token_2 : up \wedge x \wedge \forall\, ch \in C_p \bullet ch.x = x \wedge \neg ch.up$ % Feedback Token

$token_3 : \theta_p.x \neq x \wedge x$ % Execute Token

$token_4 : up \wedge \neg x \wedge \forall\, ch \in C_p \bullet ch.x = x \wedge \neg ch.up$ % Complete Token

Functions

$update_m() := \{v \in \mathbb{R} \mid v \text{ is independent of the algorithm}\}$

$choose(P' \subseteq P) := \{i \mid p_i \in P' \wedge \forall q \in P' \bullet p_i.m = \max(q.m)\}$

$critSection()$: Access Critical Section

Guarded Commands (c_i : *guard* $\longrightarrow$ *action*)

Root Sub-Algorithm

1 : $token_2 \longrightarrow \ell := choose(\{p\} \cup C_p);\ m := p_\ell.m;\ x = \neg x;$

2 : $token_4 \wedge \ell = id \longrightarrow$ ***critSection()***; $m := update_m();\ x = \neg x;$ % Privileged

3 : $token_4 \wedge \ell \neq id \longrightarrow m := update_m(); x = \neg x;$

Inner Process Sub-Algorithm

4 : $token_1 \longrightarrow m := update_m();\ up := \top;\ x := \neg x;$

5 : $token_2 \wedge \neg token_3 \longrightarrow \ell := choose(\{p\} \cup C_p);\ m = p_\ell.m;\ up := \bot;$

6 : $token_3 \wedge \theta_p.\ell = id \wedge \ell = id \longrightarrow$ ***critSection()***; $up := \top;\ x := \neg x;$ % Privileged

7 : $token_3 \wedge \theta_p.\ell = id \wedge \exists q \in C_p \bullet p.\ell = q.id \longrightarrow up := \top;\ x := \neg x;$

8 : $token_3 \wedge \neg(\theta_p.\ell = id \vee \exists q \in C_p \bullet q.\ell = q.id) \longrightarrow \ell := id;\ up := \top;\ x := \neg x;$

9 : $token_4 \wedge \neg token_1 \longrightarrow up := \bot;$

Leaf Sub-Algorithm

10 : $token_1 \longrightarrow m := update_m();\ \ell := id;\ x := \neg x;$

11 : $token_3 \wedge \theta_p.\ell = id \longrightarrow$ ***critSection()***; $x := \neg x;$ % Privileged

12 : $token_3 \wedge \theta_p.\ell \neq id \longrightarrow x := \neg x;$

Algorithm 2. Extending Algorithm 1

Additional Variables

$snapShot = [k_0, ..., k_{n-1}]$, where $k_i \in \mathbb{R}$ for $0 \leq i \leq n-1$

Extended Functions

$update_m([k_0, ..., k_{n-1}]) = \{v \in \mathbb{R} \mid v \text{ is dependent of } [k_0, ..., k_{n-1}]\}$

Extended Guarded Commands $(2, 3, 4, 6, 9, 10, 11)$

$2'$: ... $\longrightarrow$ ***critSection()***; $snapShot.k_{id} = k;\ m := update_m(snapShot);\ x = \neg x;$

$3'$: ... $\longrightarrow snapShot = p_\ell.snapShot;\ m := update_m(snapShot);\ x := \neg x;$

$4'$: ... $\longrightarrow snapShot = \theta_p.snapShot;\ m := update_m(snapShot);\ up := \top; x := \neg x;$

$6'$: ... $\longrightarrow$ ***critSection()***; $snapShot.k_{id} := k;\ up := \bot;\ x := \neg x;$

$9'$: ... $\longrightarrow snapShot := p_\ell.snapShot;\ up := \bot;$

$10'$: ... $\longrightarrow snapShot = \theta_p.snapShot;\ m := update_m(snapShot);\ \ell := id;\ x := \neg x;$

$11'$: ... $\longrightarrow$ ***critSection()***; $snapShot.k_{id} = k;\ m := update_m(snapShot);\ x := \neg x;$

First PIF Cycle

$token_1 \downarrow$: the root sends $token_1$. When a process p receives $token_1$, p updates m, and forwards the token to its children (c_4), until $token_1$ reaches the leaves. Each leaf l_i updates $l_i.m$, and sends $token_2$ to its parent (c_{10}).

$token_2 \uparrow$: when a process p receives $token_2$, p points to a process q, where $q \in \{p\} \cup C_p$ and q has the maximum value of m among p and its children (c_5). Then, p copies $q.m$, and switches the value of $p.up(c_5)$. With this action, each process p eventually points to a path that leads to the process with the original maximum value of m, after copying it. Eventually, $token_2$ reaches the root, and the root starts the second PIF cycle (c_1).

Second PIF Cycle

$token_3 \downarrow$: the root sends $token_3$. If a process p receives $token_3$, one of three possible cases exists:

- **Case (1)** represented by commands c_6, c_{11}: if θ_p points to p and p points to itself, then p has a privilege. p runs *critSection*() and forwards the token.
- **Case (2)** represented by c_7: if θ_p points to p and p points to one of its children q, this implies that the selected process exists in the subtree rooted by q. p passes $token_3$, while keeping $p.\ell = q.id$.
- **Case (3)** represented by c_8, c_{12}: if θ_p is not pointing to p, or p is neither pointing to itself nor to one of its children, then there is no selected process in the maximal subtree rooted by p. p sets ℓ to $p.id$, to prohibit any child from running *critSection*() after forwarding $token_3$.

Note that, if $token_3$ is directed to a subtree T', in which there is no selected process, then c_8 is enabled in each process in T' in the current PIF cycle.

$token_4 \uparrow$: Next, $token_4$ is forwarded to the root (c_9). The root receives $token_4$ which involves all its children. If the selected process is the root, then c_2 is enabled, the root runs *critSection*(), and sends $token_1$ to its children. Otherwise (c_3), the root simply starts a new PIF cycle.

Regarding the time complexity: (1) The algorithm guarantees unique process selection in d rounds, where d is the tree depth. (2) The algorithm guarantees that after at most $3d$ rounds, each PIF cycle lasts $2d$ rounds, and within any two subsequent PIF cycles, exactly one process is privileged.

3.2 Educated Selection Based on Global Configurations

We extend Algorithm 1 for educated selection based on configurations. We show the extension in Algorithm 2. In Algorithm 1, the update value of m, returned by $update_m()$, is based on the local state. In Algorithm 2, the value of m is updated according to the global configuration. This indicates that each process should know the configuration. We abstract the configuration by the vector *snapShot*, owned by each process, and defined as follows: $snapShot = [k_0, ..., k_{n-1}]$, where $k_i \in \mathbb{R}$, for $0 \le i \le n-1$, is the relevant evaluation of the local state of p_i. Now, each process p updates $p.m$ according to the value of $p.snapShot$.

The extended commands from Algorithm 1 are c_2-c_4, c_6, c_9-c_{11}. With the extension, the stable behavior is as follows: in the first PIF cycle, when a process receives $token_1$, it copies the parent's snapshot, and updates m according to the snapshot ($c_{4'}, c_{10'}$). With this action, a copy of the snapshot reaches each process. The remainder of the first PIF cycle continues normally. In the second PIF cycle, the selected process runs *critSection*(), and modifies its snapshot based on the new value of k ($c_{6'}, c_{11'}$). Next, the parent of p copies the new snapshot, and forwards it to the root ($c_{9'}$). $c_{2'}$ and $c_{3'}$ concern extended root commands.

In the above behavior, it is assumed that the snapshot sent by the root matches the values of k of all processes. If there is an incorrect value of some k, the snapshot is said to be *inconsistent*. For inconsistent snapshots: we say that a snapshot *snap* is *highlighted* iff it contains at least one *null* value of some k. We also say that *snap* is empty if it contains only *null* values.

The snapshot inconsistency is corrected in the first PIF cycle: (1) When the root propagates $token_1$ with an inconsistent *snapShot*, there exists a process p_j such that $p_j.k$ is not equal to $snapShot.k_j$. Eventually, p_j receives $token_1$. (2) When p_j copies the snapshot, p_j checks if there is an inconsistency, or if $\theta_p.snapShot$ is empty. In both cases, p_j sets its snapshot empty. (3) Next, all processes in the maximal subtree rooted by p_j set their snapshots empty, analogous to step 2, since $token_1$ reaches every process. (4) Now, starting from the leaves, for each process p that receives $token_2$, if p recognizes a highlighted snapshot in one of its children or itself, then p creates a new snapshot by merging the snapshots of its children, and adding its value of k. Now, the snapshot of p contains correct values of all processes in the subtree rooted by p, and *null* values for the processes that are not in the subtree. (5) After the root receives a feedback token ($token_2$), it merges the new snapshots, yielding a correct one.

4 Conclusion

We presented a self-stabilizing PIF algorithm for educated unique process selection for trees using the shared memory model. The algorithm ensures that a process is selected to execute an action only if it is distinguished from other processes according to some criterion, and the criterion is based on the local state of the selected process. We denote the criterion as whether or not a particular number value of a process is maximal among all processes. We extended the algorithm for selecting processes based on a global configuration by propagating a snapshot of the local states of all processes.

References

1. Dolev, S.: Self-Stabilization. The MIT Press, Cambridge (2000)
2. Dijkstra, E.W.: Self-stabilizing systems in spite of distributed control. Commun. ACM **17**(11), 643–644 (1974)
3. Segall, A.: Distributed network protocols. IEEE Trans. Inf. Theory **29**(1), 23–34 (1983)
4. Jubran, O., Theel, O.: Exploiting synchronicity for immediate feedback in self-stabilizing PIF algorithms. In: PRDC, pp. 106–115. IEEE (2014)

Coalitional Game Theory for Cooperative Transmission in VANET: Internet Access via Fixed and Mobile Gateways

Abdelfettah Mabrouk[1(✉)], Abdellatif Kobbane[1], Essaid Sabir[2], and Mohammed EL Koutbi[1]

[1] MIS Team, SIME Lab, ENSIAS, Mohammed V University of Rabat, Rabat, Morocco
mabroukdes@gmail.com, {kobbane,elkoutbi}@ensias.ma

[2] NEST Research Group, ENSEM, Hassan II University of Casablanca, Casablanca, Morocco
e.sabir@ensem.ac.ma

Abstract. In Vehicular Ad-hoc Networks (VANETs), vehicles need to cooperate with each other or with a roadside infrastructure to transmit data. In this work, we study the cooperative transmission for VANETs using coalitional game theory. Each vehicle has a desire to access Internet via gateways that can be either fixed or mobiles. The gateways can enhance the vehicles' transmissions by cooperatively relaying the vehicles' data. Moreover, due to the mobility of the vehicles, we introduce the notion of encounter and predicted lifetime to indicate the availability of forwarding between the vehicle and gateway. We model the problem as a coalition formation game with non-transferable utility and we propose an algorithm for forming coalitions among the vehicles. To evaluate the proposed solution, we present and discuss the numerical results under two scenarios: fixed gateways scenario and mobile gateways scenario. The numerical results show that mobile gateways scenario is more effective than fixed gateways scenario in term of cooperative transmission.

Keywords: VANET · Coalitional game · Cooperative transmission · Fixed gateways · Mobile gateways · Coalition formation game

1 Introduction

In order to access Internet services, VANETs must be integrated into the Internet. This integration is typically achieved by enhancing communication and routing performances in VANETs. For this reason, several routing algorithms are proposed. But due to high mobility in VANETs, it is hard to design an efficient routing algorithm for connecting vehicles to Internet with a reasonable cost. However, researchers have recently used several mathematical approaches to enhance the communication in wireless networks. While heuristic methods can be used to study the performance optimization of wireless networks, coalitional game theory is also considered as an interesting approach which provides

A. Bouajjani and H. Fauconnier (Eds.): NETYS 2015, LNCS 9466, pp. 490–495, 2015.
DOI: 10.1007/978-3-319-26850-7_37

analytical tools to model the behaviors of rational players when they cooperate, it is a powerful tool for designing robust, practical, efficient, and fair cooperation strategies and has been extensively applied in communication and wireless networks. For example, in [1], the coalitional game theory is utilized to study the cooperation between rational wireless users, and the stability of the coalition is analyzed. The authors in [2] studied the bandwidth sharing by using coalition formation games in V2R communications. In [3], the coalition formation games for distributed cooperation among RSUs in vehicular networks were studied. The authors proposed in [4] an approach based on coalitional game theory to study how to stimulate message forwarding in VANETs. Therefore, such game can be a coalitional game with transferable utility (UT), in which the total utility received by any coalition is a real number can be apportioned in any manner between the members of this coalition [5]. On the other hand a coalitional game with non-transferable utility (NUT), in which the coalition value is not a real number, but is a payoffs' vector [6], where each element of this vector represents a payoff that a player can obtain within the coalition.

In this paper, we propose a mathematical model based on coalitional game theory with non-transferable utility (NTU) to access Internet in VANETs under two different scenarios: fixed gateways scenario, in which the gateways are installed along the road and serve as internet access point as depicted in Fig. 1(a); and mobile gateways scenario, in which the gateways are special vehicles moving on the road as depicted in Fig. 1(b). In these both scenarios, two kinds of cooperation are considered. First, vehicles can form coalitions and cooperate with each other to avoid interfering transmissions. Second, the gateways can join the coalitions to cooperate the transmission of the vehicles. But, due to the highly dynamic topology in VANETs, vehicles and gateways may be very far away from each other and the cooperative transmission may be impossible. Hence, we propose the notion of encounter and predicted lifetime between the vehicles and the gateways. Before a gateway cooperates a vehicle's transmission, two conditions should be satisfied: (1) the gateway and vehicle are in the same coalition; (2) the gateway and vehicle encounter each other with a predicted lifetime of linking.

The rest of the paper is structured as follows. Section 2 present the system model. The coalitional game approach is proposed in Sect. 3. In Sect. 4, the numerical results are discussed. Finally, we conclude the paper in Sect. 5.

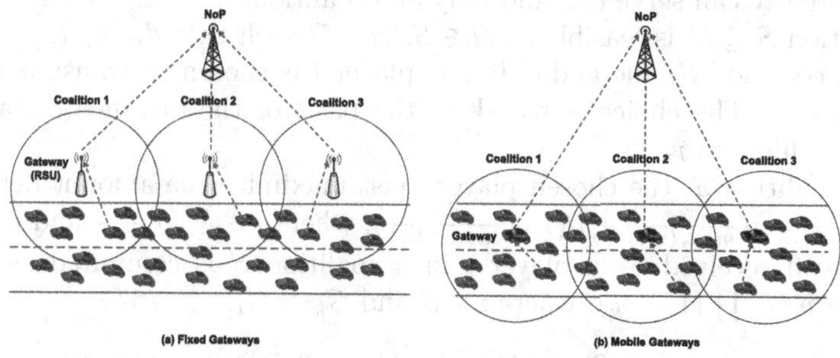

Fig. 1. Internet access via (a) fixed gateways and (b) mobile gateways

2 System Model

Considering vehicular networks depicted in Figs. 1 and 2, which consist of a network operator (NoP), N vehicles, and M gateways. The vehicles can form coalitions and the gateways can cooperate the transmissions of the vehicles when they are in the same coalition. Let $\mathbb{V} = \{1, 2, 3, ..., N\}$ and $\mathbb{G} = \{1, 2, 3, ..., M\}$ represent the set of the vehicles and gateways, respectively. For both scenarios proposed above, we assume that:

1. All vehicles are equipped with GPS receivers.
2. Each vehicle can obtain its current location and speed using GPS capabilities.
3. Ordinary vehicle is a vehicle with only WLAN capabilities (WiFi).
4. Gateway is a RSU or a special vehicle acting as a relay with both WLAN and WWAN capabilities (UMTS); vehicles access Internet through gateways.
5. A link l_{ij} can be established between vehicle $i \in \mathbb{V}$ and gateway $j \in \mathbb{G}$ only if i encounters j, i.e. the distance d_{ij} between them is inferior to R ($d_{ij} \leq R$), where R is the transmission range of the technology WLAN.
6. Any link l_{ij} has a predicted lifetime given as: $\tau_{ij} = \frac{R-|d_{ij}|}{|S_i - S_j|}, S_i \neq S_j$, where S_i and S_j represent the speed of vehicle i and gateway j, respectively. If S_i=S_j, the predicted lifetime is set to a predefined great value.
7. Two or more vehicles can not transmit simultaneously when they encounter the same gateway, the transmissions will fail due to the signal interference.

3 Coalitional Game Approach

Under both scenarios proposed above, the game applied is a coalitional game with non-transferable utility (NTU) which is defined by the tuple $(\mathcal{N}, \mathcal{F}, v)$, where $\mathcal{N}$ is a set of players, $\mathcal{F} \subseteq 2^{\mathcal{N}}$ is the set of feasible coalitions and $v(S)$, for each $S \in \mathcal{F}$, is the coalition value. It is a payoffs' vector, $v(S) \in \mathbb{R}^{|S|}$, where each component x_i of $v(S)$ represents a payoff that player $i \in S$ can obtain within coalition S. For our problem, the model is defined at each time-slot as fellow:

1. The players are the vehicles, i.e., $\mathcal{N} = \mathbb{V}$.
2. Each player i is active with a probability p_i to transmit data.
3. Each coalition has one and only one gateway as a relay to access Internet.
4. Each gateway can serve one and only one coalition.
5. A coalition $S \subseteq \mathcal{N}$ is feasible if: $\forall i \in S, \exists j \in \mathbb{G}$ such that $d_{ij} \leq R$.
6. In each coalition S, one and only one player i is chosen to transmit data to a gateway j. The choice is based on the basis of the distance d_{ij} and the predicted lifetime τ_{ij}.
7. In the coalition S, the chosen player must maximize the amount defined as follow: $G_i = \alpha \frac{\tau_{ij}}{max_i(\tau_{ij})} + \beta(1 - \frac{d_{ij}}{max_i(d_{ij})})$, where $i \in \mathcal{N}$, $j \in \mathbb{G}$ and $i, j \in S$.
8. The payoff received by a player i in a coalition S is computed as follow: $U_i(S) = p_i G_i \prod_{k \in S} (1 - p_k)$, where $i \in S$ and $G_k > G_i$.
9. The coalition value $v(S) \in \mathbb{R}^{|S|}$ is a payoffs' vector given by: $v(S) = (U_i(S))_{i \in S}$.

Generally, in a coalition formation game, the most important aspect is the formation of the coalitions in the game. In many applications, the coalition formation in the game with NTU entails finding a structure with Pareto optimal payoff distribution for the players. But, it is very difficult to achieve such a goal. The reason is that, finding an optimal partition requires complete information on all the players set $\mathcal{N}$. Hence, since the game which is applied in our scenarios is a coalitional game with NTU, and the players do not have detailed knowledge of network (incomplete information), we have proposed the following algorithm to coalition structure formation.

Algorithm. Coalition Structure Formation

At each time-slot t ***do:***
Input: $\mathcal{N}$, $\mathbb{G}$, R, α, β, $p_{i\in\mathcal{N}}$;
Output: *Coalitional structure* Π *at time-slot* t;
Begin:
1. *Compute* d_{ij} *and* τ_{ij} *for each* $i \in \mathcal{N}$ *and* $j \in \mathbb{G}$;
2. *Compute* $S_j = \{i \in \mathcal{N}, d_{ij} \leq R\}$ *for each* $j \in \mathbb{G}$;
3. *For each* $i \in \mathcal{N}$
    For each $j \in \mathbb{G}$
        If $(i \in S_j)$
            Compute $U_i(S_j)$;
        End If
    End For
    Player i *chooses* $\hat{\jmath}(i) \in \underset{S_j, i\in S_j}{\operatorname{argmax}}\, U_i(S_j)$;
   End For
4. *For each* $j \in \mathbb{G}$
    Compute $S_j^* = \{i \in \mathcal{N}, j = \hat{\jmath}(i)\}$;
   End For
5. *Return*$((S_j^*)_{j\in\mathbb{G}})$;

End.

---

4 Numerical Results

Two important metrics which were evaluated in this paper are: (1) Average coalition size; and (2) Average coalition utility.

Figure 2(a) shows that the average coalition size increases when the vehicle density increases. This can be explained by the fact that increasing the number of vehicles increases the number of nodes that join a coalition. On the other hand, Fig. 2(b) shows that the average coalition size decreases when the number of gateways increases. It is because that increasing the number of gateways increases the number of coalitions, and this regroups the vehicles in many subsets with smaller size. In addition, the average coalition size in mobile gateways scenario remains lower in comparison with that in fixed gateways scenario. The reason is that gateways mobility helps the vehicles to find many nearby gateways.

Figure 2(c) shows that the average coalition utility decreases with the increase of vehicles density in the road. This is mainly due to the fact that increasing the number of vehicles increases the size of coalitions, which naturally reduces their utilities. However, Fig. 2(d) shows that the average coalition utility increases when the number of gateways increases too. It can be explained by the fact that increasing the number of gateways in the road increases the number of coalitions, which reduces their sizes and increases their utilities. Furthermore, the average coalition utility in the mobile gateways scenario remains much better compared with that in the fixed gateways scenario. This is due to the fact that the gateways mobility increases the encounter probability between vehicles and gateways.

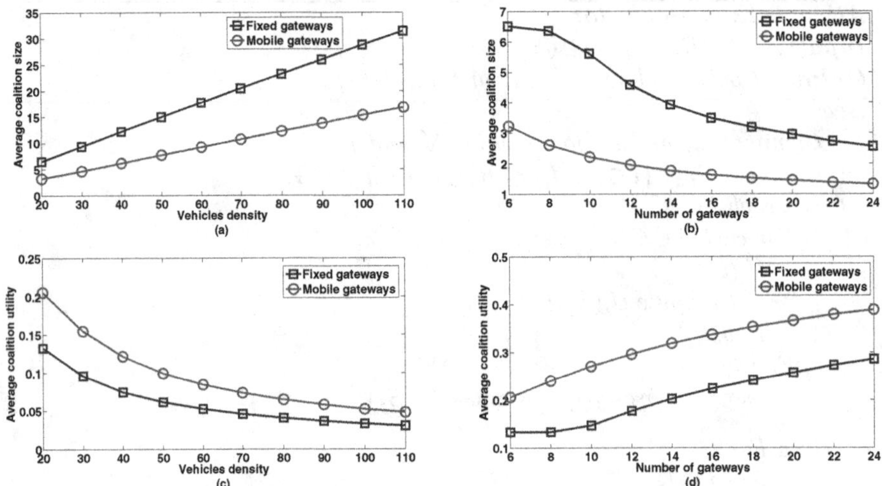

Fig. 2. Average coalition size and average coalition utility

5 Conclusion

In this paper, we have studied the cooperative transmission among vehicles using coalitional game theory in order to relay data to the Internet via fixed and mobile gateways. We have also proposed the notion of encounter in order to regroup the vehicles around the gateways. An algorithm, based on both the distance and the predicted lifetime of links established between vehicles and gateways, is proposed to form a NTU coalition structure. The obtained simulation results show that the mobile gateways scenario is more effective than the fixed gateways scenario.

References

1. Mathur, S., Sankar, L., Mandayam, N.B.: Coalitions in Cooperative Wireless Networks. J. Sel. Areas Commun. **26**(7), 1104–1115 (2008)

2. Niyato, D., Wang, P., Saad, W., Hjorungnes, A.: Coalition formation games for bandwidth sharing in vehicle-to-roadside communications. In: IEEE International Wireless Communications and Networking Conference, pp. 1–5 (2010)
3. Saad, W., Han, Z., Hjorungnes, A., Niyato, D., Hossain, E.: Coalition formation games for distributed cooperation among roadside units in vehicular networks. J. Sel. Areas Commun. **29**(1), 48–60 (2011)
4. Chen, T., Zhu, L., Wu, F., Zhong, S.: Stimulating cooperation in vehicular ad hoc networks: a coalitional game theoretic approach. IEEE Trans. Veh. Technol. **60**(2), 566–579 (2011)
5. Li, D., Xu, Y., Wang, X., Guizani, M.: Coalitional game theoretic approach for secondary spectrum access in cooperative cognitive radio networks. IEEE Trans. Wirel. Commun. **10**(3), 844–856 (2011)
6. Saad, W.: Coalitional game theory for distributed cooperation in next generation wireless networks. Ph.D. thesis, University of Oslo (2010)

Performance Evaluation for Ad hoc Routing Protocols in Realistic Physical Layer

Hassan Faouzi[1(✉)], Hicham Mouncif[2], and Mohamed Lamsaadi[2]

[1] FST, Sultan Moulay Slimane University, Beni Mellal, Morocco
faouzi.hassan.mi@gmail.com

[2] FP, Sultan Moulay Slimane University, Beni Mellal, Morocco
{hmouncif, lamsaadima}@yahoo.fr

Abstract. A mobile ad hoc network or MANET (Mobile Ad hoc NETwork) is an autonomous system of mobile platforms called nodes that are free to move about freely. This system can be isolated or have gateways or interfaces connecting it to a fixed network. Most performance evaluation models of routing protocols for ad hoc networks based on the assumption of an ideal radio channel, implying that the underlying physical phenomena are neglected. We propose to use a realistic physical layer by integrating the probability of transmission error characterized by a two-state Markov model in the different radio propagation modes. We measure the impact of such modeling to evaluate-the performance of Proactive and Reactive MANET protocols.

Keywords: Mobile ad-hoc network · Routing protocols · NS2(Simulator) · Radio channel · Throughput · Delay · Packet delivery ratio · Control overhead · Markov chain · Gilbert-Elliot model

1 Introduction

There is a lot of research studying the performance of routing protocols in ad hoc networks. However, their performance evaluation is based on an ideal radio channel hypothesis: no transmission error, no interference.

In this article we try to evaluate and compare the performance of four routing protocols for mobile ad hoc networks, DSDV [1], AODV [2], DSR [3] and OLSR [4] using the NS-2 network simulator [5] taking into consideration all the problems related to the transmission media. Packet Delivery Ratio, Average End-to-End Delay, Normalized Routing Load and Throughput are the four common measures used for the comparison of the performance of above protocols.

The rest of the paper is organized as follows: Sect. 2 presents the definition of Routing and protocol classification. Section 3 we study the media transmission error by using a two-state Markov Model. Section 4 gives an overview of different radio propagation models. The simulation environment and then the results are presented in Sect. 5. Finally, Sect. 6 concludes the paper.

A. Bouajjani and H. Fauconnier (Eds.): NETYS 2015, LNCS 9466, pp. 496–500, 2015.
DOI: 10.1007/978-3-319-26850-7_38

2 Routing and Protocol Classification

Routing protocols in ad hoc networks are essential for communication between two stations that are not in direct contact. Generally the routing protocols can be separated into two categories, proactive and reactive protocols. Proactive protocols establish routes in advance based on the periodic exchange of the routing tables, while the reactive protocols seek routes to the request.

3 Media Transmission Error

A number of researchers have studied the behavior of wireless channels. Among them, Gilbert and Elliot proposed a Discrete Time Markov Chain (DTMC) model, called the Gilbert-Elliot model [6, 7], which consists of two states (i.e., a good state and a bad state) and uses a two-by-two transition matrix to specify the state transition probabilities.

The state transition is described by the probabilities of changing from the Good state to the bad state $p_{g/b}$ and from the bad state to the good state $p_{b/g}$. This is illustrated in Fig. 1.

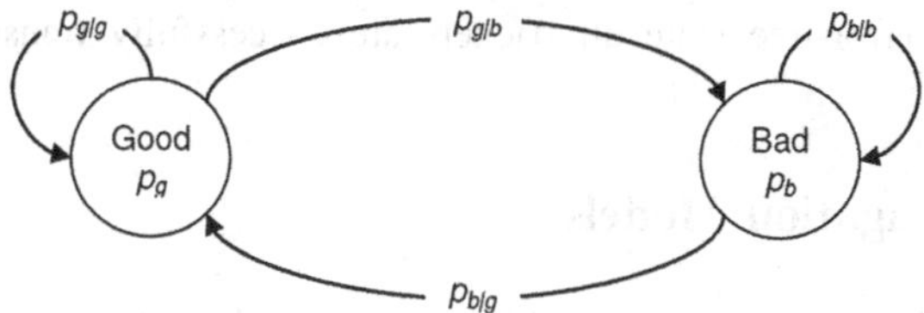

Fig. 1. Markov chain of errors on a link

The matrix transition can be expressed by:

$$P = \begin{bmatrix} p_{g/g} & p_{g/b} \\ p_{b/g} & p_{b/b} \end{bmatrix} = \begin{bmatrix} 1-p & p \\ q & 1-q \end{bmatrix} \quad (1)$$

The parameters p and q can be derived from experimental observations. Real measurements show that $q \gg p$. For example, measurements of errors on the wireless link, given in [8], show $p_{b/g} = 0.3820$ and $p_{g/b} = 0.0060$ we obtain:

$$P = \begin{bmatrix} 0.994 & 0.006 \\ 0.382 & 0.618 \end{bmatrix} \quad (2)$$

The probability of being in a good state π_g or in a bad state π_b can be calculated using a steady state:

$$\pi P = P \quad (3)$$

Therefore

$$[\pi_g \quad \pi_b] = [\pi_g \quad \pi_b]\begin{bmatrix} 1-p & p \\ q & 1-q \end{bmatrix} \tag{4}$$

And

$$\sum \pi = 1 \tag{5}$$

Than

$$\pi_g = \frac{p}{p+q} \tag{6}$$

and

$$\pi_b = \frac{q}{p+q} \tag{7}$$

When a channel is in error-state, any IP packets sent would be either lost or corrupted. In the error-free state all packets are successfully transmitted over the wireless link.

4 Radio Propagation Models

Propagation models are used to predict the propagation characteristics such as received signal power of each packet. At the physical layer of each wireless node, there is a receiving threshold. When a packet is received, if its signal power is below the receiving threshold, it is marked as error and dropped by the MAC layer. In general there are three main propagation models, firstly the Free Space model assumes the propagation conditions as ideal, and the radius of the radio signal propagation is in the form of disc, within which the reception is perfect, and that beyond no further communication is possible; secondly the Two-Ray Ground model considers the direct path propagation in addition to the reflection caused by the ground; and thirdly the Shadowing model is more realistic, since several propagation phenomena are considered, namely, reflection, diffusion and absorption, in addition, the communication radius is no longer considered a perfect disc.

5 Simulation and Results

5.1 Simulation Environment

There Simulation environment in NS2 consists of 30 mobile nodes which are placed uniformly and forming a Mobile Ad-hoc Network with nodes max moving speed of 10.0 m/s and the pause between movements is 20 s about over a 1000 × 1000 m area for 150 s of simulated time.

5.2 Simulation Results

See Fig. 2.

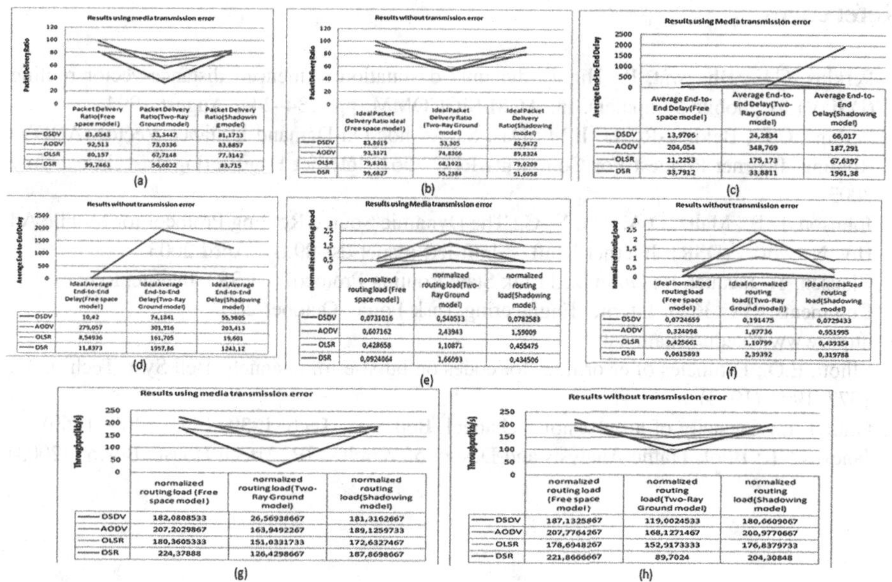

Fig. 2. Simulation Results

6 Conclusion

This paper presents the comparative study and performance evaluation of the routing protocols DSDV, AODV, DSR and OLSR. In the ideal condition of transmission we note that the protocols give good results but in reality we can't achieve them because the wireless links are characterized by high error rates caused by a variety of transmission impairments such as multi-path fading and background noise so it's normal that we note the decrease in performance of routing protocols if we take into account these effects. Make a comparison in ideal conditions don't always give the real result so we had to simulate transmission problems in wireless networks in order to get the most useful and reliable results that's why we integrated the Markov model in our simulation. Simulation results (Fig. 2(a–h)) show that all types of radio propagation models, AODV performs optimally because is a reactive protocol, which uses routing table one route per destination, sequence number to maintain route and when links break AODV causes the affected set of nodes to be notified so that they are able to invalidate the routes using the lost link, these are the major reasons for it having a good result in average Packet Delivery Ratio, End-to-End DeLay and Throughput, but has a higher Routing load because it generates more control packets. Our future work will include the modification to the basic AODV routing protocol to reduce the number of the control packets.

References

1. Perkins, C.E., Bhagwat, P.: Highly dynamic destination sequenced distance-vector routing (DSDV) for mobile computers. In: ACM SIGCOMM, pp. 234–244, August 1994
2. Perkins, C.E., Belding-Royer, E.M., Das, S.: Ad hoc On-Demand Distance Vector (AODV) Routing. Internet Request For Comments RFC 3561, Internet Engineering Task Force, July 2003
3. Johnson, D.B., Maltz, D.A., Hu, Y.-C.: The Dynamic Source Routing Protocol for Mobile Ad Hoc Networks (DSR). Internet Draft – draft-ietf-manet-dsr-09.txt, April 2003
4. Clausen, T., Jacquet, P.: Optimized Link State Routing Protocol (OLSR). Internet Request For Comments RFC 3626, Internet Engineering Task Force, October 2003
5. http://www.isi.edu/nsnam/ns/
6. Elliott, E.O.: Estimates of error rates for codes on burst-error channels. Bell Syst. Tech. J. **42**, 1977–1997 (1963)
7. Gilbert, E.: Capacity of a burst-noise channel. Bell Syst. Tech. J. **39**, 1253–1266 (1960)
8. Janevski, T.: Book Traffic Analysis and Design of Wireless IP. Artech House, Boston (2003)

Understanding Cloud Storage Services Usage: A Practical Case Study

Daniela Oliveira, Paulo Carvalho[(✉)], and Solange Rito Lima

Departamento de Informática, Centro Algoritmi,
Universidade do Minho, Braga, Portugal
pmc@di.uminho.pt

Abstract. Cloud Storage services present several characteristics that turn current classification methods insufficient or too complex to apply, namely the use of dynamic communication ports and security protocols. This paper identifies appropriate techniques for cloud traffic classification and defines a model for processing cloud services traces, taking the University of Minho (UMinho) network as a practical case study. The obtained results, using a classification approach based on Tstat tool, provide global statistics regarding the most used Cloud Storage services at UMinho and characterize the corresponding traffic.

1 Introduction

With the emergence of Cloud Services, traffic classification tasks become a deeper challenge as conventional classification rules fail to succeed. Often the ownership entity of the service is not responsible for providing it [2], making the classification even more complex. The use of dynamic ports and of security protocols for encrypting data, further stress the need for improving current traffic classification techniques.

Attending to the relevance of cloud storage for end users, Internet service providers and cloud service providers (CSP), the present work is focused on characterizing the usage of the most popular cloud storage services, studying also the inner properties of this type of traffic. The work describes a method for traffic filtering and processing able to identify and quantify the use of cloud services by the users at UMinho campus network, which is here used as a case study. In this context, the contributions of this work are threefold: (i) the discussion on challenges regarding the classification and characterization of encrypted traffic; (ii) the systematization of a method for recognizing cloud storage services based on server signatures; and (iii) the identification of useful parameters for a more comprehensive understanding of cloud services usage, allowing to guide network administrators in tuning network management and configuration.

2 Related Work

The encapsulation of applications in protocols connoted with distinct services (e.g., over HTTP), the use of security protocols (e.g., IPSec, TTLS), the growing of applications allocating communication ports dynamically, turn traditional

A. Bouajjani and H. Fauconnier (Eds.): NETYS 2015, LNCS 9466, pp. 501–506, 2015.
DOI: 10.1007/978-3-319-26850-7_39

classification techniques imprecise when based solely on transport protocol and origin/destination ports. Therefore several alternative methods for traffic classification are currently used: (i) analysis of payload resorting to, e.g., pattern matching [8] and numerical analysis [7], which are effective regarding the hit ratio but heavy and unable to classify encrypted traffic; (ii) analysis of systems or terminals behavior (host-behavior) [7], where classification is carried out analyzing the behavior of end systems instead of traffic flows, avoiding payload processing; and (iii) analysis of flows (flow-behavior), which assumes that each application presents proper statistical properties. The training phase of AI learning algorithms is crucial, and proposals exist to obtain an adequate "ground of truth" [6].

These methods can be combined to increase classification ability, for instance, in the classification of encrypted traffic [1,5]. An alternative method for classifying encrypted traffic [3] resorts to service server signatures extracted from the certificates exchanged when establishing a secure session. This classification method is explored in the present work to allow identifying the cloud service providers in use.

3 Case Study: Cloud Storage Services at UMinho

UMinho Network Infrastructure - The University of Minho has currently a population of nearly 18,000 students, 1,200 teachers, and 600 technical and administrative staff, being one of the biggest Portuguese universities. The academic and scientific activities at UMinho are developed in two campuses: Gualtar in Braga and Azurém in Guimarães, interconnected through a 768 Mbps link. The core of network operation is located in Gualtar, where the main network services are assured to users inside and outside the campus (e.g., in residences and libraries), providing a 10 Gbps access to the Internet.

Data Collection Strategy - In a first instance, traffic collection was focused on gathering secure traffic traversing the main backbone router of the University of Minho network. The traffic collection was carried out over a typical working week in May 2013, for periods of low, medium and high network activity, corresponding to more than a thousand dump files for a total of approximately 300 GB of flows data.

Data Processing Strategy - Dump files containing secure flow data must undergo several processing steps before being ready for analysis. The first step involves a preprocessing phase carried out by Tstat [4], a sniffer tool able to handle dump files, producing a set of text files (logs) on a per flow basis. Each line in a log file is related to a flow, reporting multicolumn flow data (a total of 111) [4], being relevant for the present study the following columns: Client IP addr (1); Server IP addr (45); Client TCP port (2): Server TCP port (46); Packets[C2S] (3); Packets[S2C](47); Unique Bytes[C2S] (7); Unique Bytes[S2C] (51); RTT[C2S] (29); RTT[S2C] (73); Flow duration (89); Server name (110); Common name (111). The terms C2S and S2C express the flow direction between a client (C) and a server (S). A second phase consists in processing traffic logs using R statistical environment which allows for data manipulation and calculation. Attending to the aim of the study, two broad traffic flow categories were created: Cloud Storage Flows (CSF) and other cloud flows. As mentioned above, this detection process is based on specific flow signatures, coded as an R function. Each signature aggregates the variables `server_name` and `Common Name` (`CN`), enabling R to forward the flow to the respective category. This R function compares the current values of `server_name` and `CN` against the signatures database in order to identify each flow category. The last phase aims to characterize the use of cloud storage per service provider. For this study, only flows within Cloud Storage category are used to derive new flow categories (as R objects) for each CSP to analyze. Once again the values of the variables `server_name` and `CN` of each flow determine each new CSP category.

Extracting Server Signatures - Extracting a server signature is accomplished resorting to Tstat tool, which inspects and filters the SSL handshaking phase between clients and servers, as shown in Fig. 1. In brief, SSL handshaking involves the following steps: (1) the client requests the establishment of a secure communication by sending a `Client Hello` message along with cryptographic data; (2) the server responses with a `Server Hello` message along with his digital certificate and public key, requesting also the client certificate, if applicable; (3) the client verifies the certificate and, if deemed to be a reliable communication, it proceeds sending a single session key encrypted with the public key of the server, allowing the calculation of the keys to encrypt the communication; and (4) if there is a server-side application for certifying the client, this certificate must also be validated in order to proceed with a secure communication. During step (1), Tstat extracts the value of `server_name` parameter sent within the `Client Hello` message (see RFC 3546), and during step (2) extracts the `CN` that matches a string identifying the name of the server specified in the certificate.

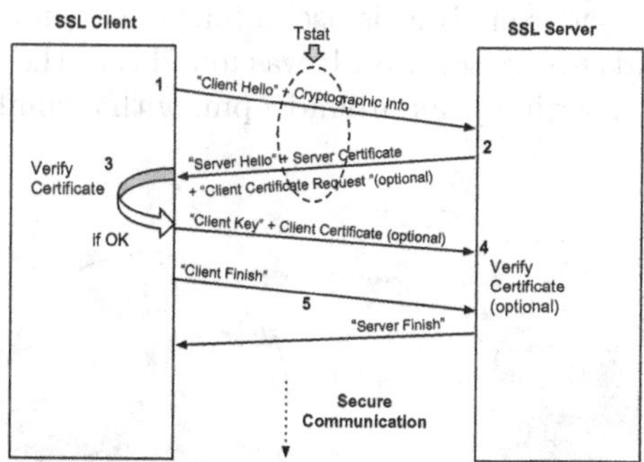

Fig. 1. Tstat filtering during SSL handshaking

4 Results of Data Analysis

Global Statistics of Secure Traffic - Figure 2 (left) illustrates the most popular user services across the university campus network, running over SSL. Currently, it is common that applications in rapid expansion resort to external servers in a Content Delivery Network (CDN) to distribute data to end users/services in a fast and reliable way. Akamai Technologies, Inc. as a CDN provider, is an intermediary for numerous applications, being therefore in the top of the list. Akamai signatures are also captured for other services such as Facebook, which use Akamai servers to store and retrieve users data.

The third most requested service relates to Google. Google Inc. began providing a search engine but quickly has expanded to a wide range of services, including email, social networking, productivity software, web browsing, among others. In this analysis, Google storage service (Google Drive) is grouped with other CSP traffic in the category Cloud Storage. The fourth most accessed service is the institutional email service within UMinho. This service still represents a fundamental means of exchanging information within the academic community, despite the compulsory use of e-learning platforms to support academic activities. With 3.1 % of accesses, Cloud Storage is in the fifth category. All other categories of no cloud flows with less than 3 % of representativeness are included in the category "Other", as they are not significative for the present study.

Characterization of Cloud Storage Flows - This section is focused on classifying and characterizing storage traffic according to each CSP.

CSP Usage - Figure 2 (right) summarizes the accesses made to cloud storage services within the campus network. According to the traffic collected, Dropbox is clearly the most popular service with 71.39 % of accesses, followed by Icloud and Skydrive. The remaining ratio of less than 1.55 % accesses, is shared by Box, Google Drive, PT Cloud, Idrive, and finally, the Ubuntu One with 0.06 % of hits. The study on the number of accesses to the more representative CSPs for the different time periods under analysis is useful for understanding the behavior of users when using cloud storage services. It was found that the number of accesses increases along the day with a peak around 7 pm, with a similar behavior for all

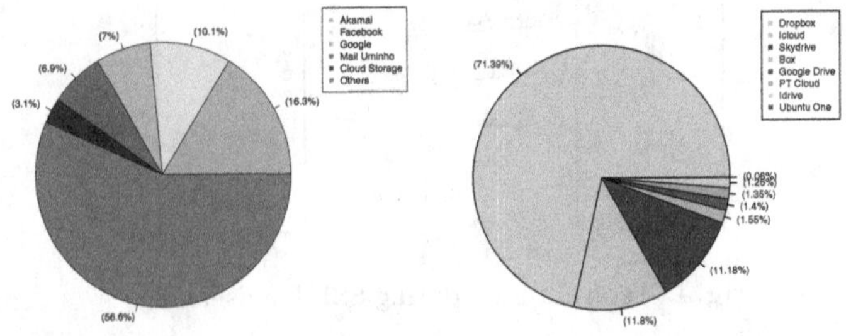

Fig. 2. Global flow classification (left); Classification of flows *Cloud Storage* per CSP (right)

Table 1. Synthesis of statistics when accessing CSP

	per IP		Average per Flow			
	Ratio of accesses (%)	External Servers	Packets	Bytes (k)	RTT (ms)	Duration (s)
Dropbox	4.6	Yes	64	49.8	139.7	12.2
Icloud	4.0	Yes	16	3.7	112.9	4.6
Skydrive	18.5	No	17	5.9	124.9	7.1
Box	26.7	No	57	32.7	119.9	3.0
Google Drive	18.7	No	23	26.6	27.6	13.0
PT Cloud	32.8	No	34	29.4	33.3	0.6
Idrive	100.0	No	8	0.7	118.2	3.9
Ubuntu One	26.5	No	24	10.0	110.1	5.4

CPS, exhibiting an access profile distinct from the typical network usage trend, which usually presents peak periods around 11 am and 4 pm.

Traffic Flow Analysis - Regarding the main CSP under analysis, Table 1 summarizes several statistics useful for the understanding of cloud storage traffic flows, such as the number packets, number of bytes, round-trip time (RTT) and flow duration. The first column in Table 1, referring to the IP address of the server with the highest number of accesses, expresses the ratio between the number of accesses per server and the total number of flows. The table also includes the indication of CSPs which resort to external servers, for instance, Dropbox and iCloud resort to Amazon and Akamai, respectively. Regarding the average flow statistics, Dropbox flows are usually larger on the number of packets and Bytes exchanged per flow, in opposition to Idrive. On average, RTT and flow duration are also larger for Dropbox. Accesses to Google Drive and PT cloud exhibit low RTTs as servers are located in the country. Regarding flow duration, taking Dropbox as example, with a 92.5 % percentile is obtained a value of 30 s, with flows spanning a range duration from 0.27 s to 1158.17 s.

5 Conclusions

The present work studied the usage and characteristics of cloud storage services within the University of Minho. As a viable alternative, a traffic classification approach based on the signatures exchanged between clients and cloud service providers was adopted, resorting to Tstat for extracting the signatures of servers during the SSL handshaking phase. The obtained results aimed at providing (i) new insights regarding the challenges on the classification of secure cloud traffic; (ii) the systematization of a method for detecting cloud services; and (iii) the study of useful characterization parameters for assisting network administrators when configuring networks and services.

Acknowledgements. This work has been supported by FCT - *Fundação para a Ciência e Tecnologia* in the scope of the project: PEst-UID/CEC/00319/2013.

References

1. Aceto, G., Dainotti, A., de Donato, W., Pescapé, A.: Portload: taking the best of two worlds in traffic classification. In: IEEE INFOCOM Workshops, pp. 1–5 (2010)
2. Bermudez, I.N., Mellia, M., Munafò, M.M., Keralapura, R., Nucci, A.: DNS to the Rescue: discerning content and services in a tangled web. In: Proceedings of the 2012 ACM Conference on Internet Measurement Conference, IMC 2012, New York, USA, pp. 413–426 (2012)
3. Drago, I., Mellia, M., Munafò, M., Sperotto, A., Sadre, R., Pras, A.: Inside dropbox: understanding personal cloud storage services. In: Proceedings of the 2012 ACM Conference on Internet Measurement Conference, IMC 2012, New York, USA, pp. 481–494 (2012)
4. Finamore, A., Mellia, M., Meo, M., Munafò, M.M., Torino, P.D., Rossi, D.: Experiences of Internet traffic monitoring with Tstat. IEEE Netw. **25**(3), 8–14 (2011)
5. García-Dorado, J.L., Finamore, A., Mellia, M., Meo, M., Munafò, M.M.: Characterization of ISP traffic: trends, user habits, and access technology impact. IEEE Trans. Netw. Serv. Manage. **9**(2), 142–155 (2012)
6. Gringoli, F., Salgarelli, L., Dusi, M., Cascarano, N., Risso, F., Claffy, K.C.: GT: picking up the truth from the ground for internet traffic. SIGCOMM Comput. Commun. Rev. **39**(5), 12–18 (2009)
7. Karagiannis, T., Papagiannaki, K., Faloutsos, M.: Blinc: multilevel traffic classification in the dark. SIGCOMM Comput. Commun. Rev. **35**(4), 229–240 (2005)
8. Ramaswamy, R., Kencl, L., Iannaccone, G.: Approximate fingerprinting to accelerate pattern matching. In: Proceedings of the 6th ACM Internet Measurement Conference, IMC 2006, New York, USA, pp. 301–306 (2006)

Towards an Optimal Pricing for Mobile Virtual Network Operators

Mohammed Raiss-El-Fenni[1](✉), Mohamed El Kamili[2], Sidi Ahmed Ezzahidi[3], Ismail Berrada[2], and El Houssine Bouyakhf[3]

[1] PACOMS, INPT, Rabat, Morocco
raiss@inpt.ac.ma
[2] LIMS, FSDM, USMBA, Fez, Morocco
{mohamed.elkamili,ismail.berrada}@usmba.ac.ma
[3] LIMIARF, UM-V, Rabat, Morocco
{ezzahidiah,bouillac.lhou}@gmail.com

Abstract. Mobile Virtual Network Operators (MVNO) provide their own subscribers, with mobile voice and data services without owning the access rights to the spectrum they use. In this paper, we study the optimal pricing decisions in the context of MVNO, through two perspectives: the user's view and provider's view. While a user have to optimally adjust its transmission parameters in order to reduce the bill to pay, The MVNO tries to establish an optimal tariff strategy. This paper introduces a mathematical analysis for the two perspectives. The formulas of optimal parameters in each case are presented and some interesting properties are investigated.

1 Introduction

Network professionals are constantly looking to optimize network resources and ensure adequate bandwidth. However, the bandwidth capacity, which is typically considered as a scarce resource, is limited. In order to provide an acceptable level of Quality of Service (QoS) to user applications, providers require efficient bandwidth management techniques.

In this paper, we consider the pricing decisions in the context of a Mobile Virtual Network Operator (MVNO). A MVNO is defined as a company that provides mobile services without owning its licensed frequency of radio spectrum. The frequency bandwidth provided by the MVNO is leased from the spectrum license after an estimation of the average demand of the secondary unlicensed users. In the lease contract, the MVNO anticipates future demands and the heterogeneities of wireless users such as different maximum transmission power levels and channel gains. Next, we will refer to MVNO simply as "provider" and secondary users as "users". A natural question arises here about the tariffs that the provider shall establish in order to obtain the maximum profit margin. A full answer to this issue requires from the provider to distinguish between the case when the average demands exceeds the offered bandwidth or not. In the first case, the provider can enhance the frequency bandwidth by leasing the extra

A. Bouajjani and H. Fauconnier (Eds.): NETYS 2015, LNCS 9466, pp. 507–512, 2015.
DOI: 10.1007/978-3-319-26850-7_40

bandwidth requested by a user. As alternatives, the provider may either look for a taxation strategy [1] or reduce the leasing cost by sensing and utilizing spectrum holes in time and space [5]. This situation is most typical in economic models of Cognitive Radio Networks [2]. From the user's view, based on the price decision of the provider, he might try to maximize his utility function (and thus reduce his bill) by choosing the optimal values for power and bandwidth matching his need.

Recently, bandwidth management schemes were the subject of several studies to improve the quality of service. The authors of [3] propose an algorithm to determine the associations between the user and the access point to achieve a fair bandwidth allocation. Different bandwidth management techniques, for WLANs using a hybrid load balancing scheme, are presented and compared in [4]. The main contributions of this paper are:

- A mathematical analysis of the user strategy for adjusting his transmission parameters, in order to reduce the bill to pay to the MVNO.
- A mathematical analysis of the pricing management strategy of the provider. In this analysis, we differentiate between the case when the requested spectrum belongs to the provider and the case when there is a need to lease band to complete the lack of bandwidth.
- Simulation results demonstrating the preference of our mathematical analysis

2 User's View: Frequency and Power Control

Let us consider the following scenario: A user would like to transmit a signal cheaper without deteriorating its quality of service. The parameter, which allows him to control the signal (resp. the quality of service) is the power P (resp. frequency bandwidth W). In this paper, we can consider the Shannon capacity minus the total payment as the user's payoff. Now, we define the net utility as the difference between the Shannon capacity and the total payment of the power used to transmit signal and the frequency bandwidth demanded from the provider, i.e.:

$$v_U(P,W) = W\ln\left(1+\frac{P}{WN_0+I}\right) - C_W W - C_P P, \tag{1}$$

where N_0 is the background noise, I is the induced noise, C_W is the frequency bandwidth cost and C_P is the power cost.

To solve this problem, we should find the derivatives of v_U on P and W. Then we have,

$$\ln(1+y) = yN_0C_P + C_W. \tag{2}$$

Note that, the Eq. (2) has either zero root, a unique one, or two roots. Namely, the following result holds.

Theorem 1. *From a user's view:*

- *If* $N_0C_P - 1 < \ln(N_0C_P) + C_W$ *then the optimal strategy is* $(P, W) = (0, 0)$*, so the user has no benefit to transmit at all.*
- *If* $N_0C_P - 1 \geq \ln(N_0C_P) + C_W$ *then the optimal strategy is given as follows:*

$$P = \frac{Iy^*}{1 - N_0C_P(1 + y^*)}, W = \frac{IC_P(1 + y^*)}{1 - N_0C_P(1 + y^*)} \tag{3}$$

where y^* *represents the SINR and it is the largest root from the two ones of the equation:* $\ln(1 + y) = yN_0C_P + C_W$.
In particular, between the optimal power P *and the frequency bandwidth* W*, there is a strong linear correlation:* $W = C_P\left(1 + \frac{1}{y^*}\right)P$.
Also, it is interesting to note that since W *is increasing by* y^* *then (3) implies that:* $W \geq \frac{IC_P}{1 - N_0C_P}$.

3 Provider's View: Tariff Control Without Leased Band

Now, we will have a look at the problem from the provider's point of view. The provider assigns the tariff C_W for the frequency bandwidth and get a profit C_WW. His objective is to maximize its profit. In this section we assume that all the requested spectrum of bandwidth frequencies belongs to the provider. Then the payoff to the provider is given as follows: $v_P(W) = C_WW$ where by Theorem 1, $C_W \in [0, 1 + N_0C_P - \ln(N_0C_P)]$.
Then, (3) implies that $v_P(W)$ depends only on y^* (SINR) and C_W as follows:

$$v_P(W) = C_W\frac{IC_P(1 + y^*)}{1 - N_0C_P(1 + y^*)}. \tag{4}$$

The optimal W is given in the following theorem by finding the derivative of $v_P(W)$ on C_W.

Theorem 2. *If the requested spectrum of bandwidth belongs to the provider then the optimal tariff which the provider assigns to bring the maximal profit is given as follows:* $C_W = N_0C_P - 1 - \ln(N_0C_P)$. *This tariff allows to demand* W^* *where* $W^* = \frac{IC_P(1 + y^*)}{1 - N_0C_P(1 + y^*)}$, *and* y^* *is the unique root of the equation* $\ln(1 + y) = (1 + y)N_0C_P - 1 - \ln(N_0C_P)$.

Finally, the maximal provider profit is

$$v_P = (N_0C_P - 1 - \ln(N_0C_P))\frac{IC_P(1 + y^*)}{1 - N_0C_P(1 + y^*)}. \tag{5}$$

4 Provider's View: Tariff Control with Leased Band

If the number of users increases or if the users demand more bandwidth to satisfy their need, the provider may exceed its capacity. In this section we consider that the requested bandwidth cannot be covered by own service band and a part of it has to be covered by leasing. It is well known that leasing cost is essential larger than the bandwidth cost which will be assigned to user. Then the payoff to the provider is given as follows: $v_P(W) = C_W W_p - C_S(W - W_p)$, where C_S is the leasing cost and $C_S \gg C_W$ and W_p is the spectrum owned by the provider. To emphasize the fact that the provider will attempt to squeeze the users' consumption to escape leasing, in the payoff we do not take into account the money obtained from user partly to cover the provider expenses.
Thus, assuming that $W > W_p$, (3) implies that $v_P(W)$ depends only on y^* and C_W as follows:

$$v_P(W) = C_W W_p - C_S \left(\frac{IC_P(1+y^*)}{1 - N_0 C_P(1+y^*)} - W_p \right). \tag{6}$$

with

$$\frac{IC_P(1+y^*)}{1 - N_0 C_P(1+y^*)} \geq W_p.$$

The optimal W is given as follows.

Theorem 3. *If the provider has to lease a part of the bandwidth, then the optimal tariff to assign to users to get the maximal profit is:* $C_W = \ln(1 + y_*) - y_* N_0 C_P$, *where*

$$\begin{aligned} y_* =& \frac{1}{N_0 C_P} - 1 \\ &+ \frac{(C_S I/(W_p.N_0))^{1/3}}{6 N_0 C_P} \left(12\sqrt{12 C_S I/(W_p.N_0) + 81} - 108 \right)^{1/3} \\ &- \frac{2(C_S I/(W_p.N_0))^{2/3}}{N_0 C_P \left(12\sqrt{12 C_S I/(W_p.N_0) + 81} - 108 \right)^{1/3}} \end{aligned}$$

5 Numerical Results

Let us consider the background noise $N_0 = 1$, the induced noise $I = 1$ and the power cost $C_p \in [0, 1]$. Figure 1 shows how optimal power and bandwidth change with increasing user's power cost. The result is quite normal and it is consistent with the fact that when a user transmit with high power, he has tendency to pay more. But greater than a certain threshold $C_p = 0.6$, we fall in the case of negative roots (first point of Theorem 1), and consequently the user has no interest to transmit at all $P = 0$. The curve of optimal bandwidth W has the same shape as the power because of the linear correlation between both them.

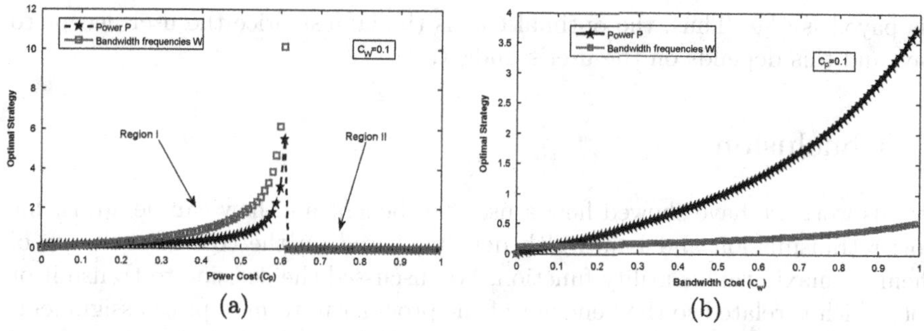

Fig. 1. Optimal user's power and bandwidth for different power and bandwidth prices.

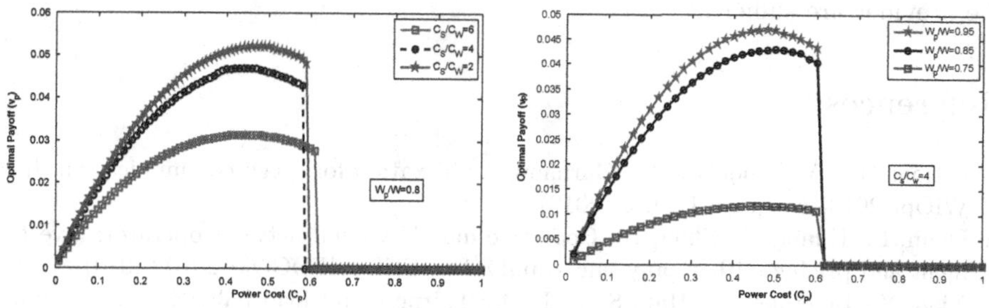

Fig. 2. Impact of leasing cost and the spectrum owned by the provider on the provider's payoff for different values of C_p.

For each power cost, Fig. 1 shows the optimal power and bandwidth that a user must use to maximize its utility function.

Figure 2 shows the provider's point of view when he tries to maximize its payoff. In the case when the provider doesn't have enough bandwidth frequencies and needs to lease a part to cover his need, the leasing cost C_S is added to the model. This cost is known to be greater than the bandwidth cost C_W. We plot in Fig. 2(a) the optimal payoff of the provider when the power cost is increasing for different values of the ratio C_S/C_W. We note that, more C_S is greater than C_W, thes more the provider's payoff is lower, for a fixed value of W and W_p. This behavior can be explained by the fact that the difference between what the provider gets and what he pays goes to zero. Also, the concavity of the function is due to the power cost. Indeed, the provider can incite users to reduce their transmission power if it exceeds certain threshold that insure a maximal payoff to the provider. Figure 2(b) shows the impact of the quantity of spectrum owned by the provider W_p on its payoff. This payoff increases with increasing W_p, because W_p is payed by a small price. In the case when the requested spectrum of bandwidth frequencies belongs to the provider, the only parameter that affect his payoff is C_W. Thus, the optimal C_W is the largest price the user accept to pay, and this depends on the user's budget.

6 Conclusion

In this work we have showed how a user can benefit and how can he adjust his power transmission and bandwidth demand based on the cost of each one of them, to maximize his utility function. We discussed the decision to transmit or not, which is related to the behavior of the provider in term of price assignment. The provider try to obtain the maximal profit. We were interested in the optimal tariff the provider has to set when there is a need in leasing extra bands to satisfy the total demand of users and also the case when the own resources of the provider are sufficient.

References

1. Altman, E., Avrachenkov, K., Garnaev, A.: Taxation for green communication. In: WiOpt 2010, Avignon, France (2010)
2. Duan, L., Huang, J., Shou, B.: Cognitive mobile virtual network operator: investment and pricing with supply uncertainty. In: IEEE INFOCOM 2010 (2010)
3. Xiao, Y., Bejerano, Y., Han, S.-J., Li, L.: Fairness and load balancing in wireless LANs using association control. In: Proceedings of MobiCom, September 2004
4. Prommak, C., Jantaweetip, A.: On the analysis of bandwidth management for hybrid load balancing scheme in WLANs. In: World Academy of Science, Engineering and Technology, vol. 54 (2009)
5. Zhao, Q., Sadler, B.: A survey of dynamic spectrum access: signal processing, networking, and regulatory policy. IEEE Signal Process. **24**(3), 78–89 (2007)

Modeling and Implementation Approach to Evaluate the Intrusion Detection System

Mohammed Saber[1], Sara Chadli[2](✉), Mohamed Emharraf[1], and Ilhame El Farissi[1]

[1] Laboratory LSE2I, National School of Applied Sciences, First Mohammed University, Oujda, Morocco
{mosaber,m.emharraf,ilhame.elfarissi}@gmail.com
[2] Laboratory Electronics and Systems, Sciences Faculty, First Mohammed University, Oujda, Morocco
chad.saraa@gmail.com
http://wwwensa.ump.ma

Abstract. Intrusions detection systems (IDSs) are systems that try to detect attacks as they occur or when they were over. Research in this area had two objectives: first, reducing the impact of attacks; and secondly the evaluation of the system IDS. Indeed, in one hand the IDSs collect network traffic information from some sources present in the network or the computer system and then use these data to enhance the systems safety. In the other hand, the evaluation of IDS is a critical task. In fact, its important to note the difference between evaluating the effectiveness of an entire system and evaluating the characteristics of the system components. In this paper, we present an approach for IDS evaluating based on measuring the performance of its components. First of all, in order to implement the IDS SNORT components safely we have proposed a hardware platform based on embedded systems. Then we have tested it by using a generator of traffics and attacks based on Linux KALI (Backtrack) and Metasploite 3 Framework. The obtained results show that the IDS performance is closely related to the characteristics of these components.

Keywords: Evaluation · IDS · Performance · Embedded system · Field-Programmable Gate Array (FPGA) · Pattern matching · SNORT · Linux KALI · Metasploite 3 framework · LAN traffic generator

1 Introduction

The evaluation of intrusion detection systems is a challenging task; it requires a thorough knowledge of techniques relating to different disciplines, especially intrusion detection, methods of attack, networks and systems, technical testing and evaluation [1]. What makes the evaluation more difficult is the fact that different intrusion detection systems have different operational environments and can use a variety of techniques for producing alerts corresponding to attacks.

Normally, before beginning any experimental test, it is extremely important to identify clearly the objectives of the evaluation. First of all, it is important

A. Bouajjani and H. Fauconnier (Eds.): NETYS 2015, LNCS 9466, pp. 513–517, 2015.
DOI: 10.1007/978-3-319-26850-7_41

to distinguish between testing the evaluation of the systems effectiveness, and testing the whole characteristics of IDS [2] (that is to say, testing components of IDS). In our case, first, we measure the performance of these components, which allows us subsequently to evaluate the systems characteristics.

In practice, most of IDSs suffer from several problems, taking into consideration the large number of false positives and false negatives, and the evolution of attacks. All these problems increase the need of implementing an IDSs evaluation system. In this context, many attempts took place [3–6]. Some of these attempts are based on classification of attacks, which aims to simplify attacks detection, or by technology, or detection range, or by the generation of attack scenarios to understand the behavior of attacks and by other criteria. But the great weakness of these assessments is their inability to cover all the characteristics of an IDS as cited in [2].

In this paper, we present an approach for IDS evaluating based on measuring the performance of its components. In this context, we have proposed a hardware platform based on embedded systems for the implementation of the IDS components (SNORT), and then we tested a system for generating traffics and attacks based on Linux KALI and Metasploite 3 Framework. The obtained results show that the IDS performance is linked to the characteristics of these components.

2 Experiment Design and Results

2.1 Network Design

To verify that our system produces the correct results, we compared it with the standard SNORT software distribution and EIDS. We have created a network (Fig. 1) in which a computer connected to our platform for the supervision operations (Test scenarios) and recovery results. The specific metrics for evaluating used are: Packets captured (**PCA**), Packets analysed (**PAN**), Packets dropped (**PDR**) and Packets detected (**PDE**).

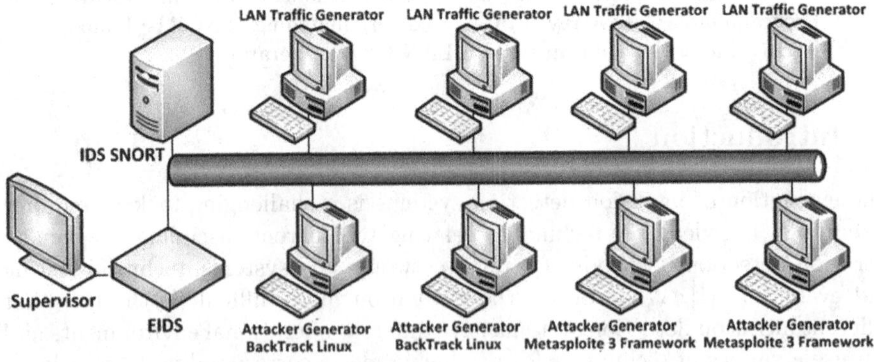

Fig. 1. Network Test

2.2 Senario 1: EIDS and SNORT Reactions to High-Speed Network Traffic

We used LAN Traffic Genarator tools to manage IP traffic in the network and the packet generator tool to send a number of IP packets in different speeds per ms. We sent 21000 packets (14000 TCP, and 7000 UDP) at different transmission time intervals (16 ms, 8 ms, 4 ms), and for each case we calculate the run time RT (seconds) for packet processing by each system (time of packets analysis). Table 1 show the EIDS and SNORT output and results of our experiments.

Table 1. Same number of packets but different transmission time intervals

Packets type	Metrics	SNORT reaction			EIDS reaction		
		16 ms	8 ms	4 ms	16 ms	8 ms	4 ms
TCP (14000)	PCA	14103	14060	14018	14080	14047	14011
	PAN	14095	10023	6121	14011	8967	3431
	PDR	8	4037	7897	69	5080	10580
	RT (s)	209.23	131.24	91.69	225.32	137.21	97.23
UDP (7000)	PCA	7097	7051	7007	7047	7011	7003
	PAN	7017	5219	4917	7001	4371	2153
	PDR	80	1832	2090	46	2640	4850
	RT (s)	189.19	101.14	66.97	201.17	117.89	81.75

2.3 Senario 2: EIDS and SNORT Reactions to Heavy-Traffic Networks

Here, the transmission rate of packets was kept to the same speed (16 ms intervals) to obtain a fair analysis of different numbers of packets (each packet carried 1024). We sent 100, 500 and 1000 packets batches at 16 ms intervals, and for each case we calculate the run time RT (seconds) for packet processing by each system. Table 2 show the SNORT and EIDS results.

Table 2. Same speed limit and different numbers of packets

Metrics	SNORT reaction to heavy traffic			EIDS reaction to heavy traffic		
	100	500	1000	100	500	1000
PCA	106	508	1023	109	505	1017
PAN	106	354	317	101	254	271
PDR	0	154	706	8	251	746
RT (s)	5.41	7.12	9.61	7.61	9.24	13.95

2.4 Senario 3: EIDS and SNORT Reactions to Large Packets

For this experiment, the number of packets was kept to the same value (18000) and the same speed (16ms) to obtain a fair analysis of different sizes (lengths) of packets. We increased the size of each packet sent started from 256 byte, to 512 bytes, and to 1024 bytes. Table 3 show the performance detection results.

Table 3. Same speed and value but different packet size

Metrics	SNORT reaction to packet sizes			EIDS reaction to packet sizes		
	256	512	1024	256	512	1024
PCA	18107	18082	18026	18090	18043	18017
PAN	18107	12314	8193	18010	11357	6791
PDR	0	5768	9833	80	6686	11226
RT (s)	269.31	195.32	162.37	317.32	232.21	207.56

2.5 Senario 4: EIDS and SNORT Reactions to Generate the Number of Alerts (Attack Detection Rate)

During the evaluation, attacks have been generated to evaluate the performance of both IDSs in a heavy and mixed traffic. The initial test was perfomed with background traffic only. This was done to confirm that both EIDS and SNORT are configured to generate the number of alerts. We then went on generating the same attacks for both EIDS and SNORT in high speeds network. The results are presented in Table 4.

Table 4. Same number of alerts but different speed

Speed	SNORT rate of attacks detection				EIDS rate of attacks detection			
	250 Mbps	500 Mbps	1.0 Gpbs	2.0 Gbps	250 Mbps	500 Mbps	1.0 Gpbs	2.0 Gbps
PDE	100 %	100 %	100 %	99,3 %	100 %	89,97 %	65.12 %	41.28 %

2.6 Discussion of results

Critical analyses were done for experiments senario1, senario2, senario3 and senario4. The obtained results show that both systems performance analysis throughput is affected by high-speed and heavy traffic, and more packets are dropped as the number and size of packets and the speed of traffic increases. Both systems had a limited time to process and analyse any traffic successfully and if a network's traffic speed limit is higher than both systems limit. This problem due to the limited characteristics of the components.

3 Conclusion

For many years attacks made on networks have risen dramatically. The major reason for this is the unlimited access to and use of software (written and uploaded to websites by technical experts) by inadequately trained people. However, an IDS is considered to be one of the best technologies to detect threats and attacks. IDSs have attracted the interest of many organizations and governments, and any Internet user can deploy them. An IDS usually features four stages to secure a computer system network: scanning, analysing, detecting, and correcting. In this paper we proposed an approach for evaluating an IDS with these characteristics. This approach based on tests to measure performance indicators of the components of an IDS. For this we chose a hardware solution based on embedded systems. Our solution is a hardware platform that gives the hand to measure the performance indicators of the components of an IDS. As a result of our approach, systems can be configured such that attacks can be thwarted more easily.

References

1. Khorkov, D.A.: Methods for testing network-intrusion detection systems. Sci. Tech. Inf. Proc. **39**(2), 120–126 (2012). doi:10.3103/S0147688212020128
2. Mell, P., Hu, V., Lippmann, R., Haines, J., Zissman, M.: An overview of issues in testing intrusion detection systems. Technical report, National Institute of Standard and Technology (2003)
3. Akhlaq, M., Alserhani, F., Awan, I., Mellor, J., Cullen, A.J., Al-Dhelaan, A.: Implementation and evaluation of network intrusion detection systems. In: Kouvatsos, D.D. (ed.) Next Generation Internet: Performance Evaluation and Applications. LNCS, vol. 5233, pp. 988–1016. Springer, Heidelberg (2011)
4. Saber, M., Emharref, M., Bouchentouf, T., Benazzi, A.: Platform based on an embedded system to evaluate the intrusion detection system. In: IEEE Xplore Digital Library. pp. 894–899 (2012) doi:10.1109/ICMCS.2012.6320253
5. Albin, E.; Rowe, N.C.: A realistic experimental comparison of the suricata and SNORT intrusion-detection systems. In: 2012 26th International Conference on Advanced Information Networking and Applications Workshops (WAINA), pp. 122–127, 26–29 March 2012. doi:10.1109/WAINA.2012.29
6. Wang, X., Kordas, A., Hu, L., Gaedke, M., Smith, D.: Administrative evaluation of intrusion detection system. In: Proceedings of the 2nd Annual Conference on Research in Information Technology (RIIT 2013) pp. 47–52. ACM, New York, USA (2013) doi:10.1145/2512209.2512216

Trust Based Energy Preserving Routing Protocol in Multi-hop WSN

Saima Raza[1(✉)], Waleej Haider[1], Nouman M. Durrani[2], Nadeem Kafi Khan[2], and Mohammad Asad Abbasi[1]

[1] Sir Syed University of Engineering and Technology, Karachi, Pakistan
saimarzaidi@gmail.com
[2] FAST NUCES, Karachi, Pakistan

Abstract. Wireless Sensor Networks (WSN) are widely used in many sensitive applications, where human deployment is almost impossible. Due to resource constraints, the network and hence the forwarded information is open for attacks. Hence, it is desirable to ensure source to sink privacy in order to maximize the network lifetime. In this paper we studied security threats and energy constraints while deploying WSN nodes. Moreover, we propose a Trust Based Secure and Energy Preserving Routing Protocol (TEPP), in multi-hop WSN. The proposed solution monitors reputation and trust worthiness of nodes and maintains a history of interaction between nodes to identify secure and trust worthy path. The effectiveness of our proposed protocol has been experimentally verified against various attacks. At the end future research directions have been highlighted.

Keywords: WSN · Trust-based · Energy efficient · Secure routing

1 Introduction

Wireless sensor network (WSN) is a network of small and smart computing devices for establishing reliable, scalable and resilient network of sensing and forwarding nodes. WSN are mainly deployed in many applications such as industrial power control, environmental monitoring, medical instrumentation and homeland security, where human intervention is difficult. In such networks, it is required to maximize network lifetime and strengthen source to sink privacy, by finding trustworthy, secure and energy-efficient route discovery and forwarding mechanisms.

As, these networks deal in sensitive data and are opened due to limited resources, it is important to make them secure against various types of attacks such as spoofing, selective forwarding, sinkhole attacks, wormholes, traffic analysis node replication and attacks against privacy. Moreover, the attackers can easily demolish the whole network by capturing the network nodes or by attacking the routing protocol. Even few computational resources are enough to shoot up fake messages, operate routing messages, attack the routing protocols and disrupt the normal operation of the network. Even more, arbitrary behavior may be induced by corrupting the intermediate nodes or planting an internal attacker into the network. Considering all these realities, the deployment of a secure routing protocol becomes a primary task; however, designing of such secure

A. Bouajjani and H. Fauconnier (Eds.): NETYS 2015, LNCS 9466, pp. 518–523, 2015.
DOI: 10.1007/978-3-319-26850-7_42

routing protocols are not easy. An important factor in this regard is energy-aware trustworthy secure routing, which is significant in ensuring smooth operation of WSNs [1]. Careful management of the network is also desired, as processing required for secure routing and communication is distributed over the nodes itself. Providing security in such networks is extremely important and challenging.

Generally, WSN system threats fall in three categories with reference to security considerations: confidentiality, availability and integrity [2]. Many researchers suggested trust management system to help in selection of trust worthy peer of same behavioral pattern [3–6]. Some of trust metrics depends upon recommendation system but our proposed algorithm doesn't support recommendation system as they may suffer from badmouthing attack. According to Xiong et al. [7] reputation is a key factor which adds value to trust certificate whereas Sen et al. [8] proposed that reputation and rating framework has several lacunas due to dishonest parties and great numbers of variables for assessing trust.

Providing an accredited vocabulary, string of trust and delegated permissions as designed in by Freudenthal et al. [9] in Role-based access control model. Several researcher proposed to integrate processing modules with in WSN for observing and calculating different parameters for selection of optimal path [10, 11]. However these protocol may magnify traffic in WSN as regular broadcast of message from BS and sensors nodes require more computing power as two computing components run on nodes. Considering the limited computational and energy constraints, in this paper we have presented a trust based routing scheme called "Trust Based Energy Preserving multihop Routing Protocol (TEPP)" for secure data transmission in WSNs in Sect. 2, followed by the performance and evaluation of our proposed protocol in Sect. 3. Afterwards conclusion is drawn with future research directions.

2 Proposed Solution

The protocol called as TEPP comprises of three phases: Neighbor Identifying Phase, *Cluster Head Selection phase and Data Sharing Phase.* It provides a secure information sharing path and controls malicious nodes by providing a mechanism of authentication and trust calculation of each node. The network consists nodes, cluster Heads and the BS. BS has a centralized control and helps to reduce the Bandwidth and computation requirements of network. Our proposed routing protocol uses Modified Closest pair-wise keys pre-distribution scheme for secure communication between two nodes [12]. All server nodes have their master keys provided by setup server and for every pair of node (IDS, IDR), a pair-wise key KS, R = PRF KR (S) is generated where PRF is pseudo random function. New sensor node has predefined keys for all sensor nodes in its transmission range. Hash Message Authentication Code (HMAC) is applied to provide message integrity and to verify sender authentication. TEPP Phases are described as under:

Neighbor Identifying Phase: In Neighbor Discovery Phase, node initiates zero messages using "Modified dynamic, zero-message broadcast encryption scheme based on Secure Multiparty Computation" [13] to discover its neighbors with in transmission range. This broadcast message has two blocks cipher block and header block. Header block has message id and list of several receiver nodes where message id is unique. Cipher block is encrypted using one-time key (OTK) which is calculated: OTK = Combine t, n (K_1, K_2, …. K_n) where Ki = H(ID message, ID RNode, Key RNode, ID SNode) where RNode is recipient node, SNode is source node and ciphers block is composed of (ID SNode, Nonce SNode) information. Interested Nodes sends reply message with in time out as follows:

$$\mathrm{ID_{RNode}} \rightarrow \mathrm{ID_{SNode}} = \mathrm{K_{R,S}}[(\mathrm{Nonce_{RNode}} \parallel \mathrm{ID_{RNode}}) \parallel (\mathrm{ID_{SNode}} \parallel \mathrm{Nonce_{SNode}})]$$

Sender Node decrypts this acceptance message using its private key and adds nodes in its neighbor list. Sharing of data within a cluster requires minimum level of energy.

Cluster Head Selection Phase: In proposed algorithm Cluster Heads are decided by applying LEACH (Low-Energy Adaptive Clustering Hierarchy) algorithm [13] under surveillance of BS. CH behaves as an intermediate channel between sensor nodes and base station, and maintains communication history table CHT shown in Table 1, of nodes located in respective cluster and calculates a threshold value of each node using formula: $T_{Th} = f(MI) + TR + EN + FP$; where, TR is data transmission range of node, EN indicates energy of node; FP is number of times sensor node participated in communication, *f* (MI) function of integrity is calculated on basis of frequency of errors, link failures, Message verification techniques thus CH and BS help a sensor node to choose best data transferring node among several alternatives. Initially, nodes have no information about their respective neighbors. To initiate trust calculation, flooding mechanism is introduced and CHT is created. During and after neighbor detection phase all sensor nodes update about malicious nodes to their respective CH, which share this information to all other nodes within and outside the Clusters. After CH is decided, it detects its surrounding CH by broadcasting a zero message encrypted using OTK after getting response message it updates CH neighbor list. BS after receiving information about CH and their neighbor calculates multipath and share secret pair keys with all CH.

Data Sharing Phase: When node wants to transmit data, it uses distance vector algorithm to find all available route towards destination and CH helps sending node in

Table 1. Communication history table (CHT)

Source	Destination	f (MI)	TR (Meters)	EN (Volts)	FP	Threshold value
A	B	01.40	60	3.2	4	68.6
B	E	01.10	50	2.2	8	61.3
B	D	00.75	45	3.5	3	52.25
E	F	01.00	56	2.4	7	66.4
D	F	01.20	60	2.4	7	70.6
F	C	01.35	45	3.1	5	54.4

deciding best among multiple route options i.e. When a node "A" wants to send information to destination node "C", it finds several alternatives path using modified distance vector algorithm.

i. A– –>B– –>E– –>F– –>C ii. A – –>B– –>D – –>F– –>C

Than Cluster Head using "CHT" works in reverse order i.e. it will forward the data on nodes with high **threshold** (trust value) for the destination node "C" which is node "F" in this sample case. We can express this path selection and data forwarding on the following expression:

$$\begin{aligned} A - - > B : HMAC\left(K_{A,B}, Data, ID_A, ID_B\right) \\ = H[(ID_A \parallel (Ku \oplus opad)) \parallel H[((Ku \oplus ipad) \parallel Data \parallel ID_B)]] \end{aligned}$$

Since only trustworthy nodes are selected in the data forwarding process, hence the impact of malicious nodes is decreased. Moreover, the energy is conserved as only trusted nodes are involved in the data forwarding process. In the next section we discuss performance of our proposed protocol against various types of attacks and their impact on the packet delivery or packet drop.

3 Performance and Evaluation

The proposed protocol provides a mechanism which keeps track of malicious behavior within network to combat unfair acts by any node and sensed data is transferred through node with high threshold value with combination of energy aware mechanism. OMNeT++ has been used to simulate the performance of our proposed protocol. Initially a test bed of 100 nodes with an average calculated threshold 54.6 was evaluated against 15 % malicious nodes involved in different types of attacks such as wormhole, selective forwarding, and de-synchronization attacks. The proposed protocol was evaluated against ATSR, GPSR and TARF routing protocols. Experimentally, it has been found that only 14 % of the packets were dropped. Further, when the numbers of malicious nodes were increased randomly to 40 % of 2000 nodes, the packet drop ratio was observed to be stable. As shown in Fig. 1, less than 33 % packets were unable to reach the destination node. In the same case, major packet drop was observed for ATSR, GPSR and TARF. It shows that the protocol is exceptionally stable under large number of attacks. Proposed TEPP compared with TARF, TEESR, Trusted GPSR protocols and analyzed that it performs better in providing defensive measures against De-Synchronization, Selective Forwarding, Wormholes attacks. Table 2 highlights the impact of different attacks on threshold value of individual node calculated using TEPP. It shows that three to four time occurrence of attack decreases threshold value of nodes thus degrading trustworthiness of that node. Also, it has been

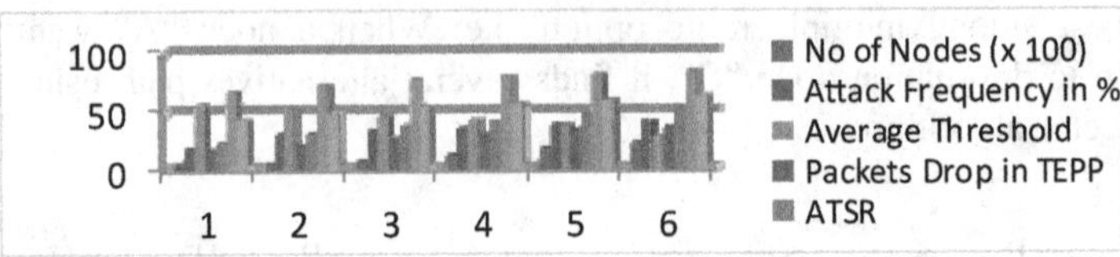

Fig. 1. Effect of security attacks on packet delivery

Table 2. Impact of different attacks on threshold value of node calculated using TEPP

Nodes	De-Synchronization			Selective Forwarding			Wormholes		
	A_F	T_H	I_F	A_F	T_H	I_F	A_F	T_H	I_F
A	5	54.6	Medium	2	58.00	Low	4	53.24	Medium
B	4	51.00	Medium	6	45.23	High	5	50.66	Medium
C	4	45.00	Medium	4	47.80	Medium	7	40.23	High
D	4	45.4	Medium	4	48.50	Medium	3	55.27	Low
E	2	60.6	Low	6	43.24	High	3	52.00	Low
F	7	34.4	High	4	40.23	Medium	8	36.12	High

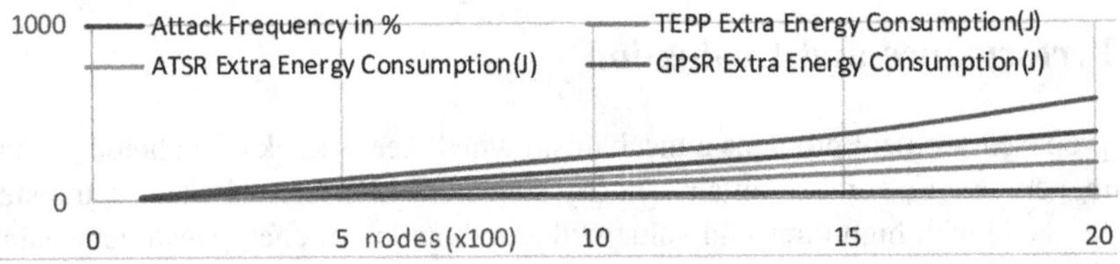

Fig. 2. Extra energy consumption (in J/×100 nodes) due to packet drop

found that for the same network when compared with other routing protocols such as TARF, ATSR and GPSR protocols also shown Fig. 2.

4 Conclusion

Due to various security challenges in WSNs, we have presented a Trust Based Energy Preserving multihop Routing Protocol that not only tends to mitigate major security risks but also provides an energy efficient data forwarding mechanism. Performance in terms of packet drop and extra-energy consumption was evaluated against various secure and energy efficient protocols. Processing power required for head nodes to maintain history and trust calculation of each node and to combat energy exhaustion required in movement of nodes between clusters is left for future research.

References

1. Stajano, F.: Security issues in ubiquitous computing. In: Nakashima, H., Aghajan, H., Augusto, J.C. (eds.) Handbook of Ambient Intelligence and Smart Environments, pp. 281–314. Springer, Heidelberg (2010)
2. Durrani, N.M., et al.: Secure multi-hop routing protocols in wireless sensor networks: requirements, challenges and solutions. In: 8th IEEE ICDIM (2013)
3. Carullo, G., et al.: FeelTrust: providing trustworthy communications in Ubiquitous Mobile environment. In: 2013 IEEE 27th International Conference on Advanced Information Networking and Applications (AINA). IEEE (2013)
4. Pirzada, A.A., McDonald, C.: Trusted greedy perimeter stateless routing. In: 15th IEEE International Conference on Networks, ICON 2007. IEEE (2007)
5. Bao, F., et al.: Hierarchical trust management for wireless sensor networks and its applications to trust-based routing and intrusion detection. IEEE Trans. Netw. Serv. Manag. **9**(2), 169–183 (2012)
6. Li, X., Lyu, M.R., Liu, J.: A trust model based routing protocol for secure adhoc networks. In: IEEE Proceedings on Aerospace Conference, vol. 2 (2004)
7. Xiong, L., Liu, L.: PeerTrust: supporting reputation-based trust for peer-to-peer electronic communities. IEEE Trans. Knowl. Data Eng. **16**(7), 843–857 (2004)
8. Sen, S., Sajja, N.: Robustness of reputation-based trust: boolean case. In: Proceedings of the First International Joint Conference on Autonomous Agents and Multiagent Systems: Part 1, Bologna, Italy, 15–19 July 2002
9. Freudenthal, E., Pesin, T., Port, L., Keenan, E., Karamcheti, V.: dRBAC: distributed role-based access control for dynamic coalition environments. In: Proceedings of the 22nd ICDCS 2002. IEEE Computer Society, July 2002
10. Zhan, G., Shi, W., Deng, J.: TARF: A trust-aware routing framework for wireless sensor networks. In: Sá Silva, J., Krishnamachari, B., Boavida, F. (eds.) EWSN 2010. LNCS, vol. 5970, pp. 65–80. Springer, Heidelberg (2010)
11. Marti, S., Giuli, T., Lai, K., Baker, M.: Mitigating routing misbehavior in mobile ad hoc. In: Proceedings of the Sixth Annual International Conference on Mobile Computing and Networking (MobiCom). ACM Press, pp. 255–265 (2000)
12. Liu, D., Ning, P.: Location-based pairwise key establishments for static sensor networks. In: Proceedings of the 1st ACM Workshop on Security of Ad Hoc and Sensor Networks. ACM (2003)
13. Soodkhah, M., Mohammadi, A., Bafghi, G.: A dynamic, zero-message broadcast encryption scheme based on secure multiparty computation. In: 9th ISC (2012)

Author Index